AUTUMN OF GLORY

AUTUMN OF GLORY

The Army of Tennessee, 1862-1865

THOMAS LAWRENCE CONNELLY

LOUISIANA STATE UNIVERSITY PRESS

BATON ROUGE AND LONDON

To FRANK E. VANDIVER, *in appreciation*
for his encouragement and trust

ISBN 0-8071-0445-0
Library of Congress Catalog Card Number 70-122353
Copyright © 1971 by Louisiana State University Press
All rights reserved
Manufactured in the United States of America
1986 printing

Acknowledgments

I AM GRATEFUL FOR THE VALUABLE ASSISTANCE PROVIDED BY THE STAFFS of the National Archives, the United States Military Academy, Harvard University Library, New York Public Library, Tulane University Library, the Library of Congress, Duke University Library, the Southern Historical Collection of the University of North Carolina, the Chicago Historical Society, Western Reserve Historical Society, Tennessee State Archives, Emory University Library, the Alabama State Department of Archives and History, and the College of William and Mary Library.

I feel special appreciation also to several institutions whose grants made this work possible, including the National Endowment on the Arts and Humanities, the American Philosophical Society, and the Mississippi State University Development Foundaton.

Many historians have offered valuable advice and encouragement. I am indebted particularly to Professor Frank Vandiver of Rice University, Professor T. Harry Williams of Louisiana State University, Professor Grady McWhiney of Wayne University, Mr. Thomas R. Hay of Locust Valley, New York, Professor Harold Snellgrove of Mississippi State University, and Professor Robert D. Ochs of the University of South Carolina.

Many other people extended valuable aid and great kindness. Lieutenant Val Husley drew upon his combat experience in army intelligence to produce the maps. Mr. Emmet A. Nichols, a National Park Service historian and ordnance expert, provided advice and logistical support while I was researching in Pennsylvania. Lieutenant Michael Vice, United States Army, and Dr. James Shoalmire gave other assistance.

Above all, my sincere gratitude is extended to my wife Sally. Her patience and abilities as a professional free-lance editor were invaluable.

Contents

Illustrations and Maps

AUTUMN OF GLORY

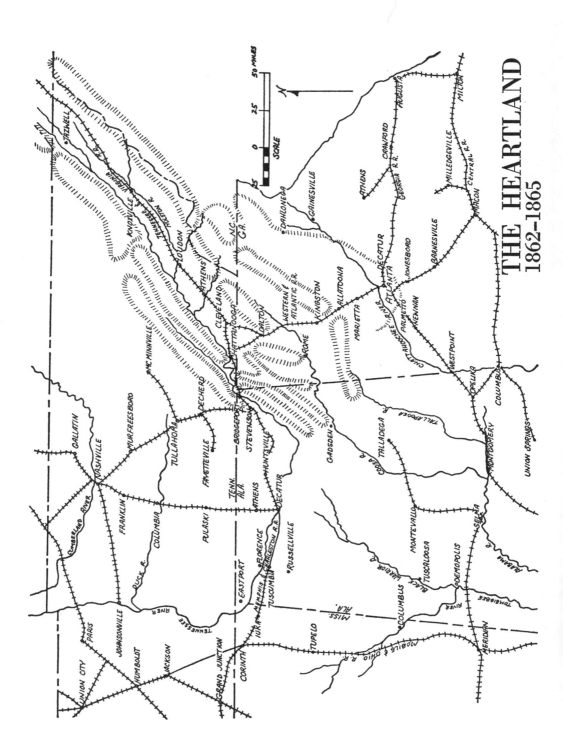

THE HEARTLAND
1862–1865

introduction

IT WAS A CRISP AUTUMN DAY IN THE CUMBERLAND MOUNTAINS, AND A FEW perceptive crows already were complaining of the oncoming winter. I stood on the rim of Broad Mountain, at the antebellum mineral spa of Beersheba Springs. With many questions yet unanswered, I had completed the first draft of this book, which continues the history of the Army of Tennessee from late 1862 until its surrender in 1865.

Beersheba Springs in autumn seemed an appropriate place to begin final work on such a project. The country here is rich with those leisurely, modest reminiscences associated with the unsung western army. The old hotel, with its long white portico and quaint courtyard, still stands on the mountain crest. Many a future western Rebel had found refuge here during yellow fever perils. The hard drinking, gambling, and dancing, the Sunday sermons of Bishop—later Confederate General—Leonidas Polk, the mob of refugees from both Rebel and Union guerillas—all are a part of the hotel's past.

Along the quiet village lane General Nathan Bedford Forrest's troopers filed past in 1862 en route to capture Murfreesboro. By the lane stands the summer home of Bishop-General Polk, just at the point where the Old Altamont Stage Road swings west to follow the mountain crest to Sewanee. Nearby is the summer retreat once occupied by General Dahlgren, who commanded the Mississippi state troops in 1861.

Just across the lane from the hotel stands a two-story log house built almost a decade before Bragg's Kentucky campaign. This house, which I now own, was looted twice by bushwhackers during the war. Sometimes I look down the lane at the Dahlgren house, conjure up a ghost or two, and think of the General's kinsman, the unlucky young colonel who died in the raid on Richmond.

The low-key nature of this Tennessee village symbolizes much of the Army of Tennessee's character. The historiographical gap between General Robert E. Lee's Virginia army and the western command has been narrowed by biographies such as T. Harry Williams' life of Beauregard

3

and Robert Hartje's recent study of Earl Van Dorn. Still, much remains to be written of the war in the West. The army of Virginia has been more often credited with bearing most of the Confederacy's load. Names such as Resaca, McLemore's Cove, and Tullahoma lack the colorful aura of Chancellorsville or the Seven Days. As a sequel to *Army of the Heart-land,* which examined the Army of Tennessee from its early organization in the late spring of 1861 until its failure in the Kentucky invasion in the autumn of 1862, this volume is intended to further close the gap.

The late autumn of 1862 seems an appropriate dividing point for the two books. One detects already that the western Confederacy had reached its peak, and was beginning to decline. The decline was to be gradual, with an occasional upsurge of hope such as was raised at Chickamauga. But, by November, 1862, the army's fortunes had turned irreversibly downhill.

Confederate weakness was more sharply evident, too, by comparison with growing Federal strength. The disparity between the Army of Tennessee and the Federal Military Division of the Mississippi had not yet reached the proportions of 1863-64. Still, Union manpower was already sufficient in the West to maintain a two-front war—a matter President Jefferson Davis did not appear to appreciate. After the sur-render at Vicksburg, this disparity of numbers would become much greater, as the total Union effort became concentrated against the Army of Tennessee.

This was ruinous enough, but there were also problems within. Much of this book deals with the internal problems of the Army of Tennessee as well as with its actual military operations. Some of the old matters which had troubled the army since its origin were still present, and had become more complicated. The chief of these was command discord. Since the summer of 1861 the army command had been troubled by a double problem—feuding and a lack of communication among its high officers.

By late 1862 the old days of the Polk-Pillow feud and Albert Sidney Johnston's troubles with his generals looked almost peaceful. Two new and more sophisticated strains were appearing in the command problem which would dominate the army's fortunes until 1865. One was the well-organized movement against Bragg within the army. The other was the political intrigue between Richmond and the military.

By September, 1863, the anti-Bragg bloc, which strongly influenced the army and the administration in Richmond, felt sufficiently powerful to abandon its covert attack against General Bragg and to openly attempt to secure his removal.

The move failed, but as a consequence military operations were impeded, and after the resulting Chattanooga disaster, Bragg left the army. Ironically, he came out of it the victor. Not a single corps leader who had risen against him in September remained with the army in December. Still, the anti-Bragg organization did not die, but retained a semblance of itself under Bragg's successors, Generals Joseph E. Johnston and John Hood. Too, the strong fight of the anti-Bragg elements in 1863 created a counter-move within the army. Contrary to popular opinion, Bragg had a strong base of support in the army, much of it derived from the officers who had served with him on the Gulf in 1861. Some generals, such as Patton Anderson, were genuine, warm friends of Bragg's. Others—Joseph Wheeler for instance—seemed more opportunists who flattered the commanding general for their own advancement.

The continuance of these two blocs was no small matter. When General Joseph E. Johnston led the army in 1864, he had little united support among his subordinates. Even old anti-Bragg men, such as Leonidas Polk and William Hardee, were among his critics. In addition, he was attacked by Bragg's friends through clandestine correspondence between Richmond and the field in much the same way Bragg's enemies had worked to undermine him.

Johnston's appearance in the West heralded the second of the two major strains of command discord evident by late 1862—the problem of who was to lead the Army of Tennessee. This question was a growing political issue of the Confederacy. By the autumn of 1862 the anti-administration faction in Congress seized upon Bragg's unpopularity as an excuse for criticizing the government. At first they championed General P. G. T. Beauregard as a successor to Bragg. But Davis' hatred of that fine officer made the Creole a poor candidate. By November, 1862, the anti-Davis congressional bloc had rallied to the standard of Joseph E. Johnston. Even while Johnston served as theater commander in the West during 1863, his supporters fought to have him replace Bragg as army commander.

By December, 1863, the matter had unquestionably become a major political issue. The anti-Bragg and pro-Johnston elements moved in separate channels through 1863 but became entangled in the fall of 1863. After Johnston was appointed to succeed Bragg in December, support or criticism of the army commander for the remainder of the war depended on one's views of the administration in Richmond. Out of this developed a peculiar caste system. In Richmond it was difficult to champion ideas of the Davis-Bragg forces without alienating the army's subordinate generals. Yet unless a commander in the field was an administration supporter, it was difficult to maintain good communication with the government.

I have also devoted close study to the "Virginia syndrome," a command issue that had become evident by late 1862. Five times between 1862 and 1865, Richmond sent officers from Virginia to the West. The motives and effects of these transfers vitally influenced the performance of these officers. Johnston, obsessed by his struggle with Richmond, felt self-pity over what he considered his subordinated position. Generals James Longstreet and John Bell Hood came to the West as corps commanders. Both were troublemakers, a factor closely related to their motives for coming. The performance of General Daniel Harvey Hill was also colored by Virginia experience. Too, in late 1864, General P. G. T. Beauregard was returned to the West and given an impossible theater command. The circumstances of his appointment and his service in Virginia probably affected Beauregard's conduct of operations.

Another continuing command matter was the increasingly rapid turnover among commanders and corps leaders. By mid-1863 the body count was becoming so heavy that keeping tabs is difficult. For example, between September and December, 1863, almost a dozen different men commanded corps in either permanent or temporary positions. Thus, as in earlier days, the high command of 1862-65 simply never solidified into a coordinated body.

The old matter of poor direction from Richmond persisted in late 1862. Attention is given to the impossible tangle of boundaries, authority, and direction in the western departmental system, a system which diverted talent and manpower from important areas. In turn, these matters were complicated by Richmond's two appointments to provide overall direction in the West—the theater commands of Joseph E. Johnston in 1862-63 and P. G. T. Beauregard in late 1864-65.

Richmond's inconsistencies continued to plague all the West. From the beginning the Army of Tennessee received second-class treatment. Richmond frequently intervened without adequate knowledge of western problems. For example, when Johnston was appointed theater commander, he supposedly had the power to coordinate affairs among several departments. Yet the government repeatedly overrode him from Richmond, as in December, 1862, when reinforcements were ordered moved from Bragg to General John C. Pemberton.

Problems of a geographical nature became more complicated in late 1862. With the loss of the upper Heartland, early in the year, a new and larger belt of munitions works, iron furnaces, and forges, and food producing areas was established in the West. This new complex was located on a broad front in East Tennessee, Central Georgia, and Central and South Alabama. By 1863, this belt, which included Atlanta, Augusta,

Macon, Columbus, and Selma, continued to make the lower Heartland the South's most vital supply area.

The army's problem of defending such essential areas was complicated by Jefferson Davis' legalistic departmental organization. Many of these installations were technically not within the authority of the Second Department and its army. The Army of Tennessee was expected to defend them, though it could draw no food, recruits, or equipment from them. For example, in the late summer of 1863 the Army of Tennessee alone faced the armies of Generals U. S. Grant and William Rosecrans. Yet East Tennessee was off limits for support because it was in the East Tennessee department. Almost all of Alabama and Mississippi was the domain of another department. Though the army was Georgia's protector, most of the state was restricted in the South Carolina-Georgia-Florida Department.

The improper management of manpower was, by late 1862, a much larger problem than any shortage of manpower. Under the departmental system, thousands of men were idle in Mississippi and Alabama while Bragg faced Rosecrans, and Joseph Johnston and Hood confronted Sherman. Frequent and long marches over the mountainous terrain of the West resulted in disciplinary problems. The mountains provided plenty of hiding places for deserters. A sixth column grew out of stragglers, deserters, civilian refugees, detached outposts, and thousands of the sick and worn.

The cavalry was becoming more important by late 1862, and thus receives increased attention in this book. Cavalry grew more vital because of the lengthening Federal communication lines, new threats on munitions areas, and the broader front of maneuvering.

Somehow western cavalry, by the end of 1862, was simply getting out of hand. Contrary to popular belief, the western army did not have cavalry officers capable of broad strategy. The cavalry was often wasted in assaults upon objectives of secondary importance which produced sensational newspaper coverage but little else. Under cavalry officers there was also a steady decline in discipline. Frequently, two-thirds of the Army of Tennessee's troopers were lost somewhere in that morass of the sixth column.

Waste was at its worst in the cavalry. There was no shortage of men; in 1863, at least forty thousand horsemen were in the field from East Tennessee to Mississippi. Of these, some were wasted in the departmental system; some were in state service and openly competed with the army for recruits. Many were lost in irregular cavalry units, an evil allowed to exist by the War Department. Hastily formed cavalry companies claimed deserting infantry or other troops attempting to escape more active service. In addition, there were always several thousand regular cavalry, such as those who, in the spring of 1864, drifted back behind the lines in Company Q, allegedly in search of horses. These examples of cavalry mismanagement, coupled with the improved Federal cavalry organization wrought by Generals David Stanley and James Wilson, seem to contradict the myth of western Rebel cavalry superiority—at least after 1862.

All of these problems—command discord, direction, geography, and waste—were tied closely to the personalities of many generals. Thus I carefully examine these personalities—commanders, corps and division leaders, and others who influenced the army. Some of the conclusions may seem somewhat unorthodox.

Emphasis is also given to the army's military operations from late 1862 until 1865, a long saga which involves many key campaigns— Stone's River, Duck River, Chickamauga-Chattanooga, North Georgia, Atlanta, Franklin-Nashville, and North Carolina. The book contains some new ideas concerning these campaigns, as well as certain particular actions within them, often questioned by historians. There are many of these, such as at Tullahoma, McLemore's Cove, and Chickamauga, and certain aspects of the Georgia campaign, Spring Hill, for example. As in the previous volume, I have relied on army intelligence in discussing military operations. In every case possible, pertinent information not then known to the army is placed in the footnotes.

Conflicting information on military operations, the difficulty of accurately assessing personalities, and the constant counter-charges found within command feuds made necessary a wide search for sources. The Army of Tennessee's official and private papers are literally scattered from California to New England. In one summer alone, I logged eleven thousand miles on my automobile speedometer, searching the eastern United States for collections that might have been overlooked. The search involved long and lonely night rides on buses and railroad coaches.

This long pursuit resulted in some unforgettable, if not sensational, memories. There were some unhurried, enlightening conversations with Mr. Thomas Hay, surely the dean of western Confederate historians. And one stormy night in an old Texas prairie farmhouse, by kerosene lamp, I pulled General Don Carlos Buell's papers from an old trunk— coincidentally on the anniversary of his death. Then there was a soggy day when that indomitable Middle Tennessee historian, Colonel Campbell Brown, led me through the cedars in search of Hood's fording point on Duck River.

I also remember a number of truckstop meals, heavily laden with grease, and many a cold chicken box supper on railroad cars. I do not begrudge the quality of these meals. The Army of Tennessee never went first-class.

THOMAS LAWRENCE CONNELLY
University of South Carolina

PART I

the bragg-johnston influence

one

A Season of Discontent

It was late October, 1862, and the chill of the East Tennessee autumn was already in the air. Down from Cumberland Gap, across Powell River at McHenry's Ford, rode General Braxton Bragg with the advance of his retreating army. Behind him the Army of the Mississippi straggled through the Cumberland Mountains. Discouraged by defeat in the Kentucky campaign, the army slogged through swollen mountain streams and along muddy roads, bound for the lush valley of East Tennessee. On October 21 Bragg, with the head of the column, cleared the last ridge and broke onto the valley floor at Morristown.

They did not pause long at Morristown. Within eight days, the army was moving southwest on the East Tennessee Railroad. Spirits rose as the lower valley towns were left behind, and the trains whistled into the Great Bend at Chattanooga. They moved forward again, through the gorge of Sand Mountain, downriver to Bridgeport, Alabama. There they ferried the Tennessee, boarded other trains, and rattled northward, up the Crow Creek gorge, through the long Cumberland Mountain tunnel, and into Middle Tennessee. The destination was the Stone's River Valley, only thirty miles south of the Federal bastion at Nashville.

Probably never had a Confederate offensive been so hastily planned, and an invading army so unready for a new campaign. Bragg had made the decision to move even while he was involved in the Kentucky invasion. In late September he had sent General Nathan Bedford Forrest with a small command back to Tennessee. Forrest's main assignment was to protect the supposedly rich Murfreesboro area from Union foraging expeditions.

13

From this modest beginning, a mania developed among military and political leaders for a mass occupation of Murfreesboro and the re-taking of Nashville. Governor Isham Harris, a volunteer aide to Bragg and constant lobbyist for such a move, excused himself from the Kentucky column. He returned to Tennessee and without any authority assumed a quasi-military command in the Murfreesboro area. Units were recruited for a strike on Nashville. More men were diverted to Murfreesboro in early October. By October 2 General John C. Breckinridge had arrived in Knoxville from Mississippi with a motley division composed mainly of exchanged prisoners and unarmed regiments. The acting commander of the Department of East Tennessee, General Sam Jones, also longed for an attack on Nashville. By October 10 Jones had succeeded both in gaining temporary jurisdiction of Murfreesboro and in diverting two thousand of Breckinridge's men for use there. Meanwhile, Tennessee congressmen were pressuring the government at Richmond to organize a full-scale invasion of Nashville.[1]

Bragg was also seized with the new offensive spirit. By October 14, two days after his own decision to abandon Kentucky, he was planning the new offensive. He ordered Breckinridge to take his division to Murfreesboro and assume command. That same day Bragg also confided to the Kentuckian that the main army would soon follow him to Murfreesboro. Seven days later, when he reached the railroad at Morristown Bragg telegraphed the government that he now planned to invade Middle Tennessee.[2]

The haphazard planning continued. Bragg, on October 23, admitted to the government that his army was so badly organized that he could not estimate its strength. Troubled by Bragg's hasty decision, that same day the government ordered him to report in person to Richmond to explain his future plans. Without any pause, Bragg ordered General

---

1 Chattanooga *Daily Rebel*, October 9, 28, 1862; Mobile *Register*, November 2, 9, 1862; Robert S. Henry, *"First with the Most" Forrest* (Indianapolis, 1944), 100–105; *The War of the Rebellion: A Compilation of the Official Records of Union and Confederate Armies* (Washington, D.C., 1880–1901), Ser. I, Vol. XVI, Pt. 2, pp. 858, 862, 888, 891, 1000, 1002–1003, hereinafter cited as *Official Records* (unless otherwise indicated, all citations are to Series I); Sam Jones to John C. Breckinridge, October 11, 1862, Jones to Braxton Bragg, October 12, 1862, Jones to Samuel Cooper, October 10, 1862, all in Letters and Telegrams Sent, Department of East Tennessee, March–November, 1862, Chap. II, Vol. 51, Confederate Records, Record Group 109, National Archives. (All records cited from National Archives are in Record Group 109); Nathan B. Forrest to Breckinridge, November 3, 1862, Bragg to Breckinridge, November 5, 1862, B. F. Cheatham to Breckinridge, November 4, 1862, E. W. Cole to Breckinridge, October 30, 31, 1862, all in John C. Breckinridge Papers, Chicago Historical Society.

2 *Official Records*, XVI, Pt. 2, pp. 974, 1000; Don Seitz, *Braxton Bragg, General of the Confederacy* (Columbia, S.C., 1924), 201, 203.

Leonidas Polk to assume temporary command of the army and to follow Breckinridge to Murfreesboro. Bragg knew so little of the Middle Tennessee terrain and the enemy's strength that he told Polk to take any position he thought desirable.[3]

During the last week of October, Bragg continued these hasty preparations. On the day that he left for the capital, Bragg asked General Edmund Kirby Smith to prepare his East Tennessee department troops for the campaign. Bitter over the command wrangling in the Kentucky expedition, Kirby Smith flatly refused. Bragg boarded the Richmond train not knowing if Kirby Smith's army would be available for support. He then remained in Richmond for a week, conferring with Davis and General Samuel Cooper. On October 31, Bragg presented a written memorandum to Davis requesting permission for the operation. Richmond gave its official consent the next day—four days after the army had already begun to move toward Murfreesboro.[4]

Bragg's haste was motivated by several factors. There had been mounting criticism by late October among border state congressmen because of the Kentucky retreat. There was a general demand as well to mitigate the Kentucky loss by an occupation of Middle Tennessee. Too, Bragg believed the fertile valleys of the Elk, Duck, and Stone's rivers would restock the army's diminishing food and storage. More important, Middle Tennessee seemed the only real choice Bragg had for continued operations. He could not remain in East Tennessee or at Chattanooga. This was Kirby Smith's domain, and the two generals had already endured constant command hassles during the Kentucky invasion. A position in North Alabama also seemed ill-advised. The terrain was a poor supplier of foodstuffs, and such a recessed position would open East Tennessee and Chattanooga to possible seizure. There seemed no alternative but to move into Middle Tennessee.

Bragg's error was not so much his choice of destination as the haste with which he committed the army. Several key problems seemed to be almost ignored. The most obvious was that the army was in no condition for another offensive move. A curious myth has long existed that Bragg departed from Kentucky laden with foodstuffs and other stores. This notion was partially the result of army politics. Kirby Smith attempted to blame Bragg for the retreat. He charged that it was un-

---

3 Special Orders No. 17, Dept. No. 2, October 23, 1862, in Leonidas Polk Papers, University of the South Library, Sewanee, hereinafter cited as Polk Papers, Sewanee; Seitz, *Bragg*, 201.

4 Edmund Kirby Smith to Bragg, October 23, 1862, in William P. Palmer Collection of Braxton Bragg Papers, Western Reserve Historical Society, Cleveland, hereinafter cited as Bragg Papers, Western Reserve; Mobile *Register*, November 1, 8, 1862; *Official Records*, XVI, Pt. 2, pp. 384, 386.

necessary, since the army had retreated with a wealth of supplies. Faced with rising criticism, Bragg tried to salvage a semblance of victory by claiming that he had returned from Kentucky with vast supplies.

Rumors generally typical of war also created the story. The public knew little of what was occurring in Kentucky in early October, due to poor communications through the Cumberland Mountains. Newspapers filled this lack with fanciful stories of Buell's army being smashed at Perryville, and Louisville being on the verge of capitulation. Even when it was known that Bragg was retreating, the rumors continued. Strange tales came out of the Cumberlands. Rumor claimed that Bragg now had a huge train of stores garnered from Lexington and Frankfort, and droves of cattle beyond number were reported. By the end of October even War Department officials believed that Bragg had a forty-mile-long train of rich stores.[5]

Not until early November was the truth known—that Bragg's men were on the verge of sheer physical collapse. They were poorly clothed and shod, and half-starved as well. The wagons mainly contained weapons Bragg had taken into Kentucky with hopes of arming the people. While some cattle were brought out and some merchandise purchased, there was no rich wagon train.[6]

Instead, the army's retreat had been one of incredible suffering—a two-hundred-mile march across rocky, muddy roads in bad weather. Many troops were barefoot and had only tattered scraps of clothing. They subsisted on parched corn and drank polluted water from roadside pools where dead livestock lay. The situation was worsened in late October by a severe snowfall which was the first October snow in the memory of East Tennessee's older residents. By November 1 six inches lay on the ground. The army possessed practically no tents or blankets, and many troops collapsed under the hardships of bad weather and little food. Widespread outbreaks of typhoid, scurvy, dysentery, and pneumonia struck the army. Emergency hospitals were hastily set up as far south as North Georgia. By November 12 fifteen thousand men were lodged in East Tennessee hospitals alone.[7]

The army had nearly starved on the retreat. Due to matters of conflicting departmental authority, General Sam Jones did not have ready, in

5 Bragg's official report of Kentucky campaign, in Bragg Papers, Western Reserve; Augusta *Chronicle and Sentinel*, October 25, November 2, 1862; Mobile *Register*, October 31, 1862; Kirby Smith, "The Kentucky Campaign" (MS in Edmund Kirby Smith Papers, Southern Historical Society Collection, University of North Carolina; all collections at University of North Carolina hereinafter cited as UNC).

6 Mobile *Register*, November 9, 11, 1862.

7 Kirby Smith to wife, November 12, 1862, in Kirby Smith Papers, UNC; Alfred J. Vaughan, *Personal Record of the Thirteenth Regiment, Tennessee Infantry, By Its Old Commander* (Memphis, 1897), 23–24.

October, the several hundred thousand rations expected by Bragg. An early fall drought had also burned many East Tennessee crops. By October 22 Kirby Smith estimated that ten thousand of his men were scattered through East Kentucky looking for food.[8]

Matters improved little when Bragg reached East Tennessee. Since the previous autumn, the government had insisted that the rich farmland of Tennessee was to be preserved for the army in Virginia. Albert Sidney Johnston had not been allowed to subsist from the Nashville depot. These supplies were reserved for Virginia, and Johnston was required to live off the country.

Also Lee's army demanded priority on food in late 1862. While Bragg was in Kentucky, Commissary General Lucius Northrop's agents had scoured Middle Tennessee for corn, beef, and hogs. By paying higher prices than Bragg's agents, Northrop's agents had stripped Middle Tennessee of food by the end of November. Thousands of bushels of wheat and barrels of flour, over 2 million pounds of bacon, thousands of heads of cattle, and almost 100,000 hogs were withdrawn to the commissary depot at Atlanta.

Desperate, Bragg sent agents as far south as Columbus, Georgia, to purchase corn. His complaints to Northrop availed nothing. Northrop insisted that the Tennessee supplies were for Lee's army alone. Bragg was expected to live off the country—one already foraged by the Federal army in the summer of 1862 and by Northrop's agents.[9]

As a result of these hardships, Bragg's army almost disintegrated even as the new campaign began. There was widespread desertion and straggling, particularly by border state troops. Although he left Bryantsville with sixteen thousand effectives, Kirby Smith, near Cumberland Gap, had only six thousand men. By mid-November some stragglers had returned. Still, one-third of Kirby Smith's East Tennessee force alone was gone, and its strength was listed as only one-half that of the summer. Bragg's own two corps were depleted by desertion, illness, and Kentucky casualties. By early November some of Bragg's regiments were reduced

8 Buell described Bragg's line of retreat as "almost a desert." D. C. Buell to Henry Halleck, October 17, 1862, in General Don Carlos Buell Papers, Fondren Library, Rice University; J. P. Austin, *The Blue and the Gray* (Atlanta, 1899), 53; Mobile *Register*, October 31, 1862; Kate Cumming, *Gleanings from the Southland* (Birmingham, 1896), 86; *Official Records*, XVI, Pt. 2, p. 962; Kirby Smith to wife, October 24, 1862, in Kirby Smith Papers, UNC.

9 *Official Records*, IV, pp. 444, 452, XXIII, Pt. 2, pp. 625, 648–49; Joseph E. Johnston to James Seddon, February 25, March 21, 1863, in Joseph E. Johnston Papers, College of William and Mary Library, hereinafter cited as Johnston Papers, William and Mary; Chattanooga *Daily Rebel*, December 20, 1862; Mobile *Register*, November 11, 1862.

to one hundred men, and he lamented that only thirty thousand men could be mustered for the new campaign.[10]

The poor condition of the army was equaled by its problems of organization. One such problem involved Bragg's relationship with neighboring departments. In October the Mississippi segment of Bragg's department was detached. The new command, called the Department of Mississippi and East Louisiana, was led by General John C. Pemberton. Bragg's Second Department's jurisdiction was now more constricted. Actually Bragg no longer had a base. Before moving to Kentucky, his headquarters had been at Tupelo, supported by depots at Meridian and Jackson. All of this now was under Pemberton's authority.[11]

Bragg felt the constriction of his boundaries elsewhere. During the Kentucky invasion his commissary and quartermaster depots had been placed temporarily at Chattanooga, which was not even in his department. He had no ordnance depot, and no place where his weapons could be repaired. With the loss of Mississippi to Pemberton and the retention of East Tennessee by Kirby Smith, Bragg's efforts in recruiting were also crippled. By October he was reduced to recruiting in Alabama, northern Georgia, and a small part of Middle Tennessee.

Yet the most acute departmental problem was Bragg's relationship to Kirby Smith. That young general's initial refusal to join the Middle Tennessee effort sorely embarrassed Bragg. He could not order Kirby Smith to cooperate, yet East Tennessee was his only genuine hope of reinforcement. Nor could Bragg even obtain the return of all of the troops loaned to Kirby Smith during the summer. Kirby Smith had returned General Patrick Cleburne's division to Bragg in Kentucky. But he made no gesture to send back General John McCown's division. Instead, McCown's seven thousand troops had been incorporated neatly into the Army of East Tennessee as the Second Division.[12]

The government moved slowly to resolve these criticial departmental differences. On October 22 Kirby Smith had sent a personal emissary to President Davis with a letter critical of Bragg's conduct in Kentucky. Seven days later, after his conversation with Bragg, Davis replied to Smith with a sympathetic but firm note. In effect he offered Kirby Smith a choice—either relinquish part of his army to Bragg, or personally go with Bragg to Middle Tennessee. Two days later, the government

10 Kirby Smith to wife, November 8, 12, 20, 1862, in Kirby Smith Papers, UNC; *Official Records*, XVI, Pt. 2, p. 975; XX, Pt. 2, p. 376.

11 *Official Records*, XX, Pt. 2. p. 394; Seitz, *Bragg*, 209–10; Robert Hartje, *Van Dorn: The Life and Times of a Confederate General* (Nashville, 1967) , 240–51.

12 Kirby Smith to Bragg, October 23, 1862, in Bragg Papers, Western Reserve; Colonel George Brent Diary, *ibid; Official Records*, XX, Pt. 2, p. 386.

gave Bragg authority to use the East Tennessee forces "for such time as the exigency of the operation may demand." [13]

The problem was far from settled even after the army was already committed. The government gave Kirby Smith the final authority as to how many troops Bragg could take. It also left to that officer's discretion the decision whether he would actually go with Bragg. Thus Bragg's own two corps left for the Murfreesboro front with no real guarantee of support. Pressured by the government, Kirby Smith offered the equivalent of a corps—McCown's division and that of General Carter Stevenson. The first of these began leaving Knoxville for Chattanooga on November 9. However, Bragg was still uncertain whether Kirby Smith planned to go with his troops.

Not until early December would the young general shelve his bitterness temporarily and rejoin his troops at Murfreesboro. His tardiness forced Bragg to delay needed reorganization until late November and early December. Until then, the old two-corps system, with Generals William Hardee and Leonidas Polk commanding, would be retained.[14] Their presence portended more trouble, for by November, the army was shaken by quarrels between Bragg and his corps leaders. Like earlier army commanders, Bragg was to experience that high echelon discord which preceded and followed each campaign.

The October-November feuds heralded the beginning of a semi-organized anti-Bragg movement within the army. The opposition group would be nurtured by the post-Murfreesboro quarrels of January and February, and the renewal of the Kentucky campaign dispute in March and April. Gradually the anti-Bragg element was to collect into three groups: Kentucky and Tennessee officers embittered by failure in the border country; various generals who fell out with Bragg for assorted reasons; and Polk, Hardee, and their admiring staffs and division officers.

Two of these elements were very much present in October. Bragg had never established good relations with border state commanders. From his first associations with them at the Corinth concentration in March, 1862, Bragg had been contemptuous of border state officers. He partially blamed the Shiloh failure on their alleged lack of discipline, and referred to them as "Polk's mob." Later he distrusted Tennesseans to the point that he disliked to brigade them together. After the Kentucky invasion he labeled Kentucky men as cowards who did not deserve liberation by the Confederates. His preliminary official report in October

13 *Official Records,* XX, Pt. 2, p. 384; also Jefferson Davis to Kirby Smith, October 29, 1862, Dr. S. A. Smith to Mrs. Kirby Smith, October 22, 1862, in Kirby Smith Papers, UNC.
14 Kirby Smith to wife, November 8, 1862, in Kirby Smith Papers, UNC.

blamed the campaign's failure on lack of support by Kentucky civilians.[15]

By November, his feelings were heartily reciprocated by Kentucky and Tennessee officers. Some were angered by the retreat, others were incensed at Bragg's explanation of failure. John Forsyth, editor of the Mobile *Register*, attempted to defend Bragg in a published account of the campaign. Forsyth echoed Bragg's charge that the Kentucky people had behaved cowardly, and reminded his readers that at Bryantsville, prominent Kentuckians such as General Simon Buckner had voted to retreat. Forsyth was answered by the popular, but nonfunctioning Confederate governor of Kentucky, Richard Hawes. Hawes, who had been unseated when the Federals seized Frankfort on the very day of his inauguration, assailed Bragg in the Richmond *Enquirer*. He maintained that the cause of failure was Bragg's own incompetence.[16]

This kind of criticism was easier to weather than the bitterness among his corps leaders. Relations between Bragg and Polk had been less than pleasant since their first service together in the Corinth concentration. Bragg had never considered Polk a soldier, had criticized his discipline procedures, and had even implied that the loss of Tennessee and Kentucky in 1861 was in large measure Polk's fault. However, it was the Kentucky expedition which provided the final break. In Kentucky, Bragg had placed Polk in immediate command of the army. Now he believed that Polk had exhibited poor generalship. Worse, Bragg was angered when Polk's November report placed the commander in a bad light. Polk charged that he had known that General Don Carlos Buell's main army was concentrating at Perryville, and had warned Bragg of this danger repeatedly.[17]

It further angered Bragg that Polk, in October, took his side of the case directly to the government. October saw Polk at his best—or worst. The fifty-six-year-old former Episcopal bishop possessed immense power both in and out of the army. His paternal manner made him a favorite with the soldiers in the ranks. More important, Polk had powerful influence due to important friendships and his background. He had

15 Bragg to wife, March 23, April 8, 1862, in William K. Bixby Collection of Braxton Bragg Papers, Missouri Historical Society, St. Louis, hereinafter cited as Bragg Papers, Missouri; Nathaniel C. Hughes, Jr., *General William J. Hardee: Old Reliable* (Baton Rouge, 1965), 119; Bragg to wife, November 9, 1862, quoted in Seitz, *Bragg*, 206–207; *Official Records*, XVI, Pt. 2, p. 1088.

16 G. A. Henry to L. T. Wigfall, October 26, 1862, in Wigfall Family Papers, Library of Congress, hereinafter cited as Wigfall Papers, DLC; Chattanooga *Daily Rebel*, December 4, 1862; James Phelan to Bragg, December 4, 1862, in Bragg Papers, Western Reserve; Hughes, *Hardee*, 133–34; H. C. Clay to "Dear Sister," December 26, 1862, in Clement Clay Papers, National Archives.

17 Bragg to wife, March 23, 1862, in Bragg Papers, Missouri; Hughes, *Hardee*, 119; *Official Records*, XVI, Pt. 1, pp. 1095, 1110.

been raised in the wealthy planter society of Columbia, Tennessee, where a row of elegant Polk family homes lined the Mt. Pleasant Pike. He had been Albert Sidney Johnston's West Point roommate and friend, and Johnston's son, William Preston, was now the President's chief aide regarding Army of Tennessee affairs. These connections plus his own warm friendship with the President strengthened Polk's power base in Richmond.

Polk was as dangerous as he was influential. He seemed to feel that his background as the army's first commander, his friendship with Davis, and possibly other factors gave him the right to transcend normal military channels. He believed himself to be the army's patriarch, the ex officio commander in chief, who could go over his commanders to take matters directly to the President. Thus, beginning in the autumn of 1862, Polk would initiate a clandestine correspondence with Richmond, designed to oust Bragg, which would continue until the following autumn.

Polk had other characteristics which would cause Bragg much grief. A man of unusual personal courage, he was also stubborn and insubordinate. He tended to disregard orders if he did not agree with them. Also, like Bragg himself, Polk was often childish, quarrelsome, and relished petty quarrels. Above all, he still possessed that amazing—and irritating—ability he had shown earlier, to emerge from a bungled operation with a minimum of criticism.[18]

Prior to the Kentucky invasion, relations between Bragg and Hardee had been cordial. But Hardee became disgusted with Bragg's generalship and aligned himself with Polk against Bragg. This alignment was the beginning of the clique which would later direct the opposition within the army during 1863. If Polk's greatest influence lay in his Richmond ties, Hardee probably had more influence among the army's officers. A former West Point commandant and author of a standard text on field tactics, Hardee was, by 1862, respected as a scholar-soldier and as an able corps commander.

Beginning in October, Hardee began to use his influence against Bragg. In a professorial manner, he enjoyed criticism of Bragg's operations, yet he disliked responsibility himself. Hardee specialized in frank

---

18 Mobile *Register*, November 9, 1862; Bragg to Jefferson Davis, May 22, 1863, in Braxton Bragg Papers, Duke University Library; Sam Watkins, *"Co. Aytch," Maury Grays, First Tennessee Regiment, or a Side Show of the Big Show,* ed. Bell I. Wiley (2nd ed.; Jackson, Tenn., 1952), 154; Walter Lord (ed.), *The Fremantle Diary: Being the Journal of Lieutenant Colonel James Arthur Lyon Fremantle, Coldstream Guards, On His Three Months in the Southern States* (Boston, 1954), 111; G. Moxley Sorrel, *Recollections of a Confederate Staff Officer,* ed. Bell I. Wiley (2nd ed.; Jackson, Tenn., 1958), 188.

conversations with his staff, division and brigade officers. In an atmosphere resembling a military academy classroom, he combined direct criticism and innuendo to demolish Bragg's reputation with the junior officers of the Second Corps.

Hardee went further than this. He credited Polk with saving the army from disaster. In November he privately wrote Davis' aide, Colonel William Preston Johnston, labeled Bragg a failure, and made no secret of his desire to see him removed. His official report, penned in December, resembled Polk's greatly. Hardee also insisted that he had known that Buell's main army was at Perryville, but could not convince Bragg to concentrate the main army there.[19]

The quarrels with Hardee and Polk, as well as with Kirby Smith, were detrimental to Bragg's planning. In the midst of preparing the expedition, Bragg was forced to visit Richmond in late October, where he discussed, among other matters, these command differences. Bragg did not know, and would not know until November 8, that Kirby Smith's envoy had preceded him with a criticism of the campaign. Bragg did know it was obvious that the cooperative effort with Kirby Smith had failed. Thus he pressed Davis to appoint an overall theater commander, and recommended General Joseph E. Johnston.[20]

After Bragg's departure from Richmond, two of his corps commanders arrived, evidently to condemn his policies. On November 4 Bragg ordered Polk to report to the capital to confer on the state of affairs in the Second Department. Bragg later maintained that he sent Polk to urge that Johnston be appointed. Polk denied this, and asserted that he went to Richmond to urge Bragg's dismissal. When Davis inquired as to his choice for a replacement, Polk recommended Johnston.[21]

Regardless of the visit's official purpose, Polk took the occasion to

---

19 "Biographical Sketch of Lieut. Genl. William J. Hardee, Selma, Ala., June 1867, by T. B. Roy" (MS in William J. Hardee Papers, Alabama State Department of Archives and History). All collections in this library hereinafter cited as Alabama; see also Jeremy Gilmer to wife, January 14, 1862, in Jeremy F. Gilmer Papers, UNC; General William J. Hardee Service Record, 1861–65, National Archives; Hughes, *Hardee*, 133–34; Hardee's official report of Perryville, December 1, 1862, in William P. Palmer Collection of Confederate Papers, Western Reserve, hereinafter cited as Palmer Papers, Western Reserve.

20 Kirby Smith to wife, October 20, November 8, 11, 20, 23, 1862, Dr. S. A. Smith to Mrs. Kirby Smith, October 22, 1862, Jefferson Davis to Kirby Smith, October 29, 1862, all in Kirby Smith Papers, UNC; Mobile *Register*, November 11, 1862.

21 Special Orders No. 29, Dept. No. 2, November 4, 1862, in Polk Papers, Sewanee; Gilbert E. Govan and James Livingood, *A Different Valor: The Story of General Joseph E. Johnston* (New York, 1956), 162; Joseph H. Parks, *General Leonidas Polk, C.S.A.: The Fighting Bishop* (Baton Rouge, 1962), 279–81; William Polk, *Leonidas Polk, Bishop and General* (New York, 1915), II, 165.

stab Bragg in the back. He discussed the Kentucky campaign with Davis, and argued that Bragg had lost the army's confidence. That same week, Kirby Smith visited Richmond at Davis' request. Like Polk, he urged that Johnston be appointed, and gave his own version of what had occurred in Kentucky.

The entire distasteful episode ended with little being accomplished. Polk left Richmond unsuccessful in his effort to oust Bragg. Hardee, through November, remained publicly hostile to his commander. Nor had Kirby Smith's views changed. He returned to Knoxville muttering that his men would desert if placed again under Bragg. Never had a general begun a campaign in the West with such little support from his lieutenants.[22]

The error of Bragg's haste in committing his army to another offensive was also evidenced in his poor choice of position. Though he knew almost nothing of Middle Tennessee topography, he had fashioned a strategy dependent upon a good choice of ground. By mid-November he directed his plans toward two aims. Scout reports repeatedly indicated that the Nashville fortress was impregnable. Thus Bragg determined to assume a defensive-offensive position at Murfreesboro, and wait for Buell to advance on him. Meanwhile, such a position would enable Bragg to collect foodstuffs and forage from Middle Tennessee.[23]

For these objectives, he had selected the worst possible defensive position. Although Murfreesboro appeared to have certain advantages, its disadvantages were far greater. It is true that the town lay in the rich limestone basin of the Stone's River Valley where foodstuffs and cattle were abundant. But Buell's army had thoroughly scoured the area in July and August, followed by the Nashville garrison in September.[24] Also while Murfreesboro appeared advantageously located astride the Nashville and Chattanooga Railroad, which led to Bragg's

22 Mobile *Register*, November 11, 1862; Govan and Livingood, *A Different Valor*, 132; Polk, *Polk*, II, 165; Parks, *Polk*, 280; Hughes, *Hardee*, 134–35; Kirby Smith to wife, November 8, 1862, in Kirby Smith Papers, UNC.

23 *Official Records*, XX, Pt. 2, pp. 416, 421; W. D. Gale to wife, October 17, 1862, in Gale–Polk Papers, UNC; Chattanooga *Daily Rebel*, October 12, 1862; "Information Received at Engineer Office, Murfreesboro, Tenn. about Entrenchments around Nashville" (MS in Bragg Papers, Western Reserve).

24 Carlton C. Sims (ed.), *A History of Rutherford County* (Murfreesboro, 1947), I, 39; United States Bureau of the Census, *Agriculture of the United States in 1860, Compiled from the Original Returns of the Eighth Census* (Washington, 1864), 136–37.

supply base in Chattanooga,[25] this too was of questionable benefit. For the link was one hundred miles long through the Cumberland Mountains, and two of its bridges at Bridgeport, Alabama, had been destroyed during summer fighting. The Federals, on the other hand, would not have to extend their line of communication since Nashville was only thirty miles from Murfreesboro via a good macadamized pike.

Bragg had no direct pike to Chattanooga for wagon transportation. The main route crossed the Cumberlands at University Place, debouched into the Sequatchie Valley at Jasper, and toiled across Walden's Ridge to the north bank of the Tennessee opposite Chattanooga.

Murfreesboro could be easily flanked. The only approach route blocked was the Nashville and Chattanooga Railroad. On the west, the Federals could advance on the fine Columbia Pike and the parallel Nashville and Decatur Railroad. Between the Columbia and the Murfreesboro pikes, a second road, the Triune Pike, led to Shelbyville. There it intersected the main pike to Chattanooga to the rear of Bragg's position. On the northeast, Murfreesboro could be flanked via the Baird's Mill–Smithville road, and farther northeast, by the pike from Nashville to McMinnville via Lebanon. It would be impossible to anticipate such flanking attempts unless Bragg chose to spread his troops across a fifty-mile-wide front.[26]

A better defensive line was available to the southeast, where the Middle Tennessee plain merged into the outlying ridges of the rugged Highland Rim. The Highland Rim, an oval belt of steep ridges, completely encircles Middle Tennessee. The segment south of Murfreesboro contains a broad front of ridges which reach elevations of thirteen hundred feet. The roads extending through the area from Nashville coursed the Highland Rim at strong gap positions such as Hoover's, Liberty, and Guy's gaps. The main pike to Chattanooga and the railroad were both thus protected, and the distance to the Chattanooga base was greatly shortened. Moreover, such a position would surrender little area in the fertile grain and livestock counties. These productive Middle Tennessee counties lay in the Duck River country and the valley of the Elk River

25 Marcus Wright Diary, October 30, 1862 (printed copy in Confederate Collection, State Archives Library, Nashville, Tennessee, hereinafter all collections in this library cited as Tennessee); Johnston to Cooper, December 6, 1862, in Johnston Papers, William and Mary; *Official Records*, XX, Pt. 2, p. 421; map of Middle Tennessee, in Benjamin F. Cheatham Papers, Tennessee.

26 Bureau of the Census, *Agriculture of the United States in 1860*, 132–33, 136–37; *Official Records*, XXIII, Pt. 1, p. 588, XX, Pt. 2, p. 421; R. S. Bassler, *Stratigraphy of the Central Basin of Tennessee*, Tennessee Division of Geology *Bulletin 38* (Nashville, 1932), 14–15.

to the south, surrounding towns such as Shelbyville, Columbia, Fayette-ville, Winchester, and Pulaski.[27]

Even if the Stone's River country was considered vital to Bragg's commissary agents, the army's presence there was unnecessary. Forrest and Breckinridge had already demonstrated that smaller units could impede Union forage expeditions. Before the arrival of Breckinridge's infantry, Forrest's modest cavalry command had reduced the Federals to foraging only in the small area between Nashville and Franklin.[28]

It is unclear if Bragg ever seriously considered any position besides the one at Murfreesboro. His engineers could offer him little aid. They were both undermanned and disorganized. The former chief engineer, Jeremy Gilmer, had been transferred to Richmond, and not until October was Bragg's department assigned a replacement, Major James Nocquet. The small, black-bearded Frenchman, a former officer in Algeria, knew little of the region's terrain. He did not even arrive in Middle Tennessee until early November, almost a month after Bragg's selection of Mur-freesboro. In mid-November Nocquet did survey the area along Stone's River, and warned Bragg that the terrain north of Murfreesboro had no natural defensive attributes.[29] But Bragg ignored this warning, and on November 24 he boasted to Davis that he was confident of victory along Stone's River.

Bragg's intelligence through early November indicated that Nashville was on the verge of collapse due to a food shortage and that Buell's army, en route there from Kentucky, was both demoralized and dis-organized. Too, Bragg learned in early November that General William S. Rosecrans had replaced Buell as commander of the Army of the Cumberland. Bragg believed this change would require more time for reorganization by the enemy, and he seemed unworried that his scouts reported Rosecrans' army to be almost twice the size of his own.

27 Buell to William B. Hazen, September 5, 1862, Buell to Halleck, October 20, 1862, all in Buell Papers, Rice; John Walker to Major Cumming, December 20, 1862, in Bragg Papers, Western Reserve.

28 James Negley to Colonel Fry, October 13, 15, 1862, Buell to Halleck, October 13, 1862, all in Buell Papers, Rice. Both Buell and Negley reported that Nashville was running low on rations. See also Forrest to Breckinridge, November 1, 2, 8, 9, 10, 1862, Bragg to Breckinridge, November 11, 1862, all in Breckinridge Papers, Chicago. On October 28, the Chattanooga *Daily Rebel* published a letter from a Nashville informant who reported that Negley's men had been living on half and quarter rations for three months. See also Mobile *Register*, November 9, 1862.

29 As late as the spring of 1863, Bragg's engineer service had only thirteen men in all positions. See "List of Officers and Assistants, Engineer Corps, Army of Tennessee, March 16, 1863," in Bragg Papers, Western Reserve; James Nocquet Military Records, Gilmer to "Dear General," October 7, 1862, Nocquet to Judah P. Benjamin, January 21, 1862, all in James Nocquet Military Records Jacket, National Archives; *Official Records*, XX, Pt. 2, p. 396.

His confidence was also based upon estimates of the Federal commissary. Prior to Rosecrans' arrival, Bragg knew the garrison at Nashville had been reduced to quarter rations. In mid-November he believed the Louisville and Nashville Railroad to be out of operation, and he knew that the low water stage of the Cumberland River prevented navigation to the city.[30]

In late November Bragg still based his strategy upon a misguided estimation of Rosecrans' commissary. By November 24 Hardee's and Polk's corps had reached Bragg's temporary headquarters at Tullahoma, prior to moving into position at Murfreesboro. At Tullahoma during the ensuing week, Bragg developed his plans. While the infantry occupied Murfreesboro, he intended for the cavalry to harass Federal supply routes. A fragile plan, Bragg's strategy placed a greatly inferior army thirty miles from the enemy's base.[31]

The heart of his planning demanded good use of his cavalry. Again, Bragg had committed his troops without sufficient attention to the basic requirements for success. Not until he arrived at Tullahoma on November 14 did Bragg begin to reorganize his haphazard cavalry system. Some improvement had been effected by Bragg after he took command in June. He had abolished General Albert Sidney Johnston's old system of assigning a cavalry regiment to each infantry brigade. Bragg had organized the scattered regiments into three effective brigades, commanded by General Nathan Bedford Forrest and Colonels John Morgan and Joseph Wheeler. Too, Bragg had been the first commander to utilize the cavalry against Federal communications with any effect. In July and August, Morgan and Forrest had completely wrecked Buell's supply line on a wide front from Kentucky to northern Alabama.

Still, by mid-November there was need for better organization. Bragg had operated in Kentucky without a chief of cavalry and had yet to form a cavalry corps. Instead, a brigade was assigned to each corps. Also, Bragg rarely massed his cavalry for any full strike on enemy communications, but kept them close in to the main army, usually employed on picket duty or for limited reconnaissance.[32]

30 *Official Records*, XX, Pt. 2, pp. 416, 421–22, 461; Negley to Fry, October 13, 15, 1862, in Buell Papers, Rice; Chattanooga *Daily Rebel*, October 12, 28, 1862; Mobile *Register*, December 17, 1863. Kirby Smith wrote of Bragg, "I believe he underestimates Rosecrantz [*sic*] strength, and does not sufficiently appreciate his enterprise." See Kirby Smith to wife, December 28, 1862, in Kirby Smith Papers, UNC.

31 *Official Records*, XX, Pt. 2, p. 421; Brent Diary, November 20, 22, 24, 1862, in Bragg Papers, Western Reserve.

32 John P. Dyer, "Some Aspects of Cavalry Operations in the Army of Tennessee," *Journal of Southern History*, III (May, 1942), 211–14, 217; David T. Childress, Jr., "Cavalry in the Western Confederacy: A Military Analysis" (M.A. thesis, Mississippi State University, 1961), 6, 18, 19.

The November reorganization still failed to provide effective cavalry utilization. Bragg revamped his now-enlarged cavalry into five brigades. Three were termed regular units, and were commanded by Generals Joseph Wheeler, John Pegram, and John Wharton. The other two, designated for partisan service, were commanded by Forrest and Morgan. Bragg then passed over his senior officer Forrest, and appointed his protégé General Joseph Wheeler as chief of Cavalry.

Small of statue with the air of a bantam cock, Wheeler was only twenty-five years old. He had limited cavalry experience, his service having been in the artillery and infantry until April of 1862. Wheeler's performance thus far did not merit the appointment. He had practically no experience in extended raiding. In Kentucky, where his duty had been mainly reconnaissance, he had not done well. It was Wheeler who, in September, had allowed Buell to approach Bragg near Green River without proper warning. By his own admission, Wheeler had given Bragg what proved to be the erroneous intelligence that Buell was flanking the Confederates from their position near Munfordville. Again, at Bardstown, Wheeler had failed to give adequate warning of Buell's approach, and at Perryville he did not provide adequate intelligence of the size of the Federal column.

Several factors caused Bragg to select Wheeler over Forrest. Bragg considered the non-professional Forrest a mere partisan, with few capabilities for high command. But Wheeler, a West Point graduate, possessed a suavity, love of drill, and a vocabulary that outshone the rough-hewn Forrest. Too, Wheeler probably knew how to manipulate Bragg. He had done so in the earlier days at Pensacola in 1861 when he served under Bragg as an artillery officer. At first, Bragg had resented Wheeler's direct promotion from lieutenant to colonel, a move pressed by influential Alabama friends. But Wheeler's penchant for drill and ceremony won Bragg over. Too, he was devoutly loyal to Bragg. Repeatedly undercut by his subordinates, Bragg relished Wheeler's friendship.[33]

Wheeler probably gained Bragg's favor also because he managed to receive a better press than did some other officers. A facile writer, the young Wheeler's reports could transform a moderately successful, limited strike into a massive raid. His field reports often contained phrases of bravado which contrasted with the awkward, more realistic appraisals

33 T. C. De Leon, *Joseph Wheeler: The Man, the Statesman, the Soldier* (Atlanta, 1899) , 120; John W. Du Bose, *General Joseph Wheeler and the Army of Tennessee* (New York, 1912) , 113; William C. Oates, *War between the Union and the Confederacy and Its Lost Opportunities with a History of the Fifteenth Alabama Regiment* (New York, 1905) , 469–70; John P. Dyer, *Fightin' Joe Wheeler* (Baton Rouge, 1941) , 24–25, 28, 70.

of Forrest. In fact, despite his mediocre performance in Kentucky, Wheeler was hailed as a hero of the campaign by November. He was remembered for the only real service he had performed, that of skillfully guarding the retreat through Cumberland Gap.[34]

The reorganized cavalry under Wheeler brought about slightly better order, but serious problems remained. Wheeler was forced to divide his time between being chief of cavalry and commanding his own brigade. Bragg's system of attaching one regular brigade to each corps meant that often Wharton, Pegram, and others reported not to Wheeler but to infantry commanders. Too, Wheeler was inexperienced in both strategic planning and administration. Lacking time or ability, or possibly both, he refrained from venturing any strategic proposals, and behaved more as a clerk. Bragg, now also troubled with problems of infantry reorganization, evidently was giving less attention to his cavalry in late November, and as a result those brigades were misused.

Since mid-October Bragg had planned to take the Murfreesboro position, and, by use of his cavalry, to stymie a Federal thrust. Yet not until mid-December did he begin to deploy cavalry against Rosecrans' communications—the very tactic he considered essential to Confederate success. Bragg's delay—which gave the new Union commander a month's reprieve to store rations at Nashville—occurred despite intelligence warnings as early as mid-November that long supply trains were crossing the Cumberland River into Nashville.[35]

When Bragg did decide cavalry policy, his plans seemed vague and contradictory. In late November, Pemberton appealed for aid in interrupting General U. S. Grant's communications along the Mobile and Ohio and Mississippi Central railroads. Whereupon, Bragg informed Davis on November 21 that he was throwing a large force commanded by Forrest into West Tennessee. Three days later, Bragg had outlined a vague and different plan whereby Forrest and Morgan would operate against Rosecrans' communications. Neither plan was put in operation in November.[36]

Bragg's December planning seemed equally vague. Heavy recruiting swelled his cavalry to seven brigades. None of them was used directly to stall the collection of supplies at Nashville. Instead, Bragg either dispersed them or held them on picket duty. On December 10 Bragg changed plans again and sent Forrest into West Tennessee on a fifteen-

[34] See Bragg's Perryville report, May 20, 1863 (MS in Bragg Papers, Western Reserve) ; *Official Records*, XVI, Pt. 1, p. 1112, Pt. 2, pp. 965, 971.

[35] Forrest to Breckinridge, November 10, 1862, in Breckinridge Papers, Chicago; Childress, "Cavalry in the Western Confederacy," 27.

[36] *Official Records*, XX, Pt. 2, p. 421; Seitz, *Bragg*, 209–10.

day raid. For most of December, Morgan's troopers did little more than harass unimportant Federal outposts northeast of Nashville. Then Morgan returned to Murfreesboro to prepare for his December 14 wedding. While "hosannas to the heroic Morgan" were sounded through some camps, and gold braids, cake, and wine were readied, the cavalry remained idle. Through December, Wheeler, Pegram, and Wharton were kept on outpost duty along the Stone's River.

With Forrest absent, Morgan seemed the logical cavalry commander to interrupt Rosecrans' communications. On December 22 Morgan, with thirty-one hundred of Bragg's best horsemen, drove northward into central Kentucky, He severely damaged the Louisville and Nashville Railroad, north of Green River, but the raid, probably Morgan's best, was too late. Already the Nashville commissary depots were full, and one-half of Bragg's cavalry was absent from Middle Tennessee.[37]

37 James Chalmers, "Forrest and His Campaigns," *Southern Historical Society Papers,* VII (1879), 460; hereinafter cited as *SHSP; Official Records,* XX, Pt. 1, pp. 62, 155–56; Charles E. Robert, "At Murfreesboro Just before the Battle," *Confederate Veteran,* XVI (December, 1908), 632; Hughes, *Hardee,* 138; John A. Wyeth, *That Devil Forrest: Life of General Nathan Bedford Forrest* (New York, 1899), 92–125; George Winchester Diary, December 8, 1862, in Confederate Collection, Tennessee.

two

The Grand Design Falters

It was bitterly cold along Stone's River during early December. Snow had begun to fall on November 28, and on that same day, Bragg's infantry had reached Murfreesboro from its temporary camps along the Duck River. By December 5 a thick layer of snow covered the cedar glades around Murfreesboro. There, Bragg's infantry, woefully short of winter clothing, awaited Rosecrans' advance from Nashville.

In December two new, serious command problems beset the western army. The more pressing of the two was the complete disorganization of Bragg's infantry. The second was Confederate political intrigue.

On November 22 Bragg had reoganized his infantry into three corps, commanded by Polk, Hardee, and Kirby Smith. To this new force, Bragg had affixed the title it would wear for the war's duration—the Army of Tennessee.[1]

At first it appeared that Bragg had brought together a well-organized command system. Polk's First Corps contained three divisions, all led by veterans. The rough, nonprofessional General Frank Cheatham had commanded a division since the Shiloh battle. He was joined by General Jones Withers, an old Bragg ally who had served with the general in 1861 at Pensacola. General John C. Breckinridge—a former Kentucky senator, Vice-President, and 1860 Presidential candidate—led the third division. By April of 1862 Breckinridge had risen to the rank of major general, a promotion due more to politics than ability. Tall, handsome,

1 *Official Records*, XX, Pt. 2, pp. 411, 417.

30

dapper, and tremendously popular in Kentucky, Breckinridge was a useful propaganda instrument.[2]

Hardee's corps also had veteran officers. The first division was commanded by the Irish immigrant General Patrick Cleburne. Cleburne in December replaced General Simon Buckner, who was transferred to the garrison at Mobile. Already distinguished as a brigade commander, Cleburne would later be known as the West's finest division leader. His division was a model of discipline, cleanliness, and competence under fire. Cleburne himself was an enigma. A former British soldier and Helena, Arkansas, lawyer, he had joined the army as a private in 1861; by December, 1862, he was a major general. No other officer seemed to possess so intense a desire to improve himself and his command. Cleburne had some mystical driving force, labeled by his enemies as ambition and by his friends as sheer devotion to the Confederacy. Shy and tightlipped, he was not easy to know, save perhaps, by his close friend Hardee.[3]

Hardee's other division leader, General Patton Anderson, was also competent. Anderson's prewar career had been varied—a Mississippi physician, a United States marshal in the Washington Territory, and a member of the Florida secession convention. He was among that cadre of hardcore Bragg supporters who had served with the general at Pensacola and Mobile.[4]

A third corps was organized from the troops Kirby Smith had loaned from East Tennessee. In early December Kirby Smith arrived to join the two divisions he had sent a few weeks before. General Carter Stevenson, commanding the first division, had been a West Point classmate of Hardee and Beauregard, and had served in East Tennessee since early 1862. General John McCown, commanding the second division, had been with the Tennessee army since May of 1861, when it had still been under state control.[5]

Scarcely had this organization been effected, however, when, early in December, it fell apart. On December 12 to achieve better balance among

2 "Benjamin F. Cheatham's Military Record" (MS in Cheatham Papers, Tennessee); James D. Porter, *Tennessee*, Vol. VIII of Clement Evans (ed.), *Confederate Military History* (Atlanta, 1899), 302–303; Austin, *The Blue and the Gray*, 47; Joab Goodson to "Niece," September 28, 1863, in Joab Goodson Correspondence, Chickamauga–Chattanooga National Military Park Library; Bragg to Davis, December 1, 1863, in Braxton Bragg Letters, Houghton Library, Harvard University.

3 William Hardee, "Biographical Sketch of Major-General Patrick R. Cleburne," *SHSP*, XXXI (1903), 161–62; George W. Gordon, "General P. R. Cleburne," *ibid*, XVIII (1890), 269; Irving A. Buck, *Cleburne and His Command*, ed. Thomas R. Hay (2nd ed.; Jackson, Tenn., 1959), 19–64.

4 "General Patton Anderson," *Confederate Veteran*, IX (August, 1901), 340–41; Seitz, *Bragg*, 79.

5 Porter, *Tennessee*, 321.

Polk's and Hardee's corps, Anderson's division was broken up between the two corps, and Breckinridge's division was assigned to Hardee's command. With Buckner's departure and with Cleburne's assignment as well, the new structure gave Polk the divisions of Withers and Cheatham, and Hardee now had Breckinridge's and Cleburne's divisions.

Worse, the entire third corps was abolished in December. On December 15 the government ordered Bragg to detach General Carter Stevenson with ten thousand troops to reinforce Pemberton in Mississippi. Since this left only one division in the corps, Kirby Smith's command was eliminated. McCown's division was temporarily attached to Hardee's command, and Kirby Smith returned to East Tennessee.[6]

The confusion of internal reorganization was minor compared to the problems imposed by sweeping change in the overall western command. On November 24 the army became part of a broad new theater commanded by General Joseph E. Johnston. Johnston was assigned the territory between the Blue Ridge Mountains of North Carolina and the Mississippi River. He was to lead the departments of Kirby Smith, Bragg, and Pemberton.[7]

Johnston's appointment was the outcome of several considerations. By the late autumn of 1862 Davis was reassessing his departmental strategy. Prior to the summer, departmental organization was based upon fairly rigid lines of operation. Each department possessed a certain territory to defend and a particular objective.

The transition began with the invasion of Kentucky. That campaign was a joint effort by three departments: Bragg's, Kirby Smith's, and the Mississippi commands of Generals Earl Van Dorn and Sterling Price which were incorporated into a new department in October. Cooperation between the departments had failed badly, a fact President Davis admitted in late October. By early November, Davis and the western leaders sensed the need for some overall planning.[8]

This need became more acute by November because of rising Federal strength in the West. Bragg, with a scant 40,000, faced a reported 60,000 at Nashville under Rosecrans, who allegedly had 35,000 supporting troops on the railroad to Louisville. Bragg's only hope of reinforcement was the garrison of less than 10,000 left by Kirby Smith in East Tennessee. On the Mississippi front, Pemberton commanded only 25,000

6 Seitz, *Bragg*, 79; Special Orders No. 7, December 15, 1862, in Johnston Papers, William and Mary; *Official Records*, XX, Pt. 2, pp. 412, 461; W. L. Clay to "Dear Sister," in Clement Clay Papers, National Archives.

7 Special Orders No. 275, November 14, 1862, in Johnston Papers, William and Mary. This copy is incorrectly dated. See Johnston to Wigfall, December 3, 1863, in Wigfall Papers, DLC.

8 Davis to Kirby Smith, October 29, 1862, in Kirby Smith Papers, UNC.

men opposed to the combined armies of Generals U. S. Grant and William Sherman. On a wide front from Memphis to Corinth, Grant and Sherman had a force estimated to be between 60,000 and 100,000 men, while General Nathaniel P. Banks was reported to have another 30,000 troops in southern Louisiana. To combat such odds, Davis and others now believed that a supervisory officer was needed to deploy western strength.[9]

By November there was much pressure on Davis to make such an appointment. Bragg, Polk, and Kirby Smith had recommended it. Davis' Secretary of War, George Randolph, also supported the plan. Too, Davis might have believed such an appointment would silence critics in the army and in Congress and enable Bragg to retain his position.[10]

Who would be chosen to lead the western army? Only three available officers outranked Bragg—Generals Robert E. Lee, P. G. T. Beauregard, and Joseph E. Johnston. With Lee busy in Virginia, Davis must choose between his two chief enemies among the military. His relations with Beauregard had been poor since the fall of 1861. The bad feelings intensified in June of 1862 when Davis removed the Louisiana officer from command of the Army of Tennessee at Tupelo. To Beauregard's supporters, Davis' explanation that Beauregard had technically deserted his post while on an unauthorized sick leave was a guise for the President's hatred of the general. [11]

At first, most supporters for a theater commander favored Beauregard. In September a delegation of some sixty senators and representatives petitioned Davis for his appointment. They asserted that Beauregard's health was improved enough for him to resume command.

But Davis had no intention of reappointing Beauregard. On September 13 when Senators Edward Sparrow and T. J. Semmes of Louisiana presented the petition, Davis was adamant, stating flatly that it was out of the question. He reiterated this determination on October 29 in a letter to Kirby Smith, declaring that in his opinion Beauregard

9 Archer Jones, *Confederate Strategy from Shiloh to Vicksburg* (Baton Rouge, 1961), 105–107; John C. Pemberton to Johnston, December 4, 1862, Johnston to Cooper, December 5, 6, 1862, all in Johnston Papers, William and Mary.

10 Phelan to Bragg, December 4, 1862, in Bragg Papers, Western Reserve; W. L. Clay to "Dear Sister," in Clement Clay Papers, National Archives; Davis to Kirby Smith, October 29, 1862, in Kirby Smith Papers, UNC; Mobile *Register*, November 8, 1862.

11 Alfred Roman, *Military Operations of General Beauregard in the War Between the States 1861 to 1865* (New York, 1883) I, 411–19; Beauregard to Thomas Jordan, July 13, 1862, in P. G. T. Beauregard Papers, Duke.

had been tried, had failed, and had left the army in a demoralized state.[12]

By October the remaining candidate was Johnston. The origins of the Davis-Johnston dislike, which later would greatly influence the fate of the Army of Tennessee, were ascribed to several causes. Some attributed the men's mutual dislike to an alleged fight when both were West Point cadets. Others cited an incident in 1854 when Secretary of War Davis turned down Johnston's application to be appointed the colonel of a new regiment. Still others blamed an 1860 episode, when Senator Davis opposed Johnston's appointment as Quartermaster General. A social quarrel in 1861 between their wives was also said to have sparked the dispute.[13]

If the men had not been enemies before the war, their differences in 1861 would have created a rift. Early in that year, while Johnston commanded in Virginia, the two disagreed over the need to concentrate troops there. After the battle of Manassas, a fight began concerning Johnston's rank in the Confederate Army. Because of the rank he had held in the United States Army, Johnston had expected to be named ranking officer in the Confederacy. But Davis disagreed, and on August 31 placed both Lee and Albert Sidney Johnston ahead of the general in his list of nominations sent to Congress. Johnston considered this a personal affront, and on September 6 sent Davis a famous note insisting that he deserved the rank of first general, to which Davis replied, with an equally stiff note of refusal, and the dreary, war-long quarrel had commenced. [14]

Their ill feeling mounted during early 1862. Repeatedly Davis and Johnston disagreed about strategic matters in Virginia. Johnston also feuded with the new Secretary of War, Judah P. Benjamin, over what the

[12] Thomas Semmes, "Notes of an Interview with the President relative to transferring back General Beauregard to the command of Department No. 2," in *Review of Certain Remarks Made by the President When Requested to Restore General Beauregard to the Command of Department No. 2* (Charleston, 1863), 17–19 (Copy of pamphlet in South Caroliniana Library, University of South Carolina, hereinafter all collections cited as South Carolina). See also Charles Villeré *et al.,* to Jefferson Davis, n.d., *ibid.,* pp. 15–16; Davis to Kirby Smith, October 29, 1862, in Kirby Smith Papers, UNC.

[13] Ellsworth Eliot, Jr., *West Point in the Confederacy* (New York, 1941), 81; John W. Du Bose, "Chronicles of the Canebrake," *Alabama Historical Quarterly,* IX (Winter, 1947), 539.

[14] Johnston to Davis, July 24, August 3, November 10, 1861, all in Joseph E. Johnston Papers, Duke; Johnston to Wigfall, April 3, 1865, in Wigfall Papers, DLC; Johnston to "Dear Colonel," in Georgia Portfolio, Duke; Davis to Johnston, September 12, 1861, in Varina Davis, *Jefferson Davis, Ex-President of the Confederate States* (New York, 1890), II, 154, see also pp. 138–59; Davis to James Lyons, August 30, 1878, in Dunbar Rowland (ed.), *Jefferson Davis, Constitutionalist, His Letters, Papers and Speeches* (Jackson, Miss., 1923), VIII, 257; J. A. Early to Fitzhugh Lee, May 14, 1877, in Rowland (ed.), *Davis,* VII, 554–55.

general considered the secretary's improper methods of dealing with problems in the army. More disagreement with Davis followed in April, over the defense of Richmond. [15]

Johnston's severe wounds at the Battle of Seven Pines, in May, forced a showdown. During his several months of recuperation in Richmond, Lee commanded the army. Although Lee evidently considered his command only temporary, pending Johnston's recovery, Davis apparently did not agree. For with Beauregard's removal from the command of the western army in June, the South's two main armies were again under the control of friends of the Davis administration.

Johnston remained in Richmond until November when he was considered well enough to return to active service. His recuperation followed closely on the pleas of Bragg, Kirby Smith, and others for his appointment, and probably because he had no other man available, Davis, on November 24, finally gave Johnston the command of the western theater.[16] Five days later, after being feted at a breakfast given by his congressional supporters, Johnston left on the arduous five-day rail trip to Chattanooga and the new experiment in command.

Johnston's appointment heralded the beginning of the Army of Tennessee's second basic problem during the 1862-65 period—Confederate political intrigue. Gradually, beginning in December, Johnston began to represent in the West the aims of the anti-Davis faction in Congress. The effect of the army's involvement in political matters would not be strongly felt until late 1863, after the Chattanooga campaign.

Clearly, Johnston had powerful friends in Congress who were opponents of the administration. Whether these men were more interested in Johnston's success or Davis' failure is uncertain. Some, like Senator Henry Foote of Tennessee, had been unfriendly to Davis before the war. Some, including Senators R. M. T. Hunter of Virginia and Edward Sparrow of Louisiana, became alienated from Davis in 1862 and gradually drifted into the Johnston camp. Senator Louis Wigfall of Texas, was among those who seemed to have genuine confidence in Johnston. A former brigade commander under the general, Wigfall had become his Richmond confidante by the autumn of 1862. Johnston had recup-

15 Bradley T. Johnston, *A Memoir of the Life and Public Service of General Joseph E. Johnston* (Baltimore, 1891), 254–55; Eliot, *West Point in the Confederacy*, 82–84; Robert Douthat Meade, "The Relations between Judah P. Benjamin and Jefferson Davis: Some New Light on the Working of the Confederate Machine," *Journal of Southern History*, V (November, 1939), 473.

16 Govan and Livingood, *A Different Valor*, 158–62, 165; Johnston, *Johnston*, 305; Johnston to Wigfall, January 26, 1863, in Mrs. D. Giraud Wright, *A Southern Girl in '61—the War-Time Memories of a Confederate Senator's Daughter* (New York, 1905), 122–23.

erated from his wounds in Wigfall's home, and shared a warm friendship with the Texan. Frequently Johnston asserted that Wigfall was his only true political friend in Richmond.[17]

Even Wigfall may have been using Johnston. Although he was John ston's champion in December, in September he had been in Beauregard's camp. Perhaps Wigfall and others turned to Johnston only after Davis had declared in September that he would not reappoint Beauregard if the whole world requested it.

Wigfall had fallen out with Davis in November when he learned that his recommendation for a successor to George Randolph, who had resigned as Secretary of War, apparently was given no consideration. For this he never forgave Davis.[18]

Meanwhile, Johnston's most pressing problem was the ambiguous nature of his command. Both in geographical scope and authority, his command was confusing. Johnston soon discovered that the western departments were geographically misaligned. He was responsible not only for the three main western departments, but for the District of the Gulf as well. Yet this Gulf command, which embraced parts of Georgia, Alabama, and Florida, was under Bragg's jurisdiction though it was closer to Pemberton. The two main departmental armies, Bragg's and Pemberton's, were separated by several hundred miles of sparse terrain, Grant's army, and the Tennessee River. Any combined operations had to rely on a circuitous rail route from Jackson via Mobile, Atlanta, and Chattanooga, to Murfreesboro.[19]

On the day he was assigned, Johnston, had complained of these matters, arguing to Cooper that Bragg's and Pemberton's armies were too widely separated for effective coordination. Johnston pointed out that Bragg was closer to Lee than to Pemberton, and contended that his own command was thus miscast. Instead, Johnston averred that he should command the Mississippi Valley, with control over armies in Arkansas, Missouri, and Mississippi. Again, after arriving at Chattanooga, John-

[17] James Lyons to W. T. Walthall, July 31, 1878, in Rowland (ed.), *Jefferson Davis,* VIII, 215; John Reagan, *Memoirs with Special Reference to Secession and the Civil War,* ed. by Walter McCaleb (New York, 1906), 161; John Gonzales, "Henry Stuart Foote, Confederate Congressman and Exile," *Civil War History,* XI (December, 1965), 385–86; Johnston to Wigfall, December 15, 1862, January 26, 1863, in Wright, *Southern Girl,* 105–106, 123.

[18] Reagan, *Memoirs,* 162; Edward A. Pollard, *Life of Jefferson Davis, With a Secret History of the Southern Confederacy* (Philadelphia, 1869), 419; Wilfred B. Yearns, *The Confederate Congress* (Athens, Ga., 1960), 220–21.

[19] Johnston to Cooper, December 4, 6, 1862, in Johnston Papers, William and Mary; Johnston to Wigfall, January 8, 1863, January 26, 1863, in Wright, *Southern Girl,* 107–108, 122; Johnston to Wigfall, August 12, 1863, in Wigfall Papers, DLC.

ston, on December 4, protested to both Cooper and Wigfall that it would be impossible to control both Bragg and Pemberton.[20]

After his first conference at Murfreesboro with Bragg on December 5, Johnston felt even more convinced of this misalignment. Rebel estimates gave Rosecrans a potential 100,000 troops in Nashville and southern Kentucky. At best, Johnston believed it would require a month to shuttle troops between Pemberton and Bragg. The threat seemed obvious to Johnston. If Bragg tried to heavily reinforce Pemberton, Rosecrans could overrun Bragg before the reinforcements sent to Mississippi became effective there. Fearful, Johnston again appealed from Murfreesboro to have his command altered, and urged Wigfall to use his influence with the new Secretary of War, James Seddon.[21]

Johnston might have salvaged some order from the loose geographical nature of his command if his authority had been more clearly defined. There seemed good cause for Johnston's belief that the government deliberately gave him a nominal command with little power, but with heavy responsibilities. The November 24 order directed him to establish his headquarters at Chattanooga or any other place deemed desirable by Johnston. He was empowered to go in person to any part of his command "whenever his presence may, for the time, be necessary or desirable." [22]

The main advantage of having a theater commander to superintend moves in a vast area was destroyed when Richmond allowed department heads to continue their reports directly to Richmond. Under this arrangement Johnston could never be sure of being completely informed. And also, although Johnston was empowered to visit any of his field armies, the order did not specify whether this was to be done on his own initiative or at the government's discretion. Too, it left unsaid whether Johnston was to give direct orders to field commanders when he was not present with the army.[23]

Not until the spring of 1863 would Richmond clarify some of these problems. Even then, the government's inconsistent policy could only

[20] Johnston to Wigfall, December 15, 1862, in Wigfall Papers, DLC; Johnston to Wigfall, December 4, 1862, in Wright, *Southern Girl*, 98–99; Johnston to Cooper, November 24, December 4, 1862, in Johnston Papers, William and Mary.

[21] Johnston to Cooper, December 4, 5, 6, 1862, and two telegrams, December 4, 1862, all in Johnston Papers, William and Mary; Wigfall to Seddon, December 8, 1862, in Wright, *Southern Girl*, 101–102; *Official Records*, XX, Pt. 2, p. 444.

[22] Special Orders 275, Adjutant and Inspector General's Office, November 14 [*sic*] 1862, in Johnston Papers, William and Mary; Johnston to Wigfall, February 14, 1863, in Wigfall Papers, DLC; Johnston to Wigfall, January 8, 1863, in Wright, *Southern Girl*, 107–108.

[23] Johnston to Wigfall, January 8, 1863, in Wright, *Southern Girl*, 107–108; Johnston to Wigfall, February 14, March 4, 8, August 12, 1863, in Wigfall Papers, DLC.

confuse the general. Frequently Davis issued directives garnered from his own communications with Bragg and Pemberton, communications not even seen by the theater commander. Before the end of December, Davis went over Johnston's head and ordered Bragg to reinforce Pemberton.[24]

During that first month, the seeds of other problems portended trouble. Already Johnston was disagreeing with Davis over the strategy to be used in the West. Davis insisted that Bragg and Pemberton must remain in stationary positions to defend their respective territories. He claimed that any enemy threat could be met by shuttling troops between them. Johnston urged concentration. His first plan, formulated in late November, called for concentrating Pemberton and the idle force of General T. H. Holmes in the Trans-Mississippi area against Grant. After Pemberton and Holmes defeated Grant, then Bragg and Pemberton could be united against Rosecrans. Davis rejected this idea, insisting that Holmes' defense of his own department should take precedence over any junction with Pemberton. Instead, said Davis, Rosecrans and Grant must be met by shuttling reinforcements to the most threatened point. [25]

Johnston and Davis also disagreed on the relative importance of Bragg's and Pemberton's positions. From the outset Johnston insisted that it was impossible to stall Rosecrans and Grant simultaneously. Thus he pressed the government for a commitment as to which territory should be considered more valuable, Middle Tennessee or Mississippi. Johnston viewed Tennessee as more vital. He feared its loss would demoralize Bragg's army and greatly aid Rosecrans' ability to maneuver against the lower South.[26]

Davis did not share Johnston's regard for the importance of Tennessee. In December the President believed that the Federals had only two main objectives, the seizure of Richmond and the control of the Mississippi River. He did not consider the seizure of Tennessee to be a major Federal aim. Thus, in mid-December, when Bragg protested Stevenson's transfer to Pemberton, Davis' retort was for Bragg to fight

[24] Davis to Johnston, July 15, 1863, in Jefferson Davis Papers, Louisiana Historical Association Collection, Howard–Tilton Memorial Library, Tulane University, hereinafter all collections in this library cited as Tulane; Seddon to Johnston, February 5, 1863, in Johnston Papers, William and Mary; Davis to Bragg, June 17, 1863, in Bragg Papers, Western Reserve.

[25] Jones, Confederate Strategy, 105–107, 116–22; Joseph E. Johnston, "Jefferson Davis and the Mississippi Campaign," North American Review, CXLIII (December, 1886), 585–87; Johnston to Wigfall, December 3, 1863, in Wigfall Papers, DLC; Johnston to Cooper, November 24, 1863, in Johnston Papers, William and Mary.

[26] Johnston to Cooper, December 6, 1862, Johnston to Davis, December 22, 1862, January 6, 1863, in Johnston Papers, William and Mary; Johnston, "Jefferson Davis and the Mississippi Campaign," 587.

if possible, and if not, to retreat to Alabama. Later, when Johnston asked Davis to state which was more important, Tennessee or Mississippi, the President's terse reply was simply, "to hold the Mississippi is vital." [27]

Beginning with these early disagreements in December, Bragg's army became an object of experimentation, with Johnston groping for a plan to coordinate Bragg and Pemberton. His first plan, Pemberton and Holmes united against Grant, was doomed even before Johnston reached Murfreesboro. He had presented the plan to Secretary of War Randolph on November 13, only to learn that the Secretary had been rebuked by Davis for attempting to initiate such a concentration.[28]

After Randolph's November 15 resignation, Johnston continued to advocate the plan to his successor, James Seddon. as well to Davis and Cooper. Johnston was disappointed when his November 24 orders did not mention Holmes' incorporation into the western design, and before leaving for Tennessee, he penned another request to Cooper for such a concentration.[29]

In Tennessee, Johnston's hopes flickered and then dimmed. When he arrived at Chattanooga on December 4, he received a telegram from Cooper. Pemberton had abandoned his position at Grenada, in northern Mississippi, and was retreating toward Vicksburg due to the threat of a Union flank move up the Yazoo River. Cooper informed Johnston that Holmes had been ordered to reinforce Pemberton. However, since Holmes would be slow in arriving, the government desired that part of Bragg's army be sent to Mississippi. Unknown to Johnston, Cooper actually had not ordered Holmes to cross the river, but had merely requested his cooperation with Pemberton if possible.[30]

Fired by the possibility of the Pemberton-Holmes combination, Johnston wrote Wigfall to continue to exert pressure. Then Johnston took the train to Murfreesboro for a conference with Bragg. After their

27 Davis to Johnston, January 8, 1863, in Joseph E. Johnston Papers, Miami (Ohio) University Library; Davis to Bragg, January 15, 1863, in Rowland (ed.), *Davis*, V, 418; Govan and Livingood, *A Different Valor*, 169; Jones, *Confederate Strategy*, 127; Johnston to Davis, January 6, 7, 1863, in Johnston Papers, William and Mary.

28 Davis to George Randolph, November 12, 13, 14, 15, 1862, in Davis Papers, Tulane.

29 Johnston to Wigfall, December 3, 1863, in Wigfall Papers, DLC; Johnston to Cooper, November 24, 1862, in Johnston Papers, William and Mary. The letter to Wigfall recounted a hotel meeting with Seddon over a year earlier. See also J. B. Jones, *A Rebel War Clerk's Diary at the Confederate States Capital*, ed. Howard Swiggett (New York, 1935), I, 190–91; Robert G. H. Kean, *Inside the Confederate Government: the Diary of Robert Garlick Hill Kean, Head of the Bureau of War*, ed. Edward Younger (New York, 1957).

30 *Official Records*, XX, Pt. 2, p. 435; T. H. Holmes to Cooper, November 22, 1862, Pemberton to Johnston, December 4, 1862, in Johnston Papers, William and Mary.

discussion, Johnston telegraphed Cooper, urging him to bring Holmes across the river.[31]

The *coup de grace* to Johnston's hopes was supplied by President Davis. On December 11 Davis arrived in Chattanooga en route to visit Bragg's army. This first western visit was probably motivated by reports of disaffection among Bragg's officers and general poor morale in the West. Davis was also probably disturbed by the gloomy reports he had received from Johnston.

A hasty conference was held with Johnston, who had returned to Chattanooga, and then Davis pushed on to Murfreesboro. Bands struck up "Bonnie Blue Flag" as the special train rolled out of Chattanooga, and crowds gathered at wayside stations to observe the procession. During the afternoon the train pushed through the Cumberland Mountain tunnel and into the Elk and Duck river valleys. Finally, the glimmering town lights and the ring of campfires around Murfreesboro gave Davis his first glimpse of the western army.[32]

After a colorful review of Hardee's and Polk's corps, Davis spent a day and a half talking with Bragg and his commanders. A key purpose of the visit was to ascertain Bragg's opinion of the need to reinforce Pemberton. Like Johnston, Bragg argued that reinforcements could be more easily obtained from Holmes. Davis remained unconvinced. He possessed intelligence received on December 5 which indicated that sixty thousand Federals were massing against Pemberton. Bragg rebutted that he had already detached Forrest's cavalry to sever Grant's communications, and that this move would force a retreat. [33]

Unimpressed with Bragg's arguments, Davis returned to Chattanooga to confer again with Johnston. Johnston then learned, from Davis, that Holmes had never been ordered across the Mississippi River. Holmes had been insisting that he could not cross the river, and Davis had not been inclined to order him to do so.[34]

Johnston was shaken by this news which "has blown away some tall castles in the air." [35] He seemed to pass the initiative in western planning to Davis. On December 15 Davis ordered Bragg to prepare Carter Stevenson's division for the move to reinforce Pemberton. Still, Johnston did not give up completely. On December 16 Davis and Johnston

31 Johnston to Cooper, December 4, 5, 6, 1862, in Johnston Papers, William and Mary, Johnston to Wigfall, December 4, 1862, in Wright, *Southern Girl*, 99–100.
32 Davis to wife, December 15, 1862, in Davis Papers, Tulane; Kean, *Diary*, 33; Chattanooga *Daily Rebel*, December 17, 1862; Mobile *Register*, December 18, 1862.
33 *Official Records*, XX, Pt. 2, p. 493.
34 Johnston to Wigfall, December 15, 1862, in Wigfall Papers, DLC; Johnston, "Jefferson Davis and the Mississippi Campaign," 588.
35 Johnston to Wigfall, December 15, 1862, in Wigfall Papers, DLC.

left Chattanooga to inspect Pemberton's army. While at Vicksburg, on December 21–22, Johnston again pleaded for Holmes to be transferred. He argued that even with Stevenson's division, Pemberton's effective number of men in the field army would total only thirty thousand. Johnston urged Davis to force Holmes to send at least ten thousand reinforcements in order to give Pemberton the forty thousand men Johnston believed necessary. Davis refused to do even this. Instead, on December 21, he told Holmes merely that it would be beneficial if he would send reinforcements, noting that he was trusting Holmes's discretion.[36]

By Christmas Day, Johnston's strategy for Bragg was a shambles. One-fourth of Bragg's infantry—Stevenson's division—began leaving Murfreesboro on December 18 for a three-week trip to Mississippi. Equally serious, Johnston simply lost touch with Bragg's army. The poor communication with Johnston, created by Bragg's reporting directly to Richmond, worsened because the telegraph wire between Chattanooga and Murfreesboro was out of commission during the last week of December.

The results were almost ludicrous. When Rosecrans moved against Bragg that week, Johnston was almost totally ignorant of what was happening. He had hoped to unite Pemberton's cavalry, commanded by General Earl Van Dorn, with Forrest. But he could not find Forrest. Nor could he locate Colonel Philip Roddey's cavalry brigade in northern Alabama, which he also sought to use against Grant's communications. By December 27 Johnston had also lost contact with Stevenson's division and admitted he had no idea where the expected reinforcement was. On December 27 he did receive a hint of news that Rosecrans was moving against Bragg. Although Johnston was theater commander, he considered his powers so weak that he could be scarcely more than an onlooker in the operation at Murfreesboro. He merely requested his aide, Colonel Benjamin Ewell, to keep a staff officer at Murfreesboro "until the crisis is over."[37] Johnston admitted that he did not even know if there were any reinforcements available for Bragg in East Tennessee or at Chattanooga.[38]

A thoroughly disgusted Johnston now sought relief from his obscure position. On Christmas Day he asked Davis to transfer him to another

36 Special Orders No. 7, December 15, 1862, Johnston to Sam Tate, December 19, 1862, Johnston to M. L. Smith, December 19, 1862, Johnston to Davis, December 22, 1862, all in Johnston Papers, William and Mary; Davis to T. H. Holmes, December 21, 1862, in Davis Papers, Tulane; Johnston, "Jefferson Davis and the Mississippi Campaign," 588.

37 Johnston to B. S. Ewell, December 27, 1862, in Johnston Papers, William and Mary.

38 Johnston to Davis, December 22, 31, 1862, January 6, 1863, Johnston to Kirby Smith, December 27, 1862, Johnston to Pemberton, December 31, 1862, Johnston to Bragg, December 30, 1862, Johnston to Ewell, December 27, 1862, *ibid.*

command. Davis refused on the grounds that he was needed to transfer troops during emergencies. In the light of Davis' dominance of Johnston's duties during the previous few weeks, this argument did not seem valid to the general, and on January 6 he again begged to be relieved. By that time Johnston no longer knew anything of conditions on Bragg's front; indeed, he did not even know where Bragg's army was.[39]

Despite this turmoil, a façade of calm prevailed at Murfreesboro during December. Bragg's camp hardly resembled that of an army scarcely thirty miles from a superior enemy. Wives and sweethearts flocked to Murfreesboro for holiday visits. The glitter of John Morgan's wedding was matched by other parties, receptions, horse races, and card games. A fancy banquet was held during the President's visit. On Christmas Eve, Louisiana and Kentucky officers feted the high command at a fancy ball in the courthouse. Another large ball was planned for the day after Christmas.[40]

The entire army seemed far too confident. Later Davis would be blamed for ordering away Stevenson's division. However, some of his opinions were garnered from consultations at Murfreesboro. When he returned to Chattanooga, Davis expressed only what the army's leaders seemed to believe—that Rosecrans probably would not advance on Bragg. Davis confided to Seddon that Rosecrans indicated only defensive purposes. Even should the Federals advance, Davis recalled that Bragg's officers were highly confident of victory.[41]

Bragg evidently shared these views. By December 20, he seemed convinced that Rosecrans would not advance. Instead, he thought perhaps the Federals might abandon Nashville and retreat to Kentucky. If Rosecrans did not do this, Bragg expected him to go into winter quarters at Nashville.[42]

Bragg's overconfidence was mainly a result of poor intelligence reports. The army still lacked any well-organized group of scouts, and Bragg was forced to rely upon rumors, reports from citizens, newspapers, and other media. The need to watch the many roads leading south from Nashville forced Bragg to disperse Wheeler's brigades for picket duty only. With Morgan and Forrest absent, Bragg simply lacked enough cavalry for

[39] Johnston to Davis, January 6, 1863, *ibid;* Johnston, "Jefferson Davis and the Mississippi Campaign," 588–89; Govan and Livingood, *A Different Valor,* 172–73.

[40] Robert, "At Murfreesboro Just before the Battle," 631–32; Stanley Horn, *The Army of Tennessee* (2nd ed.; Norman, Okla., 1955), 195–96; Bromfield Ridley, "Echoes from the Battle of Murfreesboro," *Confederate Veteran,* XI (February, 1903), 65.

[41] Davis to wife, December 15, 1862, in Davis Papers, Tulane; *Official Records,* XX, Pt. 2, pp. 449, 457.

[42] *Official Records,* XX, Pt. 2, pp. 449, 457; see also Brent Diary, December 19, 1862, in Bragg Papers, Western Reserve; E. T. Sykes, "General Braxton Bragg—A Cursory Sketch of His Campaigns," *SHSP,* XI (1883), 471.

both reconnaissance and picket duty. Instead, Wheeler, Wharton, and Pegram were spread on a wide front extending from the Franklin Pike on the west to the McMinnville Road east of Murfreesboro.[43]

This dispersal not only failed to provide information, but also made it impossible for them to effectively strike Rosecrans' communications. There is little indication that Bragg actually knew that by late November Rosecrans had a good supply line in operation. Apparently Bragg did not know that Rosecrans, by November 26, had the Louisville and Nashville Railroad in working order from Nashville to the Ohio River. If Bragg did know, he did nothing to disrupt it until Morgan was ordered into Kentucky on December 22.[44]

The meager intelligence reports Bragg did receive were confusing and misleading. On December 10 Wharton relayed a warning from a private citizen who said that Rosecrans was readying to advance. Three days later a similiar report came from Wharton. But on December 17 he came up with another Nashvillian who said Rosecrans was preparing to withdraw to Kentucky. This news seemed to jibe with the report Bragg had received on December 16 of Lee's victory at Fredericksburg. Other scattered reports spoke of a retreat, and by December 19 Bragg seemed convinced that Rosecrans would withdraw for lack of supplies.[45]

Finally, Wharton and Wheeler were ordered forward on December 20 for more information. Their fresh reports were confusing. General George Thomas' corps had arrived at Nashville, large stockpiles of supplies were in the city, and Rosecrans' entire army had been moved to the south bank of the Cumberland. Still, Bragg remained unmoved. Supremely confident, he boasted to Kirby Smith that he expected to be in Nashville soon.[46]

43 Edwin C. Bearss, "Cavalry Operations in the Battle of Stone's River, Part One," *Tennessee Historical Quarterly*, XIX (March, 1960) , 25; *Official Records*, XX, Pt. 2, p. 455.

44 *Official Records*, XX, Pt. 1, p. 189 Pt. 2, p. 421; William D. Bickham, *Rosecrans' Campaign with the Fourteenth Army Corps, or the Army of the Cumberland* (Cincinnati, 1863) , 87, 120–21; Forrest to Breckinridge, November 10, 1862, in Breckinridge Papers, Chicago.

45 Brent Diary, December 16, 19, 1862, in Bragg Papers, Western Reserve; Sykes, "Bragg's Campaigns," 471; *Official Records*, XX, Pt. 2, pp. 445, 448, 452, 457, 468.

46 *Official Records*, XX, Pt. 2, pp. 457–58, 462; Kirby Smith to wife, December 23, 1862, in Kirby Smith Papers, UNC.

three

Confusion in the Cedars

ON THE DAY AFTER CHRISTMAS, THE FINE, BALMY WEATHER THE TROOPS had enjoyed for a week disappeared. By dawn a hard rain was falling along Stone's River, and the roads between Nashville and Murfreesboro became quagmires of knee-deep mud.

Out of the heavy mist and fog the Federals began to appear in force on every major road. Wharton's left wing on the Nashville Pike was struck early that morning, and by 9 A.M. his outpost at Franklin had collapsed. On the Triune Pike, by 7 A.M. blue columns were pouring through the knobby hill country. They pushed at Wharton's main outpost at Nolensville. Unable to hold the weak position, Wharton abandoned the village and fell back to tough Knob Gap between Nolensville and Triune. There the Texan deployed his men on the high ridges north of Triune, and a long artillery fight commenced which could be heard at Bragg's headquarters.[1]

---

[1] Rosecrans was moving against Bragg with full knowledge of the Rebel predicament. He knew that Forrest, Morgan, and Stevenson had been detached. Nashville newspapers had even published accurate descriptions of Morgan's strength and destination. With this information and with supplies accumulated, Rosecrans judged that by December 26 the time was "opportune" to move on Bragg. With an effective force of 43,400, Rosecrans' three corps moved south on December 26. General George Thomas' corps moved first by the Franklin Pike and from there by crossroads to Nolensville; General A. M. McCook's corps moved directly from Nashville toward Nolensville on the Triune Pike. General T. L. Crittenden's corps was to move on the Nashville-Murfreesboro Pike as far south as Lavergne. Rosecrans was not yet sure where he would fight. His flexible plan called for McCook, aided by Thomas, to attack Hardee at Nolensville. If Hardee fell back and Bragg centered his resistance on the Murfreesboro-Nashville Pike, Thomas would move cross-country behind McCook and form on Crittenden's right for a fight along the Nashville Pike. See *Official Records,* XX, Pt. 1, pp. 191, 201; Bearss, "Cavalry Operations," 26–29.

44

Bragg was also in trouble on a third road, the Nashville-Murfreesboro Pike. By early morning, Wheeler's vedettes along Hurricane Creek north of Lavergne were being beaten back. Wheeler left his headquarters at Stewart's Creek and rushed his entire brigade to Lavergne, no more than fifteen miles north of Murfreesboro. A tough fight ensued throughout the day as Wheeler strove to hold the heavy Federal lines north of Hurricane Creek. In the afternoon General George Maney's brigade arrived to help him. Wheeler and Maney hastily conferred and agreed this was a genuine advance. By 2 P.M. Wheeler reported to Bragg that Rosecrans' entire army was advancing on the Triune and Nashville pikes. Meanwhile, Bragg's telegraph operator at Wheeler's headquarters at Stewart's Creek excitedly reported that heavy cannonading could be heard on the Nolensville and the Lavergne fronts.[2]

Bragg's surprise at the advance was equalled by his concern for how he could concentrate his widely scattered forces. When he had moved into Murfreesboro in late November, he scattered his army across a fifty-mile-wide front to protect all road approaches. This dispersal made part of his army vulnerable to being cut off. All of Hardee's corps, except for one brigade, was at Eagleville, on the Nashville-Triune-Shelbyville Road. Hardee had kept General S. A. M. Wood's brigade at Triune, north of Eagleville, to support Wharton. The Federal push which drove Wharton out of Nolensville now threatened to cut Bragg off from Hardee. Triune was at the junction of the Nashville-Triune-Shelbyville and the Murfreesboro-Franklin roads. Wharton and Wood could scarcely be expected to contain the advance. If the Federals seized Triune, they would be only sixteen miles west of Murfreesboro. At Eagleville, Hardee's most direct road to Murfreesboro was the twenty-four-mile Salem Pike.[3]

The remainder of Bragg's army was also scattered. Polk's corps was concentrated at Murfreesboro, almost twenty-five miles east of Hardee. The right wing, General John McCown's lone division of Kirby Smith's defunct corps, was twelve miles east of Murfreesboro at Readyville, on the McMinnville Road. The left wing of Wharton's brigade was still floundering near Franklin, almost thirty miles west of Murfreesboro. Fifteen miles north of the town on the Nashville Pike, Wheeler's and Maney's brigades were threatened with isolation from Bragg by a direct road which joined Nolensville with the Nashville-Murfreesboro Road south of Stewart's Creek.[4]

During the night of December 26 and through the early hours of the

2 Stewart's Creek operator to Bragg, December 26, 1862, Wheeler to Bragg, December 26—2 P.M., 1862, all in Bragg Papers, Western Reserve; Du Bose, *Wheeler*, 122.
3 Hardee's Murfreesboro report, in William Joseph Hardee Papers, 1863–71, Duke.
4 Bragg's Murfreesboro report, in Bragg Papers, Western Reserve.

following day, Bragg groped for information. He was not yet sure this was a real advance. If it were, he was still unsure where the bulk of Rosecrans' force lay. At midnight he ordered McCown to hasten back to Murfreesboro, but refrained from ordering Hardee off the Triune Pike until more news could be obtained at headquarters. The news soon came. During the cold, drizzling dawn hours of December 27, Bragg realized his army was in deep trouble. Late on December 26 Wheeler reported that prisoners had confirmed that Rosecrans' entire army was on the move. Shortly after 2 A.M., Wheeler again reported the advance was certain. Wheeler insisted that Bragg could expect a general attack at Murfreesboro by as early as the night of December 28. Shortly after 4 A.M. Hardee reported a large Yankee column on the Triune Road. Finally, about daylight, Wheeler reported the enemy still in force before him.[5]

Still unsure of Rosecrans' aims, Bragg on the twenty-seventh began drawing together his army. Hardee was ordered to hurry to Murfreesboro. This was no easy task. All day on December 27, while Hardee marched northeast to Murfreesboro, Wharton and Wood desperately sought to hold the Triune junction lest Hardee be taken in the flank. Through a cold, misty rain, Wharton and Wood managed to hold the high hills north of the junction. During the afternoon, however, the fog lifted temporarily and the superior Federal artillery drove the Confederates out of Triune. By nightfall Wood and Wharton had been driven south to Eagleville, where they too disappeared into the foggy night to Murfreesboro.[6]

On the early morning of December 28, a council was held at Bragg's headquarters on the Nashville Pike. Corps, division, and brigade commanders met to discuss what should be done. As the cold rain fell, the noise of artillery northward toward Lavergne drew closer. Bragg, motivated by Wheeler's warning of an early attack, drew up a hasty defensive line. He outlined the dispositions to his generals, and by nightfall the troops began moving into position along Stone's River.[7]

5 Wheeler to Brent, December 26—9 P.M., 1862, December 27—5:40 A.M., Hardee to Brent, December 27—4 A.M., 1862, Smyrna operator to Bragg, December 27, 1862, Bragg's Official Report, Brent Diary, December 27, 1862, all in Bragg Papers, Western Reserve; *Official Records*, XX, Pt. 2, p. 464.

6 Murfreesboro correspondent to *Register*, December 27, 1862, in Mobile *Register*, January 3, 1863; Hardee's Murfreesboro Report, Duke; Bearss, "Cavalry Operations," 35–38.

7 Bragg's Murfreesboro Report, "Memoranda for General and Staff Officers, December 28, 1862," all in Bragg Papers, Western Reserve; David Urquhart, "Bragg's Advance and Retreat," in Robert Johnson and C. C. Buel (eds.), *Battles and Leaders of the Civil War* (2nd ed.; New York, 1956), III, 605; A. D. Kirwan (ed.), *Johnny Green of the Orphan Brigade: the Journal of a Confederate Soldier* (Lexington,

Between December 28 and December 31, Bragg did not know where Rosecrans' army was or from which direction the Federals would approach the town. His cavalry was too badly scattered to provide information. Wheeler was busy on the Nashville Pike. Wharton's brigade was still at Eagleville and Salem. Fearful of an advance from Lebanon, Pegram's brigade had been posted ten miles north of Murfreesboro on the Lebanon Road. The only other available cavalry was General Abraham Buford's small brigade, which was in the process of moving from McMinnville to Rover on the Nashville-Shelbyville Pike.

Murfreesboro was, of course, a poor site from which to conduct the new campaign. On December 28 Bragg faced attack by way of five possible routes. He still feared a wide flanking move via the Salem Pike from the southwest. A heavy column was known to be astride the Franklin Pike, west of Murfreesboro, at Triune. The Wilkinson Pike, which joined Murfreesboro and Nolensville, was in Federal hands. Another force was pushing Wheeler back on the Nashville Road. Also, there seemed to be a genuine threat on the Lebanon Pike, which led due north from Murfreesboro. Intelligence on December 28–29 indicated a column was using a lateral road, the Liberty Pike, to move from the Nashville Road to the Lebanon Road. The Liberty Pike was a thorn for Bragg. It provided Rosecrans with a fine west-east connection from Franklin via Nolensville, thence to Stewartsburg on the Nashville Pike, and then through Jefferson to the Lebanon Pike.[3]

The need to defend all of these approaches forced Bragg to accept a poor defensive line around Murfreesboro. Geography had made this town almost undefendable. The only advantage provided by the terrain was that it did protect the roads. However, it held many disadvantages. Among the worst was the split in half of Bragg's line by Stone's River, which flowed north and then northeast just west of the town. Because of a peculiar bend in the river just northwest of the town, the Nashville Pike and the Nashville and Chattanooga Railroad ran parallel to the river for a considerable distance before crossing the river into Murfreesboro. Thus,

1956), 65. The general impression in the army was that Rosecrans would attack by daybreak of the 29th. Bragg later termed Wheeler's warning as "premature." See *Official Records*, XX, Pt. 2, p. 4468; also see Murfreesboro correspondent to *Register*, December 28, 1862, in Mobile *Register*, January 4, 1863; see also William Mitchell to father, December 28, 1862, in William Mitchell Letters, Chickamauga–Chattanooga National Military Park Library.

8 Middle Tennessee map in Cheatham Papers, Tennessee; Troop position maps, Stone's River National Military Park Library; Bragg's Murfreesboro Report, Wheeler to Brent, December 29—1:30 P.M., 1862, all in Bragg Papers, Western Reserve.

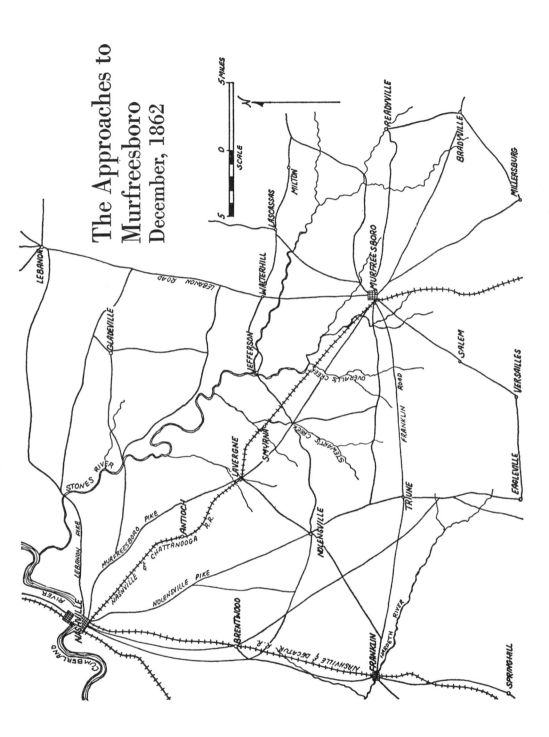

The Approaches to
Murfreesboro
December, 1862

to contest an advance along the Nashville Pike, Bragg must place his left wing on the west bank of the river.[9]

Other defensive problems became obvious as the army moved into position late on December 28 and early the following morning. Hardee's corps was to occupy a semicircular line between the Lebanon Pike and the river. This space of over a half-mile in length was filled by Breckinridge's division, and Cleburne's division formed a second line. Because Bragg feared an advance from the direction of Lebanon and Jefferson, Hardee's corps did not even face the Federal approach from Nashville. Instead, it was aligned facing almost due north. This alignment surrendered the only high ground on Bragg's line. On the east bank of the river, between the Nashville Pike and the mouth of Sinking Creek, a series of limestone bluffs bordered the river. From these bluffs Hardee could enfilade the Federals across the river. Also, should the Federals cross the river at any of the several good fords between the Nashville Pike and Sinking Creek, Hardee's line would be enfiladed. [10]

Conditions were no better on the west bank, which was occupied by Polk's corps. To protect the several road approaches from the west and northwest, Polk was forced to deploy in a long semicircular line. His first line was General Jones Withers' division. Withers' right flank rested on the river bank opposite Breckinridge. His line then extended on a long curve across the Nashville and Wilkinson pikes. Cheatham's division formed a second line along the banks of the river.

The country west of the river offered few defensive advantages. The valley here was a mixture of open fields, cedar forests, and rocky glades. If Bragg elected to attack, Polk would lose heavily. Withers' position was confronted by a series of open fields between the Franklin and Wilkinson roads. North of the Wilkinson Pike, the country was a morass of thick cedar forests and limestone outcroppings. This rugged terrain threatened

[9] General William Preston termed the Murfreesboro line as "utterly worthless, so far as attaining any advantage of position." See Preston to William Preston Johnston, January 26, 1862, in the Mrs. Mason Barret Collection of Albert Sidney and William Preston Johnston Papers Tulane; for other comments on the weakness of the position, see Polk, *Polk*, II, 180–81. Bragg's chief engineer, James Nocquet, stated there was "no advantageous position between town and the river." *Official Records*, XX, Pt. 2, p. 396. One correspondent wrote, "It is not a little remarkable that in the selection of our battle ground, the very worst position was chosen . . . while the cedar woods, and all the elevated and commanding positions were left for the enemy to secure. . . ." Correspondent to Richmond *Examiner*, January 26, 1863, in Richmond *Examiner*, February 25, 1863.

[10] Bragg's Murfreesboro report, "Memoranda for General and Staff Officers," all in Bragg Papers, Western Reserve; *Official Records*, XX, Pt. 1, pp. 781–82.

to break up the order of any frontal assault, and provided excellent positions for a defender.[11]

Even as the two corps moved into position on December 29, Bragg was unsure of the location of Rosecrans' main column. The previous night Wharton reported from Salem that the enemy threat on the road from Eagleville had disappeared. Most of Bragg's information pointed to a threat against his right wing, between the Nashville Pike and the Lebanon Road. He received news on the twenty-ninth that a column was moving through Jefferson to reach the Lebanon Road and swing around on Hardee's right. During the evening, as artillery rumblings grew louder on the Franklin Road, the news came that Wheeler had been forced back across Overall Creek, only five miles from Murfreesboro. Later in the evening, Wheeler's weary horsemen slowly fell back within Bragg's line, pursued by enemy skirmish lines which felt out Withers's right wing near the Nashville Road. [12]

That afternoon, other activity on Hardee's front had indicated the main threat to be on the right wing. During mid-afternoon Breckinridge noticed that a key hill some six hundred yards in advance of his left brigade was unoccupied. This eminence, Wayne's Hill, commanded the river fords opposite Breckinridge's left, and also enfiladed Withers's right flank across the river. Except for Bragg's fears of a threat from the Lebanon Road, Wayne's Hill rightfully should have been the anchor of Hardee's left, with his center and right occupying the high ground along the river bank northward to Sinking Creek. The enemy's desire for Wayne's Hill was obvious by late afternoon. About 3 P.M., Breckinridge ordered several regiments from General Roger Hanson's brigade to take an advance position on the hill. Shortly before dark, the enemy, in brigade strength, forded the river and rushed through the cornfield against the hill. The defenders beat back the attack, but that night the hill still remained an isolated position.[13]

Bragg's plans faced more revision. Late on the twenty-ninth, Bragg ordered Wheeler to move his brigade via the Lebanon Road and Liberty Pike to strike Rosecrans from behind. Bragg was as anxious to discern the enemy's strength on Hardee's front as he was for Wheeler to destroy supply wagons. In less than twenty-four hours, Wheeler rode completely around Rosecrans' army and en route destroyed the reserve wagon train

11 *Official Records*, XX, Pt. 1, pp. 705, 753–54; Polk, *Polk*, II, 180–81; Troop Position Maps, Stone's River Library.

12 Wheeler to Bragg, December 29—1:30 P.M., 1862, Bragg's Murfreesboro Report, all in Bragg Papers, Western Reserve; Du Bose, *Wheeler*, 138–43; Ridley, "Echoes from the Battle of Murfreesboro," 149; *Official Records*, XX, Pt. 2, p. 467.

13 Hardee's Murfreesboro Report, Duke; *Official Records*, XX, Pt. 1, p. 782; Troop Position Maps, Stone's River Library.

of General A. M. McCook's corps. More important, by daylight of December 30 Wheeler reported from near Jefferson that the Lebanon Road and Liberty Pike appeared to be clear. As this threat to his far right dwindled, Bragg received discomfiting intelligence from his left. News received on the night of December 29 indicated a heavy Federal column was moving toward Murfreesboro along the Wilkinson Pike. Still puzzled by Rosecrans' evasive maneuvers, Bragg committed his only genuine reserve, McCown's division, to extend Withers' left wing across the Franklin Pike.[14]

More changes had to be made on the thirtieth. As the cold, drizzling rain continued to fall, heavy firing erupted out the Wilkinson Pike near Overall Creek. Wharton's brigade, which had just arrived on Withers' flank, was pushed back into the Confederate lines by a massive infantry force. During the afternoon, this new threat began to deploy in front of Withers and McCown, to form a continuous line from the Nashville Road across the Franklin Pike. By nightfall, Bragg sensed that the bulk of Rosecrans' strength seemed to be concentrated west of the river in front of Withers and McCown. The long line of campfires which flickered through the mist between the Wilkinson and Franklin pikes indicated a heavy concentration there.[15]

That night, Bragg called Polk and Hardee to his headquarters to discuss what should be done. The accounts of this meeting and those of general affairs during the evening are contradictory. Hardee and Polk neglected to mention the council in their reports. Instead, Hardee noted that during the afternoon, Bragg ordered him to move Cleburne's division across the river to form a second line behind McCown, and that he was ordered to take personal command of the far left. Hardee implies that Bragg ordered the attack of the thirty-first "during the night." Bragg's account indicates that he moved Cleburne to the left as a move preparatory to attacking Rosecrans the following morning.[16]

Other accounts agree with neither officer. Bragg's aide, Colonel David Urquhart, recorded that Bragg called Polk and Hardee to his headquarters after sundown. After it was agreed that Rosecrans was massing on Bragg's left for an attack, it was also agreed that Bragg should attack

14 Bragg's Murfreesboro Report, Wheeler to Bragg, December 30—4 A.M., 1862, all in Bragg Papers, Western Reserve; Du Bose, *Wheeler*, 138-43; Dyer, *Wheeler*, 81-82.

15 Bearss, "Cavalry Operations," 46-47; Bragg's Murfreesboro Report, Western Reserve; Hardee's Murfreesboro Report, Duke; *Official Records*, II, Pt. 1, pp. 705, 754.

16 Hardee's headquarters indicated as early as 3:30 P.M. that he had orders to cross Cleburne's division. See Roy to Breckinridge, December 30—3:30 P.M., 1862, in Breckinridge Papers, Chicago; Bragg's Murfreesboro Report, in Bragg Papers, Western Reserve; Hardee's Murfreesboro Report, in Hardee Papers, Duke; Urquhart, "Bragg's Advance and Retreat," 606.

first. Then Bragg did give Hardee command of the left and ordered Cleburne to move across the river. Yet another staff member, Colonel George Brent, wrote in his diary that Cleburne had been ordered across prior to the council. Brent noted that Bragg did not favor an attack against Rosecrans' right wing along the Franklin Pike, but first favored an assault on the Federal left opposite Breckinridge. Polk opposed this plan, Bragg gave in to Polk's desire for an attack on the Federal right, and then Bragg gave Hardee the command of the left wing.[17]

More important than the sequence of events was Bragg's decision to attack. Bragg's tactics called for McCown to begin the attack at daylight, supported by Cleburne. As he moved forward, McCown was to begin a wheel to the right. Each successive brigade on Withers' front was then to take up the attack and also wheel. By this tactic, Bragg hoped to jack-knife Rosecrans' right wing, and force the Federals back into the angle between the Nashville Pike and Stone's River. These tactics seemed suited neither to Bragg's strength nor to the terrain. McCown and Withers must charge across open fields into thick cedar forests. Bragg's alignment did not possess the power to successfully make such a move. Cleburne's and McCown's divisions together could amass only 11,430 men, while Polk's corps totaled only 14,118 men. Across the river, Breckinridge had only 7,000 men. Bragg's only reserve was a meager 800-man brigade under General J. K. Jackson. Under Bragg's assumption that Rosecrans had at least 60,000 men, the Confederates had too few reserves to bring off such a wheeling maneuver.[18]

Equally serious, Bragg made no disposition to utilize Breckinridge's division during the early hours of the attack. Together with Jackson's and Pegram's brigades, Breckinridge could muster ten thousand men. With these men Breckinridge could have done either of two things. He could have demonstrated against Rosecrans' left in order to keep back reserves

---

[17] Urquhart, "Bragg's Advance and Retreat," 606; Johnston Diary, December 30, 1862, in Bragg Papers, Western Reserve.

[18] "Tabular Statement Showing the Number Present for Duty on the morning of the 31 Dec. 1862, the number of killed, wounded and missing, and the percentage of loss in the battle of Murfreesboro" (MS in Bragg Papers, Western Reserve) ; Bragg's Murfreesboro Report, *ibid.* Bragg's strategy was almost the same as Rosecrans'. By the night of December 30, Rosecrans' three corps had assembled before Murfreesboro. Crittenden's corps held the left, from the river across the Nashville Pike. Thomas' corps comprised the center, with James Negley's division across the Wilkinson Pike and Lovell Rousseau's division in reserve. McCook, on the right wing, held the ground from Wilkinson Pike, stretching south across the Franklin Pike. Rosecrans' tactics called for McCook to hold his position while T. J. Wood's and H. P. Van Cleve's divisions of Crittenden's corps crossed Stone's River and attacked Bragg's right wing. That Bragg attacked first was due less to his speed than to a lack of understanding at Rosecrans' camp as to the precise order in which the corps were to attack. See Kenneth Williams, *Lincoln Finds a General* (New York, 1956) , IV, 261–65.

from the Federals on Hardee's front. Or he could have realigned his division on a line parallel with Withers, in order to seize the high ground on the east bank of the river. On December 31 the only segment of this high ground held by Breckinridge was Wayne's Hill. Bragg gave no orders for either movement, however, and Breckinridge took no initiative. His later explanation was that such a move would have exposed him to an attack from the Lebanon Road. This explanation appears rather feeble, considering that Wheeler already had swept through this route the previous day without opposition. Also, Breckinridge had Pegram's cavalry brigade on hand, which could have observed the road. [19]

The lethargy on Breckinridge's side of the river was matched by the confusion on the west bank. A cold, pelting rain drenched Polk's and Hardee's shivering troops. Bragg had ordered that no fires be made, so many sought warmth in piles of cornstalks and in haystacks. While the troops huddled for shelter, the army's high command experienced that chaos which colored its operations before other battles. The trouble began late that night as Cleburne and McCown were moving into their final positions. Cleburne had trouble in fording the river, and did not even move into position behind McCown until 1 A.M. McCown was also having trouble. About sundown on December 30, Hardee had discovered that McCown's line was not aligned properly. McCown was holding the ground on the south side of the Franklin Pike, and was supposed to link with Withers' left on the north side of the road. Hardee ordered McCown to move up his only reserve brigade, that of General Evander McNair, to fill the gap. The hot-tempered McCown bickered with Hardee, who argued for the move to be made during the night lest it bring on a Federal assault. Hardee persisted, but McCown delayed in completing the move until after daylight the following morning.[20]

McCown's troubles were not over. He did not seem to understand just when he should begin the attack. Bragg had vaguely suggested that he attack at "daylight," which Bragg later argued was 5:00 A.M. Hardee, too, had ordered McCown to be ready at daylight. But Hardee had muddled the issue by stating that he would be on the field to superintend the move, and would meet McCown at 5:45, before the assault. Shortly after midnight Hardee sent Cleburne slightly different orders for the morning's attack. Cleburne in turn issued orders to his brigade commanders to be ready to attack at 4:30 A.M. It is not clear, however, whether Hardee himself specified this hour, for Cleburne merely stated that he was basing his

19 Official Records, XX, Pt. 1, p. 782.

20 Hardee's Murfreesboro Report, Duke; Roy to E. L. Drake, November 8, 1878, in Hardee Papers, Duke; H. W. Walter to John McCown, June 5, 1863, in Bragg Papers, Western Reserve; Official Records, XX, Pt. 1, pp. 917–18, 844.

order on one received from the general. The result of these minor disparities was that Hardee was not ready to begin the attack until after six o'clock. [21]

Light was slow in coming along Stone's River on the early morning of December 31. A cold drizzle continued, and a heavy mist clouded the river bottom. Out of this mist, shortly after 6 A.M., McCown's division advanced along the Triune Pike. Crossing a cornfield, McCown's brigades dashed into a large cedar forest where the enemy was rousing. The surprise was almost complete. Only a frantic picket firing warned the Federals, who were engaged in cooking breakfast.

The morass of confusion in the ensuing battle was created by the impossible terrain and by command disorder. From the outset, Bragg's plan to throw Rosecrans' right wing back upon his left ran into trouble. McCown, successful in his first attack, then proceeded in the wrong direction. Instead of wheeling to the right, his brigades continued straight west out the Franklin Road. Soon he was flanked on the right, where he thought Withers' troops would be, and he suffered heavy losses.[22]

The reaction to this first failure of Bragg's fragile tactics echoed down the line. McCown's supporting division—Cleburne's—pushed northwest across the Franklin Pike as expected. Scarcely had Cleburne reached the pike when a sheet of fire from behind rail fences and large boulders ripped through his division. A surprised Cleburne soon discovered that instead of McCown he was facing General Jeff C. Davis' division of McCook's corps. Cleburne pushed Davis north of the pike and continued to wheel around toward the Wilkinson Road.

Again the tactics stalled. While driving Davis back toward the Wilkinson Pike, Cleburne's men were hit by an enfilading fire on their right flank. This time the culprit was Withers' division, which had not advanced promptly. Hardee was forced to commit Cleburne's only reserve brigade, that of General S. A. M. Wood, to fill the gap. Again Cleburne swept forward on a four-brigade front, with the commands of Generals St. John Liddell, Bushrod Johnson, Lucius Polk, and Wood. They scrambled through the cedar brakes and rock outcroppings toward the Wilkinson Road. The force of Cleburne's assault drove the Federals back to the road. By 9 A.M., with little support from McCown, Cleburne had

21 Bragg's Murfreesboro Report, in Bragg Papers, Western Reserve; Hardee's Murfreesboro Report, Duke; *Official Records*, XX, Pt. 1, pp. 917–21, 844; Walter to McCown, June 5, 1863, in Bragg Papers, Western Reserve.

22 *Official Records*, XX, Pt. 1, pp. 912, 926–27, 922, 944.

forced McCook back to a new line along the Wilkinson Road. Now the Confederates faced northward instead of westward. [23]

Matters were confused to Cleburne's right. On the eve of the battle, Polk had revamped his command structure because of the broken terrain and the width of his front line. The result was an unwieldy system in which General B. F. Cheatham was to take charge of the two left brigades in Withers' line, and his own two left brigades in the second line. Withers was to superintend his own two right brigades and the two supporting brigades in Cheatham's line.

Cheatham's attack was a piecemeal affair. The far left brigade on Withers' front, that of Colonel J. Q. Loomis, did not even more forward until 7 A.M. Crossing a cornfield and open woods, Loomis was thrown back by what was ascertained to be the left of McCook's line, the division of General Philip Sheridan. Sheridan's men, posted in a thick cedar grove, decimated Loomis' brigade and wounded its commander. Part of the trouble here was that the brigade on Loomis' right, that of Colonel A. M. Manigault, did not even move forward until 8 A.M. Because of this delay, Cheatham had to commit both of his supporting brigades in the first hour of the fight, those of Generals A. J. Vaughan and George Maney. By 9 A.M. Cheatham also had shoved the Federals back to the Wilkinson Pike line.[24]

By 9 A.M. Bragg's tactics seemed to be succeeding. The Federal right and center had been driven back into a sharp right angle, and the Federal right now faced south along the Wilkinson Road. However, the victory was more superficial than real. Because Bragg's intricate wheeling tactics failed to be executed properly, Cleburne's and Cheatham's front line brigades had already lost heavily, and both had already committed all of their reserves.

Equally heavy losses were sustained shortly after 9 A.M. in the attempt to break the new Federal line. Aided by the arrival of McCowan's errant division, Cleburne charged across cotton and corn fields, crossed the Wilkinson Road, and fell upon McCook's men posted in a large cedar grove. Cleburne lost heavily here because his right wing was flanked. Cheatham was having difficulty in crossing the Wilkinson Road. The Yankee defenses on his front were imbedded around the Harding farmhouse and a

23 Buck, *Cleburne*, 119–20; *Official Records*, XX, Pt. 1, pp. 844–53, 856–57. McCown's attack had struck the brigades of General Edward Kirk and General August Willich of General Richard Johnson's division of McCook's corps. Cleburne's attack struck the middle division of McCook's corps, that of General Jefferson C. Davis. *Official Records*, XX, Pt. 1, pp. 193, 255–56, 264, 296.

24 *Official Records*, XX, Pt. 1, pp. 706–707, 734–35, 744, 754–55; see also Murfreesboro reports of J. Q. Loomis' brigade, Captain David D. Water's Alabama Battery, in Bragg Papers, Western Reserve; see also Troop Position Maps, Stone's River Library.

nearby brick kiln on the south side of the road. Cheatham's brigades were badly mauled here by massed artillery, and the ground around the farmhouse and kiln was strewn with the dead and wounded. [25]

By 10 A.M. the Federal right and center collapsed. While Cheatham and Cleburne attacked northward, Withers at last entered the fight. About 9 A.M. General Patton Anderson's brigade was rushed west along the Wilkinson Pike to strike the Federals on the flank. Despite terrific losses from massed artillery, Anderson broke the lines and seized two batteries. He learned that the force on his front and Cheatham's right belonged to the corps of General George Thomas. This combined assault proved too much for McCook and Thomas. Shortly after 10 A.M. the second Federal line melted away, and the weary Union defenders drifted back through the cedars to the Nashville Road. It appeared that Bragg was on the verge of complete victory. Rosecrans' line by late morning was forced into the angle between Stone's River and the Nashville Pike. The Union left faced northeast along the river, and the right and center faced northwest along the Nashville Pike.[26]

Out of this precarious Federal situation of midday stemmed the questionable legend that all Bragg had needed for total victory was Stevenson's absent division. Bragg's success was more illusory than genuine. He had gained the captured ground at awful cost. Both Hardee's and Polk's corps were shattered. By 10 A.M. Hardee had already lost one-third of his strength. Six of his brigade and regimental commanders were killed or wounded. Polk's corps was also badly mauled. Maney's and Loomis' brigades had been decimated in the first attacks along the Franklin Road. On Polk's right, the brigades of Generals James Chalmers and Daniel Donelson had suffered terribly, about 10 A.M., when they first went into action against the new line. Donelson's Eighth Tennessee Infantry had lost its commander and 306 of its 472 men, the Sixteenth Tennessee had lost 207 of 402 men, and his other regiments had lost almost as heavily. By noon, Chalmers' brigade was completely broken up and its commander wounded. [27]

How well Bragg would have done with the help of Stevenson's division might be indicated by the poor use he made of the reinforcements he did

25 *Official Records,* XX, Pt. 1, pp. 706–707; J. A. Pollard Diary, December 31, 1862, Tennessee State; Murfreesboro report of Water's Alabama Battery, in Bragg Papers, Western Reserve.

26 *Official Records,* XX, Pt. 1, pp. 688–89, 707, 725, 735, 744–45, 755–56, 763–64; see also Murfreesboro reports of Forty-fifth Alabama Regiment, Twenty-seventh Mississippi Regiment, Twenty-ninth Mississippi Regiment, Twenty-fourth Mississippi Regiment, Thirtieth Mississippi Regiment, all in Bragg Papers, Western Reserve.

27 Hardee's Murfreesboro Report, Duke; *Official Records,* XX, Pt. 2, pp. 690, 711–12, 714–45, 756.

have. From noon until the evening of the thirty-first, Bragg seemed to use his replacements in the wrong place and manner, and at the wrong time. He had available over fourteen thousand reinforcements. Wheeler and Wharton, each with twenty-five hundred troopers, were in position behind Hardee's flank on December 31. Across the river, Breckinridge's division and Jackson's brigade promised almost eight thousand fresh infantry, and Pegram could muster an additional sixteen hundred cavalry.

With these reserves Bragg could have done either of two things. He could have thrown them on Hardee's left to overlap McCook's extended right wing along the Nashville Pike and seize the road. With five thousand cavalry available on his left, it appeared that Bragg was in a good position to do so. This had been demonstrated during the morning by Wharton's brigade. As Hardee swept forward, Wharton was ordered to move his brigade around McCook's right and attack the enemy's rear on the Nashville Road. In a wild, Indian-style open field charge, Wharton reached the pike and overran a large supply train beyond Rosecrans' right flank. The Rebel cavalry then chased the train's defenders north for another mile on the pike across Overall Creek. All that Wharton needed to hold the pike was support. [28]

That support could have been provided by Wheeler. The young chief of cavalry was slow in returning from his flashy ride around Rosecrans and thus almost rode himself out of the battle. At 9 A.M. when Hardee was pushing McCook back from the Wilkinson Pike, Wheeler was still far west at Petersburg, between Franklin and Triune. He did not arrive on Hardee's left until the early afternoon. Though he had received orders from Bragg early that morning to attack the enemy's rear, Wheeler chose not to support Wharton. Behaving more like a single brigade commander than cavalry chief, Wheeler struck north on a country road which led from the Wilkinson Pike to the Nashville Pike near Overall Creek. He accomplished nothing and was beaten back by Federal cavalry. Meanwhile, in the early afternoon, Wharton alone sought to hold the Nashville Road northwest of McCook's right but was forced back by superior numbers. If Wheeler had exercised his command to unite his brigade, Wharton's, and the newly arrived small brigade of General Abraham Buford, Rosecrans' supply line to Nashville might have been severed. At least, if he had fought dismounted as Forrest had done at

---

28 "Tabular Statement Showing the Number Present for Duty on the Morning of the 31 Dec. 1862" (MS in Bragg Papers, Western Reserve); Bearss, "Cavalry Operations," 118–23; W. D. Pickett, "Reminiscences of Murfreesboro," *Confederate Veteran*, XVI (September, 1908), 451.

Shiloh, Wheeler could have provided Hardee with reinforcements on his weak left.[29]

Bragg's other and better choice was on Hardee's front. The bulk of Rosecrans' power was obviously concentrated in front of Polk's right and center, at the angle formed by Stone's River and the Nashville Road. Here Polk knew he was confronted by parts of Thomas' and T. L. Crittenden's corps. The Federal left here was guarded by the river and by the deep cut of the Nashville and Chattanooga Railroad. The angle of Rosecrans' left and center was protected by a four-acre stand of cedars on both sides of the railroad just north of the Nashville Pike. This grove, known as the Round Forest, stood on an eminence of ground confronting Polk's center and right. To reach the angle, Polk's men must emerge from the protective cedar groves south of the pike, and cross open fields against the high ground. In addition, Rosecrans had massed artillery both in the Round Forest and northward along the high ground west of Stone's Road. The weakest segment of Rosecrans' line was opposite Hardee. Here McCook had been forced to extend his lines for over a mile and a half, and did not have the massed artillery protection afforded Thomas and Crittenden at the angle. A strong push by Hardee's left could possibly force McCook's right back into the pocket formed by the river.[30]

Yet Bragg neglected both of these opportunities. By noon of December 31 command supervision seemed to be breaking down. Despite repeated pleas by Hardee for reinforcements to overlap McCook, Bragg sent none. Instead, the General chose to hammer at the Round Forest throughout the afternoon in a series of sporadic attacks. Not only did Bragg choose to attack the strongest position on the line, but he also did not mass enough troops to promise any hope of victory. Rather, beginning with an assault by Chalmers about 10 A.M., Polk's right wing was gradually chewed up by a series of such isolated attacks. After Chalmers was thrown back, Polk sent in Donelson's brigade, which also suffered frightful losses. Then the brigades of Generals A. P. Stewart and George Maney were thrown at the angle. Meanwhile, during the early afternoon, Hardee's weakened corps hurled three separate attacks against the Nashville Road. Weary, short of ammunition, and lacking reserves, Hardee's men could do nothing.[31]

[29] Wheeler to Bragg, December 31—8:30 A.M., 1862, December 31—9 A.M., 1862, in Bragg Papers, Western Reserve; Bearss, "Cavalry Operations," 125–28; Dyer, *Wheeler*, 84.

[30] Polk, *Polk*, II, 180–81; Hardee's Murfreesboro Report, Duke; Pickett, "Reminiscences of Murfreesboro," 451; Major Joseph Cumming Reminiscences (MS in Joseph Cumming Papers, UNC).

[31] Roy, "Hardee Sketch," in Hardee Papers, Alabama; Hardee's Murfreesboro Report, Duke; *Official Records*, XX, Pt. 2, pp. 689–90, 711–12, 735, 725, 756.

Bragg also misused the reserves he had available across the river. Not until after 10 A.M. did Bragg move at last to use Breckinridge. Then commenced a long series of order and counter-orders which stymied any successful use of the Kentuckian's division. Shortly after ten o'clock Bragg sent his aide, Major William Clare, across the river to Breckinridge. Clare galloped to Breckinridge's headquarters with an order for the general to advance his entire division. Exactly what Bragg wanted Breckinridge to do is not clear. Bragg's battle report mentioned only that Breckinridge was ordered to reinforce Polk. But Clare later recalled the verbal order was simply for Breckinridge to move forward. Clare's account is bolstered by the recollections penned in 1863 by two of Breckinridge's staff officers, Theodore O'Hara and John Buckner. Both agreed that the initial order was for a forward move east of the river.

To Breckinridge this seemed impossible. Repeatedly during the morning, Pegram sent information that the enemy was crossing the river at the lower fords near Sinking Creek, and were advancing in battle line. Clare hastened back to Bragg to inquire what Breckinridge was to do. Again the accounts conflict. Clare claimed that Bragg told him to order Breckinridge to advance unless he was sure the enemy was advancing east of the river. Yet O'Hara contended that Bragg's initial order to advance was included in a statement that the enemy was crossing and that Breckinridge should attack first. [32]

When Clare rode back to Breckinridge, he met a second officer sent by Bragg, Colonel Stoddard Johnston. By now Bragg had information from other sources that the enemy definitely was crossing the river in Breckinridge's front. Bragg reiterated his order for Breckinridge to strike before he was attacked himself. Scarcely had Breckinridge advanced a half mile when further delays occurred. About 11:30 A.M. new instructions came from Bragg. This time the order to advance was countermanded. Breckinridge was now told to fall back on the defensive and send support to Polk across the river. No one seems to agree even on how much reinforcement was requested. Bragg indicated the request was for two brigades; Breckinridge argued that it was for one, or for two if they

---

[32] Bragg's Murfreesboro Report, in Bragg, Western Reserve; William Clare to Bragg, June 2, 1863, John Buckner to Breckinridge, May 20, 1863, Theodore O'Hara to Breckinridge, January 16, 1863, all in Breckinridge Papers, New York Historical Society; Breckinridge to Bragg, December 31 (10:10 A.M.), 1862, in Bragg Papers, Western Reserve; *Official Records*, XX, Pt. 1, pp. 781–82. Pegram's reconnaissance, which Breckinridge termed as careless, had observed General Horatio Van Cleve's division of Crittenden's corps crossing the river in the first phase of Rosecrans' planned attack against Bragg's right wing. But when Bragg attacked first on the opposite end of the field, Van Cleve's crossing was halted. His brigades were ordered to recross the river, and the bulk of his division was moved to the Nashville Pike. For some unexplained reason, Pegram failed to report this withdrawal.

could be spared. O'Hara agrees that two were ordered, while Buckner indicates that only one was requested but that Breckinridge generously ordered two. Nevertheless, by 11:30, Breckinridge had ordered the brigades of Dan Adams and John Jackson to cross and aid Polk.

By noon Bragg had changed his mind again. At 11:30 Breckinridge reported a heavy infantry force advancing along the Lebanon Road. True to his performance of the entire morning, Breckinridge relied on scout reports, and apparently did not send staff officers to ascertain the truth of the reports of Federal activity on his front. Other news received by Bragg placed the mysterious force only five miles from Breckinridge's flank. Bragg hastily ordered Pegram to learn the truth, and countermanded the instructions for Adams and Jackson to join Polk. Instead, Bragg prepared to reinforce Breckinridge with two brigades from Polk.[33]

As the early afternoon dragged on, Bragg changed his mind once more. Shortly before one o'clock, Breckinridge reported that Pegram's reconnaissance might have been hasty. As yet, no enemy was advancing east of the river. Bragg's own sources had also proved Pegram's warnings to be false. No force was advancing on the Lebanon Road, and, except for some sharpshooters, none was across the river on Breckinridge's front. About 1 P.M. Bragg at last moved to get Breckinridge into action. He ordered the entire division across the river, except for Hanson's brigade, which was to retain Wayne's Hill.

The harm caused by the long delay in using Breckinridge was matched by the haphazard deployment of his four brigades. None were sent to reinforce Hardee though Breckinridge was in Hardee's corps. All were handed over to Polk, who wasted them in repeated small assaults against the Round Forest. Polk did not wait for all of them to arrive but sent them into action as they arrived. Adams' and Jackson's brigades were across the river by noon. By the time Breckinridge arrived after 1 P.M. with the brigades of Generals Gideon Pillow and William Preston, his other two brigades had already been used up. Jackson's brigade, the first across the river, had been ordered by Polk to break the angle. Jackson moved past the burned hulk of the Cowan house along the Nashville Pike where he was met by close-range artillery fire from the Round Forest. After several charges, Jackson fell back with a third of his command gone. Then Polk sent in Adams to attack the angle. Adams moved past the Cowan house, but was hit at 150-yard range by withering ar-

[33] Breckinridge to Bragg, December 31—11:30 A.M., 1862, Breckinridge to Brent, December 31—12:50 P.M., 1862, Buckner to Breckinridge, May 20, 1863, O'Hara to Breckinridge, January 16, 1863, Clare to Bragg, June 2, 1863, all in Breckinridge Papers, New York Historical Society; Bragg's Murfreesboro Report, Pegram to Bragg, December 31—10 A.M., 1862, in Bragg Papers, Western Reserve; *Official Records*, XX, Pt. 1, p. 783.

tillery fire from the massed guns at the angle. Adams, too, lost a third of his command.

Just as Adams' brigade was reeling back, Breckinridge arrived. Polk immediately threw both brigades against the angle. Again, the results were disastrous. The two brigades were broken up by the fences and out-buildings surrounding the Cowan house. Instead of reaching the forest on a two-brigade front, Pillow and Preston could muster only a few separate regimental charges in which they suffered heavy losses. By late afternoon, when his troops on the left were too worn out to continue, Hardee hurried to the right to learn what was transpiring. Observing the useless slaughter at the angle, he ordered Breckinridge to cease firing. By nightfall only occasional artillery or musket fire could be heard, as both armies halted to count their losses.[34]

The night of December 31 and the following day produced more discord in the high command. Obviously hungry for a victory after the Perryville criticism, Bragg telegraphed Richmond and theater commander Johnston that he had won a brilliant victory. Bragg seemed convinced that Rosecrans would retreat to Nashville that night, and boasted to Johnston that he would pursue. His confidence seemed to be shared by the high command and the troops, who thought Rosecrans surely would retreat.[35]

On New Year's Day Bragg learned he was mistaken. An early morning reconnaissance indicated that Rosecrans had abandoned only that sharp angle of his line in the Round Forest. Obviously confused, Bragg exhibited one of those personality traits that had plagued him in Kentucky —the inability to adjust to a new situation. Several times in Kentucky, he had shown, as he also did in later battles, that he had ability to plan tactics but little ability to adapt to the contingencies of a battle. Characteristically, almost from the outset of the day's fighting on the thirty-first, Bragg had been somewhat isolated from events on the field. His only attempt to assume command direction had been the Breckinridge debacle. Bragg's entire strategy for Murfreesboro had been to force Rosecrans to retreat in a single day's action. For this he had pushed his army

34 Roy, Hardee Sketch, in Hardee Papers, Alabama; Pickett, "Reminiscences of Murfreesboro," 451; Polk, *Polk*, II, 192–93; Hughes, *Hardee*, 144; Hardee's Murfreesboro Report, Duke; *Official Records*, XX, Pt. 1, pp. 690–91, 783–84, 793, 795; Polk to Breckinridge, March 31, 1862, in Breckinridge Papers, New York Historical Society.

35 *Official Records*, XX, Pt. 1, p. 662; Bragg to Johnston, January 1, 1863, in Johnston Papers, William and Mary. For other evidence of the Confederate confidence that Rosecrans would retreat, see: Chattanooga correspondent to *Register*, January 6, 1863, in Mobile *Register*, January 10, 1863. On January 1, Governor Isham Harris dispatched to the *Daily Rebel* that Rosecrans was evidently retreating. See Chattanooga *Daily Rebel*, January 3, 1863; see also Ridley, "Echoes from the Battle of Murfreesboro," 153; Pickett, "Reminiscences of Murfreesboro," 452.

to its limits. By the end of the day, Cheatham's division had suffered nearly 36 per cent casualties, with over two thousand losses. With nearly twenty-four hundred men lost, Withers had 28 per cent casualties. Cleburne's loss of over two thousand men meant losses of almost 30 per cent, while Withers had lost one-fourth of his men.[36]

Now Bragg found himself unable to revise his plans. Evidently he had prepared no plans in case there should be a second day's battle. Instead, on New Year's Day, he seemed at a loss as to what to do. He ordered the infantry to disperse for the menial tasks of picking up captured Federal equipment and war trophies. Meanwhile, Wheeler and Wharton harassed Federal ambulance trains on the Nashville Road.[37]

Bragg's apparently confused state continued on the morning of January 2. A hard rain began early in the morning that soon turned to sleet. Wharton's and Wheeler's troopers sloshed into Murfreesboro after a day's harassment on the Nashville Pike. The cavalry brought only bad news. Rosecrans was definitely not retreating. Instead, it appeared that he might be reinforced.

Other bad news was received that morning. In his lethargic state of January 1, Bragg had overlooked an obvious threat across the river. The long ridge along the east bank of the river, from which Polk's corps could be enfiladed, remained unoccupied. The only deployment Bragg had made in this area on January 1 was to return Breckinridge with a single brigade to the east bank. Even then, Breckinridge had no orders to advance and hold the ridge. Bragg learned that during the inactivity of the previous day, Federals in division strength had crossed and seized the high ground on the east bank near McFadden's Ford. Polk's line was open to enfilading artillery fire.[38]

Stunned, Bragg hastily decided that Breckinridge should attack and take the heights. Bragg did not bother to consult either Polk or Hardee in this decision. During the morning, he had sent staff officers to the east bank to reconnoiter the Yankee position. Their findings confirmed Bragg's fears that Polk's flank was vulnerable. Oblivious of Bragg's hasty

[36] Bragg's Murfreesboro Report, in Bragg Papers, Western Reserve; "Consolidated Report of Killed & Wounded at the battle of Murfreesboro, December 31, 1862" (MS in *ibid.*); "Recapitulation of Casualties, First Division Polk's Corps, Army of Tennessee" (MS in Cheatham Papers, Tennessee).

[37] Ridley, "Echoes from the Battle of Murfreesboro," 157; Wheeler to Bragg, January 1—1:30 P.M., 1863, Wheeler to "Dear General," January 1, 1863, Wheeler to Polk, January 1—6 P.M., 1863, all in Bragg Papers, Western Reserve; DuBose, *Wheeler*, 143; Bragg's Murfreesboro Report, in Bragg Papers, Western Reserve; Bearss, "Cavalry Operations," 132–35.

[38] Kirwan, *Orphan Brigade*, 67; Brent Diary, January 2, 1862, Bragg's Murfreesboro Report, Breckinridge to Bragg, December 31—7 P.M., 1862, all in Bragg Papers, Western Reserve; *Official Records*, XX, Pt. 1, pp. 784–85.

designs, Hardee, Polk, and Breckinridge were conversing shortly before noon. Soon after staff officers recalled Polk and Hardee to their head-quarters for other matters, a staff officer from Bragg requested that Breckinridge come to the General's headquarters. About noon Breckinridge, accompanied by Hardee's staff officer, Colonel W. D. Pickett, arrived at Bragg's camp.

To a surprised Breckinridge, Bragg announced his intention of using the Kentuckian's division to seize the high ground. Breckinridge, who already had spent several hours observing the position with his own staff, protested that the attack would be suicidal. He argued that the high ground west of McFadden's Ford commanded the eminence on the east bank, and that his troops would be hit by artillery as they attacked.

Bragg was adamant. Evidently without even consulting Breckinridge's superior, Hardee, Bragg planned the attack. Breckinridge was to advance at 4 P.M. A preliminary artillery barrage by Polk's guns across the river was to precede the advance. Breckinridge was to use his brigades, which were withdrawn from the west bank. He was assigned the battery of Captain Felix Robertson and a section of Captain Henry Semple's battery to supplement his own three batteries. After the slope had been won, the artillery was to be planted on the crest in order to enfilade Rosecrans' line across the river.[39]

The resulting attack was chaotic, largely because of Bragg's hasty planning. Polk, who opposed the plan, did not even know of the plans until Bragg rode over to talk with him about 3:00 P.M. Thus, the Bishop had less than an hour to prepare his artillery support, which was supposed to open at 3:45 P.M. Bragg also moved no troops across the river to support Breckinridge, and left the Kentuckian no hope of immediate reinforcement.

Two command feuds at the very hour of the attack also helped to doom the venture. When Robertson moved his guns across the river, he and Breckinridge argued as to how they were to be used. Robertson maintained that Bragg's instructions were for the infantry first to clear the crest on the east bank, and then for the artillery to hasten up and be planted in position. Breckinridge disagreed, insisting that the guns should advance between his two lines of infantry. Robertson refused, and Breckinridge offered a compromise—that the artillery advance immediately behind the second line of infantry. Robertson refused again, maintaining that such an alignment would crowd the field and offer too good

39 Pickett, "Reminiscences of Murfreesboro," 452; Bragg's Murfreesboro Report, in Bragg Papers, Western Reserve; *Official Records*, XX, Pt. 1, p. 787; Horn, *Army of Tennessee*, 207; O'Hara to Breckinridge, January 16, 1863, in Breckinridge Papers, New York Historical Society.

a target for the Yankee artillery concentrated across the river in the Round Forest. Without settling anything, Robertson kept his guns well in the rear as Breckinridge prepared to move forward.[40]

A worse command error was Breckinridge's failure to move his right wing into the battle. Because of the width of the ground on his front, Breckinridge needed additional support on his right flank to prevent being overlapped. Bragg designated Wharton's and Pegram's cavalry brigades to advance as Breckinridge's two right brigades.

For some reason, neither Wharton nor Pegram was in position to advance when the attack began. Openly angry at being ordered to make the attack, Breckinridge seemed to make only a halfhearted attempt to find the two officers. About 1 P.M. a message to Pegram indicated a movement was afoot. No time was given for the attack, however, and Pegram was ordered merely to arrange his lines along with Wharton's so as to "cooperate" with this move. By 3 P.M. Breckinridge still had received no reply from Pegram. About that time, General Gideon Pillow questioned him as to whether he had established communications with the two men. After receiving a negative reply, Pillow urged that this be done immediately. Between that hour and the beginning of the attack at 4 P.M., Breckinridge finally sent two staff officers to look for the cavalry, but they could not find them.[41]

Because of this confusion, the cavalrymen probably did not know an assault was in progress. Wharton declared he had received no news that an attack was even contemplated, and did not learn of it until he observed Breckinridge's infantry moving forward. Pegram may have known of the attack, but was not in position and did not tell Wharton. In the early afternoon, a member of Pegram's staff, Captain H. B. Clay, had been sent by Bragg to Pegram with orders to be ready to advance by 3 P.M. Although Clay maintained after the war that he was back at his command's headquarters before 3 o'clock, Pegram was not in position when Breckinridge attacked. [42]

These command disagreements doomed the advance. Timing was crucial, for Breckinridge needed to seize the heights on the east bank and plant his artillery before the Federals could mass firepower on the opposite bank. About 4 P.M. his division moved forward toward the desired slopes some one thousand yards away. Scarcely half the distance had

[40] Report of Felix Robertson, February 18, 1863, in Breckinridge Papers, New York Historical Society; *Official Records*, XX, Pt. 1, pp. 691, 785; Polk, *Polk*, II, 194.
[41] Brent to Pegram, January 2—1 P.M., 1863, Bragg's Murfreesboro Report, in Bragg Papers, Western Reserve; Brent to Bragg, March 15, 1863, in Breckinridge Papers, New York Historical Society; *Official Records*, XX, Pt. 1, pp. 785–86.
[42] H. B. Clay, "On the Right at Murfreesboro," *Confederate Veteran*, XXI (December, 1913), 588; *Official Records*, XX, Pt. 1, p. 969.

been covered when Breckinridge learned that his right wing was badly overlapped because of the absence of Wharton and Pegram. Breckinridge was forced to halt his advance until a battery could be brought up to cover that sector. This costly delay gave the Federals across the river time to mass artillery above McFadden's Ford. Even before the Kentuckians reached the slope on the east bank, they were losing heavily.

When the slope was finally reached, more confusion ensued. The Federal defenders were overrun and driven off the crest down into the river bottom. Breckinridge's first line, out of control, swarmed over the low bluff and down into the ford. Artillery massed on the high ground west of the ford, and southward from the Round Forest poured a terrible fire into the closely packed masses. Although he had seized the heights, Breckinridge was unable to locate Robertson's guns to set up a counterbarrage. Twice he unsuccessfully sent a staff officer to locate Robertson, who had waited in the rear for the infantry to take the heights. Robertson's artillery never arrived. Breckinridge's left flank, which had been dependent on Robertson to offset the enfilading fire from the area of the Round Forest, thus proved especially vulnerable.[43]

Even had Robertson been available, the assault would probably still have failed. When the crest was taken and Breckinridge's first line poured into the river at McFadden's Ford, the fire from the massed artillery above the bank there confused them. The front line recoiled onto the second line, which had halted on the east bank. More fire was poured into the mixed lines. The brigades in the second line panicked and fired into their own men during the confusion. By 4:45 P.M. the fight was over. Breckinridge's demoralized troops streamed back to their old lines. When Bragg saw the rout, he hurried Patton Anderson's brigade to halt the flight. By then it was getting dark, and the Federals did not pursue. There was little for Anderson to do but to interpose a fresh line between Breckinridge and the river. This move gave Breckinridge an opportunity to restore some semblance of command to his shattered troops. Of the forty-five hundred men who had attacked, over thirteen hundred were lost.[44]

43 John Buckner to Breckinridge, May 20, 1863, in Breckinridge Papers, New York Historical Society; Clay, "On the Right at Murfreesboro," 589; *Official Records*, XX, Pt. 1, p. 786; Du Bose, *Wheeler*, 146.

44 Report of Robertson, February 18, 1863, in Breckinridge Papers, New York Historical Society; E. T. Sykes, "A Cursory Sketch of General Bragg's Campaigns— Paper Number Two," *SHSP*, XI (1883), 472–73, Bragg in his report gave Anderson credit for saving Breckinridge's division. See Bragg's Murfreesboro Report, in Bragg Papers, Western Reserve. Anderson denied this, stating that "General Bragg founded his report upon exaggerated statements of some partial friends of mine and hence attributed to me more than I deserved." See "Autobiography of General Patton Anderson," *SHSP*, XXIV (1896), 68; see also *Official Records*, XX, Pt. 1, pp. 668, 765–66, 793, 797, 808, 812–13.

On the night of January 2 Bragg again appeared uncertain as to what should be done. Sleet fell during the night, freezing clothes to bodies and causing great suffering among the wounded on the field. Churches and practically every home and public building in Murfreesboro were filled with the wounded. Prisoners stood shivering in the streets, awaiting a trek southward to Confederate prisons. About 10 P.M. the corps and division leaders huddled at Bragg's headquarters. Little developed from this meeting, however. Earlier that evening, Bragg had ordered McCown's and Cleburne's divisions to cross the river and reinforce Breckinridge, lest the Federals follow up the repulse. This move left only Cheatham and Withers on the west bank with scarcely seven thousand effectives, and they were separated from the east bank by a rapidly rising, rain-swollen river. Unable to decide anything else to do, the council adjourned and Bragg retired. [45]

During the early hours of January 3, troubling news was heard from all quarters. Shortly after midnight a courier awoke Bragg with a report from a cavalry outpost on the right wing. The enemy reportedly was making threatening moves in that sector. During the night Bragg ordered Hardee personally to take charge on that bank. Scarcely was this done when a disturbing note was received from Polk at about 2 A.M. Polk enclosed a note written directly to Bragg from Cheatham and Withers. These two generals were concerned about their isolated position and heavy casualties. They were also concerned about a warning received shortly before midnight from Patton Anderson. Anderson, still detached from Polk's corps, reported from the east bank that the lines were too thin. He warned that a gap of eight hundred yards, fronted by the enemy, existed on his left, and another gap was on his right. Cheatham and Withers wrote a hasty note to Bragg and sent it via Polk's headquarters. They urged a retreat, and argued that there were only three brigades in the army that could be considered reliable. With his customary evasiveness, Polk sent the note on to Bragg with no direct statement as to whether he agreed. Bragg was roused by Polk's aide, Lieutenant W. B. Richmond, who bore both notes. Although Polk did not commit himself on the re-

45 Du Bose, *Wheeler*, 147; Kirwan, *Orphan Brigade*, 69; Polk, *Polk*, II, 194; Ridley, "Echoes from the Battle of Murfreesboro," 67; Sykes, "Cursory Sketch of General Bragg's Campaigns," 473–74; "Tabular Statement of the 'Present for Duty' on 31st Dec. 1862, the number of killed, wounded and missing and the percentage of loss in the brigades of Breckinridge's division at the battle of Murfreesboro" (MS in Bragg Papers, Western Reserve) ; "Tabular Statement Showing the Number Present for Duty on the morning of the 31 Dec. 1862, the number of killed, wounded and missing, and the percentage of loss in the battle of Murfreesboro" (MS in Bragg Papers, Western Reserve) ; "Statement of Lt. Col. Urquhart AAG to the location of General Hardee and Breckinridge on the night 2nd Jan 63, during operations at Murfreesboro" (MS in Bragg Papers, Western Reserve) .

treat, he did add that he feared the consequence of another battle at Murfreesboro on January 3. He also hinted that if a retreat were handled properly, the army might escape.[46]

At first Bragg refused to consider the matter. He snapped a reply to Richmond to tell Polk to hold his position despite all hazards, and then went back to bed. Unsatisfied, Polk about 3 A.M. sent Richmond with the notes to Hardee. Polk enclosed a third note to Hardee stating that he thought Bragg's decision was not wise. This was the first mention of a retreat that Hardee had heard during the campaign. He could offer no advice other than to tell Polk that nothing could be done that night anyway.

By the following morning Bragg had changed his mind. Another council was held at his quarters at 10 A.M. He now favored a retreat. During the night he had been brought General A. M. McCook's papers, which had been captured on the field. The strength of McCook's corps, listed as eighteen thousand, convinced Bragg that Rosecrans must have more men on the field than he had believed. Now Bragg feared he was confronted with seventy thousand men. During the morning, more reports from Wheeler indicated Rosecrans was being reinforced. Bragg could muster barely twenty thousand effectives, and the heavy rains threatened to isolate Cheatham and Withers on the west bank. Other problems were evident. The army was beginning to straggle. Many officers and men were so exhausted from exposure and the battle that they were being placed in hospitals in the rear. Trains to Chattanooga were crowded with the wounded. There was no disagreement now—Bragg, Polk, and Hardee concurred that a retreat was imperative.[47]

During the afternoon the baggage and ordnance trains were moved southward down the pikes to Shelbyville and Manchester. All wounded who could walk trailed behind. While rain and sleet alternated during the cold night, Bragg and his generals met for a final council and hesitated again. To abandon Murfreesboro meant the surrender of seventeen hundred men—the sick and wounded, and medical officers. The question was whether to hold the town for another twenty-four hours in an

46 Bragg's Murfreesboro Report, in Bragg Papers, Western Reserve; Hardee's Murfreesboro Report, Duke; Cheatham and Withers to Bragg, January 3—12:15 A.M., 1863, in Cheatham Papers, Tennessee; Polk to Bragg, January 3—1:30 A.M., 1863, in Breckinridge Papers, New York Historical Society; Anderson to Major Huger, January 2—10:45 P.M., 1863, in Bragg Papers, Western Reserve.

47 Hardee to Bragg, January 12, 1863, Breckinridge to Bragg, January 12, 1863, all in Davis Papers, Tulane; Polk to Bragg, January 3—1:30 A.M., 1863, in Bragg Papers, New York Historical Society; Official Records, XX, Pt. 1, pp. 700–701; Bragg's Murfreesboro Report in Bragg Papers, Western Reserve; Brent Diary, January 3, 1863, Bragg Papers, Western Reserve; Ridley, "Echoes from the Battle of Murfreesboro," 67; Pickett, "Reminiscences of Murfreesboro," 452; Du Bose, Wheeler, 147.

attempt to evacuate more of the wounded. The generals voted to retreat immediately. Intelligence indicated that already Rosecrans had transferred a large part of his army to the front occupied by Polk's two weak divisions. Across the river, Rosecrans had probed during the day at Breckinridge's front, and there were indications of a flanking move on the east bank as well. Shortly after 7 P.M. the final decision was made. Polk would begin his retreat that night on the road from Murfreesboro to Shelbyville. Hardee would leave at daylight the next morning, and would move via Manchester behind Duck River to Tullahoma.[48]

The problem of command direction which had doomed the Murfreesboro campaign from the outset flickered one last time. In his haste to bring his command to the untenable line at Murfreesboro, Bragg had made no provision for retreat, so he did not really know where his army was going. He knew that he must hasten, for continual reports on January 4 warned of an advance by Rosecrans. Vaguely Bragg envisioned a line somewhere southward along the Elk River, but he also was pondering some defensive position in the Duck River Valley. While his army, weaker by ten thousand men, slogged southward into the Highland Rim country, Bragg hurried south to search for a new position.[49]

[48] Polk, *Polk*, II, 196; Bragg's Murfreesboro Report, in Bragg Papers, Western Reserve; Hardee to Bragg, January 12, 1863, Breckinridge to Bragg, January 12, 1863, all in Davis Papers, Tulane; Kirwan, *Orphan Brigade*, 70.

[49] Johnston Diary, January 3, 4, 5, 6, 1863, in Bragg Papers, Western Reserve; Special Orders, January 3, 1863, Wheeler to General, January 4, 1863, C. M. Blackburn to Breckinridge, January 4, 1863, Wheeler to Roy, January 4—1 P.M., 1863, Roy to General, January 5, 1863, all in Wheeler Papers, Chicago; Wheeler to Bragg, January 4, 1863, in Bragg Papers, Western Reserve.

four

The Rise of the Anti-Bragg Men

ALL NIGHT ON JANUARY 3 BRAGG AND HIS STAFF TRAVELED THROUGH A cold rain. In the early morning the party reached Shelbyville, on the north bank of the Duck River. Still uncertain where to place his army, Bragg pushed on to Winchester in the Elk River Valley. By January 6 he seemed to favor a line along the Elk River, but by the following day he had changed his mind. Bragg halted his retreating corps and took up a line in the Duck River Valley, behind the sheltering ridges of the Highland Rim.[1]

Bragg's six months stay on this line was a curious and unfortunate one. While the army remained inactive, its numbers were bolstered to a strength never attained previously, and organization, drill, and discipline were improved. At the same time bitter quarrels finally demolished all esprit which remained in the high command, and the army also experienced a complete internal collapse. No plan of strategy was formulated, no strong defensive line drawn. As a result of these consumate failures, in early July Bragg lost Middle Tennessee with scarcely a shot being fired.

Failure could be laid to Bragg and to Joseph Johnston. Bragg's whole attention seemed wrapped up in the power struggle within the Army of Tennessee. Johnston failed to take hold and produce a workable strategy

---

1 W. L. Clay to sister, December 26, 1862, in C. C. Clay Papers, National Archives; Richard Taylor, *Destruction and Reconstruction: Personal Experiences of the Late War* (New York, 1879), 99–100; Oates, *War Between the Union and the Confederacy*, 319–20; W. W. Mackall to wife, September 29, 1863, in William W. Mackall, *A Son's Recollections of His Father* (New York, 1930), 178–79; John Buie to I. E. Buie, September 30, 1862, in John Buie Papers, Duke.

for Bragg's army, and Richmond's dream of unified command became chaos under his direction as theater commander.

Even as Bragg's horsemen retreated from Murfreesboro, clashes began between him and his generals. The old familiar Bragg—dull, sour, pedantic—seemed unable to inspire his officers. Even his letters home to his wife resembled battle reports and lacked any semblance of affection. He had little social life in the army, and his personal mannerisms, which his own chief of staff later termed repulsive, failed to incite enthusiasm or warmth. The men respected his abilities as a drillmaster and disciplinarian, but little else.

Bragg's lack of compassion made it difficult for him to deal with individuals. A hard worker, thoroughly devoted to the war effort, Bragg did not seem to understand people. He was irritable and impatient, even with his friends. Also, he possessed an amazing sense of poor timing. With feeling against him running high among the Kentucky troops prior to Murfreesboro, Bragg executed a young deserter from the Second Kentucky Regiment despite pleas from the Kentucky officers. In early January, when bitterness over Murfreesboro's defeat was obvious in the army, he opened himself to abuse by inviting the written opinions of his staff as to his abilities.[2]

As for Bragg's difficulty in dealing with his friends, although John Forsyth, editor of the Mobile *Register,* had risked personal criticism by publishing a strong defense of the Kentucky campaign, Bragg was not appreciative. Instead, he complained to Forsyth over some petty technicalities of the article.[3]

If Bragg could irritate a friend, he could infuriate an enemy. He never left his enemies any escape mechanism, but instead relished complete victory in any dispute. Within the army, he drove his enemies to the wall, humiliated them, and forced them into the anti-Bragg element. Then he never let the matter subside. He showed a paternalistic manner toward all dissenters. He often spoke of his officers' not meeting his expectations, of their shortcomings, and of how they "winced" under his blows. Always the same theme persisted—Bragg was right and his generals wrong. Thus, beginning with Perryville, he sought scapegoats for every mistake. He never admitted to fault, except to say that he had entrusted generals with tasks they were not good enough to perform.

And always he ignored the matter of pride. Bragg never understood that his army was a series of cliques, each based around some general with a regional or personal attraction. Each of his corps and division

2 W. W. Mackall to wife, September 29, 1863, in Mackall, *Recollections,* 178–79.
3 J. Stoddard Johnston to John Forsyth, December 22, 1862, in J. Stoddard Johnston Military Papers, Filson Club Historical Society.

leaders, such as Polk, Hardee, Cleburne, Breckinridge, Cheatham, and others, had a cadre of surrounding officers and staff members. In turn, these groups were often backed by geographical combines, such as Cheatham's following of Tennessee troops. To these men, preserving face was all important. Bragg never realized this. On several occasions, beginning in the spring, he publicly humiliated his generals by arrest, damnation in reports to Richmond, and by other devices. Several times in 1862, Bragg had demonstrated his penchant for openly embarrassing his officers. During that summer he had stated that many of his brigadier generals were dead weight and that Hardee was his only decent major general. To a visitor, General Richard Taylor, Bragg had further elaborated that he had only one or two men fit for high command.[4]

Other familiar personality quirks were evident during the Duck River stay. On and off the field, Bragg was indecisive. In both previous campaigns, he had shown ability in preparing plans, only to waver at the final moment. He seemed to lack the strength to make a final commitment. In Kentucky and again at Murfreesboro Bragg seemed unable to carry through his plans. He seemed good only for a day's battle. When it became obvious that Rosecrans would fight another day, Bragg lost his balance, fumbled for a solution, and hastily settled on the suicidal attack by Breckinridge.

Paradoxically, Bragg was as rigid as he was indecisive. Once he had made a decision in his field tactics, he seemed unable to adjust to a changing confrontation. In Kentucky, he did not count on Buell's rapid advance from Louisville, and for several days remained unable to reassess. At Murfreesboro, Bragg seemed hard pressed to devise a new strategy to meet Rosecrans' continued advance since his rigid plan called for a one-day battle.[5]

During the spring of 1863 other aspects of Bragg's overall poor mental and physical condition became evident. He had been nervous for years, a victim of headaches, dyspepsia, and assorted ailments. Matters of health were frequently discussed in his letters home. By 1863 Bragg was suffering from the beginnings of a nervous and physical breakdown. His suspicious, nervous temper, battered by criticism over Kentucky, grew worse after Murfreesboro. In June Bragg himself admitted that he had suffered "a general breakdown" caused by "the long-continued excitement of mind and body." [6] In early July Bragg conceded that he was utterly broken down. This collapse, often underrated by historians, was

4 Hughes, *Hardee*, 119; Taylor, *Destruction and Reconstruction*, 99–100.
5 William Polk to Archibald Gracie, December 18, 1911, in Polk Papers, Sewanee; Oates, *War Between the Union and the Confederacy*, 320.
6 *Official Records*, III, Pt. 2, p. 499.

so serious that at that time his corps leaders considered him unable to examine a battle line, much less to take command in the field.[7]

Although his spirit broke in one sense, in another sense he became more aggressive. Previously, Bragg had been relatively docile in his reaction to the Kentucky criticism. By February, however, he changed abruptly. He felt committed to purge the army of its malcontents. Bragg explained to President Davis, "Assailed, myself, for the blunders of others, and by them and their friends, my mind is made up to bear no sins in the future but my own." [8]

In his new aggressiveness, Bragg seemed to enjoy verbal contests. Beginning with the first clash in January, concerning Murfreesboro, Bragg pounced on any scrap of evidence of poor generalship with the fervor of a forensic debate student. This is why most of his time along Duck River was expended not in preparing strategy or defenses but in preparing briefs for his personal cases. In fact, he was accused of preferring to win one battle in Richmond more than two in the field.[9]

Bragg now seemed to underrate his enemies in the army much as he had previously underestimated his Union opponents. Not until the fall of 1863 did Bragg seem to realize that the sentiment against him, if not well organized was widespread. Until then, he tossed it off as the handiwork of only several disgruntled officers and nothing more. He believed some aspired to his command. Others, he thought, were only trying to hide their own faults. Thus, Bragg considered this discontent to be a passing thing which could be eliminated by punishment of the particular dissenter. He did not seem to understand that a strike against Cheatham would be considered an affront not only to Polk but also to the proud Tennessee troops. An attack on Hardee would involve Cleburne, and criticism of Breckinridge would involve other Kentucky officers.[10]

Self-pitying letters written by Bragg in January revealed his notion that he had become a martyr to Davis' failing policies—that he was being harassed by evil men for doing his duty. Such friends as General John K. Jackson fed these beliefs. In January, Jackson warned Bragg he had suspected for some time that some generals desired "to sweep you away." [11] Other friends augmented Bragg's suspicions. As early as December, Sen-

[7] Arthur Noll (ed.), *Doctor Quintard, Chaplain, C.S.A.* (Sewanee, 1905), 87; Hardee to Polk, July 1, 1863, Polk to Hardee, July 1, 1863, in Polk, *Polk*, II, 222–23.

[8] *Official Records*, LII, Pt. 2, p. 426.

[9] William Preston to William Preston Johnston, January 26, 1863, in Barret Collection, Tulane.

[10] For evidence of Bragg's change of thinking, see *Official Records*, LII, Pt. 2, pp. 407, 426; XXIII, Pt. 2, p. 652; Bragg to Davis, May 22, 1863, in Braxton Bragg Papers, Duke.

[11] John K. Jackson to Bragg, January 17, 1863, in Bragg Papers, Western Reserve.

ator James Phelan of Mississippi warned of rumblings against Bragg in Congress. Later, another congressional supporter, James Pugh of Alabama, warned of "an organized effort to break you down." [12] Bragg's self-righteous posture was further encouraged by his former medical director, Dr. A. J. Foard, who noted that the general would finally be sustained by all who were honest in their opinions.[13] A more rabid supporter, Confederate surgeon J. C. Nott, added more fuel by stating that Bragg had no general capable of leading more than a brigade, and that "justice may not be done you till the world learns how necessary your presence is to that army." [14]

By mid-January Bragg's popularity and the army's morale seemed at a new low. The outcry over Kentucky had not abated, and after Murfreesboro, dislike of Bragg was widespread in the army. Public dissatisfaction over Murfreesboro equalled that following Perryville. He was severely criticized, particularly in the newspapers. His first dispatches from the field on the night of December 31 had been distorted into a great victory. The Augusta Chronicle noted that the victory on the thirty-first was so great that it was impossible to throw it away. The Chattanooga Rebel exulted that Murfreesboro would put Bragg in a new light.[15]

When the truth of the battle was known, the strongest attack yet was aimed at Bragg by the newspapers. Some of these criticisms were expected. The Winchester correspondent for the anti-Davis Richmond Examiner charged that there was no "exercise of military genius" by Bragg. The Augusta Chronicle implied that he had misled the public by his reports. Even the more moderate publications joined the attack. Bragg was surprised when he was attacked in the Mobile Register. He was more angered to learn how the attack had been instigated. A correspondent for the Register had befriended Breckinridge's adjutant general, Theodore O'Hara. O'Hara bore a grudge against Bragg, who had discharged him in 1861 at Pensacola "as a disgrace to the service." O'Hara had them drifted into Beauregard's camp until a Bragg warning prompted the Creole to expel O'Hara from the army. At Murfreesboro, O'Hara had been rebuffed in an attempt to befriend Joseph E. Johnston, but had taken a job as Breckinridge's adjutant. Evidently he furnished the cor-

12 Phelan to Bragg, December 4, 1862, J. L. Pugh to Bragg, March 5, 1863, ibid.

13 A. F. Foard to Bragg, January 31, 1863, ibid.

14 J. C. Nott to Bragg, January 31, 1863, ibid.

15 Augusta Daily Chronicle and Sentinel, January 4, 1863; see also ibid., January 6, 1863; Irving A. Buck to sister, January 13, 1863, in Irving Buck Letters, UNC; Chattanooga Daily Rebel, January 3, 4, 6, 11, 1863; Richmond Examiner, February 25, 1863.

respondent with information from the army's records which was used in several critical articles on Bragg in the *Register*.[16]

An even sorer spot was the Chattanooga *Rebel*. This newspaper had prophesied trouble three days after the battle, when the populace still thought Bragg had won. It editorialized that if Bragg had lost, "he would have been damned from one end of the South to the other; he would have been jeered and hooted from the service." When the news of his retreat was learned, the *Rebel* published a series of critical editorials. They insisted that he was not popular in the army, that he had alienated many of his generals, and that the troops felt no confidence or affection for him. Then followed a stronger statement which charged that the retreat from Murfreesboro had been against the advice of his generals. Moreover, noted the newspaper, Bragg would be soon removed from command.[17]

The last bit of news proved to be the final straw. Bragg moved to instigate his first personal battle. On January 10 he assembled his staff and read the newspaper editorial aloud. Already there were rumors in the high command that Bragg would be replaced by Beauregard. Bragg, having heard that Kirby Smith had been summoned to Richmond for a conference, evidently believed that officer would replace him. Determined to squelch any such move, Bragg asked his staff if it were true that he had lost the army's confidence. He declared, as he had many times before, that if he had lost such confidence, he would resign his command. After the morning meeting, the staff caucused and reported back. They informed Bragg that under the existing circumstances it would be best if he would ask to be relieved of his position.[18]

The following day Bragg took the matter further. He composed a circular letter to send to all corps and division leaders. Bragg wrote two versions of the note. The first draft stated that some were accusing him of retreating from Murfreesboro against the advice of his junior officers, and asked the generals to verify in writing that they had advised a retreat. With even less discretion, he also asked if the generals believed the army had lost its confidence in him.

Some of his staff, fearful of the answers, begged him not to send his first note. Bragg finally wrote a second note omitting his request for a

16 Richmond *Examiner*, February 25, 1863; Augusta *Daily Chronicle and Sentinel*, January 6, 1863; Bragg to W. W. Mackall, February 14, 1863, in W. W. Mackall Papers, UNC.

17 Chattanooga *Daily Rebel*, January 6, 1863; Johnston Journal, January 10, 1863, Bragg Papers, Western Reserve.

18 Irving Buck to sister, January 18, 1863, in Buck Papers, UNC; Brent Diary, January 10, 1863, in Bragg Papers, Western Reserve; Bragg to Johnston, January 11, 1863, in Seitz, *Bragg*, 254–55.

statement of the army's confidence, but he left himself vulnerable by declaring that he would resign if he had lost the confidence of his generals.[19]

The replies received by Bragg were not what he had hoped for. Polk was on a trip to the North Carolina Blue Ridge, and did not receive the January 11 note until six days later. A curious succession of events followed. When Polk read the note, his own interpretation was that Bragg was asking two questions: had Polk advised a retreat from Murfreesboro, and did he think Bragg had the army's confidence? Instead of answering directly, Polk shrewdly hedged. He took advantage of Bragg's request that he consult his subordinates before replying. Polk merely dispatched a note stating he would return in a few days and furnish a reply. Meanwhile, in Polk's corps Withers and Cheatham seemed more unsure than the Bishop as to what Bragg wanted. Desiring to consult Polk before they committed themselves, the two officers responded only to the retreat question in a note sent by Cheatham. On January 31 Cheatham sent a brief note assuring Bragg that he had been one of the first to suggest a retreat, and had repeatedly said so since the army had fallen back to Duck River.[20]

When Polk came back in late January, he still refused to commit himself. Instead, on January 30 he felt out Bragg's intentions in an awkward note. Polk admitted that he had seen two questions in the original circular, but said that his division commanders had seen only one—the question regarding a retreat. Thus, "to avoid being placed in a false position," Polk asked Bragg if his own interpretation of a request for two answers was correct. Bragg quickly replied that same day by stating that the Bishop's interpretation was wrong. Bragg insisted that he had never intended to ask for a statement of confidence. The following day, Polk hedged again, and merely answered that he had favored a retreat.[21]

After receiving the frank replies from Hardee's corps, Bragg was not anxious to hear Polk's opinion of his abilities. Hardee and his generals interpreted the message as Polk did. The day after receiving the note, Hardee wrote Bragg a stiff reply, informing him that he had conferred with Cleburne and Breckinridge and that all three had agreed the army needed a new commanding general. Moreover, Hardee denied both that

19 Bragg to Polk, Hardee, Breckinridge, Cleburne, and Cheatham, January 11, 1862, copy of circular letter in Breckinridge Papers, New York Historical Society; Brent Diary, January 11, 1862, in Bragg Papers, Western Reserve.

20 *Official Records,* XX, Pt. 1, p. 698; Cheatham to Bragg, January 13, 1863, in Bragg Papers, Western Reserve.

21 Polk to Bragg, January 30, 1863, in General Leonidas Polk, Letters and Telegrams Sent, 1861–64, National Archives; Bragg to Polk, January 30, 1863, Polk to Bragg, January 31, 1863, in Breckinridge Papers, New York Historical Society.

he had advocated a retreat at Murfreesboro, and that his officers had made any disparaging statements regarding the nature of the retreat since falling back to the Duck River line.[22]

The replies sent by Hardee's division command were even more infuriating to Bragg. That same day, Breckinridge also replied. He had conferred with his brigade commanders, and all had agreed that Bragg did not possess the army's confidence. Like Hardee, Breckinridge denied any part in the decision to retreat. The next day Cleburne sent another sharp note to Bragg. He, too, had consulted his brigade commanders, and all had agreed that Bragg did not have the army's confidence to a degree which would ensure success.[23]

The repercussions of this episode were to have important effects. Not only did it herald the beginning of a long season of disputes, but also motivated Bragg to retaliate harshly against his subordinates. Intended or not, his January 11 circular had been interpreted by most of his officers as an assurance that he would resign if he discovered that the army did not have confidence in his leadership. Certainly he had implied this to Joseph E. Johnston in a private letter on January 11, where, commenting on a rumor that Kirby Smith might replace him, he noted that if a better man for the job were found, he would cheerfully step down. Three days later, in a letter to Johnston's chief of staff, Colonel B. S. Ewell, Bragg reiterated his claim.

Bragg was now trapped in a dilemma of his own making. To avoid resigning he must justify his mistakes. He was convinced that the dissidents among his officers were few, and from them he would select a number of scapegoats. Since Hardee's officers had been the more aggressive in their criticisms, Bragg, in February, would move against Hardee's generals.[24]

In early February Bragg seemed convinced the army's discontent was confined to these few generals. He apparently did not know that the ill feelings were shared by Polk and his generals. He probably knew nothing of the private conversation in late January between Polk and Joseph E. Johnston, in which the Bishop told Johnston that he and his generals had no confidence in Bragg. Nor did Bragg seem to know that on February 4, after evading an answer to Bragg for four days, Polk wrote the first of a series of clandestine letters to Davis urging that Bragg be replaced by Johnston.[25]

22 Hardee to Bragg, January 12, 1863, in William J. Hardee Papers, Alabama.
23 Cleburne to Bragg, January 13, 1863, in Bragg Papers, Duke; Breckinridge to Bragg, January 12, 1863, in Jefferson Davis Papers, Louisiana Historical Association Collection. Tulane.
24 *Official Records*, XXIII, Pt. 2, p. 652, LII, Pt. 2, pp. 426, 407; Johnston to Davis, February 3, 12, 1863, in Johnston Papers, William and Mary.
25 Polk to Davis, February 4, 1863, in Polk, *Polk*, II, 206–207; Johnston to Davis, February 12, 1863, in Johnston Papers, William and Mary.

Perhaps Bragg also did not know that Cheatham had deep resentment for him. Aside from Polk, Cheatham had been the only recipient of the circular note who had not attacked Bragg. Yet, privately Cheatham shared the views of Hardee's men. Shortly after Murfreesboro, Cheatham declared that he would never serve under Bragg in the future and was only calmed down by his friend Governor Isham Harris.[26]

Bragg's new policy of dealing with dissension was strengthened by a second crisis in late January. Richmond was aware of the general military and public disapproval with Bragg. Davis had also learned of Bragg's circular note, a maneuver the President considered to show extremely poor judgment. By some means, Davis had also learned that the responses to Bragg's note had condemned that officer. Anxious to learn the full truth of the matter, Davis, on January 21, telegraphed Joseph E. Johnston, at Mobile where he was inspecting defenses, to hurry to Bragg's army. Davis was in such haste that he sent no explanatory letter. Instead, Johnston was to receive further orders while passing through Chattanooga en route to Tullahoma. He left immediately for Chattanooga but found no letter of instructions there. He was told to push on to Tullahoma, where, on January 29, he finally received a letter from the President.[27]

Whatever Davis expected Johnston to do after he arrived at Tullahoma was not clarified in the President's letter. He told Johnston to confer with Bragg and his generals and to "decide what the best interests of the service require." [28]

He gave Johnston no authority to supersede Bragg, but ambiguously told him to direct the army's operations "and do whatever else belongs to the General commanding." [29]

Johnston's views on two generals operating at the same headquarters were well known to Davis. Throughout December and early January, Johnston had maintained that it was impossible for two commanders to oversee the same army. This had been his key argument in late December at Jackson when Johnston asked the President to relieve him. Johnston had argued that he had no alternative to taking command of one of his armies, "which, as each had its own General, was not intended or desirable." [30] Later, in mid-January, Johnston had again expressed to

[26] Pillow to Major Clare, March 9, 1863, in Bragg Papers, Western Reserve; William Preston to William Preston Johnston, January 26, 1863, in Barret Collection, Tulane; Johnston to Davis, February 12, 1863, in Johnston Papers, William and Mary.
[27] Davis to Johnston, January 22, 1863, in Johnston Papers, William and Mary; *Official Records*, LII, Pt. 2, pp. 410, 418.
[28] Davis to Johnston, January 22, 1863, in Johnston Papers, William and Mary.
[29] *Ibid.;* see also Johnston to Wigfall, February 14, 1863, in Wigfall, DLC.
[30] Joseph E. Johnston, "Jefferson Davis and the Mississippi Campaign," 589.

Richmond his hesitancy over taking actual charge of one of the armies.
Johnston noted that in such a case he "should deprive an officer, in whom
you have confidence, of the command for which you have selected him." [31]
In late January, Johnston repeated these fears in correspondence with
his friend Wigfall.[32]

This was not merely a matter of discomfort for Johnston. He feared
that if he took immediate command of Bragg's army, his motives might
be misconstrued. His repeated complaints of the past two months to the
government and to Wigfall that his command amounted to nothing, his
avowed desire for a field command, his complaint to Davis that he was
nothing more than a spectator—all placed him in a delicate position.
Also, he had asked Wigfall to help him to obtain a field command, and
indicated he thought Bragg's job was a more desirable position than his
own.[33]

Now, in late January, Johnston seemed concerned lest he be accused
of seeking Bragg's command. In his preliminary report from Tullahoma
on February 3, Johnston asserted that if Davis had in mind to remove
Bragg, no one connected with the investigation should take his place. In
his second report on February 12, Johnston wrote specifically that if
Davis chose to remove Bragg, that he should not be considered for the
position. Later, Johnston admitted to Wigfall that this fear that his
motives would be misconstrued was very much on his mind at the time.[34]

Johnston's concern in his February observations was also influenced
by the obvious attitudes of anti-Bragg friends. By February Johnston
knew that his congressional supporters were lobbying for his replacement
of Bragg. Johnston also knew that Wigfall was converting Seddon to the
anti-Bragg side. Throughout February, sometimes in late night meetings,
Wigfall pressed the Secretary for Bragg's removal. By late February, Wigfall could boast to Johnston that the general only had to let him know
what command he wanted and "I believe I will be able to accomplish
your wishes." [35] Wigfall also assured Johnston that he could have Bragg's
post if he wanted it.

Less than a week after arriving at Tullahoma, Johnston received a
confidential note from Secretary Seddon flatly offering him Bragg's posi-

31 Johnston to Davis, "written between January 10 and 31st 1863," in Johnston
Papers, William and Mary.
32 Johnston to Wigfall, January 26, 1863, in Wright, Southern Girl, 122.
33 Johnston to Wigfall, February 14, 1863, Johnston to Wigfall, December 15, 1862,
in Wigfall Papers, DLC; Johnston to Wigfall, January 8, 1863, in Wright, Southern
Girl, 107–108; Wigfall to Johnston, February 28, 1863, in Joseph E. Johnston Letters,
Henry E. Huntington Library.
34 Johnston to Davis, February 3, 12, 1863, in Johnston Papers, William and Mary;
Johnston to Wigfall, March 4, 8, 1863, April 1, 1864, in Wigfall, DLC.
35 Wigfall to Johnston, February 28, 1863, in Johnston Papers, Huntington.

tion as army commander in Tennessee. He suggested that Johnston might establish permanent headquarters with Bragg's army and relegate Bragg to chief of staff. Better, suggested Seddon, might Johnston not be happier by taking complete command of the army and being rid of Bragg? While he was at Tullahoma, both Polk and Hardee told him that they had asked Davis for Bragg's removal and Johnston's appointment.[36]

Yet Johnston's glowing report of Bragg's abilities were not totally due to that general's fear of being called a Brutus. Long before the inspection trip, Johnston had expressed great confidence in Bragg. On his trip to Murfreesboro in December, Johnston saw no evidence of the lack of confidence in Bragg of which he had heard at Richmond, and considered the army to be in fine condition and spirits. After Murfreesboro, Johnston continued to support Bragg. He thought Bragg had "done wonders" [37] at Stone's River, and believed Bragg was entitled to "high reward" [38] for his performance. Since Johnston thought Bragg's Murfreesboro defeat was the fault of the government, he considered it "criminal" [39] to deprive him of his command. Johnston maintained that "more effective fighting is not to be found in the history of modern battles" than that done by Bragg at Murfreesboro.[40]

His first report to Davis on February 3 was hastily researched, consisting only of interviews with Bragg, Hardee, Polk, and Governor Harris. All four told Johnston that there was trouble in the army. Bragg termed it a passing matter inspired by a few generals. Polk and Hardee admitted they had no confidence in Bragg, and Hardee indicated his generals had none either. Harris also agreed that the feeling existed. In the face of these avowals, Johnston sent a vague report. On one hand he praised Bragg's Murfreesboro campaign and said it would be unfortunate to relieve him. Yet on the same page he urged Davis not to consider him for Bragg's post should Davis decide to remove him.[41]

Johnston's second report was more obviously a stall. He did not seem to carry out Davis' instructions of January 22 to determine the army's confidence in Bragg, In his entire investigation, Johnston questioned only Bragg, Polk, Harris and Hardee, interrogating none of the division or brigade commanders. He seemed almost fearful of finding the truth.

36 Johnston to Wigfall, December 27, 1863, in Wigfall, DLC; Seddon to Johnston, February 5, 1863, in Johnston Papers, William and Mary; Johnston to Wigfall, January 26, 1863, in Wright, *Southern Girl,* 121–22.
37 Johnston to Wigfall, January 26, 1863, in Wright, *Southern Girl,* 121–22; see also Johnston to Wigfall, December 15, 1862, in Wigfall, DLC.
38 Johnston to Wigfall, December 27, 1863, in Wigfall, DLC.
39 Johnston to Wigfall, April 15, 1864, in *ibid.*
40 Johnston to Wigfall, February 14, 1863, in *ibid.*
41 Johnston to Davis, February 3, 1863, in Johnston Papers, William and Mary.

With the same ambiguity of the first report, he stated that "some or all of the general officers" lacked confidence in Bragg, then he again praised the Murfreesboro campaign, and suggested that Bragg not be removed.[42]

Occurrences at Tullahoma during the first two weeks in February probably influenced this final report. Aside from Polk's and Hardee's informing him that they had asked Davis to place him in command, Johnston was probably embarrassed by Seddon's similar offer. Also, Johnston still believed that he had no real authority except as some sort of inspector general. Seddon in early February tried to convince Johnston that he was wrong, stating that Johnston was empowered to assume the "supreme command" of any imperiled army.[43] Two weeks after this statement, Johnston was complaining to Wigfall that he had no real authority. Johnston seemed embarrassed at even being with Bragg's army. He left Tullahoma as soon as he sent his second report, having spent only two weeks with Bragg. While there, he certainly declined to assume any "supreme command." According to Bragg, Johnston told him that he would not give an order or assume "one particle" of direction.[44] When Bragg told Johnston that he would call on him if the prospect of a battle appeared, Johnston replied that he would come and serve on Bragg's staff, but not as commander. Later, after returning to Chattanooga, Johnston wrote Bragg that if he were needed, "I will be back to assist you." [45]

At Tullahoma, Johnston had assured Bragg that he had the best organized, armed, equipped, and disciplined army in the Confederacy. He agreed with Bragg that the trouble was caused by some generals who sought only to hide their own failures, and that the complaints were "generally totally unfounded." [46] Bragg gloated over this praise and Johnston's congratulatory order which praised both Bragg and the army. Strengthened by Johnston's agreeable visit, Bragg felt that this "completely knocked the pegs" from the "scoundrels who were abusing me." [47]

On February 23 he completed his official report to Davis on the Murfreesboro campaign. It was dispatched to Richmond by Colonel John Sale, Bragg's close friend. Sale was to deliver the report and to supply Davis with some verbal answers. Bragg wrote Davis a short accompanying

42 Johnston to Davis, February 12, 1863, in *ibid.*
43 Seddon to Johnston, February 5, 1863, in *ibid.*
44 Bragg to Mackall, February 14, 1863, in Mackall Papers, UNC.
45 Johnston to Bragg, March 8, 1863, in Joseph E. Johnston Papers, Duke. Johnston's aloof policy toward controlling Bragg was illustrated by a letter to General Earl Van Dorn on February 24 when he stated "the movements in General Bragg's theater of operations will be necessarily under his control." *Official Records*, XXIII, Pt. 2, p. 646. See also Johnston to Wigfall, February 14, 1863, in Wigfall Papers, DLC.
46 Bragg to Mackall, February 14, 1863, in Mackall Papers, UNC.
47 *Ibid.*

letter boasting that his report "tells the whole truth." Also, one of Bragg's staff officers, Colonel Stoddard Johnston, prepared lengthy notes on the Kentucky campaign which defended Bragg's position.[48]

Bragg moved first against McCown. He had never liked the Tennessee general. As early as the summer of 1862, he had considered McCown unfit and incapable of high command. He had criticized McCown's performance at New Madrid and was probably displeased at his service as East Tennessee's commander during the Kentucky episode. Yet McCown was entrenched in the army. One of the oldest officers in terms of service, he had commanded the artillery corps in the old state army of Tennessee. He had powerful congressional allies, such as Senators Gustavus Henry and Landon Haynes of Tennessee.

Despite McCown's influence, Bragg was determined to be rid of him. He was angry over McCown's failure to complete the wheeling maneuver at Murfreesboro on December 31, and blamed him for delaying the morning attack. Here Bragg was somewhat reinforced by Hardee's official report, completed on February 28, which also criticized McCown for the delay. McCown did not help his own cause. He talked openly against Bragg, and some of the comments got back to headquarters. In one early March conversation with Pillow, McCown abused Bragg and labeled the Confederacy as "a damned stinking cotton oligarchy" run by cliques.[49] Gradually McCown's comments got back to Bragg's staff in a letter from Pillow to one of Bragg's staff officers.[50]

Even before the conversation with Pillow, Bragg had moved against McCown. Bragg ordered him arrested and relieved him of his command. The charge was a technical one—on several occasions McCown had defied army regulations by ordering details of men and officers to Charleston and other points. While McCown awaited his fate in Chattanooga, his Richmond friends petitioned for a speedy court-martial. This was granted on March 16, and Bragg won his first victory. A court composed of friends and enemies of Bragg, including Cleburne, Withers, and Patton Anderson, found McCown guilty. He was suspended from his command for six months.[51]

Bragg now turned on Breckinridge. He had been critical in October of Breckinridge's failure to reach Kentucky in time to be of service. It was

48 Sale to Bragg, March 5, 18, 1863, in Seitz, *Bragg;* Bragg to Davis, February 23, 1863, in Davis Papers, Tulane; Bragg to Mackall, February 14, 1863, in Mackall Papers, UNC.

49 Pillow to Major Clare, March 9, 1863, in Bragg Papers, Western Reserve; see also Hardee's Murfreesboro report, in Hardee Papers, Duke.

50 Pillow to Clare, March 9, 1863, in Bragg Papers, Western Reserve.

51 *Official Records,* XXIII, Pt. 2, pp. 653–54, 673, 698, 713, 722; Walter to McCown, June 5, 1863, in Bragg Papers, Western Reserve.

believed in Breckinridge's camp that some of Bragg's dislike was because the Kentuckian and some of his brigadiers were politicians turned soldier. Some of these brigade officers, such as General William Preston and Colonel Randall Gibson, were old enemies of Bragg. After Murfreesboro, differences grew. In his official report of Stone's River, Bragg blamed much of the loss on Breckinridge. He criticized his failure to promptly reinforce Polk on December 31. Bragg also blamed him for not ascertaining, on January 2, whether Pegram and Wharton were in position. Bragg was embittered by Breckinridge's reply to his circular letter, and considered the Kentucky officer one of the army's key troublemakers.[52]

The attack on Breckinridge in his official Stone's River report opened a long, bitter quarrel. The Kentucky generals, already angry over the failures of the late summer, urged Breckinridge to resign from the army and challenge Bragg to a duel. They believed that Breckinridge had been selected as a scapegoat for Bragg's own errors. Breckinridge disregarded their advice and chose to fight back in his official report. Bragg hesitated before forwarding the report to Richmond. Colonel Sale had warned that Breckinridge's Kentucky friends in Congress were demanding to see the subordinates' reports of Murfreesboro. Thus Bragg took time to compile an appendix of letters which he affixed to Breckinridge's report. These letters, which challenged Breckinridge's version of affairs on December 31 and January 2, seemed necessary to Bragg since he considered that general's own report to contain "errors and misapprehensions." [53]

When Bragg forwarded the Kentuckian's report on March 11, more trouble ensued. Breckinridge was angry that Bragg's own report of Murfreesboro had evidently been sent to Richmond before his own report had reached Bragg's headquarters. Thus, on March 31 Breckinridge appealed to Cooper for a court of inquiry. The following day Breckinridge demanded that Bragg furnish him with a copy of his Murfreesboro report, which Bragg refused to do. Meanwhile Breckinridge busily accumulated statements from staff members to refute Bragg's charges.[54]

[52] Bragg to Davis, October 2, 1862, in Bragg Papers, Western Reserve; Bragg's Murfreesboro report, in *ibid.;* Bragg to Mackall, February 14, 1863, in Mackall Papers, UNC.

[53] Bragg to Cooper, March 11, 1863, in Breckinridge Papers, New York Historical Society. See also Eliot, *West Point in the Confederacy*, 24; William Preston to William Preston Johnston, January 26, 1863, in Barret Papers, Tulane; Kirwan, *Orphan Brigade*, 77; William Preston to P. G. T. Beauregard, in Beauregard Papers, National Archives.

[54] Breckinridge to Cooper, March 31, 1863, in Barret Papers, Tulane; Breckinridge to Polk, April 2, 1863, Brent to Breckinridge, April 2, 6, 1863, Polk to Breckinridge, March 31, 1863, O'Hara to Breckinridge, January 16, 1863, John Buckner to Breckinridge, May 20, 1863, in Breckinridge, Papers, New York Historical Society; see also *Official Records*, XX, Pt. 1, p. 694.

Bragg was busy accumulating his own evidence. Captain Felix Robertson had commanded the batteries detached to Breckinridge's division for the January 2 attack. His first report of January 12 had not been critical of Breckinridge's poor alignment for the assault, so, on February 16, Bragg requested a revised report. This time Robertson was ordered not to send his report via the normal channel through Breckinridge's headquarters. Bragg reminded poor Robertson that he "exercised a special command under my orders," ordered him to make a "special report," and prompted the officer to report in such a way as would "do justice." [55]

Robertson understood what Bragg wanted. He wrote a denunciation of Breckinridge's conduct on January 2, charging that the Kentucky general had knowingly disobeyed Bragg's orders. Robertson also had strong criticism for the conduct of the division after the battle, stating that he had never seen troops so broken.[56]

Bragg collected other evidence. In March he came up with a statement from one of his staff, Colonel George Brent. Brent remembered the conversation he had overheard on January 2 between Pillow and Breckinridge. He recalled that Pillow had urged Breckinridge to make sure the cavalry understood their part in the attack. Pillow, an old hand at playing the opportunist, came up with his own statement. In a conversation with Bragg at Tullahoma, for which he supplied Bragg a memorandum, he criticized Breckinridge's alignment on January 2. Pillow also expressed surprise that Breckinridge had had available Wharton's and Pegram's cavalries, stating that Bragg's mention of it in the conversation was the first he knew of it. This last bit of information did not exactly jibe with Brent's own account of the conversation he had overheard between Pillow and Breckinridge regarding the cavalry.[57]

Bragg's Richmond emissary, Colonel Sale, had made certain that Bragg's report of Murfreesboro was published, an act which infuriated Breckinridge. Angry because Bragg's report was published while his request for an inquiry was stalled, Breckinridge in early May asked Richmond to publish his letter requesting the inquiry. Bragg, on May 13, passed this request on to Richmond but tried to stymie it by stating that there were statements in the letter "not in accordance with my understanding of the facts." [58] The effort to suppress the letter failed, however.

55 Bragg to Robertson, February 16, 1863, F. H. Robertson's Murfreesboro report, January 12, 1863, in Breckinridge Papers, New York Historical Society.

56 Robertson to Breckinridge, April 6, 1863, F. H. Robertson's Murfreesboro report, February 16, 1863, in ibid.

57 Brent to Bragg, March 15, 1863, in Bragg Papers, Western Reserve; Official Records, XX, Pt. 1, p. 809.

58 Breckinridge to Cooper, May 6, 1863, with endorsement by Bragg, May 13, 1863, in Letters, Telegrams and Orders Received and Sent, General J. C. Breckinridge's Command, December 1861–November, 1863, CCCXI, Chap. 2, National Archives.

In early May a Richmond friend of Breckinridge's talked General Samuel Cooper into supplying him with a copy of the letter and granting permission for its publication. Bragg was furious when he saw it in print and complained to Cooper. A chagrined Cooper tried to soothe Bragg by explaining that Breckinridge did err in publishing it, but that this could be explained by "the want of professional training" on Breckinridge's part.[59] The Bragg-Breckinridge controversy finally ebbed into a bitter stalemate. In late May when Breckinridge was transferred to Mississippi, the active fight between the two generals stopped, but Bragg never overcame his hatred of the Kentucky elements in the army.

Even while the quarrels with McCown and Beckinridge were rampant, Bragg attacked a third general. Bragg had never considered General Frank Cheatham a professional soldier, but no open clash arose between the two men until the spring of 1863. The origin of the dispute was Cheatham's penchant for liquor while in battle. During the Murfreesboro battle, Hardee allegedly informed Bragg that Cheatham had been drunk on December 31. From other sources Bragg had reports that Cheatham had been so intoxicated that a staff officer was compelled to hold him on his horse. After the battle Bragg mentioned the matter to Polk. Polk supposedly agreed that he had heard this from other sources, and added that he had already announced his displeasure to Cheatham. This did not satisfy Bragg. After reaching Winchester in early January, Bragg ordered Polk to rebuke Cheatham in writing. Before he submitted his own official report of Murfreesboro, Polk informed Bragg that it had been done and that Cheatham had apologized. But upon seeing the report, Bragg was angered to see that, in his opinion, Cheatham had been commended by Polk above his other generals on the field.[60]

In his own official report, Bragg rebuked Cheatham in two separate passages. He blamed Cleburne's heavy casualties of the morning of December 31 on Cheatham's failure to attack promptly. He also omitted Cheatham's name from the long list of corps and division commanders who were commended.

Bragg explained to Richmond that the latter rebuke was a mild punishment for Cheatham's intemperance. It was not considered mild to Cheatham's friends, who included such influential politicians as Henry Foote and Gustavus Henry. When Bragg's report was released, it caused a storm

59 Breckinridge to Cooper, May 6, 1863, in *ibid*; Bragg's endorsement on Breckinridge report, May 26, 1863, in Bragg Papers, Western Reserve; Cooper to Bragg, May 31, 1863, in Breckinridge Papers, New York Historical Society.

60 Bragg to Cooper, April 9, 1863, in Bragg Papers, Western Reserve; Bragg to Davis, December 1, 1863, in Braxton Bragg Papers, Harvard; Bragg to E. T. Sykes, February 8, 1873, in Polk, *Polk*, II, 312–13. See also W. M. T. Rogers Diary, December 31, 1863, in Roy Black Papers, UNC.

of protest among his political connections and among the Tennessee
soldiers with whom Cheatham was tremendously popular. Cheatham was
dissuaded from resigning, but the feud continued.[61]

Largely as an outgrowth of the public clamor produced by Bragg's
report, Davis, on March 9, ordered Joseph E. Johnston back to Tullahoma. This time he instructed him to relieve Bragg, take charge of the
Army of Tennessee, and order Bragg to report to Richmond.[62]

Johnston's ambiguous report on Bragg in late February had, whatever
Johnston's intent, weakened the President's confidence in Bragg. The
House of Representatives was even threatening to hold up a resolution
to compliment Bragg and the army on the campaign.[63] And though Davis
knew of Johnston's reservations about succeeding Bragg, he ordered him
to effect the replacement.

Upon arriving at Tullahoma on March 19, Johnston felt all his old
trepidations about his situation.[64] He still feared being accused of covet-
ing Bragg's job.[65] He was still convinced two men could not command the
same army. And although he had received a letter at Mobile from Davis
on February 19, better defining his powers as theater commander, he
still maintained that he did not understand his authority.[66] Richmond
even assured him that he could avoid embarrassment at taking over, by
retaining a command for Bragg. Whatever his reasons, he stubbornly
refused to assert complete command.[67]

Johnston's discomfort was increased when he learned that Mrs. Bragg
was critically ill with typhoid fever. Johnston had Seddon give Bragg a
copy of the order placing him in command, but out of feeling for
Bragg's distress over his wife, he withheld the order which removed Bragg

[61] —— to "Dear Sir," March 27, 1863, in Polk Papers, Sewanee; Bragg to Cooper,
April 9, 1863, in Bragg Papers, Western Reserve; Bragg's Murfreesboro report, in
Bragg Papers, Western Reserve.
[62] Seddon to Johnston, March 9, 1863, in Johnston Papers, William and Mary.
[63] For evidence of clamor against Bragg, see Liddell to wife, February 18, 1863,
in St. John Liddell and Family Papers, Louisiana State University, Department of
Archives; Irving Buck to sister, January 13, 1863, in Buck Papers, UNC; Phelan to
Bragg, March 6, 1863, J. L. Pugh to Bragg, March 5, 1863, J. C. Nott to Bragg, March 1,
1863, in Bragg Papers, Western Reserve; —— to "Dear Sir," March 27, 1863, in Polk
Papers, Sewanee; Austin, *The Blue and the Gray*, 69. See also Davis to Joseph E.
Johnston, February 19, 1863, in Johnston Papers, William and Mary.
[64] Wigfall to Johnston, February 27, 28, 1863, in Johnston Papers, Huntington;
Official Records, XXIII, Pt. 2, p. 658.
[65] Johnston to Wigfall, March 4, 1863, in Wigfall, DLC.
[66] Johnston to Wigfall, December 26, 1863, in *ibid.*; see also Johnston to Wigfall,
March 8, 1863, *ibid.*
[67] Davis to Johnston, February 19, 1863, Johnston to Davis, February 3, 12, March 2,
1863, in Johnston Papers, William and Mary; Johnston to Wigfall, March 4, 8, 1863,
in Wigfall Papers, DLC; Johnston, "Jefferson Davis and the Mississippi Campaign,"
589.

to Richmond. Johnston took nominal command, but refused to issue a public announcement of the change. As he assumed this timorous command, several factors caused Richmond's attitude toward Johnston to soften. For one thing Davis and Seddon were probably content not to remove Bragg once they felt Johnston was secured as commander. In this mood they were not receptive to Polk's March 30 appeal that the President oust Bragg.[68]

Mrs. Bragg's health improved, and there was no longer any call for gentler treatment on her account. But as she recovered, Johnston himself suffered a recurrence of illness resulting from his Seven Pines wounds. On April 10 he reported to Davis that he was physically unfit for field duty and that as a consequence, Bragg's presence was vital to the army. Almost by default Bragg resumed command, and although Johnston remained there until early May when he was ordered to Pemberton's army, Bragg was in control again.[69]

A strong factor in Bragg's apparent return to the administration's favor was a report Davis received after sending, on March 12, his aide-de-camp, Colonel William Preston Johnston, to inspect the Army of Tennessee. The son of Davis' longtime friend, Albert Sidney Johnston, William Preston had fought in the Virginia army until sickness disabled him for field duty. Then, in April of 1862, shortly after his father's death at Shiloh, young Johnston was commissioned as Davis' aide-de-camp, usually functioning as an investigator. Earlier, when the army was under Beauregard at Tupelo, Davis had sent Johnston to inspect the command.[70]

The warm friendship between William Preston Johnston and Bragg, which continued after the war, was already evident in 1863. Another bond was their mutual distaste for Beauregard, whom young Johnston considered responsible for the Shiloh defeat.

On the other side, two of his father's former staff members, General William Preston and Colonel Randall Gibson, were brigade commanders in Breckinridge's division. Preston was young Johnston's uncle as well as his namesake and was an outspoken foe of Bragg. Gibson, a longtime friend of Johnston's late father, was hated by Bragg, who considered Gibson a coward and had only recently removed him from his command. Egged on by Hardee, Gibson appealed to Richmond, and also complained

68 Seddon to Johnston, February 5, 1863, in Johnston Papers, William and Mary. See also Polk to Davis, March 30, 1863, in Polk Papers, Sewanee; *Official Records,* XXIII, Pt. 2, pp. 708, 745.

69 Govan and Livingood, *A Different Valor,* 185; Johnston to Davis, April 10, 1863, in Johnston Papers, William and Mary; Johnston, "Jefferson Davis and the Mississippi Campaign." 591.

70 Arthur Marvin Shaw, *William Preston Johnston: A Transitional Figure of the Confederacy* (Baton Rouge, 1943), 70–75.

to William Preston Johnston that Bragg wanted to drive him from the army.[71]

Also, Johnston's mission was complicated by the presence of Polk, another warm friend of his father. When he arrived at Tullahoma, Johnston spent several days at Polk's headquarters, during which time the Bishop maintained that the army had lost confidence in Bragg and that Joe Johnston should be put in command. He heard the same story at Hardee's headquarters. General William Preston advised his nephew that Bragg had once told President Davis that Albert Sidney Johnston had lost the army's confidence after Fort Donelson fell. Young Johnston had heard this before, and Davis had assured him that Bragg had made no such statement. But now Hardee, anxious to rekindle the story against Bragg, evidently put Preston up to writing young Johnston in March that Hardee swore he had heard Bragg state it.[72]

Johnston's April 15 report resulting from these pressures was vague, telling little of the army's basic trouble and leaning in Bragg's favor. Davis' instructions had been for Johnston to make himself acquainted with the condition of the army, but he avoided reporting the conditions he knew to exist. He did send excellent reports of the army's logistical and ordnance affairs. But as to the Bragg feud, nothing was said save two cryptic statements. With faint praise, Johnston commended Bragg's talents for organization. The only negative hint was his comment that the army lacked no material needed for success.[73]

Bragg believed that he had again won a victory over his enemies. The support he had received from the two Johnstons was reinforced in March by the news from Richmond that his congressional friends, such as James Pugh and Clement Clay of Alabama, were counterattacking the anti-Bragg faction by waving copies of a complimentary letter from Joe Johnston to Davis. By mid-March, Bragg's information indicated that the combination of his Richmond support and his own Murfreesboro report was stifling the opposition. Particularly well circulated in Richmond was Johnston's comment to Davis that there was no man able to take Bragg's place.

With new confidence, Bragg, in late March, occupied himself with a new charge, this time against his two corps leaders, Polk and Hardee, his

71 William Preston to W. P. Johnston, January 26, 1863, Randall Gibson to "Dear Will," March 9, 1863, William Preston to W. P. Johnston, March 13, 1863, William Preston to Thomas Jordan, March 29, 1863, Randall Gibson to "Dear Will," March 1, 1863, all in Barret Collection, Tulane.

72 William Preston to W. P. Johnston, March 13, 1863, ibid; W. P. Johnston to "Dear Rosa," April 3, 1863, ibid.; Official Records, XXIII, Pt. 2, pp. 757–58; Polk to Davis, March 30, 1863, in Polk Papers, Sewanee.

73 Official Records, XXIII, Pt. 2, pp. 757–73.

adversaries in the argument over the Kentucky campaign. Bragg's Richmond friends had warned that the Kentucky delegation in Congress was threatening to block a vote of thanks for the Murfreesboro campaign and to instigate an investigation of the Kentucky campaign. Already the Senate had requested that Davis furnish copies of the reports of the Kentucky expedition by Bragg and his generals. In early April, attacks on Bragg for the Kentucky defeat continued to sound on the Senate floor.[74]

Polk's report on Kentucky irritated him for several reasons. On October 3 at Bardstown, Polk had notified Bragg that he had called a council of war which had voted to disobey Bragg's order to attack. Polk promised to explain this later, but in his official report, he did not even mention the Bardstown council. On the other hand, Polk did mention a second council held at Perryville on October 8, which had also voted to veto a Bragg order to attack. This revelation angered Bragg, as well, for it was the first knowledge he had of such a council. Polk's report left the impression that he knew the enemy's main army was at Perryville on October 7 and 8, that Bragg did not, and that Polk had unsuccessfully tried to warn him of such.

Hardee's report also miffed Bragg. Hardee did not mention the Bardstown council, nor even the Perryville council. He did severely criticize Bragg for not knowing that Buell was on the Perryville front on October 8. Hardee maintained that he did know, because on several occasions he had warned Bragg of it. This accusation particularly angered Bragg since he had received a note from Hardee on October 2 indicating that the bulk of Buell's force was not threatening Polk and Hardee but was moving against Bragg's right wing at Frankfort. Also, Bragg could find nothing in the private letters sent to him by Hardee from Perryville which bore out the claims made by that general in his report.[75]

Bragg reacted with a poorly timed attack on Polk and Hardee. With the army's morale already depleted, he sent out another circular letter, a device which could only solidify opposition against him. He addressed the letter to the fourteen brigade, division, and corps commanders who had been present at Perryville and Bardstown. Curiously, Bragg emphasized only one particular complaint in his attack, the matter of the two councils. The manner in which he presented the letter also would only cause anger. After noting the October 3 note received from Polk, and the ex-

74 Sale to Bragg, March 5, 1863, in Seitz, *Bragg*, 284–86; J. L. Pugh to Bragg, March 5, 1863, in Bragg Papers, Western Reserve; Fifty-Eighth Congress, Second Session, *Senate Document Number 234, Journal of the Congress of the Confederate States of America*, III (Washington, 1904), 106.

75 Bragg to Davis, May 22, 1863, in Bragg Papers, Duke; *Official Records*, XVI, Pt. 1, pp. 1110, 1120; Hardee to Bragg, October 2, 1862, in Bragg Papers, Western Reserve.

cerpt from the Bishop's official report of the Perryville council, Bragg backed his generals to the wall. He reminded the recipients of his circular that Polk's accounts indicted them as sustaining a disobedience to orders, and asked them to what extent thay had done so.

With his usual lack of finesse, Bragg had cornered his generals. His circular accused Polk outright of a disobedience of orders. The other generals could alienate themselves with Bragg by refusing to answer, or they could admit to participating in the councils, which by Polk's own admission were held, and thereby validate Bragg's charge that Polk had disobeyed orders.

If Bragg hoped to divide his enemies, he was unsuccessful. An almost united front was presented in reply to his note. Polk ignored the letter, having been warned by Hardee that any answer could be used by Bragg in a court-martial. Hardee, usually a fine officer, played the affair with an exhibition of two of his more obvious flaws—his dislike of final responsibility and his love of army intrigue. On April 16, after announcing to Bragg that he did not want to shirk any responsibility, Hardee declined to answer. Hardee gave as one reason for his ducking the issue that any answer of his might re-open the Kentucky argument, a strange reason, considering that the campaign's arguments had already been opened. Hardee also flattered the Bishop that he could "tear Bragg to tatters" in any discussion of the campaign.[76]

Cheatham also refused to answer. Buckner, now commanding the Department of the Gulf, replied with a sensible message, praising Bragg's abilities, but he urged Bragg to forget the entire matter since he had already been sustained by the government and any pursuance of the matter would only open old wounds. Patton Anderson's reply indicated the difficult position in which Bragg had placed his generals. An old friend of Bragg's, Anderson also felt loyalty to his commander Polk. Anderson admitted that the Bardstown council had decided to disobey Bragg's order. Disturbed by being forced to testify against Polk, Anderson not only sent a copy of his answer to the Bishop, but met with him later to compare recollections of the council.[77]

Bragg refused to let the issue die and continued the fight through late

[76] Bragg to Hardee, Cheatham, Buckner, Anderson, Withers, Donelson, Maney, Preston Smith, Stewart, Cleburne, Liddell, Johnson, Brown, and Adams, circular letter, April 13, 1863, in Bragg Papers, Western Reserve; Hardee to Bragg, April 16, 1863, in Hardee Papers, Alabama; *Official Records*, XVI, Pt. 1, p. 1098.

[77] Cheatham to Bragg, April 20, 1863, Buckner to Bragg, April 26, 1863, Bushrod Johnston to Bragg, Arpil 17, 1863, John C. Brown to Bragg, April 15, 1863, S. A. M. Wood to Bragg, April 17, 1863, all in Bragg Papers, Western Reserve; see also *Official Records*, XVI, Pt. 1, pp. 1099–100; Patton Anderson to Bragg, April 17, 1863, in Bragg Papers, Historical Society of Pennsylvania.

April and May. He brought no formal charges against Polk, but did severely criticize him in his official report. Ironically, Bragg's own rigid sense of military propriety induced him to withhold some of his most incriminating information from his offical report—that concerning Hardee's letters of October 2 and 7 which contradicted that general's version of what he had advised. Bragg's reasoning, as explained to Davis, was that Hardee's letters did not constitute part of the official record because they were private letters not sent through the normal chain of command.

Bragg's opposition continued to fight him. Expecting to be arrested, Polk accumulated evidence for his defense. Without authorization from the War Department, he also had his Murfreesboro and Perryville reports published in the Knoxville *Register,* and this act drove the final breach between Bragg and his corps leaders. In late May, Bragg admitted to Davis that "it will not be possible for the cordial official confidence to exist again." [78]

Aside from the neglect of military matters, a factor that would soon be obvious, the spring quarrels produced other important results. On the surface it appeared that Bragg, by the end of May, had emerged the victor. The government had supported him, two observers had praised his efforts, and several of the dissenters had been weeded out. Breckinridge and his division, replete with Bragg enemies, were transferred to Mississippi in May. McCown was under suspension, and his division likewise was sent to Pemberton. General William Preston had been transferred to a command in southwestern Virginia.

Yet the discord remained cemented in a strong anti-Bragg opposition united behind the corps commanders. Polk and Hardee were supported by the Kentucky elements both in and out of the army. Bragg's attacks on Cheatham and Polk had garnered powerful support for them from the Tennessee troops. Hardee's popularity with his staff had pulled in others such as Cleburne and St. John Liddell. And this opposition's power was yet to reach its full fury. Polk, who had closer ties with Richmond than Hardee had, managed affairs on that front via his private letters to the President. Hardee who had a better military reputation in the army than Polk, apparently led the opposition within the army itself. Together the two generals engaged in activities which sometimes amounted to insubordination. Shortly after Murfreesboro, they, together with Preston and Buckner, plotted with Captain R. W. Wooley, a staff officer in Preston's brigade, to write a pamphlet derogatory to Bragg. The pamphlet covered

78 Bragg's report of Perryville, in Bragg Papers, Western Reserve; Bragg to Davis, May 22, 1863, in Bragg Papers, Duke; W. B. Richmond to Seddon, June 15, 1863, Richmond to Colonel Dupree, May 5, 8, 1863, in Polk, Letters and Telegrams Sent, 1861–64, National Archives.

Perryville and Murfreesboro. It criticized Bragg on both occasions, and even lambasted the retreat to Tullahoma. The pamphlet, when it was finished, was considered too strong an attack to publish and was laid aside.

Like Bragg himself, the opposition disliked any sign of agreement with the other side. Thus they were angered when Joseph E. Johnston complimented Bragg. Hardee complained that Johnston seemed a "decided partisan" of Bragg's. They undoubtedly were peeved that Johnston did not indulge in the backstairs conversation and correspondence which marked their efforts. Hardee, too, complained that Johnston would not confide in him.[79]

Both Bragg and his opponents maintained lobbies in the Confederate capital. In early March, Bragg's selection of John Sale to confer with his supporters in Richmond was a careful choice. Sale had important political ties among Alabama and Mississippi congressmen, the core of Bragg's support. In Richmond, Sale talked with Davis, Cooper, and congressional supporters including Phelan, Clay, and Pugh. He furnished Bragg with advice as to which reports to hasten to Richmond. Davis participated in the intrigue by furnishing the congressional leader of Bragg's defense, Phelan, with valuable documents such as copies of Bragg's report and a private letter from Johnston. Meetings were held between Sale, Phelan, and other allies while another Bragg envoy, Captain Felix Robertson, circulated on the Senate floor explaining Bragg's conduct. Robertson, who had endeared himself to Bragg with his revised report of Breckinridge's activities had been rewarded with the post of lobbyist in Richmond.[80]

Though the opposition in the army had no such lobby, they had powerful allies among the anti-Davis congressmen. Wigfall continued to lead a dual fight to oust Bragg and appoint Johnston. He was supported by other anti-Davis stalwarts who seemed less interested in the Army of Tennessee than in criticizing the administration. And while undoubtedly some congressmen, like Gustavus Henry, were primarily interested in the Army of Tennessee, everyone's motives were suspect. The anti-Davis faction was irritated with Johnston's laudatory reports of Bragg's conduct, fearful that Davis would use the reports against them. In turn, Johnston was irked with them, stating, "The friends who have been irritated by my

---

[79] Cooper to Bragg, May 26, 1863, Bragg to Hardee, May 23, 1863, Bragg to Mackall, May 23, 1863, in Bragg Papers, Western Reserve; R. W. Wooley, "An Apology for the Campaign in Kentucky and Middle Tennessee" (MS in Polk Papers, Sewanee); Wooley to Mrs. Polk, September 22, 1868, ibid.; Hardee to William Preston Johnston, April 12, 1863, in Barret Collection, Tulane.

[80] Sale to Bragg, March 5, 1863, in Seitz, Bragg, 284–85; Phelan to Bragg, March 6, 1863, J. L. Pugh to Bragg, March 5, 1863, in Bragg Papers, Western Reserve.

expressions of opinion are less my friends, I take it, than the President's enemies." [81]

Johnston, possibly as a by-product of the quarrels, became an object of Bragg's dislike, by the end of May. This was not Johnston's fault, for even Bragg's congressional allies praised Johnston's treatment of Bragg, and averred that his reports stifled criticism of Bragg. Bragg knew in March of a private letter from Johnston to Wigfall that had praised him. Moreover, during his second visit to the army, Johnston had leaned over backwards to avoid the appearance of taking command. Until May 9, when he was ordered to Mississippi, Johnston had exerted only scant authority.

But, for a man of Bragg's disposition, the matters were too delicate not to incur his resentment. Bragg had known the previous fall of the pleas from within the army for Johnston's appointment. He could hardly have escaped knowledge of the same pleas during the spring by newspapers and congressmen. Johnston's warm friendships with Bragg enemies such as Beauregard and Wigfall hardly helped his feelings. Though he said very little of Johnston's popularity, Bragg's comment on Johnston's departure from Tullahoma portended continued trials. To a friend, Bragg remarked that Johnston was kept at Tullahoma "to watch me too long." [82]

81 Johnston to Wigfall, December 27, 1863, in Wigfall Papers, DLC; Wigfall to Johnston, June 8, October 6, 1863, March 17, 1864, in Johnston Papers, Huntington.
82 Noll, *Quintard,* 70; J. L. Pugh to Bragg, March 5, 1863, in Bragg Papers, Western Reserve.

five

Failure of an Experiment

GENERAL JOSEPH JOHNSTON STILL COULD NOT DETERMINE WHAT RICHMOND
desired of him in the West, and they gave him no guidelines as to which
areas of his vast command were the most vital. By January, Johnston had
seen that some areas must be sacrificed for longer-range gains because his
four departments were widely scattered, undermanned, and outnumbered.
Bragg's army in January consisted of fewer than forty thousand effectives
of all arms, while his opponent Rosecrans was believed to have twice as
many and to be receiving periodic reinforcement. The tiny East Tennessee
department had fewer than ten thousand troops of all types, while the
even smaller Department of the Gulf at Mobile had only three thousand
effective infantry. Pemberton had scarcely thirty thousand available for
field service to cope with those forces under Grant and Sherman estimated
at well over twice that number.

Yet the problem was not so much a shortage of Rebel manpower in
the West as it was a lack of agreement on how Johnston should use his
eighty thousand effectives. The basic difference in philosophy of western
defense, obvious in the winter, continued until June of 1863. Johnston
argued that some ground must be temporarily surrendered, and periodically asked the government which areas were considered more vital.
Davis and Seddon refused to designate specific areas and maintained the
official position that Johnston had ample troops to shuttle among the
most threatened areas in his command.[1]

1 Johnston to Davis, January 7, 1863, Davis to Johnston, January 8, 1863, in
Joseph E. Johnston Papers, Miami (Ohio) University Library; Johnston to Seddon,
June 12, 15, 1863, John Pettus *et al.,* to Davis, June 18, 1863, in Johnston Papers,
William and Mary.

Beginning in January Johnston tried to convince Richmond that Pemberton, Bragg, and the two smaller departments were too widely spread to provide the mutual support intended by the government. With Pemberton falling back toward Vicksburg and Bragg retreating toward Duck River, Davis still refused to admit that all areas could not be defended simultaneously. In early February, Seddon asserted that Johnston's armies were not too remote from one another to provide such support.[2]

The disagreement continued during March. On March 2 Johnston had intelligence that Rosecrans was being heavily reinforced from the Virginia front. He suggested similar help from some of Lee's divisions, but Davis and Seddon only sent blank replies with vague promise of reinforcement.[3]

Again, in mid-March, Johnston pointed out that Lee was closer to Middle Tennessee than Bragg was to Pemberton. Ignoring this logic, Davis, on March 17 and March 20, maintained that the enemy could not simultaneously assault all areas of Johnston's command. Johnston insisted to Richmond that this strategy of mutual support looked good on paper, but that it was unworkable. The distance by rail between the Middle Tennessee and Mississippi fronts was so great that an enemy attack on either Bragg or Pemberton could not be anticipated in time to shuttle reinforcements successfully. Bragg's case particularly was acute. Rosecrans' army at Murfreesboro was less than twenty miles from Bragg's Duck River line. Should Rosecrans advance, Bragg would have time only to draw from the thin East Tennessee garrison.[4]

The argument continued in April while Johnston was at Tullahoma. On April 6 a despondent Johnston warned that Bragg, greatly outnumbered, might have to abandon Middle Tennessee. Johnston's discouragement was heightened by intelligence received in late March that General Ambrose Burnside's entire corps had been withdrawn from the Virginia front to Kentucky, and that Grant was moving reinforcements from the Mississippi front to Rosecrans. After receiving another vague promise of reinforcement from Davis, Johnston on April 10 reiterated that unless Bragg were reinforced, Middle and perhaps East Tennessee as well would be lost. He argued that communications between Bragg's and Pember-

2 Davis to Johnston, January 5, 1863, Seddon to Johnston, February 5, 1863; in Johnston Papers, William and Mary; Davis to Johnston, January 8, 1863, in Johnston Papers, Miami.

3 Johnston to Seddon, March 12, 1863, Davis to Johnston, March 6, 17, 1863, in Johnston Papers, William and Mary; *Official Records,* LII, Pt. 2, p. 428, XXIII, Pt. 2, pp. 646, 656, 674.

4 Davis to Johnston, March 17, 1863, Johnston to Davis, March 28, 1863, Johnston Papers, William and Mary; Davis to Johnston, March 20, 1863, in Johnston Papers, Miami; Johnston to Wigfall, March 8, 1863, in Wigfall Papers, DLC.

ton's headquarters were so poor that the Federals could transfer an entire army from Pemberton's front to Nashville before Johnston knew it was in motion. While this was probably an exaggeration, it was no overstatement that a corresponding move by the Confederates would have required six weeks to complete. In December the vanguard of Stevenson's division had taken a month to reach Pemberton from Murfreesboro. In late April, only a few days prior to his being ordered to Mississippi, Johnston issued his last appeal for reinforcements for Bragg. Again his warning that Middle Tennessee might be lost was not heeded.[5]

Johnston's being ordered to Mississippi on May 9 was closely related to a second area of general misunderstanding with Richmond. Even if, as Davis repeatedly argued, Johnston had ample troops in the West, the command structure made the government's strategy completely unworkable. From December of 1862 until he was formally relieved of command over Bragg on July 22, 1863, Johnston never understood his duties. Several facets of this confusion negated any hope of success in the mutual reinforcement of Bragg and Pemberton envisioned by President Davis. One problem was Davis' policy of allowing departmental commanders to report directly to Richmond. Often Johnston did not have the general theater intelligence prerequisite to the manipulation of these troops. Pemberton's department was a particular problem. In mid-December Pemberton had asked Johnston whether his departmental papers should go directly to Richmond or through Johnston's office. Though Johnston told him to send his papers through the theater commander's office, Pemberton communicated directly with Richmond. Thus, from late January until mid-May, Johnston knew little of affairs on Pemberton's front. Possibly, Pemberton assumed incorrectly that when Johnston twice was ordered to Bragg's army in the spring, Johnston relinquished his control over Mississippi.[6]

In February when Johnston complained to Richmond of Pemberton's failure to communicate, he received nothing but Davis' regrets that the general was so uncommunicative. In March, Johnston complained bitterly to Davis' aide, Colonel William Preston Johnston, that he had received no intelligence from Pemberton. The climax of this fiasco occurred in late April. Early that month Pemberton had been convinced that Grant was reinforcing Rosecrans. By April 17, however, Pemberton's brief telegrams to Johnston changed in nature. Between April 17 and April 28,

5 Johnston to Cooper, April 2, 6, 1863, Johnston to Davis, April 2, 10, 1863, Johnston to Seddon, April 28, 1863, in Johnston Papers, William and Mary; *Official Records*, XXIII, Pt. 2, p. 736.

6 Pemberton to Ewell, December 12, 1862, in Johnston Papers, William and Mary; Jones, *Confederate Strategy*, 132–33, 163, 175–76, 224–25; Govan and Livingood, *A Different Valor*, 188–89.

Pemberton merely telegraphed extensive lists of Federal ships which had passed the Vicksburg batteries. Not until April 28 did Johnston learn that Grant had troops on the west bank of the Mississippi opposite Grand Gulf. On April 30, unknown to Johnston, Grant moved the bulk of his force to the east bank and occupied Grand Gulf, below Vicksburg.

Although Pemberton kept Richmond informed, Johnston did not know until May 7 that Pemberton had engaged Grant on the east bank and had been defeated. Even then, Johnston still did not know that Grant's main army had crossed the river. Also unknown to Johnston, Davis was sending Pemberton contradictory advice from Richmond. Johnston advised Pemberton to concentrate against Grant, but on May 7 the President urged that Pemberton should maintain the garrisons at Port Hudson and Vicksburg. Not until he arrived in Jackson, Mississippi, a few days later, did Johnston learn that his advice had not been followed and that Grant's army was interposed between Pemberton at Vicksburg and Johnston's force at Jackson.[7]

Davis' personal directive to Pemberton was symptomatic of another element of the breakdown of communication between Johnston and the government. Continually, Richmond disregarded the very purpose of the western theater command—that of personal supervision. Orders were repeatedly issued without Johnston's knowledge or consent. The ordering of Stevenson to Mississippi in December, the dispatching of Johnston to Bragg's headquarters in January and March—all violated the repeated assurances given by Davis and Seddon that Johnston had full authority in the West to move freely from department to department and to disperse reinforcements at will.

Other examples of this inconsistent policy served to keep Johnston off balance. Davis and Seddon insisted during the early spring that Johnston had the authority to reinforce Bragg with the troops in East Tennessee. Yet Richmond's intervention frustrated this aim. In February, Seddon attempted to plan directly with the East Tennessee commander, General Daniel Donelson, a large cavalry expedition into Kentucky, although Johnston was counting on those troops as a ready reinforcement for Bragg. In March General Samuel Cooper commenced more planning with Donelson for another cavalry expedition to be led by General Humphrey Marshall into eastern Kentucky. Johnston had already con-

---

[7] Johnston, "Jefferson Davis and the Mississippi Campaign," 591; Pemberton to Johnston, April 17, 1863, p. 182; Pemberton to Johnston, April 17, 1863, pp. 183–184, Pemberton to Johnston, April 28, 1863, p. 191, all in Sarah A. Dorsey, *Recollections of Henry Watkins Allen* (New York, 1866); Johnston to Davis, February 12, 1863, Davis, to Johnston, February 19, 1863, in Johnston Papers, William and Mary; Jones, *Confederate Strategy*, 176; Govan and Livingood, *A Different Valor*, pp. 192–96, 198.

templated a combined infantry-cavalry expedition into the same area to hold back reinforcements from Rosecrans. When he learned of Cooper's meddling, he sarcastically remarked, "If the Department will give me timely notice when it intends to exercise my command, I shall be able to avoid such interference with its orders." [8]

In April, Marshall was sent into Kentucky. Johnston intended that a sizeable infantry column should accompany him, but due to Davis' intervention, Marshall's column of three thousand cavalry went alone and accomplished nothing. By April 22 a bitter Johnston again lashed out at the government's policy. He complained to Seddon, "By attempting occasionally to regulate details in this department by direct orders, the government can do little . . . but will certainly impair discipline by bringing General Bragg's authority and mine into contempt." [9]

On May 9 the War Department ordered Johnston to leave Bragg's army and take command in Mississippi. This hardly coincided with Davis' earlier assurance that he "had felt the importance of keeping you free to pass from army to army in your Dept." [10] Also, this directive included further contradiction by ordering Johnston to send 3,000 more reinforcements from Bragg to Pemberton. Scarcely had this contingent, McCown's division, been ordered to Mississippi, when Davis again interfered. On May 23 Davis asked Bragg for more reinforcements for Pemberton. Again Bragg sent a division, this one Breckinridge's 6,000-man unit. Likewise the government obtained 2,500 cavalry from Bragg for Pemberton. Within the month of May, Bragg sent 11,500 men to Pemberton. [11]

This chaotic command situation culminated in June. Communication between Johnston and Richmond had so completely broken down that he misunderstood the government's order to go to Mississippi. Johnston believed that the May 9 directive gave him a new position, limited his authority to Pemberton's department, and removed Bragg's department from his control. [12]

Almost a month after leaving Tullahoma, Johnston was startled by a

8 Johnston to Cooper, March 27, 1863, in *Official Records*, XXIII, Pt. 2, p. 726.
9 Johnston to Seddon, April 22, 1863, in Johnston Papers, William and Mary; see also *Official Records*, XXIII, Pt. 2, pp. 634, 655, 660–62, 705, 740, 751–53, 774.
10 Davis to Johnston, February 19, 1863, in Johnston Papers, William and Mary.
11 Bragg to Hardee, May 23, 1863, Bragg to Mackall, May 23, 1863, Hardee to Bragg, June 2, 1863, Bragg to Johnston, May 25, 1863, Cooper to Bragg, May 26, 1863, all in Bragg Papers, Western Reserve; Cooper to Johnston, May 26, 1863, Bragg to Johnston, May 23, 1863, in Johnston Papers, William and Mary; see also Seddon to Johnston, May 9, 1863, in Davis Papers, Tulane.
12 Davis to Johnston, June 15, 1863, Johnston to Davis, July 5, 1863, in Johnston Papers, William and Mary; Johnston to Seddon, June 12, 1863, in Davis Papers, Tulane.

June 8 note from Seddon suggesting that more reinforcements should be ordered to Pemberton from Bragg. On June 12 Johnston replied that he had not considered himself commanding in Tennessee since coming to Mississippi, and thus did not feel authorized to take troops from Bragg. Immediately Davis replied that Johnston's being sent to Mississippi did not end his authority over Bragg. On June 30 Davis criticized Johnston's "strange error" in thinking that he no longer controlled Bragg. Johnston replied pointedly that the War Department's habitual ordering of reinforcements from Bragg in May "would have convinced me had I doubted" that loss of control.[13] Although Davis maintained there was no ground for this confusion, he contradicted himself in late June when he again directly sought to obtain more reinforcements from Bragg for Pemberton.

Johnston was as disturbed over the failure to reach an understanding with Richmond as he was by his unsuccessful attempt to obtain reinforcements for Bragg. Throughout the spring, Richmond generally ignored Johnston's warnings of a massive troop build-up on the western front. In January, with Bragg commanding only some thirty-five thousand effectives, field intelligence obtained at Murfreesboro indicated Rosecrans had between sixty thousand and seventy thousand men. By January 8, Yankee prisoners and deserters reported that Rosecrans was being reinforced heavily from Kentucky. By mid-January Bragg's intelligence indicated that Rosecrans had received twenty-five thousand reinforcements, and again Johnston asked Richmond for reinforcements.[14]

By late February the situation on Bragg's front had become critical, and once more Johnston asked for assistance. By February 25 Bragg's intelligence reported that General Jacob Cox had arrived at Nashville the week before with a division from Virginia, and that General Franz Siegel's division from the eastern front had also just arrived in Middle Tennessee. Johnston pressed Seddon with a familiar argument—that these moves should be followed by comparable Confederate moves from Virginia.[15]

During early March the situation became even more grim. By March 2 Bragg's information indicated that since Murfreesboro, Rosecrans had been reinforced by five divisions, two of them from the Virginia front. Even with the western department's large body of irregular cavalry in Middle Tennessee and North Alabama, Bragg was still considered out-

[13] Johnston to Davis, July 5, 1863, in Johnston Papers, William and Mary; see also Davis to Johnston, June 15, 30, 1863; *ibid.;* Johnston to Seddon, June 12, 1863, in Davis Papers, Tulane.

[14] *Official Records,* XX, Pt. 1, p. 662, Pt. 2, p. 498; Bragg to B. S. Ewell, January 8, 1863, Johnston to Davis, January 9, 1863, in Johnston Papers, William and Mary.

[15] Johnston to Davis, March 2, 1863 in Johnston Papers, William and Mary; *Official Records,* XXIII, Pt. 2, p. 646.

numbered by more than two to one. Thus, on March 2, Johnston again appealed to both Seddon and Davis to transfer troops west from Virginia. On March 12 Johnston begged Seddon to restore the balance by shifting troops from the eastern theater to Bragg. Again on March 28 he appealed to Davis to send aid from Virginia.[16]

The Middle Tennessee situation worsened. By April 1 Johnston had intelligence that more troops were being sent from the Virginia front to oppose Bragg. He learned that General Ambrose Burnside's corps had left Baltimore in late March for Kentucky. Davis himself that same day passed on to Johnston a dispatch the government had received from an "entirely trustworthy" gentleman which indicated that twenty thousand men under Burnside were moving west along the Baltimore and Ohio Railroad to Kentucky. On April 2 Johnston retaliated by urging that a similar move from Lee to Bragg would be in order. Davis admitted on April 6 that Burnside's presence in Kentucky negated any hope that a cavalry raid from East Tennessee could keep Rosecrans from receiving reinforcements. Still, Davis promised only that he would reinforce Bragg when practicable.[17]

By May, shortly before Johnston left for Mississippi, a new threat to Bragg arose. Davis' old argument that the enemy could not simultaneously press Bragg, Pemberton, and East Tennessee appeared to be crumbling. General Simon Buckner, who now commanded in East Tennessee, had plentiful intelligence which foretold that Burnside planned to move against East Tennessee. Such a move would make reinforcement of Bragg from East Tennessee impossible. Johnston again pleaded for help from Virginia. And although the West was now threatened by three full-scale armies, the government sent nothing.[18]

The departure of Johnston for Mississippi doomed any hope of reinforcement for the Army of Tennessee. For practically a month, from mid-May until mid-June, a genuine command gap existed. Unaware that he was still responsible for Middle Tennessee, and busy with affairs in Mississippi, Johnston provided no strategic direction for Bragg. Though Davis himself admitted that the design of funnelling reinforcements to needed areas in the West was difficult while Johnston commanded directly in Mississippi, no changes were made. During May and June, Bragg's army was extremely vulnerable as a source of reinforcement for Pem-

16 Johnston to Davis, March 2, 28, 1863, Johnston to Seddon, March 12, 1863, in Johnston Papers, William and Mary; *Official Records*, XXIII, Pt. 2, p. 656.

17 *Official Records*, XXIII, Pt 2, p. 736; Johnston to Cooper, April 2, 1863, in Johnston Papers, William and Mary; Davis to Johnston, April 6, 1863, in Davis Papers, Tulane.

18 Johnston to Davis, March, 28, 1863, in Johnston Papers, William and Mary; *Official Records*, XXIII, Pt. 2, pp. 791, 800, 823, 836, 868.

berton, despite intelligence reports of a heavy build-up on the Murfrees-boro front. After he reached Mississippi, Johnston busied himself as-sembling a meager force of twenty-three thousand to oppose Grant's army, which was threatening the Vicksburg and Port Hudson garrisons. Believing himself relieved of the command in Tennessee, Johnston be-came less anxious for that section and behaved more as a typical army commander attempting to bolster his own forces. He did not protest the withdrawal of over eleven thousand men from Bragg in May, despite his earlier avowals that Bragg was heavily outnumbered. Moreover, during June, he concentrated solely on finding succor for his own army. Thus his dispatches to Richmond in May and June were completely one-sided, stressing the need for aid to Mississippi, leaving Bragg with no one to plead his army's case in Richmond. The government, assuming that Johnston still oversaw Bragg's needs, responded during this month by weakening the Tennessee army to aid Johnston.[19]

Another factor in the government's failure to reinforce Bragg was the absence of a strong western lobby in Richmond. By May, in the gov-ernment's view, Bragg's army was evidently considered a bad risk for rein-forcement. During the spring, only a handful of people campaigned for a large concentration on Bragg's front. Some of these were administration enemies, while others, after an initial support of Bragg, backed away to support a policy of an eastern offensive.

Beauregard was concerned for the Middle Tennessee position, but lacked the Richmond influence to accomplish anything. Since early 1862 the Creole had urged a Napoleonic concentration on the Tennessee front against one of the enemy's multiple lines of advance. As early as February, 1862, Beauregard had contended that not all areas in the West could be held simultaneously, and that some points must be temporarily sacrificed. After he was removed from the command of the Army of Tennessee, Beauregard, in July, 1862, offered this same advice to Bragg, urging him to concentrate against one of General Henry Halleck's lines of operation. Through the fall and winter of 1862, he preached this same philosophy to congressional allies, fellow generals, and close friends.

In May, 1863, Beauregard again came forward with a grand strategy for Bragg's army. Beauregard proposed to Johnston and to Wigfall that Rosecrans could be defeated and Grant forced to retreat by a concentra-tion on Bragg's front. Beauregard suggested that Lee maintain a defensive in Virginia, while twenty thousand men under Longstreet hurried to

19 Govan and Livingood, *A Different Valor,* 198; From Mississippi, Johnston wrote that "I have not considered myself commanding in Tennessee since assignment here . . ." Johnston to Seddon, June 12, 1863, in Johnston Papers, William and Mary.

Middle Tennessee. With other reinforcements from the West, Bragg would then have between sixty thousand and seventy thousand troops. With this force Rosecrans could be attacked and defeated at Murfreesboro, and driven into Kentucky. Such a retreat would jeopardize Grant's extended communications down the Mississippi River basin and would force a retreat there. The shabby Confederate infighting was illustrated by Beauregard's caution to Wigfall that he should present the plan to Seddon anonymously, lest the government know its author.[20]

For a time Beauregard's plan did receive the support of General James Longstreet. As early as January, Longstreet had suggested the same strategy to Lee. Exactly what Longstreet's motive was in making this suggestion is not certain. Perhaps he hoped to take over Bragg's command. Certainly in late January and in February Wigfall was pushing Longstreet as a possible replacement for Bragg. Longstreet corresponded with the Texas senator on the matter, and noted that he wanted to go West because there seemed "opportunities for all kinds of moves to great advantages." [21]

In May, after a period of service in southeastern Virginia, Longstreet revived his plan. On May 6 he met in Richmond with Seddon and proposed the same strategy as Beauregard had—that his corps be rushed to Tullahoma to join reinforcements from Mississippi. Such an army would drive Rosecrans back into Kentucky, and then could force Grant to retreat by veering into his West Tennessee line of supply.

Yet within a week, a visit with Lee in Richmond had completely reversed Longstreet's view. The Virginia general had rejected Longstreet's plan because he intended to take the offensive into Maryland, and as Longstreet explained to Wigfall later, his own plan had been predicated on an idle army in Virginia. If Lee went into Maryland, no men could be spared from the East.[22]

The ultimate blow to Bragg's hopes for reinforcements came from Davis and Seddon, who in May simply turned their attention to the more promising front—Virginia. Bragg whose growing distractions now included his command disputes, his wife's critical illness, his being tempo-

20 Beauregard to Bragg, July 28, 1862, in Buell Papers, Rice; Beauregard to Bragg, September 2, 1862, in Bragg Papers, Western Reserve; Beauregard to A. Dawson, July 15, 1862, Beauregard to Augusta Evans, January 1, 1863, Beauregard to J. E. Brown, October 31, 1862, Beauregard to Pierre Soulé, December 8, 1863, all in Beauregard Papers, National Archives; Beauregard to Wigfall, May 16, 1863, in Wigfall, DLC; *Official Records*, XIV, p. 955, XXVIII, Pt. 2, pp. 173–74, XXIII, Pt. 2, pp. 836–37.
21 Longstreet to Wigfall, February 4, 1863, in Wigfall, DLC.
22 Seddon to Longstreet, May 3, 1875, in James Longstreet Papers, Emory University Library; Longstreet to Wigfall, February 4, 1863, in Wigfall, DLC; Jones, *Confederate Strategy*, 206–209.

rarily relieved by Johnston, and his own indisposition, filed uninspired reports maintaining his contention that he could not take the offensive but must await Rosecrans at Duck River. Tennessee seemed a risky area, to Davis and Seddon, to concentrate troops.

The government's change of attitude was also probably a reaction to their disappointment in Johnston. Until April, Johnston, too, had presented little in the way of a design for Bragg's troops save to suggest, as Bragg had, that the army must stand on the defensive. Throughout January, February, and March, most of Johnston's letters to the government were concerned with a series of complaints as to the structure of his command, the problem of coordinating Bragg and Pemberton, and other matters. Justified or not, Johnston's continual assertions that practically nothing could be done in the West were bound to lessen his chances of being entrusted with heavy reinforcement. By April 6 Johnston was already talking of the routes to be used in a retreat from Middle Tennessee, and throughout that month, retreat, and not advancing or even holding the line was the subject of his reports.[23]

Also, Davis and Seddon may have become disgusted with Johnston's personal attitude. Seddon particularly had staked much on Johnston's appointment. In February the Secretary had placed himself dangerously close to the anti-Davis people by his open offer of Bragg's army to Johnston. In essence, Johnston rebuffed him by praising Bragg during the first visit to Tullahoma. In March, Seddon again offered Johnston the position, whereupon he was again rebuffed. Evidently Seddon was among Johnston's Richmond "friends" who Wigfall had reported were angered by Johnston's praise of Bragg. Seddon complained to Wigfall that just as he obtained Davis' consent to remove Bragg, Johnston's endorsement "upset the whole arrangement and prevented the removal."[24] The lengthy correspondence between the two men ceased after the March refusal by Johnston to assert his authority over Bragg, and by May, Seddon seemed disinterested in the Tennessee situation. But in June, bickering reopened between the two over the number of reinforcements being sent by the government to Johnston in Mississippi.

In other ways, Johnston's general attitude probably annoyed the government. While he personally seemed to inspire his troops, Johnston did not come off well in letters. His messages to Richmond often were sarcastic and pedantic, and sometimes even childish. In his correspondence

---

23 Johnston to Cooper, April 6, 1863, Johnston to Davis, April 10, 1863, Johnston to Seddon, April 28, 1863, in Johnston Papers, William and Mary.

24 Wigfall to Johnston, March 17, 1864, in Wigfall, DLC; Seddon to Johnston, February 5, 1863, in Johnston Papers, William and Mary; *Official Records*, XXIII, Pt. 2, p. 658.

with Davis, Seddon, Cooper, and Wigfall, Johnston exhibited a general air of defeatism. From the beginning he had made it clear that he disliked his position, thought it was nominal, and considered it unworkable, and undoubtedly left the impression that he saw little use in trying to make it succeed.[25]

This despair was particularly noticeable in his basic strategic disagreement with Davis as to whether all western areas could be defended at the same time. Johnston complained to his brother Beverley that the government could not understand "that by attempting to defend all valuable points at once he exposes his troops to being beaten everywhere."[26] To Beauregard and Wigfall, he also criticized this policy of dispersion. Still, Johnston himself never actually proposed a heavy concentration at one specific point. Likewise, though he criticized the government for maneuvering reinforcements between his armies, he never utilized these powers himself to concentrate a large force on one line of advance.

Other factors in Johnston's personality probably annoyed Richmond. He seemed to possess a stubbornness that grated on the government. In February and March, Johnston's persistent claims that any removal of Bragg would reflect upon himself seemed dogmatic. So, too, did his refusal to seize the alternative offered by the government, to leave Bragg in charge and exercise departmental authority. His letters could be interpreted by some as being realistic, by others as a mixture of argumentation, complaints, self-pity, and pessimism. He gave the appearance that nothing pleased him and that whatever future arrangement was made probably would not please him either. Johnston's letters were always unpolitic accounts of food shortages, troop shortages, transportation problems, and other equally dreary matters. Though the accounts were not inaccurate, they inspired no enthusiasm in the capital for risking more men in the West.

Apparently this habitual pessimism had a reverse effect upon the government. By April Richmond officials may have thought that Johnston had overrated the threat to Bragg. During the first few days of April, Pemberton repeatedly warned Johnston at Tullahoma that his scouts had indicated a heavy reinforcement of Rosecrans by Grant. Spy reports re-

25 For examples of increasingly strained relations, see Johnston to Seddon, June 3, 4, 10, 12, 18, 24, 1863, Johnston to Davis, May 23, 27, 31, June 1, 9, 1863, Johnston to Cooper, May 18, 1863, Seddon to Johnston, June 21, 1863, all in Johnston Papers William and Mary; see also Seddon to Johnston, June 3, 5, 8, 14, 16, 1863, Johnston to Seddon, June 3, 11, 1863, in Davis Papers, Tulane. On June 7, Johnston wrote a friend that he considered success in Mississippi as "impossible," and failure as "inevitable." Johnston to Mackall, June 7, 1863, in Mackall Papers, UNC.

26 Johnston to Beverley Johnston, May 7, 1863, in Robert M. Hughes (ed.), "Some War Letters of General Joseph E. Johnston," *Journal of the Military Service Institution of the United States*, L (May–June, 1912), 319–20.

ceived from Kentucky and Nashville during the first week of April by
Bragg's headquarters also indicated a heavy buildup at Murfreesboro. On
April 3 Pemberton reported the first of a series of warnings that transport
activity on the Mississippi indicated such action by Grant. On April 6
Johnston warned Richmond that Grant was making such a move, and
that if he were not reinforced, Bragg would lose Middle Tennessee.[27]

Richmond seemed impressed by these reports. Seddon asked Lee to
lend two or three brigades to Bragg. Davis went further and asked Lee
for General George Pickett's entire division to be sent to Tullahoma.
Then on April 16 Pemberton reported that his earlier dispatches were in
error and that no sizeable force had left Grant. Whether the government
was angered by this unwarranted crisis is not clear. It is certain that this
was the last time before Rosecrans advanced on Bragg in June that Richmond showed any interest in strengthening Bragg's army from the East.[28]

In May the administration decided to allow Lee to undertake an offensive in the East. Since he had assumed command in Virginia, Lee had
exhibited a one-way policy toward the West—quite willing to draw heavy
reinforcements, but unwilling to offer his own troops. This attitude was
evident in September of 1862, when Bragg was confronted by the armies
of Halleck in Mississippi and West Tennessee, and Buell in North Alabama and Middle Tennessee. Lee then suggested that Bragg's army
should be transferred to Virginia to protect that state while Lee invaded
Maryland. Three months later Lee once more showed a willingness to
strip the West of manpower. In early December, while both Bragg and
Pemberton were heavily outnumbered, Lee proposed that the West be
left only with a token force. Instead, he wished to send the bulk of the
western armies to Virginia to help combat Burnside's menacing movements north of Fredericksburg.

Consistently, Lee fought every proposal to aid the West. He had rejected Longstreet's January suggestion that his corps reinforce Bragg. In
March, after being warned by Johnston that heavy Federal reinforcements
were being sent to the western theater from Virginia, Lee conferred with
Davis relative to countering that move by sending a corps to Bragg. Lee
rejected both the idea of such a transfer and the belief that Burnside's

27 Pemberton to Johnston, April 3, 1863, in Dorsey, *Recollections of Henry Watkins
Allen,* 178; Pemberton to Johnston, April 9, 1863, *ibid.,* 178; Pemberton to Johnston,
April 10, 1863, *ibid.,* 178–79; Pemberton to Johnston, April 11, 1863, *ibid.,* 179;
Pemberton to Johnston, April 11, 1863, *ibid.,* 179–80; Pemberton to Johnston, April
12, 1863, *ibid,* 181; Pemberton to Johnston, April 14, 1863, *ibid.,* 181; Pemberton to
Johnston, April 16, 1863, *ibid.,* 181; Pemberton to Johnston, April 7, 9, 11, 13, 17,
1863; Johnston to Cooper, April 5, 6, 1863, in Johnston Papers, William and Mary.
28 Lee to Seddon, April 9, 1863, Lee to Cooper, April 16, 1863, in Davis Papers,
Tulane; Jones, *Confederate Strategy,* 201–203.

corps was moving to the West. In early April, even after his own scouts reported that five Yankee divisions were being sent to the West from Baltimore, Lee opposed any transfer of his men. His April 9 reply to Seddon's request for a few brigades to aid Bragg was typical of the logic Lee exhibited in April and May. Lee's statements seemed more a mishmash of objections to his aiding the West than a statement of his plans for the East. To Seddon he claimed to believe that the summer climate would force Grant to suspend operations against Vicksburg. Thus Grant would send part of his army to reinforce Hooker in Virginia. Lee evidently overlooked the operations in Mississippi in 1862, which had continued throughout the summer. In another equally illogical objection, Lee contended that while his reinforcing Johnston would be "the most natural way" to aid the West, the Federals could move troops between departments more rapidly than could the Confederates. Also, argued Lee, the idea of shuttling troops between departments was not workable. Yet twice in 1862 Lee had thought nothing of stripping the western department for service in Virginia.[29]

On April 16 Lee again fought the idea of sending his men to the West. During the false crisis of early April, Davis ordered Cooper to write Lee and request the transfer of Pickett's division to Bragg. Lee objected, repeating his argument that the danger to Vicksburg would be eased by the summer weather. In early May, when the War Department again asked for Pickett's division to reinforce Johnston in Mississippi, Lee refused. In letters to Seddon and Davis, Lee once more revealed his lack of understanding of the mounting problem in West. He contended that the June climate in Mississippi would force Grant to retreat and render Pickett's move a useless maneuver. Also, Lee seemed obsessed with the idea that the Federals would make only one great effort in the early summer, that this main thrust would be in Virginia, and that he, not the West, needed reinforcing.

Yet the most telling part of Lee's argument was his reminder to Seddon that it was the War Department that must decide which area was more imperiled, Virginia or Mississippi. For Lee's spectacle of successes, when compared with the morass of misunderstanding between Johnston and the government, in effect doomed any hope of Bragg receiving outside aid. By late May the government was talking instead of an invasion across the Potomac.[30]

[29] Lee to Davis, September 3, 1862, in Clifford Dowdey and Louis Manarin (eds.), *The Wartime Papers of R. E. Lee* (Boston, 1961), 292–94; Lee to Davis, December 6, 1862, *ibid.;* Jones, *Confederate Strategy,* 199–205, 295–97; Lee to Seddon, April 9, 1863, in Davis Papers, Tulane.

[30] Lee to Seddon, May 10, 1863, in Dowdey and Manarin (eds.), *Wartime Papers,* 482; Lee to Davis, May 11, 1863, *ibid.,* 483; Lee to Cooper, April 16, 1863, in Davis papers, Tulane.

Johnston was even unsuccessful in obtaining men for Bragg from within the western theater. His first attempt was to move several cavalry brigades from Pemberton's department in February. Johnston planned to send six thousand cavalry to Bragg's left flank at Columbia. They were to be joined with some of Bragg's own troopers to form an interdepartmental force commanded by General Earl Van Dorn.

Such a contingent, would protect the supply areas in the Columbia vicinity, could threaten Grant's communications in West Tennessee, and could operate against Rosecrans' supply line. By February 20 the Mississippi contingent, commanded by the short, dapper, yellow-haired Van Dorn, arrived in Columbia. Van Dorn assumed command of a cavalry corps, six thousand strong, composed of his own and Forrest's divisions. Yet this strategic move actually furnished Bragg little material aid. Van Dorn did not bring the six thousand as Johnston had hoped, but scarcely thirty-four hundred. And in early May, after a delegation of influential Mississippians asked President Davis for more reinforcements for Pemberton, Van Dorn's troops were returned.[31]

Johnston's second attempt to aid Bragg involved the initiation of a "pipeline" system of reinforcement. Unable to secure outside aid, Johnston in March and April attempted to devise a mutual system of reinforcement between his four departments. If Bragg were threatened, Pemberton, Buckner at Mobile, and East Tennessee would temporarily send modest reinforcements.

Yet this system could not work. Even unincumbered with wagons, Pemberton would require three weeks to reach Tullahoma with infantry, while Rosecrans could reach Bragg in less than two days. Johnston might have done better by keeping a division of Pemberton's troops at some overland half-way point, such as Florence, Alabama. But the poor food and forage in northwestern Alabama made this route impossible.

The impracticality of Pemberton's aiding Bragg was demonstrated during the false crisis in early April. Pemberton had the misinformation about Grant's supposed move by April 3, whereupon Johnston asked for the return of Stevenson's division to Bragg. Pemberton sent only two brigades. Their advance was still in Georgia on April 18 when the episode had passed. This same distance problem also made Johnston's pipeline from Mobile to Tullahoma unworkable. The meager three thousand in-

---

[31] Johnston to Earl Van Dorn, February 24, 1863, Johnston to Bragg, January 11, 1863, Johnston to Davis, January 17, 1863, Johnston to Seddon, March 12, 1863, in Johnston Papers, William and Mary; Henry, *Forrest*, 494; *Official Records*, XXIII, Pt. 2, pp. 646, 650–51; Edward Dillon, "General Van Dorn's operations between Columbia and Nashville in 1863," *SHSP*, VII (1879), 144–46; Johnston to Polk, March 3, 1863, in Polk Papers, Sewanee.

fantry at the Gulf city simply could not reach Bragg in time to fend off an advance by Rosecrans.[32]

The brightest hope of reinforcement was the Department of East Tennessee. By April this small department contained almost fourteen thousand troops. The previous month, Johnston had reached an agreement with the departmental commander, General Daniel Donelson, on a plan of reinforcement for Bragg. Donelson was to form a large reserve of troops freed from regular duties of protecting railroad bridges and mountain gaps and garrison duty. These reserves would be at several points along the East Tennessee Railroad, ready to be rushed to Tullahoma when needed. By April 10 the new East Tennessee commander, General W. G. M. Davis, assured Johnston that such a force was available and could reach Tullahoma within forty-eight hours.

For several reasons, however, East Tennessee never supplied the aid that Johnson had wanted. One reason was, of course, the perpetual state of command confusion in the area. Between August of 1862 and July of 1863, nine men commanded the department. Each commander seemed to instigate a new policy. Donelson agreed with Johnston's idea of keeping a reserve stationed near the railroad, but he considered the launching of a long cavalry raid into Kentucky to break up any potential Federal threat would be the best policy. His successor, W. G. M. Davis, favored still another policy. Davis advocated a weak defense of the multiple mountain passes into Kentucky. Instead, the department's cavalry would remain on constant patrol on the Kentucky side of the Cumberland Mountains, and the infantry would be concentrated along the railroad. By May another commander, General Dabney Maury, favored a defensive-offensive, whereby Knoxville would be fortified as a central garrison, and infantry would be released for offensive operations against any invading force.[33]

The chaotic command situation was also caused by the poor geographical alignment of the department. The two-hundred-mile stretch from the Virginia border to Georgia was too long to patrol with such a small force. The lower part of the valley below Knoxville rightfully belonged in Bragg's department. After much agitation, Bragg in January finally did get control of the base at Chattanooga, but not of the lower part of the valley below the Little Tennessee River until June. Equally serious, a duplication of effort with the neighboring Department of Western Virginia produced a waste of manpower. Both departments merged in south-

---

[32] Johnston to Davis, March 28, April 10, 1863, Johnston to Pemberton, April 11, 1863, Johnston to Cooper, April 6, 1863, Johnston to Seddon, March 12, 1863, all in Johnston Papers, William and Mary; Govan and Livingood, *A Different Valor,* 190–91; Robert C. Black III, *Railroads of the Confederacy* (Chapel Hill, 1952), 192.

[33] *Official Records,* XXIII, Pt. 2, pp. 746, 798, 821, 831, 843; Jones, *Confederate Strategy,* 177.

western Virginia near the salt works at Saltville, and technically both were responsible for that region's defense. As a result, a considerable segment of the East Tennessee troops was immobilized in the area east and northeast of Cumberland Gap to block an invasion of the salt area.

This waste of manpower in East Tennessee was the crux of the situation. The department had almost fourteen thousand men in May, but only four thousand were considered available to reinforce Bragg. The remaining troops were pinned down for a number of reasons. One whole brigade of two thousand men was held in southwest Virginia. The entire departmental cavalry force, three thousand strong, was utterly useless to Bragg. It was a tatterdemalion outfit of poorly armed and undisciplined mountain units. Because of a lack of forage north of Knoxville, and the need to anticipate an advance by Burnside, all the department's cavalry was compelled to operate across the mountains in East Kentucky. Other troops were busy guarding the multiple bridges along the East Tennessee railroad. The need to defend the many gaps along the Kentucky border also sapped the small army. When General Simon Buckner assumed command of the department in May, he discovered that one thousand men were guarding Cumberland Gap, while additional forces watched other major routes such as Big Creek Gap.[34]

The result was that in May and June, East Tennessee had only four thousand men available for Bragg's reinforcement. And even these welcome additions were stymied by the combined advance of Rosecrans and Burnside in late June, for contrary to Richmond's expectations this advance now became a reality. Bragg got his only East Tennessee reinforcement when, in answer to his request, Buckner unselfishly dispatched all the men he could spare, three thousand infantry and two batteries. He sent the help knowing, through intelligence, that part of Burnside's force had penetrated Tennessee and was at Jamestown across the Cumberlands from Knoxville via Big Creek Gap. So great was the pressure on Buckner's front that his small reinforcement could not leave Knoxville until June 27, and by July 7 it was back in East Tennessee.[35]

Bragg's only other hope of obtaining men was by a more vigorous conscription and by a strong policy on the acute problems of absentees and deserters. Many Kentucky and Tennessee troops habitually deserted whenever their home territory was given up by the army. Also, Bragg was operating amidst some of the Confederacy's most disaffected areas. A sizeable number of Bragg's men were from nearby Unionist regions such

34 *Official Records*, XXIII, Pt. 2, pp. 821, 831, 843, 855, 868, 871; Johnston to Bragg, January 9, 1863, Johnston to Ewell, January 11, 1863, Johnston to Bragg, January 11, 1863, in Johnston Papers, William and Mary.

35 *Official Records*, XXIII, Pt. 2, pp. 885, 887, 889, 893.

as East Tennessee, the Cumberlands of Tennessee, the North Georgia Appalachians, and the northern Alabama mountains. Not only was a short route home available to many, but there was also shelter for stragglers and deserters from other areas. An estimated ten thousand deserters and absentees were reportedly sheltered in the northern Alabama mountains during the spring of 1863. Another fifteen hundred absentees and evaders of conscription were in the very heart of Bragg's army at Shelbyville, and another three thousand were at nearby Fayetteville.

The War Department had tried to improve conscription procedures by establishing the Bureau of Conscription. This organization, headed by General G. J. Rains, was badly attuned to Bragg's geographical locale. While the new system was an improvement over state conscription, it lacked the force needed for the tough Unionist-deserter country almost completely surrounding Bragg. The Unionist-deserter-bushwacker complexities of the upper South so completely intimidated the bureau's efforts during the spring, that Bragg complained in April of having received only fifty conscripts under the new system.

To return these absentees, stragglers, and deserters, and to enforce conscription laws, Johnston believed an organization backed by military pressure was imperative. Hence, in January, Johnston appointed General Gideon Pillow to head the new Volunteer and Conscript Bureau of the Army of Tennessee. Pillow was empowered to use military force to obtain conscripts, return absentees, and organize recruits.[36]

The two months of the new bureau's operation embodied Pillow's finest hour. His pedantic, tin-soldier nature fitted well into his new position. Distrusted because of his miserable performance on the Tennessee front in 1861-62, Pillow seemed to find himself in the paper work of his new job, where he controlled companies of cavalry rather than a division of infantry. Between its organization shortly after January 14, and its abolition by the War Department about April 1, Pillow's bureau greatly strengthened Bragg's army. He zealously scoured the counties of southern Middle Tennessee and northern Alabama, backed by small squads of irregular cavalry. Exactly how many men Pillow obtained during those two months is not certain. His boast that he added 12,000 men within the first month was no doubt an exaggeration. Bragg estimated that by April 1, Pillow had provided 10,000 men. Whatever the exact figure, the change was obvious. Pillow's activities saw the army's effective strength increase by 9,414. Within ten days after his bureau ceased to

36 *Ibid.*, XX, Pt. 2, pp. 496, 497; *ibid.*, Ser. IV, Vol. II, pp. 361–62, 387, 680, 741; Albert B. Moore, *Conscription and Conflict in the Confederacy* (New York, 1924), 191–92.

function, a marked decrease of over 5,000 men in Bragg's effective strength was noted.

As head of the bureau, Pillow was repeatedly warned by the War Department to stop meddling with the process of conscription. While no doubt Pillow did use extra-legal means to obtain men, such as denying some exemptions, he did succeed—a matter which perhaps also annoyed the Central Bureau. Finally, on March 2, Seddon directed Johnston to make Pillow stop all conscription activities. Seddon, by his directive, unintentionally wrecked Johnston's plans to bolster Bragg's army. Not only did Pillow have to stop conscripting men, but his recruiting activities, as well as the conscription activities of the Central Bureau for Bragg's army, were restricted to the limited area of central and North Alabama and to Mississippi. The restriction of conscripts and recruits to this area was a crucial blow to Bragg's manpowers. Already Pemberton had absorbed nearly all Mississippi conscripts, and Governor John Pettus of Mississippi had thirteen cavalry companies in the state recruiting for Pemberton. North and Central Alabama, the heart of the Unionist activity east of the Mississippi River, would scarcely heed the passive tactics of the Central Bureau's enrolling officers. Other areas such as West and Middle Tennessee, North Georgia, East Tennessee, and Kentucky, which had previously supplied men, were off limits to conscription and recruiting for Bragg's army.[37]

By late April, Bragg had built his army to a peak strength of over fifty-two thousand effectives. In May, however, the government withdrew over eleven thousand men from Bragg when McCown's and Breckinridge's infantry divisions and Pemberton's cavalry division were sent to Mississippi. In June the unauthorized raid by General John Morgan into Indiana and Ohio sapped another two thousand men. The late spring detachment of General Philip Roddey's cavalry brigade to protect the Florence-Muscle Shoals area of northwestern Alabama cost Bragg another sixteen hundred men. As a result, Bragg's force had eroded to the point by late June that it had barely thirty thousand effective infantry, practically the same sized army he had immediately after the battle at Stone's River.[38]

Early on the morning of May 10 Johnston left Tullahoma for Mississippi, thus ending his frustrated tenure over Bragg's force. Although he was responsible for the Army of Tennessee until mid-July, Johnston by his own misunderstanding thought Bragg was no longer under his jurisdiction. Johnston's period of command in Tennessee had not been outstanding, and the general's own prophecy that no army could have two generals was probably true. Because of Johnston's viewpoint on his theater authority in Tennessee, from February until May, the Army of Tennessee had in effect had an excess of commanders and a lack of command direction. In other areas he had failed. Unsuccessful in presenting Bragg's case in Richmond, Johnston had been equally unsuccessful in devising any strategy for the Tennessee front. Save for some vague comments on Bragg's necessity of standing on the defensive, and some April comments on possible routes of retreat from Tennessee, Johnston had not produced any strategic policy for Tennessee. Likewise, Johnston's personality and his poor communication with Richmond had stifled any coordination of the various western departments. By May, save for his temporary success with Pillow's bureau, Johnston clearly had done little to bolster Bragg's weak army.

six

The Road to Chattanooga

HAVING COMMITTED HIS TROOPS TO A DEFENSIVE LINE ALONG THE DUCK River, Braxton Bragg also decided upon a strategy from which he never wavered—that because of Rosecrans' strength and his own weakness, he must maintain a defensive position and stave off a Federal attack.

But the attack was not stemmed. Weakened by six months of discord, the army in June was swept out of its Duck River line and sent retreating hastily toward Chattanooga. The advance by Rosecrans coincided with a total breakdown of communication among Bragg's high command.

The defense of the Duck River line was made difficult by problems of both geography and logistics. From Murfreesboro the Union army had a number of routes by which Bragg could be flanked out of his new line. On Bragg's far right flank, two roads led from McMinnville across the Cumberland Mountains to the Sequatchie Valley near Jasper. If Jasper were seized, Bragg's main line of retreat from Middle Tennessee would be severed.

There were several other ways of threatening Bragg on his immediate right flank, which was anchored on the main pike from Murfreesboro to Manchester. The Murfreesboro-Manchester Road led through strategic Hoover's Gap in the Highland Rim, across the Duck River, and thence to Manchester. From Manchester, Rosecrans almost at his leisure could select his choice of routes to entrap Bragg along the Duck River. A road led south to ascend the Cumberland Mountains to University Place. Here the main road from Middle Tennessee to Chattanooga, via Murfreesboro, Shelbyville, Tullahoma, and Jasper, crossed the mountains. Or Rosecrans could move more southwest and seize the village of Dec-herd, twelve miles south of Bragg's headquarters at Tullahoma. Decherd was a strategic point, since it lay both on the Chattanooga Pike and on the Nashville and Chattanooga Railroad. Also, Rosecrans could advance directly on Bragg's base at Tullahoma. The loss of Tullahoma would entail the loss of the entire position. The Nashville and Chattanooga Railroad and Chattanooga Pike both passed through this village. Here also intersected a key branch line of the railroad which led northeastward through Manchester to McMinnville. Rosecrans could thence move directly down the branch line, only eleven miles from Manchester to Tullahoma.

Even should the Confederates strongly defend Hoover's Gap, there remained another threat to Manchester. To the east of the main Murfreesboro-Manchester road, an alternate route led from Murfreesboro via Bradyville. This route, less than thirty miles in length, led through Gillie's Gap in the Highland Rim, to debouch in the Duck River Valley at Manchester.[1]

On Bragg's immediate front in the Tullahoma area, there were also several routes by which Rosecrans could advance. A good road led through the Highlands from Murfreesboro via Liberty Gap to Wartrace on the Nashville and Chattanooga Railroad. The seizure of Wartrace would both cut the railroad and threaten the line of retreat to Chattanooga of any forces west of Wartrace. This was so because the main Chattanooga Pike via Shelbyville veered southeast to cross the Duck River only about eight miles south of Wartrace. Thus, if Wartrace were to fall, any position at Shelbyville would collapse as well.

On Bragg's left front at Shelbyville, Rosecrans could advance from Murfreesboro on the main Chattanooga Pike. It was a mere twenty-four miles from Murfreesboro through the Highland Rim at Guy's Gap to Shelbyville, which lay on the north bank of the Duck River. In turn, if Shelbyville fell, any positions west of this key town would also be forced back.[2]

The geographical problems were thus extremely difficult. To avoid a flanking maneuver, Bragg would have to maintain a watch along a front seventy miles wide. Also, to protect the immediate routes to Chattanooga via Hoover's, Liberty, and Guy's gaps would, at the same time, require the bulk of the army at the center of the line.

While it might have been more desirable to concentrate in the Shelbyville-Manchester area, the lack of food presented a problem. By June the

[1] Cheatham's map of Middle Tennessee, in Cheatham Papers, Tennessee; George Reynolds, "Sewanee and the Cumberland Plateau in the Civil War" (Typescript in University of the South Library, Sewanee), 11.

[2] Gilbert C. Kniffen, "Maneuvering Bragg out of Tennessee," in *Battles and Leaders,* III, 636; *Official Records,* XXIII, Pt. 1, pp. 404–405.

army was suffering from short rations. Thus Bragg was forced to disperse along a wide front from Columbia to McMinnville, not so much to protect the multiple road approaches as to feed the army. During the spring of 1863 the Commissary Bureau applied the same rules that had so disrupted the Army of Tennessee's food supply during the previous hard autumn in East Tennessee. Commissary agents denuded the Duck and Elk river valleys of corn, hogs, and beeves, which were placed in the central depot at Atlanta for the use of Lee's Virginia army. Bragg's army in fact was forced to defend the area from which Lee derived his rations while his own men lived a hand-to-mouth existence.

As this crippling food shortage worsened in March and April, Bragg's mobility even in his own defensive territory became limited. The army ran completely out of meat; in one two-week period, Bragg was 400,000 rations short. Though both Bragg and Joseph E. Johnston protested to Richmond, little was done to aid them. The depot commissary officer at Atlanta, Major J. F. Cumming, grudgingly allowed the army only 60,000 pounds of meat from Atlanta, scarcely three days' supply. Meanwhile during March, the Atlanta depot, which had eight million pounds of salt meat and several thousand head of cattle on hand, was shipping Lee a half million pounds of meat per week. In his April report to Davis, Colonel William Preston Johnston lashed out at the government's treatment of Bragg and warned that the army had a bare subsistence.[3]

Richmond did not realize that Bragg was immobilized because of transportation difficulties. The Nashville and Decatur Railroad could have drained stores from the rich country around Columbia and Pulaski except that the Duck and Elk River bridges and several smaller bridges had been destroyed. Wagon transportation was in worse condition. In May, Bragg was almost immobilized because of a shortage of wagons and animals. The problem was a vicious cycle of wagon and forage shortages. Bragg literally wore out his wagons and teams during the spring by hauling forage. Hardee's corps was posted in the Wartrace area, east of the Nashville and Chattanooga rail line. By the first week in March the forage supply east of the line was exhausted. From then until July Hardee had to obtain his forage from the Columbia-Pulaski region and from north Alabama. This involved long wagon hauls of up to 150 miles. Polk's corps, in the Shelbyville vicinity, also had to draw forage from as far west as Pulaski.

[3] Seddon to Johnston, March 3, 1863, Johnston to Seddon, April 28, 1863, Bragg to Ewell, March 16, 1863, in Johnston Papers, William and Mary; John Walker to Major Cumming, December 20, 1862, George Brent to Van Dorn, March 30, 1863, in Bragg Papers, Western Reserve; Official Records, XXIII, Pt. 2, pp. 657, 661, 674, 680, 688, 695, 700, 702, 708, 759, 764–65 769.

By March the food supply between Shelbyville and Manchester was used up, and Bragg was forced to reach even beyond Columbia and Pulaski to Franklin. This involved wagon hauls of forty miles at a minimum, sometimes more than one hundred miles. Meat was obtainable only from central Kentucky; this haul of several hundred miles around Rosecrans' left flank was all but impossible. By mid-April, the only remaining bread source for the army was on the far left, in the vicinity of Fayetteville, Columbia, and Pulaski.

This was the kind of hauling that completely wore out the wagons. Hardee estimated in May that if the army retreated, there were not even enough wagons to carry off the baggage. Richmond may not have grasped this situation. Colonel William Preston Johnston's report in April had estimated that Bragg's entire army, including cavalry and outposts in Alabama, had 2,276 wagons. But Johnston overstated the case. This was not an accurate description of the wagons, horses, and mules possessed by Bragg's two corps of infantry. Hardee and Polk had only 1,225 wagons available for hauling baggage, forage, food, and other items. Of this number, only thirteen were genuine forage wagons, and not even all of the 1,225 vehicles had a team of mules or horses.[4]

The livestock problem was also severe. By 1863 the western army's mule and horse supply was depleted by the loss of the rich Kentucky and northern Middle Tennessee counties. Also, the animal quality was noticeably poorer. Corn was so scarce that some units could not provide a daily issue, while others drew only two or three ears per day. Hardee's corps thus had only 2,654 animals for all headquarters, baggage, forage, ordnance, ambulance, and food vehicles. The bare requirement for the backbone of the food supply, the six-, four-, and two-horse wagons alone, would have required 2,118 animals.[5]

The combination of geography and failing supply pinned Bragg to the Duck River line during the spring. He believed he was too weak in men and rations for an offensive on Murfreesboro. Intelligence reports from January until June consistently showed that Rosecrans was well reinforced and well entrenched on Stone's River. Yet as long as he had stayed on the Duck River, Bragg consumed only the sparse local food and forage supply. Unable to draw from the Atlanta depot, and faced with failing transportation, Bragg was forced to place the army on a defensive and dispersed line.

4 "Returns in Detail of Army of Tennessee Allowances of Transportation, March 1863," in Bragg Papers, Western Reserve; "Consolidated Report of Means and Allowance of Transportation," *ibid.*; Brent to Van Dorn, March 30, 1863, *ibid.*; *Official Records*, XXIII, Pt. 2, pp. 732, 759–60, 764, 821.

5 "Returns in Detail of Army of Tennessee Allowances of Transportation, March, 1863," in Bragg Papers, Western Reserve; *Official Records*, XXIII, Pt. 2, pp. 764, 769.

This defensive cordon, which stretched from Columbia to McMinn-ville, was intended to encompass both food production areas and road approaches toward Bragg's base at Chattanooga. The left wing was established at Columbia and Spring Hill under General Earl Van Dorn. Van Dorn's cavalry corps, six thousand strong, consisted of the divisions of Generals Will Martin, William Jackson, and Nathan Bedford Forrest. The left center, manned by Leonidas Polk's infantry corps, was placed to contest any advance via Shelbyville. During the spring, Polk's men began constructing a large semicircular line of entrenchments that stretched from Duck River on the west, across the north side of Shelby-ville, to the Highland Rim on the east. Will Martin's cavalry division was detached from Van Dorn and was placed two miles north of Shelby-ville at Guy's Gap.

The right center, that region traversed by the roads through Liberty Gap on Wartrace and Hoover's Gap on Manchester, was manned by Hardee's corps. Hardee was ordered to take his position on the railroad at Tullahoma, where the roads from Manchester and Wartrace merged with the main pike to Chattanooga. Hardee, too, was ordered to dig elaborate entrenchments, while his advance was to be covered by General John Wharton's cavalry division of Wheeler's corps. Wharton was to picket the general area to the north of Hoover's and Liberty Gaps. The far right flank, from the Murfreesboro-Manchester Road northeast to McMinnville, was guarded only by two small cavalry divisions of Wheeler's corps, his own and that of General John Morgan.[6]

This new line, with barely thirty-eight thousand effectives covering a seventy-mile front, promised disaster. Furthermore, Bragg and his two infantry corps leaders had not reached an understanding as to what the army was to do. By June, Bragg was more concerned with the most direct road approaches on his Chattanooga base, via Shelbyville, War-trace, and Manchester. Never did either Bragg or Johnston fear a massive move via Columbia, but instead always considered that Rosecrans would feint in that direction in order to make the Rebels more nervous over their food supply. There was a time in April when Bragg feared an advance as far east as McMinnville, but by June the possibility of this route had been discounted by Rebel intelligence. Instead, the heaviest Union activity centered on the Shelbyville, Wartrace, and Manchester fronts.

To guard against this expected march, Bragg had prepared only a hazy plan, so vague that Colonel William Preston Johnston voiced con-

6 Johnston to Wigfall, March 24, 1863, in Wigfall Papers, DLC; *Official Records,* XXIII, Pt. 2, pp. 754, 760; Brent Diary, January 68, February 2, 1863, in Bragg Papers, Western Reserve.

cern to the President about it. Prior to April, Bragg and Johnston had agreed only on a vague offensive-defensive. They would await Rosecrans' approach on the right center, and then would move Polk's infantry from the left wing to strike the Federals on the flank. As spring progressed, it became obvious that the two generals were not thinking along the same lines. Johnston approved the building of extensive earthworks at Tullahoma, but did not envision a battle there. Instead, he held to the idea of striking Rosecrans on the flank with one of the army's wings.

In March, Bragg seemed to agree that they should not fight in the Tullahoma fortifications, and held to the idea of a flank move. By June, however, he had changed his mind. He then seemed unsure as to what the army should do. He envisioned a hazy plan whereby Polk's corps at Shelbyville would still make a flank attack, but Hardee's corps at Tullahoma would make a stand in the Tullahoma entrenchments.[7]

This ambiguous plan, never understood by Polk or Hardee, was based on the erroneous idea that Rosecrans could be stalled at Tullahoma long enough for Polk to move against him from Shelbyville. As early as January 26 Hardee saw the fallacy in this idea. A master at discerning topographical matters, Hardee warned Bragg that a line at Tullahoma would not hold. It was so far west of the key approach via Hoover's Gap on Manchester, that Rosecrans could bypass Tullahoma and seize the Chattanooga Pike and the railroad at Bragg's rear. Rosecrans could move from Manchester, cross the Duck River, and cut both the railroad and the pike at Decherd. [8]

Bragg's two corps leaders were confused not only by his vague plans for the operations regarding Tullahoma, but by his entire strategy. Until Polk ordered its execution on June 26, the Bishop seemed to have known practically nothing of Bragg's idea of a flank attack from Shelbyville. Polk was not only surprised to learn of the plan, but strongly opposed it. He felt it was impossible for his corps to march north from Shelbyville, and then turn east through the rugged Highland Rim ridges to strike Rosecrans on the flank as he marched toward Liberty or Hoover's Gaps. Also, Bragg's notion of having Hardee make a stand at Tullahoma evidently was not even discussed with Polk before the crisis arose on June 26. [9]

[7] Johnston to Polk, March 3, 1863, in Polk Papers, Sewanee; Polk, *Polk*, II, 219; "Notes of Lieut. W. B. Richmond, aide-de-camp to Lieutenant-General Polk, on movement of the Army of Tennessee from Tullahoma to Chattanooga, June 26–July 7, 1863" (MS in Polk Papers, Sewanee), June 26, 1863, Hereinafter cited as "Richmond Notes." *Official Records*, XXIII, Pt. 2, pp. 724, 760–61.

[8] Hardee to Bragg, January 26, 1863, June 5, 1863, in Hardee Papers, Alabama.

[9] "Richmond Notes," June 26, 1863; W. W. Mackall to Polk, June 26—5 P.M., 1863, in Polk Papers, Sewanee; Polk, *Polk*, II, 218–19.

Nor did Hardee understand what was expected of him. The lack of communication between Bragg and Hardee created another problem—the failure of Bragg to strengthen his defenses on the Hoover's Gap front. Why did this position remain so weak in June, though both Bragg and Johnston feared a potential attack from that direction? Not until April 21 when intelligence of a move against Hoover's and Liberty Gaps was received, did Bragg let Hardee even move to the north side of the Duck River to Wartrace. And then Bragg allowed Hardee to place only a single brigade on the Murfreesboro-Manchester Pike to block the Hoover's Gap pass. The remainder of the corps was posted south of Liberty Gap in the vicinity of Wartrace.[10]

This startling weakness on the right flank continued through June. After the departure of Breckinridge's division for Mississippi, Hardee was left with only one good division—Cleburne's. To replace the Kentucky division, Hardee was given a hastily formed, small division headed by a former mathematics professor, General Alexander Stewart. Even then, only one of Stewart's brigades remained on the Murfreesboro-Manchester Road. The remainder of Stewart's division was posted some ten miles southwest, toward Wartrace.

By the end of June, Hoover's Gap remained almost undefended. The gaps itself was actually a four-mile-long pass between eleven-hundred-foot ridges dividing the waters of the Stone's and Duck rivers. The pass was so narrow that two wagons could hardly pass side by side, and it was commanded by the surrounding ridges. Strong entrenchments had been prepared in the gap, but in June they were manned by only a single cavalry regiment of Wharton's division. The nearest—and only—support on the Manchester Road was General William Bate's brigade, stationed three miles to the south at Beech Grove. Since Murfreesboro lay only eleven miles north of Hoover's Gap, it was possible for Rosecrans to reach the gap before Bate was informed of the extent of the Federal threat. Why Stewart did not compel Bate to maintain a heavier force in the entrenchments is not explained. Evidently Bate was relying upon sufficient warnings from the lone cavalry regiment in the gap.[11]

Gillie's Gap, on the Murfreesboro-Bradyville-Manchester Road, was

10 *Official Records*, XXIII, Pt. 2, p. 780.

11 James Connolly to wife, July 5, 1863, in Paul M. Angle (ed.), *Three Years in the Army of the Cumberland*, by James A. Connolly (Bloomington, Ind., 1959), 89–91; George Wildon, "Wilder's Brigade of Mounted Infantry in the Tullahoma Chickamauga Campaign," in Military Order of the Loyal Legion of the United States, Kansas Commandery, *War Talks in Kansas* (Kansas City, Missouri, 1906), 50; John T. Wilder, "The Battle of Hoover's Gap," in Ohio Commandery of the Military Order of the Loyal Legion of the United States, *Sketches of War History, 1861–1865* (Cincinnati, 1908), VI, 169; *Official Records*, XXIII, Pt. 1, p. 611.

even more poorly defended. Hardee on June 5 warned Bragg that this route could flank his troops, yet neither Bragg nor Hardee posted any force there save a small patrol of cavalry.

Why were the approaches on Manchester neglected? One major cause was that Hardee simply did not know what Bragg wanted him to do. By June, Hardee believed that Bragg did not plan to contest any Federal passage into the Duck River Valley at any point east of Liberty Gap. Instead, Hardee believed that should Rosecrans' move via Hoover's Gap, his infantry was to fall back into the Tullahoma defenses. In fact, Hardee even suggested that unless Bragg wanted to control Hoover's Gap, Bate's brigade should be withdrawn completely to the Wartrace front. Bragg did not bother to correct Hardee's interpretation. On June 24, when Rosecrans first threatened Hoover's Gap, Hardee thus ordered Stewart not to contest the Manchester front, if hard pressed, but to fall back to Wartrace. Since Hardee knew the weakness of the Tullahoma defenses, and had warned that any capture of Manchester would enfilade Bragg, why did he not take personal action to shore up Bragg's right wing? No doubt Hardee was confused by Bragg's lack of any specific plan. Too, disputes had intensified the animosity between the two men until by June communication had simply broken down.[12]

In addition to all the confusion about the Manchester front, Bragg, during June, lost track of Rosecrans. Since February the Confederates had been confused by a series of parries which befuddled Rebel intelligence. The first major Federal threat came on March 10. A force estimated at twenty thousand drove Van Dorn out of his Spring Hill headquarters in full flight for Duck River. By night Van Dorn was almost entrapped on the north bank of the rain-swollen Duck opposite his Columbia base. With no bridge and his pontoons awash, the flashy cavalryman came close to losing an entire cavalry corps before slipping away during the night.[13]

By mid-March, the threat on the far left vanished. Instead, by March 15, Wharton's scouts were bringing strange tales of a Yankee retreat from Murfreesboro. Citizens brought news that the Federals were abandoning

12 *Official Records,* XXIII, Pt. 2, p. 884. For evidence that Hardee believed the Tullahoma defenses were weak, see Hardee to Bragg, January 12, 1863, also Hardee to Bragg, January 26, June 5, 1863, Hardee to Mackall, April 25, 1863, all in Hardee Papers, Alabama.
13 *Official Records,* XXIII, Pt. 2, pp. 677, 679, 681, 683, 686; Van Dorn to Philip Roddey, March 10, 1863, Lucius Polk to Leonidas Polk, March 10, 1863, Van Dorn to Polk, March 10, 1863, Van Dorn to Bragg and Polk, March 10, 1863, Roddey to Polk, March 10, 11, 1863, all in Dispatches from the Front, 1863, Polk's First Corps, Army of Tennessee, Chap. II, Vol. 53 3/4, National Archives, hereinafter cited as Chap. II, Vol. 53 3/4, National Archives; Richmond to Mrs. Rayner, March 9, 1863, in Polk Papers, Sewanee.

their line on Stone's River and were withdrawing to Nashville. The number of these reports had become so extensive by March 18 that a full-scale cavalry reconnaissance was ordered by Bragg. The reconnaissance produced only chaos. Van Dorn insisted on March 20 that his scouts reported part of Rosecrans force had withdrawn to Nashville. That night he relayed another interesting tale—the troops were withdrawing from Nashville for Kentucky. Yet, the next day, Van Dorn revised his account, and reported that fifty thousand fresh troops from Virginia were expected at Nashville in a few days. Moreover, it appeared that Rosecrans was preparing for a general offensive.

The other cavalrymen provided equally confusing intelligence. Wheeler on March 20 said that troop trains were already rolling north from Nashville en route to Kentucky, and that men and supplies were being withdrawn from Murfreesboro. Yet a reconnaissance by Will Martin produced a different story. Martin penetrated as far north as the pike between Nashville and Stone's River; he reported that no Federals had left the Stone's River line. From near Lebanon, General John Morgan reported also that Rosecrans was not falling back; the much-heralded troop trains seen en route to Kentucky were only carrying a detachment to guard against Confederate raiding parties on the Louisville and Nashville Railroad. Yet General John Wharton on March 20 insisted that heavy artillery and supply trains were leaving Murfreesboro for Nashville and that the infantry was expected to follow.[14]

In late April Rosecrans again confused Bragg. On April 21 heavy Federal columns struck on a wide front from Shelbyville to McMinnville. One force, estimated to be seven regiments, held Will Martin's division at Guy's Gap. A second force drove through Hoover's Gap and penetrated as far south as Beech Grove before being driven back. A third column, with an estimated fifteen hundred men, skirted Hoover's Gap and wrecked the key spur line between Manchester and McMinnville. To the north, an alleged twelve thousand troops drove back Morgan's outpost on the Nashville-Knoxville Pike at Liberty. Then, all units quickly retreated

14 ——— to Van Dorn, March 21, 1863, Wheeler to Polk, March 20, 1863, Col. Baxter Smith to John Wharton, March 24—5 P.M., 1863, S. C. Ferrill to Wharton, March 28, 1863; Van Dorn to Polk, March 20—9 P.M., 1863, Post Commander to Wharton, March 16, 1863, Martin to Thomas Jack, March 19, 1863, W. P. Johnston to Polk, March 16, 1863, Wharton to Polk, March 19, 20, 28, 1863, Roddey to Polk, March 19—7 P.M., March 20, 1863, Wheeler to Polk, March 20, 1863 all in Chap. II, Vol. 53 3/4, National Archives; "Martha" to Frank Cheatham, March 30, 1863, in Cheatham Papers, Tennessee; *Official Records*, XXIII, Pt. 2, pp. 695–99, 703–704, 709, 713–17, 725, 728, XXIII, Pt. 1, pp. 151–52, 162.

to Murfreesboro after demonstrating the vulnerable nature of Bragg's right-center.[15]

By June there was no doubt that the Federals were about to move in one direction or another. Forrest's scouts penetrated the cordon of Nashville defenses to report that either a retreat or an advance was about to begin. Other scouts on June 2 reported a concentration of cavalry at Murfreesboro. Other information indicated that reinforcements were being sent to Grant from Middle Tennessee. Befuddled, Bragg warned Buckner in East Tennessee that Rosecrans was readying an advance on his Tullahoma base, yet that same day he spoke of a retreat by Rosecrans from Murfreesboro to Nashville or parts unknown.[16]

Unsure of what the Federals intended, Bragg, on the afternoon of June 2, ordered Polk and Hardee to inch forward on the Shelbyville, Wartrace, and Manchester roads toward Murfreesboro on a general reconnaissance. This two-day reconnaissance netted only more confusing intelligence. On June 3 Hardee reported that Rosecrans had allegedly sent twenty-four regiments to Grant. That same day Forrest and spies in Nashville reported that forty carloads of infantry from Kentucky were passing through Nashville to Murfreesboro. Also, the Nashville and Franklin garrisons were being stripped of troops who were being hurried to Murfreesboro. These menacing activities were made more impressive by news on June 5 that Burnside with thirteen regiments was advancing across the old battleground around Mill Springs toward East Tennessee. Buckner's headquarters warned Bragg that spies had heard talk of a simultaneous advance by Burnside and Rosecrans.[17]

By June 6 Bragg at last realized that an advance was imminent, for scout reports and interrogation of prisoners taken during the reconnaissance confirmed Bragg's fears. Rosecrans was not reinforcing Grant. Instead, within the past few days, four thousand fresh infantry troops from Kentucky had arrived at Murfreesboro. Hardee was hurriedly pulled back

15 *Official Records*, XXIII, Pt. 2, pp. 782, 784–86; Martin to Jack, April 21, 22, 29, 1863, Mackall to Polk, April 22, 1863, Kinloch Falconer to Polk, April 21, 1863, Martin to Mackall, April 22—3 P.M., 1863, Mackall to Martin, April 22, 1863, all in Chap. II, Vol. 53 3/4, National Archives; Falconer to Hardee, April 21, 1863, Mackall to Hardee, April 21, 1863, Falconer to Ben Hardin Helm, April 21, 1863, Falconer to Helm, April 21, 1863, all in Bragg Papers, Western Reserve.

16 *Official Records*, XXIII, Pt. 2, pp. 856–57; Hardee to Bragg, June 3, June 3—3 P.M., 1863, Bragg to Mackall, June 2, 1863, Forrest to Bragg, June 1, 1863, Bragg to Cooper, June 2, 1863, Bragg to Martin, June 2, 1863, Roddey to Bragg, June 3, 1863, Bragg to Hardee, June 3, 1863, Bragg to Buckner, June 2, 1863, all in Bragg Papers, Western Reserve.

17 Bragg to Mackall, June 6, 1863, Mackall to Polk, June 8, 1863, Hardee to Bragg, June 4, 1863, all in Bragg Papers, Western Reserve.

to Wartrace while Polk was hastily sent into the fortifications at Shelby-ville.[18] Then Bragg awaited the expected advance, declaring to Joe Johnston, "We shall watch him." [19] But by late June he had lost them again.

The final stroke in this Rebel command morass was misuse of cavalry. After the February organization, Bragg's cavalry in the corps of Wheeler and Van Dorn seemed to at last attain cohesion. Too, by early May, the troopers numbered sixteen thousand effectives, almost one-third of the army's strength.[20]

Yet, during the spring, neither corps had been well handled. Wheeler evinced little ability in long-range planning. He seemed more intent on leading the traditional Rebel cavalry dash against targets of lesser im-portance. In January he raided a steamboat landing on the Cumberland River below Nashville. In February Wheeler led an unwise attack in an attempt to recapture Fort Donelson. Rebuffed by Bragg for suggesting another visionary scheme, the capture of Louisville, Wheeler in April led a small, unsuccessful raid on the Louisville and Nashville Railroad north of Nashville. Aside from these activities, the young cavalryman seemed unable to devise effective plans for crippling Rosecrans' line of com-munication.[21]

On the Columbia front, Van Dorn's corps was also ineffective. From his arrival there in February until his murder in May, Van Dorn was un-sure exactly what his duties were. He had been brought to Tennessee by General Joseph E. Johnston, who failed to make clear the purpose of Van Dorn's mission. On February 22 Van Dorn admitted to Johnston that he was unsure of his duties. Van Dorn did not even know where he was expected to take position, or who would serve under him. Johnston's clarifying order was confusing. Van Dorn had been summoned to operate on Rosecrans' communications should the Yankee commander advance. If the Federals remained idle, Van Dorn might raid Kentucky. But who would plan his movements? Johnston left this unsaid, save for a vague statement that the general's actions in the Second Department would be

18 Bragg to Mackall, June 6, 1863, Bragg to Ewell. June 6, 1863, Mackall to Polk, June 8, 1863, Bragg to Wheeler, June 4, 1863, Hardee to Bragg, June 4, 1863, Jack to Withers, June 8, 1863, Bragg to Hardee, June 6, 1863, in Bragg Papers, Western Reserve; see also *Official Records*, XXIII, Pt. 2, pp. 861, 864, 870, 881.

19 Bragg to Johnston, June 6, 1863, in Johnston Papers, William and Mary.

20 Wheeler to Bragg, June 6, 1863; Bragg to Forrest, June 2, 6, 1863, Bragg to Martin, June 6, 1863, Wheeler to Bragg, June 6, 1863, all in Bragg Papers, Western Reserve.

21 Du Bose, *Wheeler,* 151–54; William C. Dodson, *The Campaigns of Wheeler and His Cavalry* (Atlanta, 1899) , 61–63.

controlled by Bragg. Any moves out of that department would be controlled by the theater commander, Johnston.[22]

Confused by these orders, Van Dorn did little to sever Rosecrans' communications between February and May. His only significant raids included two unimportant cavalry fights north of Spring Hill in March, and Forrest's brilliant pursuit and capture of Colonel Abel Streight's raiders in Alabama in April.

Much of this lack of deployment was due to increasing personality conflicts among Bragg's cavalry officers. There was little *esprit de corps* in the cavalry, but much rivalry among generals did exist. Relations between Forrest and Wheeler had worsened during the February attack on Fort Donelson. Forrest, who had opposed the assault, later lashed out at Wheeler and swore that he could never take orders from the Alabamian again. Soon Forrest was transferred to the new corps under Van Dorn.[23]

Relations between Forrest and Van Dorn were little better. Forrest probably resented the personality of the flashy Van Dorn, once described by Fitzhugh Lee as resembling a game cock. Van Dorn had come to Tennessee under criticism both for his way with the ladies and for his questionable military ability. Forrest may have regarded him as less a soldier than a Southern hotspur.

The spark which generated their mutual dislike was Forrest's success in two limited engagements at Brentwood and Thompson's Station in March. Van Dorn seemed angry at the credit given to Forrest by press and public for the two victories. He believed that Forrest had connived to have favorable articles published describing the engagements in the Chattanooga *Daily Rebel.* Van Dorn was also irritated that Forrest had commandeered much of the captured property for his own outfits. The accounts of the ensuing quarrel in April are varied, but all seem to agree that the generals very nearly challenged each other to a duel before tempers cooled. Soon afterward Forrest rode south to halt the raid of Colonel Abel Streight in Alabama. Van Dorn was murdered on May 7 at his Spring Hill headquarters, allegedly by a jealous husband.[24]

The ill feeling spread to the other flank of Bragg's troopers. Wheeler seemed totally unable to control Morgan. Morgan's behavior during the

22 Johnston to Bragg, January 11, 1863, Johnston to Davis, January 17, 1863, Johnston to Van Dorn, February 24, 1863, in Johnston Papers, William and Mary; *Official Records,* LII, Pt. 2, p. 425.

23 Henry, *Forrest,* 123–26; Du Bose, *Wheeler,* 157–58.

24 Fitzhugh Lee statement, August 9, 1901 (MS in General Earl Van Dorn Papers, Alabama State Archives) ; Sterling Price to Van Dorn, October 13, 1862, General Orders Number 3, May 7, 1863, Van Dorn staff to editors, Mobile *Advertiser and Register,* May 15, 1863, Van Dorn to Emily Miller, April 1, 1863, all in *ibid.;* Van Dorn to Davis, ——— 8, 1862, in Davis Papers, Tulane; Henry, *Forrest,* 142–43.

spring and early summer indicated the general felt he was losing status. Always eager for public acclaim, Morgan found himself, through the spring, bound to the unromantic task of picketing Bragg's far right wing in front of the McMinnville-Murfreesboro and the Nashville-Knoxville pikes. Though Morgan constantly sought permission to dash into Kentucky, Bragg refused and held him to picket duty on the right flank. The public and Morgan's friends wondered at Bragg's change of attitude toward Morgan during the spring. Some speculated that Morgan's December marriage had caused the Kentuckian to lose his touch as a raider. One Nashville newspaper humorously compared Morgan to Samson shorn of his locks by Delilah. Morgan's friends' only explanation was that Bragg was mistreating him out of prejudice against Morgan's nonprofessional background. It was true that Bragg and Hardee had lost confidence in Morgan. By March, Bragg was convinced that Morgan's new division command was simply too large for him. The general condition and discipline of Morgan's division were notorious, and Hardee warned that they were growing worse.

There were other matters which may have affected Morgan's conduct. Like Forrest, Morgan disliked serving under Wheeler. Too, constant service in the McMinnville locale had reduced Morgan's horse supply until his command was filled with many dismounted men. When Bragg ordered these men brigaded as infantry until mounts were available, Morgan became further dissatisfied. Then, the late April Federal advance no doubt embarrassed Morgan. His McMinnville headquarters was overrun, his wife captured, and Morgan himself barely escaped.[25]

By June, Morgan grasped for some electrifying plan that would restore his reputation. The Copperhead activities during 1863 in Ohio, Indiana, and Illinois, and the general dissatisfaction with the slowness of the Union war effort in the West seemed to promise great things north of the Ohio. Morgan envisioned a raid into Ohio with a consequent move into either Pennsylvania or Illinois. At last, in early June, he went to Bragg to obtain permission. Bragg refused him permission to cross the Ohio, and apparently not remembering the earlier lessons of his cavalry dispersion, told Morgan that he could raid in Kentucky where he pleased.

Bragg's haphazard approach to the Kentucky raid was indicative of the subsequent absence of over-all direction. Morgan left the meeting determined to disobey Bragg's orders not to cross the river, and so told his brother-in-law, Basil Duke. He began his move on June 13. Under the guise of making an attack on Louisville, he requested permission from

25 *Official Records*, XXIII, Pt. 2, pp. 656, 824; W. Simms to Morgan, March 12, 1863, W. W. Ray to Morgan, April 16, 1863, in John Hunt Morgan Papers, UNC; Austin, *The Blue and the Gray*, 70, 97–98.

Wheeler to move into Kentucky. After conferring with Bragg, Wheeler gave Morgan permission to take fifteen hundred men into Kentucky, but gave no specific instructions as to where he should go or when he should return. Morgan then lobbied for more men. On June 15 he requested two thousand troops instead of fifteen hundred. Though Bragg had repeatedly stated in the past few days that he believed an advance by Rosecrans was imminent, on June 18 he acceded to this additional drain on the cavalry. Still neither Bragg nor Wheeler gave Morgan any specific instructions, save for a hope that he would, "as far as possible," destroy the Louisville and Nashville Railroad. Morgan quickly seized on this as *carte blanche*. Mustering even more men than Bragg had authorized, Morgan on July 2 crossed the Cumberland River determined to reach Ohio.[26]

With Morgan's departure, the dissolution of the cavalry command was nearly complete. One corps commander, Van Dorn, was dead. Van Dorn's Mississippi contingent had been returned to Pemberton in May and the corps was theoretically abolished. Probably because of the bad feeling between them, Wheeler had practically no communication with Forrest, who had assumed control of the left wing on the Columbia Pike.

Morgan's departure signaled more than command confusion. By the last of June, Bragg's cavalry manpower and logistics had dwindled steadily. The loss of Morgan's division in June, the May transfer of Van Dorn's troops back to Mississippi, and the assignment of Roddey's brigade to Alabama reduced Bragg's effective cavalry strength by almost one-half. Instead of the sixteen thousand horsemen he had had in the spring, Bragg, in July, had fewer than nine thousand.

The cavalry had also declined in quality and in morale. Bragg knew that he had reduced the western Federal cavalry to fewer than thirty-four hundred men in 1862. He did not know that in the spring of 1863 Rosecrans' troopers, under the direction of General David Stanley, were reorganized. By late spring Rosecrans' mounted force consisted of two divisions of regular cavalry and a brigade of mounted infantry under the intrepid General John Wilder—all together over twelve thousand men.[27]

Confederate governmental policy required that each horseman provide his own mount. Policy also required that the cavalrymen furnish their own rations and forage. Prior to the summer of 1862 the supply of horses

26 *Official Records*, XXIII, Pt. 1, pp. 817–18; Dee Alexander Brown, *Bold Cavaliers: Morgan's 2nd Kentucky Cavalry* (Philadelphia, 1959); Basil Duke, *A History of Morgan's Cavalry*, ed. Cecil F. Holland (Bloomington, 1960).

27 *Official Records*, XXIII, Pt. 1, pp. 410, 418, Pt. 2, pp. 737, 758, 764, 919, Wilder "Battle of Hoover's Gap," 168; Dyer, "Some Aspects of Cavalry Operations," 213–14; W. F. Carter, *History of the First Regiment of Tennessee Volunteer Cavalry* (Knoxville, 1902), 59–60; Mackall to Wheeler, April 23, 1863, Mackall to Wharton, April 23, 1863, Brent to Van Dorn, April 4, 1863, in Bragg Papers, Western Reserve.

posed no problem since Bragg's troopers could locate mounts from the rich supply in Kentucky and Middle and West Tennessee.

With that supply gone and Bragg now long immobilized, the scarcity of mounts became so serious that Bragg began putting cavalrymen without horses into the infantry. The men, desperate to remain in the cavalry, brought in any available horses—frequently spindly-legged farm animals, half-starved by the food shortage—that compared poorly with Rosecrans' improved cavalry mounts. These Confederate problems culminated on the right wing where Wharton's and Wheeler's men were expected to defend the Woodbury-McMinnville area.[28]

With this state prevailing, Bragg assigned Wheeler a key role on June 6. Since the coming Federal attack was now almost certain, he ordered Wheeler to concentrate his troops at once and to assume the responsibility for defending the area from Hoover's Gap eastward. Bragg then turned his full attention to Union activity on the Shelbyville and Wartrace fronts.[29]

During the last week of June, however, Wheeler neglected his duties on Bragg's right wing. Already the position east of Liberty Gap had been weakened by the stationing of Martin's division in support of Forrest at Columbia. Instead of staying with his assignment on the Hoover's Gap front, Wheeler, on June 22, abruptly began moving his division to the Shelbyville front where heavy Federal strength had been reported. The right wing was almost left bare of cavalry. Only a single brigade of Wharton's command covered the long front from Liberty Gap to Hoover's Gap. A long regiment, the First Kentucky, was left by Wheeler to guard Hoover's Gap.[30]

Late on the morning of June 24, in a drizzling rain, an overpowering Union force swept over the meager defenders of Hoover's Gap. Stewart's division was totally unprepared for the attack. Bate's brigade, the nearest aid, was four miles southward near the village of Beech Grove with many of its officers away at a Masonic picnic.[31]

Confusion ensued in the Confederate ranks during the afternoon. Bate did not learn of the attack until 2 P.M., at least an hour after it had been reported to General Bushrod Johnson, whose brigade was encamped farther away toward Wartrace. Not until the late afternoon did Bate attack the Federals entrenched at the south end of the gap. The rapid

28 Duke, *Morgan's Cavalry.*

29 Bragg to Wheeler, June 4, 6, 1863, in Bragg Papers, Western Reserve; *Official Records,* XXIII, Pt. 2, p. 866.

30 Dodson, *Wheeler,* 86–90.

31 James Connolly to wife, July 5, 1863, in James Connolly, *Three Years in the Army of the Cumberland,* 89–92; Wilder, "Battle of Hoover's Gap," 169–73; *Official Records,* XXIII, Pt. 1, pp. 611, 602.

fire of the enemy rifles convinced Bate that he was facing overwhelming numbers. Still, his men repeatedly stormed the gap amidst a murderous fire that cost Bate 25 per cent of his command. By nightfall it was clear that Hoover's Gap was lost to the enemy's control. [32]

The next forty-eight hours saw further confusion in the Rebel high command. Late on the night of June 24, shortly after his arrival at the south end of Hoover's Gap, Stewart received instructions from Hardee setting forth that general's interpretation of Bragg's strategy. If Stewart were hard pressed on the twenty-fifth, he was not to contest the Manchester Pike, but was to withdraw southwestward to join the remainder of the corps between Beech Grove and Wartrace. Thus, during the next day, Stewart offered only slight resistance as the enemy pushed his division away from the Manchester Road.

Again, late on June 26, Hardee repeated his order that Stewart not contest heavily any force on the Manchester Pike, but fall back on Wartrace if threatened. This last note was unnecessary. By midday of June 26 Stewart had completely given up the Manchester front. Meanwhile, unknown to the Confederates, the Union advance penetrated to within six miles of Manchester by the evening of June 26. By 8 A.M. on June 27 Manchester had fallen, and Bragg's Duck River line was enfiladed. [33]

Bragg knew little of this impending disaster. Wheeler's poor cavalry direction and the general lapse of high level accord created a communications blackout. Between June 24 and June 26, Bragg's Shelbyville headquarters was almost completely out of touch with Stewart's division on the Manchester Pike front. And Wheeler's fruitless dash across the Shelbyville front had helped mislead Bragg as to Rosecrans' main point of attack.

Acting on information received from Wheeler, Bragg until July 26 believed that Rosecrans' main advance was against Shelbyville and Liberty Gap. Since June 23 Wheeler had been fighting a strong Yankee cavalry force northwest of Shelbyville. A large Federal infantry column had pressed Wheeler's pickets north of Guy's Gap on the Shelbyville-Murfreesboro Pike.[34]

By June 25 Bragg had revised his opinion slightly. The threat to Polk on the Shelbyville Road had diminished. Still, no substantial news had been received from the Manchester Road. Instead, Bragg by this time believed the main thrust was to be through Liberty Gap. There seemed to be good reason to believe this. On the evening of June 24, in a pouring

[32] *Official Records*, XXIII, Pt. 1, pp. 602, 611.

[33] *Ibid.*, Pt. 2, pp. 884, 886, 888, Pt. 1, p. 459.

[34] "Richmond Notes," June 26, 1863, in Polk Papers, Sewanee; Dodson, *Wheeler*, 86–90; Polk, *Polk*, II, 218–19.

rain, a strong Union infantry force loomed out of the mist at Liberty Gap, overwhelmed Liddell's two small regiments, and seized the gap. Throughout the next day, Cleburne's attempts to win it back were unsuccessful. Convinced that at least a division held the narrow gap, Cleburne fell back to a line of hills a mile south of the gap to await further developments.

With the absence of news from the right wing, Bragg on June 26 was convinced that the main Union army was drawn up in front of Liberty Gap. He envisioned a strike similiar to that he had planned for Polk months before on the Bardstown front. That afternoon Bragg summoned Polk to his Shelbyville headquarters and ordered him to execute the flanking maneuver through Guy's Gap, striking eastward against the force confronting Cleburne at Liberty Gap. Polk's protest that the rough topography made this plan unworkable was unheeded. A dissatisfied Polk returned to his headquarters in the late afternoon and prepared for the attack. [35]

Suddenly, in the early evening of June 26, Bragg discovered that he had been duped and that his army was in serious danger. At 5 P.M., after his meeting with Polk, Bragg at last received news from Stewart. All of Bragg's plans now were shattered. Stewart had been swept aside from the Manchester front by a force estimated to be as large as Hardee's corps. Not only was the Manchester Road open, but the enemy appeared to be driving Stewart through Fairfield onto Wartrace. As Fairfield was only five miles east of Wartrace, there was a danger that Cleburne's division now concentrated at the southern approach to Liberty Gap, would be encircled. Worse, the seizure of Wartrace would threaten to isolate Polk on the north bank of the Duck at Shelbyville.

Bragg saw little to do other than to hasten his troops to the south bank of the Duck, already swollen by incessant rains. Later that night, another dispatch from Stewart's front indicated that both his flanks had given way, and the threat to Wartrace heightened. Quickly, at 11 P.M., Bragg ordered both Hardee and Polk to fall back across the river to the entrenchments at Tullahoma. At daylight the corps began their withdrawal. Even as Polk's corps crossed the river southeast of Shelbyville, the enemy was at Wartrace, only five miles northward. The roads were so muddy that the infantry did not reach Tullahoma until the early morning of the

---

35 Buck, *Cleburne*, 130–31; Carter, *First Tennessee*, 74; "Richmond Notes," June 26, 1863, in Polk Papers, Sewanee; Polk, *Polk*, II, 219; *Official Records*, XXIII, Pt. 1, pp. 586–90; Pt. 2, pp. 886.

twenty-eighth, and the rear guard and trains did not arrive until late that afternoon.[36]

Bragg seemed thoroughly confused, and the morning of the twenty-ninth found the army at Tullahoma in a grave state. As early as June 27 Bragg knew that Rosecrans had seized Manchester and thereby had endangered Tullahoma. By moving across the Elk River the Federals could both destroy Bragg's railroad supply line to Chattanooga and block his line of retreat through Decherd. Or, by moving from Manchester through Hillsborough, Rosecrans could seize the main Chattanooga Road at University Place, or he could cut the pike and railroad at Cowan, twenty-two miles south of Tullahoma. A seizure of Cowan would be fatal. The village lay beneath the northern face of the Cumberland Mountains, astride both the Chattanooga Pike and the railroad. About two and a half miles south of Cowan, the railroad could easily be blocked at the famed twenty-two-hundred-foot Cowan Tunnel, an engineering feat carved during the eighteen-forties by several hundred slaves. Another possibility was that Rosecrans could leave Manchester, cross the Elk River, and move down its southern bank to seize Bragg's crossings between Tullahoma and Decherd.[37]

By one of these routes Rosecrans, by June 29, threatened to cut Bragg off from the south bank of the Elk and his Chattanooga base. That morning Bragg had information that the Elk was no longer fordable. The matter of bridging points now became critical. There were only three bridges in the vicinity whereby Bragg could cross. One, upstream on the Elk at Pelham, was known to be in Federal hands. South of Tullahoma, only a few miles apart, there were the road bridge at Bethpage near Estill Springs, and the railroad and pike bridges at Allisonia, which lay on the south bank of the river opposite Estill Springs.[38]

Already this thin line of river passages was in great peril. Due to Wheeler's being out of position on the Shelbyville front, Bragg's communication line to Chattanooga was almost totally unguarded. Wheeler and his division, as well as those of Forrest and Martin, did not even

36 Mackall to Polk, June 26—5 P.M., 1863, Jack to Cheatham, June 26—11:30 P.M., 1863, Jack to Withers, June 26—11:30 P.M., 1863, David Urquhart to Polk, June 27—5:30 A.M., 1863, Mackall to Polk, June 27—10 P.M., 1863, Cleburne to Hardee, June 27, 1863; "Richmond Notes," June 26–27, 1863, all in Polk Papers, Sewanee; *Official Records*, XXIII, Pt. 1, p. 583.

37 "Richmond Notes," June 27–29, 1863, Mackall to Polk, June 29, 1863, in Polk Papers, Sewanee.

38 Reynolds, "Sewanee and the Cumberland Plateau in the Civil War," 11; Statement of Urquhart, June 29, 1863, of meeting at Bragg's headquarters, (MS in Bragg Papers, Western Reserve) ; *Official Records*, XXIII, Pt. 2, p. 894; Pt. 1, p. 583; Howard M. Hannah, *Confederate Action in Franklin County Tennessee* (Sewanee, 1963), 19, 26.

leave Shelbyville until late on June 27, and they spent the next day falling back with Bragg's wagon train to Tullahoma. With Bragg's cavalry absent, the Federal horsemen struck hard at his communications. On June 28 a heavy Federal cavalry force overran the small Confederate picket holding the Elk River Bridge at Phelan. Seizing that bridge for future use, the Union cavalry then moved unopposed on Decherd, Bragg's important rail and supply center on the main Nashville and Chattanooga Road only twelve miles south of Tullahoma. The feeble Rebel garrison of eighty men was no match for the Federal repeating rifles. By night the railroad was destroyed around Decherd, valuable Confederate stores were burned, and Bragg's communications with Chattanooga were severed.[39]

On June 29 Bragg's confusion was complicated by intelligence received during the dawn hours that Rosecrans was advancing on the Manchester Pike against Tullahoma, and that by 5 A.M., he was within five miles of the town. About 9 A.M. a conference between Polk and Bragg produced only disagreement. Bragg felt he should stand and fight at Tullahoma despite the intelligence that part of Rosecrans' force was at his rear at Decherd. Moreover, Bragg intended to recall the infantry sent to Estill Springs to protect the bridgepoints, in order to use it to defend Tullahoma's entrenchments. Polk's protest that to fight at Tullahoma, cut off from his base of supplies, was dangerous, was of no avail. Around midday, Polk sought out Hardee to tell him of his fears for a fight at Tullahoma.[40]

More indecision resulted during the afternoon. About 3 P.M., both corps leaders visited Bragg, only to arouse further disagreement. Bragg held out for fighting at Tullahoma, arguing that his communications line south of the Elk could be protected by Wheeler's cavalry, which had come up during the day. Polk demurred, claiming that Bragg did not have enough cavalry to hold the long communication line across the Elk and through the Cumberlands. Instead, he said, if his supply line were cut, Bragg might be forced to retreat to Chattanooga via a circuitous route through the barren country around Fayetteville, Tennessee, and Decatur, Alabama. Such a route promised starvation for the army and a possible seizure of Chattanooga by Rosecrans.

While Polk talked, a new development created additional uncertainty. A telegram arrived from Bragg's battered outpost at Decherd, indicating that the damage to the railroad was not as heavy as was believed. Only

[39] "Richmond Notes," June 29, 1863, in Polk Papers, Sewanee; Hannah, *Franklin County*, 18–21; Mackall to Wheeler, June 29, 1863, in Wheeler Papers, Alabama.
[40] The 9 A.M. Polk-Bragg conference and the later Polk-Hardee council are recorded in "Richmond Notes," June 29, 1863, in Polk Papers, Sewanee; see also Mackall to Polk, June 29, 1863, in *ibid.*

a few hundred yards had been damaged, and it could be repaired in a few hours. With this new information, Hardee now suggested that he was not yet in favor of a retreat, but recommended holding Tullahoma until further developments were observed. While Polk agreed that the Decherd telegram made a difference, he still insisted that the army should retreat from Tullahoma across the Elk. The meeting closed with nothing settled, save that the high command would adopt a "wait and see" attitude. Throughout the remainder of the day, Polk's and Hardee's men toiled through the pouring rain to ready the Tullahoma breastworks for an attack. [41]

By the morning of June 30 Bragg had revised his views. Late on June 29 he learned of both Federal infantry and cavalry activity at his rear. That same day a strong Federal cavalry column seized his Chattanooga communications line at University Place, before it was driven back toward Manchester by Forrest. Worse, intelligence received that afternoon indicated a Federal column moving from Manchester along the north bank of the river to seize the bridges at Bethpage and Estill Springs. Unsure exactly where Rosecrans' left wing was now operating, Bragg ordered Wheeler to learn just where the threat to his communications lay.

Throughout the morning, Bragg received information. The Federal right wing loomed up on the Tullahoma front, with heavy pressure against Bragg's pickets north of the town. But the Federal left seemed to have flanked Bragg. One report indicated a column of perhaps ten thousand had driven to within three miles of the Bethpage Bridge, dangerously close to the Estill Springs-Allisonia bridges as well. If the Bethpage Bridge fell, Bragg would be limited to the crossings at Allisonia, because the rain-flooded Elk was still unfordable on June 30. Meanwhile, scouts told of another column on the road from Manchester to University Place, where the Chattanooga Road ascended the Cumberland Mountains.[42]

Thus, on the afternoon of June 30, Bragg desperately sought another position. The decision was made to abandon Tullahoma and fall back across the Elk. Though the distance to the Elk was only eight miles, the roads were knee-deep in mud, and it required almost twenty-four hours to remove the infantry and trains from Tullahoma. Not until noon of July 1 was the infantry across the river. Behind them the cavalry

41 Statement of Urquhart, June 29, 1863, in Bragg Papers, Western Reserve. Urquhart wrote a résumé of the afternoon council at Bragg's headquarters; another account of the council is given in "Richmond Notes," June 29, 1863, in Polk Papers, Sewanee.

42 Hannah, *Franklin County*, 18–23; "Richmond Notes," September 29–30; Mackall to Polk, June 30—11 A.M., 1863. in Polk Papers, Sewanee. See also *Official Records*, XXIII, Pt. 2, pp. 891–93.

slowly yielded Tullahoma to Rosecrans by noon. The cavalry was across by nightfall, and the Bethpage and Allisonia bridges were fired. Bragg's new line had been quickly established that afternoon—Hardee held the right at Bethpage Bridge, Polk the left at the Allisonia Bridge.[43]

But that same night Bragg realized he must move on beyond the Elk, for the river was falling fast, and by the next day Rosecrans would be able to ford it at a number of places beyond Hardee's right all the way to the Federal-held bridgehead at Pelham. Pelham was less than fourteen miles from Bragg's supply depot at Decherd. The peculiar curve of the Elk between Pelham and Allisonia, coupled with the slant of the Cumberlands behind Bragg, offered a wide front of maneuver to Rosecrans along a number of roads, almost all of them converging at Bragg's rear at Decherd or Cowan.[44]

Although the river was becoming fordable on July 1 and 2, it remained too high for easy passage, and Rosecrans' approach was slow and arduous. Possibly a strong defense of the Elk fords and a rapid response by Polk and Hardee could have isolated part of the Federal army on the south bank of the river. But the Confederate high command seemed to be disintegrating, and the army fell back aimlessly. Polk and Hardee by now thoroughly mistrusted Bragg's judgment. On the night of July 1 Hardee confided to Polk that Bragg seemed too enfeebled even to draw up a line of operations, and suggested that the corps commanders hold a secret meeting to discuss the subject.

Bragg seemed dazed during these critical hours. He repeatedly reversed himself. On the night of July 1 he sent a note to Polk asking him if he thought the army should fight on the Elk or retreat to Cowan. Yet that same day he had ordered engineers to begin work on a line of retreat across the mountain to Chattanooga, and had boasted to Richmond that his new Elk line was a better defensive position than was Tullahoma. Both Hardee and Polk strongly favored a retreat to Cowan, the implication being that they were hesitant to commit their troops to battle under Bragg in his current condition.[45]

By the early morning hours of July 2, Bragg had decided to retreat. Shortly after 1 A.M. orders went out for Polk and Hardee to fall back at daylight to Cowan, at the base of the Cumberland Mountains. After this

[43] "Richmond Notes," June 30–July 1, 1863, in Polk Papers, Sewanee; Axel Reed Diary, July 1, 1863, in Chickamauga–Chattanooga National Military Park Library.
[44] *Official Records*, XXIII, Pt. 1, p. 583; Pt. 2, pp. 894–95; Hannah, *Franklin County*, 25–34.
[45] Hardee to Polk, July 1—8:30 P.M., 1863, "Richmond Notes," July 1, 1863, Hardee to Polk, July 1, 1863, Polk to Mackall, July 1, 1863, Mackall to Polk, July 1—7 P.M., 1863, in Polk Papers, Sewanee; *Official Records*, XXIII, Pt. 1, p. 583; Pt. 2, p. 894.

initial decision, Bragg continued to waver as to what dispositions he should make. About dawn he changed his mind and ordered the army to halt at Decherd. Shortly thereafter he reversed his order and directed the army to continue the march and halt at Cowan.[46]

Evidently, Bragg never really planned to stop and fight at Cowan, though Polk and Hardee had believed this to be his strategy when they advised a retreat from the Elk River the previous evening. Only hours after the army reached Cowan, Bragg by 4 P.M. was giving orders for a retreat to Chattanooga, his final order in the loss of all Middle Tennessee. His explanation to the government for the move was that at Cowan he had his back to the mountains, was short of rations, and could not force Rosecrans to attack him.[47]

This statement seems more a rationalization than an acceptable explanation. Rosecrans was advancing. By the afternoon of the second, Bragg knew that part of the Federal army had forced Wheeler away from Allisonia by crossing at a ford slightly downstream, and had also crossed at a ford above Bethpage Bridge. Other Federal columns were attempting to force crossings upstream at Morris Ford and Shallow Ford. By necessity, all of these routes converged on Cowan, where Bragg was in a good defensive position. Cowan offered two good routes of retreat should Bragg be defeated: across the mountain through University Place, or directly south through the Crow Creek Valley to Bridgeport or Jasper.[48]

But Bragg ordered a retreat without consulting his corps commanders. That night the army toiled up the mountain and through University Place, then descended into Sweden's Cove. On the evening of July 4 the army reached the Tennessee River. Slowly the crossings began at the mouth of Battle Creek and at Bridgeport, as the army fell back upon its main base in the Great Bend of the Tennessee at Chattanooga.

Probably such precious ground had never been bought so cheaply by the Federals. Due to accessions of men received en route to Chattanooga, Polk's corps on the march was actually several hundred stronger than it was at Duck River. Hardee's corps had suffered the bulk of the losses, since it had done the fighting at Hoover's and Liberty gaps. Still, Hardee had lost only about 1,700 men. Unknown to Bragg, Rosecrans' entire

46 Mackall to Polk, July 2—1:30 A.M., 1863, in Polk Papers, Sewanee; "Richmond Notes," July 2, 1863, *ibid.*; Mackall to Wheeler, July 2—12:30 A.M., 1863, in Wheeler Papers, Alabama.

47 Mackall to Polk, July 2, 1863, Wheeler to Polk, July 4, 1863, Jack to Wheeler, July 4, 1863, Polk to Mackall, July 5—9:30 A.M., 1863, Mackall to Polk, July 5, 1863, Jack to Cheatham, July 5—5:30 P.M., 1863, "Richmond Notes," July 2, 3, 4, 5, 1863, all in Polk Papers, Sewanee; Bragg to Cooper, July 3, 1863, Walter to officer commanding pontoon bridge, Bridgeport, July 3, 1863, in Bragg Papers, Western Reserve. Bragg to Cooper, July 3, 1863, in Davis Papers, Duke.

48 *Official Records*, XXIII, Pt. 1, pp. 584, 615; Hannah, *Franklin County*, 24–49.

army had lost only about 570 men. With this relatively inexpensive casualty list, the Federals had gained not only Middle Tennessee, but North Alabama as well. [49]

The Federals had also gained a route by which Chattanooga might eventually be taken. Bragg neglected to have Wheeler destroy the Nashville and Chattanooga Railroad behind the Confederates. The long tunnel at Cowan was left unharmed, though its destruction would have put the railroad out of operation for an indefinite length of time. South of the tunnel the railroad was almost completely undamaged. Three small bridges were burned, but the major ones were not touched. Four high wooden trestle bridges spanning deep ravines across Crow Creek were unharmed. So minor was the damage that by July 25, the railroad was operating again as far south as the river.[50]

The collapse of the Duck River line was the result of months of command instability which by July produced a paralysis in Bragg's high command. At some time during the last week of June, the army's command system just ceased to function. Bragg attempted to minimize the loss as a "trifling loss of men and materials." [51] Yet the psychological effect upon the army, the continuing warfare in the high command, Bragg's deteriorating condition, and the loss of geographical position more than counterbalanced this small loss of men and supplies.

In the first week of July, as the army crossed the river and moved into its base, ominous burdens were developing. Far up the Appalachian Valley, as Bragg's army entered Chattanooga, Lee's defeated army retreated from the battlefield at Gettysburg. And far to the West, Pemberton's tired men stacked their arms and marched out of Vicksburg. With Pemberton gone, the full Federal push in the West would now be concentrated against the weary, demoralized Army of Tennessee.[52]

---

[49] Official Records, XXIII, Pt. 1, pp. 424, 585–86; "Richmond Notes," July 7, 1863, in Polk Papers, Sewanee.

[50] Hannah, Franklin County, 48–49; Official Records, XXX, Pt. 1, p. 50.

[51] Official Records, XXIII, Pt. 1, p. 584.

[52] For evidence of Bragg's unstable condition, see Hardee to Polk, July 1—8:30 P.M., 1863, in Polk Papers, Sewanee; Noll, Quintard, 871; Official Records, XXIII, Pt. 2, pp. 920, 925; LII, Pt. 2, p. 499.

PART II

the bragg-longstreet influence

seven

A Season of Disorganization

It was dusty and hot in the parched Chattanooga country during August. Tired, ill, and despondent, Bragg had sought to rebuild his shattered health at the small mountain spa of Cherokee Springs, a few miles below Chattanooga. There, one hot Sunday morning, Bishop Charles Quintard, army chaplain and confidant to the high command, preached to a gathering of convalescents from the Duck River campaign. Bragg and his staff listened as Quintard chose his text from the saga of the Hebrew exodus from Egypt: "We are journeying on to the place where the Lord hath said I will give to you." [1]

Quintard's melancholy allusion to the search for a final resting place well suited the army's temper. A sense of aimlessness pervaded the ranks. Twice before, the Army had in good spirits marched north from Chattanooga to Kentucky and to Murfreesboro. Now they were back for a third time in the Great Bend of the Tennessee River with little to show but dwindling numbers. Plagued with illness and desertion, Bragg's effective infantry strength by July had dwindled to an alarmingly low 29,000. The retreat from Elk River had not aided the army's morale. Choosing desertion rather than serving with Bragg, hundreds of soldiers had veered southwest into the shelter of the Sand and Lookout ranges in Alabama. Bragg's own appearance would scarcely inspire confidence. Thin, gaunt, and pale, he confided to Robert E. Lee that his health was bad. On the retreat to Chattanooga, Bishop Quintard recalled that Bragg remarked, "I am utterly broken down." [2]

Bragg's disposition was not improved by intelligence received from

1 Cumming, *Gleanings from the Southland*, 121–22.
2 Noll, *Quintard*, 871; see also *Official Records*, XXIII, Pt. 2, p. 925.

Middle Tennessee during the late summer. Rosecrans was strengthening his army, preparing for offensive operations. By August he reportedly had between 60,000 and 70,000 men. Reports indicated that heavy reinforcements were being sent to Tennessee and Kentucky from Grant's idle army in Mississippi. Intelligence sources also indicated that General Ambrose Burnside's corps was in Kentucky, that he had at least 25,000 men, and that he was readying for a thrust against East Tennessee. There, departmental commander Simon Buckner could accumulate only 10,000 assorted troops, less than half of them classified as effective infantry. By late August both Bragg and Buckner feared that Burnside would coordinate his operations with Rosecrans in a dual invasion aimed at the possession of Knoxville and Chattanooga, the respective bases of the two Confederate departments. Even should he draw Buckner's entire army to Chattanooga, Bragg would have less than 35,000 infantry to oppose a combined Union force believed to be at near 100,000.[3]

The drab prospects at Chattanooga in August were intensified by the problems of holding the Chattanooga terrain and of anticipating the route of Rosecrans' advance. The Chattanooga country was a wild, turbulent region, rich in a heritage of loneliness and violence. It had been such a place since the American Revolution when the renegade Cherokee chieftain and splendid tactician Dragging Canoe seceded from the Cherokee nation. He gathered a strong band of Cherokee dissidents, Creeks, half-breed traders, and renegade Shawnee, and moved to the Great Bend of the Tennessee, where that mighty river left the tranquil East Tennessee Valley and roared through the Cumberland Mountain front. For almost fifteen years, this Indian band, known as the Chickamauga, terrorized the southwestern frontier from their stronghold towns such as Running Water and Nickajack, in the Tennessee River gorge.[4]

Once more Chattanooga was a vital stronghold. To Bragg it was both a hub of his operations and a fortress. Northeast lay the East Tennessee Railroad to Knoxville, Bristol, and Lynchburg. From the west came the Memphis and Charleston from North Alabama, and the Nashville and Chattanooga from Middle Tennessee. To the southeast ran the Western and Atlantic to Atlanta. From Atlanta, rail connections linked Bragg with Virginia via the route through the Carolinas, and with the munitions-iron centers of central Georgia and Alabama. Valuable commissary, quartermaster, and ordnance depots were at Chattanooga, as well as in

3 *Official Records*, LII, Pt. 2, pp. 491, 495, 520, 522–23; Bragg's Official Report of Chickamauga, December 28, 1863 (MS in Claiborne Papers, UNC) .

4 John C. Brown, *Old Frontiers: The Story of the Cherokee Indians From Earliest Times to the Date of Their Removal to the West, 1838* (Kingsport, 1938) , 175, 203.

the rear at Atlanta. By the late summer of 1863, Bragg's director of hospitals, Dr. Samuel Stout, had established an extensive complex of hospitals at Chattanooga which extended down the Atlanta Railroad through Dalton, Cassville, and Marietta to Atlanta itself. Too, Chattanooga was a doorway to the heart of the South. To lose it would entail the loss of the copper, saltpeter, and grain of East Tennessee, the nitre mines of North Alabama, and perhaps even the munitions complex of Alabama and Georgia.

Yet Chattanooga also seemed to be a great fortress. To the casual observer, Bragg appeared to have an impregnable position. His right flank in the valley of eastern Tennessee was protected by the dual ranges of the Cumberland Mountains—the main Cumberland front and Walden's Ridge. Any move by Rosecrans to reach this valley would require a trek over difficult mountain roads on the main Cumberland front, then down into the narrow Sequatchie Valley, and then across Walden's Ridge to debouch in the valley northeast of Chattanooga. The Federals were confronted here with several disadvantages. The plateau-like topography of both ranges required steep ascents to the crests as high as two thousand and twenty-five hundred feet divided by the deep Sequatchie Valley. Atop both ranges the land was barren, scarcely able to support subsistence farming and totally unable to sustain an army. To strike Bragg's right flank in the valley, Rosecrans would be forced to march across fifty miles of such terrain.

There were also few roads by which the Federals could gain the right. The old frontier path, Harrison's Trace, led from McMinnville across the Cumberlands to Pikeville, in the Sequatchie Valley, and then across Walden's Ridge to Washington Ferry on the Tennessee River. On the east bank, the road led through Decatur and struck Bragg's East Tennessee Railroad at Athens. A second route followed this path across Walden's Ridge, forked before reaching Washington Ferry, and struck the Tennessee at Blythe's Ferry at the mouth of the Hiwassee River. Across the river, the road led along the Hiwassee to strike the East Tennessee Railroad at Charleston. A third road crossed the Cumberlands, continued through Dunlap in the Sequatchie Valley, and ascended Walden's Ridge to debouch at Harrison's Landing, fifteen miles northeast of Chattanooga. All three roads were rough, traversed country, which was poor in both water and forage, and seemed unsure for artillery and wagon traffic.[5]

Bragg's front at Chattanooga also seemed secure. There were two approaches to Chattanooga from Middle Tennessee via the north and south

[5] Chickamauga-Chattanooga area map, in Cheatham papers, Tennessee; Chattanooga map, in General Henry Clayton Papers, Alabama State Archives.

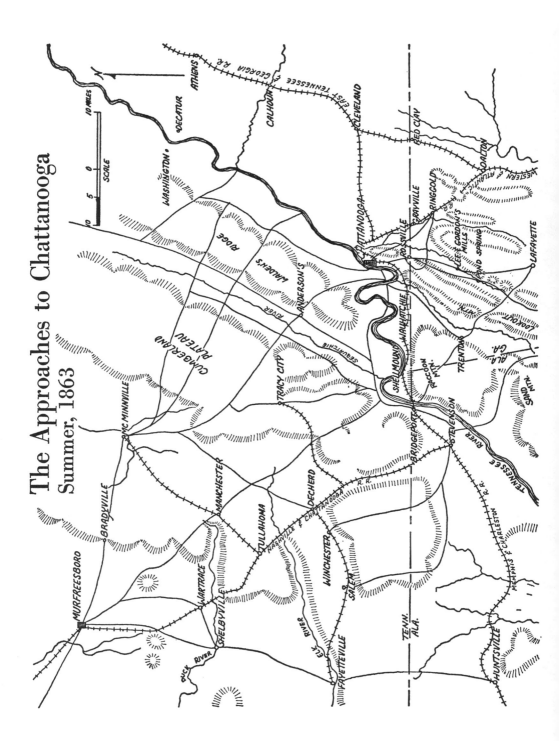

The Approaches to Chattanooga
Summer, 1863

banks of the Tennessee River. Any approach from the north bank would again have to contend with the dual ranges of the Cumberlands and Walden's Ridge. The Cumberlands lay some thirty miles north and west of Chattanooga, forming the west wall of the Sequatchie Valley, and then extended across the Tennessee River into the upper northwest corner of Alabama. The east wall of the Sequatchie was the Walden's Ridge which was especially rugged where it struck the river directly west of Chattanooga. Here the southern butt of the ridge, Signal Point, formed the north wall of the precipitous Tennessee River gorge.

The road approaches through this maze on the north bank were few and impossible. Because of the many curves in the river west of Chattanooga, one could not approach Chattanooga by clinging to the river bank and avoiding the mountains, without crossing the river at least four times. Thus, one must deal with Walden's Ridge. There were only three roads on the north bank. One could march north up the Sequatchie Valley from Jasper to Therman, and climb Walden's Ridge on the Anderson Pike. But the Anderson Pike was extremely rough, unsuited to wagon traffic, and could be commanded either on the western end of the ridge or at Signal Point on the eastern slope where it entered the environs of Chattanooga.

Haley's Trace was an even more difficult road. This trail left the Sequatchie Valley near Jasper, and cut a road across Walden's Ridge to descend to the Tennessee River near the mouth of Suck Creek. From thence the road wound beneath Walden's Ridge along the north bank of the Tennessee River gorge and ended opposite the town of Chattanooga. Haley's Trace was almost impossible as a route of advance. It was impassable for wagon traffic, and was also commanded by either artillery or infantry fire from the south bank of the gorge, atop Raccoon Mountain.

A third approach to Chattanooga from the north bank seemed even worse. The old Kelly's Ferry Road struck the Tennessee River near Jasper. It then followed the north bank of the river on a long circuitous route until it crossed the river at Kelly's Ferry. Here the route became even rougher, as the road had to cross Raccoon Mountain in order to debouch into the valley of Lookout Creek. From that point, two choices were available. One could follow the road across the north face of Lookout Mountain into Chattanooga. This road, however, was completely commanded by troops on the mountain. An easier route was to move north up Lookout Valley and recross to the north bank of the Tennessee at Brown's Ferry. Once on the north bank, one would be in the river bottom known as Moccasin Bend, directly opposite both Lookout Mountain and Chattanooga. Aside from its tortuous route, the Kelly's Ferry road was also defensible. The ferry was commanded by the west slope of Raccoon Mountain, as was the road across the mountain itself. Down in Lookout Valley, the road from Kelly's Ferry to Brown's Ferry was commanded from Raccoon and partially from Lookout Mountain itself.[6]

On the south side of the river, the approaches to Chattanooga also seemed secure. Here the city was protected by a dual mountain system which extended Walden's Ridge over seventy-five miles across the tip of Georgia into Alabama. On the west was the Raccoon-Sand Mountain range. Raccoon Mountain, more than twelve miles wide, formed the south rim of the river gorge opposite Signal Point. It extended southwest across the tip of Georgia into northern Alabama, where it merged into the long Sand Mountain front. At Chattanooga, Raccoon Mountain overlooked to the east the narrow valley of Lookout Creek.

The eastern rim of this valley was formed by massive Lookout Mountain. Lookout in the 1860's was still a mysterious land of deep gorges and waterfalls, prehistoric Indian fortifications and campsites of Spanish conquistadores. The Indians called it Chatanuga Mountain, which allegedly meant "rock coming to a point." Like a huge spear point, Lookout did extend over eighty miles from near Gadsden, Alabama, to strike the Tennessee River at Chattanooga. Less than a mile wide at Point Lookout in Chattanooga, the mountain broadened to a width of nine miles and reached an elevation of almost twenty-four hundred feet some twelve miles below Chattanooga.

The combined Raccoon and Lookout ranges seemed to command all approaches to Chattanooga along the south bank. This was because all these routes converged either at or near the village of Wauhatchie, in the northern end of Lookout Valley, directly beneath Lookout Mountain. From Wauhatchie, the only route to Chattanooga was the old Summertown Toll Road, which led across the northern brow of the mountain and down into Chattanooga. This road could be commanded completely from Lookout Mountain.

Wauhatchie was a vital junction of several roads which led to Chattanooga along the south bank. From the west came the Kelly's Ferry Road from Jasper. Also from the west ran the main road from Middle Tennessee, via Tullahoma and University Place, to the mouth of Battle Creek. From here the Tennessee River could be crossed at Alley's Ferry near Jasper, or further south at Long Island in the Tennessee at Bridgeport, Alabama. The Confederates had destroyed the railroad bridge at Long Island. Yet the presence of this island, known to the colonial

6 Carter Patten, *Signal Mountain and Walden's Ridge* (n.p., 1962), 24–26; Chickamauga-Chattanooga area map, in Cheatham Papers, Tennessee.

Indians as the "Great Crossing," made the building of pontoon bridges easier. Both the Alley's Ferry and the Bridgeport crossings converged on the railroad at Shellmound. Then the road led across Raccoon Mountain through the gorge of Running Water Creek, and down into the valley of Lookout Creek at Wauhatchie.

Another key route to Chattanooga lay far to the southwest at Stevenson, Alabama, the junction of the Nashville and Chattanooga and the Memphis and Charleston rail lines. There were three important ferries near Stevenson—Caperton's, Shallow Ford, and Cameron's. The roads from all converged and then cut across the top of Raccoon Mountain to the southern end of Lookout Valley at Trenton, Georgia. From Trenton the road led up the valley to Wauhatchie. A railroad was also available from Trenton to Wauhatchie; the Wills Valley Railroad, a branch line of the Nashville and Chattanooga, coursed the valley.

These approaches along the south bank of the river seemed relatively safe. Since all converged at Wauhatchie, they could be commanded from Raccoon Mountain, from the head of the valley, and partially from Lookout Mountain itself. The single road across the face of Lookout into Chattanooga was easily commanded from the crest of the mountain. Too, stubborn resistance could be made either at the Tennessee River crossings, or atop Raccoon Mountain before the roads broke into Lookout Valley.

Far to the southwest of Chattanooga, Bragg's left flank seemed even more secure. Here the mountains both widened and multiplied, until any thrust by Rosecrans against Bragg's communication line to Atlanta would require crossing four separate mountain ranges totaling fifty miles in width. Both the Raccoon-Sand and the Lookout ranges widened as they extended across the tip of North Georgia into northeastern Alabama. The width was intensified by two key spur ridges which branched off Lookout Mountain south of Chattanooga from the east side. Chattanooga lay in the narrow valley of Chattanooga Creek, between Lookout and Missionary Ridge, which reached heights of one thousand feet, and dominated the rail approaches into Chattanooga from East Tennessee and Georgia. The Western and Atlantic from Atlanta skirted the north end of the ridge near the river, to follow the curve of Chickamauga Creek into Chattanooga. The Chattanooga branch of the East Tennessee road cut through Missionary Ridge in a long tunnel.

The other spur range, Pigeon Mountain, was also an impressive barrier. Often exceeding two thousand feet in elevation, Pigeon Mountain branched northeast off Lookout, some twelve miles south to the point where Missionary Ridge branched from the main range. Then Pigeon Mountain extended to the northeast, jutting some fifteen miles out into the valley of Chickamauga Creek. The head of the valley, formed by the pocket of Lookout and Pigeon, was known as McLemore's Cove.

Rosecrans would be confronted with another barrier east of Pigeon Mountain. Taylor's Ridge also protected Bragg's rail line to Atlanta. This long front, over seventy miles in length, extended from East Tennessee into Alabama. Sometimes it reached a height of thirteen hundred feet. Still, its width was more impressive. It embraced a wide series of spur ridges which created a mountain front ten miles wide between the railroad and the valley of Chickamauga Creek.

The combination of the Sand, Lookout, Missionary Ridge, Pigeon, and Taylor's Ridge fronts seemed to guard well Bragg's left flank and his rear. This seemed especially true in the immediate area of his left flank below Chattanooga. There were few roads by which Rosecrans could cross the Sand-Lookout front with comparatively little difficulty. From the crossings at Bridgeport and Stevenson, roads converged on the east side of Raccoon Mountain. The road then led down into the valley of Lookout Creek, south of Trenton, Georgia. From there, the road veered south and east, to ascend Lookout Mountain at a giant indentation in its west face known as Johnson Crook. From Johnson Crook two roads led across Lookout Mountain to Bragg's rear. The north road cut across the face of Lookout to descend into the northern end of McLemore's Cove at Cooper's Gap. The south road descended into the cove at Stevens' Gap. From McLemore's Cove, the road from Stevens' Gap cut across Pigeon Mountain via Dug Gap to La Fayette, beneath the east slope of Pigeon Mountain. The road from Cooper's Gap led across the cove, then cut through Pigeon Mountain at Catlett's Gap, also to debouch at La Fayette.

A second general approach to Bragg's rear was some forty miles south of Chattanooga. From Stevenson, a road crossed Raccoon Mountain into the valley of Will's Creek at Valley Head, Georgia. Will's Valley was actually the same valley as Lookout Valley to the north. A bit of high ground on the valley floor separated the two creeks. From Valley Head a road crossed Lookout Mountain at Winston's Gap, and descended to the east side at Alpine, Georgia. The seizure of Alpine would threaten Bragg's communications with Atlanta, since the road led eventually to Kingston, only forty-four miles north of Atlanta.

Still, these few roads across Sand and Lookout were rough and steep. Distance was also a factor. An advance from Bridgeport or Stevenson through McLemore's Cove would take Rosecrans almost fifty miles from his line of supply on the north bank even before he cleared the east crest of Lookout. By crossing at Bridgeport and moving across Lookout

Mountain via McLemore's Cove to La Fayette, Rosecrans would extend his own communications almost ninety miles across four mountain ranges before striking Bragg's supply line to Atlanta.[7]

Despite the maze of mountain barriers, the safety of the Chattanooga position was precarious. Because of the northeast-southwest position of the river and mountains, a wide front of maneuver was open to Rosecrans. The area of operations resembled a giant triangle stretching across the Cumberlands. Rosecrans' base in the Cowan-Decherd area was the apex; the base of the triangle was the long front, well over one hundred miles by road, between Washington Ferry near Athens, Tennessee, and Stevenson, Alabama. The Federals could thus penetrate Bragg's line at any point on this front and still be relatively the same distance from their base. Also, even should Bragg learn the Federal path of march once they moved, the actual destination would be hard to discern. This was so because many possible invasion routes branched from others en route. For example, from Stevenson, Rosecrans could either move against Chattanooga up Lookout Valley, westward through McLemore's Cove against Bragg's rear end line of supply to Atlanta, or southwest against Bragg's railroad link via Alpine and Kingston, Georgia.

This problem of ascertaining Rosecrans' destination was particularly acute if Bragg let the Federals get through the mountains. For example, on the right or northeastern flank, once Rosecrans cleared Walden's Ridge, he could maneuver along good parallel roads to cross the Tennessee River at a large number of fords and ferries between Washington Ferry and Chattanooga. By using an ancient Indian road running hard by the west bank of the river, known as the Poe Road, the Federals could maneuver so as to conceal their crossing unless Bragg guarded every potential crossing place. This task in itself was almost impossible. During the summer, Bragg's engineers warned that from Blythe's Ferry near Charleston, Tennessee, and Harrison's Landing just above Chattanooga, a distance of twenty-one miles, there were ten crossings that Rosecrans might use. The problem was obvious. To insure control of the right flank, Bragg must hold Walden's Ridge to prevent a debouching onto the Poe Road; this could only be done by controlling the mountain at its western edge overlooking the Sequatchie Valley.

The problem of maneuver was also present on Bragg's immediate front at Chattanooga. Unless Bragg held that part of Walden's Ridge on the north bank known as Signal Point, he could not prevent an advance from Jasper and the Sequatchie Valley. Yet if he placed a force to control

[7] Robert Sparks Walker, *Lookout: the Story of a Mountain* (Kingsport, 1941), *Official Records*, XXX, Pt. 1, pp. 48–53; Govan and Livingood, *Chattanooga Country*, 222–23.

the approaches on the north bank, such troops would be threatened unless the crossings at Kelly's Ferry, Alley's Ferry, and Bridgeport were also held. Yet any force holding these three crossings would in turn be in danger of entrapment if the crossings near Stevenson were not guarded also.[8]

The terrain was complicated, and the problem of defending it was more difficult than was immediately obvious. There were over twenty-five major potential crossings of the Tennessee on this long front, and over twenty major roads by which the Federals could bypass or move on Chattanooga. In short, the one-hundred-mile defensive front resembled many dominoes. The collapse of defenses opposite Bridgeport would isolate those opposite Stevenson. The failure to defend properly the northern routes across Walden's Ridge to East Tennessee would threaten to isolate any force guarding Signal Point opposite Chattanooga. It was not that Chattanooga was not defensible. However, one of Bragg's major weaknesses was his failure to appreciate the advantages and perils of terrain. He had one general, William Hardee, who understood such problems. In July, Hardee, an old Bragg enemy, was transferred to Johnston's department in Mississippi.

Hardee's departure was indicative of the continuing problem in the army's echelons—that peculiar combination of poor relationships and poor communication. Faced with a possible advance from somewhere near the Great Smoky Mountains to northern Alabama, Bragg needed badly two factors—a well-coordinated high command and dependable intelligence. But in August of 1863, after the army was established at Chattanooga, he lacked both.

The high command's long metamorphosis continued, with a new arrangement promised for the fall. And other change was in the wind. The scheme of western concentration, so often advocated by Beauregard but ignored by the government, was slowly evolving. Even now this idea came not from the government, but from within the western command. Bragg was determined by July that a concentration of his and Johnston's armies was necessary lest both be defeated in succession. Just when Bragg became converted to this view is unknown. In July he confided to Beauregard that he had desired such a unity in the spring, but had been unable to impress the idea upon "others who control." [9] Yet a few weeks earlier, he had confessed to Johnston that he, like most of the Confederate leadership, had been tardy in seeing that western concentration was the key. Bragg even ventured to state, "How we can now see

[8] "Report of Reconnaissance of Fords and Ferries on Tennessee River between Harrison & Hiwassee River, Distance 21 Miles" (MS in Bragg Papers, Western Reserve) ; *Official Records*, XXX, Pt. 1, pp. 48–49.
[9] Bragg to Beauregard, July 21, 1863, in Seitz, *Bragg*, 321.

the folly of last spring's operations in diverting you from your aims." [10]

Bragg's new interest in concentration was motivated by fear and disgust. He feared the Rebel Heartland would be caught in a giant pincer move. And he was deeply irritated when after twice retreating to the Great Bend, he applied to Richmond for some instructions and received no reply.

In the meantime, Johnston in mid-July retreated across the Pearl River to escape a flanking maneuver by Sherman. With scarcely twenty-three thousand effectives, Johnston had taken a new position at Morton, Mississippi, on the Southern Railroad between Jackson and Meridian. With his back to the industrial-railroad area of Alabama, Johnston faced a Federal army of sixty thousand led by Grant and Sherman. Bragg feared not only for the munitions area, but also for the Tombigbee Valley of northeastern Mississippi and southwestern Alabama. After the loss of Tennessee, the area from above Columbus, Mississippi, to below Demopolis, Alabama, was vital to Bragg's food supply.

With no encouragement from the government, Bragg on July 17 took the initiative and proposed a bold plan of concentration. He urged Johnston to strike against Grant while Rosecrans was busy reorganizing for a move on Chattanooga. Bragg believed that Rosecrans would not be ready to move before the first of September, and so offered his entire army to Johnston, save for a few infantry brigades and the cavalry, which would garrison Chattanooga. Bragg urged Johnston to implement the plan, and argued that "our success can only result from concentration." [11]

Though Johnston, engrossed in a post-Vicksburg feud with the government, did not respond, other forces were at work. In July, Polk began an extensive correspondence designed to bring about a concentration in the West. On July 26 he urged President Davis to accept basically the plan which Beauregard had proposed that spring—that the Mississippi and Tennessee armies be concentrated against Rosecrans, and that a resulting victory would force the retreat by Grant from Mississippi. Polk also urged that Buckner's East Tennessee garrison be added to the concentration. Four days after writing Davis, Polk proposed the plan to his friend Hardee, who was then temporarily commanding Johnston's department. His argument was basically the same as that he sent to Richmond—that a combination of Bragg, Johnston, and Buckner would muster about eighty thousand effectives against Rosecrans.[12]

10 Bragg to Johnston, June 22, 1863, in *ibid.*, p. 308.
11 Bragg to Johnston, July 17, 1863, in Johnston Papers, William and Mary.
12 Polk to Hardee, July 30, 1863, in Polk Papers, Sewanee; Polk to Davis, July 26, 1863, in *Official Records*, XXIII, Pt. 2, p. 932.

For a time in early August, there was a flickering of interest in the ideas of Polk and Bragg. Davis in mid-July had expressed a fear that Rosecrans and Grant might combine against Bragg and advance against Chattanooga. This fear seemed realized on July 30, when Hardee reported that Grant's army was withdrawing from Vicksburg and was moving either to Mobile or to Tennessee. Two days later General Samuel Cooper wired Bragg and asked whether he would attack Rosecrans if he were given the bulk of Johnston's infantry. Bragg wired back that he was interested in the scheme and invited Johnston to confer with him on the matter. Meanwhile, the War Department asked Hardee what forces were available to aid Bragg. Hardee passed the dispatch to Johnston, who agreed to send all of his infantry save for two brigades if Bragg reportedly were threatened.[13]

Here the concentration scheme stalled. Johnston seemed almost completely engrossed in defending his operations in Mississippi against official criticism. During this time, his correspondence with the government and his friend Wigfall rarely mentioned the war effort. Others seemed to have lost their enthusiasm for such a move. By August 2 Davis was talking of using Johnston's army not to reinforce Bragg but to reinforce Beauregard, who was besieged at Charleston.

Bragg, too, was losing interest. By August 5 he had learned from Hardee of the true condition of Johnston's army, which consisted of only slightly over 18,000 effective infantry. Bragg was convinced that an offensive was impossible. Even with Buckner and Johnston, he could muster less than 40,000 effectives against a possible 90,000 to 100,000 under Rosecrans and Burnside. Instead, Bragg spoke more in terms of a defensive position in Chattanooga. Polk, too, bowed out of the scheme. On August 9 he explained to President Davis that his earlier plan had been based on a much more optimistic estimate of the size of Johnston's army. After he learned the truth from Hardee, Polk thought the plan was good but not feasible unless Bragg could get reinforcements from elsewhere.[14]

The importance of this general change of attitude was great. When Rosecrans advanced against Bragg on August 21, Bragg was still badly outnumbered, and no general scheme of concentration from any quarter had been adopted. It was only after the Federals began shelling Chattanooga on the twenty-first that reinforcements from all directions began to be directed in haphazard fashion toward Bragg's army. This much

---

13 Davis to Johnston, July 18, 1863, in Rowland (ed.), *Davis*, V, 569; Johnston to Seddon, July 30, 1863, in Johnston Papers, William and Mary; Seitz, *Bragg*, 323; Hughes, *Hardee*, 159; *Official Records*, LII, Pt. 2, p. 936.

14 Seitz, *Bragg*, 323–25; Polk to Davis, August 9, 1863, in Polk Papers, Duke.

heralded concentration at Chattanooga, often praised by historians, was actually only a hasty, hodgepodge arrangement. Desperate for aid, Bragg, on the twenty-first, telegraphed Johnston. Johnston asked Richmond what he should do. The government did not order him to aid Bragg, but merely told him to do so if he were able. The result was a half-hearted effort. Johnston had promised Seddon earlier that if Bragg were threatened, he would send him some nine of his eleven infantry brigades. Instead, though matters on his front were idle, Johnston sent only six brigades in two divisions, totaling some nine thousand men. He specified they were a loan and were to be promptly returned. Meanwhile, another nine thousand infantry and over six thousand cavalry remained idle in Mississippi. One of the two divisions was that of Breckinridge, which rightfully belonged to Bragg anyway. The other was commanded by General W. H. T. Walker. Not only was the reinforcement small, but it was also slow. They required six days to reach Chattanooga. Not until the twenty-eighth did Breckinridge and Walker arrive. By then Rosecrans had been across the Tennessee River for a week.[15]

During that week Bragg received aid from another source. In early August, Buckner's small East Tennessee department was merged into Bragg's, and was renamed the Third Corps of the Army of Tennessee. On the same day that Rosecrans shelled Chattanooga, Bragg learned from his new corps commander that a feared joint move by Burnside and Rosecrans had begun. Buckner learned on the twenty-first at his Knoxville headquarters that Burnside was advancing into the valley of East Tennessee. By the twenty-third it was obvious that Buckner would have to evacuate Knoxville. The bulk of Burnside's corps, reportedly an army of twenty-five thousand men, seemed to be moving through Big Creek Gap to strike the East Tennessee Railroad at the Loudon Bridge, between Buckner and Bragg.

Buckner could not defend East Tennessee. He had only five thousand badly disciplined and poorly armed infantry. Thus, by the twenty-fourth it was decided to withdraw Buckner's corps to the south bank of the Tennessee at the railroad bridge at Loudon. Though Bragg well could have used Buckner's men to aid in finding Rosecrans' path of march, the East Tennessee corps was wasted. Bragg held Buckner at Loudon until August 30. He was then withdrawn only as far as Charleston, on the south bank of the Hiwassee River. Another idle week went by until Buckner was moved still further south to Ooltewah, where the main East Tennessee-Georgia Railroad intersected with the branch to

15 Johnston to Bragg, August 22, 24, 1863, Johnston to Davis, August 22, 1863, Johnston to Cooper, August 22, 1863, in Johnston Papers, William and Mary; *Official Records*, XXX, Pt. 4, pp. 529–30, 538, 540–41, 547, 695.

Chattanooga. Not until September 8, after he had given orders to abandon Chattanooga, did Bragg finally order Buckner to join the main column in Georgia.[16]

Other sources of aid for Bragg were developing slowly. As with Buckner's arrival, the help was too little and too late. Not until the day after Rosecrans had opened his offensive did Richmond show interest in aiding Bragg. Then on August 22 Davis and Cooper merely told Johnston's department to send aid if possible. Two days later, Davis sent his aide Colonel James Chesnut to confer with the governors of Georgia and Alabama about sending the home guards to defend Chattanooga.[17]

The government's dilatory attitude was seen also in the decision to send aid to Bragg from Lee's army in Virginia. This idea had been advocated repeatedly by Beauregard since 1862 and was urged twice by Longstreet in early 1863. By August of 1863, Longstreet had revived this plan. In mid-August he pressed Seddon to detach at least part of his corps to the West while Lee held a defensive line on the Rapidan. By late August, Longstreet even approached Lee with the idea. After this conference, Lee went to Richmond to confer with Davis on overall Confederate policy. While there, Lee received another request for the move from Longstreet. On September 2 he urged Lee to leave two corps in Virginia and transfer one to Chattanooga.[18]

Even as Davis and Lee conferred during the last week of August and through early September, grim news came from the West. Knoxville had fallen, and by September 3 Burnside's corps had marched into the town through streets lined with cheering Unionists. The vital railroad to East Tennessee was lost: by September 6 all of East Tennessee was gone save for that small region south of the Hiwassee. Worse, the western threat most feared by Davis, a combination of Burnside and Rosecrans attacking Chattanooga, now seemed likely. By September 5 Davis was convinced that such a junction, which entailed a Federal command of almost 100,000 men was planned. Meanwhile, urgent appeals for aid came from the Tennessee delegation in Congress and from the State's governor, Isham Harris.

16 Brent Diary, August 23–24, 30–31, September 5, 6, 8, 1863, in Bragg Papers, Western Reserve; Buckner to Seddon, September 2, 1863, Buckner to Wooley, August 31, 1863, in Davis Papers, Tulane.

17 Davis to Alexander Stephens, August 31, 1863, in Rowland (ed.), *Davis*, VI, 20; Davis to James Chesnut, August 31, 1863, *ibid.*, p. 19; Davis to Hardee, August 22, 1863, *ibid.*, p. 597; *Official Records*, LII, Pt. 2, pp. 516–18, 520–21.

18 Lee to Longstreet, August 31, 1863, Longstreet to Lee, September 2, 1863, in James Longstreet, *From Manassas to Appomattox* (Philadelphia, 1893), 435. See also *ibid.*, pp. 433–34; Douglas S. Freeman, *Lee's Lieutenants, a Study in Command* (New York, 1942–44), III, 220, 222.

Still, Davis stalled in his decision, probably because of Lee's unwillingness. Lee evidently had not gone into the Richmond conference advocating such a reinforcement. In fact, as late as August 31, from Richmond he ordered Longstreet to prepare the army for offensive operations against Meade. In the conference he suggested that he take the offensive in Virginia, and argued that Meade's army had been weakened by sending reinforcement to the besieging forces at Charleston. Lee and Davis also evidently toyed with the idea of opening a third front in Southwest Virginia. They discussed the possibility of operating against the rear of Burnside's column either by using the small army of General Sam Jones in Southwest Virginia, or by sending a combined Jones-Longstreet expedition southward into the upper East Tennessee Valley.[19]

The final alternative, that of sending considerable reinforcement from Lee to Bragg, was agreed upon about September 5. Delay ensued while they determined who would command and how the West could be reached. Each seemed to have a different idea. Lee favored the detachment of part of Longstreet's corps; by September 4 he was inquiring of that general how long it would take his corps to move to Chattanooga. But Davis wanted Lee to go to the West and assume command. In their Richmond conversations, Lee squelched this idea, on the ground that he was ignorant of the country and that some officer already at Chattanooga could do better. And although Lee supposedly abandoned this idea on September 6, Davis left the matter open as late as September 8 in case Lee changed his mind.

Longstreet held a different opinion. His great interest in the concentration scheme during the spring and late summer gives credence to the suspicion that Longstreet hungered for Bragg's command. On September 5 he laid his cards on the table and proposed that he be sent to command Bragg's army. He suggested to Lee that Bragg could then come east to command Longstreet's corps in Virginia. But two days after his suggestion to Lee, that general was on his way back to his headquarters on the Rapidan where he ordered Longstreet with two divisions to move at once to reinforce Bragg at Chattanooga.[20]

[19] Davis to Bragg, September 5, 1863, in Rowland (ed), *Davis*, VI, 23, Davis to Bragg, September 10, 1863, in *ibid.*, p. 30; Digby Gordon Seymour, *Divided Loyalties: Fort Sanders and the Civil War in East Tennessee* (Knoxville, 1963), 85; *Official Records*, XXIX, Pt. 2, pp. 565–66, 660, 664–65, 720, 726; Lee to Davis, August 30, 1863, in McWhiney (ed.), *Lee's Dispatches*, 125; Lee to Longstreet, August 31, 1863, in Longstreet, *Manassas to Appomattox*, 435.

[20] Lee to Davis, September 6, 1863, in Dowdey and Manarin (eds.), *Wartime Papers*, 596; *Official Records*, XXIX, Pt. 2, p. 699; Freeman, *Lee's Lieutenants*, III, 222–24; Jones, *War Clerk's Diary*, II, 32–33; Davis to Lee, September 8, 1863, in Rowland (ed.), *Davis*, VI, 26.

The two weeks of deliberation at Richmond almost doomed the entire project. Not until September 9 did the first of Longstreet's men depart from Orange Court House for the long trek through the Carolinas to Atlanta and eventually to North Georgia. The original plan had called for Longstreet to use the East Tennessee railroad. The fall of East Tennessee forced his two divisions to go south via the long, circuitous route via Charlotte and Wilmington to Augusta, and from there to Atlanta. The trip was a disaster. His two divisions led by Generals John Hood and Lafayette McLaws, most recently engaged at Gettysburg, experienced numerous delays due to varying gauges, shortages of rolling stock, and lack of supplies. They moved on coal, platform, passenger, and baggage cars. From Kingsville, South Carolina, more delay ensued because only a single track linked them with Atlanta.

The concentration at Chickamauga, often eulogized by historians, is more myth than genuine fact. Only two of Longstreet's divisions reached Bragg; of these, only five brigades, totaling five thousand effectives, had reached Georgia by September 20, in time to participate in the battle of Chickamauga. The other brigades and Longstreet's entire artillery battalion trailed far behind, across eastern Georgia and the Carolinas. Furthermore because of the delay in the final decision and the resulting haste, Longstreet brought no wagons or horses.[21]

The haphazard nature of this reinforcement indicated the deeper problem—lack of central control. Ironically, when the West had an overall theater commander during the spring, the government had chosen not to concentrate there. Now there was no central control and little communication with Richmond during late August and early September. Johnston's theater command was abolished in July. Richmond seemed to have an inflated estimate of Bragg's forces. Government officials believed in early September that Bragg, exclusive of Longstreet's troops, had over 76,000 men. Actually, Bragg, including Buckner's and Johnston's reinforcements, had barely 40,000, of which only about 28,500 were infantry.[22]

This misunderstanding was symptomatic of the communication lag between Davis and Bragg, which by September 21 was so serious that Davis determined to go West personally and see what was happening. Davis commented several times during early September on his lack of knowledge of western affairs, and he knew little of the situation prior to dispatching Longstreet. In late August the president believed that

21 *Official Records*, XXX, Pt. 4, p. 526, XXIII, Pt. 2, p. 964; Freeman, *Lee's Lieutenants*, III, 227, 229; Oates, *War Between Union and the Confederacy*, 253–54; Black, *Railroads of the Confederacy*, 187–88.
22 *Official Records*, XXX, Pt. 4, pp. 518–19, XXIX, Pt. 2, pp. 720–21.

Rosecrans would join Burnside before moving on Chattanooga. Thus, as late as September 10, Davis was suggesting to Bragg that perhaps he should detach part of his army to strike Burnside before such a junction was made. At that time Rosecrans was across the river, already maneuvering to get around Bragg.

The heart of the matter was that both Davis and Lee seemed more concerned with East Tennessee than with the threat of Rosecrans driving into North Georgia. Lee admitted that the reason he detached Longstreet was to keep the East Tennessee rail link open. After Knoxville and Chattanooga fell, Lee bemoaned his sending Longstreet. He admitted that if he had known Burnside was moving on Knoxville, he would have sent Longstreet through Southwest Virginia in an independent move and not as a reinforcement to Bragg. Davis agreed with Lee. He confided to the general that had he known of Chattanooga's fall before detaching Longstreet, he would have sent that general on a Virginia campaign and not to reinforce Bragg.

Two days after Bragg abandoned Chattanooga, Davis still believed that Rosecrans would pause and unite with Burnside before any future operations. He never seemed to grasp that the main invasion column was that of Rosecrans. Thus, on September 16 Davis announced that he was disappointed in Chattanooga's abandonment because an opportunity to entrap Burnside was lost. He also continued his belief that the main Federal objective was a union of the two columns and a seizure of East Tennessee. Not until late September, after Chickamauga, did Davis seem to realize that the main threat was Rosecrans' move against the Chattanooga-Atlanta rail link. His delay in recognizing the real Federal objective in Georgia was partly responsible for the slowness and smallness of the reinforcements sent to Bragg in August and September.[23]

With the reinforcements came that total reorganization so traditional with the Western army prior to a crucial campaign. But the army had never been compelled to adjust to so many changes in the high command at one time. By late September, with the addition of Buckner and Longstreet, the army would have a new system of four corps instead of the old two-corps arrangement. Adjustments did not merely involve reorganization; but also complicated personnel relationships. All four of Bragg's corps leaders under the new arrangement had personal dislikes or ambitions which threatened to demolish the command.

A sad commentary on Bragg's new command situation was that his best relationship was with his old enemy in the First Corps, Polk. During

[23] Davis to Bragg, September 10, 1863, in Rowland (ed.), *Davis*, VI, 30; Davis to Lee, September 16, 21, 1863, in Davis Papers, Tulane; *Official Records*, XXIX, Pt. 2, pp. 720–21.

the summer, the Bishop had declared a semi-moratorium on his campaign to oust Bragg, for sagging Rebel fortunes everywhere disturbed him. In July and August he used his Richmond influence to beg Davis for aid to Bragg.[24]

But this particular incident did not do much to help the command problems in Bragg's corps. The old hatred between him and Polk remained. Also, Bragg lost one of his two seasoned division commanders in the First Corps. On July 22 General Jones Withers was assigned a less rigorous task of superintending the reserve forces in Alabama, due to his failing health. He was replaced by General Thomas C. Hindman. Hindman's service had been primarily in the trans-Mississippi region. He knew nothing of the Tennessee-Georgia terrain, or of the army's troops. And unfortunately he fell in naturally with the anti-Bragg forces, since, in the pre-war days, he had been a staunch friend of General Patrick Cleburne.

More radical changes were made in Hardee's Second Corps. In one of the most serious misuses of talent in the West, Hardee in July was transferred to Johnston's command. The transfer evidently had been at the behest of influential Mississippians seeking more aid for Johnston. The loss of Bragg's best corps leader was particularly acute because of Hardee's knowledge of western topography. It was also frustrating, because Hardee was wasted in Mississippi. For weeks he performed the menial tasks of minding Johnston's department while that general toured various areas of the command. Then, in late August, when Bragg badly needed him, Hardee was given an even less important role—that of commanding the paroled Louisiana and Mississippi troops from Vicksburg. Evidently miserable in his new department, he confided to Polk, "I wish I were back at Chattanooga with my corps." [25]

Bragg would soon wish the same. On July 14, when Hardee was ordered to Mississippi, the government promoted General Daniel Harvey Hill to lieutenant general and sent him to Bragg to replace Hardee. Hill's arrival in Chattanooga on July 18 was both melancholy and foreboding. It was a sad confrontation of old friends, some of whom were now enemies. A number of Hill's classmates at West Point in the class of 1842 were now across the river in the Federal lines. One of these was Rosecrans. Another classmate, General A. P. Stewart, was with Bragg at Chattanooga; two others, Longstreet and McLaws, were soon to arrive.

24 Polk to Kenneth Rayner, August 15, 1863, in Polk Papers, Sewanee; see also Polk to Hardee, August 30, 1863, *ibid.*; Polk to Davis, August 9, 1863, in Polk Papers, Duke; *Official Records*, XXIII, Pt. 2, p. 932.

25 Hardee to Polk, July 27, 1863, in Polk Papers, Sewanee; Hughes, *Hardee*, 158–61; Buck, *Cleburne and His Command*, 20; *Official Records*, XXX, Pt. 4, p. 495, XXIII, Pt. 2, p. 925.

There were other old friends on both sides of the river. As a young second lieutenant in 1845, Hill had maintained a close relationship with the messmates in his company, George Thomas, John Reynolds, and Braxton Bragg. Now, General George Thomas led a corps in Rosecrans' army, Reynolds had been killed at Gettysburg, and Bragg was Hill's superior.

But from their first conference on July 19, matters were not friendly between Hill and Bragg. Somehow in that conference, their personalities, both frayed by disputes in their respective armies, clashed, and Hill left the meeting troubled. Hill's personality too, was unpredictable, and he was sometimes gloomy and often sarcastic. His lifelong spinal ailment, which seemed to trouble him in damp weather, may have agitated his evident states of mental depression. Like Bragg, Hill was a single-minded individual, inflexible in his opinions, and usually convinced he was right. His rigid Presbyterian upbringing, his long practice of personal self-discipline, and his pre-war extremism in anti-Northern sentiment made Hill an uncompromising person.

Hill's career in the army had, like Bragg's, involved a continuous series of command quarrels. His record as a combat officer at Seven Days, Second Manassas, and Sharpsburg had been outstanding but stormy. After Malvern Hill, a quarrel with a brigade commander, General Robert Toombs, had resulted in a duel challenge. Hill had been critical of Lee in his Seven Days and Sharpsburg reports. For whatever reason, Lee had passed over him for promotion to lieutenant general in the fall of 1862. Later in 1863 Lee expressed some lack of confidence in Hill's abilities. In the spring of 1863, while Hill commanded the North Carolina Department and the Petersburg defenses, there had been further tension between them. There was an unusually sharp exchange among Hill, Lee, and Davis in late May regarding Lee's desire to have certain of Hill's brigades transferred to his army.

Hill brought his personality problems to the West. He seemed to provoke disputes with his fellow officers. Nervous, irritable, and easily affronted, Hill tended to point out freely the flaws in any command situation. His intense desire to reform was dominant in his personality. From the time of his arrival at Chattanooga, he slowly began to comprehend the army's opinion of Bragg and to form his own views of that General's military ability. By September Hill was also in the anti-Bragg camp.[26]

26 *Official Records*, XXIII, Pt. 2, p. 918; for comments on Hill's personality see Lafayette McLaws to Hill, January 23, 1864, in Daniel Harvey Hill Papers, North Carolina State Archives, hereinafter cited as NCA; Bragg to Davis, September 25, 1863, in Georgia Portfolio II, Duke; see also Hal Bridges, *Lee's Maverick General* (New York, 1961), 6, 146–54, 195–201; Daniel H. Hill, "Chickamauga—the Great Battle of the West," *Battles and Leaders*, III, 638–41.

There was more trouble for Bragg in the Second Corps than the addition of Hill. With complete reorganization of the corps, Cleburne's division was the only remnant of Hardee's old command. On September 1 General A. P. Stewart's division was transferred from the Second Corps to Buckner's corps. To fill Stewart's place, an old enemy of Bragg was reassigned to it. On August 28 General John C. Breckinridge's division from Mississippi was put back in the Second Corps. Thus, with Hill in command, and Cleburne and Breckinridge as division commanders, the Second Corps was completely dominated by Bragg enemies.[27]

The quarrel that erupted between Bragg and Buckner in the summer had begun back in the spring, over boundaries of commands.[28] In May, 1863, after a long spring of wasted effort by multiple commanders, East Tennessee was turned over to Simon Buckner. On May 19 he proposed to Bragg an end to the waste that had characterized the use of East Tennessee troops. He called for more cooperation between himself and Bragg, and suggested that it was regrettable a single officer did not control both departments. Obviously Buckner, too, assumed that Johnston's removal to Mississippi in mid-May ended his jurisdiction over the two departments.[29]

Buckner's frank letters to Bragg and the War Department in May proved to be his undoing. Slowly, his authority drifted away. Johnston had already suggested in January that the East Tennessee Department be merged into Bragg's. In early May he reiterated this proposal. In early June Bragg, probably prompted by Buckner's letter of May 19, also suggested that some central authority was needed. A few days later an indication of things to come occurred when Bragg's limit of authority was readjusted, with Buckner's approval, to include the southeastern segment of East Tennessee as far north as the Tennessee River crossing at Loudon.[30]

Matters reached a climax on June 17. Prompted by Bragg's complaint that Buckner refused to cooperate in coordinated efforts, Johnston on June 16 suggested to Davis that Bragg's authority be extended over East Tennessee. Davis immediately wrote Buckner and Bragg for their opinions of this arrangement. The letter to Buckner was particularly persuasive, since Davis reminded the Kentuckian that he had made an earlier

27 *Official Records*, XXX, Pt. 4, p. 561.

28 *Ibid.*, XX, Pt. 2, pp. 491, 493–95, 463; Johnston to Bragg, January 9, 1863, Johnston to Ewell, January 11, 1863, in Johnston Papers, William and Mary.

29 *Official Records*, XXIII, Pt. 2, pp. 843–44, 855.

30 *Ibid.*, pp. 826, 857, XX, Pt. 2, p. 495.

statement that he would accept any arrangement that insured coopera-tion.[31]

The result was a complete and confusing reorganization of Bragg's department on the eve of the new campaign. The government by July 22 had definitely decided to extend Bragg's jurisdiction over East Tennessee. Other important changes were made that day. Johnston's theater com-mand was abolished, and Bragg's department was renamed the Depart-ment of Tennessee. Davis thought it was necessary to shift territory to add more ground to Johnston's Department of Mississippi and East Louisiana. The result was a serious constriction of Bragg's territory in those areas. On July 25 Bragg's department was allowed to retain control of only that part of Alabama north of the Tennessee River and the tier of counties bordering the river on the south bank. Bragg's new command included East Tennessee and the upper quarter section of Georgia bounded by the railroads from Chattanooga to Atlanta, and from Atlanta to West Point, on the Georgia-Alabama border. From West Point, the dividing line between Bragg and Johnston was extended northward along the state border to the counties on the south bank of the Tennessee River.[32]

Much was wrong with this new arrangement. Bragg had lost practically all of Alabama, upon which he had depended for logistical and man-power resources. With almost three times the number of men Johnston had, Bragg had been restricted to an area of subsistence less than one-third that of Johnston's. Also, in Georgia, Bragg was responsible for the defense of the south-central industrial complex from Augusta through Macon to Columbus. Yet he could draw neither men nor rations from the area. Beauregard's vast Department of South Carolina, Georgia, and Florida was allowed to extend its domain as far north as the east side of the Chattanooga-Atlanta Railroad, into the Blue Ridge Mountains. Yet Beauregard's much smaller army was concerned only with coastal de-fense, and did not require such a vast area for subsistence.

The allotting of the smallest subsistence territory to the Confederacy's only genuine western army created problems with Buckner's command also. The government could not decide whether to allow Bragg to retain control of Buckner. This hesitation abetted the serious personal feud between the two men which erupted after Chickamauga. On July 22 the War Department announced that Bragg now controlled Buckner's depart-ment. But the government did not say whether the East Tennessee de-partment was abolished, and it befuddled matters by allowing Buckner,

[31] Davis to Bragg, June 17, 1863, in Bragg Papers, Western Reserve; Davis to Buckner, June 17, 1863, in Rowland (ed.), *Davis*, V, 522–23; Arndt M. Stickles, *Simon Bolivar Buckner: Borderland Knight* (Chapel Hill, 1940), 220.
[32] *Official Records*, XXIII, Pt. 2, pp. 924, 926, 931, 952–53.

allegedly under Bragg, to continue to correspond directly with Richmond. Three days later, it was announced that the Department of East Tennessee was being merged into Bragg's department, but again no clear statement was made as to whether it formally had been abolished.

In August, matters became more confusing. Bragg on August 6 formally took charge of Buckner's department, finally serving official notice that the name "Department of East Tennessee" was abolished. While the East Tennessee troops were now designated as the Third Corps in Bragg's army, Buckner still was to control administrative affairs in East Tennessee. The retention of the Department of East Tennessee as a distinct administrative organization confused Buckner. He did not understand how he could maintain a separate administration, communicate directly with Richmond, and still be considered in Bragg's department. Disgusted, on August 11 he appealed to Cooper to either place him on an equal footing with Bragg's other corps leaders, relieve him of his administration duties, or else to allow him to command a separate department with authority as a departmental commander.[33]

In late August the situation became more involved and even ludicrous. On August 21 General Samuel Cooper inquired of Bragg whether the Department of East Tennessee might not be reestablished, so that Buckner could have control of administration. Bragg agreed and the department, on August 28, announced a new arrangement. Now there was to be and there was not to be an East Tennessee Department. The department was to exist for "administrative duties" but was also to be considered part of the Department of Tennessee.[34]

As a result of this entanglement, a serious dispute between Bragg and Buckner began. Both generals moved toward their junction below Chattanooga in September with varying ideas of authority. Bragg believed that since Buckner had left the confines of his old department, he had surrendered both strategic and administrative control. Hence, when Buckner joined him, Bragg proceeded to reorganize his command. Buckner came with a different interpretation. He conceded that Bragg had the power to direct military operations, but did not believe Bragg could transfer his troops to another command or could relieve his officers. In Buckner's view, the organization he brought to Georgia was frozen and not under Bragg's authority.[35]

Other problems in the Third Corps portended trouble. Buckner's com-

33 *Ibid*, pp. 954, 962–63, XXXI, Pt. 3, pp. 657, 963.
34 *Ibid.*, XXX, Pt. 4, p. 562, XXXI, Pt. 3, p. 658, XXIII, Pt. 2, pp. 962–63.
35 *Ibid.*, XXXI, Pt. 3, pp. 657–64, 651, XXX, Pt. 4, p. 703; Buckner to Brent, October 20, 25, 1863, in Buckner Papers, Huntington; Bragg to Davis, October 22, 1863, in Davis Papers, Emory.

mand was new and had not had time to solidify before the Rosecrans offensive. On September 1 Bragg transferred Stewart's division to Buckner. Buckner thus had two divisions—Stewart's and the single unit he brought from East Tennessee, that of General William Preston's troops. Preston was an old campaigner in the anti-Bragg faction, who had seen service under Breckinridge during the spring quarrels. He had been detached to command in southwestern Virginia. Preston was now back, and the Virginia mountain air had not quenched his dislike of Bragg.[36]

Bragg's relationship with Longstreet, the leader of the Fourth Corps, was no better than with Polk, Hill, and Buckner. If any success in North Georgia were not already doomed by the lack of rapport between Bragg and the other three corps leaders, the arrival of Longstreet may well have provided the *coup de grace*. On the surface, the situation looked optimistic at last. Longstreet was Lee's senior corps commander and had a fine reputation in the eastern army, second only to that of his commander. On the Peninsula, at Second Manassas, at Sharpsburg, and Fredericksburg, Longstreet, known for his reliability, hard fighting, and tenacity, had earned the sobriquet "Lee's old war horse." The onus of the accusations that he delayed on July 2 at Gettysburg was yet in the future. In fact Longstreet, in September of 1863, was still immensely popular in Virginia. He was not yet saddled with the image of a stubborn, slow man, which arose after his alignment with the Republicans during Reconstruction.

Longstreet brought with him to the western army many close ties with that area. He must have had sentimental thoughts as the rickety trains clattered through the pine barrens of the Carolina-Georgia Piedmont. He would now face in battle his West Point roommate Rosecrans. En route from Virginia, he passed through his native South Carolina, and through Augusta, Georgia, where he had received his early education. Ahead was a reunion with his classmates of 1842, Harvey Hill and Alexander Stewart. West of Chattanooga, on the edge of the mountainous northern Alabama terrain was Huntsville. Longstreet had lived there as a young man, and from Alabama had received his appointment to West Point.[37]

Longstreet's two divisions would also bring experienced leaders and troops to the campaign. His lead division was commanded by the gaunt, blond-bearded Kentuckian John Hood. By the fall of 1863 young Hood was established as one of Lee's hardest hitting division commanders. His reputation was established on such fields as Antietam, where his First

36 *Official Records*, XXX, Pt. 4, p. 578; Preston wrote of his relationship with Bragg, "I have a dull future before me with Bragg—No approval or praise if I win, ruin and censure if I lose. I intend to get away if I can." William Preston to William Preston Johnston, October 3, 1863, in Barret Collection, Tulane.

37 Glenn Tucker, *Lee and Longstreet at Gettysburg* (Indianapolis, 1968), 160–62, 168.

Texas Regiment lost 82 per cent of its strength on the field. Hood himself had suffered a severe arm wound at Gettysburg. When his division entrained at Richmond for the trip to Georgia, his men cheered as they saw their slim commander, arm in a sling, unexpectedly board the train to accompany them. With him were three well-seasoned brigades. The former Georgia lawyer, General Henry "Rock" Benning led a brigade of Georgians. General Evander Law's Alabama brigade had suffered heavily in the action at Gettysburg on July 2 near Round Top and Little Round Top, as had the men in Hood's third brigade, the Texas brigade. This outfit was led by General Jerome Robertson, father of the young artillery captain so useful to Bragg in the post-Murfreesboro controversy with Breckinridge.

Behind Hood trailed the division of General Lafayette McLaws. For McLaws, also, there was rendevous ahead with old classmates from 1842— Rosecrans, Hill, and Stewart. Like Hood, McLaws was an established fighter, especially renowned for his defense of Marye's Heights at Fredericksburg against the assaults by Burnside's men. Burnside, too, was in the West now, maneuvering somewhere up the valley from Chattanooga. The South Carolina brigade, led by the able South Carolinian General Joseph Kershaw, came directly from combat in the Peach Orchard at Gettysburg. The Mississippi brigade, now commanded by General Benjamin Humphreys, had also been there.[38]

It might have been better for the Army of Tennessee had Longstreet never come to Georgia, for during his three months' stay with the army, he created more problems than he solved. His relationship with Bragg deteriorated from the outset, and by October the Virginia officer had allied himself with the dissidents. By virtue of his prestige, rank, and other factors, Longstreet may well have instigated the October revolt which completely destroyed the army's morale. Following this revolt, feelings between Longstreet and Bragg worsened. Their inability to coordinate matters might well explain the collapse of the siege at Chattanooga, and the virtual secession of Longstreet from Bragg's army in his East Tennessee campaign.

Though these matters were in the future, the seeds of trouble probably were already there as Longstreet's trains rolled through the Carolinas. Like some other Virginia officers who came West, Longstreet's future conduct was probably affected somewhat by his motives for coming to Bragg's army. What was Longstreet after in the western army? No doubt he was dismayed at the government's policy of defending all areas simultaneously, a strategy that was destroying the West in segments. He spoke

[38] Glenn Tucker, *Chickamauga: Bloody Battle in the West* (Indianapolis, 1961), 94.

of this to Lee on September 2, and insisted that failure would result unless they concentrated.[39]

Also, Longstreet may well have thought that short work could be made of the western Federals. Like some others of the Virginia army, he seemed to have a cavalier attitude toward the West. Some observers considered the West and its chief army to be rough, second-rate, and defended by second-rate generals. The fact that Williamsburg was two centuries old before Memphis was incorporated probably motivated such allusions as Mrs. Chesnut's description of western battles as bloody street brawls. Her view of the Confederate Heartland as the "frontier" was shared by other eastern folk. Western battles seem to have come across partially as comic operas. How much Longstreet shared this view is unknown, though some of his officers and men chose to compare the armies of Lee and Bragg. Lee obviously believed that quick work could be made of Rosecrans and that Longstreet's men would be the deciding factor.[40]

If Longstreet coveted Bragg's command, he concealed it skillfully by striking the pose of the unselfish officer committed to an unpleasant task. In fact, many of his August and September statements were characterized by an almost pietistic tone of sacrifice. When Lee asked him in August if he would take command in the West, Longstreet stated he would do so only on the assumption that he could gain the army's confidence, win a decisive victory, and follow up with aggressive offensive operations. On September 5, when suggesting that he be put in Bragg's place, Longstreet assured Lee that he was influenced by no personal motive and would cheerfully give up the command "when we have a fair prospect" [41] of holding the West. Later, on September 12, Longstreet promised that if allowed to do anything in the West, "it shall be done promptly," and he advised Lee to recall him if it was not done. Longstreet then stated, "If I did not think our move a necessary one, my regrets at leaving you would be distressing to me. . . . Believing it to be necessary, I hope to accept it and my other personal inconveniences cheerfully and hopefully." [42]

Longstreet's pose as the unwilling suitor, and his declarations of hu-

39 Seddon to Longstreet, May 3, 1875, in Longstreet Papers, Emory; Jones Confederate Strategy, 206–209; Official Records, XXIX, Pt. 2, p. 699.

40 Mary Boykin Chesnut, A Diary from Dixie, ed. Ben Ames Williams (Boston, 1961), 429, 445. One government official commented that western battle accounts "are generally exaggerated." See Jones, War Clerk's Diary, I, 171, also pp. 49, 229. See also Charles Blackford to wife, October 29, 1863, in Susan Leigh Blackford (ed.), Letters from Lee's Army or Memoirs of Life In and Out of the Army in Virginia During the War Between the States (New York and London, 1947), 226; Official Records, XXIX, Pt. 2, pp. 713–14, 749.

41 Official Records, XXIX, Pt. 2, p. 699; see also Longstreet, Manassas to Appomattox, 434.

42 Official Records, XXIX, Pt. 2, pp. 712–14.

mility and sacrifice appear something less than credible in the light of his later conduct on the Tennessee front. General Lafayette McLaws later wrote Bragg that Longstreet wanted the army's command. McLaws on another occasion contended that Longstreet deliberately stalled during the move toward Knoxville so that he would not have to return to Bragg's command. However, McLaws was no impartial observer. Both documents were probably written after McLaws was relieved of his command by Longstreet in December of 1863.[43]

There is stronger evidence from Longstreet himself that he was after Bragg's job. In August, Longstreet admitted that he would take the command if it were offered. On September 5 he became more direct and suggested to Lee that he be given Bragg's position. In this note Longstreet gave his low estimate of Bragg, stating that the general had no confidence in either his troops or himself and that he was not likely "to do a great deal for us." [44] Rebuffed in his proposal, Longstreet seemed disgruntled and confided to Wigfall that he did not think he should be under Bragg's command. Longstreet hinted that he would openly oppose being placed under Bragg if he did not fear that someone would accuse him of wanting the job. Regardless of what Longstreet secretly wanted, it is apparent that his attitudes toward Bragg and the West were probably fixed weeks before the Virginia troops arrived in northern Georgia.[45]

Command disunity was not the only problem which would make it difficult to discern Rosecrans' route of advance once the campaign opened. In August and September, Bragg's intelligence service seemed to be falling apart. The system had never functioned well. Bragg derived his intelligence chiefly from two sources. He had a modest network of spies and scouts under the direction of the chief of his secret service, Colonel Alec McKinstry. Under McKinstry's supervision, several groups were organized, usually loosely and with poor effect. The most notable group was the Coleman Scouts, led by Captain H. B. Shaw. Until he was captured in November, 1863, Shaw operated from the Highland Rim country below Nashville. He obtained information and Federal newspapers from the city and relayed them by couriers to Bragg's headquarters. By the fall of 1863 this system was on the verge of collapse. The loss of Middle Tennessee had greatly increased both the distance and the danger. At its shortest point, Bragg's courier line now extended over 120 miles of territory heavily guarded by cordons of Union picket lines and cavalry

43 Lafayette McLaws undated manuscript on East Tennessee campaign, McLaws to Bragg, n.d., in Lafayette McLaws Papers, UNC; Archer Anderson to Brent, April 14, 1864, in Davis Papers, Tulane.

44 *Official Records*, XXIX, Pt. 2, p. 699; see also Longstreet, *Manassas to Appomattox*, 434.

45 Longstreet to Wigfall, September 2, 1863, in Wigfall Papers, DLC.

patrols. Too, McKinstry's scouts had no special training. They were simply men who were detached from various divisions for that service because they knew the country.[46]

This system might have performed better had Bragg not consistently relied upon his cavalry for the bulk of his intelligence, thereby limiting the possible growth and effectiveness of his secret service. For in August, 1863, his cavalry failed him. The causes were bad organization and poor troop placement. During the summer, Bragg reorganized his troopers into two corps, commanded by Wheeler and Forrest. Wheeler's corps included Martin's and Wharton's divisions, and the independent brigade commanded by Colonel Phillip Roddey. Forrest's corps contained his old division now commanded by General Frank Armstrong, and a division of Buckner's cavalry from the East Tennessee department, commanded by General John Pegram. By August this new organization had replenished the cavalry until Bragg boasted over ten thousand troopers. With these, Bragg could have controlled the north bank of the river, anticipated Rosecrans' march route, and learned the Federal destination on the south bank.

Instead, Bragg placed his cavalry where it would be impossible for them to ascertain Rosecrans' route of advance. Forrest was sent to East Tennessee to picket the ferries and fords northeast of Chattanooga as far north as Kingston. But in so doing, Bragg in effect surrendered control of the entire north bank of the river above Chattanooga. No cavalrymen were placed on Walden's Ridge or on the north bank.

The worst placement was on the west side of Chattanooga. In late July, Wheeler was ordered to guard the Tennessee River fords west of Chattanooga. Wharton and Martin were to picket the river from Chattanooga as far west as Gunter's Landing, eight miles away. Roddey's brigade was to picket the river from Gunter's Landing to Florence. There were many things wrong with this arrangement. Bragg reduced Wheeler to a defensive position on the south bank and thus conceded the crucial areas such as Jasper, Stevenson, Bridgeport, and the Sequatchie Valley. Bragg also ordered Wheeler to place his headquarters at Gadsden, Alabama. This was completely out of position to control the river west of Chattanooga, for Gadsden was eighty miles southwest of Stevenson and further away from Bridgeport. Hence, the line of communication from

46 Mabel Baxter Pittard, "The Coleman Scouts" (Master's thesis, Middle Tennessee State College, 1953), 17–20; R. B. Anderson, "Fellow Scout of Samuel Davis," *Confederate Veteran*, III (July, 1895), 202; H. B. Shaw to Alex McKinstry, November 18, 1863, in Bromfield Ridley (ed.), *Battles and Sketches of the Army of Tennessee* (Mexico, Mo., 1906), 260–61; R. B. Anderson, "Secret Service in the Army of Tennessee," *Confederate Veteran*, XXI (July, 1913), 345; P. N. Matlock, "Sam Davis and Others Visited Nashville," *Confederate Veteran*, XIII (April, 1905), 168–69.

Wheeler's scouts on the river to his headquarters and then to Bragg's headquarters at Chattanooga was well over 160 miles in length.[47]

There were other factors not to be blamed on Wheeler. The retreat from Tennessee had shattered Wheeler's cavalry in hard rearguard fighting. Also, there was a general decline in the number of horses because of the increasing difficulty in troopers furnishing their own mounts as required by the government. Desertion was commonplace in the cavalry as well. Thus, by August, Bragg, on paper, boasted over twenty-six thousand cavalry, while only about ten thousand were present for duty. Wheeler's corps particularly showed the effects of the long stay on the Alabama front. Though his aggregate was over nineteen thousand men, Wheeler had only about sixty-six hundred present for duty in August of 1863.[48]

Yet Wheeler must share the blame for the cavalry's misuse, because he had failed to obey orders. When the Federals began to move in late August, he did not heed Bragg's orders to watch the river crossings and to supply intelligence. Instead, he placed his troopers out of position. Only a single regiment guarded the fifty-seven-mile front from Bridgeport through Stevenson to Gunter's Landing. Another lone regiment protected the crossings downstream from Gunter's Landing to Decatur, a fifty-mile-wide front. Instead, Wheeler withdrew his two divisions to replenish and refit them. Wharton's division was moved across both the Sand and Lookout Mountain ranges to Rome—over seventy miles from the river. Martin's division was also withdrawn across both mountain ranges to Alexandria, Alabama, almost eighty miles south of Stevenson. Thus, except for two cavalry regiments, Bragg had no one guarding the many crossings of the Tennessee west from Bridgeport.[49]

This void could have been supplied partially by infantry. Instead, Bragg's deployment of his infantry in late August wrecked any possible chance of anticipating Rosecrans' approach. The army was thrown to the right, surrendering two vital areas. No effort was made to control the north bank, even that part which was immediately opposite Chattanooga. This neglect occurred despite Bragg's admission in July to his medical director, Dr. Samuel Stout, that if the enemy took the opposite bank of the river, Chattanooga could not be held. Bragg explained to Stout that a comparatively small force on Walden's Ridge could bombard the town and drive out any defenders there. Therefore, Bragg warned him to begin to evacuate his hospital facilities southward toward Atlanta.

47 *Official Records*, XXX, Pt. 2, pp. 519–20, XXIII, Pt. 2, pp. 925–26, Pt. 4, p. 715; Henry, *Forrest*, 169.
48 *Official Records*, XXIII, Pt. 2, p. 957.
49 *Ibid*, XXX, Pt. 2, pp. 519–20; Special Orders 179, Army of Tennessee, July 7, 1863, Special Orders 189, Army of Tennessee, July 18, 1863, Mackall to Roddey, July 19, 1863, Walter to Pillow, July 19, 1863, in Bragg Papers, Western Reserve.

Nor were dispositions made to protect against either an approach to the town from the south bank, or a flanking move around Bragg's left flank via Bridgeport or Stevenson. Only a single infantry brigade, that of General Patton Anderson, was posted west of Chattanooga. Anderson was placed opposite the crossing at Bridgeport. But the remainder of Polk's corps was at Chattanooga, while Hill's corps was stationed northeast of the town to watch a 100-mile front of river crossings extending to Loudon.

Thus did Bragg concede the crossings west of Chattanooga, and did so despite some advice to the contrary. As early as January his chief engineer, Major James Nocquet, had emphasized that two of the most threatened routes west of Chattanooga were at Kelly's and Alley's ferries near Jasper. As late as August 21 General Thomas Hindman had argued that a modest artillery emplacement could hold Kelly's Ferry at the river landing while a position on Raccoon Mountain would command all roads in the sector. By late August Bragg controlled only one—the crossing at Bridgeport. Kelly's and Alley's ferries upstream were unguarded, while downstream from Bridgeport, the ferries at Stevenson were not picketed, though Bragg knew as early as July 23 that Rosecrans had repaired the rail link to Stevenson.[50]

Thus did the army's old problems—command discord and disorganization, misuse of cavalry, and Bragg's lack of appreciation for terrain— loom up at Chattanooga. By late August it was not certain if these problems could be corrected before the expected Federal advance in September. It was certain that when President Davis decreed August 21 as a day of fasting and prayer for the Confederacy, no one needed it more than Bragg's ill-starred force at Chattanooga.

50 *Official Records*, LII, Pt. 2, p. 417, XXX, Pt. 4, p. 523, XXIII, Pt. 2, pp. 911, 913, 923, Brent Diary, August 21, 1863, 925–26; in Bragg Papers, Western Reserve.

eight

The Search for Rosecrans

ON AUGUST 21 THE TENSIONS RESULTING FROM PROBLEMS OF GEOGRAPHY, disunified command, and poor intelligence reports tore at the army. Most of Bragg's officers joined the civilians of Chattanooga in flocking to churches in response to the President's request for a day of prayer. But most of the sermons in the warm, packed churches were cut short. About nine o'clock artillery fire opened from the north bank of the river. As shells roared into the town, a steamer at the Chattanooga wharves was sunk and another disabled, a pontoon bridge was sunk, and some of Bragg's own artillery on the south bank was silenced.

Buell's unexpected shelling from across the Kentucky River had caught Bragg unaware at Frankfort. Now ten months later and four hundred miles southward, Bragg seemed equally unprepared for this surprise attack on the army's main base. The town was close to panic. Everyone seemed convinced that Rosecrans' main army was readying to cross the river. Hundreds of civilians fled to the woods south of town while others crowded onto every available train chugging south to Atlanta. Business houses were closed, and factories began the task of moving precious ordnance machinery to the safety of North Georgia.[1]

By the evening of August 21 Rosecrans' troops seemed to loom up everywhere. Scouts reported that he was hastily building pontoons near Jasper, at the mouth of Battle Creek. Others claimed he was readying to cross at Alley's Ferry near Jasper. Hindman reported Federal infantry in motion along old Haley's Trace, on the north bank of the river opposite Raccoon Mountain. From his position opposite the crossing at

[1] Brent Diary, August 21, 1863, in Bragg Papers, Western Reserve; Noll, *Quintard*, 88; Govan and Livingood, *Chattanooga Country*, 218–19.

Bridgeport, General Patton Anderson warned that a heavy column of blue infantry was moving down Sweden's Cove toward Jasper. Another sighting of a large force was made opposite Lookout Mountain, near Brown's Ferry. Still others said that Federals were moving to cross at Stevenson and Bridgeport.[2]

There was no doubt the Federal advance was genuine, and Bragg sent hasty appeals to Richmond and to Johnston for reinforcement. But where was Rosecrans? Despite the numerous warnings of Federal maneuvering on a long front from Stevenson to Jasper, Bragg seemed to ignore the danger signs west of Chattanooga. Though he learned on August 22 that the Federals were crossing at Shellmound, no strength was concentrated to oppose any crossings in the area west of Lookout Mountain. Instead, on the night of August 21, the last brigade west of Chattanooga was withdrawn to the town. By the next day, practically all of Bragg's infantry was concentrated from Chattanooga northward to Harrison's Landing, some ten miles distant.

Bragg instead turned his attention upriver. Between August 21 and 28, he, Polk, Hill, and Buckner were certain the crossing would be there. There seemed good reason for this, for even on the day Chattanooga was first shelled, disturbing news was received from that quarter. Rosecrans' army was said to be moving via Dunlap and Pikeville to strike the roads across Walden's Ridge leading to the river. That same evening, Buckner reported that the dreaded double offensive seemed to have begun. His scouts on the Cumberland front reported that the Federals under Burnside were moving in heavy force through the gaps northwest of Knoxville.

By August 23 Bragg seemed more convinced that Rosecrans was to cross above the town. The previous day he had received some strong reports which indicated a combined move by Burnside and Rosecrans. General A. P. Stewart was convinced Rosecrans would cross directly above Chattanooga at the mouth of Chickamauga Creek. Bragg's engineers made a hasty survey further upstream and came back with disquieting news. Federals in brigade numbers were already at Blythe's and Doughty's ferries, near the mouth of the Hiwassee River. That night General Henry Clayton, commanding one of Harvey Hill's brigades, sent more intelligence. Posted to observe the Hiwassee crossings, Clayton warned that several thousand Federals were already at the river, on a front from Washington's Ferry downstream to the mouth of the Hiwassee at Blythe's Ferry. Where would they cross? Clayton speculated that in all probability they would cross at Washington to join Burnside, but he did not rule out

<hr />

2 *Official Records*, XXX, Pt. 4, pp. 523–25; Polk, *Polk*, II, 233–35.

the possibility that Rosecrans might attempt to cross as far south as Harrison's Landing.[3]

More news from Knoxville on the twenty-third confirmed the fears of a junction with Burnside. Buckner's scouts had learned that Burnside's main column would probably join Rosecrans' left wing somewhere in the vicinity of Kingston or Loudon. Buckner had also learned that prior to the actual union of the two columns, Rosecrans planned to cross the river at some point north of the mouth of the Hiwassee. Fearful that Buckner's small corps would be trapped at Knoxville, Bragg on the twenty-third ordered him to abandon Knoxville and fall back to the Tennessee River bridge at Loudon.[4]

But suddenly, by August 25, Rosecrans seemed to disappear. Practically all activity ceased. There were still scattered reports of a Federal crossing below the town. One told of a pontoon bridge being constructed at the mouth of Battle Creek near Jasper; another even warned that some Federals had already crossed at Bridgeport and Shellmound. These were regarded as questionable by Bragg and his corps leaders. They believed the reason for the delay in crossing was that Rosecrans was now waiting for Burnside to reach the East Tennessee Valley. So, during the last week in August, the Rebel high command considered that Rosecrans' main army was northeast of Chattanooga.

This view seemed to be sustained by information received between August 25 and 28. On the twenty-fifth, Buckner telegraphed a detailed report from one of his most reliable spies, who gave Burnside thirty-two thousand men. Twenty thousand of these were moving on Big Creek Gap, and conversations with Federal officers indicated that the move was in unison with one by Rosecrans, as Bragg had feared. Apprehensive of such a concentration, Bragg, on the twenty-seventh, even ordered Stewart's division to move ninety miles up the East Tennessee Railroad to reinforce Buckner at the Loudon bridge.[5]

But by the twenty-ninth, something appeared to have changed. Scouts had come to Bragg's headquarters the previous night with disturbing news. Rosecrans' headquarters was not northeast of Chattanooga, but instead was to the southwest, at Stevenson, Alabama. Moreover, the bulk of the Federal army was stretched from Jasper to Stevenson, Alabama. Then, on the twenty-ninth, one of Wheeler's scouts reported a brigade crossing

[3] *Official Records*, XXX, Pt. 4, pp. 532–33; Brent Diary, August 22, 1863, in Bragg Papers, Western Reserve; "Report of Reconnaissance of Fords and Ferries on Tennessee River between Harrison & Hiwassee River, Distance 21 miles" (MS in Bragg Papers, Western Reserve).

[4] *Official Records*, XX, Pt. 4, pp. 526, 531–35.

[5] *Ibid.*, pp. 554, 561; Polk to wife, August 25, 27, 1863, in Polk Papers, Sewanee; Brent Diary, August 24–28, 1863, in Bragg Papers, Western Reserve.

at Bridgeport, and other forces crossing at Shellmound. The next day, reports of Federal crossings at Wauhatchie, Trenton, Georgia, and Shellmound were received.

But the Rebel command continued to underestimate these signs. Bragg still placed Rosecrans northeast of Chattanooga. Polk also maintained that the real attack would be in that quarter. Harvey Hill was convinced that the main thrust would be against Harrison's Landing, where the bulk of his corps was posted. Too, on the twenty-ninth, one of Bragg's most highly regarded regimental commanders, Colonel Ben Hill, sent a concise opinion from his post at Thatcher's Ferry, about midway between Harrison's Landing and the mouth of the Hiwassee River. Hill was an old mountain man who knew the region between McMinnville and Chattanooga well. His scouts had scoured the foreboding country north of the Tennessee, with interesting results. Crittenden's corps was moving across Walden's Ridge toward Blythe's Ferry at the mouth of the Hiwassee. Crittenden's own headquarters was in the Sequatchie Valley at Dunlap. Behind moved the remainder of Rosecrans' army. Rosecrans himself was with Crittenden at Dunlap. Thomas' corps had been at Bridgeport but was now either already at Dunlap or moving on to cross north of the mouth of the Hiwassee at Washington Ferry. But what of the several days of shelling experienced in front of Chattanooga? Again Hill's scouts came up with a plausible sounding bit of intelligence. This was nothing more than a demonstration by a small part of McCook's corps. One of his divisions was still at Murfreesboro, while the remainder were scattered from Stevenson to Bridgeport.[6]

Armed with a report which seemed to explain the maneuvering southwest of Chattanooga, Bragg by August 30 was more convinced than ever of Rosecrans' location. Quickly he ordered Buckner's corps to withdraw to the south bank of the Hiwassee at Charleston. Forrest's cavalry was to fall back with Buckner, and then to picket the river from the mouth of the Hiwassee to Chattanooga. Hill's corps was aligned to guard the crossings between the Hiwassee and Chattanooga, supported by the division of W. H. T. Walker, a new arrival from Mississippi.[7]

Yet even Bragg's most reliable intelligence reports were more speculation than fact. Bragg, badly needing some reconnaissance, had no cavalry to cover his front. Though he had over eleven thousand cavalry present for duty on August 31, barely five hundred were protecting the river

6 "Memo furnished by Col. B. J. Hill, 35th Tenn. Regt., August 29, 1863" (MS in Bragg Papers, Western Reserve); Brent Diary, August 28-30, 1863, in *ibid.; Official Records*, XXX, Pt. 4, p. 564.
7 *Official Records*, XXX, Pt. 4, pp. 531–35, 556–57, 570; Brent Diary, August 30, 1863, in Bragg Papers, Western Reserve.

crossings below Chattanooga. Forrest's corps was held northeast of Chattanooga. Though Wheeler's corps allegedly had the responsibility of observing the river west of the town, little was accomplished here. Wheeler was totally out of position to watch the crossings. He did not order Martin's division north from Alexandria, Alabama, into Lookout Valley until August 27. Martin's force was so badly organized that he could bring only twelve hundred men. Bragg did not consider the division fit for field duty. The first of Martin's troops, five hundred men under Lieutenant Colonel T. H. Mauldin, did not reach the valley until August 29. Instead of having Mauldin guard the passes leading from the river through Sand Mountain, Wheeler sent him northward to watch the road from Kelly's Ferry into Chattanooga. Wharton's division was equally mishandled. He was not ordered to move north from Rome, Georgia, until August 29. Even then Wharton was ordered to report to Hill at Chattanooga. By September 1 Wharton had not arrived in Chattanooga, and the bulk of Martin's force was yet to reach Lookout Valley. In effect, Bragg had no reconnaissance on the river west of Chattanooga, and no troops guarded the Sand and Lookout Mountain passes at the army's rear. Not until September 2 did Wheeler begin to get his troopers under control. At last, Wharton was ordered to picket the gaps through Lookout Mountain, and Martin was sent to patrol the northern end of Lookout Valley. Even then, the Stevenson-Trenton front was almost overlooked.[8]

Wheeler's efforts were too little and too late. By the night of August 31 Bragg and his generals realized they had made a costly mistake. It was not one of Wheeler's men, but a resident of Stevenson who came to Bragg's headquarters with a disturbing story. A heavy column was crossing the Tennessee River near Stevenson at Caperton's Ferry, and was moving across Sand Mountain to Lookout and Will's valleys. By the next morning, Wheeler's own men had reported the same, with an additional bits of news—the force crossing in the Stevenson-Bridgeport area was reportedly Rosecrans' main army. By the morning of September 2, Bragg and his corps leaders now realized that the main Federal army was crossing on the far left.[9]

Again the ghosts of Harrodsburg and Perryville shadowed the high command. Bragg and his commanders appeared dazed, unsure, and unable to recoup the initiative. Bragg held a council of war on the second at his headquarters at La Fayette, Georgia. Neither he nor his corps and

8 *Brent Diary*, August 30–31, September 1, 1863, in Bragg Papers, Western Reserve; *Official Records*, XXX, Pt. 4, pp. 565, 580, Pt. 2, p. 520.

9 *Official Records*, XXX, Pt. 4, pp. 579, 583–85; Brent Diary, September 1–3, 1863, in Bragg Papers, Western Reserve; Robert Shook, "Timely Information to General Bragg," *Confederate Veteran*, XVIII (July, 1910), 39.

division commanders could do much but offer more intelligence reports indicating the advance was actually west of the town. Bragg did not even order Wheeler to block the Sand Mountain passes into Will's and Lookout valleys. Not until September 5 did Bragg even order Wheeler into the two valleys to drive in the enemy and to develop his strength and position.

In the days following the council, more uncertainty developed. On September 3 Harvey Hill sent over a vague note to Bragg stating his belief that the Federals would push northeast and try to take Chattanooga and then join with Burnside. But Hill offered no plan, begged his ignorance of the terrain, and apologized for his "too little confidence" in his own judgment. Bragg studied Hill's note on the fourth, but replied only with an equally vague plan of his own. By the fourth, Bragg's information was that Crittenden's corps was on the north bank opposite Chattanooga, while Thomas' and McCook's corps had crossed in the Bridgeport-Stevenson area. One of these two corps was in the Lookout Valley near Trenton, while the other was farther south, moving down Lookout Valley. Already this second corps had advanced to the head of Winston's Gap, the route via Alpine, Georgia, either to the manufacturing installations at Rome or to the Atlanta Railroad at Kingston. Though Bragg hurried W. H. T. Walker's division to Rome, little else was done. Bragg pondered ordering Hill to cross the Tennessee and strike Crittenden, but hesitated to commit himself. Instead, he asked Hill's advice concerning a countermeasure whereby the Federals themselves might be drawn across the river above Chattanooga. Unsure of exactly what to suggest, Bragg urged Hill to seek Cleburne's opinion and remarked that "we must do something and that soon." [10]

But on September 5 Bragg seemed ready to commit his troops. A spy had garnered some fresh reports from Rosecrans' headquarters which indicated a grand plan of operations between the two invading Federal columns. Burnside would hold Buckner's attention while Crittenden crossed above Chattanooga and trapped Buckner. Meanwhile, McCook's and Thomas' corps were to move across Lookout Mountain to Rome, to threaten Bragg's communications. Rome had been selected, according to the new information, because the Federals believed that Bragg's main army had been withdrawn there.

On the afternoon of the fifth, Bragg envisioned a new plan. Buckner was ordered back from the Hiwassee to the comparative safety of Ooltewah, only thirteen miles east of Chattanooga. He would face northward, with his flank on the west being guarded by Forrest, who would picket

10 *Official Records*, XXX, Pt. 4, p. 594; see also *ibid.*, p. 595; Brent Diary, September 2–4, 1863, in Bragg Papers, Western Reserve.

the Tennessee between Chattanooga and the mouth of the Hiwassee at
Blythe's Ferry. Meanwhile, on the fifth, the other two corps were concentrated at Chattanooga, and early the next morning were given orders
to march southward to Rome, where Bragg hoped to meet the Federals as
they debouched from Lookout Mountain north of Rome at Alpine.[11]

Yet, characteristically, Bragg again seemed unable to make the final
commitment. The intelligence received of the two Federal corps south of
the river was so sparse that Bragg considered abandoning his Chattanooga
base. The army was again sorely lacking in good cavalry intelligence.
Forrest's whole corps was being held on picket duty north of Chattanooga.
Wheeler's absence was less excusable—he simply disobeyed Bragg's orders.
On the fifth, he had been told to move from Lookout Mountain down
into Will's Valley and Lookout Valley. Wheeler was to drive in the enemy
pickets and learn both enemy strength and plans. The order was firm:
Wheeler must do this "even at the sacrifice of troops." [12] But Wheeler,
who was at Alpine, did not receive the order until the afternoon of the
sixth. Then Wheeler disobeyed the orders, a matter that Bragg's headquarters did not even learn of until the following day. Wheeler's explanations seemed feeble—he had so successfully fortified the Lookout passes
that he could not move through them, that he could learn no more in
the valley than he could atop Lookout, that his animals were weak and
the Federal pickets in the valley were in strong positions.[13]

Therefore, by nightfall of the sixth, Bragg wavered in his decision to
abandon Chattanooga. Was the reported movement in Lookout Valley a
ruse to force the abandonment of Chattanooga and facilitate a Rosecrans-
Burnside junction? That same day Buckner's scouts had warned that
Burnside already was moving slowly down the East Tennessee Valley
toward the Hiwassee. Too, heavy demonstrations were being made against
the Confederate outposts on the northern tip of Lookout Mountain at
Chattanooga by forces in the valley to the west. Unable to make the commitment, Bragg by 8 P.M. had directed a suspension of his orders to march
to Rome, and the army still waited at Chattanooga.

On September 7 Bragg wavered again. No one seemed to agree on
whether the Federal threat west of Lookout Mountain was Rosecrans'
main army. Wheeler's explanation for not making the ordered scout was
received, as well as the cavalryman's estimate that the enemy was "in
force" west of Lookout. But Bragg had sent one of his staff members,
Major Pollock Lee, to Alpine. Lee reported a different story; he doubted

11 *Official Records*, XXX, Pt. 4, pp. 599–600, 610–11; Brent Diary, September 5, 1863,
in Bragg Papers, Western Reserve.
12 *Official Records*, XXX, Pt. 4, p. 602.
13 *Ibid.*, pp. 614–15.

that the enemy was in force west of the mountains. Meanwhile, in the late morning the Federals opened strong artillery fire again on Chattanooga from the north bank, while another force estimated at eight regiments skirmished against the northern tip of Lookout.[14]

What was to be done? Both Polk and Hill had advised the cessation of the withdrawal. Like Bragg, they were confused as to Rosecrans' whereabouts. Should Bragg abandon the town on the sparse intelligence he had received? Or should he leave Buckner's corps to hold the town while the remainder of the army marched to Rome? Was Rosecrans actually flanking Bragg, or was the move a trick to force the abandonment of Bragg's base and the possible ensnarement of Buckner's men?

By the afternoon of September 7 Bragg revised his plans once more. During the late afternoon the threat on the Rome flank appeared more definite. At nightfall the decision was made; Bragg would abandon Chattanooga, unite with Buckner's corps, and retreat to Rome where he expected to meet Rosecrans. Hill's corps was ordered to take the direct road from Chattanooga, via Rossville and La Fayette, which ran east and parallel of Pigeon Mountain. Buckner's corps and a new makeshift reserve corps under W. H. T. Walker would follow a parallel road westward via Ringgold, which joined the main road north of La Fayette. By nightfall Hill's corps took up the march over roads so dusty that the teamsters could not see to drive, while the troops trudged through the intolerable dust. Early on the eighth, with Bragg and his staff in the van, Polk's corps made the hot, dusty march. By night Hill had already reached La Fayette, twenty-two miles south of Chattanooga, while Polk encamped along Chickamauga Creek in Crawfish Valley, some ten miles north. Buckner and Walker still trailed behind on the alternate Ringgold Road. Wheeler's two divisions, those of Will Martin and John Wharton, picketed the passes in Lookout Mountain from directly south of Chattanooga all the way to Gadsden, Alabama, while Forrest's corps brought up the rear of Buckner's column in the vicinity of Dalton, Georgia.[15]

There are some peculiar bits of mythology regarding Bragg's retreat from Chattanooga. Beginning with Colonel Archer Anderson's 1881 address at a reunion of the Army of Northern Virginia, the legend arose that when he left Chattanooga, Bragg knew well the badly divided condition of the Federals, and failed to capitalize upon it. The assumption was that Bragg knew that Crittenden's corps was on the north bank, that Thomas' corps was twenty miles southward moving across Lookout Moun-

14 Brent Diary, September 6–7, in Bragg Papers, Western Reserve.
15 *Ibid.*, September 7, 1863; "Richmond Notes," September 6–7, 1863, in Polk Papers, Sewanee.

tain toward La Fayette, and that McCook's corps was still twenty miles farther south en route to Rome via Alpine.[16]

Much of this seems to be erroneous. As late as the night of September 8, the army's high command seemed as confused as ever regarding Rosecrans' location. Bragg's giving up of his base had been initiated under the assumption that the Federals were divided into only two groups: Crittenden's corps opposite Chattanooga, and the other two corps en route to Rome from the Trenton-Bridgeport area.

In fact, instead of moving to entrap Rosecrans, it appeared by late on September 8 that Bragg himself might be on the verge of being trapped on the road from La Fayette to Chattanooga. Late on the eighth and throughout the morning of September 9, confusing and disturbing scout reports were received. Early on the eighth, Colonel Will Martin warned Wheeler that his pickets on Lookout Mountain had been driven from Cooper's Gap and Stevens' Gap down across McLemore's Cove and onto the top of Pigeon Mountain. During the night of the eighth, Bragg belatedly received Martin's note. Other reports identified the threat as being Thomas' whole corps moving through Cooper's Gap into the cove. Still others indicated a force of between four and eight thousand men was in the cove by the morning of September 9.[17]

Thus, on September 9, Bragg was faced with revising his plans to meet Rosecrans at Rome. McLemore's Cove lay only five miles across Pigeon Mountain from La Fayette. Three roads led to La Fayette, via Blue Bird, Dug, and Catlett's gaps. Hill was now placed in danger east of the mountain. Though Wheeler had been told to obstruct the gaps, Martin had warned that if the enemy attacked in force, they could not be held.

Through the day Bragg pondered what to do. Until the evening the sketchy reports from the force in McLemore's Cove gave little information. Frustrated, Bragg called a halt to the march on Rome until he received more news. Meanwhile, at his headquarters, heavy firing could be heard from Chattanooga, and by noon Bragg learned that his rear guard had been forced out. This increased the danger of encirclement. With Crittenden on the road from Chattanooga only twelve miles to the north, Bragg was in danger of being trapped on the La Fayette Road. The cavalry seemed scattered. Pegram's division of Forrest's corps was in flight from Chattanooga. The remainder of Forrest's corps was scattered from near Dalton to La Fayette. Wharton's division was watching the lower passes in Lookout Mountain on a long front from Gadsden, Alabama, to

16 For illustrations of this approach, see Archer Anderson, "Campaign and Battle of Chickamauga," *SHSP*, IX (1881), 398; Horn, *Army of Tennessee*, 249–50.

17 Brent Diary, September 8–9, 1863, in Bragg Papers, Western Reserve; *Official Records*, XXX, Pt. 2, pp. 522–23.

Rome, Georgia. Wheeler was far south near Alpine, while Martin's division was immobilized behind the fortifications on Pigeon Mountain. With accuracy, one of Polk's aides remarked that as far as the location of Rosecrans was concerned, "we are in utter darkness." [18]

Not until about midnight of September 9, did Bragg begin to get a better understanding of the situation. Wharton's scouts confirmed that McCook's corps was in Will's Valley, evidently still moving toward Rome. Other intelligence indicated that Thomas' corps was probably en route to McLemore's Cove via Stevens' and Cooper's gaps. Five thousand Federals were at Stevens' gap on the west side of the cove, evidently preparing to cross the small valley and strike toward La Fayette through Dug Gap. Another force of undetermined size was slightly to the north at Cooper's Gap. Crittenden appeared to be moving slowly southward from Chattanooga on the La Fayette Road.[19]

Bragg later would be castigated for his handling of the force reported in McLemore's Cove. But his critics would have facts that he did not have on the night of September 9. Even when he ordered the move, Bragg did not know for certain that Thomas was there and that McCook was en route to Alpine. Some reports were contradictory, pinpointing Thomas both in the cove and also as turning up Chattanooga Creek to join Crittenden. With two-thirds of his cavalry absent between September 8 and 10, Bragg was sorely in need of reconnaissance.

He struck blindly on the night of September 9. He believed that the Federals in McLemore's Cove were preparing to strike La Fayette. To prevent this, he determined to interpose a force in the cove at the critical Davis' crossroads, where the road from Stevens' Gap to Dug Gap crossed the north-south road through the cove. That night General Thomas Hindman was called to Bragg's headquarters at Lee and Gordon's Mill. There, a plan was outlined to entrap Thomas. Hindman would take his division through Worthen's Gap on Pigeon Mountain into the northern end of the cove, then turn south down the cove until he reached Davis' crossroads. Meanwhile, Cleburne's division of Hill's corps would cross Pigeon Mountain at Dug Gap and join Hindman at the crossroads. Hindman was to take command of both divisions, and then attack the enemy believed to be at the base of Lookout Mountain at Stevens' Gap. Later that night Hindman's instructions were repeated in writing, and a copy of them was sent to Hill. Hill was ordered to either send Cleburne or to take personal charge of the column.

18 "Richmond Notes," September 9, 1863, in Polk Papers, Sewanee.
19 *Ibid.*, September 8–9; Falconer to Hindman, September 9—11:45 P.M., 1863, in Thomas C. Hindman Papers, National Archives; *Official Records*, XXX, Pt. 4, p. 620; Brent Diary, September 8–9, 1863, in Bragg Papers, Western Reserve.

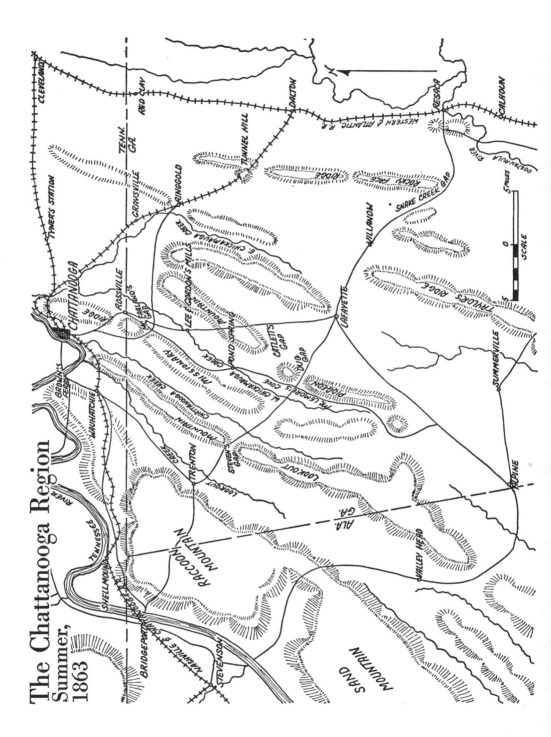

The Chattanooga Region
Summer, 1863

Though apparently fairly well outlined, the orders to Hindman and Hill promised only trouble. Bragg was probably expecting too much from his new command organization, placing them in a situation where they were to use their own initiative. This was significant because Bragg's tendency to blame subordinates for failures had already created a reluctance in the high command to take initiative without specific instructions from the commanding general. Both Hindman's and Hill's orders contained minute but important omissions by which a timid officer could excuse his lack of initiative. No mention was made in Hindman's orders as to whether he was to open communication with Hill's column prior to reaching the crossroads, though Hindman's verbal instructions did mention this. No instructions were given Hindman as to how he would deal with the force reported on his flank and to his rear at Cooper's Gap. Hill's orders also contained such minor omissions. He was not given a specific hour to start for the crossroads, but merely told to join Hindman in the morning. Also, he was vaguely told that "if unforeseen circumstances" prevented his move, he should notify Hindman.[20]

From the beginning the plan faltered. Hindman was in motion by about 1 A.M. of the tenth, and by daylight had covered nine of the thirteen miles to Davis' crossroads. But at 6 A.M., within four miles of his destination, he stalled. He had heard that the Pigeon Mountain gaps were blockaded, and he worried lest Hill could not reach him. His fears were intensified because he had heard nothing from Hill. Scouts had warned him that a Federal division was in the vicinity of Davis' crossroads, and another division was allegedly between the crossroads and Stevens' Gap. Though Hindman admitted these were rumors, he determined to move no farther until he learned that Hill was in motion. He notified both Hill and Bragg, and waited for orders.[21]

Hill was having his own problems. The courier bearing Bragg's orders had difficulty in finding him. Hill did not receive a copy of the orders until five hours later, at 4:30 A.M. As soon as he read them, he dispatched a list of reasons to Bragg explaining why they could not be obeyed. Cleburne had been ill all the previous day, and a third of his division was posted along Pigeon Mountain at the blockaded gaps. It would require hours to reopen Dug Gap to allow the troops to march into the cove. Again, delay was a factor. Though his reply to Bragg was sent about

---

20 Falconer to Hindman, September 9—11:45 P.M., Mackall to Hindman, September 9—10 P.M., in Hindman Papers, National Archives; Mackall to Hill, September 9—11:45 P.M., in Hill Papers, NCA; Bragg's official report of Chickamauga campaign (MS in Claiborne Papers, UNC); *Official Records*, XXX, Pt. 2, p. 292.

21 Hindman to Hill, September 10—6 A.M., 1863, Hindman to Mackall, September 10—6:30 A.M., 1863, in Hindman Papers, National Archives.

4:30 A.M., Bragg did not receive it until 8:00 A.M. In addition, Hill did not bother to notify Hindman of the delay until almost noon.[22]

Bragg accepted Hill's explanation and ordered Buckner's corps to prepare to make the move. About 8 A.M., on September 10, Buckner was ordered to march via Hindman's old route to Davis' crossroads, and to attack the enemy. By 5 P.M. of that day, Buckner had arrived at Hindman's headquarters at Morgan's, some four miles north of Davis' crossroads.[23]

Even while Buckner's men toiled over Pigeon Mountain, the command problem was becoming more complex. During the mid-afternoon, Hindman showed a remarkable disinterest in taking the initiative. In fact, he seemed more interested in the possibilities of retreat. He had deliberately halted his division at Morgan's so that he could be sure of maintaining a hold on a line of retreat via Catlett's Gap; the road to the gap intersected the valley road at Morgan's. About 5 P.M., when Buckner came up, Hindman had him bivouac his men a mile farther north, so that the road through Worthen's Gap could also be held. Then, in the late afternoon, he received dispatches from Hill which were forwarded through Bragg's headquarters. Hill had sent a note shortly after noon reporting that the Federals had already crossed McLemore's Cove and were skirmishing at Dug Gap. About an hour later, Hill sent a second note to Hindman. He urged Hindman to advance to the rear of Dug Gap and attack the enemy, as Cleburne was being moved toward the gap from the other direction.

Again the difficulties of the new command system thwarted success. Although he knew Hindman was untried in the army and knew nothing of the terrain, Bragg attached no specific orders to this new information. Instead, the notes were forwarded to Hindman for his "information and guidance." As he later explained, Hindman interpreted this merely as a suggestion and not an order. Why Bragg did not order him to hurry to the crossroads and entrap the Federals between his own and Cleburne's column approaching Dug Gap is not certain. Hindman showed no interest in the plan, though his scouts had already reported the Federals as being between Dug Gap and the crossroads.[24]

Bragg's reluctance to send Hindman more direct orders was due to his own uncertainty as to the relative strength and positions of the Federals

22 Hill to Mackall, September 10—4:25 A.M., 1863, Hill to Hindman, September 10—11 A.M., Brent to Hindman, September 10—8 A.M., in *ibid.*

23 *Official Records*, XXX, Pt. 2, p. 293; Brent to Hindman, September 10—10 A.M., 1863, in Hindman Papers, National Archives; Bragg's Chickamauga report, in Claiborne Papers, UNC.

24 S. A. M. Wood to Captain Buck, September 10, 1863, Hill to Mackall, September 10—1:30 P.M., 1863, in Hindman Papers, National Archives.

in McLemore's Cove and southward toward Alpine. By night he still did not know where these forces were, but finally did understand where Crittenden was. About half of Crittenden's corps was believed advancing on La Fayette on the direct road from Chattanooga via Lee and Gordon's Mill. The other half was moving through Ringgold and down the Crawfish Springs Road. This road intersected the La Fayette Road at Rock Spring Church, several miles south of Lee and Gordon's Mill. The danger here was obvious. With Hindman gone, Polk had only one division, Cheatham's, at the mill. Now Cheatham was in danger of being trapped between the two prongs of Crittenden's corps. Accordingly, at 7:30 P.M. on September 10, Bragg ordered Cheatham and the corps train back to Anderson's, a few miles north of Rock Springs Church. Here Polk could control both approaches to the intersection at Rock Springs Church, and could also guard Hindman's line of retreat from the cove, via Worthen's Gap to Anderson's.

Still, Bragg was confused as to the location of Thomas' and McCook's corps. Throughout September 10 and even the following day, Wheeler's scouts brought very confusing intelligence. It seemed to indicate that the bulk of the Federal column was not in McLemore's Cove but, instead, was moving northward toward La Fayette from the Alpine vicinity. By the night of September 10 the Federal column supposedly had penetrated to within seven miles of La Fayette. From McLemore's Cove. Hindman that day argued that the Union force in the cove was no more than a ruse designed to draw Bragg's attention from the south. Hill, on September 10, expressed this same belief, and Bragg himself seemed convinced. On the night of the tenth, after ordering Polk to pull Cheatham back to Anderson's, Bragg and his staff hurriedly moved to La Fayette, where he thought the danger lay.[25]

Though Bragg was not yet certain that Thomas' entire corps was moving through McLemore's Cove, he was determined to entrap the portion that was there. Therefore, at 6 P.M. that night, he had already sent Hindman a hasty note ordering him to finish the work in the cove "as rapidly as possible." An hour and a half later, he repeated his admonition to hurry. Hindman was assured that the enemy was divided and that he should move to crush the enemy in the cove. Yet Bragg again committed his oft-repeated sin of allowing discretion to officers of unknown caliber. Though Hindman that day had showed an obvious lack of enthusiasm in pressing the attack, Bragg still did not directly order

25 Brent to Wheeler, September 10—10:30 A.M., 1863, in Wheeler Papers, Alabama; Brent Diary, September 10, 1863, in Bragg Papers, Western Reserve; "Richmond Notes," September 10, 1863, in Polk Papers, Sewanee.

him to go to the Davis' crossroads or order an attack at a specified time or place.[26]

Hindman took advantage of this looseness of orders. He had received both dispatches by 8 P.M. that night. After reading them, he called a conference with Buckner and his brigade commanders. It was reminiscent of the Bardstown and Perryville conferences, where Bragg's generals had rebelled against orders. Hindman had assembled a mass of reasons why he should not march the last four miles to Davis' crossroads. Another Union column of some unknown size was at Stevens' Gap. Crittenden might cut his line of retreat through Worthen's Gap. He feared that he would be isolated in the cove because Dug and Catlett's gaps were blockaded.

Again Bragg's wishes were ignored by his subordinates. The council voted to disobey his orders until more information was received. Instead, Hindman dispatched a series of extremely confusing letters to Bragg. While the council was still meeting, Hindman, at 9 P.M., wrote Bragg promising to attack promptly at daylight, unless something unforeseen developed. The remainder of the note was a listing of developments that would probably make an attack impossible. Some were simply contradictory. Hindman argued that a Federal column was at Davis' crossroads; yet in a note sent to Hill that same night, of which Bragg received a copy, he said nothing of this and suggested that Hill meet him at the crossroads. There were other curious statements. Hindman argued that the force in the cove was a skeleton column, masking the real approach from the south. Yet in the same paragraph, he voiced the fear that if he moved toward Dug Gap, he would be attacked by a strong force at Stevens' Gap.[27]

An hour later, about 10 P.M., Hindman changed his mind. He sent a second note to Bragg. He informed him of the council's decision not to attack at daylight. Now Hindman had established his own criteria for the move. He had written a letter to Hill, a copy of which was dispatched with Bragg's letter to the commanding general. Hindman asked Hill several questions. The answers to these questions, he informed Bragg, would influence his further activities. If Hill could not answer them favorably, Hindman suggested that they call off the whole effort and attack Crittenden instead. The letter to Hill was confusing. Hindman again mentioned the threat from Stevens' Gap. Then he suggested that Hill might attack the enemy at Dug Gap while Hindman attacked them at

26 Falconer to Hindman, September 10—6 P.M., September 10—7:30 P.M., 1863, in Hindman Papers, National Archives.

27 Hindman to Brent, September 10—9:10 P.M., 1863, in *ibid.* This letter is cited in the *Official Records*, XXX, Pt. 2, p. 301, as having been written at 7 P.M. This is erroneous. Hindman asserted that he wrote it at 9:10 P.M.; see *Official Records*, XXX, Pt. 2, p. 294.

the rear. Better yet, could not Hill cut his way through the force confronting him at Dug Gap and join Hindman at Davis' crossroads? Hindman favored this latter plan though he did not explain how it would accomplish any ensnarement of the Federals. Nor did Hindman explain
what he and Buckner would be doing while Hill was doing all of the
fighting.[28]

During the night of the tenth, the command confusion intensified.
Bragg reached La Fayette shortly before midnight. Despite the contradictory reports of the location of McCook's and Thomas' corps sent by
Wheeler, Bragg now seemed more certain that the two Federal corps were
not both moving northward from Alpine. He had received a fresh report
that evening from one of Wheeler's division commanders, Will Martin.
Martin seemed to make more sense than some others. He assured Bragg
that Thomas and McCook were divided and that already as many as
eleven thousand of Thomas' men were in McLemore's Cove.[29]

Scarcely had he reached La Fayette with this information when Bragg
confronted Hindman's emissary, Major James Nocquet. Hindman had
sent Nocquet there to lobby for a suspension of the cove operations and
to contend that the Yankee force in the cove was a ruse covering the real
concentration of Thomas and McCook at Bragg's rear at Alpine. Hindman could not have picked a worse messenger. Nocquet and Bragg were
already on bad terms. The Frenchman may have been angry over his
removal in November of 1862 as Bragg's chief engineer, a post he held for
only one month. He had been openly abusive of Bragg, of the Rebel war
effort, and of democracy in general. After his brief stint as Bragg's chief
engineer, he had been assigned to Buckner's staff as chief engineer, and
thus had gone into McLemore's Cove with Buckner. Since coming to the
western Confederacy, Nocquet had spent most of his time in the construction of defensive works at Chattanooga, Bridgeport, and elsewhere,
and seemed unusually ignorant of overall topography. Furthermore, he
could barely speak English.

Thus a curious meeting occurred about midnight of the tenth at Hill's
headquarters. There Bragg, Hill, and several line and staff officers listened
to Nocquet's somewhat incoherent version of why the attack in the cove
should be called off. Hindman's key point, relayed by Nocquet, hinged
on the argument that the Federal force in the cove amounted to little but
a trick to mask the genuine operations to the south. Bragg then called in
Will Martin. Martin argued that there was nothing to what Nocquet said.
Instead, he said, Thomas was definitely moving toward the cove and was

<hr />

[28] Hindman to Hill, September 10—8 P.M., 1863, Hindman to Brent, September
10—10:15 P.M., 1863, in Hindman Papers, National Archives.

[29] Martin to Bragg, undated, 1867, in *SHSP*, XI (1883), 203–204.

not moving northward from Alpine with McCook. Bragg grew irritated with the Frenchman, and ordered him to report only what he knew as fact. Nocquet backed down quickly, and admitted that Hindman's information was based only on hearsay and that it could not be termed reliable. Bragg snapped back that this amounted to nothing. No orders would be changed. Instead, Bragg hurried off a courier to Hindman with positive orders. Hindman was to attack as soon as he could see daylight on the eleventh. He was to push toward Dug Gap, where Hill would attack as soon as he heard Hindman's guns. Nocquet was ordered to return to Hindman with verbal instructions as well. Hindman was not to change his plans but was to carry out those orders he had received from Bragg.[30]

Exactly what Nocquet told Hindman on his return is uncertain. Though at 4:00 A.M. he had received Bragg's midnight order directing a daylight attack, Hindman chose to disregard it until he heard from the Frenchman. Finally, about 6:30, well after daylight, Nocquet appeared in the cove. Again, Bragg's giving leeway to subordinates was to cause trouble. Instead of sending written orders with Nocquet, Bragg's instructions had been verbal. This factor gave Hindman an outlet. He maintained that the orders given Nocquet by Bragg were for Hindman to use his own discretion. According to Hindman's account, Bragg told Nocquet to tell him to execute his own plans, a statement which Hindman boasted "conceded to me the discretion . . . ." [31]

Though Hindman later used this verbal order as an excuse for his failure to attack on the eleventh, it is doubtful if such discretion was ever given. Bragg denied it, and none of the witnesses at the midnight council in La Fayette recalled such discretion being given. Martin remembered Bragg's emphasizing to Nocquet that Hindman must carry out the orders he had received. One of Bragg's staff officers, Colonel David Urquhart, recalled Bragg's remarking that Hindman was to attack even if he lost his command in so doing. For other reasons, Hindman's explanation is dubious. If he genuinely believed on the eleventh that he possessed the discretion he claimed for himself, Hindman would not have moved forward at all, but would have retreated, since he was completely opposed to the operation. Instead, less than thirty minutes after Nocquet's return, Hind-

---

30 *Ibid.;* Bragg to Sykes, February 8, 1873, in Claiborne Papers, UNC; Brent to Hindman, September 10—12 P.M., 1863, in Hindman Papers, National Archives; James Nocquet, Military Records Jacket, Record Group 109, National Archives; Austin, *The Blue and the Gray,* 49; Fitzgerald Ross, *Cities and Camps of the Confederate States,* ed. Richard B. Harwell (Urbana, 1958), 123; Statement of Urquhart, November 21, 1863, in Bragg Papers, Western Reserve; Bragg's Chickamauga report, in Claiborne Papers, UNC.
31 *Official Records,* XXX, Pt. 2, p. 297.

man ordered his and Buckner's men to move forward toward Davis' crossroads. Hindman's later use of the discretionary orders to Nocquet was particularly convenient. His explanation was not forwarded to Bragg until the last week in October. Shortly after the battle of Chickamauga, Nocquet disappeared. He evidently left with $150,000 in funds earmarked for bridge construction. Dressed in civilian clothing, he disappeared through the enemy lines into Tennessee. He was later labeled a deserter.[32]

Regardless of what Nocquet told Hindman, the latter knew on the morning of the eleventh that the trap for the Federals had been set. Numerous scouting parties were sent out by both Hindman and Buckner toward Stevens' Gap, Davis' crossroads, and Dug Gap. The reports indicated that since the night of the tenth, Federals had been constantly marching through the crossroads toward Dug Gap. By the morning of the eleventh, Hindman knew that they were definitely between the crossroads and the gap. All that was needed was for him to seize the crossroads and bottle them up between Hill and his own column.

But Hindman never sprang the trap. His conduct on the morning of the eleventh indicated instead that he wished to avoid contact. From his headquarters at Morgan's, Hindman had only a four-mile march to Davis' crossroads. Yet his approach to the crossroads was one of the war's slowest marches. By 11 A.M., almost seven hours after receiving Bragg's order to attack at daylight, Hindman had covered only a mile and a half. He seemed fearful of what he would find there. Repeatedly he sent out more scouts, and set Buckner's engineers to work clearing a line of retreat through Catlett's Gap. A small contingent of Federal cavalry pickets encountered between Morgan's and the crossroads seemed to paralyze him.

By the early afternoon Hindman was only some two miles from the crossroads. A fresh report from Bragg's headquarters placed the number of Federals between the gap and the crossroads at between twelve thousand and fifteen thousand, far more than the original estimate of between four thousand and five thousand. Hindman and Buckner had between fifteen thousand and twenty thousand troops, while at Dug Gap, Cleburne, who was supported by Walker's reserve corps, and Breckinridge's division, had some twenty thousand. Yet nothing was done.

Instead, Hindman called another council of officers during the late afternoon, which resulted in a vote to retreat through Catlett's Gap. Finally, as he was preparing to retire, Hindman learned from scouts that

32 *Ibid.*, pp. 295–97, 351; Gilmer to Cooper, October 7, 1864, in Nocquet Military Records Jacket, National Archives; Urquhart statement, November 21, 1863, in Bragg Papers, Western Reserve; Bragg's Chickamauga report, in Clairborne Papers, UNC; Buckner to Hindman, September 16, 1863, in Buckner Papers, Huntington; Martin to Bragg, undated, 1867, in *SHSP*, XI, 206.

the enemy was in retreat across the cove toward Stevens' Gap. Only then, about 5 P.M., did he order an advance, almost thirteen hours after receiving Bragg's original order. While Buckner unsuccessfully pursued the enemy toward Stevens' Gap, Hindman rode to Davis' crossroads, where he encountered an enraged Bragg.[33]

The stormy meeting at the crossroads, at which Bragg lashed out at Hindman for the failures of the day, was the culmination of a frustrating day for the commanding general. Shortly after the midnight meeting with Nocquet, Bragg had ordered Cleburne to clear the obstructions from Dug Gap and to be ready to attack when he heard Hindman's guns open at daylight. Through the night Cleburne's men toiled to clear the obstructions not only at Dug Gap but also at Catlett's Gap. By daylight Cleburne was ready to attack. He even established a courier line northward along Pigeon Mountain to Catlett's Gap, to inform him if they heard Hindman's guns open.

But no guns were heard. Bragg and Hill joined Cleburne at Dug Gap about daylight. Through the day Bragg angrily paced back and forth. Still, not until about an hour before sunset did Cleburne hear guns in the valley. An immediate advance found not an enemy in sight. To Bragg's chagrin, the enemy had retreated. The guns heard early that evening were not Hindman's attack, but were those of his pursuit of the enemy to Stevens' Gap. When Bragg met Hindman at the crossroads about 6 P.M., the enemy had vanished.[34]

What had gone wrong? Though Bragg later completely blamed Hindman, the day's failures went much deeper than that officer's overcautious attitude in the cove. Without giving positive orders, Bragg had again entrusted an important task to a subordinate whose judgment was questionable. The dispatches Bragg sent on the eleventh did give wide discretion to Hindman and did not order an attack. A note sent at 11 A.M. did not even mention the need to attack. Instead, Bragg discussed a retreat from the cove, and gave Hindman the authority to retreat via Catlett's Gap if he found the enemy in such force to make an attack imprudent. Later, Bragg sent a staff officer to discuss again the subject of retreat via Catlett's Gap. In the early afternoon, another dispatch from Bragg did not mention an attack. Bragg merely estimated the Federal strength in front of Dug Gap as between twelve thousand and fifteen

33 *Official Records*, XXX, Pt. 2, pp. 296–97; Buckner to Hindman, September 16, 1863, in Buckner Papers, Huntington; Buckner to Hindman, September 10—10 A.M., 1863, in Hindman Papers, National Archives; Gale to wife, September 21, 1863, in Gale-Polk Papers, UNC.

34 Buck, *Cleburne and His Command*, 38–41; Sykes, "Cursory Sketch of General Bragg's Campaigns," SHSP, XI, 492–93; Bragg's Chickamauga Report, in Claiborne Papers, UNC.

thousand men, warned that Crittenden was moving south to La Fayette, and urged Hindman to tell him his plans.

In short, Bragg himself seemed unwilling to make the final commitment to an attack in McLemore's Cove. Although Hindman was only slightly over an hour's ride from Dug Gap, Bragg made no disposition to direct the attack personally. And although a line of couriers had been established that morning between Bragg and Hindman, communication between them had been sparse. At Dug Gap, Bragg even seemed unsure about whether to commit Cleburne's troops. Once, about midday of the eleventh, he had ordered Cleburne to advance without waiting to hear Hindman's guns, but then countermanded the orders.[35]

Bragg's own hesitation probably was caused by his uncertainty as to Rosecrans' location. As late as the night of the eleventh, Bragg still remained unsure of exactly where McCook and Thomas were. Throughout the eleventh, conflicting reports were received. Bragg seemed haunted by the idea that Hindman and Hill might have been right in their assertions on the tenth that the main body of Thomas' corps was massing south of La Fayette with McCook. If so, a main thrust through McLemore's Cove might not trap the enemy, but instead trap Bragg. This danger seemed very real on the eleventh. Hill repeatedly sent Bragg warnings which he had received of a heavy force approaching from the south. Bragg's cavalry could offer little help in solving the mystery. Forrest's entire corps was committed on the tenth and eleventh to slowing Crittenden. Martin's division of Wheeler's corps was sent by Bragg, on the eleventh, to reinforce Hindman in McLemore's Cove. This left only a single division, that of Wharton, to obtain information on the long front from Cooper's Gap southward to Alpine. Wharton's division was so depleted from picket and detail duty that Wheeler had only seven regiments accessible. With these, Wheeler, on the tenth and eleventh, had sent confusing dispatches. He had warned that McCook was moving on La Fayette, then placed him as moving on Rome, and finally, by the eleventh, placed McCook at Summerville, probably readying to move northward. By the night of September 11, Wheeler all but admitted that he had not the slightest idea what McCook was doing. He was not alone. Intelligence received from the unsuccessful foray in the cove on the evening of the eleventh indicated only two of Thomas' brigades had actually been in the cove. Where were

35 Mackall to Hindman, September 11, 1863, Mackall to Hindman, September 11—"half past," 1863, in Hindman Papers, National Archives; Buck, *Cleburne and His Command,* 140–41; *Official Records,* XXX, Pt. 2, p. 296; Bragg's Chickamauga report, in Claiborne Papers, UNC.

Thomas and McCook? Neither Bragg nor his generals seemed to know.[36]

When he returned to La Fayette on the night of the eleventh, the only thing Bragg was sure of was that Crittenden was isolated from Rosecrans' other two corps. Crittenden had continued to advance toward La Fayette on both the main road from Chattanooga via Lee and Gordon's Mills and the Pea Vine Road. Because of the threat of these columns converging at the road junction at Rock Springs Church, Bragg, on the night of the tenth, had withdrawn Cheatham's division to Anderson's crossroads. Here Cheatham commanded both the Rock Spring intersection and a cross-country road which connected the road via Lee and Gordon's Mill with the Pea Vine Road. But late on the tenth and on the eleventh, when Bragg's intelligence indicated a heavy build-up south of La Fayette, he pulled Cheatham back further to La Fayette. Early on the eleventh, Polk was ordered to march with Cheatham to join the remainder of the army there. Though Bragg may have seen this as a necessary step for keeping his army concentrated against any threat from the south, actually it was both unnecessary and unwise. Since La Fayette was only eight miles south of the Rock Spring Church intersection, Bragg would have done well to keep Cheatham at the intersection to prevent a junction of Crittenden's two columns. Instead, Cheatham was withdrawn, and Forrest's corps was given the task of slowing Crittenden.[37]

But Forrest could not hold back Crittenden, whose forces loomed up on several fronts. By the early afternoon of September 11, while Bragg waited at Dug Gap for Hindman's attack, a division of Crittenden's corps reached Lee and Gordon's Mill. General Frank Armstrong tried to hold them on the north bank of the Chickamauga but by 3 A.M. was forced to retreat. Matters were no better on the Pea Vine Road. Pegram's division, too, was steadily driven from Ringgold back toward Rock Spring Church.[38]

Bragg sensed a second opportunity to strike while Rosecrans was divided. Envisioning a strike against Crittenden, Bragg, at 3 A.M. of the twelfth, ordered Polk to march to Rock Spring Church with Cheatham's division. Later in the early afternoon Hindman's division and Walker's reserve corps were ordered to make the eight-mile march. During the day the plan developed further. A dispatch from Pegram on the Pea Vine Road indicated that one of Crittenden's divisions perhaps had over-

36 Brent Diary, September 10–11, 1863, in Bragg Papers, Western Reserve; "Richmond Notes," September 10–11, 1863, in Polk Papers, Sewanee; Martin to Bragg, undated, 1867, in *SHSP*, XI, 204; *Official Records*, XXX, Pt. 4, p. 636.

37 Bragg's Chickamauga report, in Claiborne Papers, UNC; "Richmond Notes," September 11, 1863, in Polk Papers, Sewanee; Polk, *Polk*, II, 239–40.

38 Henry, *Forrest*, 178–79; "Richmond Notes," September 11, 1863, in Polk Papers, Sewanee; *Official Records*, XXX, Pt. 2, p. 530.

stepped itself. The division was reported to have advanced to Pea Vine Church, on the Graysville Road, only two miles from Rock Spring Church. Excited at the prospect of bagging a single division with three of his own, Bragg, at 6 P.M. on September 12, enclosed Pegram's note and suggested that Polk would do well to attack that lone division on the Pea Vine-Graysville Road. Then, as if he remembered the debacle of the previous two days, Bragg at 8 P.M., dispatched specific orders to Polk. He was to attack that contingent on the Pea Vine Road at daylight on the thirteenth.[39]

But command confusion plagued this second attempt to strike the Federals while they were scattered. Though Polk received the orders before daylight, and Cheatham's men began marching at 7:00 A.M., the Bishop did not arrive at Rock Spring Church until after dark. Others were equally tardy. Hindman was ordered to join Cheatham at 1:30 P.M. But his orders were again discretionary in that he was to move only when his troops were "refreshed." Despite prodding by both Bragg and Polk, Hindman was so slow that he did not show up at Polk's headquarters at Rock Spring Church until 4:30 A.M. of the thirteenth, only an hour before the ordered attack. Walker's small reserve corps, ordered during the afternoon to join Polk, did arrive about 8:00 P.M. of the twelfth.

Quickly, other things went wrong. After he arrived at Rock Spring Church, Polk reconnoitered the position and disliked what he found. His intelligence pinpointed a Federal division on each of the three roads converging at the church. Van Cleve's division was allegedly on the Lee and Gordon's Mill Road, within two miles of the church; Palmer's division was on the Pea Vine Road within two miles of Polk, and Wood's division on the Ringgold Road, the same distance away. Though Bragg had ordered a daylight attack on the contingent on the Pea Vine Road, Polk stalled. He did not think he had enough men to make the attack, and so wrote Bragg asking for reinforcements. Also, Polk seemed to cast aside Bragg's orders. He told his commander that he could not possibly attack at daylight, and would attack later if he were not first attacked. Not only did Polk notify Bragg he would not obey orders, but the Bishop, though penning the note at 8:00 P.M., did not send it by courier from his headquarters until 10:25 P.M. Only the swift thirty-five-minute ride by Lieutenant W. B. Richmond enabled Bragg to receive the dispatch by eleven that night.[40]

39 "Richmond Notes," September 11–12, 1863, in Polk Papers, Sewanee; Brent Diary, September 11, 1863, in Bragg Papers, National Archives; Polk, *Polk*, II, 240.

40 *Official Records*, XXX, Pt. 4, pp. 640–41; "Richmond Notes," September 12, 1863, in Polk Papers, Sewanee; Bragg's Chickamauga report, in Claiborne Papers, UNC; Polk, *Polk*, II, 240–41.

Bragg was not pleased with Polk's disregard for the finer points of his orders. Some time after writing the original 8 P.M. attack order, Bragg sent a second note urging that the morning attack should be "quick and decided." Now, about midnight, he sent Polk a third message. It was a curious one, of that vague and ambiguous language often employed by Bragg. Despite his orders in the previous two dispatches for Polk to attack, Bragg now said that Polk's position seemed to be a good defensive one, but that he hoped Polk would not maintain the defensive "unless the enemy attacks early." He discounted Polk's fears that Crittenden had received heavy reinforcements from Chattanooga, insisting that the bulk of Rosecrans' army lay southward at McLemore's Cove and Alpine, but he did promise to send Buckner's corps the next morning as a support. Then, despite a brief lecture on how action alone could save the army, Bragg again neglected to give a specific order to attack.[41]

Armed with this new set of vague instructions, Polk chose not to attack. About daylight, Bragg and his staff rode ahead of Buckner's division to Polk's headquarters at Rock Spring Church. But no guns were heard. When he arrived about 9 A.M., Bragg discovered that Polk as yet did not have his troops ready for an assault along the Pea Vine Road. Polk had pulled back his three divisions, those of Cheatham, Hindman, and Walker, onto a long, semicircular defensive line extending all the way from Anderson's crossroads on the Lee and Gordon's Mill Road, across the Pea Vine and Ringgold roads. Finally, about the time of Bragg's arrival, as Polk was completing his arrangements, intelligence from Pegram on the Ringgold Road indicated there was no enemy there, but that Crittenden appeared to be moving cross-country toward Lee and Gordon's Mill.

Slowly, on the morning of September 13, Polk moved to feel out the enemy toward Lee and Gordon's Mill, still ignoring the Pea Vine Road front. Cheatham's division finally made contact shortly after noon, but there was only desultory firing. Not until about 2 P.M., was Walker's reserve corps at last ordered to advance on the Pea Vine Road. But as Walker prepared to move forward, scouts reported that this road was bare of Crittenden's men. By mid-afternoon, it was learned with certainty that Crittenden's divisions on the Pea Vine front had escaped. A member of Polk's staff interrogated a local citizen who told that on the previous night he had guided Crittenden's divisions across the Chickamauga, to the vicinity of Lee and Gordon's Mill.[42]

41 Polk, *Polk*, II, 240–41.; *Official Records*, XXX, Pt. 2, p. 49; Bragg's Chickamauga report, in Claiborne Papers, UNC; "Richmond Notes," September 12, 1863, in Polk Papers, Sewanee.
42 Bragg had been badly served by his intelligence during the days, September 11–13. Crittenden was never where Bragg believed him to be. On September 11,

Twice within a week Bragg's attempts to strike a divided Rosecrans force had failed. Now there was to be a third failure. By the evening of September 13, two full corps and the smaller reserve corps, almost thirty thousand men, were concentrated at Rock Spring Church. Within five miles, across the Chickamauga, was Crittenden's corps. The Federals in McLemore's Cove were well over ten miles distant, and those at Alpine, thirty miles distant. Yet Bragg, that evening, abandoned any plan to catch an isolated Crittenden. Instead, late on September 13, Bragg began ordering his army back to La Fayette. From late that evening until the evening of September 16, Bragg essentially passed the initiative to Rosecrans and chose to take the defensive at La Fayette.[43]

Why had Bragg chosen to give Rosecrans an opportunity to unite his scattered corps? The basic reason was that Bragg's command structure had collapsed. After the failure on the thirteenth, Bragg seemed to enter a phase of emotional doldrums, so much so that his change in conduct was noticeable. Perhaps his shaky emotional condition of the spring was still in effect. More likely, Bragg simply gave up because he had lost faith in his officers, whom he thought had failed him. Whom could he trust? Prior to this latest operation, Bragg had quarreled with almost every corps and division commander in the army.

Now, he again believed they had let him down. He was disappointed in Hill for his failure to cooperate with Hindman in the initial phase of the McLemore's Cove arrangement. He was angry with Polk for the slowness in attacking in the Rock Spring plan. Though Bragg did not know that Crittenden was not there, he believed after the incident that only Polk's slowness had prevented victory. He was already at odds with Buckner over the Department of East Tennessee matter before Buckner performed badly in McLemore's Cove. Thus, all three corps commanders, as well as Hindman, had in Bragg's eyes failed him.

Bragg's lack of confidence was reciprocated. His generals simply did not trust him on two counts. Too many times, when he had issued vague or discretionary orders, his generals had been stung when they were blamed

---

a single division, Wood's, was at Lee and Gordon's, ten miles west of Van Cleve's and Palmer's divisions, which were at Ringgold. That day, Rosecrans ordered Crittenden to hasten and unite at Lee and Gordon's. At 5 A.M. of September 12, Crittenden's other two divisions moved from Ringgold to the north bank of the creek, and were at the mill by the night of September 12. See *Official Records*, XXX, Pt. 1, pp. 604–605; Pt. 4, pp. 645–47; Gale to wife, September 15, 1863, in Gale-Polk Papers, UNC; Captain J. F. Wheless, "Confederate Data: Reminiscences of the Battle of Chickamauga" (MS in Wheless Papers, Confederate Collection, Tennessee); Bragg's Chickamauga report, in Claiborne Papers, UNC; Polk, *Polk*, II, 242.

43 "Richmond Notes," September 13–14, 1863, in Polk Papers, Sewanee; Brent Diary, September 14–16, 1863, in Bragg Papers, Western Reserve.

for their failure. Thus, by September, 1863, his high command was afraid to take the initiative. Bragg's officers also had no confidence in his abilities. Even when Bragg gave specific orders, they were disregarded sometimes because his generals did not think he was capable of high command. The army's brief annals were filled with rump councils called by his generals, such as at Perryville and in McLemore's Cove, which voted to disregard an order. In short, by mid-September matters were at an impasse, with Bragg no longer trusting his officers to independent operations, while they both feared such responsibility and at the same time mistrusted his direct orders as being potentially disastrous.[44]

This command impasse was not the only reason for the army's seeming paralysis between September 13 and 16. The Confederate leadership still did not know where the Federals were. McCook's location was completely a mystery. On the thirteenth, while he was with Polk at Rock Spring, Bragg received an urgent note from Hill. Hill warned that McCook was advancing to within a few miles of La Fayette. Buckner's corps was hurried back to La Fayette, but no McCook appeared. In fact, Will Martin reported the same day that McCook was nowhere near Hill, but was now retreating toward Alpine. Then on the fifteenth, Wheeler reported that McCook was shifting his base from Alpine to unknown parts. The McCook affair was typical. Reports of Rosecrans' location came "as thick as autumn leaves . . . from all quarters and in all directions."[45] No one was even sure that Crittenden was concentrated at Lee and Gordon's Mill. Some denied his presence there. Thomas' location too was unknown. Meanwhile the enemy by the sixteenth had reoccupied McLemore's Cove, and was threatening Dug and Catlett's Gaps.[46]

Perhaps Bragg now considered himself the hunted instead of the hunter. With Crittenden holding the Chattanooga road at Lee and Gordon's Mill and McCook holding Alpine, Bragg's army was compressed into the narrow valley between Pigeon Mountain and Taylor's Ridge. By September 13 rations were running low and there was increasing con-

---

44 General St. John Liddell remarked, "It struck me that Bragg did not know whom to trust—He was not popular with his generals and hence I feared, that zealous cooperation on their part was wanting." See Liddell reminiscences, in Claiborne Papers, UNC. Captain Frank Wheless of Polk's staff remarked of Hill that his "natural acidity of temper" made for him "a most unenviable reputation during his short stay with the Western Army." See Wheless, "Confederate Data," in Wheless Papers, Tennessee; Bridges, *Hill*, 200–201; Hill, "Chickamauga—The Great Battle of the West," 639–46. On September 15, one of Bragg's staff remarked that "Genl Bragg seems sick and feeble. The responsibilities of his trust weighs heavily upon him." Brent Diary, September 15, 1863, in Bragg Papers, Western Reserve; see also Polk, *Polk*, II, 307.

45 Brent Diary, September 13, 1863, in Bragg Papers, Western Reserve.

46 *Ibid.*, September 13–16, 1863; "Richmond Notes," September 13–14, 1863, in Polk Papers, Sewanee; *Official Records*, XXX, Pt. 4, p. 648.

cern at headquarters over the army's lines of communication. The Atlanta railroad was difficult to reach from the valley. Because a bridge was out south of Ringgold, trains on the Western and Atlantic could penetrate only to the small rail siding at Catoosa Station. From there, any supplies must be transported a hard twenty-five miles via Ringgold and across Taylor's Ridge to La Fayette.

Nor was Bragg even certain how many men he would have for an all-out fight with Rosecrans. Historians' depiction of a vast concentration of men on the Chickamauga to crush the Federals is more romanticism than fact. Bragg seemed to have heard almost nothing of any reinforcement by Longstreet, until rumors reached him on September 13 that some Virginia troops had arrived at Atlanta. But how many were coming? The aid was unexpected, Richmond had sent no official word, and the size of the relief force was unknown. Not until September 15 did Bragg learn that three brigades of Longstreet's corps had definitely reached Atlanta, and that all three would be expected to reach the Ringgold-Catoosa Springs area by late that night. Yet his intelligence indicated that the three brigades, those of Generals Jerome Robertson, "Rock" Benning, and Evander Law, brought only forty-five hundred reinforcements.

Also, the slowness of these small units in arriving cast doubts on whether Bragg could rely on any additional aid from Longstreet. The much-heralded stream of reinforcement from Virginia was actually a mere trickle. Benning's brigade had first reached Atlanta on the evening of September 12, but was so badly in need of food and shoes that it was unable to leave for Ringgold until the night of the fourteenth. Congestion was heavy on the Western and Atlantic line north of Atlanta, and there was even competition between commissary agents and Bragg's staff members over who would use empty trains. The wheezy, ramshackle engines could scarcely make the mountain grades. One train was forced to make three running starts before it climbed Allatoona Mountain near Cartersville. The remainder of Longstreet's reinforcement of two divisions was strung across Georgia and the Carolinas. The next stage of reinforcement, the brigades of Generals Joseph Kershaw and Benjamin Humphreys, did not even reach Ringgold until September 19. Three other brigades trailed behind, as well as all of Longstreet's artillery.

Though Bragg knew little of the multiple delays, he did know by September 15 that he could not count on much aid from either Virginia or Mississippi. Aside from the men under Robertson, Law, and Benning, expected to be assembled at Ringgold by the sixteenth, Bragg's only hope was a small additional reinforcement from Johnston's department. By September 11 Bragg learned that two more small brigades from Johnston had reached Atlanta. But his intelligence indicated that these brigades, commanded by Generals John Gregg and Evander McNair, promised only thirty-four hundred reinforcements. The reports Bragg had received exaggerated the strength of the reinforcements of McNair, Gregg, and the Virginia troops. Actually, McNair and Gregg brought only twenty-six hundred effectives. The three brigades of Longstreet's command, which reached Ringgold by the eighteenth, though listing forty-five hundred men, together with those of Kershaw and Humphreys trailing behind, could muster only five thousand effectives.[47]

Bragg's belief that a large disparity of numbers existed partially explains his paralysis from September 13 to 16. Intelligence from both Huntsville and Atlanta hinted at wholesale reinforcement from Grant to Rosecrans, and even a shift of troops from Meade to match that from Longstreet. By the fourteenth Bragg had "very reliable" intelligence from Huntsville which stated that twenty thousand of Grant's men had already passed en route to Stevenson, Alabama. Intelligence from Clarksville, Tennessee, indicated that large numbers of troops were being shipped by boat to Clarksville, marched to Nashville, and then entrained for northern Alabama.

Even if these were unreliable rumors, some were more substantial. Bragg believed Rosecrans to have seventy thousand effective infantry. In addition there was the matter of Burnside's twenty-five thousand men in East Tennessee. When Buckner abandoned the region, he left General John Frazier with a force of some twenty-five hundred men to hold Cumberland Gap. Frazier boasted that he could hold the gap for at least a month under siege. But Frazier did not hold for two days, and on September 15 Bragg learned that the garrison had surrendered on September 9. The loss of twenty-five hundred men was far less important than the effect on operations between Burnside and Rosecrans. This disaster relieved all pressure on Burnside's communications with Kentucky, and released his entire corps for service on the Chattanooga front.[48]

Bragg's multiple problems, personal and otherwise, continued to con-

[47] A. P. Stewart to C. T. Quintard, October 18, 1895, in C. T. Quintard Papers, Duke; Bragg's Chickamauga Report, in Claiborne Papers, UNC; Brent Diary, September 13, 1863, in Bragg Papers, Western Reserve; "Richmond Notes," September 16, 1863, in Polk Papers, Sewanee; Freeman, *Lee's Lieutenants*, III, 229; *Official Records*, XXX, Pt. 4, pp. 538, 547, 619, 647, 652, 672, 518–19, Pt. 2, pp. 202, 301, 419, 497; Black, *Railroads of the Confederacy*, 186–91; Sorrel, *Recollections of a Confederate Staff Officer*, 180–81.

[48] *Official Records*, XXX, Pt. 4, p. 648, LII, Pt. 2, p. 522; Bragg's Chickamauga Report, in Claiborne Papers, UNC; Atlanta *Appeal*, September 17, 1863, Huntsville *Confederate*, September 16, 1863, in scrapbooks, Joseph Jones Papers, Louisiana Department of Archives and History; Brent Diary, September 16, 1863, in Bragg Papers, Western Reserve; "Richmond Notes," September 16, 1863, in Polk Papers, Sewanee.

strain him. Not until September 15 did he rouse slightly from his defensive posture. He then called a war council of his corps commanders at La Fayette. Noticeably feeble in appearance, he discussed prevailing problems with Polk, Hill, Walker, and Buckner. They agreed on a plan for attempting to flank Rosecrans on the north, interposing the army between the Federals and Chattanooga. This strategy could force Rosecrans either to fight to protect his communications with Chattanooga, or else to retreat across Lookout Mountain to the Tennessee River. Somewhat cheered, Bragg telegraphed Richmond after the meeting that he was turning toward Chattanooga.[49]

Instead, he hesitated, giving Rosecrans another day to concentrate. Not until the day after the council did Bragg issue any marching orders. Even then, the orders did not go into effect until the morning of the seventeenth, and thus another day was lost. Even when his orders were issued on the sixteenth, they did not take into account the region's topography. His old lack of appreciation of terrain now was to take effect. He had chosen to make the movement in the valley of West Chickamauga Creek. The creek was a long, meandering stream which flowed out of McLemore's Cove and thence northward along the east side of Missionary Ridge to the Tennessee River. To accomplish his purpose of cutting Rosecrans off from Chattanooga, Bragg needed to seize at least one of the road approaches. Only two roads gave Rosecrans access to Chattanooga. The main road from La Fayette crossed Chickamauga Creek at Lee and Gordon's Mill, then extended north up the valley between Missionary Ridge and the creek. The road then turned to the northwest and crossed Missionary Ridge at Rossville Gap. Below the gap lay the village of Rossville, and Chattanooga was only about five miles distant. Rosecrans' only other link with Chattanooga was via the Dry Valley Road. This road emerged from McLemore's Cove, and led north up the valley between Missionary Ridge and the main La Fayette Road. Then it turned across Missionary Ridge at McFarland's Gap, led up the west side of the ridge to join the main La Fayette Road at Rossville.[50]

In order to cut off Rosecrans from Chattanooga, it was critical to cross the Chickamauga and at least seize control of the main La Fayette Road and Rossville Gap, just east of where the Dry Valley and La Fayette roads converged. To do so necessitated controlling the key fords and

49 Bragg to Cooper, September 15, 1863, in Bragg Papers, Duke; Johnston Diary, September 15, 1863, in Bragg Papers, Western Reserve.

50 *Official Records*, XXX, Pt. 4, p. 657; Chickamauga map in Cheatham Papers, Tennessee; Andrew Brown, "The Chickamauga Campaign 1863 and Geology," *Geotimes*, VIII (March, 1964), 17–21; Anderson, "Campaign and Battle of Chickamauga," 402; Chickamauga and Chattanooga National Military Park Commission, *The Campaign for Chattanooga* (Washington, D.C., 1902), 6–8.

bridge points on the Chickamauga. Despite its deceptively sluggish appearance, the Chickamauga was deep and blue, with steep, bluff-like banks. On either side, the land was flat, with an almost unbroken forest of scrub oak, cedar, and pine with hardwood stands of hickory and oak. Only occasionally was the thicket broken by small farms.

Several key fords and bridges led into this forest between the creek and the La Fayette Road. The northernmost was on the main road from Rossville to Ringgold, where the road crossed at the Ringgold Bridge and the Red House Ford. The crucial route led directly to Rossville Gap. About two miles south, Dyer's Bridge and nearby Dyer's Ford provided access to the La Fayette Road south of Rossville Gap. A mile farther south, the Reed's Bridge Road crossed the creek at Reed's Bridge and then led only two and a half miles to the La Fayette Road. The junction of the Reed's Bridge Road and the La Fayette Road was a critical one. Here also intersected a west-east ridge road which climbed Missionary Ridge and struck the Dry Valley Road at McFarland's Gap. If Bragg moved along the Reed's Bridge Road, a trek of only five miles would be required to seal off both lines of retreat to Chattanooga, via the La Fayette and Dry Valley roads. About a mile south of Reed's Bridge, a road crossed at Byram's Ford and intersected the La Fayette Road. Slightly over a mile further south, the Alexander's Bridge road crossed the creek at Alexander's Bridge, from which it was only three miles to the La Fayette Road. Still another mile south was a good crossing at Thedford's Ford, from which a road intersected with the La Fayette Road. Even further upstream, a road led across Dalton Ford and joined the road from Thedford's Ford. There were other less desirable crossings, but these seven promised access to the west bank for Bragg's artillery and wagons. They also all intersected the La Fayette Road in the rear of the supposed position of Crittenden's corps at Lee and Gordon's Mill. Two of them, the Ringgold Bridge and the Reed Bridge crossings, offered direct routes to seal off the gaps on Missionary Ridge.[51]

Yet Bragg's orders, when finally issued on the sixteenth, frustrated his own design to flank the Federals. His orders called for a mere defensive posture far out of contact with what he believed the Federal position to be. No infantry crossings of any ford or bridge were ordered. In fact, only four crossings, Reed's Bridge, Byram's Ford, Alexander's Bridge, and

[51] Chickamauga map in Cheatham Papers, Tennessee; J. D. Smith, "Walthall's Brigade at Chickamauga," *Confederate Veteran*, XII (October, 1904), 483; John Coxe, "Chickamauga," *Confederate Veteran*, XXX (July, 1922), 292–93; Henry Campbell Journal, September 17, 1863, in Chickamauga-Chattanooga Military Park Library; Cumming, *Gleanings from the Southland*, 84; Major Joseph Cumming Recollections, in Joseph Cumming Papers, UNC; Tucker, *Chickamauga*, 123.

Thedford's Ford, were ordered to be seized by the cavalry. The critical crossing at the Ringgold Bridge was left untouched. Also, the infantry was not even aligned to make any crossing of the creek or to threaten communications on Chattanooga. Hill's corps was to remain at its vigil on the Pigeon Mountain front. Polk's corps occupied the center of the new line. Polk was not even aligned to face the enemy at Lee and Gordon's Mill, but was placed on a defensive position with his left on the creek below Lee and Gordon's Mill and his right at Pea Vine Church. But it was on the right wing that the most serious error was made. Buckner's and Walker's reserve corps were totally out of position to accomplish what Bragg intended to do. They were nowhere near the crossings of the Chickamauga, but were to anchor their left on Pea Vine Church, and then extend northward along Pea Vine Creek, several miles east of the parallel Chickamauga Creek.[52]

Scarcely had Bragg given these strange orders when his old tendency to vacillate took over. About 3 A.M. of September 17, only a few hours before the troops were to march, he countermanded the orders. Another day was given for the enemy to concentrate, since he waited until the afternoon to order a resumption of the march. By that time, he had made some changes which made his design to cut off the enemy from Chattanooga even more impossible. His new alignment was motivated by cavalry reports received from Wheeler on the seventeenth. The previous night Wheeler had been ordered to probe through Dug and Catlett's gaps in Pigeon Mountain and see what lay in McLemore's Cove. On the seventeenth, Wheeler's troopers drove through the two gaps, shoved back Federal horsemen, and suddenly faced long lines of blue infantry in battle order. Prisoners who were interrogated told an interesting tale. Practically all of Rosecrans' army was in the cove. McCook and Thomas were there, joining onto Crittenden's corps which held the left flank.[53]

The news on September 17 seemed to convince Bragg that the Federal left wing extended no further north than Lee and Gordon's Mill, if that far. Though Forrest's entire corps was posted on the Pea Vine Creek front, Bragg ordered no probe on either the sixteenth or seventeenth to see where Rosecrans' left wing was. Instead, he now aligned his infantry on the assumption that the Federals extended from Lee and Gordon's Mill to McLemore's Cove. This new alignment destroyed any hopes of flanking the Yankees from Chattanooga. Now, in the new orders issued on the seventeenth, the right wing under Buckner and Walker was not even to extend beyond Lee and Gordon's Mill, but was placed on a

52 *Official Records*, XXX, Pt. 4, p. 657.
53 *Ibid.*, p. 662, Pt. 1, p. 520; Brent Diary, September 16–17, 1863, in Bragg Papers, Western Reserve.

curious line facing northward from Rock Spring Church east to Pea Vine Church. Polk still held the center, extending from Glass's Mill to Rock Springs while Hill kept the gaps on Pigeon Mountain. The only bright spot in the new alignment was that Hill was ordered to begin withdrawing from Pigeon Mountain at daylight on the eighteenth, and move northward behind Polk toward Lee and Gordon's Mill.[54]

Late on the night of September 17 Bragg changed his plans again. That evening he had moved his headquarters from La Fayette northeast to Leet's Mill and Tanyard on Pea Vine Creek. After another hot, sultry day in the Chickamauga valley, a cool night by the deep, wide mill pool impregnated with pepperment seemed to revive his spirits. He worked feverishly through the night preparing new plans for the eighteenth. His intelligence reports placed Crittenden's left at Lee and Gordon's Mill, with the Union front then extending down into McLemore's Cove. Due to the shifting of Hill from Pigeon Mountain, Bragg's own army now flanked Rosecrans' left flank. Some time after midnight Bragg appeared to have at last decided to commit the army to a flanking move and cross the Chickamauga north of the Federals, between Chattanooga and the Union left.

But his old inability to take the final step intervened. His orders issued during the night of the seventeenth called for no strong blow across the Chickamauga against Crittenden's rear. When he composed his official report of the action, he substituted for the orders issued on the night of September 17 a document he had actually issued hours later on the eighteenth. The directive issued that night merely ordered a crossing at two points with no hint of action. At 6:30 A.M. of the eighteenth, Walker's division was to cross at either Alexander's Bridge or Bryam's Ford, while Buckner on Walker's left was to cross at Thedford Ford. Meanwhile, Polk would occupy Crittenden's attention at Lee and Gordon's Mill. There were several things wrong with the new plan. Buckner and Walker were given no instructions as to what to do once they crossed. There was not enough power in the move, for Walker's and Buckner's were the army's weakest corps. Also, the crossings were not planned far enough in the rear of where Bragg believed Crittenden to be. The northernmost crossing, that of Walker at Alexander's Bridge, would bring him onto the La Fayette Road only about three miles behind Lee and Gordon's Mill.[55]

[54] Brent Diary, September 17, 1863, in Bragg Papers, Western Reserve; *Official Records*, XXX, Pt. 2, pp. 139–40.

[55] *Official Records*, XXX, Pt. 2, pp. 139–40, Pt. 4, p. 633; Bragg's Chickamauga Report, in Claiborne Papers, UNC; Brent Diary, September 17, 1863, in Bragg Papers, Western Reserve; Anderson, "Campaign and Battle of Chickamauga," 403.

Thus, early on the eighteenth, Bragg realized that he must again revise his plan, and the delay cost him yet another day. The new plan did appear to remedy some of the faults of the earlier one. Bragg shifted his crossing points so that he would cross as far north as Reed's Bridge, some seven miles northeast of Lee and Gordon's Mill. There General Bushrod Johnson's division would cross, then turn south and sweep toward Lee and Gordon's Mill. To the south, Walker would cross at Alexander's Bridge, make the left wheel, and also push toward Crittenden. On Walker's left, Buckner's corps would cross at Thedford's Ford and also bear left against Lee and Gordon's Mill. As before, Polk would occupy the enemy at Lee and Gordon's, and hold himself ready to reinforce.

Yet this new plan, made about dawn of the eighteenth, revealed Bragg's haste. Buckner's and Walker's corps were nowhere near the crossings of the creek, but instead were still far to the south near Pea Vine Church. The hour when they should move had not been specified. The two corps were required to move north on the same dirt road until they reached their respective crossings. The result was an entanglement which took most of the morning to clear up. Not until the early afternoon of the eighteenth did they even reach the planned crossing points.[56]

There was other confusion. Bragg had now extended the crossings as far north as Reed's Bridge, where Bushrod Johnson was to cross. Johnson and his brigade had been kept at Ringgold, about six miles west of the Chickamauga, to protect the Atlanta line of communications. There, during the past few days, he had assembled a hodgepodge division composed of his own brigade, the two brigades sent from Mississippi, and the three brigades which had arrived from Virginia. Johnson's first set of orders, received during the night, had said nothing of the crossing, but had ordered him to march to Bragg's headquarters. He had already marched several miles from Ringgold toward Leet's Mill, when one of Bragg's staff handed him his new set of orders. Johnson was forced to retrace his steps through Ringgold. Then, shepherded by five of Forrest's cavalry brigades, Johnson began the six-mile march to Reed's Bridge.

Nothing went right for Johnson. Because of various minor delays, he had only marched half the distance to the Chickamauga by 11 A.M. Then, heavy Union cavalry resistance was met on the Reed's Bridge-Ringgold Road beginning at Pea Vine Creek. Forrest personally came up to drive back the force protecting Reed's Bridge. It was something of a reunion for the former slavetrader, Forrest, and the former college professor, Johnson. Both had refused to surrender at Fort Donelson and had slipped

56 Cumming Recollections, UNC; Bragg's Chickamauga Report, in Claiborne Papers, *Ibid.; Official Records*, XXX, Pt. 2, p. 357.

through the Federal lines to Nashville. When he observed Johnson's column stalled at Reed's Bridge, Forrest unleashed his troopers and drove the Federal cavalry across the bridge by noon. But the Federals hung on at the western end of the rickety, narrow wooden structure. Not until sometime between three and four in the afternoon did Johnson push back the resistance and begin to cross.[57]

Matters were no better to the south. Due to the tangle with Buckner, W. H. T. Walker's corps did not even arrive at Alexander's Bridge until about noon. To his chagrin, no bridge remained, since Federal defenders on the opposite bank had torn out the flooring. Faced with forcing a crossing against artillery and repeating rifles, Walker elected to retrace his path to Bryam's Ford, about a mile and a half to the north. It was already sundown when his men waded the creek and plunged through the thick underbrush on the west bank. Still farther south, Buckner did not even cross the Chickamauga. Though he had reached Thedford's Ford by 2 P.M., he hesitated, hoping for news from Walker. Hearing nothing, Buckner bivouacked for the night on the southeast bank.[58]

Again Bragg had failed in his avowed purpose to strike behind the enemy. His formation on the eighteenth made this impossible. Practically all of the army's power had been kept on the left and center. Hill's corps, containing the veteran divisions of Cleburne and Breckinridge, had been held on the far left to observe the enemy between McLemore's Cove and Lee and Gordon's Mill. Polk's corps with Cheatham's and Hindman's divisions, had been kept idle the entire day, demonstrating at Lee and Gordon's Mill. The only respectable force committed at all to the flanking move was Buckner's two divisions. These were the divisions of Generals John Preston and Peter Stewart, ten thousand strong. Yet Buckner actually had been ordered to cross in the center, at Thedford's Ford. Thus, fewer than ten thousand men were committed to the main purpose of the eighteenth. Johnson's division, thirty-six hundred strong, was an unknown quantity of hastily assembled brigades. Walker's reserve corps, a corps in name only, totaled only about six thousand men in two small divisions, those of Generals St. John Liddell and Walker. Almost three-fourths of Bragg's infantry had been kept on the left and center during the eighteenth.

As might be expected under the command confusion, the army's organization was already coming unhinged. Bragg's attack orders had omitted the key necessity—to seize the line of retreat to Chattanooga.

57 *Official Report*, XXX, Pt. 2, pp. 451–52; Henry, *Forrest*, 181–82.
58 *Official Records*, XXX, Pt. 2, pp. 239, 357, Pt. 4, p. 664; Cumming Recollections, UNC; B. L. Ridley, "Southern Side at Chickamauga," *Confederate Veteran*, VI (September, 1898) , 408; Smith, "Walthall's Brigade at Chickamauga," 483.

He mentioned nothing of moving to seize the La Fayette Road, but instead gave only vague orders to sweep southward after crossing the Chickamauga. The result was confusion on the west bank. Though Bushrod Johnson had crossed well in the rear of where Rosecrans was assumed to be, he did not remain in the vicinity of Reed's Bridge. Instead, Johnson's column moved south and completely marched across Walker's front, which was bivouacked near Alexander's Bridge. This reversal not only placed Walker on the far right, but placed Johnson's troops between Walker and Thedford's Ford, almost a mile in front of Walker's own line. Only a single infantry brigade, that of General Evander McNair, had been left to hold Reed's Bridge.

This reshuffling of position was partially due to a new command arrangement. Bragg's organization had become dangerously unwieldy. He had begun the day with a four-corps army, and by nightfall had the same number of men but in five corps. During the afternoon of the eighteenth, rumors swept the field that General John Bell Hood had arrived to direct his three brigades personally. The tall, handsome Hood, his arm sling symbolizing his Gettysburg heroism, had ridden out from Catoosa Station to meet Bushrod Johnson as he was preparing to cross Reed's Bridge. There Hood took command of the three brigades in his old division, of Johnson's own brigade, and of the two sent from Mississippi. It was not merely that Hood, fresh from Virginia, knew nothing of western topography or the interworkings of Bragg's command. Now Bragg held five corps of infantry of vastly unequal sizes, strung along a line almost twenty miles long.[59]

Such problems did not seem to worry Bragg that night. His intelligence reports still placed Rosecrans where he desired him to be, with Crittenden on the far left at Lee and Gordon's Mill, Thomas in the center opposite Glass's Mill, and McCook further south toward McLemore's Cove. That Bragg believed he still badly outflanked Rosecrans was evident in his orders issued that night for the nineteenth. No general attack order was issued, but merely a series of vague instructions. These instructions sent no strong force to the right, as Polk had advised as early as the seventeenth. Instead, Bragg concentrated on the area immediately around the Federal position supposedly at Lee and Gordon's Mill. Buckner's corps, followed by Cheatham's division of Polk's corps, was to cross the Chickamauga at daylight, just above Lee and Gordon's Mill. Hill's corps

---

59 J. H. Martin, "Longstreet's Forces at Chickamauga," *Confederate Veteran*, XX (December, 1912), 564; Ridley, "Southern Side at Chickamauga," 408; *Official Records*, XXX, Pt. 2, pp. 239, 452–53; Polk, *Polk*, II, 246; J. B. Hood, *Advance and Retreat: Personal Experiences in the United States & Confederate States Armies,* ed. Richard N. Current (2nd ed., Bloomington, 1959), 120.

was to remain idle on the far left, while Polk with Hindman's division was merely to demonstrate in front of Lee and Gordon's Mill. And what of the far right? No new force was sent there, and no orders were given. Bragg apparently planned to visit Walker's position and so sent no orders to attack in the morning. Nor did Hood appear to receive orders to attack at a specific time.[60]

It turned cold on the Chickamauga that night, and few fires were allowed to warm the shivering troops huddled in the creek-bottom forests. The night was eerie, as strong cold winds pushed threatening clouds across the sky and swirled the dust in the roads. This dust had been the object of comment much earlier in the day. One of Will Martin's scouts, perched atop Pigeon Mountain, had sent an interesting report not credited by Bragg. He reported long lines of infantry were kicking up heavy dust clouds as they marched north out of the cove, up the Chickamauga and toward Lee and Gordon's Mill.[61]

[60] Anderson, "Campaign and Battle of Chickamauga," 403–404; Bragg's Chickamauga Report, in Claiborne Papers, UNC; Polk, *Polk*, II, 245; *Official Records*, XXX, Pt. 2, pp. 51, 240, 246, Pt. 4, p. 667; Hood, *Advance and Retreat*, 62.

[61] *Official Report*, XXX, Pt. 4, p. 666; Henry Campbell Journal, September 18, 1863; Journal of A. C. Griest, July 26, 1862–July 6, 1865 (September 18, 1863), Diary of John Ely, September 19, 1863, all in Chickamauga-Chattanooga National Military Park Library.

nine

The Chaos of Chickamauga

ON THE FROSTY MORNING OF SEPTEMBER 19, THE CLASH BETWEEN BRAGG and Rosecrans finally began. For two days in the damp creek-bottom thickets of the Chickamauga one of the greatest battles ever fought on the American continent raged, with some thirty-four thousand casualties. Historians have depicted it as a near repeat of Shiloh, an "almost" situation in which only Bragg's bungling on the evening of the second day prevented a total Confederate victory. Yet, it seems that from the very opening of the battle, the Confederates were doomed to attain only a partial victory at best. For the Confederate command structure was falling to pieces when the battle began, and Bragg never brought his bulky force under control.

Bragg that morning envisioned a sweep up the Chickamauga to crush the Federal left at Lee and Gordon's Mill. To accomplish this, Buckner and Cheatham were to cross the creek early on the nineteenth, slightly above the Union left, where they would take position to form the Confederate left wing. Hood's corps, having marched in front of Walker the previous night, was now facing southward and constituted the front line of the right wing. Behind Hood was Walker's reserve corps, now the second line of the right. Buckner would cross the creek and wheel into position as the front line of the left, with Cheatham taking position behind him as the second line.[1]

This plan disintegrated from the outset. Bragg issued no specific orders. Though Buckner was to cross at daylight at Thedford's, he had no further orders regarding combined moves with Hood. Walker and Hood

---

[1] Polk, *Polk*, II, 247; Bragg's Chickamauga Report, in Claiborne Papers, UNC.

were also without orders. In fact, early on the nineteenth, they sat together on a log at Hood's headquarters waiting for some word from Bragg. Too, Buckner was late in getting into position; it was almost noon before his divisions slid into position on Hood's left. Cheatham, who experienced difficulty in the crossing, did not align behind Buckner until mid-morning.[2]

And where was Bragg during the early morning? He left his headquarters at Leet's tanyard and moved to watch Buckner and Cheatham cross the Chickamauga at Thedford's Ford. Cheerful, Bragg seemed lulled by his belief that even the position at Thedford's, so near Lee and Gordon's Mill, overlapped the Union left. Consequently, no additional power was sent downstream, nor were orders given to seize the La Fayette Road to Chattanooga. During the morning Bragg's only disposition on the right was to order Frank Armstrong to send his cavalry brigade far downstream to the Ringgold-Rossville Road crossing at Red House Ford. But Armstrong had no orders to seize the La Fayette Road. Too, Bragg seemed lax in his disposition of command during the morning. From dawn until noon, no understanding existed on the field as to who was to exercise the general command on the left and right flanks.[3]

Above all, Bragg still believed that the Federal left extended no farther north than Lee and Gordon's. He had laid aside the dispatches from Hill's front on the night of the eighteenth. Then, early on the nineteenth, other ominous news was received from the left flank. Polk rushed a messenger to Bragg's headquarters at Leet's. Unable to find the general, the courier pushed on to locate him on the northwest bank of Chickamauga Creek. There an unruffled Bragg heard that all the previous night, Federal infantry had been marching northward down the Chickamauga to a point opposite Bragg's right wing. Bragg ignored the warning, and merely sent Polk instructions that when the Bishop heard Bragg begin the attack, he was to move the rest of the command toward Thedford's Ford as a reinforcement. As for his own plans, Bragg vaguely remarked that he was moving to attack the enemy where he could find him.[4]

But instead, the enemy swiftly located Bragg. Polk's messenger had not even returned to the Bishop's headquarters when heavy firing broke out far down the creek. Unexpectedly, a heavy Union infantry column had

2 Cumming Recollections, UNC; *Official Records*, XXX, Pt. 2, p. 357; Captain W. J. Morris to William Polk, n.d., in Polk Papers, Sewanee.

3 Wheless, "Confederate Data," in Wheless Papers, Tennessee; Brent to Armstrong, September 19—9 A.M., 1863, in Wheeler Papers, Alabama; Brent Diary, September 19, 1863, in Bragg Papers, Western Reserve.

4 Wheless, "Confederate Data," in Wheless Papers, Tennessee.

severely attacked the rear of Walker's corps and Forrest's cavalry corps, which guarded Walker's right and rear at Reed's Bridge. A startled Walker left his breakfast session with Hood and galloped back to his corps only to find that it was being shoved back toward the Chickamauga. So heavy was the Union attack that by noon Walker had been driven back a mile and a half, and was in real danger of being driven across the Chickamauga. Only then did help arrive, as Cheatham's division burst through the underbrush near Alexander's Bridge on Walker's left to stymie the Union assault. [5]

The four-hour delay in sending aid to Walker typified the confused state of affairs. The celerity of Rosecrans' attack forced Bragg to revise his plans. With his hopes of flanking Rosecrans dissolving, Bragg seemingly had two choices: either to attack what now appeared the Union center in the vicinity of Lee and Gordon's, or else to reinforce strongly the right and thus flank Rosecrans. But Bragg chose a middle course and sent his troops into action piecemeal. Not until about noon did Bragg order Polk to march Hindman's division to reinforce the right, and Polk himself to assume command of the right wing. Cheatham's division was the only reinforcement sent to Walker during the morning. Meanwhile, the force of the Union attack had completely turned Bragg's position until it faced westward with Walker the right, Hood the center, and Buckner the left. During the morning, Hood's corps remained idle in the center, facing the La Fayette Road, as did Buckner's corps on the left. Nor was Hill hurried to the right. Bragg did not call Hill to come until 3 P.M. Then Hill was ordered to bring only one division, Cleburne's, while Breckinridge's division was to be posted opposite Lee and Gordon's Mill. [6]

The result of these halfway measures was a series of sporadic attacks which only sapped Bragg's strength and enabled Rosecrans to locate the Rebel position. While Buckner and Hood were idle, Cheatham's division was sent to Walker shortly after noon. Although he temporarily stopped the Union drive on Alexander's Bridge, within two hours Cheatham himself was being outflanked and forced back toward Chickamauga Creek. Then in the early afternoon, curiously, Bragg ordered Stewart's division of Buckner's corps to pull out of the line on the left, march around Hood, and reinforce Cheatham. A haphazard state of command on the field was evident. Bragg's orders were vague: Stewart was simply to march to where firing was being heard. Dissatisfied with this, Stewart sought out Bragg

5 Cumming Recollections, UNC.

6 Anderson, "Campaign and Battle of Chickamauga," 408–409; Hill, "Chickamauga— the Great Battle of the West," 651; W. W. Carnes, "Chickamauga," *SHSP*, XIV (1886), 399–400; *Official Records*, XXX, Pt. 2, p. 240.

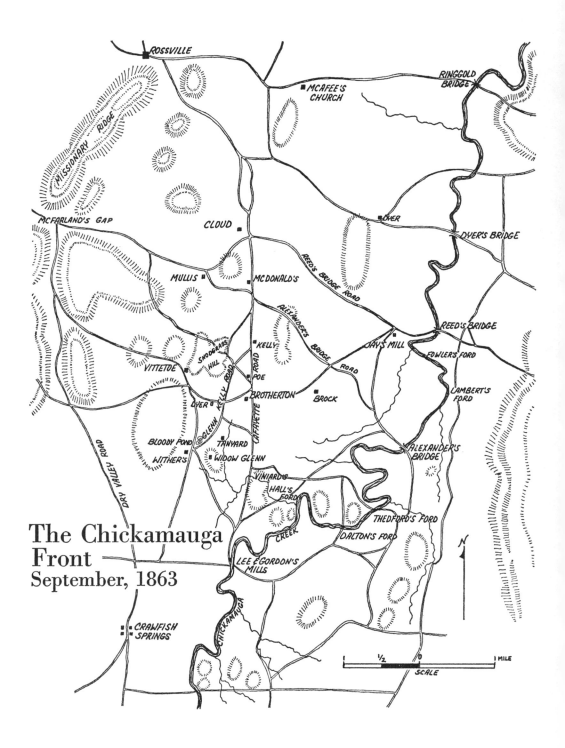

ROSSVILLE

MCAFEE'S CHURCH

RINGGOLD BRIDGE

MISSIONARY RIDGE

MCFARLAND'S GAP

CLOUD

DYER

DYER'S BRIDGE

MULLIS

MCDONALD'S

REED'S BRIDGE ROAD

REED'S BRIDGE

SNODGRASS HILL

KELLY

ALEXANDER'S BRIDGE

DAY'S MILL

FOWLER'S FORD

VITTETOE

POE

ROAD

ROAD

LAMBERT'S FORD

DYER

KELLY ROAD

BROTHERTON

BROCK

BLOODY POND

GLENN

TANYARD

LAFAYETTE

ALEXANDER'S BRIDGE

WITHER'S

WIDOW GLENN

VINIARD'S

DRY VALLEY ROAD

HALL'S FORD

THEDFORD'S FORD

The Chickamauga Front
September, 1863

CREEK

DALTON'S FORD

N

LEE & GORDON'S MILLS

CRAWFISH SPRINGS

CHICKAMAUGA

½   0   1 MILE

SCALE

near Thedford's Ford and asked for more specific orders. Bragg retorted that he had just assigned Polk to command on the field and had further orders for Stewart. But Polk was nowhere to be found, since he had not yet arrived from his former position across the creek. Stewart did find Polk's aide, Lieutenant W. B. Richmond, who could offer little help because he was also looking for him. Disgusted with the lax state of command, Stewart, on his own initiative, continued his march around Hood's corps, and finally got into action about 2:30 P.M.[7]

Stewart's ensuing success during the afternoon indicates that the Rebels probably could have won the battle on September 19 had commands been more wisely handled. Intelligence received by Bragg during the morning had indicated that Rosecrans was marching troops across Buckner's and Hood's front to reach the new Union left at the Kelly farm on the La Fayette Road, centered some three and a half miles north of Lee and Gordon's Mill. The crucial zone seemed to be this stretch of over three miles between the Kelly farm and the mill, where Buckner and Hood remained idle. Here the Dry Valley Road from Crawfish Springs swept within a half mile of the main La Fayette Road before veering northwest across Missionary Ridge. Thus, a strong attack by Hood and Buckner might have carried both the La Fayette and Dry Valley roads, and cut off Rosecrans from Chattanooga. Too, Federals marching from the Union right toward Kelly's farm had only two routes, each within striking distance of the Confederate left-center. On the east lay the main La Fayette Road. To the west, between the Dry Valley and La Fayette roads, was a small north-south cut-off road, the Glen-Kelly Road, which left the Dry Valley Road at Widow Glenn's, and joined the La Fayette Road near the Kelly farm. A strong attack against the La Fayette Road would take in flank any force Rosecrans was moving toward the left and perhaps would carry as far as McFarland's Gap.[8]

Unable to find any instructions for a coordinated effort, Stewart marched to Cheatham's left, wheeled, and drove his three brigades straight across the La Fayette Road and through the Union center. By 4 P.M., the Federal line was severed in half. On the right, General William Bate coolly drove his Georgia and Tennessee troops across the La Fayette Road within a half mile of the Glen-Kelly Road. On the center and left, Generals John C. Brown and Henry Clayton stormed across the La Fayette Road and penetrated across the Glen-Kelly Road, within a quarter mile of the Federals' second line of retreat, the Dry Val-

---

[7] *Official Records*, XXX, Pt. 2, pp. 361–62.

[8] Troop position maps, Chickamauga-Chattanooga National Military Park.

ley Road. The Federal defenders were hurled back to the Dry Valley
Road and Glen-Kelly Road intersection at the Widow Glenn's.

But Stewart could not hold. Buckner and Hood did not move to his
support. Bate had lost half his brigade, Clayton and Brown were badly
decimated, and a fresh Union division now struck from the vicinity of the
Widow Glenn's. Another Union division struck Bate's right flank across
the La Fayette Road. Unsupported, Stewart's men sullenly gave up their
hold on the Federal center, and by 4 P.M. were retreating to the east
side of the La Fayette Road. [9]

Only then did Hood come into action on Stewart's left. Hood's situation during the day also suffered from the lax command structure.
While Stewart was penetrating to the Glen-Kelly Road, Hood and
Buckner stood idle without orders. Had Hood timed an advance with
Stewart, the Dry Valley Road would have been taken, both lines of retreat to Chattanooga captured, and the Federal line split in half. But
Hood had no orders. Bragg and Polk evidently misunderstood who was
to have supervision. About noon, Bragg sent Polk a dispatch ordering
him to cross the creek and to take command "on our right." Evidently,
Bragg intended that the Bishop oversee matters on the entire northwest
bank, from Buckner to Walker. He was interpreting the Confederate left
as the earlier Polk-Hill position on the south bank. Polk, however, understood that he was being ordered to supervise only Walker and Cheatham.
As a result there was virtually no command on the left-center throughout
the day, certainly not from noon until nightfall. General A. P. Stewart
later remarked that he did not even see any Confederate officer above
division rank on the field. [10]

It was only on his own initiative that Hood about 4 P.M. ordered a
belated assault across the La Fayette Road. With his old three Virginia
brigades and Bushrod Johnson's division, Hood seized the road and penetrated to the west side of the road at Viniard's Farm. By dark, however,
he was driven back by a strong flank attack from fresh Union troops
marching from the direction of Lee and Gordon's Mill. Why did Buckner
not aid the assault by coming up on Hood's left? Also without orders,
Buckner had gone into a semi-siege position along the west bank of the
Chickamauga. Late in the afternoon, after being assaulted on the flank,
Hood called to Buckner for aid, but the Kentuckian sent only a solitary

9 Carnes, "Chickamauga," 399–400; *Official Records*, XXX, Pt. 2, pp. 361–62,
370–73, 383–84, 401, 403; Anderson, "Campaign and Battle of Chickamauga,"
408; W. J. McMurray, "The Gap of Death at Chickamauga," *Confederate Veteran*,
II (November, 1894), 329.

10 Polk, *Polk*, II, 249; *Official Records*, XXX, Pt. 2, p. 361; Bragg's Chickamauga
Report, in Claiborne Papers, UNC.

brigade to the front, while the remainder of Preston's division remained idle.[11]

Other opportunities were neglected in the late afternoon. While Hood attacked without Buckner's support, Hindman's division remained idle behind Hood and Buckner. Hindman had crossed the Chichamauga at 3 P.M., but having no orders, he remained in reserve. Cleburne also was not used properly. At 3 P.M. Bragg had finally called upon Hill to send one of his divisions to the right. Cleburne was ordered to make the six-mile march to Thedford's Ford, cross, and move on to the far right to report to Polk. Cleburne's men waded the chest-high, cold waters of the creek while Hood's men were being hard pressed on their immediate front. But having orders to move northward, Cleburne turned and reported to Polk behind Walker's position. It was almost dark when Cleburne moved to replace Walker in the front line. Walker's weary men cheered as the Irishman's smart brigades marched through their lines to attack toward the La Fayette Road. A weird fight ensued in the misty darkness. Cleburne pushed back the Federal right about a mile, but did not break the enemy hold on the La Fayette Road. The night, the dense woods, and the thick smoke made further penetration impossible, so Cleburne called a halt and bivouacked. [12]

That awful night on the Chickamauga was long remembered by the soldiers who slept on the frosty ground holding their guns. It was extremely cold, but no fires were allowed. A thick smoke hung over the dark field. Thousands of wounded lay in the creek bottom, groaning in pain and begging for water. Save for the creek there was little water available. The country had experienced a long drought which had sapped wells and springs. Also hard on the morale of the bivouacked Confederate soldiers was the sound of axes, as the Federals felled trees for breastworks.[13]

Bragg's inability to readjust his plans had cost him heavily. He had never admitted that he was wrong about the location of Rosecrans' left wing and that as a result he bypassed two splendid opportunities. During the day Bragg might have sent heavy reinforcements to Walker and attempted to roll up the Union left; or he could have attacked the Union center where he knew troops were passing from to the left. Unable to

11 Tucker, *Chickamauga*, 164–75; Carnes, "Chickamauga," 400; Hood, *Advance and Retreat*, 62; *Official Records*, XXX, Pt. 2, pp. 510, 517–18.
12 Hill, "Chickamauga—the Great Battle of the West," 651; Ridley, "Southern Side at Chickamauga," 515; Hindman's Chickamauga Report, in Hindman Papers, National Archives; Cleburne's Chickamauga Report, in Cheatham Papers, Tennessee; Buck, *Cleburne and His Command*, 144–45; *Official Records*, XXX, Pt. 2, p. 160.
13 Ely Diary, September 20, 1863, Griest Diary, September 19, 1863, in Chickamauga-Chattanooga National Military Park Library.

decide on either, Bragg tried to do both, wasting his men in sporadic assaults. Now his army was crippled and in no better position than that morning. Walker had, in the day's fighting, lost over 20 per cent of his strength, while Stewart and Cleburne had lost 30 per cent. Gone, too, was any hope for the advantage of a surprise blow against Rosecrans. Now Bragg's army was back on a three-mile-long defensive line with its back to the Chickamauga, stretching from Reed's Bridge on the north to near Lee and Gordon's Mill on the south. [14]

Matters became worse that evening. In the face of the enemy, Bragg unexplainably decided upon a total reorganization of the army, and upon a tactical plan which only held disaster. Some time during the early evening, Bragg notified Polk that he desired his presence at headquarters later that evening. Bragg also stated that he was sending couriers to the other corps commanders. About 9 P.M., the Bishop finally arrived at Thedford's Ford, where he heard Bragg's bizarre plan. During the early evening, Bragg had learned that Longstreet had arrived at nearby Ringgold and would soon join Bragg at headquarters. Now, Bragg explained to Polk, he was dividing the army into two grand wings. Polk was to keep his right wing, where Cheatham's division, Walker's reserve corps, and Hill's corps were now assembled. On the left, Longstreet would command Buckner's corps, Hindman's division, and Polk's corps.[15]

While order was badly needed on the field, this reorganization plan was extravagant. Longstreet could not arrive until almost midnight, yet he was expected to begin an attack at daylight. He knew nothing of the terrain or of his subordinates save for his old comrade Hood. Worse, too much reshuffling had to be effected. Hindman's division had to be joined into Buckner's corps; meanwhile, Stewart remained under Buckner's command but was aligned on Hood's right flank, detached from the corps. Hood was to command a makeshift corps of General Bushrod Johnson's division, one division of Hood's three Virginia brigades already on the field under Law, and a third division of two brigades en route from General Lafayette McLaws' division. McLaws was still in Atlanta, but two of his brigades, those of Generals Joseph Kershaw and Benjamin Humphreys, were already marching from Catoosa Station to the Chickamauga. Kershaw would command this new division.[16]

The problem on the right wing seems to have been one of an excess of lieutenant generals. Exactly what to do with Longstreet may have been

14 Joseph Jones, "Medical History of the Confederate States," *SHSP*, XX (1892), 125; Cleburne's Chickamauga Report, in Cheatham Papers, Tennessee; *Official Records*, XXX, Pt. 2, pp. 373, 388.
15 Wheless, "Confederate Data," in Wheless Papers, Tennessee; Polk, *Polk*, II, 254–55; Bridges, *Hill*, 206.
16 *Official Records*, XXX, Pt. 2, p. 502; Polk, *Polk*, II, 256.

a source of embarrassment. Even with the arrival of Kershaw and Humphreys on September 20, only five brigades from the Virginia army were on the field. Yet, because of his prestige as second in command in Virginia, a place must be found for Longstreet. He might well have declined the wing command to which he was assigned, pleading ignorance of the terrain and of his subcommanders. Also, Longstreet's assignment as commander on the right forced one lieutenant general, Hill, to assume a secondary position as corps commander in Longstreet's wing.

The full story of Hill's being passed over as wing commander is still a mystery. According to the account later written by Polk's son, the Bishop upon visiting Bragg's headquarters heard the commanding general launch a tirade against Hill. Bragg was irritated at Hill for the McLemore's Cove failure, labeled him as insubordinate, and stated that to avoid trouble in the high command, he would simply ignore Hill. The accuracy of Polk's son's account of the council is debatable. While relations between the two had been strained since the Chattanooga meeting, there is little other evidence that Bragg at this time blamed Hill for McLemore's Cove. Polk's own son-in-law and aide-de-camp, Colonel W. D. Dale, confided to his wife just after Chickamauga that during the crisis in McLemore's Cove, Bragg was enraged at Hindman. General Will Martin's account of the midnight meeting at La Fayette between Bragg, Hill, and Nocquet related no anger at Hill, though Bragg after the war claimed that his staff noticed this anger.[17]

Bragg evinced a peculiar attitude, not only toward Hill, but the entire command situation that night. Perhaps because he was worn down by past failures and bad health, Bragg's preparations for the morning seemed spotty. Hill was not notified by Bragg that he was now in a subordinate position. Evidently Bragg chose to let Polk tell him. All of Bragg's general preparations for battle were vague. Earlier in the evening Polk had sent a courier to Bragg asserting that Rosecrans' main army seemed concentrated in front of the Rebel center-right. According to his son's account, Polk repeated this assertion at the night council. Even had Bragg not been given these reports, the near collapse of his right wing that morning should have warned him that Rosecrans' power had shifted.[18]

Yet Bragg did not take heed and readjust his plans. He did not plan to cut off the Federals by moving northward and seizing the pass to Chattanooga. Instead, he stuck to his basic plan of trying to turn the Federal left and drive Rosecrans back into McLemore's Cove. The plan would

17 Bridges, *Hill*, 207; Polk, *Polk*, II, 255; Bragg to Sykes, February 8, 1873, in Claiborne Papers, UNC; Martin to Bragg, undated, 1867, in *SHSP*, XI, 204; Gale to wife, September 28, 1863, in Gale-Polk Papers, UNC.
18 Polk, *Polk*, II, 249, 256.

have been workable if he had placed power on the right flank. But as at Murfreesboro, Bragg placed no special strength where it was needed. Only a single division, that of Breckinridge, occupied the far right in front of Reed's Bridge. Hill's other division, Cleburne's, was on Breckinridge's left. Walker's reserve corps was supposedly held in reserve on the right, but actually was on the left-center. The right brigades in Walker's line barely extended to cover Cleburne's left. More of his line was actually massed behind Cheatham's division, in the center, almost as far south as Alexander's Bridge.

The position of the left wing, under Longstreet, was almost incredible. Because of the curvature of the creek and also as a result of the morning's fight, the left and right wings were jammed together at Cheatham's point in the line, and Polk's line was badly overlapped here by Longstreet's. The left was composed of Buckner's and Hood's corps. Buckner held the far left with Preston's division anchored on the Chickamauga near Lee and Gordon's. The left center was held by Hood's corps, with Stewart's detached division on Hood's right. But Hood's entire corps overlapped the left of Polk's wing, so much so that Confederate strength in the left-center of the line was five divisions deep: Johnson, Law, and Kershaw of Hood's corps, Cheatham, and then Liddell's. Yet on the far right, where Bragg ordered the attack to begin, the line was only one division deep.

Bragg ordered the attack to start at daylight and by divisions, beginning with Hill and then those on the center and on the left wing. Yet Polk's line was recessed over three-fourths of a mile behind that of Longstreet. Since Polk's right front, composed of Breckinridge's command, was only a single division deep, there was danger that the right would be stalled or used up before the battle really took shape. Also, delay and confusion could only result from Longstreet's overlapping of Polk. Hood's corps, on Longstreet's right front, overlapped Polk by a two-division front.

Typifying the general looseness of the battle plans, Polk left the council with no written orders, but only with verbal instructions for Hill's corps, Walker's corps, and Cheatham's division to attack at daylight. Polk was given complete responsibility for communicating with these generals, and no check was made by Bragg's staff during the night to see that the orders had been received by each. [19]

Affairs on the left wing were left equally unsettled. When Bragg pre-

---

[19] Bragg's Chickamauga Report, in Claiborne Papers, UNC; Sykes, "Cursory Sketch of General Bragg's Campaigns," *SHSP*, XI, 493; E. T. Sykes, *Walthall's Brigade: A Cursory Sketch, With Personal Experiences of Walthall's Brigade, Army of Tennessee C.S.A. 1862–1865* (n.p., n.d.), 533.

pared to retire about 10 P.M., Longstreet had not yet arrived, nor had his two left-wing corps commanders, Buckner and Hood, been given any orders. Not all of the left wing was even on the field, since Kershaw's division had yet to arrive from Catoosa Station. Despite this laxity, Bragg went to sleep. It was not until about 11 P.M. that Longstreet rode into Bragg's headquarters.

This tall, striking officer was not in a good humor. His staff had disembarked from the Atlanta train at Catoosa at about 3 P.M. To Longstreet's chagrin, no escort or courier awaited him. Through the night, he and his staff had made their way across country toward the battlefield, sometimes following the unreliable advice of civilians and at other times the sound of the guns. En route, the general was almost captured by a roving Federal cavalry patrol.

Also, Kershaw's men had not arrived when Longstreet reached the Chickamauga, though they were to be used the next morning. When Kershaw did arrive, this would mean that five Virginia brigades were on the field. In effect, the mass Virginia reinforcement had failed. Porter Alexander with Longstreet's artillery, and four additional brigades were still en route through the Carolinas and Georgia. Longstreet was very likely miffed that his arrival in the West was not accorded more ceremony. The lack of a greeting at Catoosa Station apparently irked him. His reception at Bragg's headquarters was equally non-ceremonial. Bragg, who was asleep in his ambulance, was roused, and the two men began an hour's private conversation.[20]

This glum session marked the high point in a relationship soon to collapse into intense hatred. Bragg gave Longstreet a map of the region, told him of his assignment to the left wing, and explained the plan to roll back the enemy's left. Evidently weary of travel, the Virginia general did not bother to seek out his command that night. After the meeting with Bragg, branches were cut from trees, beds were made, and Longstreet fell asleep. With the army due to attack at dawn, Buckner and Hood still had no attack orders from Longstreet, who himself did not even know where his command was.[21]

The whole night was filled with tangled situations and misunderstandings. Harvey Hill, hearing nothing from Bragg regarding orders for the next day, rode to where Bragg's headquarters had been announced—at Thedford's Ford. What occurred upon his arrival has been complicated

[20] Longstreet, *Manassas to Appomattox*, 437–39; E. P. Alexander to Longstreet, December 17, 1881, in Confederate Miscellany File, Emory; Sorrel, *Recollections of a Confederate Staff Officer*, 183–84; Ellison Capers to wife, September 18, 1863, in Ellison Capers Letters, Duke.
[21] Longstreet, *Manassas to Appomattox*, 439.

by post-campaign bitterness. In his official report, Hill claimed that he reached Thedford's to find that Bragg was not there. But Hill's accounts are contradictory. His official report states he left his position for the five-mile ride to Thedford's at 11 P.M., and gives no hint of the time of his arrival. Yet in a letter to Polk a few days later, he stated that he reached the ford by 11 P.M. Two later postwar accounts placed his time of arrival at after midnight. Exactly why Bragg and Hill failed to make contact is uncertain. Possibly Hill mistook another ford for Thedford's, since there were eight fords on the Chickamauga between Reed's Bridge and Lee and Gordon's Mill. The heavy smoke, dark night, and thick underbrush make this a possible explanation. Yet he insisted that he was at Thedford's and that Bragg's headquarters were not there. Several of his staff officers who accompanied him insisted that he was at the right ford. One of them, Hill's adjutant-general, Colonel Archer Anderson, signed an affidavit that he met Hill at Thedford's Ford.

The record is clouded by Hill's allegation that he reached the ford sometime around 11 P.M. Longstreet and Bragg both placed the Virginia general's time of arrival at eleven. It seems unlikely that Hill could have missed Bragg had he arrived at eleven. Since Longstreet and Bragg remained in counsel until after midnight, it is curious, also, that Hill could have missed them if he arrived after midnight. [22]

Probably Hill was at Thedford's Ford, but arrived after midnight when Bragg and Longstreet had retired, and simply made no effort to locate them. His subsequent activities give strength to this theory. About midnight Colonel Archer Anderson of Hill's staff rode to the creek ford. He had just left a chance meeting with Polk, while the Bishop was en route to his headquarters at Alexander's Bridge. According to Anderson, Polk ordered him to tell Hill that he wished to see him that same night at his headquarters. Polk said that Hill had been placed under Polk's command, and assured him that Hill should go to Alexander's Bridge where a courier would be posted to guide him. Polk later claimed that in this meeting with Anderson he also relayed Bragg's orders for an attack at daylight. However, several witnesses to the conversation denied this. Anderson issued an affidavit stating that Polk did not mention the daylight attack, as did two other staff officers in Hill's corps who happened to be on the scene, Lieutenant J. A. Reid and Major A. C. Avery. Also, General John Breckinridge, who was present, assured Hill in a letter a

22 For varying versions of the time of his arrival, see Hill to Polk, September 30, 1863, in Daniel Harvey Hill Papers, Virginia State Library; Hill to Davis, October 30, 1886, in Rowland (ed.), *Davis*, IX, 498; undated certificate of Archer Anderson, in Hill Papers, NCA; *Official Records*, XXX, Pt. 2, p. 140; Hill, "Chickamauga—the Great Battle of the West," 652. See also Bridges, *Hill*, 208–209; Longstreet, *Manassas to Appomattox*, 438; Bragg's Chickamauga Report, in Claiborne Papers, UNC.

month later that the subject of the daylight attack was not mentioned.

If Polk failed to furnish Hill with the attack order, Hill himself seemed to be disinterested in finding Polk. Instead of searching for Polk, Hill said that he was too tired, and shortly after midnight, decided he would rest at Thedford's Ford until about 3 A.M., and then look for Polk. This proved to be a mistake. He could have at least dispatched one of his several staff officers to locate Polk and secure his orders for the morrow. His careless attitude may also explain why he did not find Bragg at Thedford's Ford. Bragg well may have been asleep a short distance away while Hill took his three-hour nap.[23]

Polk's conduct shortly before midnight was no better than Hill's careless manner. The order for Hill to attack at daylight could have been sent either via Colonel Anderson or by Lieutenant Reid, who also left Polk and rode to join Hill at his headquarters at Thedford's Ford. Instead, Polk chose to ride back to his headquarters at Alexander's Bridge about 11:00, and by 11:30 had dictated the orders for the twentieth. Hill and Cheatham were to attack simultaneously at daylight, with Walker's corps in reserve. After writing the orders, Polk dispatched one copy to Cheatham, who received it that night. Walker rode to Polk's camp and received his copy personally. Another courier, one John Fisher, was sent with Hill's copy of the plan.

In a statement made a few days after the battle, John Fisher swore that he got the order from Polk at midnight and then went in search of Hill. He could not locate him, he reported, though he did meet Cheatham and Breckinridge during his search. Fisher insisted that he looked for four hours, then gave up and returned to camp.

There were several things wrong with his story. As Hill's biographer later pointed out, Fisher never swore that he went to Thedford's Ford; instead, he had been informed that General Hill "was near Thedford's Ford." If he had gone there, it would have been somewhat crowded, with Bragg and Longstreet asleep, Hill resting nearby, and Fisher looking for Hill. Apparently, Polk made a bad choice in couriers. He was not a staff member, but an enlisted man in the Orleans Light Horse Troop, Polk's escort. His credentials were placed in some bad light by his conduct after he failed to find Hill. He did not report that he had not found Hill to Polk's assistant adjutant, Colonel Thomas Jack, because Jack's clerk indi-

23 Certificates of Lieutenant J. A. Reid and Major A. C. Avery, Breckinridge to Hill, October 16, 1863, in Hill Papers, NCA; Bridges, *Hill*, 209; Hill, "Chickamauga—the Great Battle of the West," 453; Polk to Brent, September 28, 1863, in George Brent Papers, Duke; Hill to Polk, September 30, 1863, in Hill Papers, Virginia State Library.

cated that Fisher was not to disturb the officer.[24] Polk should have sent more than one courier with such a crucial dispatch.

Polk perhaps made another serious error that night that could have prevented Hill from finding him, had he chosen to look. Early in the evening he had directed a staff officer, Captain W. J. Morris, to locate his headquarters for the night on the south side of the stream in the vicinity of Alexander's Bridge. Yet no records agree on where Polk's headquarters actually were, only that they were hard to find. Morris later wrote Polk's son that he rode to the rear, found Polk's headquarters ambulance at the bridge, and directed the driver to turn into the woods to the right a short distance from the bridge. Morris maintained that the bivouac was within 150 feet of Alexander's Bridge.[25]

But a private from Polk's bodyguard placed the camp one hundred yards in the rear of the bridge, in a cedar thicket to the left of the road. Almost fifty years later another member of Polk's escort, L. Charvet, came up with yet a different story. Charvet had been ordered by Polk to be one of the couriers near Alexander's Bridge to guide Hill. Charvet maintained in a statement made less than two weeks after the battle that Polk's headquarters were at least a half mile east of the bridge and perhaps three-fourths of a mile. Even then, they were not on the main road but on a small side trail some one hundred yards off the road.[26]

Such small details of geographical difference became significant in the events of the night. Charvet's account seems more plausible. Polk himself admitted his headquarters was east of the bridge and in such a position that several couriers were assigned places to burn fires to guide Hill. If Polk's headquarters wagon, which Morris described as being surrounded by staff members, had been within 150 feet of the bridge, it seems unlikely that Polk would have stationed a courier at the bridge or at the fork in the road, or that Hill could have missed them. The truth seems to be that Polk simply did not take great pains to make sure Hill could find him. According to Morris, by 11:30 P.M. a heavy fog was settling over the Chickamauga. In some places, the combined fog and thick smoke reduced the visibility to less than ten yards. This condition, coupled with

24 Deposition of John Fisher, September 29, 1863, in *Official Records*, XXX, Pt. 2, p. 57; Statement of Lieutenant Colonel Thomas Jack, September 29, 1863, *ibid.*, p. 57; see also *ibid.*, p. 47; Bridges, *Hill*, 210; Hill to Polk, September 30, 1863, in Hill Papers, Virginia State Library.

25 Statement of Captain W. J. Morris to William Polk, n.d., in Polk Papers, Sewanee.

26 Deposition of L. Charvet, September 30, 1863, in *Official Records*, XXX, Pt. 2, p. 58; Dr. Y. R. LeMonnier, "Gen. Leonidas Polk at Chickamauga," *Confederate Veteran*, XXIV (January, 1916), 18.

Polk's concealment in a thicket off the road, necessitated that Hill be more properly furnished with guides than he was.[27]

Polk stationed one courier at Alexander's Bridge. He was to keep a fire burning through the fog and act as a guide for Hill. A second courier was stationed at the point where the road to Polk's headquarters branched from the main road to Alexander's Bridge. But Polk's orders were vague. The courier at the bridge was J. A. Perkins, a member of the Orleans Light Horse Troops. A week after the battle, Perkins made a sworn statement that Polk only told him to stay there looking for Hill "for an hour or so." Thus, Perkins remained only for two hours, until 2 A.M., when he built up the fire and left. Polk also ordered the other courier, L. Charvet, to keep watch at the fork of the main road from Alexander's Bridge and that which led off to Polk's wooded retreat. Yet Charvet apparently did not remain at his post past 2 A.M., at which time someone at Polk's headquarters evidently ordered all couriers to cease their duties. Thus, after 2 A.M., there were no men available to guide Hill to Polk. [28]

Polk made another mistake during the night. Although Bragg had ordered a daylight attack, part of the right wing was delayed by the Bishop's own decision. About 10 P.M. Breckinridge's division of Hill's corps had crossed the Chickamauga at Alexander's Bridge. Earlier that evening, Hill had sent a staff officer, Lieutenant J. A. Reid, to await Breckinridge's creek crossing and then guide him into position on the far right. That Breckinridge be in position was vital, since his division, located on Hill's right front, was to begin the attack, which was to be taken up successively by divisions.

However, Polk made no disposition to ready Breckinridge. The two met as the division was crossing. Breckinridge pleaded that his men were tired and asked permission to allow them to bivouac where they were, which was some one and a half miles behind their assigned point in the battle line. By this time Reid had arrived with Hill's orders for Breckinridge to follow Reid's guidance. But Polk overrode Reid, insisted he was now in command of the right, and gave Breckinridge permission to bivouac for the night near Alexander's Bridge.

It was a characteristic performance for Polk. Breckinridge remained at Polk's camp until two hours before sunrise. According to Breckinridge,

27 Polk to Brent, September 28, 1863, in Brent Papers, Duke; Morris to William Polk, n.d., in Polk Papers, Sewanee.
28 Morris to Polk, n.d., in Polk Papers, Sewanee; see also Deposition of J. A. Perkins, September 30, 1863, in *ibid.*; Deposition of L. Charvet, September 30, 1863, in *Official Records*, XXX, Pt. 2, p. 58.

all that night Polk did not mention the fact that the Kentuckian was supposed to begin the army's attack at daylight. Only as he was leaving early in the morning was he told by Polk that he should attack as soon as possible—but with no specific mention of orders for daylight. Thus, Breckinridge, like Hill and Cleburne, did not know they were to attack at dawn. Not until the early morning did Breckinridge begin to move his troops into position. He did not even reach the front line until after daylight, and then it took considerable time to get into position. Not until after daylight would Breckinridge learn that he had been expected to begin an assault at dawn.[29]

Meanwhile, Hill finished resting at Thedford's and with three staff officers moved on at 3 A.M. to find Polk's headquarters. The thick fog slowed their procession along the narrow road through the forest to Alexander's Bridge. When they were within two hundred yards of the bridge, Hill sent forward one of his staff officers, Captain J. Coleman, to the bridge. Coleman returned and said that no one was there. Here, Hill appears to have further contributed to the already ridiculous situation. Evidently Hill himself never went to the bridge, nor did he leave one of his several staff members there. Instead, he ordered another aide to search for Polk's headquarters, while Hill and the others went on to the battle front. Riding to the front, Hill reached Breckinridge's and Cleburne's positions just before daylight, still ignorant of the order to attack.

As Hill reached the front, matters were becoming even more confusing in the rear. Just what happened at Polk's headquarters at daylight has never been determined. Only after Polk arose about daybreak did he seem concerned whether Hill had received any orders. A call went around Polk's camp for John Fisher, who had supposedly carried the order to Hill the previous night. Fisher was found warming himself at a fire near Alexander's Bridge, on the north bank of the creek. About five o'clock, Polk learned that Fisher had never delivered the order. At five-thirty, Polk dictated direct orders for Cleburne and Breckinridge to attack, and dispatched them to the field by Frank Wheless, a staff officer.[30]

While Wheless galloped the mile and a half to the front, a courier from Bragg appeared at Polk's headquarters. It was almost an hour and a half after sunup, and Bragg, now thoroughly aware of Polk's slowness, wanted to know why the attack had not begun. Bragg had waited near the Thedford house on the north bank of the creek for Polk's guns to

29 *Official Records*, XXX, Pt. 2, p. 198; Breckinridge to Hill, October 16, 1863, undated certificate of Lieutenant J. A. Reid, in Hill Papers, NCA.

30 Statement of J. Frank Wheless, September 30, 1863, in *Official Records*, XXX, Pt. 2, p. 61; LeMonnier, "Gen. Leonidas Polk at Chickamauga," 17; Polk, *Polk*, 259; Bridges, *Hill*, 211–212.

open. After considerable pacing, he had sent Major Pollock Lee to investigate the delay. According to the account Lee gave Bragg, he had found Polk about an hour after sunrise, sitting on the porch of a farmhouse three miles behind the lines, reading a newspaper, and waiting for breakfast. Polk then told Lee that he did not know why the attack had been delayed, as he had not yet ridden to the front.[31]

There seems no doubt that Lee gave Bragg this story. It was quoted to Hill by Bragg about 8 A.M. after the commanding general himself rode to find out the cause of delay on the right wing. Also, in two private letters, both written to his wife within a week after the battle, Bragg repeated the story.[32]

The story, however, does not coincide with the version of several witnesses, and some two weeks after the battle, Lee himself allegedly denied telling Bragg such a tale. Polk's headquarters was in a forest clearing, only some twelve hundred feet behind Walker's reserve corps on the opposite bank, and there was no farmhouse nearby. There is also strong evidence that after arising at his headquarters, Polk breakfasted, sent the attack order to Breckinridge and Cleburne, and then rode steadily to the front. Polk's son contended that he saw Lee deliver Bragg's message at the camp as Polk was mounting to ride to the front. A member of Polk's bodyguard later recalled that Polk was in the saddle at daybreak, steadily moving toward the west, and an aide to Cheatham later stated that on a mission to Polk, he arrived at about daylight to find Polk and his staff mounted and moving to the field. The time element of the story also does not seem to be consistent with available facts. Bragg told Hill that Polk was found sitting at the house "after sunrise." Yet in a postwar letter, Bragg placed the time the message was delivered as "an hour after sunrise." Immediately after the battle, when he wrote his wife, Bragg gave two different versions of the time: one was seven o'clock and the other, eight. None of the times given by Bragg appears to have been possible. Lee could not have found Polk about an hour after sunrise. That would have been approximately 7:00 A.M., since the sun rose at 5:47. Polk had already ridden to meet Hill and was at Hill's headquarters by 7:25. Nor could Lee have found Polk at 8:00. Bragg, who did not ride to the front until after Lee returned with the news about Polk, had reached Hill by that time.[33]

31 Bragg to Sykes, February 8, 1873, in Claiborne Papers, UNC.

32 Bragg to wife, September 22, 27, 1863, in Bragg Papers, Missouri; Hill, "Chickamauga—the Great Battle of the West," 653.

33 LeMonnier, "Gen. Leonidas Polk at Chickamauga," 17; Polk, Polk, II, 260–67; Bragg to Sykes, February 8, 1873, in Claiborne Papers, UNC; Bragg to wife, September 22, 27, in Bragg Papers, Missouri; F. McNairy to William Polk, September 18, 1885, in Polk Papers, Sewanee.

Matters on the right wing were equally confusing. When Hill reached the front about daylight, neither he, Cleburne, nor Breckinridge knew that they were to lead the attack at daylight. Upon examining the front line, Hill did not like what he saw. Two of Cheatham's right brigades were aligned at right angles to the left of Cleburne's front, so that in a simultaneous advance, they would run together. Other problems were evident. By overriding Hill's order for Breckinridge's men to move into line the previous night, Polk caused a major delay. Breckinridge's wagons had gotten lost somewhere between Thedford's Ford and the front line. Some of the men had not eaten for twenty-four hours, and Hill felt they needed breakfast. Too, Hill did not like the foreboding nature of the Federal breastworks which had been constructed during the night. He did not believe this thin line, one division in strength, could penetrate the log obstructions.

Hill soon got his chance to state his objections. Some time before 7:00 while Hill, Breckinridge, and Cleburne were conferring, Captain Wheless rode up with Polk's 5:30 orders for Breckinridge and Cleburne. Propriety demanded that Breckinridge and Cleburne read the orders first. Then they passed them to Hill along with an objection from one of the two division officers that their men first needed breakfast. Hill has been castigated for not moving to attack immediately, but this accusation does not take into consideration the full situation as Hill knew it to be. Polk's 5:30 orders did not specify a daylight attack, but merely ordered an assault as soon as the divisions were in position. With the bad angle existing between Cleburne's and Cheatham's line, Hill did not think they were in position. He feared attacking without reserves and did not know whether any cavalry would be available to cover his flank. Thus, Hill sent Wheless back to Polk with a note explaining all of these problems and stating that the divisions would not be ready to move "for an hour or more." Hill also urged Polk to examine the poor state of the battle line, particularly the right angle of Cheatham and Cleburne. He also argued that it would be impossible to take the enemy line by assault with his thin ranks, and asked Polk to advise him on what was to be done when the enemy line was reached.[34]

The timing of Hill's dispatch to Polk is something of a mystery. Hill maintained that the order from Polk was not received until 7:25, after

[34] Statement of J. Frank Wheless, September 30, 1863, in *Official Records*, XXX, Pt. 2, p. 61, see also p. 141; Bridges, *Hill*, 212–14; Statement of Major A. C. Avery, October 13, 1863, Statement of Colonel A. J. Vaughan, Jr., October 13, 1863, Statement of H. C. Semple, October 13, 1863, in Hill Papers, NCA.

which he sent a reply. This version is probably in error. Polk notified Bragg at 7:00 that he had just received a dispatch from Hill stating that he would not be ready to move for an hour or more. Too, Polk was en route to the front when he met Wheless, who gave him the reply from Hill. Wheless would hardly have required almost two hours to deliver the dispatch from Polk's headquarters to Hill on the front line.[35]

The crucial matter was that by the time Polk arrived it was two hours past daylight and the right wing commanders were still ignorant of the daylight attack order. They were to remain uninformed. When Polk first rode up, he asked Cleburne why he had not attacked. Cleburne replied that Hill had ordered him to wait until rations were issued. Polk seemed to make no protest against this. Evidently, nothing was said about orders having been given the night before for an advance at daylight. In fact, according to eyewitnesses, Polk did not mention the daylight attack.

Just what Polk did when he left the brief meeting with Hill is a mystery. Over fifty years after the war, a member of his bodyguard contended that Polk, highly incensed at the delay, galloped along the line ordering every major general to attack immediately.[36] None of the division or corps commanders recalled such orders being given. Instead, between 7:30 and 9:00, Polk drifted to the rear where he conferred with Walker at about 9:00, somewhat curious behavior for the general assigned the responsibility of beginning the battle.[37]

By now it was becoming crowded at Hill's headquarters. Shortly after Polk departed, an angry Bragg rode up. Bragg's sole information thus far had been Polk's 7 A.M. dispatch giving a somewhat distorted view of why Hill had not attacked. Polk's note said nothing about the bad angle between Cheatham and Cleburne, or about the strong fortifications on Breckinridge's front. Instead, he merely mentioned Hill's desire to have the men eat breakfast. Bragg then stormed against Hill for his failure to attack at daylight. Surprised, Hill replied that this was the first time he had even heard of the order issued the previous night for a daylight attack. When Bragg heard this, he angrily assailed Polk, and recounted the story Lee allegedly had told early that morning. Hill told Bragg he was not even certain whether he was to maintain the defensive or to

35 LeMonnier, "Gen. Leonidas Polk at Chickamauga," 17; Statement of J. Frank Wheless, in *Official Records*, XXX, Pt. 2, p. 61; see also p. 141; Bridges, *Hill*, 214–15; Hill, "Chickamauga—the Great Battle of the West," 653; Statement of H. C. Semple, October 13, 1863, in Hill Papers, NCA.

36 LeMonnier, "Gen. Leonidas Polk at Chickamauga," 17.

37 *Official Records*, XXX, Pt. 2, p. 241; Buck, *Cleburne and His Command*, 149; Statement of H. C. Semple, October 13, 1863, in Hill Papers, NCA.

attack. Bragg then ordered him to attack as quickly as possible.[38]

Almost everything went wrong that foggy night at Chickamauga. Hill was partly at fault for not making a more determined effort to locate either Bragg or Polk during the night. But critics who have castigated Hill for not leading a daylight attack apparently have not considered the full facts of that general's problem. Bragg and Polk seem chiefly to blame for the fiasco that night.

Bragg had exhibited a most familiar trait which had hurt him in previous campaigns. He could maneuver, form strategic designs, and get his troops to the designated field of battle. Yet something in his personality gave him an unwillingness to become closely involved on the field. His habit of being almost withdrawn from the field seemed more acute at Chickamauga, where his health obviously was bad. Thus, on the night of the nineteenth, Bragg gave his old nemesis Polk only verbal orders to attack, though he personally distrusted Polk and considered him to be incompetent. Nor did Bragg check during the night to make sure the verbal order got to the corps leaders on the right wing, or to see if the army were really in position.

This shunning of personal involvement on the field was evident on the left wing as well. Bragg turned over complete control to Longstreet and then retired for the night. But Longstreet had not even arrived when Bragg went to bed, and not a single commander on the left knew of the daylight order. Bragg himself knew little of the alignment on the left, since he had not reconnoitered the field. And when Longstreet rode out to his new command about 6 A.M. on September 20, he had been with the western army only seven hours. Though the general attack was to be at daylight, by 10 A.M. Longstreet still had not managed to align the left properly.[39]

Polk seems more at fault than Bragg. Polk's aloofness in making sure Hill got his orders during the night was matched by his failure to make a personal reconnaissance of the front. It was obvious to Hill, Cleburne, and Breckinridge that the Federals on Cleburne's front and on Breckinridge's left front were entrenched behind heavy log fortifications. That morning about 7:00, when Hill had sent his message to Polk, he had warned of this and insisted they could not carry the line. On Hill's own

---

38 The courier, J. Frank Wheless, later contended that when he delivered the dispatch to Hill, Cleburne, and Breckinridge that morning, he mentioned the daylight attack. See Statement of J. Frank Wheless, September 30, 1863, in *Official Records*, XXX, Pt. 2, p. 61. Yet none of the other bystanders recalled the daylight attack order being mentioned; see also Bridges, *Hill*, 215; Buck, *Cleburne and His Command*, 148; Hill to Davis, October 30, 1886, in Rowland (ed.), *Davis*, IX, 498; Hill, "Chickamauga—the Great Battle in the West," 653.

39 *Official Records*, XXX, Pt. 2, p. 288.

initiative, very early that morning he had shifted two of Breckinridge's three brigades, those of Generals Dan Adams and Marcellus Stovall, slightly more to the right, so that they overlapped the line of Federal entrenchments.

Polk neglected to rectify the angle between Cleburne's and Cheatham's lines. Nor were the right wing's reserves aligned properly. Walker's reserve corps remained chiefly behind Cheatham and behind Cleburne's left. This meant that the key position on the field, that of Breckinridge, had not a single reserve and was only a brigade in depth. Polk also had made no arrangements for cavalry to cover Breckinridge's right flank. On his own initiative, Hill had brought up Forrest's cavalry to cover Breckinridge's right flank, which extended to the Reed's Bridge Road.[40]

By 9:30 A.M. a bright sun had cleared away the dense fog, and at last Polk's wing was ready to attack.

Breckinridge's three brigades rolled forward toward the La Fayette Road shortly before 10:00. His two right brigades, judiciously placed to overlap the Federal fortifications, indicated what might have been done had Bragg or Polk placed power on the far right. General Dan Adams, the one-eyed, swashbuckling Kentuckian, skirted the Federal fortifications, seized the La Fayette Road, and turned south to take the Federal line in flank. Stovall's brigade also made the successful wheel. Shortly after 10 A.M. Bragg had in effect seized one line of retreat to Chattanooga, had flanked the Federal left, and was menacing the Glen-Kelly Road and subsequently the Dry Valley Road to Chattanooga.

But Adams and Stovall received no help and gradually were pushed back across the La Fayette Road. Polk was sending no reserves to aid on the right. Breckinridge's left brigade was commanded by General Ben Hardin Helm, Abraham Lincoln's brother-in-law. Helm, a Harvard graduate and Kentucky lawyer, decimated his brigade in a simultaneous attack against the log fortifications on his front. In this attack, he lost his own life and a third of his command. The quick repulse of Helm's brigade then freed the Federals to deal with the two lone brigades of Adams and Stovall. [41]

Where were the reinforcements? When Helm's brigade was quickly thrown back, a gap was left in the Confederate line. Hill pleaded with Polk to send some of Walker's men to the right, but an hour elapsed be-

---

40 *Official Records*, XXX, Pt. 2, p. 79; Oates, *War Between the Union and the Confederacy*, 267; Anderson, "Campaign and Battle of Chickamauga," 410–11; Statement of Major A. C. Avery, October 13, 1863, November 3, 1863, Statement of Col. A. J. Vaughan, Jr., October 13, 1863, in Hill Papers, NCA; Carnes, "Chickamauga," 401; Cleburne's Chickamauga Report in Cheatham Papers, Tennessee.

41 *Official Records*, XXX, Pt. 2, pp. 198–99, 216–17, 231; Tucker, *Chickamauga*, 233–43.

fore Walker moved up in support. During this hour, Adams and Stovall were beaten back and suffered frightful losses, and Breckinridge's entire division was shattered by noon. Had Cleburne attacked promptly, this might have been avoided. Instead, his line was committed in a confused manner. General Lucius Polk's brigade did not reach the Federal log fortifications until Breckinridge had already been repulsed. Thus, Polk was also thrown back, losing several hundred men. Cleburne's other brigades, those of Generals James Deshler and S. A. M. Wood, had moved west along the road from Alexander's Bridge to the La Fayette Road. Wood's brigade promptly collided with the right front of Longstreet's wing, Stewart's division, while Deshler became entangled with Cheatham's brigades facing in the wrong direction. Wood disengaged himself and stumbled alone to the La Fayette Road where he was promptly repulsed by a galling fire from behind the log works. Deshler's brigade also managed to reach the log works but suffered horrible losses, including its commander.[42]

It was not until almost noon that Polk sent Hill any support. About an hour after Hill's plea for aid for Breckinridge, Polk finally moved Walker's corps forward. Had Polk used these reserves well, the Federal left probably would have been smashed. Walker had three good divisions —Cheatham's, Walker's own commanded by General States Rights Gist, and General St. John Liddell's. Yet Polk never filled the gap created in Breckinridge's line by Helm's repulse, despite a second request by Hill. Cheatham was not even sent into action, but remained idle during the early afternoon. Gist and Liddell were sent into action sporadically across the entire Cleburne-Breckinridge front, but by 3 P.M. were repulsed in separate actions. In fact, by midafternoon Polk's wing had sustained over 30 per cent casualties among the men engaged, but had made no headway in seizing the Chattanooga road. [43]

The laxity of matters on the right was in contrast to affairs on the left wing. Here lay Bragg's power, where some of Longstreet's line would attack three divisions deep. Longstreet wisely had massed his own power on the left-center. Stewart's division of Buckner's corps comprised his right wing. On Longstreet's center, opposite the Brotherton farm, he had massed Hood's corps. Bushrod Johnson's division held the front line. Hood's old division, led by General E. M. Law, comprised the second line, while Lafayette McLaw's division of Kershaw's and Humphrey's brigades comprised the third line. Kershaw's and Humphrey's brigades had arrived on the field just as Hill was preparing to advance, and hastily

42 *Ibid.*, pp. 243–45; Cleburne's Chickamauga Report, in Cheatham Papers, Tennessee; *Official Records*, XXX, Pt. 2, pp. 161–62, 170–71, 177, 188–89.
43 *Official Records*, XXX, Pt. 2, pp. 241, 79–80, 245.

had been formed into a third line. The left of Longstreet's column was formed by Preston and Hindman.

Though this heavy power on the left frustrated Bragg's plans to turn the Yankee right, it could not have been better placed. During the early morning, Longstreet had carefully obtained information from residents. He seemed to sense immediately that the crucial point on his front was that segment opposite Hood's corps. From Johnson's division, it was scarcely a half mile to the La Fayette Road in the vicinity of the Brotherton farm. From the Brotherton place, the Dry Valley Road was only a scant mile through open fields and woods. And from Hindman's position on the left of Johnson, the vital road junction at the Widow Glenn's house, where the Dry Valley Road junctioned with the Glen-Kelly Road, was barely a mile and a quarter away.

It seemed, however, as if Longstreet's men would experience the same confusion as had Polk's. Longstreet's midnight understanding with Bragg had been that the attack would open from right to left; also, he understood that Stewart's division, posted on Hood's right, was under Longstreet's control. But by 11 A.M., when it was obvious that the army was not wheeling to the left as expected, Longstreet dispatched a note to Bragg indicating that he believed he could break the enemy line if he advanced without waiting for Polk's attack.

Before he received any reply, Longstreet was startled by matters on his own right wing. Becoming impatient with Polk's slowness, Bragg, about 10 A.M., had sent Major Pollock Lee down to the left wing. Without informing Longstreet, Lee rode along the front and ordered Stewart to advance immediately and attack across the La Fayette Road. Longstreet's rear division, recently arrived from Virginia, was not yet in place, so he could only watch, shortly before 11 A.M., as Stewart moved out. Stewart's men crossed the road north of the Brotherton farm, but were quickly thrown back to the east side.[44]

Even while Stewart was retreating back to his position east of the road, Longstreet ordered Hood and Hindman to advance in a mass offensive. About 11:30 A.M., Hood's lead division, that of General Bushrod Johnson, roared across the La Fayette Road, swarmed around the Brotherton house, and then continued toward the west through the fields around the house. Immediately, Johnson discovered a gap in the Union line. Because of an obvious error in the shifting of troops, the Federals had left a division-wide gap, a quarter of a mile wide, in Johnson's front. Supported by Law and Kershaw, Johnson smashed the Federal line.

44 *Ibid.*, p. 288; Longstreet, *Manassas to Appomattox*, 447; Tucker, *Chickamauga*, 261–62; Bragg's Chickamauga Report, in Claiborne Papers, UNC.

Suddenly, in one of the war's most notable scenes of panic, the entire Union right collapsed, and retreated. The impact of Johnson's assault, coupled with Hindman on his left, completely obliterated the Union right wing. The remnants of two corps hastily began a retreat toward Chattanooga on the Dry Valley Road. At least thirty guns were captured, innumerable small arms were abandoned, and equipment was strewn on the road. By 2 P.M., the fight was over on the right, and Longstreet held the Dry Valley Road, only a few miles from McFarland's Gap.

The sudden collapse had caught more than the Federals by surprise. Longstreet's original intent had been to follow Bragg's instructions to wheel to the left when he attacked. But when the Federal defenders melted toward the north, he wheeled Hindman and Hood to the right, and drove back the Union center into a sharp angle. There, by 2:00, the fight became stabilized. The Union left, known to be Thomas' corps, still held the La Fayette Road in front of Polk, in the sector between the road to Reed's Bridge and the Brotherton farm. The Union center, now bent back at right angles to the left, faced southward along a spur range of Missionary Ridge known as Snodgrass Hill. This knobby series of high hills guarded the only remaining line of retreat through McFarland's Gap. The Reed's Bridge Road crossed the La Fayette Road at McDonald's, and then ascended Missionary Ridge to join the Dry Valley Road in the gap.

Obviously, Longstreet could have controlled McFarland's Gap even if he had not carried the Snodgrass Hill position. By 1 P.M., the Federal right was in flight on the Dry Valley Road. Had a strong Confederate force pursued, McFarland's Gap could have been seized, and the only remaining line of retreat for the remnants of Rosecrans' army would have entailed moving northward in the face of Bragg's army to try to reach Rossville Gap.[45]

The failure to seize McFarland's Gap was probably the greatest mistake of the day, and again resulted from the degree of command confusion on the field. Some time in the midafternoon, probably about 2:30, Bragg called Longstreet to his field headquarters, located behind Hood's line near Chickamauga Creek, between Alexander's Bridge and Thedford's

45 The gap in the Federal line had been created when Rosecrans' headquarters had erroneously ordered General Thomas J. Wood's division to close up on the division of General Joseph J. Reynolds. Rosecrans' headquarters did not know that the division commanded by General John M. Brannan lay between Reynolds and Wood, and thus that there was no need for Wood to make the move. Instead, Wood pulled his division out of the line and created a gap between Brannan and General A. M. McCook's corps. See Tucker, *Chickamauga*, 254–59, 266–73; *Official Records*, XXX, Pt. 2, pp. 288–89, 453–56; Hindman's Chickamauga Report, in Hindman Papers, National Archives; Longstreet, *Manassas to Appomattox*, 448–50.

Ford. Longstreet hastily explained the situation. Two Federal corps were in retreat toward Chattanooga, with heavy losses in artillery and prisoners. Longstreet then urged Bragg to send to the left wing some of Polk's troops which had not been as actively engaged. With these, Longstreet could pursue up the Dry Valley Road, take McFarland's Gap and Rossville Gap, and thus cut off the remaining Federals from Chattanooga.

According to Longstreet and others, Bragg seemed to disbelieve that a victory had been won. In his own eyes, his plan for rolling up Rosecrans' left wing had failed, and he was still angry at Polk. Thus, he refused any reinforcements to Longstreet, though Cheatham's division and part of Liddell's division were fresh. Even then, Longstreet did have available one fresh division in reserve, that of Preston. But Bragg refused to authorize any pursuit. He instead ordered Longstreet to hold his position at Snodgrass Hill. The meeting was brief and somewhat bitter, with Bragg allegedly lashing out at Polk's men for having no fight left; in fact, when the conversation was finished, Bragg left the field. He told Longstreet that if anything else happened, he should communicate with him at Reed's Bridge.[46]

Bragg's attitude caused a serious command lag for the rest of the afternoon. Longstreet rode back to the left, and throughout the afternoon directed attacks against Snodgrass Hill, while at about 3:30 Polk opened a new attack on Thomas' left. By 5:00, the battle was all but over. Polk lapped the Federal left and seized the La Fayette Road to Rossville Gap. Meanwhile, Longstreet committed Preston's fresh division on the left. The combined pressure proved successful. The Federal defenses buckled, and by nightfall the remnants of Thomas' defenders were retreating through McFarland's Gap on the road from Reed's Bridge via McDonald's.

Why had the Federals escaped? For over four hours on the afternoon of the twentieth, at least three good opportunities were presented. A pursuit up the Dry Valley Road to McFarland's Gap would have sealed that route of escape and perhaps would have cut off the only line of retreat to Chattanooga. Bragg's curious refusal to allow Longstreet enough men to accomplish the job was only partially to blame. Also at fault was the old, familiar misuse of cavalry. Until late in the afternoon, Wheeler's corps was kept on the south bank of the creek toward Glass's Mill.

---

46 Longstreet to Hill, July [?] 1884, quoted in Hill, "Chickamauga—the Great Battle of the West," 658; Longstreet, *Manassas to Appomattox*, 451–52; George Ratchford, "Gen. D. H. Hill at Chickamauga," *Confederate Veteran*, XXIV (March, 1916), 121. Ratchford's father, Major George Ratchford of Hill's staff, overheard the conversation between Bragg and Longstreet. See also Buck, *Cleburne and His Command*, 151.

Though Longstreet maintained that he made repeated requests during the early afternoon for cavalry, Wheeler's corps did not arrive at Lee and Gordon's Mill until 3 P.M. Not until about 5:00 did Wheeler receive specific orders from Longstreet to pursue down the Dry Valley Road. Longstreet's order mentioned nothing of seizing McFarland's Gap, but was merely a vague note relative to enfilading the Federal right. Had Wheeler's cavalry been employed as dismounted infantry at the gap, as had Forrest's troopers with Hill, good results might have been achieved. Instead, Wheeler made only a brief two-hour pursuit which netted a thousand prisoners but did not seize the line of retreat to Chattanooga.[47]

As an alternative, Bragg could have seized either Rossville Gap via the La Fayette Road or McFarland's Gap via the Reed's Bridge Road. A single division that was comparatively fresh, such as Cheatham's, could have moved north around Polk to seal both lines of retreat at Rossville. Too, there was an opportunity to split the new Federal line in half near where the angle joined. In effect, the wings opposing Longstreet and Polk in the early evening did not join, but had a gap some quarter of a mile wide near the La Fayette Road. Polk, still preoccupied on the right with his sporadic attacks, did not notice this, nor did Longstreet. Bragg's absence from the field in the late afternoon may have cost an excellent chance to overrun the two Federal lines, since communication between Polk and Longstreet was almost nonexistent.[48]

Still, by dark, it was evident that the army had won its greatest victory. Bragg had taken over seven thousand prisoners, fifty-one guns, and almost twenty-four thousand stands of small arms. The Union panic that afternoon left stores of wagons, ambulances, and other supplies. The ambitious three-corps offensive into Georgia had been stopped and had cost the Yankees over sixteen thousand casualties.

But this success had been achieved at a high price to the Rebels. General John B. Hood had lost a leg on the field, and Hindman had been wounded in the face. Six brigade commanders were killed or wounded. Helm's brigade alone suffered the death of its commander and half its regimental commanders were killed or wounded. Twelve of Bragg's regiments lost over half their men. Longstreet's wing lost almost eight

[47] Hindman's Chickamauga Report, in Hindman Papers, National Archives; Brent to Wheeler, September 20—5 P.M., 1863, in Wheeler Papers, Alabama; Archibald Gracie to D. C. Govan, May 12, 1908, in Govan Papers, UNC; George Dolton, "Chickamauga Battlefield—Snodgrass Ridge," *Confederate Veteran*, I (December, 1893), 362–63; Bragg's Chickamauga Report, in Claiborne Papers, UNC; Anderson, "Campaign and Battle of Chickamauga," 414–16; Oates, *War between the Union and the Confederacy*, 267–68; *Official Records*, XXX, Pt. 2, p. 521, Pt. 4, p. 675.

[48] Oates, *War Between the Union and the Confederacy*, 267–68; *Official Records*, XXX, Pt. 2, p. 525.

thousand men in the September 20 attack alone, while the total losses for the army probably totaled some eighteen thousand men.[49]

The battlefield reflected the horror of the carnage. The summer drought had parched the woods, and fires during the evening burned to death many of the wounded. Hundreds were burned beyond recognition. Their screams were to be long remembered by the combatants. Battery after battery of Federal artillery had been taken, and horses mangled by rifle or artillery fire lay nearby. The clear, moonlit night illuminated the scene. Debris filled the Dry Valley Road, and the body count of defenders and attackers was heavy along the La Fayette Road. With the capture of the main Federal field hospital at Crawfish Springs, piles of mortally wounded troops were found encased in rail pens to protect them from wild animals. Other piles of amputated arms and legs were nearby, some of which were carried off by wild hogs. Lanterns bobbed everywhere along the Chickamauga Creek as the wounded were retrieved. But despite the horror of the night, there was a universal exultation in the army. The cheers lasted until well into the night. Few seemed to doubt early on the twenty-first that Bragg would pursue Rosecrans into Chattanooga and strike while the Federals were demoralized.[50]

But no pursuit was made. For this Longstreet must share the blame. After a terse conversation with Longstreet about 3 P.M., Bragg had returned to his headquarters at Reed's Bridge. Though Bragg had ordered Longstreet to keep him informed of any developments, the Virginia officer did not do so. He did not send news to Bragg that night that the entire Federal right wing had collapsed, nor apparently, did he dispatch later the news that Rosecrans' army had retreated. Longstreet did send a note at 6:15 P.M., about an hour before the Snodgrass Hill position was overrun. His note told Bragg only that "we have been entirely successful in my command today." This message was all Bragg had to go on that night from the critical left wing. Written before the Union's final collapse, the note left the impression that the enemy still held the field. Bragg could hardly have inferred anything else from Longstreet's com-

49 Griest Diary, September 20, 1863, Chickamauga-Chattanooga National Military Park Library; Henry Campbell Journal, September 20, 1863, ibid.; Ely Diary, September 20, 1863, ibid.; Jones, "Medical History of the Confederate States," 124–27; George Binford to "Cousin Bob," October 11, 1863, in George Binford Letters, Virginia Historical Society; Official Records, XXX, Pt. 2, pp. 23, 40–41.

50 Sorrel, Recollections of a Confederate Staff Officer, 186–87; Scribner, How Soldiers Were Made, 159; August Bratnober Diary, September 20, 1863, in Chickamauga-Chattanooga National Military Park Library; W. W. Heartsill, Fourteen Hundred and 91 Days in the Confederate Army, ed. Bell Wiley (2nd ed., Jackson, Tenn. 1954), 159; George B. Guild, A Brief Narrative of the Fourth Tennessee Cavalry Regiment (Nashville, 1913).

ment that he hoped "to be ready to renew the conflict at an early hour tomorrow." [51]

After the war Longstreet tried to explain why he sent Bragg no report that the Federals had apparently abandoned the field after dark. He weakly argued that he had sent no further notes because he thought the cheers on the battlefield would tell Bragg of the victory. There were cheers, particularly at that poignant moment about dark when Polk's and Longstreet's men merged in the angle at Snodgrass Hill and discovered the enemy apparently had retreated. Yet this was a poor excuse for the wing commander's failure to report. Longstreet shrugged off the matter by stating it did not "occur" to him to report to Bragg "word of our complete success." [52]

Had his own morale been healthier, Bragg probably would have sent a staff officer to inquire, called Longstreet to his headquarters for a full report, or gone personally to the front to ascertain what was happening. But in his mind he had failed because his rigid battle order to wheel to the left had failed, and his health seemed as much on the verge of collapse as at Cowan the previous summer. One of General John Pegram's staff observed a late afternoon meeting between Pegram and Bragg. Pegram passed Bragg's headquarters, dismounted, and congratulated Bragg on a "brilliant victory." Bragg, pacing nervously in front of his tent, retorted that the army was fearfully decimated and "horribly demoralized." [53]

Bragg's belief that the army still had not won was further indicated. At some time during the night, Polk and Bragg consulted. Accounts vary as to the time and place of the meeting. Polk's son-in-law, Colonel W. D. Gale, accompanied the Bishop. He contended that at about 11:00 that night Polk rode to the commanding general's headquarters and found him asleep. Earlier in the night Polk had sent a staff officer to Bragg telling of a complete victory but had received no orders in return. According to Gale's account, Bragg was awakened by Polk, heard of the victory, but argued with the Bishop that such a victory had not been won. Instead, he spurned Polk's suggestion of an immediate pursuit. General St. John Liddell later recalled a similar incident, but placed the

[51] Longstreet to Bragg, September 20—6:15 P.M., 1863, in Bragg Papers, Western Reserve.

[52] Longstreet to Hill, July——, 1864, in Hill, "Chickamauga—the Great Battle of the West," 659.

[53] A. B. Clay, "On the Right at Chickamauga," *Confederate Veteran*, XIX (July, 1911), 329.

meeting time at 9 P.M. at Polk's headquarters, and claimed that Bragg rode over to awaken Polk.[54]

Regardless of which account is correct, Bragg apparently was not convinced that a Confederate victory had been won. Liddell recalled that Polk simply could not persuade him. Early the next morning, Bragg ordered Liddell's division to advance and feel out the enemy; Liddell reported back that no enemy was there. Too, on the twenty-first, Bragg telegraphed Richmond that although the Confederates held the field, Rosecrans still confronted them.[55]

Bragg may not have been alone in thinking that the enemy perhaps remained on the front that night. There is some evidence that Polk himself did not know that the enemy was in full retreat to Chattanooga. The Bishop privately admitted this in a letter to his wife on September 21. He acknowledged that it was not until 9 A.M. of that day that he definitely knew the enemy was retreating to Chattanooga. Longstreet also may not have understood the situation as well as he later claimed. He did not send cavalry to find out whether the enemy was retreating to Chattanooga until the morning of September 21. Then, shortly before 7 A.M., he also sent forward a line of skirmishers "to find and feel" the enemy. In fact, Longstreet so strongly suspected that the enemy was still on his front, that on the morning of the twenty-first he told Bragg's headquarters that he could not leave his front line.[56]

Even if Polk and Longstreet did know the enemy's whereabouts, the breakdown of communication with Bragg was such that little was accomplished on the twenty-first. Bragg later was severely criticized for not immediately pursuing Rosecrans to Chattanooga or not flanking him out of the town. This criticism relies upon Longstreet's account of his meeting with Bragg on the morning of the twenty-first. Early that morning, Bragg rode over to the left wing. According to Longstreet's memoirs he urged Bragg to cross the Tennessee immediately, strike Rosecrans' rear to force him to retreat, and then either pursue him or recross the river into eastern Tennessee and attack Rosecrans. In his memoirs Longstreet maintained that he suggested this plan and that Bragg accepted it but changed his mind later in the morning.[57]

54 Liddell's reminiscence, in Govan Papers, UNC; Polk, *Polk*, II, 280–81; Gale to W. M. Polk, March 28, 1872, in Polk Papers, Sewanee.

55 Bragg to Cooper, September 21, 1863, in Bragg Papers, Duke; Liddell's reminiscence, in Govan Papers, UNC; Bragg's Chickamauga Report, in Claiborne Papers, *ibid.*

56 Polk to wife, September 21, 1863, in Polk, *Polk*, II, 282; Longstreet to Wheeler, September 21—5 A.M., 1863, in Wheeler Papers, Alabama; Longstreet to Bragg, September 21—6:40 A.M., 1863, in Bragg Papers, Western Reserve.

57 Longstreet, *Manassas to Appomattox*, 461.

However, Longstreet later gave several contradictory accounts of the conversation. His memoirs do not jibe with his account written to Secretary of War Seddon five days after the conversation. To Seddon he explained that he had suggested to Bragg an immediate invasion of East Tennessee, and then a lateral move into Middle Tennessee against Rosecrans' communications. A third version, given in Longstreet's official report, stated that the plan he presented to Bragg was to cross the Tennessee River above Chattanooga, and either force Rosecrans back to Nashville or invade East Tennessee. Yet twenty years after the war, Longstreet wrote Hill that his idea had been either to get between Rosecrans and Nashville or to pursue the enemy to Chattanooga. A fifth version of the conversation was supplied not by Longstreet, but by one of Hill's staff officers who had talked with Longstreet later that day. This officer recalled that Longstreet suggested that the Confederates invade Middle Tennessee and perhaps move as far as Nashville or Louisville.[58]

Despite these discrepancies, on the morning of the twenty-first Bragg apparently toyed with the idea of a bold offensive across the Tennessee and then laid aside the plan. Though Longstreet and others later waxed long on this failure, the fact was that on September 21 the army was in no condition for a long offensive drive. There was a serious food shortage due to breaks in the Atlanta Railroad and to the requisition of trains to haul Longstreet's infantry. For the past three days, Bragg's men had been on half rations, and food was now running so low that Bragg expressed concern privately. Too, any move into Tennessee would be dependent upon wagon transportation. With the remainder of Longstreet's two divisions arriving, approximately 30 per cent of Bragg's army would be Virginians, yet they brought no wagons or livestock. Bragg's own transportation system had been on the verge of collapse since early 1863.

There were also impossible problems of maneuver. Bragg had no pontoon trains to bridge the Tennessee. Also, any move into East Tennessee would expose to capture the extensive system of hospitals along the railroad from Ringgold to Atlanta, which held thirteen thousand wounded. Bragg was acutely concerned over this, because he bitterly remembered having to abandon to Rosecrans the wounded at Murfreesboro. Also, a move through East Tennessee and then laterally into Middle Tennessee,

---

58 Longstreet to Seddon, September 26, 1863, in Polk, *Polk*, II, 288; *Official Records*, XXX, Pt. 2, pp. 289–90; Longstreet to Hill, July ——, 1884, in Hill, "Chickamauga—the Great Battle of the West," 659; James Goggin to J. William Jones, January 2, 1884, in "Chickamauga—A Reply to Major Sykes," *SHSP*, XII (1884), 221.

or directly northwest through the Cumberlands toward Nashville, was almost logistically impossible due to the wagon shortage.[59]

Bragg did not even attempt a limited pursuit of the enemy as far as Chattanooga. During September 21 and 22 he was in the grip of his old indecisiveness, and he buried himself in menial details, such as gathering captured arms from the field. But there was a stronger reason for his delay in immediate pursuit. Bragg believed he could capture Chattanooga without a fight.[60]

The prospects of such a capture did seem excellent. Bragg's intelligence on September 21 clearly indicated that the enemy was withdrawing from Chattanooga. That morning General Nathan Bedford Forrest rushed Bragg a dispatch via Polk which gave the first indications of a general retreat from the town. Forrest, ordered to scout Missionary Ridge, had climbed a spur of the mountain and captured a Federal signal post. He relieved the Federal signal officers of the post at gunpoint, and then climbed to observe matters below him in the Chattanooga area.

Below him spread a panorama. He could see wagon trains churning up clouds of dust as they left Chattanooga, moving around the tip of Lookout Point and perhaps to Middle Tennessee or Alabama. Pontoon bridges floated in the Tennessee. Prisoners interrogated told Forrest that Rosecrans was planning to evacuate the town by pontoon bridges. An excited Forrest scratched off a note about 9 A.M. urging that Bragg hasten to catch Rosecrans while he was leaving.[61]

The importance of Forrest's dispatch has been overrated. Longstreet later blamed the supposed abandonment of his offensive plan on this dispatch, contending that Bragg changed his mind after hearing of it. Longstreet even claimed the message sealed the fate of the Confederacy. Yet this was only one of several such reports which Bragg received on the two days following the battle. On the night of the twenty-first, he ordered Longstreet to push a division toward Chattanooga to reconnoiter. Longstreet sent General Lafayette McLaws, who had arrived only that day from Virginia. McLaws penetrated to within two miles of Chattanooga only to report that the enemy was already crossing the river on pontoon bridges. Another courier from Forrest on September 22 reported the same activity.[62]

[59] Bragg to Davis, September 24, 1863, in Bragg Papers, Duke; Bragg to wife, September 27, 1863, in Bragg Papers, Missouri; Bragg's Chickamauga Report, in Claiborne Papers, UNC; Longstreet, *Manassas to Appomattox*, 461.

[60] *Official Records*, XXX, Pt. 2, pp. 22, 53, Pt. 4, pp. 679–82; Bragg to Cooper, September 21, 1863, in Bragg Papers, Duke; Bragg to wife, September 22, 27, 1863, in Bragg Papers, Missouri; *Official Records*, XXX, Pt. 2, p. 23.

[61] *Official Records*, XXX, Pt. 4, p. 681.

[62] Falconer to Wheeler, September 22, 1863, in Wheeler Papers, Alabama; Brent to Longstreet, September 21, 1863, in Bragg Papers, Western Reserve; Longstreet, *Manassas to Appomattox*, 461.

On September 22 came other stories of Rosecrans' retreat across the Tennessee. Early that morning Bragg ordered Polk to send a division to clear the top of Missionary Ridge overlooking Chattanooga. By noon General Frank Cheatham's division had taken the ridge, and one of his brigadiers, General George Maney, soon reported heavy dust clouds moving from Chattanooga toward East Tennessee, and around Point Lookout toward Middle Tennessee. Maney also noted that Rosecrans' wagons appeared to be crossing the river on pontoons, and stated that all evidence indicated a retreat from Chattanooga. Bragg's chief of staff, General W. W. Mackall, even telegraphed General Joe Johnston that Rosecrans was burning the town. The entire staff seemed convinced, and Bragg on September 22 gave hasty orders to Wheeler and Forrest to cross the Tennessee and cut off Rosecrans' line of retreat.[63]

By 7 A.M. the next morning the army had been put in motion. But at noon when Bragg stood atop the nine-hundred-foot Missionary Ridge to view the Federal army below him in Chattanooga Valley, he saw little evidence of any retreat. And now, scouts reported that the Federals had beefed up the old Rebel fortifications. According to them, two strong defensive lines had been thrown up around the south side of town.

Bragg now had at hand three alternatives: cross the Tennessee and outflank Rosecrans, attack the Federal defenses headlong, or starve out the Federals by establishing a siege line. By the twenty-third, Bragg was convinced that a flank move was impossible. He already knew of the army's dwindling foodstuffs, lack of pontoons, and total lack of transportation for Longstreet's corps. To attack at Chattanooga seemed unnecessary and even suicidal. By September 27 the awful toll of Chickamauga was realized more fully when Bragg received the first inclusive casualty lists. His infantry strength had now dwindled to barely thirty-six thousand effectives. Rosecrans was believed by Bragg to have twice that many men at Chattanooga. Too, reports of heavy Federal reinforcement troubled the Rebels through the weeks after Chickamauga. By September 28 Bragg knew that two corps from the Army of the Potomac were already four days en route to Chattanooga while sixteen thousand of Grant's Vicksburg troops had been for some eight days en route to Chattanooga. By October 1 the threat had worsened. General Joe Johnston warned that at least two corps from Grant's army were marching across Alabama to Chattanooga. It was not merely the disparity in numbers which Bragg feared. The myth that Bragg faced a defenseless enemy at Chattanooga

---

[63] Falconer to Wheeler, September 22, 1863, Brent to Wheeler, September 22, 1863, Brent to Wheeler, September 22—6:30, 1863, Brent to Wheeler, September 22, 1863, in Wheeler Papers, Alabama; *Official Records,* XXX, Pt. 4, pp. 690–91, 694–96.

immediately following the battle was contrived later by anti-Bragg partisans. In fact, a strong defensive line existed at Chattanooga immediately after the battle of Chickamauga, built upon the former Rebel defenses.[64]

An attempt to assault this position seemed both unnecessary and costly. For over a week after arriving at Chattanooga, Bragg still received consistent reports that Rosecrans planned to abandon the town and recross the Tennessee. Some believed his extensive fortifications erected at Chattanooga were merely a subterfuge to cover this crossing. Bragg's signal officers on Lookout Mountain on September 24 and 25 warned that the Federals were retreating. In fact, Longstreet on September 25 warned Bragg that Rosecrans was preparing for a dash against the Rebel line to cover a wholesale withdrawal from Chattanooga on that day or the following day.[65]

Faced with the several alternatives, Bragg by September 29 finally decided upon a strategy. Supplies, pontoons, and transportation would be accumulated for a crossing of the Tennessee. Until this was done, Bragg would adopt a siege posture in front of Chattanooga. He had received word that Rosecrans had only six days' rations. The occupation of the valley of Lookout Creek, west of Lookout Mountain, would cut off Rosecrans' lines of supply via Trenton and Bridgeport. Then the Federals would be thrown back on the arduous Anderson Road and Haley's Trace over Walden's Ridge on the north bank of the river. Both routes were practically impossible for wagon traffic, particularly since heavy rains were washing the area by late September. Bragg, convinced that he either would starve Rosecrans into a retreat or would force him to come out and attack the Confederates in order to secure a line of subsistence, promised the government on September 29, and again on October 3, that he was readying his troops for a flank move across the river.[66]

Though Bragg may have been justified in not immediately attacking Chattanooga or moving across the river—he was later severely castigated for the delay—he failed miserably in implementing his new strategy. Through the last week of September and the early weeks of October, the high command seemed almost paralyzed. No high-level plans were made

[64] Bragg to Davis, September 29, 1863, R. H. Chilton to Bragg, October 1, 1863, in Bragg Papers, Western Reserve; Bragg to Davis, September 24, 1863, Bragg to Cooper, September 21, 1863, in Bragg Papers, Duke; *Official Records*, XXX, Pt. 2, pp. 22–23, Pt. 4, pp. 696, 707, 711, LII, Pt. 2, pp. 530, 532–33, XXIX, Pt. 2, pp. 752–54, 756–58, 766, 769–70; Lee to Davis, September 23, 1883, in Georgia Portfolio II, Duke; Mackall to wife, September 29, 1863, in Mackall, *Recollections*, 178.

[65] Longstreet to Bragg, September 25, 1863, in Bragg Papers, Western Reserve; *Official Records*, XXX, Pt. 4, pp. 700, 701, 703.

[66] Bragg to Davis, September 29, 1863, October 1, 1863, Bragg to Cooper, October 3, 1863, Brent Diary, September 22–23, 1863, in Bragg Papers, Western Reserve.

for an offensive around Rosecrans' flank and across the river. The subject was scarcely mentioned by Bragg. Nor did he implement a genuine siege. During the last week of September his army was drawn up on a line south of Chattanooga which did nothing to halt the flow of Yankee supplies into Chattanooga. Longstreet's corps was aligned with its left flank anchored on the east side of Lookout Mountain, and the corps extended to the bank of Chattanooga Creek. On the east side of the creek, the line was continued eastward across the valley immediately below Missionary Ridge by Hill's and Polk's corps. No troops were placed on the west side of Lookout Mountain to control the line of supply from Bridgeport which Bragg on September 29 admitted was the only genuine Federal artery of subsistence.

There was a singular reason, often overlooked by historians, for Bragg's peculiar handling of the initial operations at Chattanooga, a reason which might well also explain the failures of the ensuing two months of October and November. Before concerning himself with the enemy at Chattanooga, Bragg, en route from Chickamauga Creek, had committed himself to a purge of the enemy within the army. A new cycle of command conflict, battle, and recurring command conflict began on the clear, hot night of September 22, when Bragg wrote his wife a significant letter. The letter was highly critical of Polk's conduct at Chickamauga, and its message portended future disaster for the Army of Tennessee.[67]

---

[67] Bragg to wife, September 22, 1863, in Bragg Papers, Missouri.

ten

The Fall of the Anti-Bragg Men

DURING THE LAST WEEK OF SEPTEMBER, THE ARMY'S HIGH COMMAND began experiencing its worst internal crisis under Bragg's leadership. This upheaval produced a near mutiny among Bragg's generals, and a loss of morale among the enlisted men, and culminated in the Chattanooga disaster in November. Though Bragg was labeled the instigator of this new command trouble, the blame must be shared by his corps commanders. By late September, as Bragg again sought to rid the army of his enemies, many of these officers were also plotting against their commander.

Bragg's attack on his generals was, as usual, badly timed. His mental and physical condition, which may have prompted this new outburst, had improved little since his summer breakdown. Also, the newly structured command hardly needed additional troubles on the heels of the confused situation at Chickamauga. But in his typical determination to condescendingly treat his generals as though they were children, Bragg disregarded the untimeliness of his acts.

Bragg very likely underestimated his opposition in the Army of Tennessee. He miscalculated not only their numbers but also their influence. By September 22 he had decided to move against only two generals, Polk and Hindman. Hindman he planned to hold responsible for the McLemore's Cove incident, and Polk for the failure to make the attack at daylight of September 20.[1]

On September 22 Bragg began with a stiff note to Polk demanding an early explanation of why the Bishop had delayed the attack. When Polk did not immediately reply, Bragg on September 25 again ordered him

[1] Bragg to wife, September 22, 1863, in Bragg Papers, Missouri.

to report at once. But Bragg was not delaying action while he waited for Polk's explanation. By September 25 he had sent Davis two letters. At least one was carried by a staff officer, who was to supply Davis with additional verbal explanation. Bragg's letters described the failures of Polk and Hindman, and hinted that Polk might well be replaced as corps commander.[2]

On September 28 Polk had sent Bragg a long account describing his operations on the night of September 19, and placing much of the blame for delay on General Harvey Hill. The following day Bragg tersely replied that the explanation was not satisfactory. That same day, Polk and Hindman were suspended from their commands and ordered to go to Atlanta and await further orders.

When the President heard of Polk's suspension on September 30, he immediately suggested that Bragg countermand it. Bragg refused, arguing that Polk's conduct was only a repetition of past sins. If Polk were to be restored to command, Hindman also would have to be restored, he argued. Bragg then offered Davis a way out of the embarrassment of the impasse between two old friends: Perhaps Davis would consider a swap of Polk for Hardee.[3]

But Richmond was not ready to bargain. That same day Cooper notified Bragg that he had had no authority to supend Polk. Instead, Cooper declared, Bragg's authority was limited to arresting an officer and preferring charges for trial. Evidently the government hoped that Bragg would now back down. Instead, he placed matters squarely on a collision course. He preferred two charges against Polk: disobedience of orders on the night of September 19 and neglect of duty. He also charged Hindman with disobedience of orders in McLemore's Cove.[4]

While Bragg sparred with Richmond, Polk was busily involved with his own defense. Bragg had underestimated Polk's power in the army as well as with Richmond, for the news of his suspension created an uproar. Expressions of sympathy poured in from his corps and other commands, while generals and civilians visited his Atlanta quarters to offer condolences. Bragg's chief of staff, General Will Mackall, commented that he did not know of a single contented general in the army. The anti-Davis forces in Congress had learned of the suspension, and were sustained by

2 Bragg to Davis, September 25, 1863, in Georgia Portfolio, II, Duke; Polk to Brent, September 28, 1863, in Joseph Brent Papers, Duke; Official Records, XXX, Pt. 2, pp. 54–55.

3 Official Records, XXX, p. 55; Polk to Bragg, September 28, 1863, in Polk Papers, Sewanee; Bragg to Cooper, September 29, 1863, Bragg to Davis, October 1, 1863, in Bragg Papers, Western Reserve; Davis to Bragg, October 3, 1863, in Davis Papers, Tulane.

4 Official Records, XXX, Pt. 2, pp. 55–56.

news of a conversation between Senator Louis Wigfall and the cavalry-man John Wharton. Wharton told Wigfall that dissatisfaction with Bragg was universal and that there was a general desire to have him replaced with Joseph E. Johnston.[5]

Polk played well the role of the wronged suitor. He requested a court of inquiry and collected statements from Hill, Walker, and Cheatham as to what they thought happened on the night of September 19–20. Polk labeled Bragg as a man to be pitied, boasted that repeatedly he had saved Bragg from destruction on the battlefield, and characterized himself as Bragg's wet nurse. Thus, argued the Bishop, Bragg was taking jealous vengeance upon him for the times when Polk had saved the army in difficult positions; indeed, stated Polk, the entire affair was nothing but a plan of hostility.[6]

However, Polk was not as innocent as he would have others believe. At least three days before his removal, Polk was involved in secret meetings with Longstreet, Hill, and Buckner, planning to oust Bragg from command. It was agreed that Polk and Longstreet, who possessed the most influence in the capital, would launch a letter-writing campaign. On September 26 Longstreet wrote to Seddon and urged that Bragg be replaced by Lee. Longstreet wrote Lee directly on September 26 and later in early October. Polk also wrote Lee and urged that he consider moving to Tennessee. That same day, Polk wrote his old friend Davis and characterized Bragg as not being the man for the situation. He blamed Bragg for not pursuing Rosecrans into Chattanooga and asked for Lee or Beauregard. After being sent to Atlanta, Polk on October 6 again asked Davis to remove Bragg. He admitted his part in the meeting with the other corps commanders.[7]

While Richmond studied the conflicting testimony of Bragg and his officers, the discontent within the army reached a new level of bitterness.

---

[5] Polk to wife, October 3, 1863, in Polk Papers, Sewanee; Polk to "Dear Roger," October 17, 1863, in Gale-Polk Papers, UNC.

[6] Polk to daughter, October 10, 1863, Polk to wife, October 3, 1863, in Polk Papers, Sewanee; Polk to "Dear Roger," October 17, 1863, in Gale-Polk Papers, UNC.

[7] Longstreet to Seddon, September 26, 1863, in Polk, *Polk*, II, 288–89; *Official Records*, LII, Pt. 2, p. 549; Polk to Davis, October 6, 1863, in Polk Papers, Duke; Polk to Lee, September 27, 1863, in Polk Papers, Sewanee; Polk to Davis, "In field before Chattanooga," in Leonidas Polk Papers, Harvard. The letter bears no date save "recd. October 7." In his biography of Polk, Joseph Parks indicated that the September 27 letter had not been found. Polk alluded to this letter in a second note to Davis on October 6. Actually, Polk may have written three letters. In his October 6 letter, he states that three were written, one on the 27th. This letter with n.d. was evidently the one written on September 26. In his diary, J. B. Jones noted that a letter was received from Polk on October 7 and was dated September 26. His paraphrasing is much like that in the Harvard letter. See Jones, *War Clerk's Diary*, II, 65–66.

With Polk absent, the intrigue did not abate. Instead, the mantle of leadership had fallen to Longstreet.

Longstreet's activities in late September and October indicated that he had not yet given up his hope to have the western command. Later, after his own quarrel with Longstreet in the East Tennessee campaign, General Lafayette McLaws charged that Longstreet was the ringleader of the October conspiracy. Though McLaws appeared overeager to condemn his superior, there seems to be an element of truth in his estimation of the general's ambition. Longstreet took the lead in sending the series of letters to Richmond immediately after Chickamauga. He later boasted that the other corps leaders had come to him and asked that he take the lead in this particular matter. He did request that Lee come West, but this may have been a token gesture, since he well knew that scarcely three weeks earlier, Lee had turned down the offer when Davis was considering sending a corps to reinforce Bragg prior to Chickamauga.

Longstreet did nothing to discourage the rumors that he would take Bragg's position, rumors which were circulating among his own staff and through the army. Instead, he encouraged such talk by openly criticizing Bragg's conduct of Chickamauga, and by stating what he would have done if he had held the command. Longstreet's talk was so open that General Will Mackall, Bragg's chief of staff, was distressed. No admirer of Bragg, Mackall admitted that "Longstreet has done more injury to the general than all the others put together.[8]

Longstreet's stature and his egging on of anti-Bragg sentiment seemed to be the nucleus around which evolved a secret meeting of the corps leaders on October 4. The purpose of the meeting was evidently twofold: to consider alternative commanders and to draft a petition to Davis for Bragg's removal. Little is known of this unusual meeting. Its culmination was a carefully worded, long petition to Davis asking for Bragg's removal. They were careful to include no condemnation of Bragg's military abilities or mistakes, but instead centered on only one point, that "the condition of his health unfits him for the command of

---

[8] Mackall to Johnston, October 13, 1863, in Polk, *Polk*, II, 291; see also J. W. Harris to "Dear George," October 13, 1863, in J. W. Harris Papers, Confederate Collection, Tennessee; W. H. Farr to "Dear Father," n.d., U.D.C. Bound Typescript, VIII, Georgia State Archives; Ross, *Cities and Camps*, 122, 124–25; Bridges, *Hill*, 233; Mackall to wife, October 9, 1863, in Mackall, *Recollections*, 182; H. J. Eckenrode and B. Conrad, *James Longstreet* (Chapel Hill, 1936), 220–45; Longstreet, *Manassas to Appomattox*, 464.

an army in the field." [9] The identity of the document's author is hidden in denial and counterdenial.

After General Harvey Hill's death, Longstreet in his memoirs maintained an almost childish innocence of the affair and claimed that only after the war did he learn that Hill had written the petition. Although he signed it, evidently kept it at his headquarters part of the time for others to sign, and later openly opposed Bragg before President Davis, Longstreet eventually managed to escape Bragg's blame for the petition.[10]

Hill, too, denied that he was responsible. He admitted signing it, but claimed he had nothing to do with getting it up for others. Instead, he argued after the war that Polk instigated the petition before he left for Atlanta and that Buckner wrote it. One of Hill's staff officers, Major A. C. Avery, contended later that Buckner wrote it and that Hill was even the last of the corps commanders to sign. However, said Avery, because Hill's headquarters was on a central part of the line, the petition was left there for others to sign. For this reason, Hill later was blamed as a chief instigator of the petition.[11]

There is some evidence that Buckner was the author of the document. He was still seething over the virtual elimination of his departmental authority. Bragg, apparently unaware of Buckner's hostility, was, a few days prior to the signing of the petition, preparing to nominate him for a lieutenant generalship. Yet several factors point to Buckner as author. Hill maintained that Buckner wrote it. His signature is the first on the right-hand side of the page, in the position one would ordinarily sign a letter. Opposite Buckner's name are only two entries from Longstreet's corps, while below Buckner's name are nine additional signers from his and Hill's corps. The position of the signatures indicates that it first passed through Buckner's and Hill's corps before reaching Longstreet, who had the document in his possession as late as October 12. Also, on the night of the fourth, when Bragg learned of the petition from General St. John Liddell, his staff evidently believed that Buckner was an instigator of the document. Polk's son William later stated that the petition was supposedly written by Buckner. Too, Buckner may have had more in mind than mere discontent with Bragg. A month after the

[9] Copy of Petition to Jefferson Davis, October 4, 1863, in Simon Buckner Papers, Huntington.

[10] Longstreet, *Manassas to Appomattox*, 465; Longstreet to Hill, October 12, 1863, in Hill Papers, NCA.

[11] Hill to Davis, October 30, 1886, in Rowland (ed.), *Davis*, IX, 498, Bridges, *Hill*, 235–36.

October meeting, Bragg claimed to have evidence that at the meeting it was decided Buckner would be a good successor.[12]

Regardless of its authorship, the petition was the strongest effort yet by the army to oust Bragg, and all who disliked Bragg had not signed. Some of Buckner's brigadiers evidently feared reprisals. General St. John Liddell, an admitted Bragg critic, refused to sign, as did Bragg's old enemy, General John C. Breckinridge. Polk and Hindman, away in Atlanta, did not have an opportunity to sign. Absent also was the signature of Frank Cheatham, a bitter opponent of Bragg. Still, twelve general officers signed the document, including all corps commanders save Cheatham, who temporarily commanded Polk's corps. Several old anti-Bragg generals who commanded divisions and brigades also signed including Generals Pat Cleburne, William Preston, and Randall Gibson.[13]

The depth of the anti-Bragg opposition in early October had penetrated beyond the infantry. Some corps and division commanders in the cavalry also broke with Bragg. General John Wharton, commanding a division in Wheeler's corps, was openly critical. By October 4 all infantry and cavalry corps commanders save Wheeler were strongly aligned against Bragg. Bragg's break with Forrest had occurred the previous week. On September 25 the cavalryman had been ordered to take his corps into East Tennessee, to observe Burnside's corps marching from Knoxville. The following day, however, Forrest was ordered to turn over all of his corps to Wheeler except one artillery battery and a single regiment. Bragg was contemplating the use of these and Wheeler's men on a long raid against Rosecrans' communications.

Forrest was angered for several reasons. Bragg had done something similar in the Kentucky campaign, when the command so tirelessly raised by Forrest had been given to Wheeler. Since the winter episode at Fort Donelson, Forrest's relations with Wheeler had been cool. Consequently, Forrest wired a protest immediately. But on September 28 a terse order was reissued for the transfer of Forrest's troopers to the other corps.

A stormy interview ensued between Bragg and Forrest at Chattanooga. According to Forrest's chief surgeon, Dr. J. B. Cowan, Forrest accused Bragg of persecuting him, threatened to kill him if he interfered with him further, and announced that he would no longer obey any orders

12 Bridges, *Hill*, 235; Liddell went to talk with Bragg immediately after learning of the petition. See Liddell's reminiscences, Govan, UNC; *Official Records*, XXX, Pt. 2, pp. 65–66. Bragg in November argued that Buckner was prominent in an assemblage designed to throw him out, and "was himself mentioned prominently in that meeting as the expected successor." See *Official Records*, XXXI, Pt. 2, p. 650.

13 Horn, *Army of Tennessee*, 286–87.

from the commanding general's headquarters. A few days later Forrest sent his resignation to Bragg to be forwarded to Richmond. It was only through the intervention of President Davis that Forrest was not lost to the service. On October 29 he was transferred to new duties in Mississippi and West Tennessee.[14]

The Davis intervention was part of the President's attempt in early October to soothe matters generally. In addition to correspondence relative to the command clash, he had been startled by a September 29 telegram from Bragg which gave the army's effective strength as only about thirty-six thousand. Davis wondered if a mistake had been made in the cipher, but to his chagrin he learned the following day that the statistics were correct.

Davis was disturbed at the suspension of Polk and Hindman, and by Bragg's refusal to heed his suggestion to drop the charges. He admitted that the opposition to Bragg was now a "public calamity" that jeopardized his usefulness in the western command, and evidently believed that Bragg's charges against his generals were more the product of his nervous temper than reality. Too, Davis was disturbed over the lack of general planning in Bragg's command. As early as September 21 he had declared his intention to go West if he received no better intelligence of affairs and what was planned. Lee had encouraged such a visit and argued that Davis' presence would reconcile the disputers.

But Davis hesitated, and at first sent a staff member, Colonel James Chesnut, to learn the situation. Davis probably was not prepared for the intensity of the anger against Bragg which Chesnut uncovered. The Colonel paused in Atlanta on October 3 for a talk with Polk. The persuasive Bishop seemed to convince Chesnut completely that Bragg had wronged him. The South Carolinian then hurried northward to Chattanooga, where he talked with Longstreet. Then thoroughly convinced that deep trouble existed, Chesnut telegraphed Davis on October 5 to hurry to the army. But he was too late. The previous night, the corps leaders had met.[15]

Davis now lost no time, and by October 8 he was in Atlanta. He stopped to confer with Polk, who seemed to be enjoying his role as an exile. Davis attempted to get him to return to the army, and even agreed that Bragg's charges were unfounded. But Polk would not budge. He asserted that he would resign rather than serve again under Bragg's

14 Falconer to Forrest, October 9, 1863, in Bragg Papers, Western Reserve; *Official Records*, XXXI, Pt. 3, pp. 603–604; Henry, *Forrest*, 198–200.

15 Davis to Bragg, October 3, 1863, in Davis Papers, Tulane; *Official Records*, XXIX, Pt. 2, pp. 771–72, LII, Pt. 2, p. 538; Davis to Lee, September 21, 1863, in Venable Papers, UNC.

command. He seemed somewhat disappointed that Davis planned to dismiss the charges against him. He had spent a pleasant week in Atlanta receiving sympathizers, and proclaiming Bragg to be a weakling, an imbecile, and feebleminded. Polk confided to a friend that he longed for a court of inquiry because it would give him a chance at Bragg. Polk's adamant stand on returning to Bragg's army placed Davis in an embarrassing position. But before Davis hurried north on October 9 to meet with Bragg and the other generals, Polk tactfully offered him a way out. He would, he said, accept a transfer to another department.[16]

It was a clear, cool day when Davis' train rolled into Marietta, the site of Bragg's headquarters. A large contingent of dissident generals and politicians had ridden up from Atlanta with him, including Breckinridge and Longstreet. Also on the train was General John C. Pemberton. That Davis brought Pemberton with him was indicative of his naïveté about the West. After the war Davis admitted that he had invited the Vicksburg defender along in the hope that he could find a command in Bragg's army suitable to his rank of lieutenant general. Davis should have been well aware of Pemberton's unpopularity in the West. In August, Hardee had warned Davis that Pemberton was too unpopular with the Mississippi army to be of service. Governor John Pettus of Mississippi in late August passed on a report indicating that the parolees from Vicksburg and Port Hudson would assemble only if they were convinced they would not serve under Pemberton's command.

Yet Davis stubbornly supported Pemberton and now sought a new command for him. He seemed to equate Pemberton's lack of popularity with that of Lee after Gettysburg. Enmeshed in a public quarrel with Joe Johnston over the responsibility for Vicksburg, Davis seemed to view the criticism of Pemberton and Lee as similar and unwarranted. But the Western army refused to have him. Rumors flew quickly that Pemberton had arrived to take command of Polk's corps. Senator Gustavus Henry of Tennessee dashed off a letter to Seddon, warning that the Tennessee troops would mutiny if this happened. The uproar was too much even for Bragg and Davis. General Will Mackall was given the unpleasant task of telling Pemberton that no one wanted him. A dejected Pemberton quietly left the Army of Tennessee after hearing that not a single division would have him as their commander.[17]

16 Gale to Huger, October 31, 1863, Lucius Polk to "Dear Aunt," November 5, 1863, Polk to daughter, November 15, 1863, in Polk Papers, Sewanee; Polk to Davis, October 8, 1863, in Davis Papers, Duke; Polk to "Dear Roger," October 17, 1863, in Gale-Polk Papers, UNC.

17 Jones, War Clerk's Diary, II, 70; Josiah Gorgas, The Civil War Diary of General Josiah Gorgas, ed. Frank Vandiver (University, Alabama, 1947), 163–64; Jas. Blair to Governor Letcher, August 24, 1863, in Davis Papers, Duke; Davis to Bragg, June

Davis' bringing Pemberton showed no less finesse than his unwillingness to view the anti-Bragg situation with an open mind. It was apparent
to close observers within two days after Davis' arrival that he had not
the slightest notion of removing Bragg. Even before leaving Richmond,
Davis had indicated as much to Seddon.

Davis did not consider Bragg so fine an officer. He knew Bragg's
limitations and admitted that opinion was so strong against him that it
was impairing the army's success. Still, he was determined that he could
find no replacement to take Bragg's command. Before he left Richmond
he had ruled out the only possible substitutes except Lee—Longstreet,
Beauregard, and Johnston. At Atlanta, Davis admitted to Polk that he
would not appoint any of these three, yet he did not wish to pass them
by and promote an officer of lower rank to the rank of full general.
In Longstreet's case the drawback was merely Davis' questioning of his
ability as commander. With Beauregard and Johnston it was probably
more the matter of the old personality conflicts.[18]

Davis' intractable support of Bragg was probably abetted by the bitter
dispute he had been having with Joe Johnston since the surrender of
Vicksburg. The conflict had begun scarcely two weeks after the surrender. A messenger from Davis went to Johnston's department and
presented him with a fifteen-page indictment of Johnston's conduct,
which had been prepared by Davis. The entire letter involved Johnston's
earlier contention that when he was ordered to Mississippi in May, he
considered his command in Tennessee to be ended. Stung by this letter,
Johnston retaliated on August 8 with a long, argumentative review of all
the orders pertaining to his command in the West. Johnston charged
that the government was to blame for the mix-up.

By August the feud was becoming a national matter. Wigfall on the
ninth warned his friend Johnston that Davis was "very bitter" and that
Seddon appeared to be a foe. Wigfall meanwhile scurried about Congress
making sure that Johnston allies had seen the August 8 reply to Davis.
At the same time, western newspapers began to snipe at both Pemberton
and the administration. Leading Mississippi politicians telegraphed
Davis, asking for his assurance that Pemberton would not again command that army. Morale was so low that in August the government did

---

29, 1872, in Jefferson Davis Collection, Beauvoir, Biloxi, Miss.; C. C. Clay to Wigfall,
September 11, 1863, in Wigfall Papers, DLC; *Official Records*, XXX, Pt. 4, p. 727,
LII, Pt. 2, p. 515, XXXII, Pt. 2, p. 514; Mackall to wife, October 3, 1863, in Mackall,
Recollections, 181, Mackall to wife, October 10, 1863, in *Official Records*, XXXII,
Pt. 2, p. 183, Mackall to wife, October 9, 1863, in *Official Records*, XXXII, Pt. 2,
p. 182.
18 Bridges, *Hill*, 239.

not expect to field more than six thousand parolees from Vicksburg and Port Hudson.[19]

Goaded by such incidents, the government ordered a court of inquiry to be held at Montgomery about August 15. Later the government changed the time and place, ordering it to assemble at Atlanta in early September. Members of Pemberton's staff, who generally condemned him, believed the government was holding the inquiry as far as possible from the Mississippi army in order to make it difficult for anti-Pemberton witnesses to appear. Johnston did not know such a court was to be held until two days after the original August 15 designation. He believed that it was a conspiracy against his testimony. Johnston finally obtained a leave of absence and journeyed to Atlanta in early September only to find that the government had called off the inquiry.[20]

Although the hearing was not held, the animosity between Davis and Johnston intensified. Davis' anger was stirred when several newspapers in July published a letter from Johnston's medical director, Dr. D. W. Yandell, to Hardee's medical director. Davis insisted that the letter, which defended Johnston's actions in June and July, could only have been written by one who had access to the general's official correspondence. Yandell apologized to Johnston for causing him embarrassment, and insisted that the letter had not been written for public consumption. Davis was not satisfied with this explanation, but, instead, argued that the letter had been planted deliberately. Johnston in turn denied that he had put Yandell up to writing the letter.[21]

Yet Davis was not guiltless of similar dealings. He had allowed Pemberton's Vicksburg report to be filed directly with the War Department instead of going through the proper channel of Johnston's headquarters. After the report reached Richmond, a series of articles appeared in the Richmond *Sentinel* defending Pemberton. The articles evidently had been written by one who had access to War Department records. One article even contained the original order placing Johnston in command of the West. Johnston protested to General Cooper of the "official impropriety" of such publications. Meanwhile, Davis kept the fires smoldering by writing a reply to Johnston's August 8 communication—

19 Johnston to Davis, August 8, 1863, Blair to Governor Letcher, August 24, 1863, in Davis Papers, Duke; Davis to Johnston, July 15, 1863, in Davis Papers, Tulane; C. C. Clay to Wigfall, August 5, 1863, in Wigfall Papers, DLC; Wigfall to Johnston, August 9, 1863, in Johnston Papers, William and Mary.

20 Govan and Livingood, *A Different Valor*, 230; Johnston to Mackall, August 18, 1863, in Mackall Papers, UNC; C. C. Clay to Wigfall, September 11, 1863, in Wigfall Papers, DLC.

21 Davis to Johnston, August 24, 1863, Johnston to Davis, September 9, 1863, D. W. Yandell to Johnston, August 13, 1863, in Davis Papers, Tulane; Davis to Johnston, August 1, 1863, in Rowland (ed.), *Davis*, V, 582.

a response to Davis' July 15 answer to Johnston's assertion that the government had relieved him of command of Bragg's army when he was sent to Mississippi in May.[22]

Filled with such animosity toward Johnston, the President obviously seemed unlikely to consider him as a successor to Bragg. To consider any successor might be interpreted as a hint that the government's policies had been wrong, especially if Johnston were selected. Thus, with his mind already made up not to remove Bragg, Davis on the night of October 9 turned aside Bragg's offer to resign and called for a meeting of the corps commanders at Bragg's headquarters. Exactly what transpired is something of a mystery. Davis later maintained that the conference was not called to discuss the unhappiness of the corps leaders with Bragg but to plan future military operations. After a lengthy discussion of the military aspects, Davis innocently called for any further comments, whereupon Longstreet spoke up to ask for Bragg's removal. The other corps commanders replied with similar requests.

Davis' explanation does not agree with other accounts. The discussion of Bragg's faults could hardly have been as unexpected as the President tried to make it seem. Though the petition for removal had not been sent to Richmond, Davis doubtless knew of it. It also seems that Davis initiated the discussion of Bragg's capacity to command the army. Longstreet spoke first, maintaining that if Bragg had handled the army properly after Chickamauga, the victory would have been complete. Longstreet concluded that Bragg would be of more use in another theater. Then Buckner, Cheatham, and Hill presented similar views.[23]

Much has been written of Bragg's obvious embarrassment at hearing his lieutenants condemn him. Yet the real humiliation was probably suffered by the opposition. By the night of the tenth, word had been passed that Davis would completely sustain Bragg. The President added further to the embarrassment with a speech made on the night of October 12, when a band came to serenade him. Davis asserted that Bragg was "worthy of all confidence," and that "shafts of malice" had been hurled "harmlessly" against him. Indeed, Davis had assured Bragg within twenty-four hours of his arrival that he would sustain him, a fact Bragg confided to General P. G. T. Beauregard's brother.[24]

22 Johnston to Cooper, September 12, 1863, in Johnston Papers, William and Mary; Govan and Livingood, *A Different Valor*, 230; Wigfall to Johnston, October 6, 1863, in Johnston Papers, Huntington.

23 Bridges, *Hill*, 238; Horn, *Army of Tennessee*, 287–88; Longstreet, *Manassas to Appomattox*, 465–66.

24 *Official Records*, XXX, Pt. 4, p. 734; Brent Diary, October 11, 1863, in Bragg Papers, Western Reserve; Mackall to wife, October 12, 1863, in Mackall, *Recollections*, 185.

Despite his advance decision in the matter, Davis continued to play the role of impartial observer. On October 10 he had an all-day conference with Longstreet. The two rode to the top of Lookout Mountain, often engaging in heated conversation en route. Longstreet later claimed that Davis offered the army's command to him, a statement that does not coincide with views attributed to Davis earlier. Longstreet also said he turned down the offer, which does not seem consistent with his obvious hunger for independent command. Evidently the general did suggest to Davis that he place General Joseph E. Johnston in command, a suggestion which only drew Davis' anger. The conversation ended on an uneasy note, and then Davis conferred with Buckner. The Kentuckian also gave Davis a low estimate of Bragg's capacities.[25]

Thus, the conversations with the malcontents were more for show than earnestness on Davis' part. Not only had Davis decided by October 11 to keep Bragg in command, but both he and the general seemed to agree that the opposition must be squelched. The Polk case was the key to the entire situation, since the Bishop's rebellion had placed the President between two old friends. Polk was actually indispensable to the anti-Bragg group. He not only had Davis' friendship but had been active in getting up the petition to oust Bragg. In short, the anti-Bragg men needed Polk; as long as charges were placed against him, their positions were also secure. Public and army outcry against Polk's removal had been so great that that Davis could not dare to sustain Bragg's decision to oust Polk.

Shortly after leaving Bragg however, Davis found a way to escape his burden in the matter. He visited Polk again on his return trip through Atlanta, whereupon he told the Bishop he would dismiss the charges against him, and on October 23 appointed him to service in Johnston's Alabama-Mississippi department. There he would replace second-in-command Hardee, who would return to Bragg's army. This swap was now a coup for the President. Bragg was cajoled into accepting the dismissal of charges, yet would not be embarrassed by having Davis send back a corps commander he had dismissed. Davis also was bringing back Hardee, whom he hoped would be a peacemaker for the army. He admitted to Hardee that the problem of discontent was not settled and that he was relying upon him for the restoration of "a proper feeling." [26]

25 "Interview with General Simon B. Buckner," Confederate Veteran, XVII (February, 1909) , 83; Longstreet, Manassas to Appomattox, 466.

26 Davis to Hardee, October 31, 1863, in Davis Papers, Tulane; see also Bragg to Hardee, October 25, 1863, in Bragg Papers, Western Reserve; Official Records, XXX, Pt. 2, p. 70, XXXI, Pt. 3, p. 582; Roy's sketch, Hardee Papers, Alabama.

The extreme right of the Federal line on the second day of the
Battle of Chickamauga, September 20, 1863, was at Lee and Gordon's
Mill, shown here, in northern Georgia.

General James Longstreet, corps commander at Chickamauga, was critically wounded at the Wilderness. He was with Lee at the surrender at Appomattox, April 9, 1865.

General William Joseph Hardee, former commander of cadets at West Point, served as wing commander under General Braxton Bragg in the Kentucky Campaign and as corps commander under General Joseph E. Johnston at Chattanooga.

General John Bell Hood, who lost an arm at Gettysburg and a leg at Chickamauga, succeeded General Joseph E. Johnston on the eve of the Battle of Atlanta in July, 1864.

General Joseph Eggleston Johnston, commander of the Department of the West, was assigned to succeed General Braxton Bragg after the Chattanooga debacle in November, 1863.

The northern slope of Lookout Mountain, viewed from the point where General Joseph Hooker directed his troops during the "battle above the clouds," November 24, 1863.

A United States military train at the depot at Chattanooga, 1864, with Lookout Mountain in the background.

A view of earthworks protecting the Chattahoochie River railroad bridge north of Atlanta. General Joseph Johnston hoped to force a fight with Sherman south of the Chattahoochie in the 1864 Georgia campaign.

Sutters' Row, a street scene in Chattanooga during the war.

Confederate camp, in the foreground, at Knoxville, Tennessee. In the distance across the Tennessee River can be seen East Tennessee University, later the University of Tennessee.

View of General Joseph Johnston's fortifications at the battleground near Resaca, in northern Georgia during the May, 1864, campaign.

Confederate encampment beside the railroad bridge over a pass in the Raccoon Mountain Range in northern Georgia, 1864.

Peachtree Street in Atlanta, showing the ravages of Sherman's shelling, during the commands of Generals Joseph Johnston and John Bell Hood, 1864.

Confederate palisades built on the north side of Atlanta, where General Joseph Johnston's reorganized army hoped to defend the city in the summer of 1864.

The other malcontents were not as fortunate. When Davis left Bragg's headquarters on October 14, he issued a proclamation highly complimentary to the general. This declaration, plus Davis' laudatory speeches to the army while in the West, had an important influence on Bragg's own personality. Bragg characteristically tended to savor such encounters and in the postmortem always gloated at the victory over his enemies. The Chattanooga situation was no different. General St. John Liddell, who had more rapport with Bragg than many officers, urged him now to try to cool the differences with his lieutenants. Bragg's inevitably poor sense of timing reacted against this advice. Instead, he boasted to Liddell that he wanted "to get rid of all such Generals." [27]

Bragg, after Davis' departure, was occupied with more than mere gloating over his victory. By October 14 he was committed to the idea of completely revamping his command structure to eliminate opposition. Practically every major officer who had taken part would be driven from the army. Bragg seemed to believe that Davis had given him carte blanche for such a step. In a conversation with Liddell, he insisted that Davis had authorized him to relieve "any and every officer" who did not sustain him.[28] Whether Davis went this far is not known. Davis did tell Liddell in one of three conversations which he had with that officer that the army's troubles were not the fault of Bragg but of the dissatisfied generals. Davis demanded that these men should give their "zealous, unreserved cooperation" to Bragg.[29] In a post-war letter to Bragg, Davis recalled that when he made the decision to keep him in command, it was obvious that "other changes" were necessary.[30] In short, Davis seemed to believe little if any of the trouble was Bragg's fault. He spoke openly of the dissatisfaction with Bragg, and labeled the malcontents as "wholly wrong." [31]

As the mid-October rains turned the Chickamauga and Chattanooga creek valleys into virtual lakes of mud, Bragg again moved against the opposition. He turned now on Harvey Hill. The case against the North Carolinian had been building since immediately after Chickamauga as noted in Bragg's criticism of Hill both to his wife and the President. Then Bragg's September 25 letter to Davis had struck hard at Hill's personality faults, and also criticized Hill's failure to attack promptly on the morning of September 20. What was in store for Hill was evident

27 Liddell's reminiscences, Govan Papers, UNC; Brent Diary, October 14, 1863, in Bragg Papers, Western Reserve.
28 Liddell's reminiscences, Govan Papers, UNC.
29 Ibid.
30 Davis to Bragg, June 29, 1872, copy in Davis collection, Beauvoir.
31 Liddell's reminiscences, Govan Papers, UNC.

in Davis' cryptic reply on October 3. Davis indicated that Polk's failures at Chickamauga should not be regarded "as a higher offence than the disobedience of orders by another officer of the same grade; especially when to the latter is added the other offences you specify." [32]

By the time Davis arrived on the Chattanooga line, the official view of the blame for Chickamauga was turning from Polk to Hill. When he responded on September 28 to Bragg's query, Polk blamed Hill for the failures on the morning of September 20. The following day, Polk sent Hill a long list of questions concerning where Hill was on the night of September 19. When Davis visited Polk in Atlanta, the Bishop evidently tried to shift the blame to Hill. Polk was even claiming in early October that Hill had confessed he was to blame for the failure on the morning of September 20. Too, by the time Davis arrived, Bragg knew that a petition had been gotten up and that Hill was evidently a leading force behind it. That the petition was kept for a time at Hill's headquarters seemed to implicate him further. Evidently, by the time of the President's visit, the petition had become something of a "hot potato." Longstreet on October 12 seemed anxious to remove it from his headquarters and to send it back to Hill's. [33]

Thus, by October 10, the day after his night conference with the President, Bragg made known his intention to remove Hill. Hill's alleged poor showing on the night of September 19 was not the only factor that caused his suspension. He was a convenient sacrifice to save Bragg and the government from a difficult situation. His arrest would relieve much of the criticism of Polk. Strangely, Davis did not apply the same logic to Hill's removal that he had applied to Polk's suspension. On October 3 Davis had argued to Bragg that if Polk were guilty of misconduct, then Hill was also.

Too, Hill seemed the ideal victim. Who would protest his removal? He had no body of support among either western people or the army. Several generals, including Polk and W. H. T. Walker, made no secret of their dislike for Hill's grating personality. Hill had no state following such as Polk's Tennesseans and Buckner's Kentucky elements. Nor did he come from the eastern army with the reputation of a Longstreet. [34]

32 Davis to Bragg, October 3, 1863, in Davis Papers, Tulane; see also Bragg to Davis, September 25, 1863, in Georgia Portfolio, II, Duke.

33 Longstreet to D. H. Hill, October 12, 1863, in Hill Papers, NCA; Polk to "Dear Roger," October 17, 1863, in Gale-Polk Papers, UNC; Polk to wife, October 3, 1863, Polk to Hill, September 29, 1863, in Polk Papers, Sewanee; Polk to Brent, September 28, 1863, in Brent Papers, Duke.

34 Davis to Bragg, October 3, 1863, in Davis Papers, Tulane; Polk to "Dear Roger," October 17, 1863, in Gale-Polk Papers, UNC.

The man was vulnerable, and perhaps there was much truth in Polk's assertion in early October that Bragg "wants a scapegoat" for Chickamauga.[35]

Thus was Hill singled out for the Chickamauga mistakes. On October 11 Bragg asked Davis to relieve him on the grounds that Hill "weakens the morale and military tone of his command," and because he had failed to conform to certain important orders. Two days later, while still with Bragg, Davis authorized the removal. Thus on October 15 Hill was startled to receive orders relieving him from duty and ordering him to report to Cooper in Richmond.[36]

More shabbiness was to follow. The manner in which Hill was removed indicated that Bragg and Davis desired no inquiry into the Chickamauga affair, probably because it would implicate Polk. On October 16 Hill hastened to Bragg's headquarters accompanied by his aide, Colonel Archer Anderson. Hill demanded to know why he had been removed, but Bragg merely stalled and gave no reason. He insisted that no charges would be brought against Hill, but that he was being removed to add to the army's efficiency and harmony. Anderson, who wrote notes of the conversation immediately after it was concluded, recalled that Bragg never alluded to Hill's conduct at Chickamauga, though he did mention McLemore's Cove. Instead, the tone of Bragg's reply was based more on the idea that Hill had not sustained him as commanding general. Hill responded by accusing Bragg of deliberately singling him out from among the other leading generals who had expressed the same lack of confidence. Bragg repeated that he had no charges to place against Hill, and even asserted that Hill was not being removed for any events that had occurred before the close of the battle of Chickamauga.[37]

Though Hill further attempted to uncover the reasons for his removal, he was repeatedly stalled by the government. Under a cloud of suspicion due to Bragg's curious wording in his removal request, Hill departed from the western army in late October. Before leaving he had tried to induce Bragg to put in writing the reasons for his dismissal. This attempt was blocked on October 18 when Bragg's headquarters told Hill that such a reply would not promote "the harmony and interests of the service." In Richmond, Hill was again put off. On November 13 he asked for a court of inquiry to investigate his conduct in the West,

35 Polk to wife, October 3, 1863, in Polk Papers, Sewanee.

36 Bragg to Davis, October 11, 1863, in Hill Papers, NCA; *Official Records*, XXX, Pt. 2, p. 148; Bridges, *Hill*, 242.

37 Hill to Bragg, June 11, 1864, in Bragg Papers, Western Reserve; Bridges, *Hill*, 242–44.

but Davis squelched this idea on November 17. Davis insisted that no court could be held because no charges had been preferred. It was during the Richmond visit that Hill at last learned of the wording of Bragg's October 11 note to Davis. Hill had a stormy interview with Davis in which the statements made by Bragg came out. Hill insisted, however, that he was being removed because he had expressed a lack of confidence in Bragg and for no other reason. Not until November 27 did the government furnish him a copy of Bragg's letter requesting his removal. Further efforts at redress were unsuccessful, and Harvey Hill's ties with the West were finally severed.[38]

Bragg was not content with the removal of Hill from his army. He seemed determined to rid the western army of all he considered trouble-makers. Already Polk, Forrest, Hindman, and Hill had been disposed of. In November, Bragg struck at the root of the opposition, the very organization of his corps. Evidently Davis and Bragg decided, in their mid-October conference, to reorganize the army. Davis' official explanation to Longstreet was that there were too many brigades in a single division from the same state. This, argued Davis, placed too much hardship on a community. But Bragg had earlier nourished the idea of breaking up the powerful Tennessee and Kentucky cliques in the army, and after Davis left he proceeded to do so.

The new organization, which was begun on November 12, completely broke down the old Tennessee-Kentucky blocs. General George Maney's brigade of Tennesseans was transferred from Cheatham's division to that of W. H. T. Walker, a Bragg supporter. The brigade of General John C. Brown, another Bragg opponent, was moved from Stewart's division of Hill's old corps into the neutral camp of General Carter Stevenson's division. Several of the regiments in Walker's division were transferred into the once predominantly Tennessee brigade of General William Bate. Another regiment of Walker's division was transferred to Cleburne's division.

By November the army's makeup scarcely resembled the force which

38 There is some evidence that Hill's version of Bragg's reasons for his removal was correct. Bragg later wrote that he removed Hill when he found him "engaged in mutinous assemblages." See Bragg to Sykes, February 18, 1873, in Claiborne Papers, UNC. General Lafayette McLaws wrote Hill that the real reason he was removed was his opposition to Bragg, and stated, "You were, as you always are, open and out-spoken. . . ." McLaws to Hill, January 23, 1864, in Hill Papers, NCA; Brent to Hill, November 18, 1863, Seddon to Hill, November 27, 1863, Cooper to Hill, November 20, 1863, W. R. Hill to D. H. Hill, March 25, 1864, D. H. Hill to William Graham, May 27, 1864, D. H. Hill to Cooper, November 13, 1863, Cooper to D. H. Hill, November 16, 1863, D. H. Hill to Davis, November 16, 1863, all in Hill Papers, NCA; Bridges, Hill, 244–54; Official Records, XXX, Pt. 2, pp. 149, 152–53, LII, Pt. 2, p. 562.

had risen up against Bragg after Chickamauga. Of the six wing and corps commanders present at Chickamauga, only two remained, W. H. T. Walker and Longstreet. The army was now reorganized into a three-corps system designed to disperse the dissidents. Hardee, who had arrived to replace Polk, commanded four divisions. Cheatham's division was transferred from Polk's old corps to Hardee's command, but many of his Tennessee regiments were dispersed. Cheatham himself expected to be relieved because of his efforts in the confrontation with Davis and Bragg on October 9, and did request that he be relieved on October 31.

Hardee's other three divisions were a potpourri from old commands. Cleburne's division from Hill's old corps contained only half of its original brigades. A new division, that of General Carter Stevenson, was composed of brigades gathered from two Bragg opponents, Generals Simon Buckner and A. P. Stewart. Hardee's fourth division, that of General W. H. T. Walker, was a combination of units from Walker's old reserve corps and from Cheatham's division.

A second corps was commanded by General John C. Breckinridge. The Kentuckian, a bitter enemy of Bragg, had nevertheless maintained himself in good graces by refusing to sign the petition. Breckinridge was given Stewart's old division; only one of Stewart's original brigades was left intact, while the others were placed elsewhere in the army. Stewart's new division now contained transfers from Cheatham's and Breckinridge's old divisions.

Breckinridge was also given his old division, now commanded by General William Bate. Also, on November 15 Bragg restored General Thomas Hindman to his command on the basis of his good conduct at Chickamauga, and sent his division to serve with Breckinridge.

A third corps, that of Longstreet, was also reorganized. Longstreet retained his original two Virginia divisions, those of Generals Lafayette McLaws and John Hood. Hood, still seriously wounded, was unable to assume command, and the division was headed by General Micah Jenkins. Yet several of Longstreet's divisions which had served under his command both during and after the battle of Chickamauga were taken from him. Walker's division was transferred to Hardee's corps, and Preston's division was broken up.

Bragg's new organization seemed to be an attempt to disperse the opposition. Cheatham's division had previously contained twenty-two Tennessee regiments, a hard core of Polk support; now Cheatham possessed only six Tennessee regiments. Breckinridge's division, once containing another nucleus of Kentucky and Tennessee men, was obliterated. Not a single brigade which had served in the division during the spring feud with Bragg was retained in the division. Half of Stewart's

Tennessee regiments had been taken from him in the reorganization.[39]

The most notable absence in the new organization was Buckner's corps. Like Polk, Hill, and Forrest, this corps commander was cut down in the post-Chickamauga uprising. Buckner was vocal in his opposition, and attributed the victory to Longstreet while he called for Bragg's removal. Also, Bragg learned some time in October that Buckner had been mentioned by the anti-Bragg clique as a possible successor to the commanding general.

The final stroke which severed Bragg-Buckner relations was the old squabble over the conflicting powers of their two departments. When Buckner joined Bragg in September, he had assumed that the administrative powers of the East Tennessee department were to remain with him, though Bragg was to have direction of the department's military affairs. Thus on October 20 Buckner was surprised to learn that Davis, at Bragg's request, had ordered the disbanding of the East Tennessee department. Buckner was further incensed to learn that he had lost not only his status as department commander but also as corps commander. When he left East Tennessee, Buckner had kept behind almost a full division of his command, and had actually brought only one complete division, that of General William Preston. But on October 18 Buckner learned that Preston's division had been assigned to Polk's old corps, and that his own position had been reduced to that of a division commander. On the heels of this blow came the word that his department had been disbanded and that the division of his troops on the Tennessee-Virginia border had been turned over to the western Virginia department commanded by General Sam Jones. Preston, another old Bragg enemy, was reduced to the station of brigade commander.

On October 20 Buckner counterattacked. He sent a strong note to Bragg's headquarters complaining that he had lost both his departmental status and most of his troops. Bragg was angered by the note and even more incensed when he learned that Buckner had ignored the orders to revamp his old command. Instead, he had ordered Preston to take command of his troops in southwestern Virginia. Bragg complained to Davis of Buckner's disobedience to orders, and on October 25 sent the Kentuckian a stiff note informing him he was recognized as a division commander and nothing more. This stand was backed up by Davis, who

---

[39] Longstreet to Cheatham, October 21, 1863, Cheatham to Brent, October 31, 1863, in Cheatham Papers, Tennessee; Special Order No. 294, November 12, 1863, in Bragg Papers, Western Reserve. Later, an aide to General Joseph E. Johnston asserted that the reorganization was done to break up the cliques for political purposes and to "keep down the anti-Bragg men." Richard I. Manning to mother, January 17, 1864, in Williams–Chesnut–Manning Collection, South Carolina.

asserted on October 29 that Buckner's command in East Tennessee had ended.[40]

Buckner made one last appeal to Davis on November 5 but to no avail. Bragg had succeeded in embarrassing an army opponent, and had done so by entirely legal means. That his actions were motivated by more than legal matters was indicated by Bragg's summary letter to the government on November 8 recounting the entire Buckner affair. He lashed out at Buckner's participation in "a mutinous assemblage" to remove him from command, and implied that Buckner had in mind to be the new commander of the army.[41]

By mid-November the Bragg opposition seemed to have declined. Hindman had returned, defiant but somewhat battered by the humiliation of his suspension. Cheatham's request for relief had been denied, and he too was in an embarrassing position. Buckner at last acquiesced to his new rank, and Polk and Hill were gone. General Howell Cobb, who visited the army in early November, sent an exaggerated report of harmony to Davis. Cobb argued that the anti-Bragg feeling had been overrated, and that Bragg had the confidence of most of the officers and most of the men. Still, both the Georgian and Davis knew that not all was well. A week before he received Cobb's letter, Davis had admitted to Hardee that the army still lacked the harmony essential to success. Along with his depiction of harmony, Cobb did mention one disturbing element—that relations between Longstreet and Bragg were anything but peaceful.[42]

The Bragg-Longstreet quarrel was to prove to be the army's *coup de grace*. The two months of feuding with other officers had prevented Bragg from giving rightful attention to military duties; the quarrel with Longstreet prevented good results from new policies upon which Bragg had decided. During October and most of November, Bragg lacked a general strategic plan. His late September letters to the government only vaguely had promised a crossing of the Tennessee when manpower and provisions were improved. The letters sent to Richmond by the corps commanders struck hard at this lack of planning. Lee prodded Davis to persuade Bragg to take the offensive while he still had the

40 Buckner to Brent, October 20, 21, 22, 23, 1863, in Buckner Papers, Huntington; Brent to Buckner, October 27, 1863, in Brent Papers, Duke; Bragg to Davis, October 20, 25, 1863, Brent to Buckner, October 20, 21, 1863, in Bragg Papers, Western Reserve; Ross, *Cities and Camps*, 123; *Official Records*, XXX, Pt. 4, p. 703, XXXI, Pt. 3, pp. 651, 653–55, 657–64; Bragg to Davis, October 22, 1863, in Davis Papers, Emory.

41 *Official Records*, XXXI, Pt. 3, p. 651.

42 Howell Cobb to Jefferson Davis, November 6, 1863, in Davis Papers, Emory; Cheatham to Brent, October 31, 1863, in Cheatham Papers, Tennessee; Davis to Hardee, October 30, 1863, in Davis Papers, Tulane.

initiative. The secret meeting of the corps commanders on September 26 resulted in a general agreement that a move across the Tennessee should be made at once.

This lack of action was a key reason for Davis' visit. After his October 9–10 conferences relative to the army's internal matters, he called a war council at Bragg's headquarters to develop a plan. Evidently, two conflicting proposals developed. From Charleston, General P. G. T. Beauregard had dispatched a letter to Bragg, delivered by the general's brother Armand. Beauregard's strategic proposal was similar to those he had previously expressed. The Creole called for a massive concentration from Lee and Johnston at Chattanooga in order to crush Rosecrans. Beauregard's brother reached Bragg's headquarters at the same time Davis arrived, and he had a private meeting with the general on the night of October 9. Bragg spoke warmly of the plan, and promised to present it at the meeting of the war council.[43]

Exactly what occurred at the council, probably held on October 11, is not clear. Bragg presented Beauregard's plan, but did not specify exactly where he intended to cross the Tennessee River. Longstreet later maintained that Bragg favored moving up into East Tennessee, while the Virginia general preferred operating against the Federal railroad bridges and the supply depot at Bridgeport. Longstreet recalled that Davis rejected Bragg's proposal, but accepted his and ordered the army to change its base to Rome, Georgia, prior to operating against Bridgeport.

Longstreet probably exaggerated. It seems strange that he allegedly advocated the Bridgeport plan, since only a few days earlier he had proposed to Seddon the exact plan which he claimed Bragg now presented—a move into East Tennessee. However, nothing came out of the council save the vague idea of keeping up the siege of Chattanooga while awaiting an opportunity to operate against the Bridgeport front. In fact, Bragg's cordial letter to Beauregard on October 14, and his conversation with the Louisianian's brother following the council, indicated that the whole matter was left vague.[44]

This lack of planning and the amount of time expended on the army's command problems led to disastrous results. In October and November a series of major command blunders not only lost Bragg the advantage gained by the Chickamauga victory, but placed his army in

43 Beauregard to Bragg, October 7, 1863, in Beauregard Papers, National Archives; *Official Records*, XXX, Pt. 4, pp. 734, 745–46; Longstreet, *Manassas to Appomattox*, 468–69.

44 Longstreet, *Manassas to Appomattox*, 468–69; *Official Records*, XXX, Pt. 4, pp. 745–46; Longstreet to Seddon, September 26, 1863, in Polk, *Polk*, II, 288–89.

a far worse condition than before the battle. The first error was made in allowing the Federals to open a line of supply into Chattanooga. After Davis' departure, Longstreet had returned to his position as commander of the left wing—that sector from Lookout Mountain down to Chattanooga Creek. Relations between Longstreet and Bragg deteriorated so badly that the Virginia general maintained an almost isolated command on Lookout Mountain. The two held no discussion as to how the Federals should be kept bottled up in Chattanooga. The hauling of Union provisions across Walden's Ridge became almost impossible in the mid-October rain and mud, and thousands of mules and horses perished in the effort. Gradually, Rosecrans' men were reduced to one-fourth rations. Their only possible hope lay in the critical area west of Lookout Mountain, where there was a narrow but vital gateway into Chattanooga, up the valley of Lookout Creek. Two routes converged here—the road up the valley from Trenton, and the road across Raccoon Mountain through the gorge of Running Water Creek. Both led from the supply depot at Bridgeport, and converged in the north end of the valley. By moving up these roads and crossing the Tennessee River at Brown's Ferry, Union supply trains could reach the north bank of the river opposite Chattanooga.

Yet Longstreet failed to seal off this obvious route of Federal trains. To control the Bridgeport routes, a section of his corps must hold the Lookout Creek valley. Longstreet could not command the valley from atop Lookout Mountain. The valley was four miles wide, and the road toward Brown's Ferry was out of range of Alexander's artillery atop Lookout Mountain. Also, the road to Brown's Ferry lay on the opposite side of a long series of hills which extended up the valley to Brown's Ferry. A force could move up the valley to the ferry and be almost unobserved from the mountain itself. Still, the route could be sealed off. The route via Running Water gorge could be controlled from Raccoon Mountain. Both the Trenton and Running Water routes could be bottled up if the Confederates seized the hills which lay adjacent to the road to the ferry landing.[45]

45 Samuel Kelly to wife, November 8, 1863, in William Milner Kelly, "A History of the Thirtieth Alabama Volunteers (Infantry) Confederate States Army," *Alabama Historical Quarterly,* IX (Spring, 1947), 147–48; "Lookout Valley: Memoranda of Gen. E. M. Law (MS in Carman Papers, New York Public Library); William F. G. Shanks, "Lookout Mountain, and How We Won It," *Harper's New Monthly Magazine,* XXXVII (June, 1868), 12; G. W. Brent, "Notes on the Investment and Operations around Chattanooga" (MS in Bragg Papers, Western Reserve); B. F. Scribner, *How Soldiers Were Made; or The War as I Saw It Under Buell, Rosecrans, Thomas, Grant and Sherman* (New Albany, Ind., 1887), 167–68; Sykes, "A Cursory Sketch of General Braxton Bragg's Campaigns," *SHSP,* XI, 494–96; James Harrison Wilson, *Under the Old Flag* (New York and London, 1912), I, 271; Oates, *War Between the Union and the Confederacy,* 286.

Longstreet did little to seal the route. On October 9, only at Bragg's order, he did send two regiments to the river bank below Raccoon Mountain. But these slim forces were designed to keep the Federals from using Haley's Trace on the north bank. No force was placed in Lookout Valley, and during most of October little mention of the importance of the valley was made either by Longstreet or Bragg in their sparse correspondence. Thus the Rebels began to lose their grasp on the Bridgeport route. On October 25 Bragg sent word of a scout report warning that the Federals were preparing to cross the river at Bridgeport. Longstreet was ordered to make a close reconnaissance. That same day, Major James Austin's Ninth Kentucky Cavalry had reconnoitered the pass through Raccoon Mountain, and discovered that Federal engineers were busily rebuilding trestles in the gorge of Running Water Creek.[46]

Longstreet's subsequent explanation for the affairs in late October ran counter to these reports. He argued that he sent Bragg repeated warnings of a crossing at Bridgeport but that the warnings were ignored. Longstreet's later conduct indicated that he paid much less heed to the warnings than did Bragg. Also, Longstreet would argue that he was without cavalry for reconnaissance purposes, and did not know what the Federals were doing. Repeatedly, he complained that he particularly was out of touch with the regiment commanded by Colonel Warren Grigsby. Bragg had sent several cavalry regiments into the Lookout Creek area for reconnaissance. Though Longstreet complained that he had no cavalry aid, the facts do not substantiate this. On October 30 Longstreet complained that he had not heard from Grigsby until October 27. Yet an investigation the following week revealed that Grigsby had reported to Longstreet on October 25, and that same day had received orders from Longstreet to hold his position near Trenton. Also, throughout the last week of October, Longstreet repeatedly was kept informed by Major James Austin of the Ninth Kentucky Cavalry.[47]

Longstreet's statements seem intended to explain away certain errors he made in the Lookout Valley sector during the last week of October. He did not obey Bragg's order to make the reconnaissance toward Bridgeport on October 25. He later stated that before he could do so, enemy movements at Brown's Ferry forced him to recall his reconnaissance mission. Yet nearly two full days elapsed between the original order and the Brown's Ferry attack. Too, Longstreet made no attempt to disrupt

---

[46] Brent to Longstreet, October 9, 25, 1863, Longstreet to Brent, October 26, 1863, in Bragg Papers, Western Reserve; *Official Records*, LII, Pt. 2, p. 549.

[47] Longstreet, *Manassas to Appomattox*, 473–74; *Official Records*, XXXI, Pt. 3, p. 313; Austin, *The Blue and the Gray*, 109; Brent to Longstreet, October 30, 1863, J. R. Buntwell to J. P. Jones, n.d., in Bragg Papers, Western Reserve.

the repair of the railroad bridge in Running Water pass, or to place troops either on the mountain or in Lookout Valley. Instead, Austin's warnings of heavy Federal activity in the gorge were not heeded by Longstreet.[48]

By October 24 Longstreet had received another warning which was almost completely ignored. As mentioned, Bragg had ordered him on October 9 to place sharpshooters at the foot of the Raccoon Mountain sector, to prevent Haley's Trace from being used. In his official report, Longstreet maintained that when Bragg ordered this, he sent the entire brigade commanded by General E. M. Law. Actually, Longstreet sent only two of Law's five regiments. The other three were held on the east side of Lookout Mountain. When Law saw the situation in Lookout Valley, he immediately requested an additional division. He feared the Federals would cross at Brown's Ferry to establish a link with the force reportedly moving from Bridgeport, and thus warned Longstreet that more men would be needed in the valley. All that he received were his three other regiments, which had reached the valley by October 24. No sooner had they arrived than they were taken out of the valley. On October 25, while Law was taking a leave to visit his old commander General John Hood, who was recuperating in North Georgia, the acting division commander, General Micah Jenkins, withdrew his three regiments to the east side of Lookout Mountain.[49]

That by the morning of October 26 Bragg had only two infantry regiments to close off the critical Bridgeport route indicated the lack of communication between Longstreet and army headquarters. Longstreet seemed totally disinterested in affairs west of the mountain. By October 29 he still had not planted his heavy artillery atop Lookout. The general's excuse later for the subsequent loss of Lookout Valley was his assertion that when the Federal push from Bridgeport began on October 27, he repeatedly sent Bragg warnings which the general laid aside. This claim does not jibe with known facts. Actually, as early as October 26, Longstreet had begun to advance a curious theory relating to the Federal objective. He argued to Bragg that any force moving from Bridgeport would not be bound for the mouth of Lookout Valley. Instead, he said, it would halt far short of that point and cross Lookout Mountain some

48 Longstreet did not even plan to implement Bragg's October 25 order until the night of October 26. See Longstreet to Brent, October 26, 1863, in Bragg Papers, Western Reserve; *Official Records*, XXXI, Pt. 1, p. 216.

49 *Official Records*, XXXI, Pt. 1, p. 216; Law, "Lookout Valley," in Carman Papers, New York Public Library.

twenty miles from its northern tip, to flank Longstreet's position.[50]

It would seem that by the morning of October 27, Longstreet would see the connection between Brown's Ferry and the Federal force moving from Bridgeport. On the night of October 26 a Union force of some five thousand men completely overran Law's two meager regiments in the valley. This bold marine enterprise had floated silently downstream, protected by the rainy, foggy night. By early morning they had gained the south bank, had driven back Law's pickets, and were entrenched on the hills bordering the river. Law's small force could do nothing but withdraw to the east side of Lookout Mountain.

Instead of seeing that the enemy had designs on Brown's Ferry, Longstreet on October 27 was still convinced that the Bridgeport column would cross the mountain behind him. On that day, scouts sent Longstreet word that the enemy was advancing up Lookout Valley from Trenton toward Brown's Ferry. Meanwhile, Bragg learned of the Brown's Ferry fiasco and inquired what the general intended to do. Longstreet, shrugging off the loss, argued that the attack on Brown's Ferry was merely a diversion to cover the enemy's real purpose of getting atop Lookout Mountain via Johnson's Crook, some twenty miles to the southwest. When scouts warned of the enemy's approach from Trenton that afternoon, Longstreet placed no force in Lookout Valley, but merely sent Bragg a call for aid to hold Lookout Mountain against the expected move at his rear. In so doing, Longstreet ignored two more detailed scout reports sent that day by General E. M. Law. Law warned that General Joseph Hooker, with the Eleventh and Twelfth Corps, was not marching via Trenton, but was moving through Lookout Mountain in the gorge of Running Water Creek. Moreover, Law warned that a pontoon bridge was being built at Brown's Ferry. Longstreet also did not heed several warnings sent to him and to General Micah Jenkins that day by Colonel William C. Oates, commanding one of Law's regiments. Oates warned that the Federals crossing at Bridgeport evidently intended to cross the Tennessee River at Brown's Ferry.[51]

Part of the trouble was the lack of communication between Bragg and Longstreet. The Virginia general did not bother to inform Bragg on the

[50] Longstreet to Brent, October 26, 1863, in Bragg Papers, Western Reserve; *Official Records*, XXXI, Pt. 1, p. 217; Longstreet to E. P. Alexander, October 29, 1863, in E. P. Alexander Papers, UNC; Longstreet, *Manassas to Appomattox*, 474.

[51] Law, "Lookout Valley," in Carman Papers, New York Public Library; Oates, *War Between the Union and the Confederacy*, 286. Colonel Oates, commanding a regiment in Law's brigade, insisted that he sent both Longstreet and Jenkins several messages on October 27, warning that the Bridgeport force would try to cross at Brown's Ferry. See also Longstreet to Brent, October 27, 1863, in Bragg Papers, Western Reserve; Liddell's reminiscences, in Govan Papers, UNC.

morning of October 27 that Brown's Ferry had been taken. Bragg only learned of it when he sent General St. John Liddell to Lookout Mountain after hearing heavy musket firing in that direction. Liddell reported that the ferry was captured and that a pontoon bridge was being built. Though Bragg was outraged, he did nothing to retake the position. When he received Longstreet's explanation that the seizure of the ferry was a feint, Bragg seemed pacified. He gave no orders on the evening of October 27 for Longstreet to counterattack. Instead, Bragg and Longstreet spent the evening dickering over how many men Longstreet should put on the crest of Lookout to prevent a flanking move via Johnson's Crook. The only order given Longstreet was a discretionary one sent at about 11 P.M. Longstreet was to retake Brown's Ferry the next day if he learned that a force actually was not marching north from Trenton.[52]

By the morning of October 28 the situation had become more ridiculous. Bragg ordered Longstreet to meet him atop Lookout Mountain for a council on future plans. The meeting was not a pleasant one. Bragg had recently heard a rumor that Longstreet had boasted to Davis that his own corps alone could whip Rosecrans. While the two generals talked, a messenger from the west side of Lookout Mountain brought startling news. A large Federal column was marching up the valley through Wauhatchie, headed for Brown's Ferry. Bragg and Longstreet hastily rode to the western rim, amidst the futile roar of Alexander's artillery which was unsuccessfully attempting to reach the road. Longstreet later intimated that Bragg was more surprised than he. Actually, he too must have been shocked as he saw two Federal corps under Hooker marching toward Brown's Ferry.[53]

So strong was the resentment between the two officers that they could not even carry through a plan to retrieve the lost situation. That same evening Bragg and Longstreet attempted to conjure a plan for a night attack against the forces moving up Lookout Valley. There was total confusion as to the objective of the attack and to the number of troops Longstreet was to use. Longstreet thought that the agreement was for him to attack Hooker's rearguard, estimated at fifteen hundred men strong, that had halted some three miles shy of Brown's Ferry. Bragg thought that Longstreet was planning an attack on Hooker's main force, which had arrived at Brown's Ferry.

52 Longstreet to Brent, October 27, 1863, Brent to Longstreet, October 27—11 P.M., 1863, Brent to Longstreet, October 27, 1863, Longstreet to Brent, October 27, 1863, in Bragg Papers, Western Reserve; Liddell's reminiscences, in Govan Papers, UNC.

53 Longstreet, *Manassas to Appomattox*, 474–75; Liddell's reminiscences, in Govan Papers, UNC.

Neither understood the number of men to be used. Longstreet later tried to blame Bragg for the failure of the attack on that night of October 28. He maintained that Bragg would not give him enough men to make it successful. He argued that Bragg allowed him only Jenkins' division, and held back McLaws' division, though the Virginian had been counting upon it.

Longstreet's reminiscence does not coincide with recorded facts. Several times on the night of October 28, Bragg assured Longstreet that his entire corps of three divisions, Jenkins', McLaws', and Walker's men, could be used for any offensive. Bragg had already released Longstreet's entire corps for such a battle in his orders of 11 P.M. the previous night, when he told the general to make the attack on October 28 if he learned the Federals were not actually moving north from Trenton. Also, before dark on October 28, Longstreet sent a note to Bragg indicating that he intended to make the attack with only the single division of Jenkins. This does not agree with his later assertion that he waited until midnight, expecting McLaws' division to be sent.[54]

Longstreet's blaming Bragg was probably intended to cover the blunders of the night attack. By dark, Jenkins' troops were moving down the steep Lookout Trails, accompanied by Longstreet. In the valley the command was divided. Law, with his own and Robertson's brigades, was to move to a point on the valley road about midway between Brown's Ferry and the presumed position of Hooker's rear guard. Law was to block the road, preventing any reinforcements from reaching the rear guard, which was to be attacked by the lone brigade of Colonel John Bratton, with General "Rock" Benning in a reserve status. Law protested that his seventeen hundred men could scarcely contain the twelve thousand troops believed to be encamped at the ferry landing, but was ordered to hold firm.

The engagement was a disaster. Longstreet, accompanying Jenkins with the attacking column, did not even reach Lookout Valley until about midnight. By 1:00 A.M. they reached the valley road, but found no rear guard. Disgusted, Longstreet called off the plan of attack and instead ordered Jenkins to round up stragglers and wagons. Then Longstreet returned to his headquarters across Lookout. There, about 2:30 A.M., he received word from Jenkins that Law's brigade was being attacked.

The encounter was brief. Law's and Robertson's brigades were no

---

[54] Brent to Longstreet, October 28—6 P.M., 1863, Brent to Longstreet, October 28—7:30 P.M., 1863, Longstreet to Bragg, October 28, 1863, Longstreet to Brent, October 29, 1863, Brent, "Notes on the Investment and Operations around Chattanooga," all in Bragg Papers, Western Reserve; Longstreet, *Manassas to Appomattox*, 475–76; *Official Records*, XXXI, Pt. 1, p. 218.

match for the Federal corps which had moved from Brown's Ferry to attack them. Law's position on the range of hills bordering the Wauhatchie road was overrun with little trouble. He held out for some two hours in order to give Jenkins time to pull the remainder of the division back across Lookout Mountain. For this defense, Law only received Jenkins' criticism. The two were bitter rivals, for each probably coveted the command of Hood's division. Jenkins was critical of Law in his official report, as was Longstreet. Longstreet considered placing Law under arrest, and did suspend the other brigade commander, General Jerome Robertson.[55]

The loss of the Bridgeport route forced the Confederates to take a new look at the Chattanooga siege. What ensued was another major command error attributable to a lack of rapport among the officers. By October 30 the rainy weather had not ceased. The dark, cold, and stormy weather well suited the army's temper. Hardee had returned that week, only to discover a situation which portended disaster. Bragg was blaming Longstreet for the failure to hold Lookout Valley, and was intimating to Davis that the general had disobeyed his orders. Evidently Bragg now rued praising Longstreet to Davis immediately after Chickamauga. The Virginia officer's part in the anti-Bragg move seemed to be clearer to Bragg. Thus, by October 30, Bragg once more was threatening to resign unless more heads rolled. He begged Davis to visit the army again, and hinted that he planned to suspend more generals.[56]

This personal feud formed the background for the second major command blunder at Chattanooga. The loss of the Bridgeport route meant that a line of Union supply was now open across Raccoon Mountain to Brown's Ferry. Equally serious, it meant that Rosecrans could receive reinforcements. By November 1 Bragg knew that Hooker's two corps were at Chattanooga. Bragg had known for a month that Sherman's corps was moving to Chattanooga; by October 26 Sherman was pinpointed in North Alabama, and was slowing repairing the Memphis and Charleston Railroad as he advanced. The day before, Bragg's scouts had captured a courier with a grim note. Rosecrans had been replaced by General George Thomas, and Grant himself was coming to Chattanooga to direct the combined forces of Sherman, Hooker, and Thomas. Bragg knew that Sherman had between twenty thousand and twenty-five thousand men, and believed Hooker had twelve thousand more. In addition, General Ambrose Burnside, with the Twenty-third and Ninth corps, remained in

55 Longstreet, Manassas to Appomattox, 476–77; Official Records, XXXI, Pt. 1, pp. 217–19, 226–28; Longstreet to Brent, October 29, 1863, in Bragg Papers, Western Reserve; Law, "Lookout Valley," in Carman Papers, New York Public Library.

56 Official Records, LII, Pt. 2, p. 556; Brent Diary, October 29, 1863, in Bragg Papers, Western Reserve.

East Tennessee within easy distance. Even excluding Burnside, it was clear the Federals were gathering some eighty thousand to ninety thousand men at Chattanooga.[57]

It was also clear that the siege would not work. Alexander's artillery shelled Chattanooga daily from atop Lookout Mountain, but his efforts were futile. Though he depressed the muzzles, the range was simply too far and the angle too steep. The Wauhatchie Road and Brown's Ferry were out of artillery range. So was the pontoon bridge immediately opposite Chattanooga, where supplies were brought into the city after being first crossed to the north bank at Brown's Ferry.

Desperate, Bragg's generals groped for some plan. Initially, Bragg favored attacking Hooker's two corps in Lookout Valley. Thus, about October 31, Longstreet, Breckinridge, and Hardee were ordered to visit Lookout Mountain and discuss the feasibility of such a plan. General Micah Jenkins reported that twenty thousand Federals were entrenched in Lookout Valley, dug in on the range of hills adjoining the Wauhatchie Road. Besides a few trails on the west face of the summit, there was only one road leading around the face of the mountain down into the valley and this road was under artillery fire from Federal guns in Moccasin Bend. Moreover, the road was so steep that Rebel artillery could not be safely brought down it into Lookout Valley. Any artillery must make a long detour of almost fifty miles down the gap through Johnson's Crook. All three officers seemed to agree that such a move was impossible.[58]

Their decision was a mere formality, for by October 31 Bragg had already decided on a new plan. On October 29 the President had suggested a new course of action to Bragg. Though he still favored operating toward the Bridgeport area, Davis proposed an alternative plan if matters did not go well on that front. Bragg was to send two divisions under Longstreet to deal with Burnside in East Tennessee. Davis' failure to see the seriousness of the Union concentration at Chattanooga was obvious. He did not particularly intend for Longstreet to return to Chattanooga. Instead, he saw such a move as placing the Virginian in a good position to return to Lee's army easily.[59]

Bragg's reasons for accepting this idea were mixed. He never explained the military value in detaching a corps of his army in the face of the enemy's reinforcement by three corps. Bragg did hope that the defeat of

[57] Bragg to Davis, October 26, 1863, Chilton to Bragg, October 1, 1863, in Bragg Papers, Western Reserve; *Official Records*, XXXI, Pt. 1, pp. 26, 28–29, Pt. 3, pp. 600, 681, 691, XXX, Pt. 4, pp. 720, 734.

[58] *Official Records*, XXXI, Pt. 1, p. 218; Jenkins to G. M. Sorrel, October 31, 1863, in Micah Jenkins Papers, Duke.

[59] Davis to Bragg, October 29, 1863, in Davis Papers, Tulane.

Burnside would force Grant to detach part of the Chattanooga garrison to relieve him. Yet with Longstreet's two divisions absent, Bragg would have only about thirty-six thousand infantry, scarcely enough to launch an offensive against a force feared to be at least eighty thousand men. Too, Burnside's defeat would not necessarily force Grant to retreat from Chattanooga, as it would not endanger his line of communication into Middle Tennessee.

Motives of a personal nature were strongly behind Bragg's decision to send Longstreet. Why did he select the Virginian? Others were more accessible. In mid-October, Bragg had sent General Carter Stevenson into East Tennessee. Stevenson's division, aided by two cavalry brigades, was to keep Burnside on the north bank of the Tennessee River opposite Loudon. By November 1 Bragg had reinforced Stevenson with a second infantry division, that of Frank Cheatham, whose command was held temporarily by General John K. Jackson. Thus, by November 1, Bragg already had about eleven thousand infantry and cavalry in the valley. Stevenson's men knew the country and possessed their own transportation. By his own admission, Longstreet knew nothing of East Tennessee, had no maps, and had no scouts who knew the country. He also suffered from a transportation shortage. His wagons had been left in Virginia, and his corps had a great shortage of mules and horses for their artillery. Too, Longstreet occupied the extreme left of Bragg's line, whereas Bragg more easily could have sent troops from Breckinridge and Hardee on the center and right positions.[60]

But the danger and the impracticable nature of sending Longstreet had given way to personal motives. Bragg simply wanted to be rid of the man. On October 31 he spoke to Davis of "disrespectful and insubordinate" correspondence received from Longstreet and admitted that sending him to East Tennessee would be a "great relief to me." [61] To General St. John Liddell, Bragg confided that he sent Longstreet "to get rid of him and see what he could do on his own resources." [62]

Longstreet's role in initiating the move to East Tennessee is difficult to understand. He later explained that he heard rumors that Bragg had decided to send him, but did not know definitely until he met with

[60] Bragg to Carter Stevenson, October 24, 1863, Brent to Stevenson, October 17, 1863, Brent to George Dibrell, October 17, 1863, Brent to McMicken, October 22, 1863, Bragg to Davis, October 17, 1863, in Bragg Papers, Western Reserve; Frank Armstrong to Stevenson, November 4, 1863, J. J. Morrison to Jno. Reeve, November 1, 1863, Brent to Stevenson, October 24, 1863, James Park to Stevenson, October 21— 11:30 A.M., 1863, in Carter Stevenson Papers, National Archives; Official Records, XXXI, Pt. 3, pp. 576, 600–601, 638.

[61] Bragg to Davis, October 31, 1863, quoted in Seitz, Bragg, 392.

[62] Liddell's reminiscences, in Govan Papers, UNC.

Bragg and the other corps commanders in a countil of war shortly after November 1. Longstreet subsequently claimed that at this council he urged Bragg to send him with fifteen thousand men into East Tennessee to crush Burnside, and then to return before Sherman could reach Grant. In both his official report and his later reminiscences, he maintained that he fashioned the invasion plan. He recalled that he urged Bragg to put the army in a defensive position south of Missionary Ridge, behind Chickamauga Creek, until Longstreet could bring back his troops.[63]

Longstreet's version does not agree with that of Hardee. In April of 1864 Hardee insisted that Longstreet did not arrive at the council with an invasion plan for East Tennessee, but that he urged a move across the Tennessee at Bridgeport. Only after being rebuffed by Bragg did Longstreet suggest that he be sent with fifteen thousand men against Burnside. Hardee denied Longstreet's suggesting that Bragg place the army in a safe position behind the Chickamauga until his men returned. Equally important, Hardee could not recall any agreement made whereby Long street was to return to Chattanooga after he defeated Burnside in East Tennessee. His version of Bragg's advice was that Longstreet could defeat Burnside "and if need be" return before Sherman reached Chattanooga.[64]

The variance in the two accounts was indicative of the entire lack of understanding of the East Tennessee expedition. Prior to leaving Chattanooga, Bragg and Longstreet did not reach an agreement as to whether the Virginian was to return. Bragg's orders of November 4 authorizing the move to the valley said nothing of Longstreet's returning. Bragg merely stated that the campaign's object was to drive Burnside from East Tennessee or destroy him. On November 5, while his corps was in the process of moving out of Chattanooga, Longstreet sent Bragg his views on the move and asked if they were correct. He stated that his understanding was "that I should gain possession of East Tennessee." If this could be done and still maintain rail communication with Chattanooga, that would be good. However, "to get East Tennessee and to get rid of the enemy's forces there," Longstreet warned that he would have to break rail communication with Chattanooga. That Longstreet was not planning to return was evident from his suggestion that if he were successful in East Tennessee, Bragg could launch his own offensive against Grant or move to join him in the East Tennessee valley. Though Longstreet asked Bragg to tell him whether this version of the campaign plan was correct, Bragg's November 6 reply contradicted nothing Longstreet

63 Longstreet to Buckner, November 5, 1863, in Louisiana Historical Collection of Civil War Papers, Tulane; Longstreet, *Manassas to Appomattox*, 480–81; *Official Records*, XXXI, Pt. 1, p. 455.
64 Hardee to Longstreet, April 8, 1864, in Hardee Papers, Alabama.

said and did not mention his returning to the Chattanooga area. Instead, he reiterated that the campaign's purpose was "to get possession of East Tennessee." [65]

This lack of an understanding of purpose was matched by other equally serious errors. The original orders of November 4 called for a rapid move by Longstreet's two infantry divisions, some twelve thousand men, and some five thousand cavalry under General Joseph Wheeler. Even if Longstreet were not to return, it was critical that he press Burnside hard in order that some pressure might be taken off Bragg. But his corps was in no condition to move swiftly. He possessed no commissary, quartermaster, or engineer officer who knew the country. He was forced to rely on wagons and teams supplied by Bragg to forage an unknown area. There was a shortage of trains at Chattanooga to move his command northward. Longstreet had pontoons with which to cross the Tennessee River but had no pontoon train. Not until November 9 did his two divisions even make the sixty miles to Sweetwater. More delay followed. Longstreet had expected to find a Confederate commissary depot at Sweetwater, but to his chagrin he learned that it had been sent back to Chattanooga when Stevenson left the area. He thus had to halt for four more days to find food.

The lack of transportation not only delayed Longstreet, but also forced him to revise his strategy. The initial plan called for him to strike northeast from the railroad, cross the Little Tennessee River, and occupy the heights opposite Knoxville. He believed he could drive Burnside from the Knoxville defenses with artillery, and force him to fight on open ground. Yet, without wagons to haul his pontoons, Longstreet was tied to the railroad. He was forced to move northward to the Tennessee River crossing of the East Tennessee Railroad at Loudon. Not until November 13, some two weeks after the swift blow was planned, did Longstreet reach Loudon.[66]

By the time he reached the river, Longstreet had almost completely broken ties with Bragg. The situation was reminiscent of the previous autumn, when young Kirby Smith practically seceded from Bragg's command. Either because of personal hatred or because he thought Longstreet was no longer under his command, Bragg did not keep in close touch with the general. Aside from repeated urging for Longstreet to

[65] Bragg to Longstreet, November 4, 1863, Longstreet to Bragg, November 5, 1863. Bragg to Longstreet, November 6, 1863, in Bragg Papers, Western Reserve.

[66] Correspondent of Charleston *Courier*, December 9, 1863 (MS in Alexander Papers, UNC); Sorrel, *Recollections of a Confederate Staff Officer*, 200–201; *Official Records*, XXXI, Pt. 1, pp. 455–57; M. B. McMicken to Bragg, November 15, 1863, Longstreet to Brent, November 5, 1863, Bragg to Longstreet, November 12, 1863, Longstreet to Bragg, November 11, 1863, in Bragg Papers, Western Reserve.

move faster, Bragg gave no orders. Was Longstreet still under his jurisdiction? Davis only muddled matters by telling Bragg that he hoped
Longstreet would "cooperate" with him.[67]

As Longstreet went farther from Chattanooga, he became more aloof
toward Bragg. Longstreet did not cross the Tennessee River until November 15. He lost a chance to ensnare Burnside on the north bank of
the river opposite Loudon, and instead pursued him into the Knoxville
defenses. By November 18 Longstreet was drawn up before the defenses
on the west side of town. During this delay Bragg's queries did not reflect his learning on November 18 that Sherman's reinforcements were
approaching Chattanooga. On November 20 he merely asked Longstreet
if he could keep Bragg informed "of your progress and prospects." [68]
Two days later Bragg indicated that he wished him "full success and
look to your progress with great interest." [69] By November 23, though
Bragg believed that Grant now had six corps at Chattanooga, he did not
order Longstreet back, but merely told him he wished him "speedy
success." [70] Hardee was so troubled by the obvious split of the army into
two sections that on November 22 he suggested Bragg send a staff officer
to Longstreet "to explain your views." [71] It was obvious from the tone of
his dispatches that Bragg's views did not include the belief that he could
order Longstreet back.

Nor did Longstreet care for his old commander's views. Slowly but
surely, Longstreet on November 4 had begun a policy that would lead to
secession from Bragg's army—the building of an independent command
for his expedition. Gradually he lost concern for Chattanooga's fate. That
day he requested that Stevenson's division be retained in East Tennessee
as part of his invasion force. Angered when Bragg replied that such had
never been intended, Longstreet suggested that the remainder of Bragg's
forces at Chattanooga, even without Stevenson's division, would equal
the size of Grant's army. Later, Longstreet indicated further not only that
he was disinterested in Bragg's problems, but that the East Tennessee
expedition might take longer than expected. He warned Bragg that
Burnside had twenty-three thousand men, too many for his force alone to
defeat. Thus, Bragg must send him another division if he hoped for any
results. On November 11, when he learned from Bragg that Sherman
with twenty thousand men was within six days of Chattanooga, Longstreet's call for more men did not stop. He argued on November 18 that

67 Davis to Bragg, November 25, 1863, in Davis Papers, Tulane.
68 Brent to Longstreet, November 20, 1863, in Bragg Papers, Western Reserve.
69 Brent to Longstreet, November 22, 1863, in *ibid.*
70 Bragg to Longstreet, November 23, 1863, in *ibid.*
71 *Official Records,* XXXI, Pt. 3, p. 737.

Grant was probably reinforcing Burnside. On November 20 his secession-ist attitude led him to take unreasonable positions. When he heard that Grant was massing troops on Bragg's flank in Lookout Valley, Longstreet characterized the operation as a mere feint to force Bragg to retreat. Longstreet argued that the Federals themselves would retreat if they learned that Bragg did not intend such. Moreover, if they attempted to flank Bragg, he could beat them easily. Such reasoning does not correlate with his late September declarations to the government of the great danger Bragg faced at Chattanooga, at a time when his own corps was present and those of Sherman and Hooker were not.[72]

Longstreet was not solely to blame for the communications breakdown. After Knoxville was invested, Bragg still did not order the general either to return or even to explain what he planned. When Longstreet tele-graphed for more men on November 20, Bragg was angry and com-plained that he "has not advised me of any part of his operations." [73] Davis termed Longstreet's failure as "unaccountable." [74] On November 23 Bragg suddenly gave in to Longstreet's demands for more men. Though he knew nothing of the general's intentions at Knoxville, Bragg prepared to send him two more divisions, those of Generals Cleburne and Buckner. Bragg's befuddlement was indicated by his plans to send the reinforcement after he learned of Sherman's arrival at Chattanooga. Too, Bragg knew that the railroad bridge across the Hiwassee River had been washed away, making a speedy return impossible, and knew as early as November 18 that Grant was concentrating Hooker's two corps in Look-out Valley. Still, completely subdued by the Virginian, Bragg prepared to send eleven thousand more men. This addition would give Longstreet twenty-eight thousand men to combat an estimated twenty-three thou-sand under Burnside, and would leave Bragg's effective force at slightly over twenty-eight thousand men to contest at least eighty thousand be-lieved to be massed by Grant at Chattanooga. Thus, by the last week of November, Longstreet had gained much of what he probably had desired all along, including an independent command, freedom from Bragg, and the promise of more reinforcement. For all purposes, by November 20 the Virginia general had bowed out of the Chattanooga campaign.[75]

The loss of Lookout Valley and the division among Bragg's forces were no more serious command errors than that of allowing Rosecrans' supply

[72] *Ibid.*, pp. 671, 707, 733, 739; Longstreet to Bragg, November 4, 5, 11, 1863, Bragg to Longstreet, November 5, 1863, in Bragg Papers, Western Reserve.

[73] *Official Records*, XXXI, Pt. 3, p. 723.

[74] *Ibid.*, LII, Pt. 2, p. 562.

[75] Brent Diary, November 18–23, 1863, Bragg to Longstreet, November 20, 23, 1863, in Bragg Papers, Western Reserve.

route to function almost unimpeded. The Yankee supply line from Chattanooga to Kentucky was a slim thread of a single-track rail line. The long 151 miles from Chattanooga to Nashville was especially vulnerable. West of Chattanooga, the railroad cut through Running Water gorge in Raccoon Mountain, where vast trestle works invited destruction. The railroad then crossed to the north bank of the river on two long wooden trestle bridges at Bridgeport. North of Stevenson, where the rail line veered toward Middle Tennessee, a series of trestles spanned deep ravines across Crow Creek. North of these trestles was the long Cowan Tunnel which led into Middle Tennessee. North of the tunnel, the rail line repeatedly bridged the main streams and tributaries of Elk, Duck, and Stone's rivers before reaching Nashville. In October of 1863 the Federals had almost no defenses for the Nashville and Chattanooga Railroad. The massive blockhouse construction which dotted the line during Sherman's Georgia campaign was yet to be constructed; only scattered detachments guarded the entire line.[76]

Too, where the railroad emerged from the Cowan Tunnel and swung eastward toward the crossing at Bridgeport Island, it was exposed to heavy forces of Rebel horsemen. In Alabama, Johnston's department boasted 11,000 cavalry under General Stephen D. Lee. Lee had several seasoned division commanders, including Forrest, "Red" Jackson, and James Chalmers. In addition, that portion of the Tennessee department in Alabama, north of the river, held another 1,000 men in the division of General Philip Roddey. Also, by October, Wheeler had some 13,620 cavalrymen present for duty at Chattanooga, in the divisions of Generals Will Martin, Frank Armstrong, and John Wharton. With this force of 25,000 cavalry available, Johnston and Bragg could have operated against the Nashville and Chattanooga railroad, or against the Memphis and Charleston line, which was being rebuilt by Sherman as he moved eastward across northern Alabama toward Rosecrans' besieged army.

Yet never had Bragg's cavalry been so poorly utilized. During October and November there was no coordinated effort to strike either Sherman's approaching columns or the Nashville supply line. Instead, a complicated command tangle ensued. On September 29 Bragg had asked Johnston for cooperation in cutting Rosecrans' rail line. Johnston agreed, but he and Bragg prepared two completely different plans. Johnston planned

76 W. E. Merrill, "Block-Houses for Railroad Defense in the Department of the Cumberland," in Ohio Commandery, *Sketches of War History 1861–1865,* III, 390–93. Sherman later wrote, "Our greatest danger is from cavalry, in which arm of service the enemy is superior to us in quantity and quality, cutting our wagons or railroads." Sherman to wife, May 22, 1864, in M. A. DeWolfe Howe (ed.), *Home Letters of General Sherman* (New York, 1909), 293; Carter, *First Tennessee,* 161–62.

to send General Stephen Lee across the Tennessee River, and wanted Bragg to have Roddey join him near Decatur, Alabama. Meanwhile, Johnston suggested that Bragg also send part of Wheeler's cavalry across the river. Consequently, on October 2, Johnston ordered Lee to cross the Tennessee and strike the Nashville and Chattanooga rail line, preferably the bridges across the Elk and Duck rivers.[77]

But the grand sweep envisioned by Johnston did not develop. Bragg did not send Roddey to join Lee. On September 30 he ordered Roddey on his own raid across the river to strike Rosecrans' wagon road up Sequatchie Valley and over Walden's Ridge. Also, elements of Wheeler's corps were not sent to join Lee. On September 29 Wheeler was ordered to take Martin's and Wharton's divisions, and part of Forrest's old command, for a strike at the wagon road in the Sequatchie Valley.[78]

These three separate moves accomplished nothing of any lasting importance. Wheeler did destroy a train of eight hundred wagons in the valley, but the success of this raid has been distorted. Wheeler all but wrecked his command by sending it on a long sweep into Middle Tennessee, penetrating almost to Nashville, and then recrossing the Tennessee River near Decatur. After a defeat on October 7 by Federal cavalry at the battle of Farmington, Wheeler was pursued into North Alabama. By the time he recrossed the river on October 9, his command was in no condition to aid Lee.

Nor did Lee and Roddey accomplish anything. Lee was not too enthusiastic about crossing the river, but did push his horsemen to Decatur by October 12. There he suddenly decided to abandon the scheme, relying upon a discretionary phrase in Johnston's orders which had provided for the plan's abandonment if he deemed it too hazardous. Lee had two objections. First, Roddey had not joined. In fact, no one knew where he was. By October 9 Bragg was sending out search parties, and by October 17 he still did not know Roddey's location. He was finally found on October 21, when, after an abortive crossing of the Tennessee, Roddey admitted that he had done little. He had barely crossed the river and entered Tennessee when he heard that Wheeler was retreating from the state. Immediately, Roddey ordered a retreat to the south bank of the river.[79] Bragg was angered and berated Roddey for the "limited and

[77] Bragg to Johnston, September 29, 1863, in Bragg Papers, Western Reserve; *Official Records*, XXX, Pt. 4, pp. 713, 724.

[78] Brent to Roddey, September 29, 30, October 1, 1863, in Bragg Papers, Western Reserve; *Official Records*, XXX, Pt. 2, p. 722.

[79] *Official Records*, XXX, Pt. 2, pp. 723–25, 729, XXXI, Pt. 1, p. 25, XXX, Pt. 4, pp. 740, 724. Brent to Edward Dillon, October 9, 1863, Brent to commanding officer of cavalry, Trenton, October 17, 1863, Brent to Roddey, October 17, 1863, in Bragg Papers, Western Reserve.

partial results of your expedition." [80]

Also, the condition of Wheeler's cavalry forced Lee to abandon his plan. He had not actually expected to meet Wheeler in North Alabama, and saw the meeting as a mixed blessing. Though Wheeler was there, he declined to recross the river with Lee, arguing that his command was not in condition for another immediate expedition. Too, Lee was disturbed at the prospect of tangling with the estimated six thousand to eight thousand Federal troopers believed in pursuit of Wheeler. Thus, on October 26 the project died as Bragg ordered Wheeler back to Chattanooga.

Wheeler's recall ended efforts to strike the Federal line of communication. Bragg had assumed when Wheeler left that Lee would remain in North Alabama for such purposes. But this small bit of interdepartmental cooperation did not work well. Lee was insistent that he could not cross the river. He offered a host of reasons—abundance of Federal cavalry there, a lack of horseshoes, and rising waters on the Tennessee. Consequently, after a brief skirmish against Sherman's corps during the last week of October, Lee announced on the thirty-first that he was returning to Mississippi. His leaving was matched a few days later by Bragg's sending of Wheeler's cavalry with Longstreet. Two full divisions and part of a third, led personally by Wheeler, marched into East Tennessee. Bragg was left with only five hundred cavalry.[81]

There remained time for one more major command error. With Longstreet absent, Bragg attempted to defend an impossible line, weak both in men and geographical advantages. Longstreet's place on the left wing was taken by General Carter Stevenson, whose division occupied Lookout Mountain. The mountain's strength was a myth. A few hundred feet below the crest, which was a craggy summit, ran a terrace-like shelf from the west side overlooking Lookout Valley to the east side overlooking Chattanooga. It was impossible to hold this position. The terrace, only some 250 feet wide, was commanded by Federal artillery in Moccasin Bend, and it was almost impossible to hold by either Confederate infantry or artillery. Stevenson did place a battery on the mountain crest, but the guns could not be depressed enough to reach the base of the mountain. Too, there were numerous trails on the west side which led to the shelf held by Stevenson's three brigades. General Micah Jenkins had warned earlier that within four miles of the point of the mountain, there were five trails whereby the Federals could reach the shelf. Also,

80 Brent to Roddey, October 26, 1863, in Bragg Papers, Western Reserve.
81 Bragg to Johnston, October 26, 1863, Brent to Wheeler, October 14, 17, 24, 26, 1863, Brent to Lee, October 26, 1863, in Bragg Papers, Western Reserve; *Official Records*, XXX, Pt. 4, pp. 740–41, 763, 743, 747, XXXI, Pt. 1, pp. 25–31.

some eighteen miles to the rear, the pass through Johnson's Crook was a threat to any Rebel force atop the summit of Lookout Mountain.[82]

Bragg's center was equally weak. Cheatham's division held the valley, from the eastern slope of Lookout Mountain to Chattanooga Creek. Walker's division held that portion of the valley from the east side of Chattanooga Creek to Missionary Ridge. The thin line of two divisions was not enough to hold the five-mile-wide valley, through which the main Rossville Road extended around and through Missionary Ridge at Rossville Gap. A Federal penetration in the valley would both isolate Bragg's left wing and flank his right wing on Missionary Ridge.

The right wing was scarcely stronger than the center. Breckinridge's corps and Cleburne's division of Hardee's corps occupied that segment of Missionary Ridge north of the Rossville road. The strength of Missionary Ridge has been exaggerated by writers. It was more of a trap than a stronghold. Some 500 feet high, the ridge was not continuous. Instead, it was a series of hills connected by deep ravines and gullies traversed by country roads. Communication along the crests of the ridge was almost impossible. Also, the north face of the ridge was steep but was covered with rocks, ravines, and fallen trees which gave shelter to an attacker.

Other things were wrong with the ridge position. Due to its steep nature, Rebel artillery planted there had difficulty depressing the guns to reach the valley. Bragg had only promised disaster by deploying half of Breckinridge's corps at the foot of the ridge in a series of rifle pits. In the event of a retreat, Breckinridge's troops atop the summit could not fire lest they hit their own men. Also, the ridge fortifications were vulnerable to flank assaults on both north and south. On the north the ridge dwindled as it approached the valley of Chickamauga Creek. The Federals could skirt the ridge along the north bank of the creek and seize Bragg's supply depot on the Atlanta railroad at Chickamauga Station, south of Missionary Ridge. Bragg's line extended only as far as Tunnel Hill, where the East Tennessee railroad cut beneath the summit. Tunnel Hill itself was in danger; a Federal push through the tunnel could take Bragg's army from the rear. On the south end of the ridge, matters were equally serious. The loss of the Chattanooga Valley would immediately expose the left flank of the position atop Missionary Ridge in the air.[83]

[82] Micah Jenkins to G. M. Sorrel, October 31, 1863, in Jenkins Papers, Duke; Shanks, "Lookout Mountain," 1–4, 10–11.

[83] Roy sketch, Hardee Papers, Alabama; Kirwan, *Orphan Brigade*, 104; P. D. Stephenson, "Missionary Ridge," *Confederate Veteran*, XXI (November, 1913), 540; Irving Buck, "Cleburne and His Division at Missionary Ridge and Ringgold Gap," *SHSP*, VIII (1880), 464; P. D. Stephenson, "Missionary Ridge," *SHSP*, XXXIX (1911), 12–13; George Brewster, "Why Missionary Ridge Was Lost by the Confederates," *Confederate Veteran*, XXII (May, 1914), 232; Roy Kenneth Flint, "The Battle of Missionary Ridge" (M.A. thesis, University of Alabama, 1960), 77–79.

By November 20 the weakness of the Rebel line was beginning to be realized by Bragg. That day he learned of Sherman's arrival in Chattanooga. The following day, scouts brought word that blue columns were marching up the north bank of the Tennessee opposite Chattanooga. Because of his shortage of cavalry, Bragg guessed wrong as to Federal objectives. He decided that Grant was sending a column to interpose between his own and Longstreet's forces. Thus, on the night of November 22, Cleburne was ordered to take command of his and Buckner's divisions, march them to Chickamauga Station, and hurry to join Longstreet.

Cleburne never left Chattanooga. Buckner's division was en route by noon on November 23, and Cleburne was preparing to load his own when he suddenly received countermanding orders. Bragg had misread the Union shift. Shortly after noon that day, a full Union corps marched out of the Chattanooga entrenchments and fell upon one of Breckinridge's advanced outposts on an eminence known as Orchard Knob. Immediately, Bragg began throwing strength to the right wing. Hardee was ordered from his post near Lookout Mountain and was told to take command of Missionary Ridge. Bragg ordered Walker's division to the ridge but erred in attempting to hold the entire line from Lookout Mountain across the valley with the two thin divisions commanded by Stevenson and Walker.[84]

On November 24 Federal activities further confused Bragg. During the morning he learned of a new threat. The corps which had seized Orchard Knob remained stationary. Yet to the north, pontoons and steamboats were ferrying five divisions across the river at the mouth of Chickamauga Creek. Fearful of his supply line, Bragg sent one of Cleburne's brigades to protect the East Tennessee rail bridge south of Missionary Ridge. The bulk of Cleburne's division was hastened into line to extend Bragg's defenses north across Tunnel Hill. While Cleburne's men dug in on the outlying hills around the railroad tunnel, firing was heard far off to the left.

In a cold rain and fog, Hooker's men in Lookout Valley had broken through Stevenson's thin defenses on the shelf of Lookout Mountain. It was too foggy for the battery on the mountain crest to assist him. Gradually during the afternoon Stevenson abandoned both the crest and the west and north sides of the shelf, after they were caught in a crossfire from the artillery in Moccasin Bend. He tried to establish a new line extending

84 Brent Diary, November 20–23, 1863, in Bragg Papers, Western Reserve; Braxton Bragg, "Notes of Report from Dalton of Disaster at Missionary Ridge, December 1, 1863" (MS in *ibid.*); Hughes, *Hardee*, 170; Buck, *Cleburne and His Command*, 162–63.

from the east side of the shelf down into Chattanooga valley, but to no avail. A heavy massing of Federals in the valley was reported, and Bragg at 2:30 P.M. ordered the withdrawal of all troops from Lookout Mountain and the valley. By the night of November 24 the former siege line at Chattanooga was itself under siege along Missionary Ridge.[85]

That night the high command met in an attempt to recoup, but they accomplished little. Bragg met with Hardee and Breckinridge at about 9 P.M. Hardee urged that the army should retreat across Chickamauga Creek, lest it be smothered by the combined forces of Sherman, Hooker, and Thomas. Already the Chickamauga was swollen by rains, and the possibility of being cut off on the north bank by a flank move was genuine. Breckinridge, however, favored making a stand on the ridge. He argued, and Bragg agreed, that there was not enough time that night to make a retreat without being discovered. Too, Breckinridge seemed filled with some newfound bravado. Bragg later claimed the Kentuckian had been filled with whiskey from November 23 to 27. Regardless of whether Breckinridge was drunk, his thinking was irrational. He boasted that the Missionary Ridge position was a strong one and that if the troops could not fight there, they could not fight anywhere. His thin ranks atop the ridge—his men were seven to eight feet apart—did not deter him from strongly opposing any idea of retreat.

Bragg and Breckinridge were not the only two at fault for the decision to stand and fight. Hardee, too, expressed an opinion that Breckinridge's position was strong. He urged Bragg to send reinforcements to the main point of weakness, which was, he argued, the right wing, where the Federals posed a threat to rail communication with Atlanta. Bragg agreed, and the conference closed with the decision to hold fast. Hardee would command the right wing, Breckinridge the left. It was also decided to commit heavily to Hardee's front. Stevenson's and Cheatham's divisions were marched that night to the right. By the morning of November 25, Breckinridge's three divisions, commanded by Patton Anderson, William Bate, and Peter Stewart, were to defend some two-thirds of the ridge position. On the right flank, four divisions were massed in a compact area near Tunnel Hill; Cleburne and Walker were on the front line, with Stevenson and Cheatham held in reserve. Due to illness, desertion,

---

[85] Buck, "Cleburne and His Division at Missionary Ridge and Ringgold Gap," 465; Falconer to Cheatham, November 24, 1863, in Cheatham Papers, Tennessee; A. J. Neal to "Dear Emma," November 25, 1863, in A. J. Neal Letters, Georgia Department of Archives and History; Hughes, *Hardee*, 171; Bragg, "Notes of Report from Dalton," in Bragg Papers, Western Reserve; "Original Rough Draft of Report of General C. L. Stevenson, January 2, 1863," *SHSP*, VIII (1880), 271–75.

and detachment to East Tennessee, Bragg had available only about twenty-six thousand troops to man the long front.[86]

Thin ranks were not the only hazard. By the morning of November 25 the army's morale had reached a new low. It had rained for almost two months, and the men had suffered terribly from cold and exposure. Actually, Bragg's men had occupied the Missionary Ridge position only a few days. Most of them had been encamped either in the Chattanooga or Chickamauga creek bottoms. The roads and campgrounds were seas of mud. Thousands of men were ill with fever and chills. Food had been scarce since early October, when the rains impeded wagon traffic. The corn supply was exhausted in an area of forty miles around Chattanooga, and the near starving troops consumed the seed corn picked from the feeding areas of officers' horses. Because of constant rain, it was impossible to cook in many areas of the front lines. Every three days cooked rations were brought forward, which usually were consumed within one day.

Morale was also damaged by the full knowledge of Federal power in the valley. A panorama of Yankee power, extending to the river and to the bluish Cumberland Mountains beyond, spread out before the men on Missionary Ridge. They had observed the arrival of Hooker's and Sherman's reinforcements. On November 23 they had seen Thomas' corps march out as if on dress parade to seize Orchard Knob. By the night of November 24 the Chattanooga Valley was a sea of flickering campfires. No one needed to tell the private soldier that Hooker's corps were flanking Bragg in the Rossville Gap area. The lights of the campfires only further made it apparent that there was nothing to stop Breckinridge from being flanked on the left. Small wonder that one Confederate officer who saw the awesome scene described it as "the grandest military display the eye ever beheld." [87] The spectacle's fearsomeness was not dimmed by an announcement Bragg had made to the army only a few days before. The exchange of prisioners had been abolished, and any soldier captured must look forward to a Federal prison camp.[88]

86 Liddell's reminiscences, in Govan Papers, UNC; Bragg to Davis, December 1, 1863, in Bragg Papers, Harvard; Buck, *Cleburne and His Command*, 166–67; Hughes, *Hardee*, 172; Brent Diary, November 24, 1863, in Bragg Papers, Western Reserve; Buck, "Cleburne and His Division at Missionary Ridge and Ringgold Gap," 466.

87 Austin, *The Blue and the Gray*, 111.

88 Mackall to wife, October 1, 1863, in Mackall, *Recollections*, 179; W. R. Montgomery to "Aunt," October 18, 24, 1863, in W. R. Montgomery Letters, Kennesaw Mountain National Battlefield Park Library, all collection hereinafter cited as Kennesaw; Neal to "Dear Pa," November 1, 1863, in Montgomery Letters, Kennesaw; "Diary of Turner Vaughan, Co. C, 4th Alabama Regiment, C.S.A., Commenced March 4, 1863, and Ending February 12, 1864," in *Alabama Historical Quarterly*, XVIII (Winter, 1956), entry of October 14, 1863, p. 598; R. A. Smith to "Eliza," October 9, 1863, in William Robert Stevenson, "Robert Alexander Smith," *Alabama*

The morning of November 25 was clear and cool. At daylight Hardee's fears of a Union concentration against his flank seemed about to be realized. Skirmish fire flickered among the knobby hills around the Tunnel Hill position, as Cleburne's men observed long broken lines of blue swarming over the outlying ridges. By mid-morning it seemed that the battle for Chattanooga would be made here. Repeatedly, Cleburne and Stevenson hurled back the Federal charges as they stormed the railroad cut. A weird fight lasted into the late afternoon. Cleburne could not use his artillery well because of the steep nature of the ridge. Instead, his men rolled stones down the slope, and the artillerists even lighted the fuses of shells and tossed them down by hand. The Federal artillery double-teamed their pieces, and axemen cleared the way in order to bring the guns near Cleburne's position. Showers of rocks, bullets, and fallen limbs rained down on Sherman's attackers. At intervals, Rebel brigade commanders jumped the fortifications and led their men in sorties to recover lost ground. By the late afternoon, Sherman's corps had been stopped. Tunnel Hill would hold. As the firing dwindled, cheering went up from Hardee's men.[89]

Their jubilation was premature. In the late afternoon, Bragg had called upon Hardee to send reinforcements to Breckinridge. Hardee knew there was activity on the Kentuckian's front, for heavy firing was plainly heard. Thus, in the early evening, when matters on his front were stabilized, Hardee rode to the left wing. When he reached the left of his own corps, that portion held by Frank Cheatham's division, Hardee was stunned to learn that Breckinridge's corps had been routed.

The breakthrough, although unexpected, was scarcely improbable. Throughout the day, Breckinridge's men had seen Hooker's corps massing on their left flank and marching toward Rossville Gap. Then, almost as if on a parade ground, Thomas' corps had marched from their fortifications and attacked Breckinridge's first line of defense at the foot of the ridge. By 4 P.M., the strength of Missionary Ridge was a lie. The attack hit General Patton Anderson's division. Anderson's men could not hold, and scrambled up the ridge in retreat. When Anderson gave way, the first line of Bate's and Stewart's men also crumbled. The retreating front

Historical Quarterly, XX (Spring, 1958), 49; Stephenson, "Missionary Ridge," *SHSP*, 10–11; Charles Blackford to wife, October 5, 1863, p. 213, Blackford to wife, October 11, 1863, p. 219, October 1, 1863, pp. 209–10, Susan Blackford (ed.), *Letters from Lee's Army*; John Harris to mother, November 19, 1863, in J. W. Harris Papers, Tennessee; Roy's sketch, in Hardee Papers, Alabama.

89 Bragg, "Notes of Report from Dalton," in Bragg Papers, Western Reserve; Buck, *Cleburne and His Command*, 169–71; Stephenson, "Missionary Ridge," *Confederate Veteran*, 541; Neal to "Emma," November 26, 1863, in Neal Letters, Georgia Department of Archives and History.

line prevented Breckinridge's men atop the ridge from firing. When the jubilant Federals pressed close behind and reached the top, Rebel resistance melted away. Anderson's and Stewart's men scurried down the south side of Missionary Ridge into the Chickamauga valley. Bate's division held on to buy some time for a retreat, but was also driven off the ridge.

On Hardee's left, Cheatham observed the rout, and rearranged his line facing southward across the ridge, at right angles to his original position. This line was held till nightfall, with a second line commanded by Cleburne placed behind Cheatham. Then, about dark, Cleburne was ordered to form a rearguard while the bulk of the corps moved across Chickamauga Creek to Bragg's supply depot at Chickamauga Station.[90]

Judging from the scene at Chickamauga Station, there was no doubt that the army had met great disaster. By 9 P.M. flames were shooting upward from the railroad bridge across Chickamauga Creek, as Cleburne's rearguard fired the bridge. News of Federal pursuit by both Hooker and Thomas was abroad. The army was more a milling, frightened mob than an army. Grimy, weary regiments, totally lost from their corps, drifted into the village. Staff officers searched desperately for their commands, hoping to piece together some feeble resistance. By dawn of November 26 the remnants of the army were moved on southward, as Bragg headed for shelter at Dalton, on the east side of massive Taylor's Ridge. There, on the Atlanta Railroad, he hoped to regroup the army. While Bragg led the main column southward, Cleburne's rearguard fired large quantities of foodstuffs and supplies which were abandoned at the depot.[91]

By November 28 after trudging over muddy roads through Ringgold Gap in Taylor's Ridge, the army reached Dalton. It was cold, rainy, and dreary that day as Bragg began to assess the damage. There was little to show for the siege of Chattanooga, save for Cleburne's valor in covering the retreat to Dalton. The previous day, his tiny division had held off Hooker's corps at Ringgold Gap until the army was safely in the environs of Dalton; for this fight, Cleburne would receive the thanks of the Confederate Congress.

90 Roy's sketch, in Hardee Papers, Alabama; D. G. Godwin to Miss B——, December 1, 1863, in Godwin Letters, Confederate Collection, Tennessee; Stephenson, "Missionary Ridge," SHSP, 13–14; Cheatham to Walthall, April ——, 1876, Walthall to Cheatham, March 17, 1876, in Cheatham Papers, Tennessee; Wilson, Under the Old Flag, I, 292, 298–99; Mackall in Johnston, December 9, 1863, in Mackall, Recollections, 197–98; Watkins, "Co. Aytch," 127; Buck, "Cleburne and His Division at Missionary Ridge and Ringgold Gap," 468–69; Hughes, Hardee, 175–76.

91 Buck, "Cleburne and His Division at Missionary Ridge and Ringgold Gap," 469; Kirwan, Orphan Brigade, 111; Neal to father, November 29, 1863, in Neal Letters, Kennesaw.

There was little else to praise. The Chattanooga loss involved men, equipment, and morale. Straggling en route to Dalton had been heavy. Only thirty thousand men answered the roll calls. Some six thousand troops, mostly prisoners, had been left behind at Chattanooga. Forty pieces of Rebel artillery were captured, and thousands of small arms had been thrown away. The army was shamed by the retreat and angry at both Bragg and the President.

At Dalton, Bragg immediately relieved Breckinridge of his command. He contended that the Kentuckian was drunk from November 23 until November 27, and that on the night the army retreated through the depot at Chickamauga Station, Breckinridge was so intoxicated that he collapsed on the floor. Breckinridge was assigned to General States Rights Gist, who was ordered to make sure the general made it to Dalton with the remainder of the troops. Regardless of whether Bragg exaggerated the account, it was certain that the shameful collapse of his corps doomed Breckinridge's further service in the army.[92]

Braxton Bragg realized that he, too, was finished. On November 28 he penned his resignation to the government, and on November 30 he was ordered to turn over the army's command temporarily to General William Hardee at Dalton. Bragg left the army in much the same humor he had commanded its operations for the previous year and a half—with bitterness, and convinced that the mistakes of the campaign were made by his subordinates. In his official report and in a letter to President Davis, both written on December 1, Bragg blamed the disaster on cowardice among some in the army and on Breckenridge's drunkenness. He also urged that new command changes be made. Indomitable to the last, Bragg, without fanfare, left Dalton by train on December 2.[93]

The ride south toward Atlanta must have aroused memories in his mind. Over these same tracks in the summer of 1862, he had brought his army to undertake an invasion of Kentucky that stirred the South. He had done so after taking command of a weak army at Tupelo in the early summer of that year, and whipping it into a respectable fighting force. Later, Bragg had looked to the Atlanta Railroad for reinforcements and sustenance after the bitter retreats from Kentucky in 1862 and Middle

92 Bragg to Davis, November 30, 1863, Brent Diary, November 28–30, 1863, in Bragg Papers, Western Reserve; Bragg to Davis, December 1, 1863, in Bragg Papers, Harvard; Bragg to Sykes, February 8, 1873, in Claiborne Papers, UNC; Bragg to Marcus Wright, December 14, 1863, in Marcus Wright Papers, UNC; Buck, *Cleburne and His Command*, 174–85; Horn, *Army of Tennessee*, 301; Seitz, *Bragg*, 400; Hughes, *Hardee*, 177; Sykes, "Cursory Sketch of the Campaigns of General Bragg," *SHSP*, XII, 1–2.
93 Bragg to Davis, December 1, 1863, in Bragg Papers, Harvard; Bragg, "Notes of Report from Dalton," in Bragg Papers, Western Reserve.

Tennessee in 1863. Then again, he had stirred the South's hopes by turning on Rosecrans at Chickamauga and besieging Chattanooga. It was ironic that Bragg, who was then and later castigated by many as incompetent, had managed the army during its period of greatest success, had penetrated the enemy's territory deeper than any other western general, and had molded an efficient army. Yet something had been missing. A rapport between Bragg and his men and officers had never existed. Bragg's personality—quarrelsome, suspicious, quick to blame—had simply not been sufficient.

Although on December 2 he told Davis the army's disgrace rested "on my humble head," and spoke of putting past matters behind them, he believed none of this. He was to remain bitter during the winter of 1863–64, claiming to friends that his misfortune had been caused by a few ambitious and venal generals who desired to advance their own fortunes. Although there was some rejoicing in the army when Bragg left, he was soon to become President Davis' military adviser, a position of broad influence, and one in which he would continue to wield power over the Army of Tennessee. His actions would be colored by his firm belief that the mistakes of the army were those of his subordinates and not his own. His attitude at that time was best expressed to a friend in March of 1864, after Bragg had been called to serve with the President in Richmond. Commenting upon some of his old enemies in the western army, Bragg cryptically remarked, "We must mark the men . . . they will bear watching." [94]

94 Bragg to "Dear General," March 6, 1864, in Wright Papers, UNC; see also Bragg to Marcus Wright, December 14, 1863, February 6, 1864, *ibid.*

PART III

the johnston influence

eleven

The Dalton Impasse

ON THE MORNING OF DECEMBER 27, 1863, GENERAL JOSEPH E. JOHNSTON assumed command of the Army of Tennessee at Dalton. For the first time since receiving his severe wound on the Virginia Peninsula in 1862, Johnston was to command a genuine field army. He would hold this command until relieved by his superiors in Richmond amidst a bitter encounter in July of 1864. His removal spawned a host of myths, pro and con, as to his abilities and intents in the campaign of 1864. The most lasting was fostered by Johnston and his friends in the latter stages of the war and during Reconstruction—that at Dalton, from December until May, he had welded a strong fighting force which failed only because of the government's intervention.

This long period of inactivity immediately preceding General William T. Sherman's advance against Johnston's line was a troubling time. From the outset Johnston faced a host of problems, none of which had been actually solved when the campaign began in the late spring. In a sense, the campaign was already over and the army doomed to defeat when Sherman's blue columns began crowding against Rocky Face Ridge in early May. Johnston desperately needed good relations with the government, an understanding of their expectations, logistical support, and the support of his subordinate commanders. By May it was apparent that he had none of these.

Johnston's failure with Richmond was only a continuation of past bitterness. When Davis learned that Hardee would not take a permanent position, he faced the unhappy task of appointing either his friend Lee or one of his enemies, Beauregard or Johnston. Heavy pressure was applied for him to appoint Johnston. Polk wrote from Mississippi in early December that "there is so general a desire on the part of the army and the country" to put Johnston in command, it was Davis' duty to yield.[1]

Evidently, Davis first considered Beauregard for the post. By December 2 there were rumors in the War Department that Beauregard's appointment was imminent. Lee, apparently sensing Davis' hesitation to appoint Johnston, suggested on December 3 that Beauregard might be sent to Dalton and be replaced at Charleston by General Jeremy Gilmer. A master at knowing what Davis wanted, Lee tactfully avoided any mention of Johnston, and added that he knew "the difficulties surrounding this subject" of a replacement for Hardee.[2]

Unwilling to accept either Beauregard or Johnston, Davis at first attempted to persuade Lee to accept the command. By December 5 he had inquired of the general whether he would go to Dalton. As he had in September, Lee declined to accept the appointment. He explained on December 7 that he feared he would not receive "cordial co-operation" in Dalton, and was afraid also that a suitable replacement could not be found for him.[3] Davis was not satisfied, and on December 9 called Lee to Richmond to confer on the matter. Evidently Lee thought that his own objections would be overruled and that he would be sent to the West. Thus on December 9, before he entrained for the capital, Lee sent a warm note to General J. E. B. Stuart stating that "my heart and thoughts will always be with this army." [4]

In conference for over a week, Lee, Davis, and Seddon pondered the fate of the western army. By about December 15 Lee had convinced Davis that he should not be sent to Georgia. Exactly who Lee recommended instead is not certain. Apparently, only after he learned that Davis had rejected Beauregard as a choice, did he attempt to persuade the President to appoint Johnston. Meanwhile, Johnston's friends in Congress, particularly Senator Louis Wigfall, lobbied for his appointment. Wigfall held at least one night meeting with several other Johnston supporters in Seddon's office. Wigfall himself was not too enthusiastic about Johnston's accepting the appointment at first. He feared the government would not support Johnston. But, after the appointment of

1 Polk to Davis, December 8, 1863, in *Official Records*, XXXI, Pt. 3, p. 796; Mackall to wife, November 27, 1863, in Mackall, *Recollections*, 196–97; Gale to wife, December 8, 1863, in Gale-Polk Papers, UNC.

2 *Official Records*, XXXI, Pt. 3, p. 779.

3 Lee to Davis, December 7, 1863, in Davis Papers, Tulane.

4 *Official Records*, XXIX, Pt. 2, p. 866, also p. 861; Davis to Lee, December 8, 1863, in Rowland (ed.), *Davis*, VI, 128.

Johnston was finally made on December 16, Wigfall urged that he accept it.[5]

The manner in which Johnston was appointed helped to perpetuate the old feud between him and the government. Johnston was aware that Davis had not wanted him. Talk being passed around at his headquarters immediately after he was selected indicated that Lee was closeted with Davis for several days before he could convince him to place Johnston in command. Rumors in Richmond echoed this sentiment. Such stories could hardly have convinced Johnston that he had his government's confidence. His doubts were reinforced by Wigfall's December 18 letter urging that Johnston accept the appointment but also warning that the government would deliberately block his efforts in order to produce his downfall.[6]

Johnston's friends in Richmond evidently made him feel that they were in part responsible for his appointment. Thus, he owed allegiance to the anti-Davis faction. Reminding Johnston of this in December, Wigfall asserted that in the spring of 1863 the general's congressional friends had "moved heaven & earth to get you appointed" to command Bragg's army. Now, Wigfall insisted, he trusted that "you will not again decline this offer." [7] Wigfall did not let Johnston forget this matter. In the spring of 1864 he again chided Johnston for harming the anti-Davis bloc in early 1863 when he gave favorable accounts of Bragg's generalship. When Johnston perceptively commented that perhaps the congressmen were less his friends and more Davis' enemies, Wigfall was irritated and accused his friend of doing "great injustice." Indeed, argued Wigfall in March, "they had been moving heaven & earth to have you put in command of their army." [8] Again Wigfall reminded Johnston that he had not been placed in command earlier by Davis because he "hated you & would rather sacrifice the army and even the country than put you in command." [9] Johnston no doubt felt his indebtedness, and throughout the spring of 1864 furnished Wigfall with both correspondence and statements to be used to counter the Davis version of military operations in 1862–63 in the western command.

With Johnston's arrival under the banner of the anti-Davis forces in the Congress, Confederate politics was at last imbedded in the army's

[5] Freeman, *Lee*, III, 214–15; Wigfall to Johnston, December 18, 1863, in Johnston Papers, Huntington.

[6] Wigfall to Johnston, December 18, 1863, in Johnston Papers, Huntington; see also Richard Manning to father, January 4, 1864, in Williams–Chesnut–Manning Papers, South Carolina; Freeman, *Lee's Lieutenants*, III, 214.

[7] Wigfall to Johnston, December 18, 1863, in Johnston Papers, Huntington.

[8] Wigfall to Johnston, March 17, 1864, *ibid.*

[9] *Ibid.*

command system. Bragg's opposition had been more a matter within the army. Now, any support of Johnston was to be linked with opposition to the administration, and the enemies of the general had more at stake than their mere personal dislike or disdain for his generalship. The political furor over selecting a successor to Bragg had erupted soon after the Chattanooga fiasco. A fierce argument occurred on the Senate floor in reaction to a message sent by Davis. Obviously trying to restore Bragg's image, Davis intimated that the Missionary Ridge disaster was not caused by poor generalship but by a lack of valor on the part of some of the army's troops. This reflection upon the bravery of the Tennessee troops was too much for Senator Henry Foote. He took the floor with a wholesale denunciation of Davis' western policy, particularly his refusals to appoint Johnston. Foote maintained that Davis had kept Bragg in command despite entreaties from Congress, the army, and the people. Foote hit at Davis' interference in western matters, and snarled, "Would to God he would never visit the army again." Foote also called for committees to be appointed to investigate the losses of Chattanooga and Vicksburg. He struck hard at Davis' support of Pemberton, despite the soldiers' refusal to serve under him. Sneering that Pemberton was Davis' "bosom friend," Foote capped his argument by reminding his colleagues that wherever Pemberton was seen, the President was by his side. Indeed, argued Foote, when the two came to Tennessee, the soldiers pointed at the general and said, "There goes the traitor that sold Vicksburg." [10]

The administration responded to this attack in the House of Representatives via a Davis supporter, Representative William Swann of Tennessee. The government furnished Swann with the correspondence relative to Johnston's authority over Bragg in Tennessee in 1862–63 and also Johnston's letters to Davis giving an appraisal of Bragg's generalship. Swann's testimony was damaging, as he produced letter after letter proving that Johnston had been given the authority in early 1863 to supersede Bragg when he wanted, and also that Johnston had spoken highly of Bragg to the government during the spring. The exposure of these letters angered Johnston's congressional friends. Wigfall reminded the general that his opinion of Bragg's conduct "is quoted as authority for sustaining him after the affair at Chickamauga." Wigfall asserted that "the real harm done was the irritation of those who were real friends of yours & who hated Bragg or honestly distrusted him, who were making war on Davis for keeping him in." Johnston's letters "shielded Davis" and thus provoked his friends in Congress. Later, in 1864, he recalled

10 *Proceedings of First Confederate Congress,* in *SHSP,* L, p. 22, see also pp. 21, 23, 37.

that Johnston's friends "were provoked that Davis should have it in his power to seek protection under your name." Instead, just when the anti-Davis people thought they had proof of Bragg's incompetence, Davis "turned you up as the man who had kept Bragg in command." [11]

The argument continued to rage through December. Foote introduced a resolution that Davis be required to replace all commanders who lacked the army's and the public's confidence. That Foote and his colleagues were more interested in embarrassing the government and less in having Johnston appointed as commander was evident. Foote urged that if Johnston had been doomed "to obscurity for the rest of the war," then the government should appoint Beauregard.[12] Meanwhile, Wigfall, aided by Johnston, was preparing for possible publication a review of the correspondence of Johnston's stint as theater commander. In December the general also furnished Wigfall with several long letters defending his part in the Vicksburg expedition and explaining why he had supported Bragg that spring. Wigfall was grateful for the letters, asserting "they are entirely satisfactory & have done immense good." [13]

Johnston himself was much at fault for the spring arguments which laid the groundwork for later misunderstandings in May, June, and early July. Essentially, Johnston was much like Bragg in his obvious relishing of the contest with Davis. Although there was jubilation at his headquarters in January, where all seemed to consider his appointment a major victory for the anti-Davis faction, he could not be satisfied. Throughout the spring, he and his governmental supporters kept the fires of alienation burning, and he contributed little toward making the government understand his Dalton position. In February, after observing that the correspondence between Cooper, Davis, Seddon, and himself for the Vicksburg campaign had been published, Johnston urged his brother Beverley to launch a rebuttal. Johnston wanted his own correspondence for the period of November, 1862, through July, 1863, to be published to prove that the government had given him no real authority. Thus, he urged his brother to approach Wigfall and other anti-Davis men in Richmond to have it published.[14]

In March and April, Johnston still did not attempt to cool his allies' attack on the administration. In March his report of Vicksburg was

11 *Ibid.*, pp. 55–59; Wigfall to Johnston, December 18, 1863, March 17, 1864, in Johnston Papers, Huntington.

12 *Proceedings of First Confederate Congress*, 61.

13 *Ibid.*, pp. 50, 60–61; Wigfall to Johnston, December 18, 1863, in Johnston Papers, Huntington; Johnston to Wigfall, December 3, 27, 1863, in Wigfall, DLC; Johnston to Wigfall, December 14, 1863, in Wright, *Southern Girl*, 161–62.

14 Johnston to Beverley Johnston, February 19, 1864, in Wigfall, DLC; Manning to mother, December 22, 1863, in Williams–Chesnut–Manning Papers, South Carolina.

published in the anti-Davis Richmond *Examiner,* a document which placed the blame for Vicksburg's surrender on Pemberton. In April Johnston's anger was stirred by an article in the Richmond *Enquirer,* published while his aide Colonel B. S. Ewell was on a mission to Davis. Ewell related to Johnston that the editor of the newspaper published a rebuttal of Johnston's Vicksburg report, "at the special request of a member of the cabinet." [15] The editor also told Ewell that he had refused a request by a cabinet member to publish some correspondence between Seddon and Pemberton. Written the previous fall, the correspondence would have strengthened Pemberton's version of the Vicksburg matter. Angry, Johnston urged Wigfall to publish his long letter of August 8, 1863. This letter was Johnston's reply to Davis' famous July letter which gave the government's version of Johnston's command authority in the West. Johnston also wanted Wigfall to publish his correspondence with the government from the time he assumed command in November, 1862. Also, in April he carried on a lengthy correspondence with Wigfall concerning the old matter of his having endorsed Bragg as commander during the spring quarrel of 1863.[16]

What kind of a man was Johnston? His true character remains an enigma. One reason for this is that hardly anyone had mild feelings toward Joe Johnston. Thus, there are few unbiased accounts. Davis and other enemies considered him a troublemaker, overrated, and excessively proud. His friends, such as General Richard Taylor, considered him the "beau ideal of a soldier." [17]

Johnston often seemed inconsistent. To his friends the small, cocky, gray-haired general with the well-trimmed Van Dyke beard was a warm, tender man, but at the same time aloof, hard to know, and easily irritated. He was considered a charming dinner guest who regaled his hosts with talk of great military campaigns. Yet with friends and subordinates he was closemouthed as to his own military plans. Rarely did Johnston seem to consult his junior officers. The sight of the dapper Johnston riding through the lines could excite cheers from the troops. Yet this outward show of paternalism contradicted the inner man, who seemed sarcastic, eschewed self-pity, and possessed a fierce sense of pride and honor. There seemed to be two Johnstons: openly, the figure of bearing, who excited military *elan,* and privately, the troubled man who seemed bitter and despondent.[18]

15 Ewell to Johnston, April 16, 1864, in Johnston Papers, William and Mary.
16 Johnston to Wigfall, April 1, 5, 30, 1864, in Wigfall Papers, DLC.
17 Taylor, *Destruction and Reconstruction,* 42.
18 *Ibid.,* 43; Wise, *End of an Era,* 449; Oates, *War between the Union and the Confederacy,* 459; DuBose, *Wheeler,* 222–24; "Reminiscences of Col. Archer Anderson," in Johnston, *Johnston,* 309–13, 315; Johnston, *Narrative,* xiii-xiv.

In some ways Johnston resembled Albert Sidney Johnston. Like his dead predecessor, Joseph E. Johnston came to the army with broad military experience. His impressive credentials included service in the Seminole, Black Hawk, Mexican, and Mormon wars. He had served in the cavalry, artillery, and with the topographical engineers. Also, he had been Quartermaster General of the United States Army. Like Albert Sidney, he had risen fast in Confederate esteem, and was made a full general in August of 1861.

In yet another similarity, his reputation has seemed to rest upon a peculiar mystique nourished by his friends during the war and by his own memoirs and by sympathetic biographers. Johnston's standing was based more upon what he allegedly could have done if he had been given the opportunity than by any real achievement. By 1864 this mystique was pervasive. Johnston was stereotyped by his many admirers as one who was held in the wings by the government. Their version had Johnston's failures resulting either from accidents or from the government's hostility. Thus, they said, his crushing of McClellan's army on the Peninsula in 1862 had been cut short by his Seven Pines wound. His theater command in the West in 1862–63 had produced disaster only because the government had not given him real authority. The twin disasters of Vicksburg and the loss of Middle Tennessee in July, 1863, had come about because Davis would not listen to Johnston's strategic views and would not give him enough authority as theater commander to coordinate effectively the two areas. The Missionary Ridge disaster partially resulted from Davis' refusals to heed the demands that Johnston replace Bragg in October, 1863. Later, the mystique also included the belief that Johnston was on the verge of destroying Sherman's army when he was removed in July, 1864. Always the argument was the same —the government had bridled him, perhaps deliberately, and had thus kept a great general inactive. This constant theme was repeated on the floor of the Senate and in Johnston's letters to Wigfall from the dusty camps of Middle Tennessee in 1863.

Even though Johnston at last was given a field army in 1864, after the campaign his retreat into Georgia was called tactically brilliant. He and his friends later argued that he would have fought Sherman when circumstances were right, but that his removal ended hope of success. The fact that prior to crossing the Chattahoochee, he passed up several opportunities to fight Sherman, and that it was not certain he would fight at Atlanta did not matter to his supporters.

In the spring of 1864, some features of Johnston's behavior were at odds with his popular mystique. Urged by Richmond to take the offensive, the general, from December until May, argued that his army was in no condition to move forward. From a logistical and strategic standpoint, his avowal to await Sherman on the defensive at Dalton seemed sound. Still, underlying this decision was a Johnston characteristic which became clearer after he was forced into the field in May. Essentially a pessimist, his letters to Richmond that spring tended to negate any mentioned plan without offering a substitute. None of the multiple offensives suggested seemed to please him, yet he rarely offered ideas he considered better. Almost as a schoolmaster would mark a student's paper, Johnston dismembered the parts of any proposal until it seemed that he did not grasp the whole. His detailed objections to any plan resembled those he gave the government in early 1863 when directed to command Bragg's army; they seemed a shield against accepting the final responsibility. Johnston allowed the legalities of a situation, whether of an administrative or logistical nature, to halt his efforts.

Other personality quirks also alienated him from the government. He was simply not communicative. Although he was more in touch with Richmond in the spring than in the summer, Johnston never met the government halfway. Most of his correspondence consisted of not very detailed rebuttals to their proposals. Johnston was also tight-lipped in his relationship with his corps leaders during the spring. This lack of communication also became a far more serious problem after the May campaign began.

A distrust of the government—an almost childish quality—had been apparent in the general during the 1862–63 theater command. Now Johnston seemed to think that he was again being martyred. In February he insisted that "there is no reason why I should be a martyr." Again in April he confided to his friend Wigfall that he did not believe the government intended to send him any assistance at Dalton. Many of his personal letters were filled with reminiscences of how he believed the government had wronged him in his theater command. Johnston almost seemed to prefer that they did not strengthen him, for he seemed to enjoy his old role as a powerless general placed in a situation of heavy responsibility by an old enemy who desired his downfall.[19]

Because of the manner of his selection, the current anti-administration war with Davis, and Johnston's own personality, an almost impossible situation existed by 1864. Confederate politics was now so deeply involved with the army's high command that in order to receive the administration's full support—or at least maintain good communication

19 Wigfall to Johnston, December 18, 1863, in Johnston Papers, Huntington; Johnston to Beverley Johnston, February 19, 1864, Johnston to Wigfall, April 1, 5, 30, n.d., in Wigfall Papers, DLC.

with Richmond—the commander almost had to be considered a supporter of Davis. Yet if this were done, that officer would not receive
the support of the anti-Davis and anti-Bragg elements within the army.
Johnston epitomized this new caste system that existed in the spring of
1864 at Dalton.[20]

The enmity between Johnston and the government involved more
than bitterness between factions. During the winter and spring of 1863–
64, Johnston and Richmond never were able to reach an understanding
as to the army's strategic policy. Even after Sherman began his advance
in May, the quarrel over strategy continued.

The problem was obvious even before Johnston arrived at Dalton
on December 27. Davis and Seddon had already obtained a grossly
exaggerated view of the army's condition from the temporary commander, Hardee. A most complex officer, Hardee was a splendid or-
ganizer and corps leader. On November 30 he shunned the assignment
as permanent commander on the grounds that he did not have the
abilities for the position. However, there were other reasons for his
turning down the offer. His chief of staff, Colonel T. B. Roy, later explained that Hardee believed either Beauregard or Johnston would do
more to rebuild the army's morale. Also, Hardee seemed to thing that
the command should be offered first to Johnston because he outranked
him as a senior officer.

Despite these meritorious explanations, it appears that Hardee's refusal was more likely motivated by his old dislike of bearing final
responsibility. For almost eighteen months he had been one of Bragg's
chief critics. Now, when it seemed that Bragg's burdens might be his
own, Hardee drew back from the task, although he was quite capable.
Hardee also could have seen the occasion as a means to take one final
stab at Bragg, by giving the appearance that he had rebuilt an army
ruined by his predecessor.[21]

For whatever reason, Hardee's December reports were extremely optimistic and gave the government a false impression of the Dalton situation. Matters were not helped when Davis' aide-de-camp, Colonel Joseph
Christmas Ives, arrived in Georgia in early December. Ives seemed a
poor choice to make an evaluation of the problems Johnston would face.
He had seen no combat experience; his entire military career from 1861
until early 1863 had been in work on coastal defenses in the Carolinas
and at Savannah. A New Yorker, Ives knew nothing of the geographic
area in which Johnston would operate. There were doubts also as to

20 Chesnut, *Diary from Dixie*, 392, 430; Jones, *War Clerk's Diary*, II, 252.
21 Roy Sketch, in Hardee Papers, Alabama; *Official Records*, XXXI, Pt. 3, p. 764;
Hughes, *Hardee*, 184–86.

whether his report would give Johnston a fair shake. His northern birth made Ives suspect with some Confederates. Johnston's own outspoken hostility toward northern officers was well known in Richmond. Too, Ives was an old friend of Davis. Before the war, he had worked at the War Department with the President for three years on the Pacific Railroad surveys.[22]

The Hardee-Ives assessment was bound to trouble Johnston. Their combined reports indicated that the army's condition was not nearly as bad as had been supposed. As early as December 11, Hardee boasted to Davis that the army was in good spirits and was "ready to fight." Thus, on December 17, Hardee even proposed that the army be reinforced and that it take the offensive. In several notes and conversations with Davis and Ives, Hardee left the impression that Grant was all but abandoning Chattanooga, and asserted that only twenty thousand Federals remained there. He spoke of large numbers in retreat to Nashville, and hinted that part of Grant's army might even be en route to Virginia. The final blow, however, was Hardee's Christmas Eve report, which was delivered by Ives to Davis. In this document, Hardee probably did unwitting damage to Johnston's efforts. He boasted that the army's strength was now greater than it had been prior to Missionary Ridge. Also, the field artillery lost there had been replaced, and a "sufficiency of serviceable field artillery" existed. Also, any problems of transporting supplies from the interior to Johnston's army had practically been eliminated. In the future, such shipments would be prompt and regular. With a last flourish of pride, Hardee admitted "great pleasure" in turning over to Johnston the army in "fine condition." [23]

Some discrepancies in Hardee's exaggerated report became obvious during the spring. Though he took pride in replacing the lost field guns, by March of 1864 the army still had only 111 pieces of artillery. Of these Lee's artillery chief, General William Pendleton, estimated on a March inspection that only sixty-nine were considered reliable. The rest were six-pounders, which Pendleton labeled as useless, and twelve-pound howitzers, which he considered to be scarcely more effective.[24]

The force at Missionary Ridge, to which Hardee compared the force assembled in December, was a poor measuring stick. On December 3 the army still had scarcely thirty thousand effective infantry, and by Christmas the number had increased to only thirty-six thousand. Aside from those sick and wounded and detailed for special duty, there were some

22 Chesnut, *Diary from Dixie*, 430; Johnston, *Narrative*, 269.
23 *Official Records*, XXXI, Pt. 3, p. 860, see also pp. 803, 839, LII, Pt. 2, pp. 573–74, 581.
24 Pendleton to Cooper, March 29, 1864, in Davis Papers, Tulane.

thirty-four thousand men absent from the army. Too, Hardee dwelt long on infantry and artillery, but scarcely mentioned the cavalry. There was little to mention. On November 24 Bragg had ordered Wheeler back to the army, but had not ordered his cavalry. The day after the Missionary Ridge disaster, Bragg asked Longstreet to return his cavalry. The Virginian, falling back into upper East Tennessee, declined. The result was that by January of 1864, the army had only twenty-four hundred cavalry. At least two-thirds of the army's cavalry remained with General Will Martin under the command of Longstreet.[25]

Hardee's exaggerated assertions of high morale in the army in December simply do not agree with accounts of private soldiers. Desertion rates were high, discipline was lax, and the general morale was low. In fact, not only was good morale lacking under Hardee, but not until February did Johnston himself gain the army's confidence by implementing a series of reforms in troop organization, discipline, and other matters.[26]

Nor did Hardee's assessment of the Federal weakness seem correct. Hardee repeatedly left the impression that the Chattanooga area was being abandoned as a major field of emphasis. Though he admitted that some of these reports were not "altogether reliable," their emphasis on the abandonment of Chattanooga, withdrawal to Nashville, and possible wholesale reinforcement of Virginia from the West would prove damaging to Johnston. Sometimes Hardee himself was not consistent. To Davis he reported that there were only twenty thousand Federals at Chattanooga. But after Johnston arrived, Hardee told the general that some eighty thousand Federals were in the Chattanooga-Stevenson-Bridgeport area.[27]

Still, the government was greatly impressed with the Hardee-Ives evaluation. Even before Johnston arrived, the continuing pressure for him to take the offensive was implemented. On December 18 Seddon sent a letter which Johnston received at Dalton. Seddon tossed off Johnston's army's problems with the naive statement that the army was "somewhat disheartened and deprived of ordnance and materiel." Seddon then

25 "Field Return of the Effective Strength, Army of Tennessee, December 20, 1863," in Miscellaneous Field Returns, Duke; "Statement of the Strength of the Army of Tennessee, December, 1863" (MS in Map Division, Confederate Collection, Tennessee; *Official Records,* XXXI, Pt. 3, pp. 795, 850, 890; Johnston to Davis, January 2, 1864, in Georgia Portfolio II, Duke.

26 Austin, *The Blue and the Gray,* 118–19; Watkins, "*Co. Aytch,*" 131–32; Johnston, *Johnston,* 303; Manning to mother, January 17, 28, 1864, in Williams–Chesnut–Manning Papers, South Carolina; Neal to "Dear Ella," December 6, 1863 (U.D.C. Bound Typescripts, II, Georgia State Archives) ; "Reminiscences of Thomas B. Wilson" (MS in Confederate Collection, Tennessee) .

27 Johnston to Davis, January 2, 1864, in Georgia Portfolio, II, Duke; *Official Records,* XXXI, Pt. 3, p. 809, LII, Pt. 2, p. 575.

lectured Johnston on the evils of remaining idle, and expressed the hope that "as soon as the condition of your forces" allowed, Johnston would assume the offensive.[28]

Davis followed with a long note on December 23. He quoted freely from Hardee's and Ives's reports, and intimated that he knew more of the army's condition at Dalton than Johnston did. The Missionary Ridge losses were not severe, the artillery and transportation were in adequate condition, and the army was in good spirits. In fact, Davis argued that "the effective condition of your new command, as thus reported to me, is a matter of much congratulation." Johnston needed to regain the territory lost with "prompt and vigorous action." Both Seddon's and Davis' letters contained that same disturbing theme—all that prevented an offensive was Johnston himself.[29]

On the heels of Wigfall's December 18 warning to him, Johnston must have considered the Richmond letters as naive if not sinister. His own replies to Seddon on December 28 and to Davis on January 2 were equally significant. Five months before actual campaigning was to begin, the impasse in strategic thinking was created. In these letters, Johnston set forth two salient principles from which he rarely wavered that spring. He argued that the army was in no condition even to think of an offensive. The enemy at Chattanooga numbered well over twice his own command, and he had almost no cavalry. There were not enough wagons for an offensive, barely enough to remain on the defensive. The artillery was not in good condition, and the system of funnelling food to the army at Dalton via the Atlanta railroad was not working properly.[30]

Even if the army could move, where could it go? Johnston reminded Davis that there were only two possible destinations—Middle and East Tennessee. The general considered both impossible. Invasion of Middle Tennessee would involve a long march of over 130 miles through barren country before striking the fertile Elk and Duck river valleys. From Dalton, a march across the barren Sand-Lookout ranges to the Tennessee River would be required. The supply problems here were obvious, since Johnston lacked enough wagons to carry both subsistence and equipment. Too, the Tennessee River had to be crossed. Already Hardee had admitted to Richmond that the Federals were strongly entrenched along the river in northeastern Alabama, from Stevenson to Bridgeport. A crossing would have to be made in central or northwestern Alabama. A pontoon

28 Seddon to Johnston, December 20, 1863, in Johnston Papers, William and Mary; the copy in *Official Records*, XXXI, Pt. 3, p. 842 is dated December 18.
29 Davis to Johnston, December 23, 1863, in Johnston Papers, Miami.
30 Johnston to Seddon, December 28, 1863, in Johnston Papers, William and Mary; Johnston to Davis, January 2, 1863, in Georgia Portfolio II, Duke.

train would be required; 150 wagons were needed to haul the pontoons for a single bridge across the Tennessee.

There were other problems in invading Middle Tennessee. The long march to the Tennessee River would place Johnston's flank in danger from the estimated eighty thousand Federals in the Chattanooga area. Even if he could slide around this force and cross the river west of Stevenson without contact, this move would open up to Federal raids the Georgia-Alabama munitions area from Augusta to Selma. Then, once across the river, Johnston must cross the barren, wide belt of the Tennessee Cumberlands, a mountain region long on poor roads and short on provisions.

An invasion of East Tennessee was even more unrealistic. Johnston flatly told Davis that such a move was also impossible. He reminded Davis that Bragg at Chattanooga had spurned such a plan even before Sherman had reinforced Rosecrans and before Longstreet was detached. In his letter to Davis, Johnston hinted at a major point which the government did not comprehend. East Tennessee was a trap, a proverbial dead end for any army entering the valley from North Georgia. Where could the army go? After Chickamauga, Longstreet had proposed that the army enter the valley and veer west across the Cumberland Mountains toward Nashville. For both logistical and military reasons, this was absurd. At Chattanooga, the Federals, utilizing the railroad, would be on the interior line of communications. Johnston would have only poor roads across seventy-five miles of mountainous, barren terrain. It was not merely a shortage of wagons. Such a move would completely jeopardize the Georgia-Alabama manufacturing complex. Also, there was a possibility that the army in East Tennessee could not return to Georgia if necessary. With the Federals holding Chattanooga, the south end of the valley was controlled. The only hope of returning would be to disperse the army in the rugged Blue Ridge of North Georgia. Longstreet had realized this in December of 1863. He had shrugged off proposals that he attempt to rejoin the army at Dalton and argued that it was impossible to do so.[31]

Johnston's sense of the danger in attempting an offensive into Tennessee motivated a second principle which he expounded to Seddon and Davis in these first letters. He stated flatly that he had no intention of taking the offensive. Instead, he would await Sherman at Dalton in a defensive-offensive pattern, defeat him, and then advance into Tennessee on the heels of a Federal retreat. A few days after his January letter to Davis, Johnston elaborated on this strategy in a letter to Beauregard. The

---

[31] Johnston to Davis, January 2, 1863 in Georgia Portfolio II, Duke; see also Johnston to Beauregard, January 13, 1864, in Johnston Papers, William and Mary.

Creole had urged a concentration at Dalton and an offensive. Johnston reiterated the problems of such a move, and stated that any chance of an offensive "depends on the enemy's first making the attempt upon us. In that event we should be ready, if we defeat them, to press on through Tennessee." Later, he further explained his strategy to his Georgia supporter, Howell Cobb. The Federals would advance into Georgia, be beaten, and then be pursued into Tennessee. Johnston's letter indicated the seriousness of the fast developing impasse between the general and the government. Johnston argued that he was surprised to learn "that anybody is crazy enough to think of another invasion of the North." [32]

The serious nature of the impasse was also exemplified by a crisis in early February. Upon Johnston's departure for Dalton, Polk had been placed in command of the Mississippi-Alabama department. By February 1 it was obvious to Polk that Grant had shifted a large segment of his troops under Sherman to operate through central Mississippi toward Mobile. On February 3 the campaign began as Sherman, with an estimated thirty-five thousand infantry, marched east from Vicksburg. By February 14 Sherman had reached Meridian, and Polk was pleading for aid from the government and from Johnston. Three days later the government ordered Johnston to send all of Hardee's corps but one division to reinforce Polk's feeble infantry force of only nine thousand men. By February 21 the head of Hardee's column began to arrive in Montgomery, but soon a change in plans of grave importance occurred. On the night of February 22 Johnston received intelligence reports of a projected Federal advance against Dalton. With half of his infantry gone with Hardee, Johnston pleaded for their return. The next day, while General George Thomas' corps skirmished west of Dalton with Johnston, the government ordered Hardee's move countermanded. By the next day, the affair had ended. Thomas withdrew to Ringgold, while Sherman was already retreating from Meridian.[33]

This brief encounter demonstrated the basic difference in Johnston's and the government's strategic policy. In early February, when Richmond first inquired as to how many men Johnston could send Polk, Davis evidently still did not believe that Federal power in the West was great

32 Johnston to Beauregard, January 13, 1864, in Johnston Papers, William and Mary; see also Johnston to Seddon, December 28, 1864, *ibid;* Johnston to Davis, January 2, 1864, in Georgia Portfolio II, Duke; Johnston to Cobb, February 2, 1864, in R. P. Brooks (ed.), "Howell Cobb Papers," *Georgia Historical Quarterly,* VI (December, 1922), 368.

33 Johnston to Davis, February 13, 23, 1864, Johnston to Longstreet, February 23, 1864, Johnston to Cooper, February 10, 1864, in Johnston Papers, William and Mary; Polk, *Polk,* II, 321–35; *Official Records,* LII, Pt. 2, pp. 621, 624, 627, XXXII, Pt. 3, p. 716.

enough to launch simultaneous moves against two areas. Johnston was well aware of this. No doubt he remembered the episodes in December of 1862 and May of 1863, when troops were sent from Bragg, not enough to give Pemberton an advantage, but enough to weaken the former's position, and he argued against it now, as he had then. Davis had insisted the reverse—that both areas could not be threatened at once.

Again in February of 1864, the old argument was revived. Johnston on February 13 argued that he could not give Polk sufficient reinforcements and still hold the Atlanta front. Instead, it would require two-thirds of the army's infantry to give Polk's feeble army enough aid to throw back Sherman. Davis on February 15 insisted that if Sherman were attacking through Mississippi, no force could be threatening in Georgia.

On February 16 Johnston repeated his old argument—that "we cannot both hold this route to Georgia & effectually aid Genl. Polk now." But Davis was adamant. The day after receiving this telegram, Davis ordered Hardee's corps to move to reinforce Polk's army.[34]

There was more at stake in this brief February encounter than merely a difference of strategic opinion. During January and February, there was a noticeable lack of correspondence sent to Johnston from Richmond regarding an offensive move. In fact, the lag in correspondence was so obvious that on February 27 Johnston wrote the government asking what their plans were. He recalled the first Seddon and Davis letters regarding an offensive, and asked whether such an offensive was still planned.[35]

The government indeed had plans for an offensive, but was not bothering to consult Johnston. Unknown to the general, a feverish amount of discussion and correspondence had ensued during January and February. Davis and Seddon had plotted Johnston's future course with the new commander in chief Bragg and even with Lee and Longstreet. The planning for Johnston's army had been initiated by Longstreet and Lee in January.

Longstreet in January seemed to be suffering from the pangs of lost prestige. His campaign against Knoxville had been a miserable failure, culminating in a bloody repulse by the Knoxville garrison in a November 29 battle. Longstreet's popularity had slipped badly because of this fiasco, as well as by his subsequent removal of three of his officers. In December after reaching winter quarters in upper East Tennessee, Longstreet had relieved General Lafayette McLaws of his division command and ordered him to proceed to Georgia, on the grounds that in the Knoxville

---

34 *Official Records*, LII, Pt. 2, p. 619; Johnston to Davis, February 13, 16, 1864, in Johnston Papers, William and Mary.
35 Johnston to Bragg, February 27, 1864, in Johnston Papers, William and Mary.

campaign McLaws had failed to show confidence in Longstreet's plans. Charges were also filed against one of Hood's brigade commanders, General Jerome Robertson, for also expressing a want of confidence in Longstreet. Then, on December 19, General E. M. Law had tendered his resignation as brigade commander. Law, who had hoped to succeed to the command of Hood's division, was evidently angry that Longstreet had recommended General Micah Jenkins for the promotion. Later, Longstreet accused Law of going to Richmond under improper circumstances to lobby to have his brigade transferred to the Alabama front. Charges were drawn up against Law for a variety of reasons, such as obtaining leave under false pretenses and creating discontent among his command.[36]

Longstreet was probably not prepared for the repercussions of his action. Public sentiment was against McLaws' being relieved. The government was more annoyed since, as Cooper informed Longstreet, he had no right to relieve the general but was instead, to place him under arrest and file charges. McLaws appealed to Richmond and charged that the real reason for his dismissal was Longstreet's old grudge against him which arose after Chickamauga. He maintained that Longstreet headed the conspiracy against Bragg, and that when he refused to take part, Longstreet was embittered. Bragg, who by February had assumed his Richmond duties, was impressed by McLaws' statement, as well as by some long documents furnished him by the general which indicted Longstreet for deliberately delaying the campaign so he would not have to return to Chattanooga. Thus, Bragg, on March 4, informed McLaws that he would back up the beleaguered general with "ample" evidence in his possession concerning disobedience of orders, neglect of duty, and lack of support after Chickamauga.[37] Longstreet's anti-Bragg activity had boomeranged.

Then in February, final approval was given for General Edmund Kirby Smith's promotion to full general, an act designed to give him adequate rank for his command of the Trans-Mississippi department. Longstreet, whose commission as lieutenant general was given on the same date as was Kirby Smith's, was irked by the situation. He considered that he outranked Kirby Smith because he had a superior rank in the United States

36 E. M. Law to McLaws, April 29, 1864, McLaws to Sorrel, December 27, 1863, Longstreet to Cooper, December 30, 1863, in McLaws Papers, UNC; Archer Anderson to George Brent, April 14, 1864, in Davis Papers, Tulane; Official Records, XXXI, Pt. 3, p. 866, XXXII, Pt. 3, p. 652; Oates, War between the Union and the Confederacy, 338–39.

37 Official Records, XXXI, Pt. 2, p. 893, LII, Pt. 2, p. 633; McLaws to Bragg, February 25, 1864, in Bragg Papers, Western Reserve; Longstreet to Cooper, December 30, 1863, McLaws to Bragg, n.d., in McLaws Papers, UNC.

Army before the war. Longstreet later remarked bitterly that the occasion "seemed to demand resignation." [38]

Seemingly desperate to regain lost face, Longstreet in January began experimenting with strategy-making in the West. On January 10 he suggested to Lee a somewhat unrealistic invasion of Washington, whereby his corps would be mounted on mules. Accompanied by Lee's cavalry, they would penetrate behind Meade's army and reach Washington while Lee occupied Meade's attention. By the next day, however, Longstreet revised his planning and suggested to Lee that he be allowed to mount his corps on horses and mules and invade Kentucky to strike the Louisville and Nashville Railroad. Lee did not discourage his thinking on the latter project. Though he questioned whether Longstreet could obtain that many animals, he cryptically noted, "let us both quietly and ardently set to work." [39]

By early February Longstreet appeared to be making some headway. Lee made inquiries to Richmond as to how much livestock and equipment could be sent to Longstreet. Lee also broached the subject to Davis. He asserted that if Longstreet were allowed to make the raid against the Federal communication line in Kentucky, the Federals at Chattanooga would be forced to detach men for his pursuit. This, argued Lee, would enable Johnston "to take the offensive and regain the ground we have lost." Meanwhile, Longstreet enlarged upon his own plans. On February 2 he proposed a fantastic revision of his original plan to Lee. Now his mounted corps was to penetrate Kentucky while all the cavalry in Johnston's and Polk's departments were to invade central Kentucky and join Longstreet's column. Lee was to join Longstreet in East Tennessee, while Johnston's army was to be shifted to Virginia to take Lee's place.[40]

This last proposal by Longstreet provoked not only the end to his hopes for a Kentucky invasion, but a significant shift in Lee's Kentucky invasion interests as well. By mid-February Lee was backing away from the dismal prospect of having Longstreet's infantry, mounted on mules, riding through the mountains of eastern Kentucky. In a letter veiled with courtesy, he listed several disadvantages, such as the fact that he could supply only five hundred horses for Longstreet's corps. Instead, Lee gave spark to a new theme in Richmond which quickly developed—combined operations between Longstreet and Johnston. He inquired,

[38] Longstreet, *Manassas to Appomattox*, 525.

[39] *Official Records*, XXXII, Pt. 2, p. 541; Lee to Longstreet, January 16, 1864, in Confederate Miscellany, Emory.

[40] *Official Records*, XXXII, Pt. 3, pp. 654, 657; Lee to Davis, February 3, 1864, in Davis Papers, Tulane.

"Could you project a movement in connection with Gen'l Johnston to drive him from Tennessee?"[41]

The next day, still unknown to Johnston, the new strategy for him was taking shape. Lee stirred Davis' desire for a Johnston offensive by commenting, "it is very important to repossess ourselves of Tennessee," and also, "to take the initiative before the enemies are prepared to reopen the campaign." This last statement would be Richmond's basic policy for Johnston throughout the spring—the need to advance before Sherman concentrated and was ready to advance.[42]

Still, Longstreet continued to fight for a Kentucky invasion by his corps. On February 21 and 22 he pleaded with Seddon and Lee for authority to make the move. At least six thousand reinforcements should be sent to East Tennessee, he insisted, and then he could move into Kentucky to get on the railroad between Louisville and Nashville. Longstreet argued that such a move would force the enemy to abandon Tennessee and allow Johnston to advance and regain it. Even after receiving Lee's letter of February 17, Longstreet still insisted that "the easiest and most rapid" way to regain the two states was to send his mounted corps into Kentucky. Anxious to pursue his plan, Longstreet telegraphed Davis on February 29 to ask if he had permission to implement the plan. Again, on March 4, he repeated his plan to Lee. He urged that Lee move into East Tennessee, while Johnston's army be sent to hold Virginia in his absence, until Kentucky could be occupied.[43]

But the government had other plans for Longstreet's corps. Unknown to Johnston, Bragg and Davis had fashioned a new offensive strategy for the West by the first week of March. Johnston was to invade East Tennessee and join Longstreet's column somewhere near Madisonville, about forty miles below Knoxville. The two columns then were to unite and invade Middle Tennessee, by crossing the Tennessee River at Loudon and moving through the Cumberland Mountains via Sparta and McMinnville. By March 5 Davis had sent an officer to Longstreet's headquarters to confer with the general regarding the plan. No mention of the plan was made to Johnston by the government. In reply to his February 27 query as to whether the government had some offensive in mind, Johnston was told practically nothing. Instead, on March 4 Bragg sent a brief note indicating that Johnston was "to have all things in readiness at the earliest, practicable moment for the movement indicated." Three days later Bragg added another vague note which stated that "the enemy is not prepared

---

41 Lee to Longstreet, February 17, 1864, in Confederate Miscellany, Emory.
42 Lee to Davis, February 16, 1864, in Davis Papers, Tulane.
43 *Official Records*, XXXII, Pt. 3, pp. 502, 788, 791, 818.

for us, and if we can strike him a blow before he recovers success is almost certain." [44]

Serious matters were involved in the new plan. In his original December 23 letter to Johnston, Davis had urged the general to communicate freely with him and promised him all aid the government could give. Bragg on March 4 also had urged Johnston to "communicate your wants to me freely." Johnston's "chief want" was to know what was going on. By March 12 he still had received no communication regarding any offense plan. Thus, he complained to Bragg that day that he had no idea what the "movement indicated" was.

In addition to being cryptic with Johnston, Richmond was being unrealistic. Bragg, exhibiting short memory, was expecting Johnston to do things he himself had previously considered impossible. In August of 1863, when Richmond suggested that he take the offensive from Chattanooga after being reinforced by Johnston's army, Bragg had argued that it was impossible to invade Yankee-held territory with half the enemy's strength. Also, he insisted it would be impossible to march the army across the Cumberland Mountains, which he classified as "destitute even of vegetation." Again, in October of 1863, Bragg had turned down the possibility of flanking Rosecrans out of Chattanooga because he considered it logistically impossible to march his army across the Tennessee River and through the Cumberlands.[45]

Bragg's fears had been well founded. But the problems he would have faced operating from Chattanooga were nothing compared to those that would be faced now by a combined move from East Tennessee. Longstreet had an even greater deficiency of wagons and animals than did Johnson. To cut loose from the Atlanta railroad would have required Johnston to march from Dalton into the East Tennessee valley, which was devoid of forage. Longstreet himself had insisted that there was nothing between Chattanooga and upper East Tennessee to sustain an army. Forage was so short in Longstreet's corps that a single day's supply was not on hand in March. His men had already been living on short rations because the valley's corn crop had been harvested and taken by the Federals. No forage existed for his transportation animals, and the cavalry was able to obtain it only on the far reaches of his command. [46]

Without supplies in the valley, Johnston would have been required to maintain his army completely from his sparse wagon transportation. Once across the Tennessee River at Loudon, the route was a long dirt

---

[44] Johnston to Bragg, February 27, 1864, Bragg to Johnston, March 4, 7, 1864, in Johnston Papers, William and Mary.

[45] *Official Records*, XXXII, Pt. 2, p. 514, XXX, Pt. 4, p. 726.

[46] *Ibid.*, XXXII, Pt. 3, pp. 648, 655, 667.

road ninety miles across the Cumberland Mountains to Sparta. It was impossible to obtain subsistence on the mountains for even a modest force, much less for the concentrated elements of Johnston and Longstreet. Hence, Johnston's trek from Dalton to Sparta would have required a dependence upon wagon transportation for 170 miles.

However, Richmond proceeded to prepare for this unrealistic strategy without informing Johnston that it was in the offing. Four days before Johnston's March 12 complaint that he had heard of no plan, Longstreet was en route to Richmond for conferences with Davis, Bragg, Lee, and Seddon. There, unknown to Johnston, they planned his army's strategy. Longstreet spoke out against the planned concentration, and reminded Bragg that he had rejected such a proposal after Chickamauga. But Davis and Bragg seemed determined that Johnston should take the initiative. When the conference adjourned, the strategy remained for Johnston to march to some rendezvous point south of Knoxville, join Longstreet, and then cross the Tennessee River and the Cumberland Mountains to strike the enemy's supply lines and Nashville.[47]

The government's insistence on the plan was probably based on more than distrust of Johnston's word. The mood for an offensive was in the air. Longstreet's earlier proposals no doubt had stirred Bragg's memories of the 1862 Kentucky invasion. Longstreet himself seemed to be playing both sides of the game. Though he admitted to Johnston that the government's plan was not workable, Longstreet's alternative was neither realistic nor conducive to the government's apparent desire for an offensive. When he went to the Richmond conference, Longstreet had a revised version of his former Kentucky plan. It called for a three-pronged invasion of Kentucky which was reminiscent of the 1862 effort. Beauregard and twenty thousand men were to be brought from the Carolinas. Beauregard was to march into eastern Kentucky via the passes in southwestern Virginia, while Longstreet's column penetrated via the Cumberland Gap area. When the enemy retreated, Johnston then was to march into Kentucky and the three columns were to join near the Ohio River.[48] Though Beauregard rejected such a proposal, he also added to the frenzy in March when he suggested a massive concentration in either East Tennessee or Georgia and a subsequent invasion of Middle Tennessee and a push toward the Ohio River.[49]

Other plans also stirred Richmond's imagination. In mid-February a Tennessee Congressman had sent Seddon a plan proposed by one of Long-

47 Freeman, *Lee's Lieutenants*, III, 308; Longstreet, *Manassas to Appomattox*, 544–45.
48 Longstreet, *Manassas to Appomattox*, 544.
49 *Official Records*, XXXII, Pt. 3, pp. 627, 656, 679, XXXI, Pt. 3, p. 812.

street's cavalry commanders, Colonel George Dibrell. The colonel's mis-leading document proposed that Longstreet cross the Cumberlands to-ward Nashville while Johnston pursued behind the retreating enemy. This proposal left the impression that ample supplies would be found on the Cumberland Mountain route. The Congressman, John Murray, ar-gued that no portion of Middle Tennessee produced more supplies than that section just west of where the army would emerge from the Cum-berlands.[50]

Thus, by the time of the Richmond meeting, government leaders seemed obsessed with the idea of an offensive. Even before Longstreet reached Richmond, Davis maintained that the true strategy was for Longstreet and Johnston to join below Knoxville and move into Middle Tennessee. He stressed the importance "of our taking the initiative." Lee favored the plan as well. He labeled it "the most feasible plan," though he admitted that he was not acquainted with the country through which the armies would be forced to march. [51]

Not until March 18 did Johnston at last learn what Lee, Bragg, Davis, and others had decided for his troops. Bragg had dispatched Colonel John Sale to Johnston's headquarters with a letter explaining the details of the offensive. Johnston had been forewarned in a letter from Long-street, about March 13, describing the initial conversation Longstreet had had on March 4 at his East Tennessee headquarters with the emissary from Richmond, General Porter Alexander. Yet Longstreet's somewhat pessimistic appraisal of the plan's general outlines did not prepare John-ston for the shock of what the government actually intended for him to do.

In effect, what Richmond envisioned was merely a raid into Middle Tennessee. Johnston was to cut loose from his Atlanta communications and join Longstreet south of Knoxville. They would then cross the Ten-nessee River in the Loudon-Kingston area, march across the Cumberland Mountains, and seize Nashville before the Federals at Chattanooga had time to withdraw. To achieve this, Johnston would be allotted sixty thousand infantry. Aside from his own thirty-three thousand, he would have Longstreet's twelve thousand, plus five thousand reinforcements from Polk and ten thousand reinforcements from Beauregard. With the old Confederate dream of the Ohio River line still evident in his think-ing, Bragg spoke of the move as "reclaiming the provision country of Tennessee and Kentucky." [52]

---

50 *Ibid.*, XXXII, Pt. 3, p. 744.

51 *Ibid.*, p. 594, LII, Pt. 2, p. 634.

52 Bragg to Johnston, March 12, 1864, in Johnston Papers, William and Mary.

Johnston immediately saw the fallacies of the plan. His own food and transportation systems were barely able to supply a static army at Dalton. Already Longstreet had warned that his own army was on half rations, that no supplies existed between his position in upper East Tennessee and the proposed site of the rendezvous, and that once the columns joined, his own army would have to rely on Johnston's commissary. This meant that Johnston, himself badly short of wagons and teams, would have to feed his army on the 104-mile march from Dalton to Kingston, then still have enough rations in his wagons for twelve thousand more troops on a long, barren 65-mile trek through the Cumberlands to the headquarters at the Caney Fork River at Sparta. In addition, Johnston must provide over 150 wagons to carry the pontoon train for crossing the Tennessee River. Already Johnston was so short on animals that many of the artillery pieces normally drawn by six horses were being drawn by only four.[53]

Bragg's promise of reinforcements from Polk and Beauregard seemed shaky. They were not to join Johnston at Dalton, but were to be ordered to him "just as soon as you may be able to use them." This vague promise, which sounded almost like blackmail, portended only disaster. Though Bragg spoke of concentration, he was, in effect, advocating dispersal of forces. Three columns under Johnston, Polk, and Beauregard were to enter Tennessee. Just how these scattered units could dodge Grant's far superior forces at Knoxville, Chattanooga, and Nashville and unite across the Cumberland Mountains was not explained. Bragg could not even guarantee they would be sent. The dismal prospect of invading Tennessee without support was left open by Bragg's statement that they would be sent "if nothing shall occur to divert them." From his own experience in the Kentucky campaign, Bragg should have remembered the unwieldy nature of several invading columns attempting to combine operations, and the pain of waiting for promised reinforcements which did not arrive.[54]

The government's plan seemed to take lightly the Federal strength in Tennessee. Bragg stressed that Johnston would be advancing amidst the "scattered forces" of the enemy. Yet Johnston's intelligence indicated that the Federals had massed some 103,000 troops in the Chattanooga-Nashville sector alone. How could Johnston force the abandonment of Chattanooga as Bragg indicated? Bragg asserted that Johnston, moving between these scattered columns at Nashville, Chattanooga, and Knoxville, could seize Nashville before the Federals at Chattanooga had time to fall

[53] Longstreet to Johnston, March 5, 1864, *ibid; Official Records,* XXXII, Pt. 3, pp. 800, 817.
[54] Bragg to Johnston, March 12, 1864, in Johnston Papers, William and Mary.

back to that city. The absurdity of this was obvious. From Chattanooga, Nashville was merely hours away by the Nashville and Chattanooga Railroad. Once Johnston and Longstreet left Kingston, their route would be obvious. Also, it involved a long march of 159 miles to Nashville, half of which was through the mountains.[55]

Too, how was Longstreet to evade the Federal force at Knoxville (which in February was estimated as four corps in strength) and join Johnston near Kingston? Only two routes were available. He could move across the French Broad River east of Knoxville, then cross the Little Tennessee, swing south of the city, and unite with Johnston on the south bank of the Tennessee near Kingston. Also, this route, because of the configuration of the Unaka Mountains, would force him to swing within twenty-five miles of Knoxville. If he chose to unite by moving to the north side of Knoxville, Longstreet would have to cross the Holston River and await Johnston on the north bank of the Tennessee at Kingston. The lack of a pontoon train would make this difficult. If the Federals at Knoxville attempted to impede Longstreet and prevented the junction, what would Johnston do? Trapped in the East Tennessee Valley between Chattanooga and Knoxville, he then could escape only by dispersing his army through the Blue Ridge of North Georgia.

Johnston's attempt to explain these objections was unsuccessful. On March 19 he replied to Bragg's letter and listed the reasons why he thought the plan was not feasible. He still argued that the best strategy was to await the Federals on the south bank of the Tennessee in northern Georgia. Yet Johnston did not rule out an offensive. He suggested that if Richmond wanted to invade Middle Tennessee, it would be much easier to do so by moving through North Alabama. Longstreet also had decided that a union in East Tennessee was impracticable. On March 16 he sent a long letter to Davis explaining the risks of such a junction.[56]

However, Longstreet was doing Johnston no good. He seemed to be playing off one strategic proposal against another. In that same letter to Davis, Longstreet still maintained that a junction in East Tennessee would force the enemy to abandon Knoxville and Chattanooga, to withdraw to Nashville and perhaps even into Kentucky. If the enemy chose to fight, he claimed, the Confederates "ought to be able to win a glorious victory." [57] The truth was that Longstreet still was lobbying for an in-

[55] *Ibid;* see also Longstreet to Johnston, March 5, 1864, *ibid; Official Records,* XXXII, Pt. 2, pp. 637–41.

[56] Johnston to Bragg, March 19, 1864, in Johnston Papers, Duke; Johnston to Longstreet, March 13, 1864, in Johnston Papers, William and Mary; *Official Records,* XXXII, Pt. 3, pp. 637–41.

[57] *Official Records,* XXXII, Pt. 3, p. 639.

dependent move. He admitted to Davis also that a concentration of Polk's and Beauregard's troops with Johnston at Dalton would be advantageous, while his own corps invaded Kentucky. Longstreet argued, however, that the best solution still would be to bring Beauregard to join him for a dual invasion of Kentucky from upper East Tennessee. That same day Longstreet reiterated the proposal in a letter to Lee. The critical point in Longstreet's suggestions was that he rarely advised that Johnston was unable to take the offensive. Instead, to Richmond he preached an offensive and dazzled them with the prospects of regaining Kentucky.[58]

Longstreet's push for an offensive was not lost on Richmond. On March 21 Bragg sent a reply to Johnston's objections, telling him flatly that he need not expect any reinforcements at Dalton unless he agreed to take an offensive. Clearly the government did not understand Johnston's position, for he had not ruled out an offensive in his March 19 reply, but had reiterated that the better method was first to stand on the defensive and defeat the Federals, and then take the offensive into Tennessee. Neither had Johnston ruled out an invasion via North Alabama. He tried to point this out to Bragg in a reply on March 22, arguing that the only difference between his and Richmond's views was "as to details." [59]

During the spring Johnston could hardly have been accused of failing to express his objections to Richmond's plan. Bragg's letter of March 12 was delivered to Johnston by Bragg's military secretary, Colonel John B. Sale. Sale, a former staff officer with Bragg, had served the general well in Richmond during the spring quarrels of 1863 as a lobbyist with congressional supporters. Now Bragg sent him to Atlanta to deliver the offensive plan and to confer with Johnston. The two officers had a long discussion, and Johnston outlined to Sale his objections to the proposed plan. He argued that Longstreet should reinforce him at Dalton, and with additional reinforcements, the Federals could be brought to battle on the south bank of the Tennessee River. By sending a detachment to sever communications between Knoxville and Chattanooga, Johnston planned to force the Federals at Chattanooga to advance and fight him. He believed this move would draw out the enemy, and they could then be defeated. Johnston stressed that the proposed concentration and invasion of Middle Tennessee would jeopardize his army. A defeat on the north bank of the Tennessee would probably destroy his force. However, if they met a reversal in North Georgia, the army could remain intact and fall back along the Atlanta Railroad. Too, Johnston at length

58 *Ibid.*, pp. 637–42; Longstreet to Johnston, March 16, 1864, in Johnston Papers, William and Mary.
59 Johnston to Bragg, March 22, 1864, in Johnston Papers, William and Mary; see also *Official Records*, LII, Pt. 2, p. 644.

reiterated the logistical problems of the Longstreet-Johnston combination. Also, in his conversation with Sale, Johnston insisted that he was not ruling out a flat offensive campaign. He suggested, however, that if Richmond demanded such, it should be done through North Alabama, where fewer mountains would be encountered. Still, Johnston stuck to his basic principle. With his shortages of manpower, supply, and transportation, he probably could not advance before Grant was ready to do so. He considered this a Confederate advantage, since it would draw the Federals toward Dalton where they could be defeated and then pursued into Tennessee.[60]

Unimpressed with Johnston's explanations, Richmond sent a second envoy to Johnston in March. Despite Hardee's previous boastings of the artillery's fine condition, Johnston had insisted throughout the spring that guns and better horses for officers were needed. By late February, the artillery was short six hundred horses, and Johnston estimated that at least sixty-four of his guns could not be maneuvered during a battle because of the shortage of horses. Lacking an artillery commander, Johnston had applied to the government to have General Porter Alexander sent as chief of artillery. By the end of March Johnston still had no officer who had commanded more than twelve guns.[61]

Dubious of Johnston's objections, Richmond ordered Lee's chief of artillery, General W. N. Pendleton, to inspect Johnston's field guns. Pendleton arrived in Dalton on March 12 and remained a week. By March 29 he had prepared his report, which he presented in person at a Richmond conference with Bragg, Cooper, Seddon, and Davis. Probably Pendleton did not say what the government wished to hear. Johnston had only 111 guns, he reported. Of these, Pendleton labeled 15 as "nearly useless," while 27 others were "scarcely more valuable." Johnston's animals were "certainly thin" and he needed five hundred horses to have his army in combat shape.[62]

Richmond did not consider Pendleton's report as conclusive evidence, particularly since Johnston's artillery, as he described it, was no worse than other commands "at all similarly situated." Any effect Pendleton's visit had in convincing the government of Johnston's weakness was stymied when the artilleryman returned to his command with Lee. The two officers conferred at length, and Lee happily reported to Richmond

60 Memorandum of J. B. Sale, March 19, 1864 (MS in Davis Papers, Tulane).

61 Johnston to Bragg, March 16, 30, 1864, Johnston to A. R. Lawton, February 28, 1864, in Johnston Papers, William and Mary; *Official Records*, XXXII, Pt. 3, pp. 697–98.

62 Pendleton to Cooper, March 29, 1864, in Davis Papers, Tulane; *Official Records*, XXXII, Pt. 3, pp. 687–709.

that Pendleton's report of general conditions in Johnston's army "gave me unalloyed pleasure." Lee questioned Johnston's objections to the campaign, one which he claimed offered "the fairest prospects of valuable results." Even so, Lee was forced to admit that he could not properly judge those objections Johnston made in regard to the enemy's position and the topography of East Tennessee. Almost simultaneously with Lee's observations came another letter from Longstreet which stirred the Richmond spirit for an offensive. On March 16 Longstreet insisted that he had tried to instigate another campaign against Knoxville, but that Johnston had given no cooperation.[63]

Evidently convinced that Johnston's arguments over a weakness of artillery had been discounted, Richmond then in early April sent a third envoy to Johnston. Lieutenant Colonel Arthur Cole, inspector general of field transportation, was sent to ascertain the true condition of Johnston's transportation. Cole produced evidence of startling deficiencies. After ten days' work, he informed the government that the planned offensive could not be made with Johnston's current wagon transportation. Cole argued that rations for between fifteen and twenty days would be needed to last through the 250 miles of barren country before Johnston broke through into the Middle Tennessee plain. To accomplish this, Johnston needed a much larger reserve wagon train. Cole estimated that Johnston could not consider the move without an additional nine hundred wagons and teams for supply transport alone. He would require three thousand mules, not counting those animals needed for the artillery. Even while Cole was still at Dalton he learned something of the sparse animal supply in Johnston's Georgia-Alabama command. His district officer at Augusta did not believe that within two months Johnston could obtain a thousand mules from the entire district. [64]

But Richmond disregarded this impartial advice of their own agent, and still insisted that Johnston was able to make a long offensive. Thus, a fourth envoy was sent in early April, this one to encourage Johnston to advance immediately. By March 30 the government was convinced that the main Federal concentration would be against Lee in Virginia, because Grant was now known to have returned to Virginia. Deaf to the warnings that the Federals had enough men to operate simultaneously in the West and the East, Lee that day urged Davis to have Johnston take the offensive in the West in order to hold back reinforcements to Grant. On April 5 Lee repeated his basic theme, that "the great effort in this

---

63 *Ibid.,* p. 736; Longstreet to Davis, March 16, 1864, in Johnston Papers, William and Mary; Pendleton to Cooper, March 29, 1864, in Davis Papers, Tulane.

64 *Official Records,* XXXII, Pt. 3, pp. 753, 772–74.

campaign will be made in Virginia." He reported heavy reinforcements "daily arriving to the Army of the Potomac," intimating that they came from Johnston's front. Lee insisted that this concentration could not be effected for operations against Richmond "without reducing their other armies." In such a situation, Lee argued, Johnston in the West should take advantage of the Federals' reduced forces on his front. [65]

On April 7 Lee became more specific. He sent Davis a letter filled with rumors, such as scattered reports of western Federals joining Meade. Lee admitted none of his own scouts had observed such moves. Yet the evidence was somewhat convincing. Lee reported that five western corps allegedly had been seen passing eastward toward the Virginia front. Though he on one hand described these reports as mere rumors, Lee did insist that the enemy was making "large preparations" for the Virginia campaign. He spoke of the approaching storm "which will apparently burst on Virginia," and urged that Johnston be prodded to take the offensive to divert reinforcements from Meade. The next day Lee added more reports from "our most reliable scouts" which indicated that Hooker's two corps had returned from the West. By the end of April, Lee seemed convinced that the West was in little danger, and that the main concentration was in Virginia. He admitted there was a large force in the West but added that it "is not yet concentrated" to attack. Instead, since everything indicated "a concentrated attack on this front," Johnston should be able to launch successfully an offensive against the weakened Federals in Tennessee.[66]

The Lee reports seemed to raise a barrier against communication between the government and Johnston regarding the proposed offensive. Despite the reports by Pendleton and Cole, by April the government seemed certain that nothing stood in the way of a successful offensive into Tennessee except Johnston's own reluctance. Consequently, on April 7, Pendleton was ordered back to confer with Johnston. He reached Dalton at midnight on April 14, and spent several hours the following day in conference with Johnston and his cavalry commander, Wheeler. Pendleton went over the reasons why the President desired the army under Johnston to take the offensive. The enemy in Tennessee had been weakened by heavy reinforcement to Virginia and by furloughs. Thus, the time seemed appropriate to advance in order to prevent any further concentration in Virginia and to regain the supply area of Tennessee. For

65 Lee to Davis, March 30, 1864, in Davis Papers, Tulane; Lee to Davis, April 5, 1864, in Davis Papers, Emory.

66 Lee to Davis, April 7, 1864, in Dowdey and Manarin (eds.), *Wartime Papers*, 692; Lee to Davis, April 8, 1864; *ibid.*, pp. 693–94; Lee to Davis, April 30, 1864, *ibid.*, p. 709.

good measure, Pendleton added other reasons for the move, such as preventing waste in Johnston's army due to inactivity, inspiring the country,
and defeating Sherman before the Confederates themselves might be
forced to retreat.

Pendleton evidently was not prepared for the mass of evidence with
which Johnston demolished Davis' ideas. Shrewdly, Johnston had Wheeler, a staunch Bragg ally, present at the meeting to back up his statistics
on his own and Sherman's army. Wheeler estimated the enemy at Nashville, Knoxville, and Chattanooga held a minimum of 103,000 troops,
of which 51,000 infantry were concentrated in the Chattanooga area
alone, with an additional 14,000 in close support along the Nashville
and Chattanooga Railroad. Wheeler and Johnston agreed that the
enemy had some 77,000 infantry in all, while Johnston's own infantry
force was only 34,500. This force, argued Johnston, even when joined
with the 5,000 men promised from Polk, simply was not enough for an
offensive.

Johnston and Wheeler listed other objections. Johnston reminded
Pendleton that Cole himself had admitted the army did not have the
wagon transportation required for the proposed maneuver. Too, it appeared that the Federals were also preparing to advance before the army
was strong enough to move into Tennessee. Again Johnston struck the
crucial point—the expedition was not worth the risk of a defeat north of
the Tennessee River which would open up Georgia and Alabama.

Johnston presented a modified version of his own defensive-offensive.
Actually the government had been arguing that Johnston must first take
the offensive and then that reinforcements would be sent to him en route.
Instead, Johnston proposed that he be reinforced at his present position.
Then he would advance to the south side of Chattanooga, and by threatening communications with Knoxville, would force the Federals to fight
on the south bank of the Tennessee. Meanwhile, the huge cavalry command in Polk's department could cross the Tennessee River and cut
Federal communications to Nashville and Kentucky.

By April 20 an impressed Pendleton had returned to Richmond. The
following day, he presented Davis and Bragg a written report which,
like those of other envoys, sustained Johnston's position. Pendleton stated
that he "could not but admit that the mode of attack preferred by Genl.
Johnston might on the whole prove more proper." He also admitted that
"the enemy's force here is evidently greater than has been supposed."
Pendleton strongly backed Johnston's statistics regarding the Federal
strength. Lee had contended that the Twenty-Third, Eleventh, and
Twelfth corps had gone to the Virginia front. But Pendleton asserted to
Davis and Bragg that by comparing Wheeler's scouts' reports with those

derived from Federal papers, Johnston's estimate "is probably not far from the truth." Pendleton went further to dispel another erroneous assertion made by Lee. Instead of the Federals' remaining idle in the West to concentrate in Virginia, Pendleton admitted that Wheeler and Johnston had impressive evidence that the Federals at Chattanooga were preparing "a great effort here." Thus, Pendleton discounted Davis' plan of strategy, and urged Davis to do as Johnston recommended—to concentrate western forces at Dalton.[67]

While Pendleton was en route to Dalton, Johnston sent his own envoy to the government. Communication with Richmond had been sparse since Bragg's insistence on March 21 that only by taking the offensive would Johnston receive any reinforcements. Thus, on April 8, fearful that the government did not understand his views properly, Johnston sent Colonel Benjamin Ewell, a trusted staff officer, to confer with Davis and Bragg. Ewell was to insist that Johnston had not declined to take the offensive, but intended to do so when prepared. Instead, Johnston's objections had only been against the specific plan proposed by Bragg and Davis for a combination of operations with Longstreet in East Tennessee. Johnston's preparations for his offensive had been delayed because of transportation shortages. Also, Ewell was to emphasize that the best way Richmond could insure an invasion of Tennessee was to reinforce Johnston quickly.

On the morning of April 14 Ewell held an interview with Bragg in Richmond. He had requested that Bragg grant an interview and also arrange one with Davis. He stressed that he preferred to see the general first, in order to smooth out any possible bad feelings between Bragg and Johnston. Ewell was probably surprised by Bragg's conciliatory and perhaps disarming attitude. Bragg insisted that nothing could disturb "his friendly relations with General Johnston." Indeed, Bragg depicted himself as a shield between Davis and Johnston to prevent "any interruption of harmonious relations." In fact, when Ewell contended that Johnston's views on the offensive had been misunderstood, and that the general opposed only Davis' plan and not the general idea, Bragg insisted that such an interpretation "had been done by the President and the Secretary of War; that he himself had not so understood them." Bragg even argued that he was sympathetic with Johnston's transportation problems, and desired to reinforce him.

It is not clear just what Bragg had in mind during his interview with

67 "Memorandum of Conference Held at Request of President Davis & Under His Instructions, with General J. E. Johnston" (MS in W. N. Pendleton Papers, Duke); *Official Records,* XXXII, Pt. 3, p. 755; Govan and Livingood, *A Different Valor,* 256.

Ewell. He proposed that if Johnston would agree to launch an offensive campaign, the government would supply him with fifteen thousand troops, gathered from Polk's and Beauregard's commands. Longstreet was no longer a possible source, since his corps had been ordered back to Lee's army. Pressing Ewell on this matter, Bragg asked if Ewell could assure Davis in their forthcoming interview that Johnston would take the offensive. Unwilling to commit Johnston to such a venture, Ewell at once telegraphed the general at Dalton and asked permission to tell Davis that Johnston would invade Tennessee if he had fifteen thousand additional troops.[68]

Ewell stressed that an immediate reply was needed but none had arrived when Ewell met Davis on April 14. Johnston did send a telegram that day but did not commit himself to an invasion. He argued that such an agreement would depend upon how many men the Federals had in Tennessee. Johnston further warned that at least an additional month would be needed to ready his army's supply transportation.

The importance of Johnston's reply was probably nil. In his diary and his official report to Johnston, Ewell makes no mention that the government ever saw it. Instead, by April 14, the government apparently had already decided not to send Johnston any more men. Ewell met with Davis and explained the problems which made Richmond's offensive plan impossible. Though he had not heard from Johnston, Ewell took the liberty to state that Johnston would take the offensive if he had fifteen thousand more men. But Davis had no interest in this plan. He blamed Johnston for the alleged massive concentration in front of Lee. As Ewell learned later in a conversation with Lee while still in Virginia, that general was still convinced that a minimum of three corps had been sent from Tennessee to Virginia. Davis agreed that the threat of Richmond's being attacked had been one of the main reasons why the government had planned an offensive for Johnston's army. Now, according to Davis, Johnston had delayed so long that the need for an offensive had passed, since the Federals had already concentrated in Virginia. Probably to Ewell's surprise, Davis seemed to contradict the promise Bragg had made the previous day. Now Davis insisted that any reinforcements from Beauregard must go to Lee, and that Polk's small force was too weak to send troops to help the army at Dalton. Still, he stubbornly insisted that Johnston should take the offensive. Where, asked Ewell, would he derive the troops? Davis said he would give an answer in a few days.

On April 19 Ewell received his answer from Bragg. No substantial aid

[68] "Diary of Late Official Visit to Richmond, Va. under Genl. Jos. E. Johnston's Orders" (MS in Johnston Papers, William and Mary); Ewell to Johnston, April 29, 1864, Johnston to Ewell, April 14, 1864, *ibid.*

would be sent to Johnston. Bragg explained that "the pressure at Richmond" was too great to permit aid to the West. All that could be sent was a single brigade from Mobile and a few regiments from Beauregard. Determined to salvage something from the trip, Ewell, on April 20, wrote Bragg a letter while he still was in Richmond. In this letter he outlined the verbal explanations with which Johnston had sent him to Richmond. To this report Bragg did not even bother to reply.[69]

The failure of Ewell's mission to Richmond illustrated, significantly, important government positions. Richmond still discounted the Yankee force on Johnston's front. Only two days after Colonel Ewell penned his final report to Bragg, the general sent a convincing letter to Davis arguing that Johnston had greatly overrated the Federals on his front. Bragg contended that only sixty thousand Federals could be brought against Johnston at Dalton.[70]

By the first of May, Richmond had become thoroughly convinced that a massive build-up was occurring in Virginia at the expense of the West. Lee in April repeatedly had insisted that this was happening and had warned that Meade would move against him with a minimum of 100,000 men. As late as May 13, even after Johnston had been forced out of Dalton by Sherman, Davis was insisting that Grant was to be reinforced by Sherman, and that Johnston should try to halt the proposed move from the western theater to Lee's front. Bragg, too, believed that the imbalance existed. After Johnston appealed to him for reinforcements again, Bragg, as late as May 2, argued that the concentration of Federals in front of Dalton was probably a demonstration, since scouts reported large bodies of troops coming east. An almost psychotic fear, inflamed by intelligence reports of varied character, seemed to pervade Richmond. One April 16 report passed to Major William Norris of the Signal Corps at Richmond even warned of an army of 400,000 to 500,000 opposing Lee, with vast reinforcements from the West. One of Norris' scouts stationed near Washington asserted, "Never since the Persians invaded Greece, has such a force been inaugurated and the fall of Richmond is considered sure." Seddon was somewhat impressed by the report and sent it on to Bragg on April 17. Two days later General Custis Lee forwarded to Bragg a potpourri of statistics furnished by agents in Baltimore which listed the reinforcements from the West to Meade at between 25,000 and 30,000 men. Lee himself on May 9 forwarded another report gleaned from

69 Ewell to Johnston, April 29, 1864, Ewell to Bragg, April 20, 1864, Ewell Diary, *ibid.*
70 Bragg to Davis, April 22, 1864, in Davis Papers, Tulane.

prisoner interrogations to Davis indicating that 40,000 western troops were in the process of being or would be brought to Virginia.[71]

Yet Johnston had intelligence to the contrary. In April scouts reported a massive build-up at Chattanooga, with a significant shift of troops from Mississippi and West Tennessee to Chattanooga. Johnston insisted that many of the corps that Lee contended had been moved to the East were still in the Chattanooga area. The Eleventh and Twelfth corps were still there. General John Schofield's Twenty-third Corps had not gone eastward, but by April 28 was reported to be at a position east of Chattanooga at Cleveland, on the Knoxville-Atlanta Railroad. By April 17 General James McPherson's Sixteenth Army Corps reportedly was marching across North Alabama toward Huntsville. General Oliver Otis Howard with the Fourth Corps was by April 15 reported arriving at Cleveland, while Hooker's Twentieth Army Corps on April 7 was still reported west of Chattanooga in Lookout Valley. Johnston kept Richmond well advised of these reports.[72]

The failure of the Ewell mission meant more than the restatement of Richmond's belief that the West was not as imperilled as the East. By the end of April, Richmond was evincing an increasingly peculiar attitude toward Johnston. Since their own emissaries had borne out Johnston's contention that he was not in condition to take the offensive, the government could no longer press him to do so. Yet Davis and Bragg refused to admit that they had been wrong. Instead, by the end of April they devised a clever rationale. Johnston, they said, had been in error in that he had delayed his offensive until its chief purpose—to relieve pressure on Lee—was useless, since Grant was already heavily concentrated in Virginia. Thus, had Johnston moved when he should have, Grant could not have shuttled troops to Virginia. By adopting this line, the government in effect was agreeing with their envoys that Johnston could not take the offensive, and at the same time managing to condemn Johnston.

Even in May, when Sherman advanced on Johnston and thus disproved the theory that Virginia was the main front, Richmond continued to rationalize. Critical to this new line of thinking was the belief that the main threat was in Virginia. On May 15, after Sherman had already forced him back from Dalton to Resaca, Johnston desperately telegraphed

[71] Lee to Davis, May 9, 1864, in McWhiney (ed.), *Lee's Dispatches*, 176–77; "Information recd. from Baltimore, April 19, 1864," Seddon to Bragg, April 17, 1864, "Confederate agent" to William Norris, April 16, 1864, in Davis Papers, Tulane; *Official Records*, LII, Pt. 2, p. 664, XXXVIII, Pt. 4, p. 705; Lee to Bragg, April 13, 1864, in Braxton Bragg Papers, Historical Society of Pennsylvania.

[72] J. Wills to Wheeler, March 29, 1864, in Wheeler Papers, Alabama; Johnston to Bragg, April 4, 7, 11, 15, 17, 19, 20, 24, 28, 1864, May 1, 2, 4, 1864, in Johnston Papers, William and Mary.

Richmond that "we are in the presence of the whole force of the enemy assembled from Tennessee & North Alabama." Still the government did not believe him. That same day General Josiah Gorgas in his diary criticized Johnston for not furnishing Lee with a corps, "as the enemy is evidently not to attack him and he must have 65,000 men idly waiting there." Gorgas contended that Johnston was remaining idle while "the fate of the nation is being decided" in Virginia. As late as May 20, when Johnston had retreated as far south as Cassville, Davis argued that had Johnston taken the offensive in the spring he would have held back western troops ordered to Grant. There seems little doubt that by May, Richmond considered Johnston a failure as a strategy maker for the West.[73]

In addition to quarrels and accusations from Richmond, in May, Johnston was also faced with a lack of support among his officers. Something of a myth concerning Johnston's service in the Army of Tennessee in 1864 depicts him as immensely popular with both officers and men. True, by the spring of 1864, he was apparently very well liked by the men. Yet Johnston had almost as many enemies in the high command as Bragg did. When he took command he inherited a structure containing some loyal supporters of Bragg, but he did not inherit the support of the anti-Bragg generals in the army, such as Hardee and Polk. Their suggestions in 1863 that Johnston be given the command reflected less their admiration for the general than their dislike of Bragg. This lack of support came about gradually. When Johnston took command, he found only one officer suitable to command a corps, Hardee. Breckinridge in December had been replaced by Hindman as commander of the second corps. Hindman, a major general, was only a temporary commander. Johnston not only preferred that the government send him a lieutenant general to fill Breckinridge's old position, but a third officer of that rank as well. Johnston believed that the seven infantry divisions of the army, and the hoped for reinforcements, could better be utilized in a three-corps army. The government declined to allow him to divide into a three-corps system, but in February promoted and sent west Lieutenant General John Bell Hood as corps commander. That same month Wheeler's cavalry, which had been with Longstreet, was ordered back to the army. By April the army had taken shape in this way: Hardee commanded the First Corps, comprised of Cheatham's, Cleburne's, Walker's, and Bate's divisions. Hood's Second Corps included the divisions of Hindman, Stewart, and Stevenson. Wheeler retained his post as commander of the cavalry corps, which included three divisions. Martin retained the command of his old division,

73 Ewell to Johnston, April 29, 1864, Johnston to Davis, May 15, 1864, Johnston Papers, William and Mary; Gorgas, *Diary*, May 15, 1864, p. 103; Davis to Lee, May 20, 1864, in Rowland (ed.), *Davis*, VI, 258.

while Generals John Kelly and William Humes led the remaining divisions of Wheeler's corps. The army's organization remained thus until mid-May, when Polk reinforced Johnston with three divisions from his Army of Mississippi, which comprised a third corps.

Ironically, Johnston now unknowingly was in a situation much like that of Bragg in 1863—he was distrusted by all of his infantry corps commanders. All three, Hardee, Polk, and Hood—and Wheeler as well—failed to support Johnston's case during the spring, and also damaged his efforts to convince the government of his bad situation after Sherman advanced in May.

The initial breakdown of communication between Hardee and Johnston came when Hardee had been sent as second-in-command of Johnston's Alabama-Mississippi department in the summer of 1863. Hardee was miserable because he believed he had been reduced to such menial tasks as commanding the paroled prisoners from Grant's Vicksburg victory. Critical of the manner in which Johnston operated, Hardee stated that he would not like to say "what I thought of the organization, discipline and general efficiency of his command."[74]

After Bragg's departure, there were small tiffs between Hardee and Johnston. In December, while Johnston was still in Mississippi, he desired the return of two brigades sent to Bragg prior to Chickamauga. When Hardee appealed to Richmond to allow him to keep the brigades at Dalton, he received a sarcastic reply from Johnston. Johnston chided him for referring the matter to Cooper's office, and reminded Hardee that the matter in question was entirely between them. Later, in March of 1864 the two clashed over a misunderstanding with the office of the Commissary General. Johnston was requesting seventy thousand daily rations for the army, but one of Northrop's agents informed the government that Hardee, a personal friend, had told him that Johnston had only forty thousand men. When the government inquired of Johnston as to whether he had been overdrawing on rations, the general sent Hardee a brief note on April 8 demanding to know "whether his name has been properly used for this report." Hardee quickly explained that he had been misquoted, that he had probably said the army contained only forty thousand effectives.[75]

Through the late spring and early summer, the gap between the two men widened. Johnston rarely communicated with Hardee as to strategic

[74] Hardee to Polk, July 27, 1863, in Polk Papers, Sewanee; Hughes, *Hardee*, 158–62.

[75] *Official Records*, XXXII, Pt. 3, p. 596; see also XXXI, Pt. 3, p. 809; J. L. Locke to L. C. Northrop, March 8, 1864, Hardee to Mackall, March 8, 1864, in Hardee Papers, Alabama.

policy. Miffed, Hardee, in April, privately asked Colonel George Brent to tell Bragg that he "was not consulted about any offensive," and that he was not in Johnston's confidence. Brent added his own observation that, "between Johnston and Hardee, I think there is a want of harmony." Hardee's ruffled feelings probably were due to injured pride. Johnston's repeated assertions during the spring that the army was in poor shape completely contradicted Hardee's own December reports to Richmond. Too, as the army's senior corps officer, he was hurt that he was not consulted more. Repeatedly, he complained to his wife that he was in the dark as to Johnston's plans, and that the army's operations seemed to be planned by Johnston and Hood. Evidently harboring some ill feeling toward Johnston, Hardee during the spring made no attempt to use his considerable influence with Davis to aid his commander. Instead, he may have damaged Johnston badly not only by his silence but by a note sent to Davis on June 22, when the army had fallen back near the Chattahoochee River. Hardee insisted that Johnston had suffered heavy losses in the campaign, and added the damaging supposition that Johnston probably would not fight until the army reached Atlanta "if the present system continues." [76]

Johnston's relationship with Polk was scarcely better. As with Hardee, the friction was generally under the surface. Evidently, Polk's suggestion that Johnston take command of the army, which he urged several times in 1863, was based more on his desire to be rid of Bragg than on his respect for Johnston. During the summer of 1863, Polk and Hardee had talked of Johnston's deficiencies as a general. On July 27, after reaching Mississippi, Hardee wrote his friend Polk, "Johnston is wanting in all those particulars in which you feared he was deficient." Polk evidently discussed some of these deficiencies during his second meeting with Davis in late October of 1863. When Davis proposed that Polk replace Hardee in Mississippi, the general opinion of those at the conference was that the Bishop could be satisfied in the new command, "provided old Joe Johnston is not in the way." Davis told Polk that he did not believe Johnston would impede his efforts, "but will be only too glad to have somebody of life and energy enough to relieve him of all responsibility." [77]

In early 1864 relations between Polk and Johnston were cool while the Bishop commanded the Alabama-Mississippi department. The two quarreled over whether Johnston's commissary agents had a right to secure food from Polk's department. Too, Polk was concerned over the obvious

[76] Hardee to Davis, June 22, 1864, in Davis Papers, Emory; see also Hardee to wife, June 12, 19, 20, 23, 1864, in Hardee Papers, Alabama.
[77] Gale to wife, October 29, 1863, in Gale-Polk Papers, UNC; Hardee to Polk, July 27, 1863, in Polk Papers, Sewanee.

quarrel between Davis and Johnston. He insisted that it was Johnston's responsibility to mend the failing friendship by sending the President a letter stating that he "was prepared to waive all that was past in the desire to consult the public good." Later, in February, Polk may have been irked by Johnston's delay in sending Hardee to Alabama. Polk's son later insisted that if Johnston had sent Hardee immediately when the government ordered him, Sherman might have been defeated. [78]

Once Polk joined Johnston's army, the same lack of confidence continued to exist between them. As in Hardee's case, Johnston evidently did not confer much with Polk. At least, Polk did not seem to know what Johnston's plans were. Shortly after joining Johnston, Polk on May 21 confided to his wife, "we have been falling back from point to point to find ground on which General Johnston was willing to fight them." Polk did not seem to think Johnston's army was weak. He indicated that with the addition of his forces, "we are strong enough to do all that ought to be asked of us." He admitted he knew nothing of Johnston's plans to fight Sherman. He stated that "when General Johnston will offer battle I do not know." While Johnston and Polk had few outright disagreements during the campaign, Polk made no effort to influence the President on Johnston's behalf. [79]

Johnston's relations with his cavalryman Wheeler have also been badly minunderstood. The Wheeler-Johnston relationship was closely tied to the overall pro- and anti-Johnston sentiment, throughout the Confederacy and in the army. By January of 1864 Davis was attempting to have Wheeler's nomination as major general of cavalry confirmed by the Senate. The nomination was opposed by the Texas and Kentucky delegations, particularly by some of the old pro-Johnston partisans who wanted General John Wharton to receive the post. Wharton himself had gone to Richmond after a December quarrel with Wheeler, and had spoken against his commander, apparently to Wigfall. Complaining to Johnston of Wharton's activities, Wheeler labeled him a "frontier political trickster" who only desired to head the cavalry. On January 23 Davis admitted to Johnston that he was having trouble getting Wheeler's nomination through, and asked for Johnston's aid in the form of a statement of Wheeler's abilities. Johnston immediately replied that Wheeler's nomination was essential for the betterment of his cavalry, and in a separate note argued to his friend Wigfall that Wheeler's past experience justified the nomination.[80]

78 *Official Records*, XXXII, Pt. 3, pp. 794, 803; Polk to E. J. Harvie, January 3, 1864, in Polk, *Polk*, II, 320, see also pp. 324–25.

79 Polk to wife, May 21, 1864, in Polk Papers, Sewanee.

80 Johnston to Wigfall, January 9, 1864, in Wigfall Papers, DLC; *Official Records*, LII, Pt. 2, p. 606, XXXII, Pt. 3, pp. 643–44.

Wheeler did not seem to appreciate that Johnston had gone against the sentiment of his own political allies in securing his nomination. Beginning in February, he secretly began writing a series of damaging letters to the government. There was no doubt where Wheeler stood in relation to army politics. He praised Bragg's appointment, and asserted that the army believed that "you will see that this army is not so much neglected." Intended or not, such statements were to harm Johnston. Wheeler praised Hood's appointment in the West in early March, at the same time that Hood himself was engaged in a clandestine correspondence. Wheeler asserted that Hood "will be appreciated by this army." [81]

Wheeler soon began to give his own impressions of Johnston's ability to take the offensive. On March 3 he confided to Bragg that the enemy's movements "indicated weakness" and argued that several of the Federal corps which Johnston had reported on the Chattanooga front, such as the Eleventh, Twelfth, and Twenty-third, were actually smaller than ordinary sized units. Wheeler in April related the same opinions to Bragg that he had stated to Pendleton during his visit—that if Johnston were reinforced by fifteen thousand men, he could invade by Richmond's desired route through East Tennessee and that he would not suffer any food shortages until he was practically into Middle Tennessee.[82]

In June and July, Wheeler contended to Bragg that any reinforcements the enemy received did not make up for the losses they were receiving in the campaign. Wheeler played down Federal strength, and estimated to Bragg that on July 1 Sherman had only sixty-six thousand infantry. After the army had fallen back to the Chattahoochee River, Wheeler still minimized Federal strength, and warned Bragg that Johnston was having all military materials removed from Atlanta. Too, Wheeler seemed to leave an erroneous impression with the government as to the strength and abilities of Johnston's cavalry. He continually spoke of the fine condition of his command, and intimated that he had the power to cut Sherman's line of supply if Johnston would only order him to do so.[83]

Other old friends of Bragg gave the government a wrong impression of affairs. In March, Bragg's old supporter, General E. C. Walthall, insisted that "every officer & man in this brigade is sincerely & devotedly attached to you," and boasted that his command was in "fine condition." An old ally, Colonel Felix Robertson, the commander of Wheeler's artillery, insisted in March that the artillery was ready "to do good service," and

[81] Wheeler to Bragg, February 14, 1864, in Joseph Wheeler Letters, Harvard. Wheeler to Bragg, March 3, 1864, in Bragg Papers, Western Reserve.
[82] Wheeler to Bragg, March 7, April 16, 1864, in Bragg Papers, Western Reserve.
[83] Wheeler to Bragg, June 4, 5, 1864, July 1, 1864, ibid.; Wheeler to Bragg, July ——, 1864, in Bragg Papers, Duke.

that the artillery transportation was in good condition. General William Bate furnished Bragg with another telling report in March. Bate probably had endeared himself to Bragg in the spring of 1863, when he protested to Senator Landon C. Haynes of Tennessee that if Bragg were removed, the army would "degenerate into an armed mob." Bate's letter, which praised Bragg's "character and discipline," insisted that the commander was not at fault but rather the ambitious "malcontents in the army" were. Haynes passed the letter on to Davis and to Seddon. No doubt Bragg was impressed when, in March, Bate characterized his own division as "in good condition." General A. P. Stewart, telling Bragg that his friends "were gratified at his assignment," declared the army was in "fine condition." Hindman, obviously grateful that he had been restored to command, also listed his divisions as being in good condition.[84]

The opinions of these division and brigade commanders were probably valued by the government, especially by Bragg for more reasons than their allegiance to their former commander. In January, perhaps by coincidence, a split occurred in the army between opponents and supporters of Bragg over a proposal made by General Patrick Cleburne to enlist slaves in the army. Cleburne, troubled by the army's dwindling numbers, had written in December of 1863 a long document suggesting that slaves be enlisted with the promise of "freedom within a reasonable time to every slave in the South who shall remain true to the Confederacy." Cleburne argued that slaves had become a military hazard for they were being recruited into the Union army as it overran Southern terrain. The abolition of slavery might encourage the desired recognition of the Confederacy by Europe, Cleburne suggested. After drafting the paper, he submitted it to his brigade and regimental commanders. All four of his brigade commanders signed the paper, as did ten regimental commanders and General John Kelly, one of Wheeler's cavalry division commanders.[85]

The document startled both the high command and Richmond. Through Hardee, Cleburne sent an invitation for all corps and division commanders to meet with him at Johnston's headquarters on the night of January 2. That night Johnston, Hardee, Walker, Stewart, Stevenson, Hindman, and Bate came; only Cheatham was absent from the meeting. Johnston requested that Hardee explain the meeting's purpose, where-

84 Walthall to Bragg, March 11, 1864, Robertson to Bragg, March 14, 1864, Bate to Bragg, March 17, 1864, Stewart to Bragg, March 19, 1864, in Bragg Papers, Western Reserve; Hindman to Davis, January 16, 1864, in T. C. Hindman Letters, Harvard. Bate to Landon Haynes, March 21, 1863, in *Official Records*, LII, Pt. 2, p. 442.

85 *Official Records*, LII, Pt. 3, pp. 586–92; Buck, *Cleburne and His Command*, 188–89.

upon Hardee noted that Cleburne had prepared a paper "on an important subject." After Cleburne read the paper, a serious division of opinion developed.

General W. H. T. Walker, a militant pro-slavery general led the attack on Cleburne's proposal at the meeting and expressed his intention not only to forward a copy of the document to the government but also to send a full report as to which generals seemed to support it. At first, Walker intended to send the report through the War Department, but Johnston forbade this, stating that it was not a military matter. Undaunted, Walker procured a copy of Cleburne's paper and then addressed a circular letter to each general present asking whether he had supported the measure. By January 2 a startled Davis had received these items and quickly made known to Walker that it would be best if the entire matter were suppressed, especially that it should be kept out of the newspapers. Davis also quickly had Seddon write Johnston to suppress any discussion of it. Officially this was done. Johnston on January 31 passed on the President's message in a circular letter to those who had attended the meeting. So well was this done that not until 1890 did Cleburne's document come to light, when it was found in the papers of a member of his staff. Walker's correspondence with the government was not revealed until the *Official Records* were published in 1898.[86]

Though Johnston did his part in suppressing the matter, the pro-Bragg forces did not. Walker seems to have been the chief instigator of further discussion. Walker's motives probably involved more than a distaste for freeing slaves. The Georgia general was unhappy that he had not been advanced beyond a division command. In this vein, he wrote his wife in September, "for many reasons I am disgusted but have to stand it." By December, he appeared unhappy when Cheatham was given temporary command of Hardee's corps while Hardee temporarily held the army's command. By the spring of 1864, Walker evidently felt that he might be in competition for any potential corps commands which might develop, and in July he showed disappointment at not being selected as commander of a corps after Polk was killed. In January Walker had had hopes of succeeding to a corps command. Hindman's appointment as corps commander was obviously only temporary, until a replacement could be found. Obviously there were only five candidates, Cleburne, Cheatham, Hindman, Stewart, and Walker. Walker's commission as

---

86 Buck, *Cleburne and His Command*, pp. 190–91; Du Bose, *Wheeler*, 256–59; W. H. T. Walker to Bragg, March 8, 1864, in Bragg Papers, Western Reserve; Johnston to Hardee, Cheatham, *et al.*, January 31, 1864, Walker to Davis, January 12, 1864, Seddon to Johnston, January 24, 1864, in Johnston Papers, William and Mary.

major general predated that of Stewart's, but not those of Cleburne and Cheatham, or Hindman.[87]

Thus, Walker violently attacked the latter three during the spring for their alleged part in an abolitionist conspiracy. Though Cheatham did not even attend the January meeting, Walker insisted to Bragg that he had approved of the document and had wanted Cleburne to sign it for him. He intimated that Hindman had come to the meeting with Cleburne, and reminded Bragg that the Arkansan had been Cleburne's former law partner. Moreover, Walker asserted that at the meeting Hindman had favored putting Negroes in the ranks and freeing the "most courageous." Yet Walker's greatest wrath was for Cleburne. To Bragg he labelled the Irishman as a traitor, called Cleburne's meeting nothing more than treason, and asserted that the Irishman represented an "abolition party." To bind his argument, Walker flattered Bragg, congratulating the country for having one of Bragg's "tried patriotism and soldiership" at Davis' side.[88]

There seems little doubt that the Cleburne proposal represented a victory for the pro-Bragg generals in the army. Wheeler added fuel to the controversy with another private letter to Bragg in February, in which he asserted that the conspirators were Cheatham, Cleburne, and Hindman, and that even Hardee approved the suggestion. Questioning Cleburne's loyalty, Wheeler snidely reminded Bragg that the Irish general had only been in the country some ten years, and remarked that three years earlier the citizens of his own home town would have hanged Cleburne for making such a proposal. General Patton Anderson, who the previous October had warned Bragg of a plot in the army to overthrow him, labelled the proposition to Polk as "monstrous" and "revolting." [89]

The loyalty of the Bragg supporters in rallying to the anti-Cleburne standard gave them more influence in Richmond. Bragg was greatly impressed with the controversy, labelling Cleburne and other proponents of the measure as "abolitionist men" who "are agitators and should be watched." Bragg considered the project to be a cooperative one of Hardee, Cheatham, and Cleburne, and boasted that "it will kill them." Probably it did kill much of their influence in Richmond. Cleburne, particularly, suffered from his proposal. Three times in the summer of 1863 he was passed over for corps commander and remained a division commander until his death. Too, the strong defense of the status quo by Bate,

---

87 Walker to wife, September 15, 30, December 3, 1863, July 12, 1864, in W. H. T. Walker Papers, Duke.

88 Walker to Bragg, March 8, 1864, in Bragg Papers, Western Reserve.

89 Anderson to Bragg, October 10, 1863, *ibid;* Wheeler to Bragg, February 14, 1864, in Wheeler Papers, Harvard; *Official Records,* LII, Pt. 2, p. 578.

Anderson, Walker, Wheeler, and Stewart no doubt made the government more amenable to their views during the spring. To Bragg and others, the chasm between some of the pro- and anti-Bragg generals was not merely a matter of army politics, but was one of near treason. Bragg commented in March, "We must mark the men . . . and feel that they will bear watching." [90]

By February there was a new general at Dalton to do his watching. On February 4 the thirty-two-year-old General John Bell Hood arrived at Dalton to assume permanent command of Hindman's corps. After his wound at Chickamauga, Hood had convalesced in Richmond, where he was acclaimed a hero for his part in the western campaign. Indeed, during the autumn of 1863, a Hood mania seemed to possess the capital. He was feted at presidential receptions, and hobnobbed with the President's social circle of the Prestons, Mallorys, Chesnuts and other influential families. In September his old corps commander Longstreet had recommended his promotion to lieutenant general "for distinguished conduct and ability" at Chickamauga. Seddon, who termed Hood "a true hero" and "Paladin of the fight," echoed Longstreet's sentiments. Seddon even went further to recommend the promotion if for no other reason than out of "gratitude of the Confederacy" for Hood's services. Davis was no less impressed with Hood. He, too, recommended the promotion, asserting that Hood's services "are equal to any reward." Johnston was not immune to the peculiar hero worship of Hood. He assured the young Kentuckian that "we want you much," and told Wigfall in April that his greatest comfort since arriving at Dalton was the coming of Hood to the army.[91]

Johnston would soon rue his statements of admiration for young Hood. During the spring of 1864 Hood did more than all other correspondents from the army to discredit Johnston's version of conditions at Dalton. Exactly what Hood wanted in Dalton is not easily understood. His extreme ambition was recognized even by his friends. The tone of Hood's secret letters to the government during the spring was constant—a rebuttal of Johnston's reasons for not taking the offensive, and repeated hints as to what he would have done if he had commanded the army. While in Richmond, Hood had played well the role of the restive combat officer chafing to see field action. The tall, blond, handsome Hood had immediately ingratiated himself to Davis when he was in Richmond. The

[90] Bragg to Marcus Wright, February 6, March 6, 1864, in Wright Papers, UNC.
[91] Longstreet to Cooper, September 24, 1863, Johnston to Wigfall, April 1, 1864, in Wigfall Papers, DLC; Seddon to Davis, October 3, 1864, in Hood, *Advance and Retreat*, 66, also Seddon to Wigfall, October 14, 1863, p. 67; *Official Records*, LII, Pt. 2, p. 624.

two took long carriage rides, attended parties together, and were seen together in church. He constantly discussed with Davis the need for an immediate offensive in the West. No doubt such talks pleased a President weary of hearing Johnston's reasons for not fighting according to Davis' own plan. Though after Johnston was removed Hood swore that he had not intended to seek the command, his activities both in Richmond and at Dalton indicate the contrary.

Hood's ambition may have been caused by the urgency to prove himself as a man. Despite his acclaim in Richmond's social circles, he was often morose and restless for service in the field. With an arm maimed at Gettysburg and a leg amputated at Chickamauga, his body was wrecked. He could hardly mount a horse, and rode strapped to the saddle. Enough to frustrate an ordinary man, Hood's debilitation had a special meaning by the winter of 1863. He had fallen deeply in love with one of Davis' favorite young people, Sally Preston, the daughter of General John Preston. She rebuffed him, and Hood's blatant pursuit of her became a joke in Richmond. There was nothing coy about his art of wooing. He demonstrated the same headlong aggressiveness that he had shown on the field. Sally Preston was frequently embarrassed and disgusted by his lack of finesse. However, shortly before he left for the West, she agreed to marry him, but her public statements of amusement at the matter may have driven him to prove himself further on the field.

Hood's lack of strategy in his personal life may provide a key to his behavior while in Dalton. He was a simple man, often tactless and crude, more of a fighter than a general. Confederate and Union generals alike never doubted his combative ability, but seriously questioned his abilities to direct an army strategically. In love or war, Hood's was a simple, naive code—to attack head on. Such simplicity of approach may have produced the naive interpretation of affairs in Dalton which Hood gave to Richmond in the spring of 1864.[92]

Richmond's motive in sending Hood to Johnston's army is equally difficult to understand. It is not certain that it was originally intended for Hood to keep the government posted secretly on conditions at Dalton. Hood later insisted that while under Johnston's command the "only correspondence I remember ever to have had with the authorities at Richmond" were letters to Davis on March 7, and to Bragg on April 13. This statement simply does not agree with the records. Hood carried on

92 Cumming Recollection, UNC; Halsey Wigfall to ———, March 21, 1864, in Wright, *Southern Girl*, 173; Wilson, *Under the Old Flag*, II, 45; Taylor, *Destruction and Reconstruction*, 217; Guild, *Fourth Tennessee*, 120; Hood, *Advance and Retreat*, 67; Chesnut, *Diary from Dixie*, 348–49, 361, 367, 370–77, 316, 333, 328, 335–37, 341–42, 381.

a much more extensive correspondence, with letters to Bragg and Seddon on March 10, to Bragg on April 3, and to Davis on July 14. The tone of the initial letters indicated that the government expected to hear from Hood. On March 7 he wrote Davis that he had "delayed writing you so as to allow myself time to see the condition of the army." On April 13 Hood's estimate of Johnston's plans was sent. Hood had received a letter from Bragg which evidently asked the general to press Johnston to take the offensive. Hood apologized for his failure to do so, and stated he had done "all in my power to induce General Johnston to accept the proposition you made to move forward." [93] He was also corresponding with Lee during April. That officer urged Hood to do what he could to bring about an invasion of the Tennessee-Kentucky area. Even if no agreement, however informal, was made for Hood to keep Richmond posted, the government made no attempt to silence his improper correspondence. Instead, they seemed to encourage it by corresponding directly with Hood. In letters to Johnston, care was taken in Richmond to avoid mention of the Hood correspondence, of which little or nothing was known by Johnston.

Regardless of the intent, the Hood correspondence created false impressions in Richmond. On March 7 Hood reported to Davis that Johnston could unite with Longstreet even without any additional reinforcement. The army was reported in fine condition with excellent transportation. If Davis chose to add reinforcements from Polk, Johnston would have enough men to drive the enemy completely across the Ohio River, for the enemy was "at present weak, and we are strong." Three days later Hood insisted to Bragg that the enemy in Tennessee had only about fifty thousand men, and would not advance until heavily reinforced. On April 3 Hood directly contradicted Johnston's assertions of a concentration in the West by asserting to Bragg that the "great effort" of the enemy in the campaign was to be against Richmond. After a few harsh words for generals in the field who did not cooperate with the government, an obvious allusion to Johnston, Hood insisted that he was anxious to advance, and warned that heavy Federal concentrations from the West would probably go to Virginia. Hood's motives could hardly be doubted when he wrote in this letter to Bragg, "I am fond of large engagements & hope you won't forget me." [94]

By far the most damaging letter during the spring was Hood's to Bragg on April 13. Johnston attempted, during the Pendleton and Ewell missions, to present the problems involved in an offensive. Hood related

[93] Hood to Bragg, April 13, 1863, in Bragg Papers, Western Reserve. See also Hood to Davis, March 7, 1864, in John Bell Hood Papers, National Archives.
[94] Hood to Bragg, April 3, 1864, in Bragg Papers, Western Reserve.

that, despite all of his efforts, Johnston would not be induced to take the offensive. Hood said he regretted this, "as my heart was fixed upon our going to the front and regaining Tennessee and Kentucky." Instead, Hood argued that "I am not able to comprehend" when the army would be in better condition for an offensive.[95]

The entire Confederacy seemed caught up in a mania for an offensive in the West. In addition to the government's plan, Beauregard's and those of Longstreet and Lee, Johnston was subjected to pressures from powerful geographical blocs in Alabama, Tennessee, and Kentucky. Governor Isham Harris of Tennessee lobbied during the spring and urged Bragg to give Johnston enough reinforcements to move into Tennessee. Harris blustered, "Give me Tenn & in 30 days I'll add 30,000 men to your army."[96]

Pressures were also applied from Alabama, particularly from the planters of the northern Tennessee Valley. Polk echoed their sentiments when in February he sent his own proposal that he and Johnston join in Alabama and invade Middle Tennessee. In January five Alabama senators and representatives already had petitioned Seddon to give more attention to the Alabama front. That month, another group of prominent Montgomery citizens petitioned Seddon for more concern for the Alabama theater. Similar petitions were sent to Seddon in February. Polk kept the fires stirred by proposing to Davis on February 28 that he be given part of Johnston's army for a thrust across the Tennessee River into Middle Tennessee. In April, while Ewell was conferring in Richmond, Polk reiterated his proposal to be reinforced by at least one of Johnston's divisions for his own offensive into the state.[97]

Even stronger urging was applied from the Kentucky bloc. In the winter of 1863–64 Richmond was alive with Kentucky generals of failing status and diminishing commands. In January three of the most prominent, Breckinridge, Morgan, and Buckner, joined with General J. H. Lewis in a petition to the President, which must have whetted the lingering appetite to regain Kentucky. They proposed withdrawing Kentucky regiments from their respective commands, brigading them together, and placing them in East Tennessee. There, "combining their movements with those of the main army," they could enter Kentucky. General John Morgan, who was feted in Richmond circles after his

---

95 Hood to Bragg, April 13, 1864, *ibid.*

96 Isham Harris to Bragg, undated letter, *ibid.* See also *Official Records*, XXXII, Pt. 3, pp. 514–17, 562, 609–14, 553, 619–20, LII, Pt. 2, pp. 486, 488–89, 496, 500–501; Breckinridge, Buckner, *et al.*, to Jefferson Davis, January 15, 1864, in Davis Papers, Duke.

97 *Official Records*, XXXII, Pt. 3, pp. 514–17, 790, 813, LII, Pt. 2, pp. 609–14.

successful escape from the Ohio State Prison, suffered the embarrassment of being a cavalry division commander in the Army of Tennessee, with no command left after his disastrous Ohio raid. Breckinridge, who was suffering his own embarrassment over the disaster at Missionary Ridge, was now seeking some new command in East Tennessee or western Virginia. The influence of the Kentucky bloc in Richmond was considerable. During the winter they frequently attended Richmond social gatherings. Among them were some of the few non-Virginian officers given access to the inner circle of Richmond society. One observer commented that the Kentucky generals "move as one body." [98]

On January 26 Davis' aide-de-camp, G. W. C. Lee, was ordered to inquire of Johnston whether he considered the Kentucky idea a good one. Lee's letter contained all of the old shibboleths that had sent other Kentucky invasion ideas into disaster, particularly the old promise that once the army reached Kentucky, droves of the state's men would join the Confederate army. Johnston was not impressed. When approached on a somewhat similar idea earlier, Johnston argued that the results of Bragg's campaign indicated that Kentuckians would not join the army. To Lee he offered no particular objection, provided that an equal number of men were given him to replace his Kentucky troops. Eventually the idea was abandoned, except that Morgan was sent into East Tennessee to raise a new command. Still, the January 15 petition to Davis echoed the old Kentucky dream. It resembled the promises made by Longstreet, Hood, and others of success in the Bluegrass, if only Johnston would take the offensive. [99]

By May few problems had been settled during Johnston's four months at Dalton. The 41,300 effective infantrymen in his army on May 7 amounted to barely 5,000 more than he found when he took over in December. Johnston's relationship with Davis and Bragg had further deteriorated, and the government considered him a failure because he refused to attempt an offensive.

[98] Chesnut, *Diary from Dixie*, 364; see also p. 353.
[99] Breckinridge, Buckner, *et al.*, to Davis, January 15, 1864, in Davis Papers, Duke; Seddon to Johnston, December 29, 1863, in Johnston Papers, Huntington; Johnston to G. W. C. Lee, February 12, 1864, in Davis Papers, Tulane; *Official Records,* XXXII, Pt. 3, pp. 602, 619–20, 520, 714, 811–12, Ser. IV, Vol. III, 31–33.

twelve

Will Johnston Fight?

For the First three days in May, General Joseph Johnston nervously received reports from scouts on Sherman's predicted advance on Dalton. On the fourth, when intelligence indicated there was no doubt of Yankee intent, Johnston hastily telegraphed Richmond for reinforcements.

His defensive position at Dalton, while deceptively impressive on the map, was in truth more vulnerable than even he realized. Dalton lay in the Conasauga River valley, a narrow corridor between the outlying ridges of the main Georgia Appalachian range on the east, and the broad belt of the Lookout-Sand-Taylor's Ridge ranges on the west. This corridor, part of the Great Appalachian Valley which extended from Pennsylvania into Alabama, widened greatly twenty miles southward at Calhoun, where the Conasauga flowed into the Oostanaula River. Farther south, the valley widened even more at Rome, where the Oostanaula River joined the Etowah to form the Coosa River valley, some twenty-five miles wide. To approach Johnston, it seemed that Sherman must force his way across the western rim of the Conasauga River valley, Taylor's Ridge, and then force Johnston back down the narrow corridor and across the Oostanaula at Calhoun.

It would appear that Sherman would have difficulty crossing the west wall of the valley at Dalton, which was composed of three ranges. Taylor's Ridge extended from near the Alabama border into East Tennessee. In the Dalton area, this long, rough ridge reached elevations of twelve hundred feet, with few passes offering access to Johnston's position. About five miles north of Ringgold, the mountain was bisected by Hurricane Creek Gap. Just east of Ringgold, the main pike to Atlanta, the Western and Atlantic Railroad, and the east fork of Chickamauga Creek all crowded through Taylor's Ridge at narrow Ringgold Gap. Five miles to the south, the road from Chattanooga to Dalton via Rossville and the old Chickamauga battlefield cut through the ridge at Nickajack Gap. Four miles farther south, the road from La Fayette to Dalton crossed the ridge at Gordon's Gap.

Even if Johnston chose not to defend this outer line, the gaps through Taylor's Ridge did not then admit Sherman to the Dalton area. For east of Taylor's Ridge were two other spur ranges which lay across his route of advance from Chattanooga. The Tunnel Hill Ridge-Stony Point range extended from above Ringgold southward to the Calhoun area. Seven miles northwest of Dalton, Tunnel Hill Ridge lay astride the main pike to Chattanooga. Here the Western and Atlantic Railroad cut beneath the mountain in a long tunnel constructed before the war. Tunnel Hill Ridge was extended southward by the sporadic ranges of Stony Point Ridge, Horn Mountain, and Camp Mountain, until the range ended on the north bank of the Oostanaula River west of Calhoun. While the entire range from Tunnel Hill Ridge to Horn Mountain was not as rugged at Taylor's Ridge, it should be expected to serve to slow a Federal advance, particularly in the immediate area of Dalton.

Even if Sherman were allowed to cross this second range, he still would not reach Dalton, but would only debouch into Mill Creek Valley. The west wall of the valley was the Tunnel Hill-Horn Mountain range. The east wall, which lay in a north-south direction immediately west of Dalton, was a long ridge reaching fifteen hundred feet in elevation. This ridge was known as Rocky Face Mountain in the Dalton area and as Mill Creek Mountain southward until it ended on the Oostanaula River at Resaca. This was Johnston's main mountain stronghold. There were only three gaps through Rocky Face Mountain by which Dalton and the valley could be reached. Immediately northwest of Dalton, where the Western and Atlantic Railroad cut through Rocky Face Mountain, was narrow Buzzard Roost or Mill Creek Gap. Two miles to the south the roads via Nickajack and Gordon's gaps converged to cross Rocky Face at Mill Gap. Two miles farther south, another crossing was available at Dug Gap. All three were narrow, rough crossings which seemingly would be easily defended. It seemed that even if Johnston chose not to defend the outer crossings at Taylor's Ridge and Tunnel Hill Ridge, he would have ample warning to provide a strong defense of Rocky Face Mountain.

However, these ranges, such as Rocky Face, ran in a north-south direction until reaching the Oostanaula River some twenty miles south of Dalton. Here, in the area around Calhoun, the line of retreat to Atlanta and the valley floor parted. The pike to Atlanta and the railroad continued across the outlying Appalachian ridges via Cartersville and Cassville southward. But from Calhoun, the valley veered to the southwest, and widened as it neared Rome.

This shift in the direction of the valley made Dalton essentially a most dangerous position. Johnston's line at Dalton faced westward, shielded by Rocky Face Mountain. To the west, there apparently were several ranges which shielded the Confederates at Dalton. But these ranges did not block Sherman from reaching Johnston's line of communication below Dalton. Instead, the north-south lay of these parallel ranges opened up to Sherman several routes by which he could reach the valley, even within fourteen miles of Johnston at Dalton. The closest approach was the road across Taylor's Ridge via Ship's Gap. Here Sherman could go around the north end of Horn Mountain, and enter the narrow Sugar Valley between Horn Mountain and the Rocky Face-Mill Creek mountain range. Snake Creek Gap was a narrow pass here which debouched at Johnston's rear at Resaca.

The Snake Creek Gap route was important for several reasons. Unless troops were posted in the gap, it would be difficult to discern a Federal advance in that direction due to the rugged nature of the Rocky Face-Mill Creek range south of Dalton, where the mountain was over three miles wide. Too, if Resaca were seized, Johnston's army would be completely trapped in the narrow valley between Dalton and Resaca, where the pike and railroad crossed the Oostanaula River.

There were other routes to the southwest where Sherman could enter the valley and threaten Johnston's connections with Atlanta and with Polk's army in Alabama. From Chattanooga, the road through Chickamauga Valley led south through La Fayette and Summerville to Rome. Another road from La Fayette led via Villanow to Rome.

The seizure of Rome would be serious. One of Johnston's two lines of communication with Alabama, that via the Rome Railroad and the pike to Gadsden, would be severed. The industrial complex at Rome would be destroyed. Worse, Rome lay less than twenty miles from Kingston, on Johnston's line of communications with Atlanta. The Atlanta Railroad passed through Kingston before veering southeast toward Atlanta. If Sherman pushed on east from Kingston to Cassville, which was almost forty miles south of Dalton, the pike to Atlanta would also be seized. There was a real threat that a push through the lower valley from Rome would cut off Johnston on the north bank of the Etowah River, which flowed eastward just south of Kingston.

There was danger on Johnston's right, or north, flank as well. His right flank at Dalton was completely open due to the continuation of the Appalachian Valley into East Tennessee. Dalton was a vital rail junction. Northwest through Mill Creek Gap ran the Western and Atlantic to

Chattanooga; northeast through the valley ran the East Tennessee Railroad to Cleveland and Knoxville. Here, between the northern continuation of Rocky Face Mountain, Whiteoak Mountain, and the outlying Appalachian ridges, the railroad and a good pike led only twenty-six miles to Cleveland. There were no natural barriers in the valley to impede progress. Instead, by May 1, Johnston knew that the Federals had advanced as far as Red Clay, less than six miles north of Dalton, and were repairing the railroad to that point. There seemed to be a heavy concentration on this vulnerable route. By mid-April, Johnston believed that Howard's Fourth Corps, allegedly eighteen thousand strong, was at Cleveland. By the first of May, Howard had been joined south of the Hiwassee River by Schofield's Twenty-third Corps, twelve thousand men, from Knoxville, and by a division of cavalry.[1]

On Johnston's immediate front, Mill Creek Gap did little to control the main Chattanooga-Atlanta Pike. Three miles north of the gap, Rocky Face Mountain dwindled. Here the pike to Atlanta encircled the north end of the mountain and veered southward. In effect, there was no natural barrier along this main pike into Dalton. Too, the rugged nature of Rocky Face Mountain was a mixed blessing. It was difficult to obtain information about Federal maneuvers to the west. All Johnston knew by May 1 was that a heavy Union concentration was being effected at Ringgold with an obvious plan to push toward Dalton. Intelligence indicated that this Union concentration included at least some 54,000 infantry gathering at Ringgold, exclusive of Howard's and Schofield's corps. By May 2 it was believed that Schofield, McCook, and the cavalry were also en route from East Tennessee to Ringgold. All together, Johnston believed Sherman had some 103,000 effective troops, most of whom were thought to be concentrating at Ringgold during the first week of May.[2]

After the war Johnston tried to claim that he had known of the vulnerability of the Dalton position. In fact, he almost attempted to blame the abandonment of Dalton on Bragg. Johnston argued that the position had been selected only because it was at that point the army halted in late November after the retreat from Missionary Ridge. Johnston argued that he would have retreated from Dalton had not the government written to him "of the bad effect of a retrograde movement upon the spirit of the Southern people."[3]

[1] Pendleton to Davis, April 16, 1864, in Davis Papers, Tulane; Wheeler to Bragg, April 16, 1864, in Bragg Papers, Western Reserve; Johnston, *Narrative*, 303; *Official Records*, XXXVIII, Pt. 4, p. 654.

[2] Pendleton to Davis, April 16, 1864, in Davis Papers, Tulane; Johnston, *Narrative*, 303.

[3] Johnston, *Narrative*, 278, see also p. 277.

This appears to be a hindsight approach. In his letters to Richmond from December until May, Johnston never mentioned any specific area of weakness of the Dalton position. In fact, he only mentioned the threat of a Federal move through Rome, which he admitted, would make the holding of Dalton impossible. Instead, Johnston, if he were aware of Dalton's weakness, did little to improve it. Snake Creek Gap was left totally unguarded. Some earthworks were constructed at the crossing of the Oostanaula River at Resaca, but these would not prevent the enemy from trapping Johnston at the lower end of the valley between Dalton and Resaca. As for that region southwest of Resaca toward Rome, almost no precautions were taken. As late as May 5 not a single Confederate occupied any of the front from Resaca to Rome. On that day Johnston did order up General Will Martin's cavalry division, which had been refitting on the Etowah River, to patrol this wide front. But until May 7 there was no infantry posted south of the passes through Rocky Face Ridge in the vicinity of Dalton.[4]

Johnston's criticism of the Dalton position seems more of a rationalization to explain away the fact that during the first week of May, due to a shortage of and bad deployment of cavalry, he simply lost touch with Sherman's army. Bragg has sent practically all of Wheeler's cavalry to East Tennessee, and though it was returned to Johnston in the spring, it was in deplorable condition. Although Wheeler supposedly had a complete new cavalry organization of three divisions, commanded by Will Martin, John Kelly, and William Y. C. Humes, with a total of eight brigades, this was actually only a paper force. Martin's entire division of General John T. Morgan's and General Alfred Iverson's brigades was on the Etowah River attempting to find remounts after the arduous East Tennessee winter campaign. General John Kelly's division could field only a single brigade, that of General William W. Allen. His other brigade, that of Colonel George Dibrell, was also so short on horses that it was in the rear recruiting by the end of April. Humes's division allegedly boasted four brigades, but by the end of April could field scarcely more than two. Humes's brigade and that of Colonel Warren Grigsby were at Dalton but both were badly undermanned.

Wheeler's system of keeping tally on his command, had a tendency to exaggerate his force. Already Johnston had seen fit to chide him for listing as effectives, men who had no horses. By the end of April, Wheeler was listing Grigsby as having a brigade though he had but four hundred men. The remainder of Humes's division was in even worse condition.

4 *Official Records*, XXXVIII, Pt. 3, p. 614, Pt. 4, p. 664; Johnston to Davis, February 1, 1864, in Johnston Papers, William and Mary; Johnston to Bragg, March 19, 1864, in Johnston Papers, Duke.

Humes allegedly had a new brigade sent from East Tennessee and commanded by Colonel Thomas Harrison. Yet this command, too, had been sent to the rear to find animals for their many men who were dismounted. Humes, on paper, was also credited with having a brigade commanded by Colonel Moses Hannon, which actually consisted of no more than one full regiment and an additional battalion.

So dispersed was Wheeler's command that when the crisis arose at Dalton in early May, only three full brigades, including Grigsby's tiny command, were serviceable. The remainder were still far to the south attempting to refit their cavalry. Sickness, a shortage of horses, and other problems reduced a cavalry of 10,000 to an estimated 2,392 effectives at Dalton by April 30.[5]

This thin cavalry command was assigned a massive reconnaissance job. Johnston, fearful of a move through Taylor's Ridge, ordered Wheeler to post strong pickets at Ship's, Gordon's, and Nickajack gaps on Taylor's Ridge. Then the bulk of Wheeler's command was put in an advanced position at Tunnel Hill Ridge to give warning of enemy moves, while some picketed the East Tennessee approach north of Dalton.

It was soon obvious that Johnston was sorely in need of intelligence. By May 1 his headquarters had received word of heavy Union activity at Ringgold. From which direction, however, would Sherman advance? Until May 5 nothing seemed sure save that the Federal threat was on the approaches from Ringgold and Red Clay. By May 2 Johnston had received word that Sherman was repairing both railroads, the East Tennessee to Red Clay and the Western and Atlantic to Ringgold. On the morning of the second, a heavy Federal reconnaissance of Wheeler's position at Tunnel Hill was made. By May 4 the threat shifted somewhat to the approach via Cleveland. Two days earlier Johnston's scouts had indicated that most of the troops in East Tennessee were being sent to Ringgold via Chattanooga. Yet now Wheeler's pickets were driven in on the Cleveland Road, Howard's corps was reported at Red Clay, and the Federal advance was only nine miles north of Dalton on the Cleveland Road at Varnell's Station.[6] On the same day that he telegraphed Bragg urging that he be temporarily reinforced by Polk's command, and asking

5 "Official returns obtained from War Office, Richmond, 1865, copies of returns 1863–1864," in Hood Papers, National Archives; "Returns of Army of Tennessee, May 7, 1864," in Johnston Papers, William and Mary; Wheeler to Hood, April 18, 1874, in Hood Papers, National Archives. Wheeler later estimated that, including all detached units such as Martin's division, he had only 4,299 cavalry effectives on May 6. See Wheeler to Hood, March 21, 1874, Hood Papers, National Archives; *Official Records*, XXXII, Pt. 3, p. 801.

6 *Official Records*, XXXVIII, Pt. 4, p. 663; Johnston, *Narrative*, 301–303; Johnston to Wheeler, May 4, 1864, in Wheeler Papers, Alabama.

for assistance from East Tennessee—May 4—he telegraphed Polk to ask if he would send General W. W. Loring's division to Rome, and any other brigade that might be closer to Rome than Loring's command. That day Davis gave in to Johnston's request and ordered Polk to send Loring's division "and any other available force at your command" to Rome. Polk was also ordered to leave General Stephen D. Lee in charge of his department and to accompany the relief column.[7]

Immediately Polk made his preparations. Often historians have misinterpreted Polk's intentions. He did not immediately decide to send his whole command to Johnston. He knew little of affairs at Dalton, only that in his May 4 request, Johnston had warned of a separate move by General James McPherson's corps from north Alabama toward Rome. Thus, Polk moved forward to deal with McPherson and not to reinforce at Dalton. At first Polk did not intend to send practically his whole command to Johnston. On May 4, he informed Richmond that he was only sending Loring's division to Rome. Polk's other division, that of General Samuel French, was to remain in northeastern Alabama at Montevallo.

In fact, as late as May 6, Polk's intentions were not to move toward Rome at all. Johnston's warning of a possible move toward Rome by McPherson's corps ignited Polk's old longing for an offensive into Tennessee. Thus, on May 6, he telegraphed Johnston his intention to halt his fourteen thousand troops at Blue Mountain, to fight on McPherson's flank. On May 7 Bragg complained to Polk that evidently he was moving toward Montevallo with a much larger force than had been ordered. Bragg was probably as puzzled as Johnston as to what Polk's intentions were. His telegram was in response to Polk's May 6 note to Cooper stating that he was taking ten thousand infantry and four thousand cavalry to Johnston. Regardless of where he thought Polk was going, Bragg was still angry that he was moving so many troops toward Johnston. On May 21 Bragg complained to Polk that he took with him General W. H. Jackson's cavalry division. Polk replied that he had moved toward Johnston on Richmond's orders, but Bragg countered on May 23 by arguing that no such orders were issued by himself or by Davis, and that they were "disapproved." Polk countered by arguing that the government had indicated that he use his own discretion and that he had used it.[8]

While Polk argued with Richmond, Johnston was disturbed over the

7 Johnston to Polk, May 4, 1864, Cooper to Polk, May 4, 1864, in Telegrams Received, Polk's command, 1861–64, National Archives; *Official Records*, XXXVIII, Pt. 4, pp. 659–60.

8 *Official Records*, LII, Pt. 2, p. 666, XXXVIII, Pt. 4, p. 661, XXXIX, Pt. 2, p. 585; Polk to Bragg, May 4, 24, 1864, Bragg to Polk, May 21, 23, 1864, Polk to Johnston, May 4, 4, 6, 1864, Polk to Cooper, May 4, 6, 1864, in Polk Papers, Sewanee.

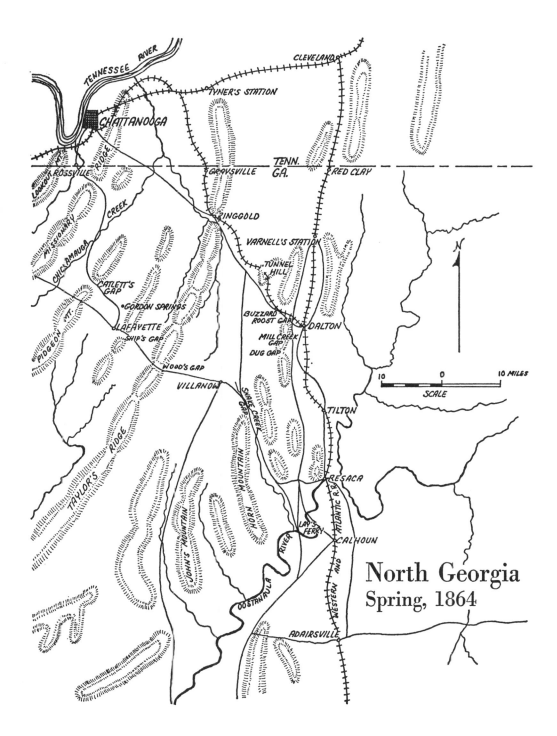

TENNESSEE RIVER

CLEVELAND

TYNER'S STATION

CHATTANOOGA

TENN.
GA.

ROSSVILLE

LOOKOUT MT.

RIDGE

GRAYSVILLE

RED CLAY

CREEK

MISSIONARY

RINGGOLD

CHICKAMAUGA

VARNELL'S STATION

CATLETT'S GAP

TUNNEL HILL

GORDON SPRINGS

PIDGEON MT.

LAFAYETTE

BUZZARD ROOST GAP

DALTON

SHIP'S GAP

MILL CREEK GAP

DUG GAP

WOOD'S GAP

VILLANOW

N

TAYLOR'S RIDGE

SNAKE CREEK

SNAKE CREEK GAP

TILTON

10   0   10 MILES
SCALE

JOHN'S MOUNTAIN

RESACA

ATLANTIC R.R.

LAY'S FERRY

RIVER

CALHOUN

OOSTANAULA

WESTERN AND

North Georgia
Spring, 1864

ADAIRSVILLE

Bishop's plans. He was upset by Polk's May 6 note. On the morning of May 7, unable to decipher Polk's note completely, Johnston expressed hope that Polk would move Loring's division on to Rome. Later that morning, when Federal designs on Dalton became more evident, Johnston again telegraphed Polk, urging the immediate concentration of his troops at Rome. Johnston argued that a concentration at Montevallo "will not do," and promised Polk that all of his troops would remain under his command. That afternoon, after learning of a new threat of a flanking move west of Rocky Face Mountain, Johnston again wired Polk that it was urgent for him to move quickly on to Rome. That night Johnston received his reply from Polk, who promised a concentration as quickly as possible. Time was now of critical importance. On the morning of May 8, Polk explained that Loring's division was still slightly beyond Blue Mountain, while French's division on the night of May 7 was still in western Alabama at Tuscaloosa.[9]

There was good reason for Johnston's urgent appeal for aid from Polk's department. On May 5 it seemed that a strong Federal push from the vicinity of Ringgold was imminent. Wheeler's cavalry, occupying the advanced position on Tunnel Hill Ridge, sent back only foreboding news. A corps believed to be Howard's had marched through Varnell's Station on the Cleveland Road, but then had veered west to link up with those Federals on the Ringgold front. Howard had aligned his troops only three miles from the northern end of Tunnel Hill Ridge facing southward. A portion of another Federal corps, reportedly Palmer's, had moved through Ringgold Gap to link up with Howard's right flank.[10]

These threats seemed to justify Johnston's alignment of his troops. Almost no troops were sent to occupy the potential crossings of Rocky Face Mountain at either Mill or Dug gaps. Instead, Johnston's left extended no further south than Mill Creek Gap. Bate's division of Hardee's corps and Stewart's division of Hood's corps were placed behind hastily erected fortifications in the gap. Cheatham's division continued the line northward along Rocky Face Mountain to a point some one mile north of Mill Creek Gap. From this point, the line bent back eastward at right angles across the valley in order to confront any force moving from the direction of Cleveland. Stevenson's division anchored on Rocky Face Mountain, and extended across the valley, joining Hindman's division which then bent back southward confronting the road to Cleveland. Dalton was held by Cleburne's division, which was posted on the north side

9 Johnston to Polk, May 7, 1864, in Telegrams Received, Polk's Command, 1861–64, National Archives; *Official Records*, XXXVIII, Pt. 4, p. 675; Polk to Johnston, May 7—9:20 P.M., 1864, May 8, 1864, in Polk Papers, Sewanee.

10 *Official Records*, XXXVIII, Pt. 4, p. 944; Johnston, *Narrative*, 304.

of town, facing the Cleveland Road, protected by Mill Creek.

Johnston's expectations of an attempted push via Tunnel Hill Ridge or the Cleveland route seemed to bear fruit. There was light skirmishing on Wheeler's front on both the fifth and the sixth. Then, at daylight on May 7, a mile-long battle line loomed up before Wheeler's thin three brigades at Tunnel Hill Ridge. Within a few hours, Johnston's advance line had been thrown back to Rocky Face Mountain. That evening, the Confederates atop the mountain watched as Sherman gradually aligned his own forces to correspond with Johnston's. The Federal line paralleled Rocky Face Mountain until its termination north of Mill Creek Gap, and then bent back eastward across the Cleveland Road. Scout and prisoner reports from Wheeler's skirmishes on May 7 seemed to confirm Johnston's theory. Wheeler's men reported that Howard's and Schofield's corps had advanced toward Dalton via the Cleveland Road, then veered west to form in battle line with Sherman's corps at Ringgold.[11]

In the early afternoon of May 7, Hood sent a note relaying news from his men at Mill Creek Gap who had observed a wagon train moving southward along the opposite side of Rocky Face Mountain. Also, that day Johnston had received word from Wheeler's scouts far westward along Taylor's Ridge. McPherson's corps was attempting to flank Dalton. Already one division was across the Chickamauga at Lee and Gordon's Mill, moving toward La Fayette, and the remainder of the corps was expected at the mill that night.

Johnston seemed to underestimate both of these distinct threats. He took lightly the possibility that a corps could slide around his left at Dalton and penetrate through Mill Gap or even farther southward at Dug Gap. Intelligence on May 5 through May 7 had accounted for McPherson's, Palmer's, Howard's, and Schofield's corps, but nothing had been seen of Hooker's corps. But Johnston on May 7 sent no troops from Dalton to either gap save for Grigsby's small cavalry brigade which was sent to Dug Gap. The only infantry forces sent to the entire region south of Mill Creek Gap toward Resaca were two regiments of General Daniel Reynolds' brigade, which had only that day arrived at Resaca. The regiments, the first of Reynolds' brigade, had been sent on May 5 by General Dabney Maury from Mobile at Bragg's order.[12]

Johnston's reaction to a possible flanking move by McPherson was also somewhat apathetic. Only two partial steps were taken to stymie such a move. On May 7 another reinforcement from Mobile, a fifteen-hundred-

---

[11] Johnston, *Narrative*, 304–305; *Official Records*, XXXVIII, Pt. 4, pp. 672, 676–77, 944.

[12] *Official Records*, XXXVIII, Pt. 4, pp. 668, 672–74; Johnston to Polk, May 7— 2:45 P.M., 1864, in Telegrams Received, Polk's Command, 1861–64, National Archives.

man brigade commanded by General James Cantey, reached Resaca. Johnston at first did not intend to leave even Cantey's brigade there, and that day ordered it to Dalton. Later in the day, however, he reversed his orders and had Cantey assume charge of the defenses built at the Oostanaula River at Resaca. Too, General Will Martin's cavalry division, now at Rome, was ordered to defend the crossing of the Oostanaula River between Calhoun and Rome.

More important was what Johnston did not do. Since McPherson's advance division by the night of May 6 had been reported within six miles of La Fayette, Johnston assumed that McPherson was sweeping wide, either to seize Rome or to get behind the Dalton position and seize the railroad south of Resaca. Thus Johnston completely ignored Snake Creek Gap, and made no inquiries as to its status. Too, on May 7, he seems not to have inquired of Wheeler as to whether his pickets were still in position at the gaps along Taylor's Ridge, particularly Ship's Gap, which lay on the route from La Fayette to Snake Creek Gap and Resaca. Cantey, who knew nothing of the country, was only told to keep a close watch on all routes leading from La Fayette to either Resaca or toward the Oostanaula River west of Resaca.[13]

On May 8 Johnston still did not grasp the significance of the reports from west of Rocky Face Mountain. That day General Cantey at Resaca forwarded a report from some of Wheeler's scouts. The Federals that day were reported around Villanow. There were two significant things in this sketchy report which Johnston might have considered. Villanow was a small community *east* of Taylor's Ridge, on the road from La Fayette toward Resaca through Snake Creek Gap. For the Federals to be at Villanow, they would have had to sweep away Wheeler's pickets, who supposedly held Ship's Gap on Taylor's Ridge. Had Wheeler withdrawn his cavalry from Ship's Gap or had they been forced out? There is nothing to indicate that on May 8 Johnston inquired of Wheeler as to just what was happening at Ship's Gap. Nor did he, after receiving this report, order a reconnaissance in force to determine the extent of the Federal menace. A second matter seemed to make such a reconnaissance imperative. If the Federals were in force around Villanow, this would indicate that McPherson was turning eastward at La Fayette toward Resaca and not southward toward Rome.[14]

Johnston's failure to see the danger to Resaca on May 8 was probably caused by the confused nature of scout reports. Badly short of cavalry,

13 *Official Records,* XXXVIII, Pt. 4, pp. 674–75, 679; Johntson to Polk, May 7— 2:45 P.M., 1864, in Telegrams Received, Polk's Command, 1861–64, National Archives.
14 *Official Records,* XXXVIII, Pt. 4, p. 678.

Johnston had only one effective scouting force west of Rocky Face Mountain, the cavalry regiment commanded by Colonel W. C. P. Breckinridge. Breckinridge's reports that day were confusing and contradictory. That morning he placed the main threat west of Rocky Face Mountain as being an infantry force slowly moving down the west side toward Dug Gap. As for the force reported pushing through Ship's Gap on Villanow, Breckinridge doubted that it was there. At Villanow, there was a critical road division. Northeast ran the road from La Fayette through Dug Gap to Dalton; southeast ran the road through Snake Creek Gap. Breckinridge believed Federal cavalry to be on the upper road, and he believed they had not come through Ship's Gap at all.

Later, in the early afternoon, Breckinridge reported two threats west of Rocky Face Mountain. Now, an infantry column was slowly moving south toward Dug Gap, immediately west of the mountain. A prisoner taken indicated that it was Hooker's corps. That cavalry force sighted on the Villanow road was shielding a force of some ten thousand infantry and cavalry apparently taking a direct route from Ringgold through Villanow to Rome, parallel to the valley road immediately west of Rocky Face Mountain, where Hooker's corps evidently lay. Nothing Breckinridge said indicated that the Confederates had even lost Ship's Gap. Nor did he mention any possible move through Snake Creek Gap. In both reports his emphasis was on the threat to Dug Gap caused by the force containing at least elements of Hooker's corps and moving slowly along the west side of the mountain. Breckinridge's report seemed to be confirmed by news received from General A. P. Stewart at Mill Creek Gap early in the afternoon of May 8. Stewart's men atop Rocky Face had sighted the enemy moving off toward the Confederate left, taking with them their wagon trains.[15]

That afternoon Johnston still ignored the potential threat to Dug Gap or even farther south at Resaca. No troops were dispatched to either point from Dalton. The results that evening were almost disastrous for the army. About 4 P.M. a heavy Union column emerged from the valley beyond Rocky Face and stormed Dug Gap. Reynolds' two infantry regiments held on stubbornly until reinforced by Grigsby's small cavalry brigade. The ridge was so steep that Grigsby's men left their horses in the valley and scrambled to the crest. Alarmed, Johnston at Dalton rushed Hardee with two of Cleburne's brigades to try and halt the attack. By nightfall the brigades of Generals Mark Lowery and Hiram Granbury had barely arrived to beat back the attack. Hardee and his men had

15 *Ibid.*, Pt. 4, pp. 677–78.

found Grigsby's horses at the foot of the mountain, mounted them, and climbed the mountain to halt any possible seizure of Dug Gap.[16]

Hooker's near success failed to rouse the concern of Johnston's high command on May 9. Attention instead was turned more toward the Mill Creek Gap-Cleveland Road front. The Federals were pushing at three points. Bate's and Stewart's divisions were hard pressed in Mill Creek Gap. To their right, at the angle where Cheatham's right wing on the north end of Rocky Face Mountain joined to Stevenson's left facing northward across the valley, at least five strong attacks were made and repulsed. Too, on the Cleveland Road, Wheeler spent much of the day driving back McCook's cavalry division, estimated at five thousand men.

In effect, Wheeler was wasted on May 9. All of his available brigades, except for that of Grigsby, were committed to the fight on the Cleveland Road, though intelligence from elsewhere was sorely needed. By 6:30 A.M. Johnston had been inquiring of Cleburne as to what was going on west of Rocky Face. About 10:00 P.M. the previous night, Cleburne had warned Johnston that it appeared the Federals were retiring from the Dug Gap vicinity and were moving on southward along the west side of Rocky Face. Confused, Johnston within an hour ordered Wheeler to try to find out where Sherman's main force lay. Johnston admitted that he did not know if the main force was now west of Rocky Face Mountain or was still on the front stretching from Mill Creek Gap north and then east toward the Cleveland Road. But instead of giving Wheeler specific orders, Johnston allowed him to use his discretion. Considering the large enemy cavalry force on the Cleveland Road, Wheeler was to take what he considered "the best and quickest mode of getting it." Wheeler, who disliked commonplace reconnaissance missions, was chafing for action. Already that morning early he had suggested to Johnston that he be allowed to ride around Sherman's army, a suggestion that was refused. Now, instead of obeying Johnston's wishes, Wheeler committed his entire command to a headlong attack on Sherman's cavalry on the Cleveland Road. This attack netted him some praise but little information.[17]

Through the day, Wheeler continued to disregard Johnston's wishes. Shortly before 10 A.M. Johnston ordered Wheeler on a more serious mission. He was to send part of his cavalry southward to cover all gaps south of Dug Gap by which the enemy could reach Resaca. Wheeler, busy on the Cleveland Road, disregarded the order, one which might have effectively blocked Snake Creek Gap had it been carried out. Still later in the day, Wheeler was again ordered to send part of his cavalry

---

16 Buck, *Cleburne and His Command*, 207; Johnston, *Narrative*, 305–306.
17 *Official Records*, XXXVIII, Pt. 4, p. 681, Pt. 3, p. 944.

to watch the passes from Dalton to Resaca, but sent none. Not all of this neglect was Wheeler's fault. On May 9 Johnston never questioned the cavalryman as to whether he still had pickets at the gaps on Taylor's Ridge. Too, when the afternoon order was sent to Wheeler telling him to send scouts to picket Rocky Face toward Resaca, Johnston's chief of staff, General W. W. Mackall, did not make the order appear to be a vital one. He stated that since Cantey's brigade and some smaller forces were there, "I do not think Resaca in any danger." [18]

That same night Johnston learned that Resaca was not so secure. By a stroke of good luck, on the night of May 8, Grigsby's small cavalry brigade had been ordered to move to Resaca to patrol the terrain west of the town near the mouth of Snake Creek Gap. Early on May 9, as Grigsby approached the mouth of the gap, he suddenly ran into McPherson's Army of the Tennessee, estimated by the Confederates as between fifteen thousand and twenty thousand strong. Grigsby was driven back into the Resaca fortifications manned by Cantey, who boasted only four thousand defenders. The Federals opened with artillery, attempting to reconnoiter the foreboding earthworks Johnston had constructed to protect the river crossing. Cantey responded with a determined fire from the fortifications. Through the afternoon, the enemy slowly moved forward. About dusk, McPherson slowly withdrew his lines into the mouth of Snake Creek Gap, as he evidently considered the Resaca works boasted a stronger force.[19]

Johnston's reaction to the McPherson threat was a curious one, based largely upon a lack of intelligence of the Federal whereabouts from May 9–11. Johnston in his official report made no mention of Cantey's defense of Resaca. Instead, he reported that during the afternoon of May 9 he learned that two corps were in Snake Creek Gap, and consequently sent Hood with three divisions to Resaca. In his memoirs, Johnston revised his story somewhat. He learned of the crisis at Resaca from two sources. During the afternoon, he had learned of two corps in the gap. Then, on the night of May 9 Cantey reported that he had been engaged all day with the Army of Tennessee. In both accounts, the emphasis was that the sending of Hood with three divisions saved the day at Resaca and that Johnston was not particularly surprised at McPherson's sudden appearance.[20]

Actually, Johnston and the remainder of the high command still

[18] Mackall to Wheeler, May 9—4 P.M., 1864, in Wheeler Papers, Alabama; *Official Records*, XXXVIII, Pt. 4, pp. 681–83, Pt. 3, p. 944.

[19] W. C. P. Breckinridge, "The Opening of the Atlanta Campaign," *Battles and Leaders*, IV, 279–81.

[20] Johnston, *Narrative*, 307; *Official Records*, XXXVIII, Pt. 3, p. 614.

seemed unable to fathom Sherman's designs. In the midnight hours of
May 9, Hood was ordered to hasten to Resaca with elements of Cleburne's, Walker's, and Hindman's divisions. Few of these troops ever arrived at Resaca. Hood and his staff were on the ground by the night of
May 9, and observed the enemy's departure. Thus, after reporting on the
morning of May 10 that the enemy apparently had gone, Hood was ordered back to Dalton. Johnston did take the initiative of ordering Hood
to halt Cleburne's and Walker's divisions at Tilton, about midway between Dalton and Resaca. But none of the relief column sent was left
with Cantey's four thousand infantry at Resaca. Johnston and his commanders still believed the main thrust would be from the north against
Dalton. As late as the afternoon of May 10, Hardee was insisting that
"there seems to be no force threatening us except on Rocky Face," and
that "all safe at Resaca." Instead, Hardee insisted the danger point was
on the road to Cleveland. Johnston's own attention that day was drawn
both to Mill Creek Gap and Stevenson's position facing northward and
guarding the pike around the northern end of Rocky Face Mountain.
Heavy skirmishing ensued all day at both positions, particularly at Mill
Creek Gap. Near nightfall a strong attack was made against Bate's division on the south side of Mill Creek Gap.[21]

Yet by the morning of May 11 Sherman loomed up again far to the
south of Dalton near Resaca. The previous night, Johnston had received
some scout reports indicating definitely that the force in Snake Creek
Gap was McPherson's Army of the Tennessee, and that it was entrenching there. This seemed to agree with an early morning report from Hardee on May 11. The force assumed to be threatening Dalton between the
northern end of Rocky Face and the Cleveland Road seemed to have disappeared. Hardee warned that the enemy appeared to be sliding around
Johnston's left behind Rocky Face, aiming at the Oostanaula River.
Finally, about 7:30 A.M., for the first time, Johnston inquired of Wheeler
as to whether Wheeler had any scouts in the area west of Rocky Face
Mountain. Johnston admitted that he did not know whether Wheeler
had ever placed scouts to observe a move through Taylor's Ridge, and
if so, he asked whether the picket line were still there. Obviously irritated
at the lack of information, Johnston ordered Wheeler to move his cavalry
around the northern end of Rocky Face Mountain and determine just
where Sherman was. Johnston's mood was not improved any by news
received from Cantey at Resaca about 8 A.M. From the lonely outpost,

21 *Official Records*, XXXVIII, Pt. 4, pp. 686–87; Johnston, *Narrative*, 307–308;
Johnston, "Opposing Sherman's Advance to Atlanta," *Battles and Leaders*, IV, 263;
Buck, *Cleburne and His Command*, 208–209.

Cantey reported that a Federal army was again emerging from Snake Creek Gap to threaten Resaca.[22]

Still, on May 11 Johnston did not shift his troops to meet the apparent threat. Wheeler was not even ordered out of Dalton until dawn of May 12. Johnston ordered him to be at headquarters at sunrise that day, at which time he was given specific orders for a reconnaissance. With Hindman's infantry division as a support, Wheeler was to circle the northern end of the ridge and learn whether Sherman was moving toward the Oostanaula. In fact, throughout the day of May 11, Johnston sent Cantey no support. After the war, he tried to explain the matter by asserting that there was no need for reinforcements at Resaca, since Polk arrived there that day with Loring's division. Since Cleburne and Walker were only some six miles north of Resaca at Tilton, their two divisions, together with Loring's and Cantey's commands, "prevented any immediate apprehension for the place." Yet, like many of the assertions in Johnston's *Narrative*, this seems to have been based on what Johnston knew later rather than what he knew at the time. In truth, he received his first warning from Cantey at 8 A.M., but only one of Loring's brigades arrived before the night of May 11. Polk did not arrive in Resaca until night either.[23]

Finally, on May 12, Johnston became convinced that Sherman was flanking his Dalton line. By 9:30 A.M., he had intelligence that Sherman definitely was moving either toward Villanow or toward Snake Creek Gap. During the morning, Wheeler's cavalry moved north out of Dalton and collided with a cavalry division learned to be that of General George Stoneman. Stoneman was driven back, which revealed that all but two divisions of Sherman's army had left the Dalton front. Johnston had received this news by nightfall, as well as a warning from Cleburne that his scouts during the day had learned that the enemy was massing in Snake Creek Gap and was fortifying Villanow as well. Still Johnston clung to Dalton until early on May 13, when he ordered Hardee's and Hood's corps to hurry to Resaca to join Polk.[24]

Johnston's delay in discerning Sherman's aims was costly, since it forced the Confederates to try to stop Sherman north of the Oostanaula River. Though Johnston later played down the crisis of May 12, the

[22] Mackall to Wheeler, May 11—7:30 A.M., 1864, Mackall to Wheeler, May 11—7:50 A.M., 1864, in Wheeler Papers, Alabama; *Official Records*, XXXVIII, Pt. 4, p. 693.

[23] *Official Records*, XXXVIII, Pt. 4, p. 694; Polk, *Polk*, II, 349; Johnston, *Narrative*, 308.

[24] Johnston, *Narrative*, 309; Govan and Livingood, *A Different Valor*, 268; Johnston, "Opposing Sherman's Advance to Atlanta," 265; *Official Records*, XXXVIII, Pt. 4, pp. 698, 700, 703.

truth was that had Sherman attacked Resaca that morning, Johnston's army might well have been trapped between the Oostanaula River and Dalton. Not until late in the morning did Hood and Hardee arrive at Resaca, to find that already Loring's division was skirmishing with Sherman west of the railroad. Behind them, Wheeler reported that Dalton had fallen, and that the cavalry was falling back slowly through the narrow valley. The peril of an attack by Sherman negated any possibility of retreating across the river.

Instead, Johnston hastily drew up a battle line. Matters were so confused that not all of his troops were even in position by nightfall. Johnston deployed his men on a ridge west of the town. Polk's single division was anchored on the Oostanaula. Hardee formed the center, and Hood's line bent back facing northward across the road from Dalton and extending to the Connasauga River, which flowed southward into the Oostanaula east of Resaca. The line was weak in several vital areas. Loring's division on the left was not advanced far enough to command a series of hills from which the Union artillery could command the railroad and pike bridges at Resaca. Only a thin skirmish line held these hills. Johnston was not aware of this weakness until May 14, when he directed his engineers to lay a pontoon bridge upstream in the event the others were enfiladed. Too, the position forced the Confederates to fight with their backs to two rivers, and the right angle position of Johnston's line promised disaster if a breakthrough occurred.[25]

After a day of skirmishing on May 13, a large battle seemed pending on the following day. Sherman then struck hard at Polk's front in an attempt to force the Rebels away from the bridges across the Oostanaula. Johnston sensed that the Federals were massing on the river front, and sent Wheeler to probe beyond Hood's position. Wheeler's reports confirmed that the Federal left facing Hood had been weakened, so about 6 P.M. Johnston ordered a strong attack by the Confederate right wing. Hood's success in pushing back the Union left before night closed in offered encouragement. During the night, Johnston shifted part of Hardee's command from the center, intending for Hood to attack again on May 15.

But later during the night Johnston called off the attack. Disturbing news was received from south of the Oostanaula. Martin's cavalry division, scouting south of the river, reported that Sherman was laying pontoon bridges across the river near Calhoun. The Oostanaula swung southwest after passing Resaca, but then made a sharp southward bend reaching within a mile of Calhoun, only six miles south of Johnston's

25 Johnston, "Opposing Sherman's Advance to Atlanta," 265; Govan and Livingood, *A Different Valor*, 268; Johnston, *Narrative*, 309–12; *Official Records*, XXXVIII, Pt. 4, pp. 706–707.

position and on the railroad and pike to Atlanta. Calhoun Ferry was only a mile west of the town, and Lay's Ferry was only about three miles from the town. Only slightly over three miles west of Calhoun, another good crossing point was available at Dobbin's Ferry. By 8 P.M. Martin's scouts reported that at least a division had crossed at Dobbin's Ferry, driving back his picket force. Later that night, the reported crossings had increased to two divisions.[26]

This news, received almost simultaneously with a report that the Federal artillery now could reach the Resaca bridges, caused Johnston to fear for his position. Quickly ordering a pontoon bridge to be constructed upstream, Johnston sent General W. H. T. Walker's division to the Calhoun area. The orders for Hood's attack were suspended, and through May 15 Johnston anxiously awaited Walker's report. In the early afternoon, Walker sent his first report which indicated that there was no truth to the rumored crossings. Johnston then ordered Hood to resume the attack planned for that morning. Hood had scarcely gotten under way when a second note was received from Walker. The Federal crossing near Calhoun was definite. Hood's orders were countermanded a second time, but not soon enough, however, to prevent Stewart's division from advancing alone and being repulsed with severe loss.

It was obvious that a retreat must be made across the Oostanaula. A conference of corps commanders was held at Johnston's headquarters after dark, and orders were given for the army to fall back across the river at midnight. Hood would cross on the pontoon bridge above Resaca, Hardee and Polk on the railroad and pike bridges at the town. They were to rendezvous just south of Calhoun.[27]

Here Johnston may well have lost his finest opportunity of the campaign. His later abandonment of a fight at Cassville would be subjected to close scrutiny. Yet his finest position possibly was in the area between Calhoun and Resaca. After the war, Johnston admitted that he had desired a line at Calhoun but had feared the demoralizing effects that spring of a retreat from Dalton. Yet later in the narrative, he recounted that upon arriving at Calhoun, he suddenly decided that the place had no good positions for defense.

Actually he could have hoped for no better place. On May 16 with a portion of Sherman's army crossing the Oostanaula west of Calhoun, and

[26] *Official Records*, XXXVIII, Pt. 4, p. 711; Johnston, *Narrative*, 311–12; "Lists of Fords and Ferries on the Oostanaula River between Rome and Resaca, Ga., W. F. Foster, December 28, 1863" (MS in Wheeler Papers, Alabama).

[27] Journal of Major Henry Hampton, acting assistant adjutant-general, Hardee's corps, May 15, 1864, in *Official Records*, XXXVIII, Pt. 3, p. 704; Polk, *Polk*, II, 352; Johnston, "Opposing Sherman's Advance to Atlanta," 266; Johnston, *Narrative*, 312–14.

part following the Confederates across at Resaca north of Calhoun, Johnston seemed in an excellent position to strike Sherman's army while it was crossing the Oostanaula. Johnston knew that geography had already divided the Federals. One column was approaching via Resaca coming out of the Dalton Valley, while a large column was debouching from Sugar Valley via Snake Creek Gap. By May 17 he had intelligence that Sherman had divided his column further by sending a corps toward Rome. Already on May 16 Hardee's corps was skirmishing with that portion which had crossed on the lower ferries west of Calhoun. Since it was fewer than six miles from Calhoun to the crossings at Resaca, Johnston might well have held that portion of Sherman's army at Resaca on the north bank while striking at that part isolated west of Calhoun.[28]

But Johnston did not intend to fight at Calhoun, and by early morning of May 17, he had ordered a retreat seven miles south to Adairsville. His later explanations for this retreat were varied. In his official report, he maintained that because some of Polk's troops were still in the rear, it was inexpedient not to give battle until better circumstances developed. Actually, only one of Polk's infantry divisions, that of General Samuel French, was still at Rome. It was held there by Johnston's orders to protect the valuable factories. In his memoirs, Johnston labeled his reason for retreating as being the unsatisfactory geographical position at Calhoun. Yet in his official report, Johnston may have struck the correct chord. He admitted that by the time he reached Calhoun, he already had committed himself to a policy of general retreat. He thus hoped to deplete Sherman's force and bide his time until many of Sherman's regiments' terms of service ran out at the end of June.[29]

Johnston also later contended that he retreated to Adairsville in the belief that it was a good position in which to make a fight. Adairsville, though it lay in the comparatively level Oostanaula River sector of the Appalachian Valley, had promise of good terrain. The town was surrounded by ridges one thousand feet in elevation, through which the valley of Oothcaloga Creek extended. Johnston's engineers had surveyed the valley and had informed him that north of the town it was narrow enough that both flanks could be anchored on the high ridges. But Johnston, after arriving on May 17, did not like the position. He thought it was too wide for the front of his army. Thus, that night he called a council of war.

28 Johnston, *Narrative*, 319; Hampton Journal, May 16–17, 1864, in *Official Records*, Vol. XXXVIII, Pt. 3, p. 704; Polk's son-in-law and aide-de-camp, Colonel W. D. Gale, recorded in his diary on May 21 that "we ought to have fought near Calhoun." See Gale Diary, May 21, 1864, in Polk Papers, Sewanee.

29 Johnston, *Narrative*, 319; *Official Records*, XXXVIII, Pt. 4, p. 615; Johnston, "Opposing Sherman's Advance to Atlanta," 267.

Hardee advocated making the fight at Adairsville. Several bits of information in Johnston's hands that night made this a promising situation. The Confederates had learned that McPherson with a corps had veered southwestward and had headed for Rome. Reinforcements for Johnston were already at hand. Polk's cavalry division, thirty-seven hundred strong, met the army at Adairsville. French's infantry division had already been ordered to join the army. Too, that night Johnston received word from General Stephen Lee in Alabama that Forrest, within a few days, would advance to attack Sherman's communication line.

Some disagreed with Hardee's plan. Hood argued that the army should retreat across the Etowah River. Johnston offered yet another proposal. He produced a map and an engineer officer who had once surveyed the country. South of Adairsville, the road and the Atlanta Railroad forked. The main Atlanta Road veered southeast toward Cassville, almost twelve miles distant. Cassville, a small college town, lay just north of the beginnings of the mountainous ridge country which formed the southeastern edge of the Appalachian Valley. The town itself was encompassed by steep ridges on the south, reaching nine hundred feet in elevation. The Atlanta Railroad did not pass through Cassville. From Adairsville, it ran south, paralleled by another pike, some twelve miles to Kingston. Here the railroad and the pike then ran east. The road joined the main Atlanta Pike at Cassville, and the railroad joined the main Atlanta Pike below Cassville. This near triangle between Cassville, Kingston, and Adairsville was a rugged isolated area embraced in the rough Cassville Mountain range, which reached eleven hundred feet in elevation. There were few roads across the triangle. The Adairsville-Cassville Road wound across barren, high country. The Adairsville-Kingston Road followed a level stretch through a creek valley with little access to the parallel pike. Hence if Sherman moved south on both roads, his columns would not only be in poor communication, but by the time they reach Kingston and Cassville, would be some seven to eight miles apart.

The topography looked ripe for an ambush, the dim outlines of which Johnston implemented before he left Adairsville. Johnston believed that Sherman would most certainly take both pikes in pursuit. To encourage this, Hardee's corps was to fall back on the Kingston Road and then march rapidly to join the other two corps at Cassville. Polk and Hood were to retreat across the Cassville Mountain range on the main road from Adairsville to Cassville. By forcing Sherman to divide his army, Johnston hoped to strike him in detail. Quickly the marching orders were consummated. On the morning of May 18, Hardee fell back toward

Kingston, Polk and Hood onto the road to Cassville. By noon, all three corps were concentrated at Cassville.[30]

By the evening of May 18, Johnston found his strategy working well. Things appeared better than even he had hoped. At least one enemy corps was certainly known to be marching toward Rome. Hardee had steadily fallen back before an enemy advance on the Kingston Road, while the rearguard on the Cassville Road reported the enemy slowly advancing toward Cassville. General W. H. Jackson, directing the rearguard on the Kingston Road, was ordered to give notice as soon as the head of Sherman's column reached Kingston, while Wheeler observed on the Cassville Road.[31]

It was a night of tension and great emotion at Cassville. After alternate days of muggy, warm weather and rain, it was clear and cool. The army was jubilant to learn that an attack was planned. French's division marched in from Rome, reporting that a heavy Federal column had been diverted toward that town. Women and children left Cassville on Johnston's orders, and no one doubted the fight would be made there. Earthworks lined the campus of the female college and Cherokee Baptist College, and the buildings on the serene campuses were turned into field hospitals.

That night about dark, Johnston called his corps commanders to a war council. Spirits were high, because a telegram had been received from Virginia indicating that Grant already had lost forty-five thousand men in his drive against Richmond. Johnston explained his plan. Two Yankee corps appeared to be advancing on the Cassville Road, the remainder on the Kingston Road. Hardee's corps was posted between Cassville and Kingston, with the left of his line facing at right angles toward the latter village. Polk was entrenched in front of Cassville. Johnston believed that when Sherman approached Hardee from Kingston, simultaneously with an approach upon Polk from Adairsville, that the Federal left would veer southwest toward Hardee and Polk. Hence, Hood's corps was directed to move the following morning out the road leading from Cassville northeast toward Spring Place. Hood would be in position to fall upon the left flank of those corps marching on the Adairsville Road, while Polk attacked in front.[32]

By the morning of May 19, it seemed that the Confederate plan was

30 Johnston, "Opposing Sherman's Advance to Atlanta," pp. 267–68; T. B. Mackall, "Journal of Operations of the Army of Tennessee, May 14–June 4," May 17, 1864, in *Official Records*, XXXVIII, Pt. 3, p. 982; Johnston, *Narrative*, 319–21.

31 Johnston, *Narrative*, 320–21; Mackall Journal, May 18, 1864, in *Official Records*, XXXVIII, Pt. 3, pp. 982–83.

32 *Official Records*, XXXVIII, Pt. 3, May 18–19, 1864, p. 983; Johnston, *Narrative*, 321.

successful. Johnston issued a stirring battle order to the troops who had cheered him as he rode the lines the previous night. Morale seemed at a high pitch, and there was good news as well. From Kingston, Jackson's cavalry reported that the Federal vanguard was reaching the town, while Hardee's signal officers warned that the enemy approaching Cassville from Adairsville was veering as had been planned toward Kingston. Probably about 9 A.M., Johnston rode with Hardee, Polk, and Hood out the Spring Place Road to show the latter where he should place his line. After seeing Polk and Hardee to their positions, Johnston returned to his headquarters and impatiently waited for Hood to begin his attack.[33]

But the planned assault did not develop. Anxious, Johnston sent his chief of staff, General W. W. Mackall, to Hood about 10:20 A.M. to urge him to begin the attack. Hood was warned that Hardee was already hard pressed. To Mackall's surprise, he found Hood in the process of ordering a retreat. Hood claimed the staff officers had located the enemy advancing toward Hood's rear via the Canton Road, and told Mackall that he was falling back to a range of hills which crossed the road. Mackall evidently accepted the report at face value, since he later admitted he saw no enemy. He sent a courier to Johnston with the news that "enemy in heavy force close to Hood on Canton Road." Johnston hastily found a map, and muttered to his staff that such a report could not be true. Still, he contended, if it were, there was nothing for Hood to do but fall back. Shortly thereafter, Mackall returned to headquarters, and Johnston sent him again to the front, to summon Hardee, Polk, and Hood. There, shortly before noon, Johnston announced that the battle plan was off.[34]

What had gone wrong? Both Hood and Johnston share the blame. Later, in his official report, written more as a refutation of Johnston's report, Hood told a curious story which does not coincide with other accounts. He argued that he was not advancing under any specific orders to make an attack on the Federal left. Instead, Hood maintained that Johnston had told him to attack "if you desire."[35] Hood argued that the reason he fell back was not because a force appeared at his rear on the Canton Road, but because he found no enemy to attack. He maintained that he knew all along what was later found to be true—that the enemy on the Canton Road was only a cavalry reconnaissance. These as-

---

[33] Mackall Journal, May 19, 1864, in *Official Records*, XXXVIII, Pt. 3, p. 983; Buck, *Cleburne and His Command*, 215; Guild, *Fourth Tennessee*, 61–62; Kirwan (ed.), *Orphan Brigade*, 130; Johnston, *Narrative*, 321.

[34] W. W. Mackall, "Memoranda of the Operations at Cassville on May 19, 1864," in *Official Records*, XXXVIII, Pt. 3, pp. 621–23; Mackall Journal, May 19, 1864, *ibid.*, pp. 983–84.

[35] *Ibid.*, Pt. 3, p. 635.

sertions, none of which seems to be substantiated, masked several of Hood's mistakes. He evidently ordered no close reconnaissance of what force had appeared on the Canton Road. Worse, Hood abandoned the battle plan and fell back two miles turning his line to face eastward along the Canton Road, without either informing Johnston or waiting for instructions after meeting with Mackall.[36]

Johnston's own conduct was questionable. He had erred in not providing written orders. When he learned from Mackall that Hood's rear was threatened, Johnston accepted the report and changed his entire strategy without sending a single staff officer to ascertain the size of the force on the road from Canton to Cassville. Too, Johnston's decision to fall back to a new line south of Cassville instead of continuing the offensive seemed premature. After the war, he explained that he decided to abandon the scheme of an attack because Hardee was already engaged on the left. Yet this was the heart of his plan—to force the enemy to concentrate against his left while Hood swung on a pivot across the Cassville-Adairsville Road.[37]

Still, Johnston hoped to redeem the morning's abortive plan of attacking Sherman. Immediately south of Cassville was a long, low ridge, rising some 140 feet above the open valley in which the town of Cassville lay. The ridge was wide enough to accommodate both Hood's and Polk's corps, and part of Hardee's. Believing that Sherman would soon attack, Johnston ordered his corps to fall back during the afternoon to the ridge. Hood held the right, and Polk the center. Half of Hardee's corps was placed on the ridge, which ended near the Atlanta Railroad. The other half was placed on low ground extending westward across the railroad on somewhat flat terrain. During the afternoon, as Sherman's artillery already duelled with that on the ridge, the line was carefully surveyed by Johnston. Save for two areas, the line looked strong. Federal troops atop a hill on Hood's front threatened to enfilade part of his line with artillery. Hardee's left also seemed to have little natural protection. Still, Johnston liked the position, and later called it "the best that I saw occupied during the war."[38] By nightfall, he was confident that the battle would take place the next morning.

That night, however, Johnston found his hopes to be dashed. General Polk had prepared a most curious supper for him. The events of the night are completely muddled by conflicting charges. No one even agrees

[36] Ibid.
[37] Mackall Journal, May 19, 1864, ibid., pp. 983–84; Hampton Journal, May 19, 1864, ibid., p. 705; see also ibid., pp. 615–16, 621–22; Johnston, Narrative, 321–22; Johnston to Gale, May 24, 1869, in Polk, Polk, II, 355.
[38] Johnston, Narrative, 322.

just how the dinner meeting originated. Johnston in his memoirs recalled that after inspecting the ridge defenses, he returned to his headquarters after dark and found in his tent an invitation from Polk to take supper with him. Yet in a postwar letter to Polk's son-in-law, Colonel W. D. Gale, Johnston recalled that Polk had sent Gale to meet him in the road as he returned to his quarters. There Gale invited Johnston to Polk's headquarters. Another postwar account, that of Polk's chief engineer, Captain Walter Morris, asserts that Johnston did not go to dinner at all, but at Polk's invitation came over to the corps leader's tent at about 9 p.m. Johnston, in a postwar conversation in 1865 with Sherman, even contradicted his other versions. This time he claimed to have met Polk and Hood on the road into Cassville, where Hood invited him to accompany the two generals to Hood's headquarters for dinner.[39]

Regardless of how the generals met that night, Johnston probably regretted the meeting. He might well have feared what Polk and Hood wished to tell him. During his afternoon inspection of the ridge defenses, Johnston had been approached by his chief of artillery, General F. A. Shoup. Shoup warned that part of Hood's and Polk's line would be exposed to enemy artillery fire from a parallel ridge on the army's front. Polk, who was present at the meeting, seemed to agree. Just how much of the ridge was exposed is not clear. Johnston later asserted that only 150 to 200 yards were singled out by Shoup as being in danger. Hood later claimed that Shoup told Johnston that a half mile of the ridge was exposed, and cited in his own memoirs a postwar letter from Shoup. Yet Shoup did not actually say this. He recalled that only in general terms did he and Polk warn Johnston of the line's vulnerability. Later in the day, after the conversation with Johnston, Shoup decided that a half-mile sector of the ridge was exposed to artillery fire from the ridge to the north where Sherman's line was being located.[40]

Out of this discussion between Polk, Shoup, and Johnston came a curious turn of events during the early evening. Polk and Hood spent much of the afternoon in conference, planning what they were to say to Johnston that night. Polk's chief engineer, Captain Morris, had arrived in Cassville that afternoon, and immediately Polk had ordered him to survey the corps line, particularly the right held by the division of General Samuel French. There is no doubt that Polk wanted evidence to support his own views. He frankly told Morris that he was convinced

---

39 Gale Diary, May 20, 1864, in Polk Papers, Sewanee; Walter Morris to William Polk, June 25, 1878, *ibid;* Johnston, *Narrative,* 323; Johnston to Gale, May 24, 1869, in Polk, *Polk,* II, 356; Sherman, *Memoirs,* II, 39–40.

40 Johnston, *Narrative,* 323; Shoup to Hood, June 3, 1874, in Hood, *Advance and Retreat,* 105–106.

French's line was untenable. Morris did not disappoint his commanding officer. By nightfall, he returned to Polk's headquarters, where Hood was still in council. Morris reported that French's section of Polk's line was untenable.[41]

By dark, Polk and Hood were ready to make their proposal. Conveniently, Hood just happened to meet General Samuel French riding near Polk's headquarters and invited him to dinner with Polk and Johnston. Thus, Hood and Polk evidently had already decided upon their plan, and had invited Johnston even before receiving the report from Morris. Morris recalled that when he came to Polk's headquarters, Hood was already there.

After the war, Morris furnished Polk's son with a long report of this whole matter which seems unusually contradictory. Obviously, Morris was attempting to show that Hood and Polk only called a conference with Johnston after receiving the engineer's report of the hazardous state of the line in front of French's position. Actually, Hood and Polk had already decided to protest the new position. Morris did not return to Polk's headquarters until after dark. He argued in his letter that only after hearing his report did Polk and Hood decide to invite Johnston. This claim is simply untrue. On his way to Polk's headquarters that evening, Hood had met French and had invited him to the talk with Johnston. Polk's aide, Colonel Gale, had been sent to invite Johnston, as he recorded in his diary, "about dark," for the express purpose of talking about the untenable nature of the line. Morris, by his own admission, did not return to Polk's headquarters until after dark. Thus the invitation to Johnston by Hood and Polk had been made already before Polk had received his engineer's report.[42]

Some time about 8 P.M., Johnston arrived at Polk's quarters, where French and Hood were also assembled. After supper, Hood and Polk got down to business. They requested Johnston to go with them to Polk's office for a conference. Johnston invited French to go along with them. There Polk and Hood argued that their line was untenable, and that a retreat should be made across the Etowah River. Johnston insisted that the line could be held. So strong was Johnston's representation that French left the council probably about 10 P.M., convinced that the fight would be made the next day. But Polk and Hood insisted that if attacked, their line would not hold. Thus Johnston relented, and announced his decision to retreat across the Etowah River. Shortly there-

41 Morris to William Polk, June 25, 1878, in Polk Papers, Sewanee.

42 Gale Diary, May 20, 1864, *ibid;* Morris to Polk, June 25, 1878, *ibid;* Samuel French, *Two Wars* (Nashville, 1901), 197; Samuel French to editor, New Orleans *Picayune,* December 12, 1893, *Two Wars,* 374.

after, Hardee arrived. He was surprised to learn of Johnston's decision, and argued that the line could be defended. Hood retorted that Polk could not hold his line forty-five minutes, and that his own line could not hold two hours. The council ended, and Johnston dictated orders for the retreat across the Etowah River that night, to begin about 12 P.M.[43]

The affairs of this council were to be clouded greatly by personality conflicts after the war. Hood's version was that he and Polk did not argue for a retreat across the Etowah River. Instead, they argued that Johnston should take the offensive the following morning. How by taking the offensive his corps would be any more shielded from the same artillery he feared on the defensive, Hood did not explain. The only evidence that such a proposal was made to Johnston, aside from Hood's avowal, was a letter furnished by Captain Morris, to Polk's son and biographer, William Polk. This long document, which also gave the account of Morris' afternoon reconnaissance, alleges that at the meeting Polk and Hood did not actually argue for the retreat across the Etowah. Instead, they pressed Johnston to take the offensive the next morning. Johnston, not Hood and Polk, desired the retreat across the Etowah, and announced his decision. Then Hardee arrived, learned of the decision, and protested. Again Polk explained that he was willing to launch an offensive the next morning, but did not think that the troops could stand on the defensive. Johnston was determined to retreat, however, and issued orders for the army to begin falling back.[44]

Morris' document was most convenient. Used by Hood and by Polk's son, it seemed to exempt Polk and Hood from the responsibility for the retreat. However, Morris' postwar recollection was full of contradictions. For instance, Johnston had already been invited prior to his giving the report to Polk. Also, Morris claimed that at the night council, Polk asserted that French did not think he could hold his position. Morris omitted any mention of French's being at the council. Actually, French was not only present, but later denied that he had made any such representation. French said instead that he was barely consulted at the meeting, and never reported that his line was too weak to hold. On the contrary, French in his diary recorded that night that he left the meeting convinced Johnston would fight the next day. A staff officer who accompanied French to the meeting later supported these assertions. He

---

[43] Morris to Polk, June 25, 1878, in Polk Papers, Sewanee; Johnston, *Narrative*, 323–24; Hardee to Johnston, April 10, 1867, in Hardee Papers, Alabama; French, *Two Wars*, 196, 198.

[44] Hood, *Advance and Retreat*, 106–109; Morris to Polk, June 25, 1878, in Polk Papers, Sewanee.

argued that French did not protest that he had a weak position, but believed it to be a strong one.[45]

Morris' recollection of the meeting, particularly his claim that Hood and Polk urged Johnston to take the offensive seems pure fabrication. It is odd that Polk's son William, who often took pains to produce documentary evidence supporting his father's good behavior on the field and his lack of mistakes, produced no supporting evidence except the letter from Morris, which he inserted in his book's appendix. In fact, Polk took great pains in his text not to mention the conference, except for including a postwar letter from Johnston. Nor did Polk's aide and son-in-law, Colonel W. D. Gale, record such a proposal in his diary of the night's events. Gale merely commented that he was sent to bring the other generals, and as soon as they met that it was decided to retreat from Cassville. French asserted that while he was present at the council there was no mention made of taking the offensive. Hardee did not recall any being made, either. After the war, Hardee only recalled that when he expressed surprise at the retreat, Hood insisted the position could not be held.[46]

Several people were at fault that night. Obviously Hood and Polk had arranged the conference beforehand, and had even attempted to accumulate some evidence of why they should not remain at Cassville. Hood was the more vocal of the two. The conference was somewhat reminiscent of Polk's old rump councils of war while Bragg was in command. Then, Polk and others had also made decisions without consulting the commander; the only difference was that in the former councils, the commanding general was absent during all deliberations.

Aside from the repercussions in Richmond in response to another retreat, there were more solid considerations for which Johnston must share the blame. He made his decision without consulting his second-in-command, Hardee—having a council of war without the presence of his left wing commander. The conference did not begin until after 8 P.M., and by the time Hardee arrived at about 10 P.M., Johnston had made his hasty decision. He might well have delayed until daylight to reconnoiter the line, since much more was at stake than the mere evacuation of the Cassville ridge. To retreat across the Etowah would mean the permanent loss of the industrial complex at Rome, which had already been seized, and the loss of the valuable Etowah Iron Works southeast of Cassville. It would mean as well a tremendous blow to the army's morale.

There were many other good reasons for not retreating across the

45 French, *Two Wars*, 198; French to editor, *Picayune*, December 12, 1893, *ibid.*, pp. 373–75; Morris to Polk, June 25, 1878, in Polk Papers, Sewanee.
46 Hardee to Johnston, April 10, 1867, in Hardee Papers, Alabama; Gale Diary, May 20, 1864, in Polk Papers, Sewanee; French, *Two Wars*, 198.

Etowah River. If Johnston had taken more time for deliberation, he might have decided that there was no need for the venture. South of Cassville, the pike and the railroad extended some nine miles to Cartersville, cut across the eastern edge of the Appalachian plateau south of Cartersville, and then crossed the Etowah River. This ridge shelf south of Cartersville was a high, steep escarpment reaching elevations of seven hundred feet. Johnston's left flank resting on the ridge would be protected by the northward curving of the river on the west side of the town and by the lack of road approaches through this area between the curve in the river and the road to Atlanta south of Cartersville. In such a position, Johnston could execute one of his two oft-planned actions against Sherman: either force Sherman to attack him in an advantageous position or strike Sherman while divided if he attempted to cross the river west of the Rebel position.

South of the river, the opportunities for such maneuvering might easily be lost due to the region's topography. On the night of May 20 Johnston's orders called for the army to withdraw south of the river to a new line on the south bank, at the head of Allatoona Pass. The terrain on the south bank was a mountainous plateau between the Etowah and the Chattahoochee rivers, the thin remnant of the once mighty Georgia Blue Ridge as it extended into Alabama. Immediately south of the river was the one-thousand-foot range of the Allatoona Mountains. The pike and railroad to Atlanta cut through the range in rugged Allatoona Pass, a narrow corridor provided by Allatoona Creek, which ran northward into the Etowah. On the north bank of the river, at the head of the pass, Johnston had already prepared fortifications.

Although the Etowah defenses were sufficient to resist a direct attack, they could easily be flanked. Neither of Johnston's ideas for dealing with Sherman could work. Unless he reversed his usual policy, Sherman would not attack Johnston head on in such a strong position. Johnston's only alternative was to strike part of the Union force as it became isolated in crossing the river. This simply could not be done from the new position on the south bank. The broad belt of the Allatoona Mountains was a mixed blessing. West of the new position Johnston had chosen, the mountains would mask any Federal crossing at the multiple fords and ferries of the Etowah within a thirty-mile area to the west. This rugged mountain country, pocked by mining attempts during the Georgia gold rush boom two decades earlier, was a heavily forested area of few good west-east roads.

Sherman would have the clear benefit of the terrain on the south bank. The principal roads extended southward from the river, through the creek and river valleys of the streams which fed the Etowah. These routes extended in a southeastward direction, gradually bearing toward John-ston's rear at Marietta. They were shielded from observation by two natural barriers. West of the creek, the range of mountains was par-ticularly steep and rugged, protecting any crossing made. For a space of over ten miles south of the river, there was only one single road across Pumpkinvine Creek and the mountains. This route, which led from the Atlanta Pike slightly north of Allatoona to Stilesboro, ran far too close to the river to be of use once Sherman was across.

Too, Johnston would have trouble finding Sherman in the rough ter-rain south of the Etowah River. There were several routes toward Atlanta which would bypass Johnston's position in the Allatoona vicinity. Sher-man could cross the river near Pumpkinvine Creek at Quinton's or Roland's Ferry, where a good road led southeast with branches to Ac-worth, Kennesaw Station, and Marietta—all at Johnston's rear. Or Sher-man could cross more to the west near Stilesboro, and move via Dallas and Powder Springs to the Chattahoochee southwest of Marietta. From Dallas, Sherman could veer east and strike Johnston's rear at Marietta.

Sherman could also cross further west and still flank Johnston. West of Stilesboro, a good route led from the river up the valley of Euharlee Creek either via New Hope Church to Marietta or directly to Dallas. Farther west, another road crossed at Wooley's Bridge and intersected the road from Rome, which led via Van Wert either to the Chattahoochee southwest of Marietta or to the main Chattanooga-Atlanta Pike near Marietta. With this morass of roads, Johnston stood in danger of losing Sherman's position.[47]

Luckily, Jackson's cavalry on May 23 pinpointed the location of the Federal crossing. Sherman was reportedly moving across the Etowah at the bridges near Stilesboro. Johnston realized that the Federals probably aimed to cross the Chattahoochee on his flank, and quickly gave orders to intercept Sherman at Dallas.

By May 25 Johnston had moved his troops into position to block Sherman's advance. Jackson had reported that Sherman had halted his advance, and had deployed with his right wing on the Stilesboro Road near Dallas. Thus, Johnston halted his army on a wide front from Dallas to New Hope Church to await Sherman's assault. Two of Har-dee's divisions, Bate's and Cheatham's, occupied the extreme left at Dallas. Polk occupied the center, while Hood's corps, prolonged by Cle-burne's addition on its right, was posted at New Hope Church.[48]

Johnston did not have to wait long for Sherman's attack. Late on the

47 Sherman, *Memoirs*, II, 42–43.
48 Johnston, *Narrative*, 326.

afternoon of May 25, Hood sent out a small reconnaissance party of regimental size, which promptly ran into an entire Federal corps a mile in the advance of Hood's position. Less than two hours before sunset, the assault by General Joseph Hooker's corps smashed into Hood's center at New Hope Church. Amidst a fierce rainstorm, Hooker's men repeatedly charged through the dense timber only to be thrown back by Stewart's massed artillery. Then, in the blinding storm, Hooker's men slowly retired.[49]

Hood's men hastily dug earthworks in the well soaked clay that night, and by morning Johnston's scouts had returned from Cleburne's front with disturbing news. Sherman had shifted his lines during the night to the northeast, and was threatening both Johnston's right and the road from Dallas to Johnston's base on the railroad at Acworth.

Until May 27 only light skirmishing occurred, while both generals paused to extend their entrenchments eastward toward the Atlanta Railroad. On the twenty-sixth, Polk was withdrawn from the Dallas area and sent to extend Hood's line and protect the dirt road to Acworth and Allatoona. But the extension by Polk's corps did not appear to be enough. Johnston learned that Sherman had again extended his line northeastward beyond Polk. By May 27 Cleburne had been shifted to lengthen Polk's right to within a half mile of Little Pumpkinvine Creek, near Pickett's Mill.

Again Sherman felt out Johnston's extended line. Late in the afternoon of May 27, an entire Federal corps launched a furious attack on Cleburne's division. The Irishman's four brigades were implanted on a low ridge above the creek valley. Several spur ridges jutting northward from the main backbone formed a natural bowl-shaped depression. From their position on the ridge, Cleburne's men poured a withering fire into the deep ravine below them and threw back the Federals with severe losses. After the fight broke off late that night, Cleburne's men picked up twelve hundred small arms on the field, and estimated the Federal casualties as three thousand killed and wounded.[50]

Cleburne's success was short lived. By the morning of May 28 Johnston had decided to once more make a fullscale assault on Sherman. Probably this decision was injudicious. Stewart's repulse of Hooker on May 25 at New Hope Church and Cleburne's victory two days later at Pickett's Mill were similar in one key respect. On both occasions, the Rebel infantry had beaten off far superior numbers because of fortifications. In this way, the stay on the Dallas-New Hope line changed the nature of the

49 Johnston, "Opposing Sherman's Advance to Atlanta," 269.
50 Jacob Cox Diary (typescript, Kennesaw), May 27, 1864; French, *Two Wars*, 199; Buck, *Cleburne and His Command*, 218–20.

Georgia campaign. Steadily, the war in the West was becoming one of entrenching, with elaborate systems of deep ditches, earthen parapets, headlogs, and sharpened abatis. The power of such fortifications had been seen in the New Hope Church fight, where only three of Stewart's brigades had thrown back an entire Union corps which had charged in deeply packed columns.

Still, Johnston determined to try a frontal assault. The reports of Sherman's continual shift eastward convinced Johnston that surely the Union right wing must be weakened. Thus on the morning of May 28, he sent forward Bate's division in a reconnaissance in force on the extreme left. Unfortunately, Bate's orders to his subordinates miscarried, and the division suffered considerable losses in a headlong assault on the Union earthworks near Dallas.[51]

Since Bate met such severe resistance, perhaps the Union left flank opposite Cleburne was not as strong as had been believed. On the afternoon of May 28, Johnston met his three corps leaders at his headquarters. A new offensive plan which Hood proposed was adopted. Hood would withdraw from his position on Cleburne's left that night and move to the extreme right. There Hood would deploy at right angles to Cleburne, facing the Union left flank. At daylight he would attack and roll up Sherman's left, while Polk and Hardee would then join the assault.[52]

Again Hood proved more sanguine in talk than in his actions. Daylight came and no sound of artillery or small arms was heard near Pumpkinvine Creek. Anxiously, Johnston and Hardee waited together until a messenger appeared at 10 A.M. with a note from Hood. The general had found it inexpedient to attack. Daylight had revealed that the Federal left was protected by a division thrown back at right angles to the main line, and heavily entrenched. For the third consecutive time, Johnston called off a planned assault on Sherman upon Hood's advice, and ordered his corps to return to their old line.[53]

It soon became obvious that Johnston could no longer remain on Pumpkinvine Creek. The Federal left again began sliding eastward, and by June 1 Sherman's cavalry had seized the railroad at Allatoona. Johnston believed his lines were too thin for a consequent shift, and on June 4 ordered the army back to a new position. Johnston's engineers had laid out a new position ten miles south of the New Hope line and more to the

51 Hughes, *Hardee*, 205; Johnston, *Narrative*, 332–33.

52 French, *Two Wars*, 199–200; Hood, *Advance and Retreat*, 118–21.

53 Johnston, *Narrative*, 333–34; Hood, *Advance and Retreat*, 121–22; Hardee to Johnston, April 10, 1867, in Hardee Papers, Alabama.

east. Johnston's new line lay squarely across the railroad, and corresponded with Sherman's eastward shift toward Acworth.[54]

Johnston soon learned that his new line could not stifle Sherman's ability to extend superior numbers beyond the Rebel flank. Through rain and mud, the army, on the night of June 4, slogged southeast toward the new position ten miles southeast of the New Hope Church line. Johnston's engineers had located the new line on a ten-mile-wide front which was almost a semicircle. The left was anchored on a high eminence known as Lost Mountain. From this lofty hill, the line curved northeast to a salient on Pine Mountain, and then curved toward the southeast across the railroad at a point five miles north of Marietta.[55]

By July 8, however, Johnston was forced to abandon such a wide line. His scouts had reported that the bulk of Sherman's army seemed concentrated on the railroad at Acworth, less than ten miles north of Johnston's right wing. Practically all of that short portion of Johnston's line east of the railroad was manned by Wheeler's cavalry. It was obvious that the line must be shortened and shifted eastward. Thus, Hood's entire corps was placed east of the railroad and the Atlanta Pike. Polk, west of the railroad and pike, occupied the center, with his back to a high summit known as Kennesaw Mountain. Hardee occupied the left, anchored at Gilgal Church, a small hamlet south of Pine Mountain. The Lost Mountain position was abandoned, and all forces were withdrawn from the vicinity of Pine Mountain save for Bate's division of Hardee's corps.[56]

But Johnston was not pleased with this line either. The low ground between Hardee's position and the center provided no particular strong defense. Too, by June 15 Sherman seemed to be massing on Hardee's front as well as on the center. Johnston still sought a position from which he could either attack Sherman with some hope of success or could force the Federals to strike a well-entrenched position.

Johnston believed he had found such a position by June 17. Two days later, his corps withdrew under cover of darkness to the new line. The new position, carefully laid out by the army's chief engineer, Colonel S. W. Presstman, seemed to remedy several defensive problems. Johnston's chief concerns were to locate a position which on the west would cover Marietta and the railroad, and on the east cover the railroad, the main Atlanta Pike, and a parallel road to Marietta via Canton. On the right, Hood's corps was aligned between the railroad and the Canton-

[54] Johnston, "Opposing Sherman's Advance to Atlanta," 270; Johnston, *Narrative*, 334–35.

[55] French, *Two Wars*, 201; Johnston, *Narrative*, 335.

[56] Johnston, *Narrative*, 336; Govan and Livingood, *A Different Valor*, 283.

Marietta Road. The center was held by Polk's corps, now temporarily commanded by General W. W. Loring. Loring's own division extended the line from the railroad west to the base of Kennesaw Mountain, a ridge-like summit which loomed seven hundred feet above the country to the north. The two remaining divisions, French's and Walthall's, were implanted on the ridge crest. Hardee's corps held the left wing. His new line was anchored at the western end of Kennesaw Mountain, and then led south across the road from Dallas to Marietta, at right angles to Hood's and Loring's position.[57]

Though strong, the new line was obtained with a serious loss. On June 14 Johnston, Polk, and Hardee had ridden to the crest of Pine Mountain to reconnoiter Sherman's position and discuss the placement of a stronger line of defense. Slowly they began to move back from the rim of the slope, which was exposed to Federal artillery fire. A shell struck nearby, and everyone hurried for cover. Polk lingered for a last look and was killed instantly by a direct hit.[58]

Sorrowfully, the small party accompanied the ambulance which bore Polk's body from the mountain. The army had suffered a severe loss. It was not that Polk had been a spectacular corps officer. His deficiencies as a commander and his personal traits of stubbornness and childishness had played no small role in several of the army's disasters in earlier times. The loss was one of morale and experience. Polk was the army's most beloved general, a representative of that intangible identification of the army with Tennessee. The army's first actual commander in the early days of 1861, Polk seemed to be a link with better times. Now this link seemed to be fading, and with it went Polk's vast experience. With no immediate replacement at hand, Johnston was forced to appoint, temporarily, the senior division commander, General Loring, to guide Polk's corps.

Polk's experience was to be needed sooner than Johnston may have thought. Johnston by June 21 discovered that Sherman had taken advantage of the cover of incessant rains to attempt again to flank the Confederates. Hardee warned that Sherman was stretching his lines to the breaking point and was close to seizing the Powder Springs Road, a key route to the Chattahoochee behind the Rebel left flank. Now that Sherman was shifting westward, Johnston, on the twenty-first, responded with a like move. Wheeler's cavalry replaced Hood's corps east of the railroad,

57 French, *Two Wars*, 203–204; Johnston, *Narrative*, 338–39; Hughes, *Hardee*, 210–11.

58 Johnston to Quintard, October 8, 1885, in Joseph E. Johnston letters, Sewanee; Govan and Livingood, *A Different Valor*, 288; Polk, *Polk*, II, 372–75; Sherman, *Memoirs*, II, 53–54.

and the Kentuckian's command was moved to the extreme left to extend Hardee's line.[59]

For several days, both Sherman and Johnston probed the opposition. With orders to prevent any further extension of Sherman's right, Hood on June 25 became embroiled in a sharp fight with Hooker's corps. After an initial repulse of Hooker's forward move, Hood replied with an unauthorized attack on the Federal breastworks. This attack cost Johnston a thousand casualties. Then, on June 24, Hardee's skirmish line, entrenched in rifle pits, beat back a strong attack. The following day, the Federals probed again against Hood's skirmishers.[60]

On June 27 the main assault came. It was no surprise, for from atop Kennesaw, Johnston could observe Sherman massing on the left and center. Then, for almost an hour that morning, a furious artillery barrage swept Hardee's and Loring's positions. The artillery ceased, and under a blazing summer sun, three Federal corps, their assault formations seven lines deep, rolled forward.

The Federals advanced quickly against what they evidently considered to be two weak points in Johnston's line. Hardee's position in the center, at right angles to Loring's position on Kennesaw Mountain, lay on relatively level ground. Hardee's right division, Cheatham's, lay at the angle, with Cleburne connecting on the south. Wave after wave of Federal infantry attempted to break the angle at Cheatham's and Cleburne's positions. Amidst terrible heat and smoke, Hardee's men poured a murderous fire from behind their powerful entrenchments, while Loring's artillery on the mountain enfiladed the Federal ranks with a vicious crossfire. By noon it was all over. The "Dead Angle" in Cheatham's line had not yielded, and the attack dwindled into desultory firing. The fight had been completely one-sided due to the intensive fortifications at the angle. Cleburne lost only 11 men and Cheatham 194. Federal casualties on Cleburne's front alone were estimated by that usually accurate officer at 1,000.[61]

To the east, Sherman's frontal assault had also failed. The attack had been aimed at a low spur of the ridge known as Little Kennesaw Mountain, and against the low ground between the main ridge and the railroad to the east. Again the Federals could not carry the extensive breastworks, and were pounded by French's artillery on the northwest summit of the

[59] Johnston, "Opposing Sherman's Advance to Atlanta," 271; Hughes, Hardee, 211.

[60] Johnston, Narrative, 339–41.

[61] Buck, Cleburne and His Command, 224–25; Hughes, Hardee, 212; French, Two Wars, 206, 208.

mountain. By noon the fight was over here as well, and Loring's line remained intact with a reported loss of only 236 men.[62]

Johnston had enjoyed the most one-sided victory of the Georgia campaign. Hood's corps and Walker's division of Hardee's command had been only lightly engaged. Together, Hardee and Loring reported a loss of only fifty-eight killed. Johnston's over-all losses were approximately six hundred. Federal losses were much heavier. Sherman later placed them at three thousand while Johnston maintained they were six thousand.[63]

Yet the victory appeared to have accomplished little. Union supply trains still whistled through Allatoona Pass, and Sherman's superior numbers could withstand such losses with relative ease. Within five days, Sherman would advance again. At his Marietta headquarters, Johnston was concerned with this threat, but by the last week of June, increasing discontent in Richmond would prove as formidable a foe as the long blue lines beyond his fortifications on Kennesaw Mountain.

---

[62] Govan and Livingood, *A Different Valor*, 293–95; French, *Two Wars*, 207–209; Johnston, *Narrative*, 341–43.

[63] Johnston, *Narrative*, 343; French, *Two Wars*, 209; Buck, *Cleburne and His Command*, 225; Hughes, *Hardee*, 212; Sherman, "The Grand Strategy of the Last Year of the War," *Battles and Leaders*, IV, 252; Govan and Livingood, *A Different Valor*, 295.

thirteen

Trouble in Georgia

BY THE TIME JOHNSTON REACHED MARIETTA, THE OLD DIVISION BETWEEN his and the government's views had broadened. The issues were varied, but generally revolved about basic disagreements which had existed since the early spring in Dalton.

By late June there was much fear in Richmond social and political circles that Johnston would eventually abandon Atlanta. This dread was based on Richmond's ignorance of Johnston's plans, for no understanding existed as to what Johnston planned to do. Not only was his strategy for opposing Sherman not understood by the government, but perhaps it was not even grasped by Johnston himself.

During May and June, Johnston implied that he expected to defeat Sherman before reaching the Etowah River, and later, before he could cross the Chattahoochee. This would be done either by attacking a portion of Sherman's columns while isolated, or by forcing the Federals to attack a strongly entrenched position. On May 20 Johnston explained to Davis that Sherman would have been attacked at Resaca had he not flanked the Confederates downstream on the Oostanaula. Johnston also explained that he would have attacked at Cassville on May 19 had Hood's misconception of a flanking threat not aborted the maneuver. Again, on May 21, Johnston argued to Davis that he had "earnestly sought for an opportunity to strike the enemy," but had been frustrated by Sherman's superior numbers and flanking techniques.[1]

---

[1] Johnston to Davis, May 21, 1864, in Joseph E. Johnston Dispatch Book, May 15, 1860–March 3, 1865, in Johnston Papers, William and Mary, hereinafter cited as Johnston Dispatch Book. See also *Official Records*, XXXVIII, Pt. 4, p. 728, LII, Pt. 2, p. 672.

After retreating across the Etowah, Johnston continued to insist that he desired to fight Sherman. On May 25 he telegraphed Davis that he was moving "to intercept him and oppose his further progress." [2] On May 28 Johnston reported that he had already fought Sherman at New Hope Church and was still "confronting the enemy." On June 8, after learning that Sherman was moving east to gain the railroad near Acworth, Johnston told Richmond that "we are moving to meet this." [3] Later, on June 27, Johnston gave Richmond his first and only detailed explanation during the campaign. Johnston explained to Bragg that he would have fought Sherman north of the Oostanaula had he not been flanked. After retreating from Calhoun he had intended to take advantage of the first good position to fight, but found no advantageous position. [4]

This same strategy was described by Johnston to Senator Ben Hill of Georgia in a conversation at Marietta on July 1. Hill had come to Johnston's headquarters at the urging of Senator Louis Wigfall, who was visiting in Georgia, and Governor Joseph Brown. Both Wigfall and Brown hoped that Hill, who was on good terms with Davis, could induce Richmond to order cavalry from General Stephen Lee's department to aid Johnston. Hill considered the situation so serious that he decided to go in person to Richmond instead of writing. First, however, he stopped at Johnston's headquarters to learn his plans. Though some of the details of Hill's conversation vary, according to when he recorded them, one factor was consistent. In his verbal report made about July 9 to Davis, in his written memorandum submitted to Seddon on July 13, and in his postwar reminiscence, Hill consistently recorded that Johnston insisted he had desired to fight between Dalton and Marietta. But Sherman had lapped his flanks constantly, and then had entrenched so as to prevent a frontal assault. [5]

Several other versions of Johnston's alleged strategy conflict with this one. In his report to Richmond submitted in late 1864, Johnston argued that he had never intended to fight north of the Chattahoochee. Any victory would have been marginal, since Sherman's army would only have retired into prepared fortifications. But defeat for Johnston, sepa-

2 Johnston to Davis, May 25, 1864, in Johnston Dispatch Book, William and Mary.

3 Johnston to Bragg, June 8, 1864, see also Johnston to Bragg, May 28, 1864, in *ibid.*

4 Johnston to Bragg, June 27, 1864, in Johnston Papers, Historical Society of Pennsylvania.

5 *Official Records,* LII, Pt. 2, pp. 693–94, 704–705. Ben Hill to ———, October 12, 1878, in Jefferson Davis, *Rise and Fall of the Confederate Government* (New York, 1881), II, 557–58.

rated from Atlanta by several rivers, would have been disastrous. Johnston especially belittled the idea of fighting in the Dalton area. There, a Federal defeat would only mean a retreat to Ringgold, whereas a Rebel defeat would mean possible disaster north of the Oostanaula. Such a statement contrasts interestingly with Johnston's May 20 telegram to Davis insisting he would have fought north of the Oostanaula had he not been outflanked at Calhoun by Sherman's crossing. In his report, Johnston repeatedly hammered at the impossibility of fighting north of the Chattahoochee. Instead, he considered drawing Sherman to the south bank of the river as his best course. There, a combination of dwindling Union numbers and Confederate cavalry attacks on Sherman's railroad line would have meant Federal defeat.[6]

This same theme, deliberate retreat in order to fight south of the Chattahoochee, was reiterated on several occasions. In a postwar article given to *Century* magazine, Johnston repeated that to fight north of the Chattahoochee would have been useless, as Sherman would not have retreated far. Instead, he planned to draw Sherman to the south bank of the Chattahoochee. Even if defeated there, Johnston would withdraw into the Atlanta fortifications. In several letters later in the war and in the postwar period, Johnston repeated this strategy. In September of 1864, he told General Dabney Maury that Sherman had lost heavily prior to reaching the Chattahoochee. "Is it not clear," Johnston argued "that Sherman would have been defeated south of the river?" To his brother, Johnston argued in August and November of 1864 that Sherman's army, weakened by losses and far from its base, would be in grave trouble.[7]

But Johnston also expounded a third plan. A few days before Senator Ben Hill visited him at Marietta, Johnston was visited by his old friend, Senator Wigfall. En route to Texas, Wigfall was disturbed by what he considered to be reliable reports in the capital that Davis planned to remove Johnston. Thus, on June 28, he visited Johnston to warn him and to learn exactly what his plans were. According to Wigfall's later memorandum of the visit, Johnston obviously did not plan to halt on the south bank of the Chattahoochee. Instead, he planned to fight Sherman on the south side of Peachtree Creek, a long, meandering stream which flowed northeast of Atlanta and emptied into the Chattahoochee. Wigfall suggested that Johnston attack Sherman as he crossed

---

6 *Official Records*, XXXVIII, Pt. 3, p. 619.

7 Johnston to Dabney Maury, September 1, 1864, in "Two Letters," *Confederate Veteran*, XXVI (September, 1918), 395; Johnston to Beverley Johnston, August 28, 1864, November 8, 1864, in Hughes, "War Letters," 321, 325.

the Chattahoochee, but the general demurred. He favored waiting until Sherman divided his columns to cross Peachtree Creek. Then the divided Federals would also have the river to their backs. If defeated, Johnston could retire into the Atlanta entrenchments.[8]

At other times, Johnston claimed that all along his plan had been to fight south of Peachtree Creek. In 1865 he reviewed his plans in a letter to Wigfall, and argued that he was in the process of implementing them when he was removed by Hood. Again, in his memoirs, Johnston reviewed his Peachtree strategy. This version was completely different from that given the government in May and June. Sherman's power made it impossible and unnecessary to fight him between Dalton and the Chattahoochee. Thus, Johnston's plan was to await Sherman, weakened in numbers, south of Peachtree Creek.[9]

There is yet a fourth version of what Johnston intended. While at Marietta in mid-June, he conferred with his chief of artillery, General F. A. Shoup. Shoup went to Johnston's headquarters to request permission to build defensive works on the north bank of the Chattahoochee. Shoup explained to Johnston that such works would enable the Confederates to hold the river crossings with only a few men, and would free the army to attack Sherman as he prepared to cross the river. Johnston and Shoup discussed the plan and the fortifications at length, and the artillery officer later recalled that Johnston agreed with his summations. Within the proposed line was ample space for maneuver, so that Johnston could mass his army to attack a single point of Sherman's line. If he learned of a crossing of the river by part of Sherman's force, Johnston could march from the fortifications and strike the portion isolated on the north bank.

Johnston liked the proposal, according to Shoup, and ordered the line prepared. By early July a thousand slaves were at work. Heavy guns were brought up from Mobile, and orders were issued for hospitals to send forward those not in condition for active field service. About a week after Shoup began construction, Johnston even contrived the idea of extending the line three miles further downstream. Thus when finished, the line stretched some seven miles, from a point a quarter of a mile upstream from the Western and Atlantic railroad bridge, to Turner's Ferry, where the road from Powder Springs to Atlanta crossed the river. According to Shoup, not until the day that Johnston retreated across

8 Govan and Livingood, *A Different Valor*, 297–98.

9 Johnston to Wigfall, August 27, 1864, in Wigfall Papers, DLC; Johnston, *Narrative*, 350, 356, 358.

the river did he learn that the plan to fight on the north bank had been abandoned.[10]

What did Johnston plan to do? By the time he reached Marietta, several things seemed evident. If he planned to retreat deliberately across the Chattahoocheee, he had misled the government. His few dispatches in May and June said nothing of retreat, but instead emphasized that he had attempted to fight Sherman. If he did believe that the best strategy was to maneuver Sherman across the Chattahoochee, he never said so to Richmond. As late as June 27, only a few days before Hill's visit, Johnston's first real explanation of what he was doing did not mention this strategy. He stated clearly that he had intended to fight north of the Oostanaula as well as north of the Etowah, and admitted that he was still trying to force Sherman to halt and fight.[11]

Probably Johnston did not intend to mislead the government. Instead, several factors in the campaign thus far indicated that Johnston had a relatively limited capacity as an overall planner, and in effect had not decided just how he would deal with Sherman. If Johnston did have a plan, he told neither Richmond nor his corps commanders. Save for his longer June 27 note to Bragg, Johnston's reports thus far had been brief telegrams which told little of his plans. Sensing this, he apologized to Bragg on June 27 for the brevity of his correspondence.

Nor did he converse closely with his lieutenants. Hardee and Polk, especially remained ignorant of Johnston's plans. Johnston evinced a somewhat cavalier attitude toward Hardee, who nominally was second-in-command. Whether Johnston felt some resentment at Hardee's glowing December reports which had misled the government or for some other reason, that officer seemed to be left out of Johnston's consultations. By Johnston's own admission, the retreat from Adairsville was discussed more closely with Hood and Polk. The decision to retreat from Cassville was made without consulting Hardee, and he noticed this isolation. During the retrograde move from Dalton, Hardee seemed irritated at being ignored, and also puzzled as to Johnston's strategy. On June 15 he admitted to his wife that "I don't know what's up." [12] According to several June letters, Hardee obviously thought the army would retreat across the Chattahoochee but knew nothing definite. He did know that Johnston seemed to confer more closely with Hood, and

10 F. A. Shoup, "Dalton Campaign—Works at Chattahoochee River," *Confederate Veteran*, III (September, 1895), 262–64; Johnston, *Narrative*, 345. Sherman called Shoup's fortifications "one of the strongest pieces of field-fortification I ever saw." Sherman, *Memoirs*, II, 66.

11 Johnston to Bragg, July 27, 1864, in Johnston Papers, Pennsylvania.

12 Hardee to wife, June 15, 1864, in Hardee Papers, Alabama.

sarcastically remarked that "Hood . . . is helping the General to do the strategy, and from what I can see is doing most of it." [13] Although at Marietta, Hardee, as well as Hood, had urged Johnston to fight north of the Chattahoochee, Johnston would say nothing definite. Hardee meanwhile speculated, "I believe we are drifting to Atlanta." [14]

Nor had there been close rapport between Johnston and Polk. After retreating across the Etowah River, there was an obvious sense of dissatisfaction at Polk's headquarters. Polk's aide and son-in-law remarked that "Gen'l J. *is not the man* we though him," and that Johnston had failed "beyond doubt and I fear beyond repair." [15] Polk was less openly critical but still did not seem to know what Johnston planned. South of the Etowah, Polk confided that he did not know when Johnston planned to fight Sherman, only that the army was falling back "to find ground on which General Johnston was willing to fight them." [16] By the time he was entrenched at New Hope Church, Polk confided that he still did not know whether Johnston would fight on the north side of the Chattahoochee. Shortly before his death, while on the Lost Mountain position, Polk still did not seem to know Johnston's plans.[17]

Johnston's uncommunicative air might be attributed to several factors. He was aware by early June that he was being criticized in Richmond for his policy of retreat. Though it would seem that such criticism would move him to explain his position, he took the opposite stand, and remained aloof. Too, his intense distrust of northern people in the Confederacy might have been a factor. Already in 1863, Johnston had expressed distrust of Generals Pemberton and Samuel French because they were native northerners. In the early summer of 1864, Johnston evidently told Wigfall that he did not dare reveal his plans because there was allegedly a spy in the war office.[18]

Johnston's personality, too, helped explain his silence. Quick to take offense, he probably was irritated at Richmond's refusals to send more infantry and to send Lee's cavalry to support him. As a result, Johnston may have seen no real use in confiding in the government. General Shoup later recalled that when he suggested Johnston request the authority to impress slaves from the department south of Atlanta to work on

13 Hardee to wife, June 20, 1864, in *ibid.;* see also Hardee to wife, June 12, 19, 1864, *ibid.*

14 Hardee to wife, June 23, 1864, in *ibid.*

15 Gale Diary, May 21, 1864, in Polk Papers, Sewanee.

16 Polk to wife, May 21, 1864, in *ibid.*

17 Polk to wife, May 27, 1864, in Polk, *Polk,* II, 364–64, Polk to wife, June 1, 1864, in *ibid.*, p. 365.

18 Chesnut, *Diary from Dixie,* 430, 445, 421–22; Davis to Johnston, June 11, 1863, in Rowland (ed.) , *Davis,* V, 511.

the fortifications, Johnston retorted that he would not ask the government for anything. Too, Johnston seemed to possess a somewhat secretive air which almost approached condescension. This was noticeable in his reply to the government upon learning that he had been removed. Johnston sarcastically remarked to Cooper that "confident language by a military commander is not usually regarded as evidence of competency." [19]

However, the reverse could also be true. Secrecy was not necessarily evidence of a great strategic mind at work. Johnston may have been so uncommunicative because he lacked any overall plan for dealing with Sherman. A disturbing looseness to Johnston's planning belies a cautious crafty general employing Fabian tactics to draw Sherman deep within Georgia for destruction. None of the four versions of what Johnston apparently intended to do gives evidence of wide-scale planning. For one who planned to dog Sherman every step and strike north of the Etowah at the first available opportunity, Johnston was ill prepared. Seemingly, he knew little of the terrain, although he had been there five months. That his Dalton position turned out to be a defensive trap was proved by Sherman's flank move. If he planned to make the fight at Dalton, as he sometimes claimed, why had he neglected to blockade both the passes in Rocky Face Mountain and Snake Creek Gap? After he retreated across the Oostanaula, Johnston seemed to be searching for terrain, which, after his long stay on the Dalton line, he should have known was there. His decisions not to stand at Calhoun and Adairsville were based on last-minute considerations which should have received forethought. His hasty decision at Cassville to abandon completely the country north of the Etowah did not indicate he had weighed the topographical disadvantages to be faced on the south bank. South of the Etowah, Sherman would be in excellent position to endanger Johnston's communications with either South Carolina or Alabama. And the Federals would have more room for maneuver. North of the river, Sherman had been restricted on the west by the angle of the Oostanaula and Etowah rivers, which united at Rome to form the Coosa.

Nor did Johnston seem to give much forethought to fighting south of the Chattahoochee, which he sometimes claimed was his plan. Not until June 10 did he give Shoup any orders to construct fortifications on the north bank. Such fortifications could enable Johnston to attack Sherman as he attempted to cross the river—the strategy which Shoup later claimed that Johnston had agreed to at Marietta. Or Johnston

19 Shoup, "Dalton Campaign—Works at Chattahoochee River," 265; Johnston to Cooper, July 18, 1864, in Joseph E. Johnston Letters, United States Military Academy Library.

could have held the entrenchments with part of his force while contesting a crossing of the river with detached units.

Much of Johnston's strategy for fighting south of the Chattahoochee depended upon strong Atlanta fortifications. At Marietta he told Wigfall that he would strike Sherman south of the river and if defeated, would fall back into the Atlanta fortifications. Several things were wrong with this plan. The Atlanta defenses protected nothing except the environs of Atlanta. The line had been under construction since the spring of 1864, under the direction of a former Georgia Railroad engineer, Lemuel F. Grant. But by mid-July, it was still uncompleted. Too, the Atlanta fortifications defended none of the critical rail approaches to the town. Johnston's supplies from Alabama were being shipped over the West Point Railroad, which entered the town from the southwest. Twelve miles southwest of Atlanta, at East Point, this railroad joined with the Macon and Western. There was not a single foot of fortifications on the front from Atlanta to East Point. In his Marietta conversation, Hill warned Johnston that Sherman could extend his lines around Atlanta and control this junction, but Johnston still did not order any fortifications constructed toward East Point until after he had crossed the Chattahoochee on the night of July 9.[20]

Johnston did not really expect to have to withstand a siege at Atlanta. Another vital part of his strategy for south of the Chattahoochee depended upon a vague hope. Since May, Johnston and others had pleaded for the government to send cavalry from Lee's department in Alabama and Mississippi to tear up Sherman's rail communications. Johnston's argument had been that his own troopers were needed for extending the infantry lines and for reconnaissance duties. The government had refused, arguing that Lee's cavalry was badly outnumbered in his own department. Still, as late as July 1, Johnston's strategy was based on outside cavalry help, which he had not the slightest promise of obtaining. As he explained to Hill in their July 1 meeting, a large cavalry strike against Sherman's rear would force him either to retreat or to fight south of the Chattahoochee.[21]

Such planning had obvious flaws. From May 12 until July 1, Sherman had already driven Johnston back seventy miles into Georgia. At this rate, there would scarcely be time to call Forrest from Mississippi or Morgan from upper East Tennessee to operate against the railroad. Hill sensed this, and asked Johnston how long he could hold Sherman

20 Hill to Seddon, July 14, 1864, in Johnston Papers, William and Mary; Shoup, "Dalton Campaign—Works at Chattahoochee River," 265.
21 Hill to Seddon, July 14, 1864, Seddon to Hill, July 13, 1864, in Johnston Papers, William and Mary.

on the north bank of the river. Johnston's exact reply is not known, since Hill's account written in July, 1864, differs with a postwar version. According to the account Hill gave Davis and Seddon on July 10–11, Johnston estimated he could hold Sherman north of the river for a month. Hill's later account placed Johnston's figure as between fifty-four and sixty days.[22]

It was not merely that Johnston did not appear to have thought out a strategic program carefully. He also did not seem to grasp the picture of the total war developing in Georgia in 1864. Johnston insisted that the best way to defeat Sherman was to surrender the territory of north-central Georgia gradually, and force Sherman south of the Chattahoo-chee. There, if necessary, Johnston later argued, he would have gone into a siege state at Atlanta which Sherman could not have turned. Johnston especially enjoyed measuring his campaign's progress with that of Lee in Virginia. He repeatedly compared the two, and insisted that he had retreated no further than Lee when removed.[23]

There was a vital difference in the retreats being conducted by Lee and Johnston, in addition to Lee's keeping in closer touch with the government. Johnston was retreating across some of the Confederacy's most valuable soil. This country was not the same as the marshy, poor land between the Rapidan and Richmond. Already Johnston had lost valuable munitions areas. The loss of Rome had involved the abandon-ment of the Noble Brothers Iron Works, which in 1861 had been the South's second largest cannon foundry. The fall of Rome had also placed in a difficult position the vast complex of Confederate iron works and nitriaries across the Alabama border in Calhoun, Cherokee, DeKalb, and Jackson counties. The loss of the north bank of the Etowah had meant the abandonment of the vast Etowah Iron Works, on the bank of the river east of Cartersville.

If Johnston retreated further southward from Marietta, more vital installations would be threatened. The extensive Roswell Mills, south-east of Marietta on the Chattahoochee, was a large-scale producer of woolen and cotton clothing. South of the river Atlanta, by the summer of 1864, had been turned into a part of that great Confederate munitions axis from Augusta through Macon and Columbus to Selma. Much of the machinery from munitions works in Tennessee had been sent to Atlanta after that state fell in early 1862. The city, which had a population of

---

[22] *Ibid.;* see also Hill to ———, October 12, 1878, in Davis, *Rise and Fall,* II, 559.

[23] Johnston to Maury, September 1, 1864, in *Confederate Veteran,* XVI, 395; Johnston to Beverley Johnston, August 28, 1864, in Hughes, "War Letters," 321; Johnston to Wigfall, August 27, 1864, February 26, 1865, in Wigfall Papers, DLC.

some twenty thousand by 1864, was a teeming industrial center. More than a mere gateway to the munitions axis, Atlanta was a town of diversified war industries. The Atlanta Rolling Mill made cannon, armorplate, and rails. Winship's Foundry, the Atlanta Machine Works, the Spiller and Burr Revolver Factory, the Withers and Solomon Foundry, and many other installations turned out artillery, small arms, naval gunplates, railroad rails, uniform buttons, and hundreds of other essential items. The central commissary depot, the Confederate arsenal, flour mills under contract to the army—all made Atlanta an industrial hub. Since the Atlanta defenses ringed the city only a mile and a half from the center of town, it is difficult to see why Johnston thought such factories would remain undisturbed by a siege.

Johnston's willingness to stand a siege at Atlanta also did not seem to take into account the vital munitions areas east, south, and southwest of Atlanta. Eighty miles northeast at Athens on the Oconee River there were key installations, such as the Confederate armory where rifles and carbines were manufactured, and the Athens Foundry where artillery and railroad wheels were manufactured. East of Atlanta at Augusta was the vast Confederate powder complex on the Savannah River, where twelve mills provided the South's main powder supply. Augusta, the northeastern terminus of the great munitions axis, also boasted installations which manufactured artillery, small arms, and other war goods. Only eighty miles southeast of Atlanta, Macon contained the central Confederate ordnance laboratory. In Macon, artillery and small arms were manufactured, as well as other items. In the Macon area were other important installations, such as a pistol factory at Griswoldville and an armory manufacturing small arms at Milledgeville. Southwest of Atlanta at Columbus were sprawling iron works, small arms manufactories, cannon foundries, and factories turning out other war goods.[24]

Johnston boasted that Sherman could never break a siege of Atlanta. But he could make no such boasts about protecting outlying munitions areas such as Augusta and Athens, as well as to Atlanta itself. Johnston might well have considered making a lateral retreat from Calhoun to Rome, where his flanks would be protected by the junction of the Oostanaula from the north and the Etowah from the south. This retreat would have forced Sherman either to halt and fight or to continue to advance, with Johnston at his flank and rear. Instead, Johnston not only determined upon a direct retreat to his base, but planned also to give

24 Walter G. Cooper, *Official History of Fulton County* (Atlanta, 1934), 115–17, 88–89; Josiah Gorgas, "Ordnance of the Confederacy: Notes of Brig. Gen. Josiah Gorgas, Chief of Ordnance, C.S.A.," *Army Ordnance*, XVI (January–April, 1936), 213–15, 284–86.

battle in the heart of the South's manufacturing area. For this decision he would be labelled a genius in the art of Fabian tactics.

Johnston seemed aloof to the rising discontent over his retreat, both in Richmond and in the army. Richmond's displeasure had been sparked in late May by a combination of his retreat across the Etowah and by his meager telegrams of explanation for the retrograde move from Dalton to Marietta. Surprised that Johnston did not fight at Calhoun, the government certainly expected him to do so before reaching the Etowah River. More disappointment was created by the brief telegram sent on May 21 by Johnston, explaining why he had retreated from Cassville and across the Etowah.[25]

This retreat kindled resentment. Johnston's chief of staff, General W. W. Mackall, confided to his wife that no doubt the move would damage Johnston in the public eye, and he was right. Rumors circulated in Richmond of panic among the Georgia populace, of a tremendous drop in morale in Johnston's army, and of the fear that he would not fight for Atlanta. Johnston's continual retreat was a constant topic of discussion at Richmond soirees attended by the cabinet set. While Johnston remained silent after Cassville, Hood did not. On May 21 Hood dispatched an aide, Colonel George Brewster, to Davis. Brewster carried a letter from Hood, as well as a prepared verbal explanation of Hood's account of the campaign thus far. Exactly what Hood's delegate told Davis is unknown, but Brewster did speak freely at Richmond social events. He referred to Johnston's lack of a plan at Dalton, to Hood's desire to fight there, and to Hood's continual frustration at Johnston's retreating. Whatever Brewster said, it was to prove damaging. Brewster later confided to Mrs. Chesnut that on his trip to Richmond, Davis told him that Johnston would have to be removed.[26]

Though Brewster's account may have been exaggerated, there is no doubt that during June, rumors circulated in Richmond both that Johnston's army was in a demoralized condition and that the government planned to remove him. As early as June 8 a member of his staff confided to a relative that Johnston was aware of Richmond's criticism but thought little of it. Only a few days before, Johnston's chief of staff, General W. W. Mackall, also commented on the government's displeasure. On June 3 Mackall wrote that "it is unjust to put a man at the

---

25 Vandiver, *Gorgas Diary*, 103, 106–108; Mackall to wife, May 29, 1864, in Mackall, *Recollections*, 211–12, Mackall to wife, June 3, 1864, *ibid.*, p. 213; Manning to mother, June 3, 1864, in Williams–Chesnut–Manning Papers, South Carolina; Davis to Lee, May 20, 1864, in Rowland (ed.), *Davis*, VI, 258.

26 Mackall to wife, May 21, 1864, in Mackall, *Recollections*, 211; Govan and Livingood, *A Different Valor*, 277; Chesnut, *Diary from Dixie*, 415, 430.

head of an army and then try to destroy his capacity for usefulness by expressing fears and distrust." [27] By late June so many stories were circulating about the loss of morale in the army that Senator Richard Walker and Representative Francis Lyon of Alabama visited Johnston at Marietta to ascertain the truth. Walker's glowing report, sent back to Assistant Secretary of War John Campbell, of the morale in Johnston's army did not halt the rumors. And on June 28 Wigfall visited Johnston with several objectives, one of which was to warn him that he had learned on good authority that Davis had decided to remove him from command. [28]

There were obvious signs of low morale within the army by the time Johnston crossed the Etowah River. The army's hopes had been lifted by his stirring May 19 proclamation asserting that battle would be given at Cassville, only to be dashed by the sudden retreat across the river. The retreat itself resembled a panic. On May 20 men, horses, and wagons jammed on the four bridges that spanned the Etowah. A feeling of alarm was sensed in the conduct of the civilian populace. Johnston's ordering his supply train to the Chattahoochee convinced some troops that the general would not fight north of that river. [29]

In his limited comprehension of the campaign, Johnston made no attempt at a total mobilization using supporting forces. Essential to his alleged strategy was the successful operation of the West Point and the Macon railroads. He had assured Hill at Marietta that Sherman did not have the force required to encircle Atlanta completely and cut off these routes. Yet he had ignored the protection of these lines west of Atlanta, particularly the Chattahoochee crossings on the border of Georgia and Alabama. He made no correlation with Lee's department to insure their safety. Only when Hill informed him did Johnston learn that the bridges were unguarded and that the Alabama militia, supposedly protecting them, had been withdrawn. [30]

Johnston's narrow administrative scope was also evident in his dealings

---

[27] Mackall to wife, June 3, 1864, in Mackall, *Recollections*, 213; see also Manning to mother, June 8, 1864, in Williams–Chesnut–Manning Papers, South Carolina.

[28] *Official Records*, LII, Pt. 2, pp. 685–86; Govan and Livingood, *A Different Valor*, 296–97.

[29] For evidence of growing army discontent, see Diary of Sergeant I. V. Moore, 37th Georgia, May 21, 1864, in Georgia State Department of Archives and History; Leonidas Mackey to family, July 5, 1864, in Leonidas Mackey Letters, Atlanta Historical Society; Neal to mother, May 20, 1864, in A. J. Neal Letters, Georgia Department of Archives and History; Mackall Journal, May 20–21, 1864, in *Official Records*, XXXVIII, Pt. 3, pp. 984–85; J. W. Hagan to wife, July 11, 1864, in J. W. Hagan, *Confederate Letters of John W. Hagan*, ed. Bell I. Wiley (Athens, Ga., 1954), 50.

[30] Hill to Seddon, July 14, 1864, in Johnston Papers, William and Mary.

with Georgia officials. His correspondence with Governor Brown and others in the campaign dealt almost solely with the need for Lee's cavalry to send some assistance. Johnston did not press for a mass calling of Georgia state troops. On his own, Brown in late May called out a three-thousand-man division of Georgia militia commanded by General G. W. Smith. Johnston thanked Brown for the use of the troops, but did not ask for all out assistance of the militia, which supposedly numbered some ten thousand men. Not until July 9, as Johnston prepared to retreat across the Chattahoochee, did Brown again at his own initiative order a general call for the militia to assemble at Atlanta. The order was tardy. General Smith, now in command of all the state forces, hurriedly tried to organize them southwest of Atlanta at Poplar Springs. But by the time of Johnston's removal in mid-July, Smith had readied only two thousand additional men.[31]

The confusion between Johnston and Richmond as to strategic plans was no greater than that of how to use the cavalry against Sherman. The great preponderance of Rebel cavalry which now stood between East Tennessee and Mississippi seemed to offer promise. Basically, two groupings were available: Johnston's own cavalry corps, and the cavalry in the neighboring departments of Alabama and Mississippi, and western Virginia and East Tennessee.

The situation seemed especially favorable because since the spring, intelligence indicated that the Federal communication line through Nashville and Chattanooga was extremely thin. Actually, Sherman had only one rail link into Georgia. From Nashville, the Central Alabama Railroad led southward across the state line to a junction with the Memphis and Charleston, on the north bank of the Tennessee River opposite Decatur. From here the Memphis and Charleston extended eastward through Huntsville, and then northeast, parallel to the river to Stevenson, Alabama. Here the main line from Nashville, the Nashville and Chattanooga, joined it. From Stevenson a single track that ran to Chattanooga and then southward on the Western and Atlantic supplied Sherman's army.

Since April the Confederates had known that this rail line was thinly guarded. That month Polk's scouts reported that the Nashville and Chattanooga was being repaired, and all supplies and troops were being brought over the single track via Columbia to the junction with the

31 T. Conn Bryan, *Confederate Georgia* (Athens, Ga., 1953), 158–59; *Official Records,* LII, Pt. 2, pp. 673, 688, 691, XXXVIII, Pt. 5, pp. 867, 878, Pt. 3, pp. 969–70, Pt. 4, p. 753; Johnston to Joseph Brown, June 4, 1864, in Johnston Papers, William and Mary; G. W. Smith, "The Georgia Militia About Atlanta," *Battles and Leaders,* IV, 331–34.

Memphis and Charleston north of Decatur. The garrisons en route were weak. A single Federal infantry division was on the road between Nashville and the junction, with only small forces of cavalry at Athens, Decatur, Columbia, and other points.

By May, as Sherman concentrated heavily at Chattanooga, the rail line became more vulnerable. Only four Union cavalry regiments protected both railroads. The garrisons at Athens, Decatur, Huntsville, Columbia, and other way towns had dwindled as troops were moved to Chattanooga. In June, Wheeler's scouts reported a further weakening of the Union guards. Only between three thousand and thirty-five hundred troops were at Nashville, and the men of all but one large regiment were convalescents. A mere thirty troops guarded the bridges near Lavergne, while Murfreesboro boasted only about two small regiments. South of Murfreesboro, a small garrison at Wartrace and a brigade scattered between Winchester, Decherd, and Tullahoma guarded the road. On the alternate road, the Alabama and Tennessee, protection was equally weak. Small guards protected the important rail bridges. Between Nashville and Athens, Alabama, there were but eight hundred troops, of which only two hundred were cavalry. By early July the demands on Sherman were so great that the railroads were again stripped, and there were rumors that the Federals would completely stop using the Alabama and Tennessee because of inadequate protection for both lines. Wheeler's scouts reported that all garrisons along the railroad were small, and manned by green, one-hundred-day troops.[32]

The Alabama and Tennessee Railroad had been well scrutinized by Confederate intelligence, and by late June, Richmond knew its vulnerabilities. There were twelve important bridges on the forty-mile stretch between Nashville and Columbia alone. The Elk River bridge south of Columbia was built of dry pine, and was manned by only fifty troops. Guarded by only a few companies, the Duck River bridge at Columbia was so extensive that it had required more than forty-two days to construct. Several miles north of Athens, a high trestle work some three hundred feet long was manned by only two companies. The force guarding the Harpeth River bridge at Franklin was so small that they did not venture out on scouting expeditions.

By the end of June the government also knew of several vulnerable points on the Nashville and Chattanooga Railroad. Only two regiments guarded the Stone's River bridge at Murfreesboro. A small garrison

32 Lee's headquarters to Polk, April 20, 1864, A. B. Coffey to Ferguson, April 21, 23, 1864, in Polk letters and telegrams sent, 1861–64, National Archives; Wheeler's scouts to Wheeler, June 22, July 4, 1864, in Wheeler Papers, Alabama; *Official Records*, XXXVIII, Pt. 4, pp. 703, 734, XXIII, Pt. 3, p. 813.

guarded the crossings of Garrison Fork Creek and Duck River near Wartrace. Further south, the long tunnel beneath the Cumberlands at Cowan and the long wooden trestle bridges over Big Crow Creek were poorly protected. There were dozens of other potential striking points, such as the creek bridges north of Athens, Alabama, the many creek crossings between the junction of the Memphis and Charleston and the Alabama and Tennessee, and Stevenson, Alabama, the Running Water Gorge near Chattanooga, the Tennessee River bridges at Bridgeport, as well as the bridges on the Chickamauga, the Oostanaula, and the Etowah south of Chattanooga. Small wonder that Sherman repeatedly confided to his wife his fears of the railroad being cut.[33]

The railroad link was also weakly garrisoned at the vast supply depot at Nashville. From here, ammunition, horses, sugar, coffee, hard bread, bacon, and other items were funnelled south, day and night, to the intermediate depot at Chattanooga. One Union officer described the Nashville installation as the largest in the world in May, 1864. Twenty-four freight trains a day left the Nashville depot bearing Sherman's supplies. By late June, Wheeler's scouts penetrated to Nashville and returned with interesting information. The stores were heavily concentrated in warehouses adjoining the depots of the two railroads. The Nashville garrison was so feeble that it seemed the warehouses could be destroyed by a quick expedition. Richmond had toyed with this idea since late April, when General George Hodge, an officer in Polk's Alabama department, proposed the plan to Davis and even brought forward an officer willing to lead such an expedition. But in early May, as Polk left the department to move to aid the army under Johnston, the interest in the project had dwindled. Now intelligence reports in late June and early July revived interest.[34]

With all this opportunity well known, the several hundred miles of railroad south of Nashville and the depot at Nashville remained almost completely untouched during the Atlanta compaign. Sherman's line could have been destroyed from two different sources: Johnston's own cavalry, and that of the nearby departments of General Stephen D. Lee in Alabama and Mississippi, and the Department of Western Virginia and East Tennessee. All told, from upper East Tennessee into Missis-

[33] James Saunders to Col. John Sale, July 5, 1864, in Davis Papers, Tulane; *Official Records*, XXXVIII, Pt. 4, p. 802; Wheeler's scouts to Wheeler, June 22, July 4, July 4, 1864, in Wheeler Papers, Alabama; Sherman to wife, June 27, 1864, June 9, 1864, June 30, 1864, May 22, 1864, in Sherman, *Home Letters*, 298, 297, 299, 292–93.

[34] Saunders to Sale, July 5, 1864, Davis to Sale, July 22, 1864, in Davis Papers, Tulane; *Official Records*, LII, Pt. 2, p. 665, XXXVIII, Pt. 4, p. 802. In his letter to Sale, Davis claimed he had been interested in the project for months.

sippi, the Confederacy had some 40,000 cavalry in the early summer of 1864. The stereotyped explanation of the failure to cut the Federal railroad link had been Richmond's refusal to order cavalry assistance to Johnston from outside his department. Both the government and Johnston, however, were responsible for the failure. The government bears the prime responsibility for not utilizing the ample troops of one of the two available sources—the East Tennessee and the Alabama-Mississippi commands. By the first of June, Lee's department comprised 15,157 effective troops. Of these, all but 1,558 were cavalry amassed in four divisions, of which General Nathan Bedford Forrest commanded two. Lee had almost 3,000 additional troopers who had no horses. In East Tennessee General Simon Buckner, now commanding the East Tennessee department, had 4,000 effective cavalry in four brigades, one commanded by General John Hunt Morgan. Not even counting the lamentable state troops in Alabama and Mississippi, the cavalry without horses, or the cavalry companies assigned to the Conscript Bureau, Lee and Buckner had available about 18,000 effective cavalry when the campaign began at Dalton.[35]

During early May, Johnston appealed first to Polk and then to Stephen D. Lee to send cavalry into Tennessee. Polk was contemplating such a move when he had to depart for Georgia. By late May, the appeals turned to Richmond. Johnston was tardy in requesting the aid. Although during Pendleton's April visit he had suggested it in general terms, not until early June did he formally request help from Richmond. On June 3 he remarked to Bragg that cavalry at the rear of Sherman's army this side of the Tennessee would do the Federals much harm.

By mid-June, Johnston became more forceful in his requests. Again, on June 12, he asked Bragg to give Lee orders for the move, and repeated his request the next day to both Bragg and Davis. On June 16 Johnston enlarged his appeal to ask for aid either from Lee or from East Tennessee. Also, Governor Joseph Brown on June 28 asked Davis to send either Forrest or Morgan. Three days later Howell Cobb appealed to Seddon, arguing that if Sherman's supplies were cut off for ten days, his army would be destroyed. Brown, on July 5 and July 7, rebuked Davis for allowing Sherman's three-hundred-mile line of supply to remain without attack. Brown hit hard at Davis' policy of dividing his forces to defend territory, and warned that this same policy of territorial defense had lost Tennessee in 1862.

In early July, after Johnston had crossed the Chattahoochee, pressure was still put on the government. On July 8 and July 12 he even asked

35 *Official Records*, XXXII, Pt. 3, p. 803, XXXIX, Pt. 2, p. 630.

for more modest assistance, four thousand men to strike the railroad somewhere south of Dalton. The assistance of Wigfall and other allies in Richmond was enlisted to convince the government of the need to send Lee against the railroad. On July 9 Hill brought back to Richmond Johnston's urging of the need for such a move.[36]

Repeatedly, Davis insisted that any potential expedition by Lee would uncover Alabama and Mississippi to seizure. The government argued that the threats of invasion via Memphis deep into the iron and munitions area of Alabama meant that Lee would be required to keep his cavalry to defend the department. This was especially true, argued Davis, since Polk's infantry had been sent, thus laying bare large stretches of territory. Howell Cobb reminded Seddon on July 1 that some territory would have to be surrendered temporarily, for if Georgia fell, all would be lost. On July 5 Governor Brown repeated the same argument: destroy Sherman, and Lee's department would be made safer. Hold to the government's policy of territorial defense via departmental command, and all would eventually be lost. Brown repeated this theme on July 7 when he rebuked Davis for keeping his forces divided. But his pleas were to no avail. Instead, Richmond's refusal to order Lee was simply another exhibition of the same policy of cordon defense which had frustrated earlier concentrations and had gradually seen the piecemeal loss of the West.[37]

The problem in the Alabama-Mississippi department was a good example of the weakness of the Confederate departmental system, and of the southern usage of cavalry in general. During the spring, Polk had talked of making a raid into Middle Tennessee with his cavalry, and Johnston had urged him to do so as early as February 13. However, the Bishop simply could not get matters organized. He had no overall cavalry commander until April 13, when Stephen D. Lee was placed in charge of all departmental cavalry. Until then, Lee nominally had been in command of the cavalry corps, but Polk had actually divided it into two departments, with Forrest to operate in West Tennessee and North

36 Ibid., XXXVIII, Pt. 4, pp. 654, 689, 692, Pt. 5, pp. 858, 868–69, LII, Pt. 2, pp. 672, 680, 687, 692; Joseph Brown to Davis, July 5, 1864, in Rowland (ed.) Davis, VI, 280; Pendleton to Davis, April 16, 1864, in Davis Papers, Tulane; Johnston to Bragg, June 3, 12, 13, 16, 1864, Johnston to S. D. Lee, June 3, 11, 16, 1964, Johnston to Ewell, June 27, 1864, Polk to Davis, June 13, 1864, in Johnston Papers, William and Mary; Johnston to Polk, May 7, 1863, in Polk letters and telegrams sent, 1861–64, National Archives.

37 Official Records, LII, Pt. 2, p. 687, XXXVIII, Pt. 5, pp. 858, 875–76, XXXIX, Pt. 2, p. 657; Brown to Davis, July 5, 1864, in Rowland (ed.), Davis, VI, 280; Davis to Johnston, July 11, 1864, in Davis Papers, Harvard; Cooper to Johnston, June 23, 1864, with notation by Davis, in Johnston Papers, William and Mary.

Mississippi, and Lee to command the central-southern part of Alabama and Mississippi.

Not until Lee assumed command of all Polk's cavalry, did it seem that some aid might be sent to Johnston. Forrest himself on April 6 had written Johnston to suggest a mass raid by the cavalry of both departments on Middle Tennessee. Then on April 15 Forrest suggested to Davis that his and Lee's cavalry be sent to break up Sherman's line of communications in Middle Tennessee and Kentucky. At first Lee was enthusiastic about the idea. On April 20 and 25 he urged Polk to consider such an expedition. On the eve of his departure for Georgia, Polk replied favorably to Lee, and indicated that he was taking the matter up with Johnston.[38]

With Polk's departure, Lee became both apprehensive and possessive of his command and gradually changed his mind. Lee was disturbed at the possibility of a Federal advance from Memphis into his new department. In February, Forrest had turned back such an expedition under General William Sooy Smith in a series of running battles between Columbus and Tupelo. Again, in late April, a second expedition commanded by General Samuel Sturgis had penetrated as far southward as Ripley, Mississippi, before abandoning the scheme to catch Forrest and retreating to Memphis on May 6. For some two weeks afterward, Lee still appeared interested in the scheme. He spoke on May 9 of hoping to launch an offensive across the Tennessee River soon, and by May 16 he had a definite plan. Forrest was ordered to concentrate thirty-five hundred men at Corinth and to march into Middle Tennessee on May 20.[39]

By the following day, however, Lee disclosed a change of plans reminiscent of the previous autumn, when he had shown timidity and an inability to organize to aid Bragg at Chattanooga. Because Forrest's scouts had warned of a new advance from Memphis, Lee on May 17 cancelled the plan to aid Johnston. Forrest, too, seemed to have lost interest. He also believed a new expedition from Memphis was in the making, and disliked the prospect of crossing the Tennessee with even 3,500 of his best men. Though only 4,500 Federal cavalry were reported to be at Memphis, and Forrest reported that in his two divisions alone he boasted 9,220 effectives, Lee on May 18 reported to Richmond that he could not assist Johnston. He did this despite his admission to Forrest on May 20 that his intelligence indicated the railroad between Nashville and Ste-

38 *Official Records*, LII, Pt. 2, p. 653, XXXII, Pt. 3, pp. 800, 822, 730, XXXVIII, Pt. 4, p. 654.
39 *Ibid.*, XXXVIII, Pt. 4, pp. 685, 719, 723.

venson was weakly guarded, and that 3,500 troops would be enough to do the job.[40]

By late May, Lee had bowed out of any designs to cut Sherman's supply line. Forrest had second thoughts on the subject, and on May 29 proposed that he could successfully raid Middle Tennessee with only two thousand men. But Lee negated the scheme and wastefully dispersed his four cavalry divisions throughout central Mississippi and Alabama which accomplished little. On May 23 Forrest's command was split in half. General James Chalmers' division was sent into central Alabama on strict defensive duty. Still Lee wavered. During the last week of May, Forrest, who now had only a single division, urged that he be allowed to raid Middle Tennessee. Lee gave his consent on May 31, and that same day Forrest laid plans to leave the following day for Russellville, Alabama. From there, Forrest intended to take some twenty-two hundred men northward along the old military road carved by General Andrew Jackson, across the river near Florence, and into Middle Tennessee.[41]

But on June 3, Lee received news of a large expedition of cavalry and infantry moving southward from Memphis under the command of General Samuel Sturgis. Immediately, Forrest was ordered to abandon the Middle Tennessee campaign, and to return to north Mississippi to repel Sturgis. This was done handsomely on June 10, when Forrest fell upon Sturgis' column at Brice's Crossroads. The Sturgis expedition ended any hope of Lee aiding Johnston. On June 18 Lee announced that as long as there was any possible threat of a move from Memphis, no invasion of Middle Tennessee would take place. And that day he ordered back from North Alabama the closest support Johnston had, the division of General Philip Roddey, which had been in position on the south bank of the river. Johnston still repeatedly asked Lee for assistance, but Richmond backed Lee's discretion as departmental commander, and on June 23 Davis informed Johnston that he "may not count on aid from General Lee." [42]

Why had Lee failed to send support? Recurring threats from Memphis do not seem an adequate reason. Aside from the industrial areas of central-south Alabama, there was simply no territory in Lee's domain whose importance equalled the need to destroy Sherman's supply line. Davis seemed to be clinging to his old assumption, which had wrecked Bragg in 1862–63, that all areas of the West could be defended simul-

40 *Ibid.,* pp. 723, 729, XXXIX, Pt. 2, p. 606.
41 *Ibid.,* XXXVIII, Pt. 4, pp. 749–50.
42 *Ibid.,* XXXIX, Pt. 2, p. 655; Cooper to Johnston, June 23, 1864, with notation by Davis, in Johnston Papers, William and Mary.

taneously. Nor did the threats from Memphis seem that awesome. There were long periods of time from April into July when Federal activity at Memphis was scant enough to allow some detachment. And Lee had not required all of his resources to repel the Memphis expeditions. By May, even after Jackson's cavalry division had been sent to Johnston, Lee still had over thirteen thousand effective cavalry. In May and June, comparatively few of these had been aligned to repel any advance from Memphis. After Chalmers' division had been sent into central Alabama in late May, only a single division under Forrest remained in North Mississippi for this purpose. The remainder of the command was scattered on strict territorial defense. Roddey's division was on picket duty in North Alabama. General Wirt Adams' division, with almost four thousand effectives, was picketing central-south Mississippi. Other smaller units were scattered from Demopolis and Selma northeast to Montevallo, Alabama.

The real reason why Lee gave Johnston no aid appears inherent in faults of the Confederate departmental system and in the cavalry organization. Although he interfered with departmental commanders when he liked, Davis generally followed a policy of allowing a commander wide discretion concerning reinforcements to another department. Such discretion had been given to Holmes in late 1862, and to both Johnston and Polk in the spring of 1864. But Lee probably lacked the desire or the ability to conduct such a grand strategy operation as striking Sherman's food link. Lee, only thirty-one years old, was an artilleryman by both training and experience. Until after Sharpsburg, he had served in Virginia. Later he commanded Pemberton's artillery at the surrender. Exchanged, Lee served first under Hardee and then under Polk as a cavalry division commander and later as commander of the department's cavalry corps.[43]

For more reasons than inexperience, Lee simply could not evaluate the comparative importance of holding Tupelo, Mississippi, and breaking Sherman's railroad. He had not wanted the job of departmental commander, nor even the command of Polk's cavalry corps. Lee had remonstrated against being placed over Polk's entire corps, particularly Forrest's command, and had stated he preferred a smaller authority. After he took command of Polk's department on May 9, Lee was not pleased. He at first asked to be relieved of the post, but was refused. Lee reasoned that he was already outranked by two infantry officers in the department, General Dabney Maury, at Mobile, and General Jones Withers, commanding the Alabama State Reserves at Montgomery.[44]

43 *Official Records*, XXXVIII, Pt. 4, p. 123, XXXIX, Pt. 2, pp. 650, 630, 702.
44 *Ibid.*, XXXIX, Pt. 2, p. 591, XXXII, Pt. 3, p. 822, XXXVIII, Pt. 4, p. 654.

However, once in authority, probably in part because he had ranking officers at Montgomery and Mobile, Lee acquiesced to a piecemeal deployment of his troops from the Tennessee border to Selma. By May, 1864, the department was full of tiny commands of regimental size. He strongly adhered to Davis' policy of territorial defense. Like most generals, once he became a departmental commander in his own right, he became possessive about lending his troops. There was also a factor of timidity. Repeatedly in the late summer and early autumn of 1863, Lee had bypassed opportunities to strike Rosecrans' supply line, often on somewhat flimsy grounds. Now, with dependable intelligence reports that the lines were weakly guarded, he still could never quite make the commitment across the Tennessee River.[45]

There was little doubt that Forrest was the popular western folk hero by the early summer of 1864. The pleas to Richmond and to Lee for assistance, which were sent by Johnston, Brown, Cobb, and others, had emphasized that Forrest was the man to send. After victory at Brice's Crossroads, he received wide public acclaim, and after his defeat of Sturgis, Forrest was idolized. Lee may have been jealous over the public's crediting Forrest with turning back Smith's expedition in the Meridian campaign of February, 1864. Later, Lee appeared jealous of the credit given Forrest for the retreat from Nashville in December, 1864. Friction between the two officers might well have hindered plans for an expedition.[46]

Underlying the failure to receive support from Lee was a basic problem; in essence, the South was being bled to death by its own cavalry. By 1864 the government was seeing the fruits of a long-standing policy of neglect and poor management of the mounted service in the West. The western policy of requiring each trooper to furnish his own mount, and the lax attention given to those who were dismounted produced large numbers of men who were listed on muster rolls as present but who were not effective. Both Johnston's and Lee's cavalries were filled with dismounted men either still in camp but inactive, or else allowed by government orders to go home on furlough to obtain another horse. Since 1863 sporadic attempts had been made to brigade these dismounted troopers as infantry, but with little success. By July of 1863 Wheeler's cavalry had only 7,896 effective cavalry, but the rolls carried 16,000 men. In the spring of 1864, when General Will Martin's division rejoined Johnston after the East Tennessee campaign, he reported only 1,500

45 *Ibid.*, XXXIX, Pt. 2, p. 608.
46 *Ibid.*, pp. 633, 639, 652, 656, 659, 666.

effectives though he was believed to have over 3,000. Martin was short on horses, as were several other of Johnston's cavalry divisions.[47]

There were worse problems. By 1864, joining the cavalry had become a convenient evasion of infantry duty. This was mainly due to the government's lax policy in allowing sporadic cavalry units to be organized. Theoretically, anyone who could organize a company of men could apply to the War Department for recognition. By the spring of 1864, Alabama and Mississippi particularly were filled with these roving bands which were romantically called partisan rangers. An estimated one thousand cavalrymen in southwestern Mississippi and East Louisiana alone were evading service in this way. Practically all western commanders complained to Richmond in 1863 and 1864 that the War Department was merely fostering evasion from the regular cavalry or infantry units. Longstreet, in December of 1863, complained that the country was completely overrun by cavalry. That same month, General Robert Ransom, commanding the East Tennessee department, also appealed to Richmond to have such organizations abolished. While heading the Volunteer and Conscript Bureau, Pillow had complained that Alabama and Mississippi were full of floating companies of cavalry. Johnston complained to Richmond that in Alabama and Mississippi such companies were merely being utilized to avoid regular service. General Stephen D. Lee complained that almost every day he heard of some new cavalry unit being organized.[48]

Georgia, Alabama, and Mississippi, by 1864, were also plagued by cavalry units organized by the state. In Alabama, General Jones Withers had twenty-one companies of fully organized state cavalry by July of 1864, and several others were then being formed. Pillow protested that Lee's department was full of such state companies which were designed to avoid conscription. Governor Charles Clark and the Mississippi State troops competed for new cavalry recruits with both the regular forces and those organizing partisan ranger forces. Sometimes the situation became so ludicrous that state and regular forces came close to a shooting war to determine who would get the cavalry recruits. The problem in Georgia was similar. An inspection officer complained to Bragg

47 Wheeler, "The effective total of the Cavalry of Genl. Wheeler in 1865" (MS in Davis Papers, Tulane); "Official Returns obtained from War Office, Richmond, 1865, copies of returns 1863–1864," in Hood Papers, National Archives; Wheeler to Hood, March 21, April 18, 1874, in Hood Papers, National Archives; *Official Records*, XXXVIII, Pt. 3, pp. 676, 679.

48 *Official Records*, XXXI, Pt. 3, pp. 849, 705, 871, 743, Ser. IV, Vol. II, pp. 758, 783.

in the summer of 1864 about the widespread shielding of cavalrymen organized in state forces.[49]

An even more serious problem was desertion from the infantry in order to join the cavalry. The problem was an old one. Though Wheeler, in July of 1863, had only 7,896 effective cavalry, an additional 1,823 were listed as deserters. Bragg had attempted to halt this trend by ordering that no more enlistments would be taken into his army's cavalry. But by the spring of 1864 such decrees were futile. A deserting infantryman from Johnston's army would find refuge in the state forces of Georgia, Alabama, or Mississippi, in the partisan troops, or even in Lee's regular cavalry.

By January of 1864 Johnston was protesting that recruiters from Forrest and Morgan were raiding his department and enticing infantrymen away. In fact, an inspection of Forrest's two cavalry divisions in May of 1864 revealed that almost a thousand were deserters from the infantry. Recruiters from Morgan's East Tennessee command were working both Lee's and Johnston's armies in the spring of 1864. Both officers asked Richmond to have this situation improved.[50]

The results of these various ills proved disastrous. Valuable horses were wasted on partisan and state groups. By May of 1864 almost half of Wheeler's cavalry was at the rear attempting to find horses. In addition, there was a severe shortage of arms, partially because they were wasted on irregular and state units. When Martin's division returned to Johnston in April of 1864, only fifteen hundred men were listed as effectives. For these, Martin reported a need for six hundred serviceable small arms. In April an inspection report of Wheeler's entire command revealed "a very great defect" of arms because of the irregularity of caliber.[51]

There was another serious problem. In both Stephen D. Lee's and Johnston's armies, it was almost impossible to make an accurate count of the cavalry. In addition to outright desertion, there was considerable marauding of the countryside by groups absent without leave, who were searching for horses and other items such as guns and food. Because of

49 *Ibid.*, XXXII, Pt. 3, pp. 784, 601, LII, Pt. 2, p. 670, XXXVIII, Pt. 2, p. 711, XXXI, Pt. 3, p. 862, Ser. IV, Vol. II, pp. 783, 758–59; Walter to Bragg, August 20, 1864, in Bragg Papers, Duke.

50 Robert E. Lee to Davis, June 20, 1864, in John Morgan Papers, UNC; Trimonthly return, July 10, 1863, in Wheeler Papers, Alabama; *Official Records*, XXII, Pt. 3, pp. 604, 621, XXX, Pt. 4, p. 718, XXXIX, Pt. 2, p. 602.

51 *Official Records*, XXXVIII, Pt. 4, p. 723, XXXIX, Pt. 2, p. 627; Johnston to Bragg, March 29, April 2, 1864, in Johnston Papers, William and Mary; Johnston to Cooper, August 9, 1864, in Georgia Portfolio II, Duke; G. A. Henry, Jr., to Col. ———, April 4, 1864, in Wheeler Papers, Alabama.

desertions from the infantry, a soldier could be listed on both cavalry and infantry rolls. Too, due to the constant organization of new cavalry commands, rolls were never stable. An inspection of Forrest's command in June of 1864 revealed regiments which the government did not even know existed. Some of his units, such as Neeley's brigade, were composed of a hodgepodge of irregular units and the debris of other old brigade organizations. Nor did there seem any stable number of men per brigade or regiment. Some of Lee's divisions totaled over 4,000 men, others barely 1,500. As a result, by June 1, although Lee's cavalry rolls listed over 27,000 men, only 13,300 were present for duty.[52]

Cavalry administration was even worse in East Tennessee, where Johnston had also asked for assistance. By May there were four cavalry brigades, supposedly totalling some 4,000 effectives. Here the horse shortage was so serious, however, that none were considered fit for field service. Two of the brigades had been sent as far southward as Asheville, North Carolina, to find horses and subsistence. Weapons were in frightfully short supply. Buckner's strongest brigade, that of General W. E. Jones, could field only an aggregate force of 1,673 men. Of these, 300 had no weapons, less than 900 could be assembled for inspection, and almost 200 were dismounted. The entire section was filled with dismounted cavalry, partisan groups, deserters, and men detached from now-destroyed commands such as Morgan's old division.[53]

The same general faults were evident in Johnston's own cavalry. Due to a shortage of horses, Wheeler, on May 1, could muster only 2,419 effectives though some 8,062 were reported as present for duty. The explanation for this discrepancy was the shortage of horses, which forced several divisions to the rear, and also encouraged desertions and leaves without permission. Though Wheeler could list only 2,419 men as effectives, there were 18,785 cavalry allegedly on his rolls.[54]

These disparities of numbers were closely aligned to the disagreement between Richmond and Johnston during the early summer, when Johnston maintained that his cavalry was insufficient to strike Sherman's supply line, while Richmond insisted that he had enough men. The problem probably originated in Johnston's laxity in keeping tabs on his forces. After his April 30 tabulation of strength at Dalton, Johnston did not call for another return until forty-two days later, on June 10. Again, another twenty days passed before he once more called for returns on June 30. During several months previous to April 30, Johnston had made careful tabulations of his strength every ten days. The effect of these

52 *Official Records*, XXXIX, Pt. 2, pp. 640, 630.
53 *Ibid.*, pp. 722–23, 698, 803–804, 678; XXXII, Pt. 3, pp. 842–46.
54 *Ibid.*, XXXVIII, Pt. 3, p. 676.

later lags was serious. Due to increased additions from Polk and the constant return of Wheeler's men who had been searching for horses, Johnston's reports to Richmond were rough estimates at best.

The problem was the Confederate method of tabulating strength. Unlike the Federals, the Confederates listed in separate categories those troops called "effectives," and others termed "present for duty." In addition, a third category known as "aggregate present" listed everyone present with the army—clerks, men detailed on special duty, those sick, and those under arrest. Always Johnston reported his strength in terms of "effectives." This method seemed to create distrust in Richmond and smacked of an attempt to underestimate the strength of his army. By the admission of Johnston's own aide, Colonel B. S. Ewell, it was possible to list only thirty thousand men as effective but to have sixty thousand men available to fight if needed. Too, the difference between those listed as effective and those listed as present for duty could be interpreted several different ways. In some Confederate armies, the term "effective" meant only enlisted men, while the term "present for duty" included enlisted men, officers, and all noncommissioned officers. But in Johnston's tabulation, all noncommissioned officers on field service were listed in the effective column. Still, it seemed to the government that he was underrating his force.[55]

The problem was especially acute in the cavalry. Wheeler was a notoriously poor administrator. More than once he had been chided by Bragg for producing returns that did not give full strength, and for his generosity in detaching men for sundry duties and listing them only under the aggregate column. So poor a roll keeper was Wheeler that he later frequently contradicted himself in attempting to explain how many troops he had in the campaign. After the war Wheeler maintained that he had never commanded more than 13,000 men in his corps aggregate present and absent. Yet on April 30 he had almost 19,000 aggregate present and absent. By June 10, after the accession of Jackson's division, Johnston's cavalry numbered over 27,000 men present and absent. Wheeler was vague on other figures as well. He later maintained that in early June he had had only 5,700 "fighting men." Yet Johnston's return for

[55] Ewell to Wigfall, March 1, 1865, in Wigfall Papers, DLC; General Jacob Cox wrote that "the introduction into the Southern returns of a column of 'effectives' as distinguished from the number of officers and men 'present for duty' led to a habitual underestimate by their commanding officers." Cox noted that when Johnston estimated his strength, "this necessarily led to an examination of his returns" by Richmond, with obvious contradictions present. See Jacob D. Cox, Military Reminiscences of the Civil War (New York, 1900), II, 285.

June 10 showed Wheeler with 8,476 officers and men listed as present for duty, and 6,366 listed as "effective." [56]

The result of this haphazard policy of roll-keeping was that Richmond completely distrusted Johnston's statistics. Part of the problem was faulty communication. In his letters to Davis and Bragg in May, June, and July, Johnston requested aid from Lee's cavalry, but he never specified exactly what his own strength was. Later, in February of 1865, he claimed to Wigfall that he had only four thousand available cavalry when the campaign began, and about eight thousand after he was reinforced by Polk. Wigfall used these figures in a March speech on the Senate floor in which he attacked Davis for allowing Johnston to confront Sherman with such weak cavalry.[57]

But from Johnston, Richmond received a different version. Although he never specified his exact number, his rolls forwarded to Richmond showed a far greater number. Thus Richmond believed, and probably accurately, that Johnston had more cavalry than he and historians later claimed. By June 10 Johnston had eleven cavalry brigades. Though he listed only 10,903 men as "effective," Johnston listed 13,446 officers and men as present for duty, and 12,328 enlisted men as present for duty. In addition to the 12,328 enlisted men, Johnston notified Richmond that an additional 4,207 were present with the army but not listed as either effective or present for duty. Also, by June 10, the total cavalry strength, present and absent, was more than 27,000 men. By July 10 this figure had not decreased. Johnston still reported over 10,000 effective cavalry, and over 12,000 present for duty.[58]

In short, Johnston and later historians exaggerated his cavalry shortages. He subsequently made much of the disparity of troopers when the campaign at Dalton began, by listing only 2,392 effective cavalry. Johnston was not even clear on this number, since in 1865 he revised it to 4,000 cavalry. His Dalton figures are misleading. Several of his divisions were at the rear obtaining horses, and joined Johnston north of the Etowah River. Polk's cavalry division also joined the army between the Oostanaula and the Etowah. Thus, Richmond quarrelled with his statistics. Bragg, on June 29, pointed out to Davis that Johnston was listing over 12,000 cavalry as present for duty. In subsequent letters to Johnston and Governor Joseph Brown, Davis hit at the same theme—that

[56] Wheeler to Hood, March 21, April 18, 1874, in Hood Papers, National Archives; *Official Records*, XXXVIII, Pt. 3, pp. 676–77.

[57] Johnston to Wigfall, February 26, 1865, in Wigfall Papers, DLC; Johnston, *Narrative*, 590–91.

[58] *Official Records*, XXXVIII, Pt. 3, pp. 677, 679.

Johnston was no more outnumbered than any other army, and should use his own cavalry.[59]

While Richmond bears the main blame for not sending outside help from Lee or from East Tennessee, Johnston also is to blame for not breaking Sherman's communications. For one who later claimed repeatedly that his strategy was based on such railroad destruction, Johnston seemed relatively passive about implementing it. During the long winter and spring at Dalton, he took no steps to forestall a build-up of food at the vast Chattanooga depots, and scarcely mentioned the need for a cavalry strike. Also during the spring, Johnston may have bypassed an opportunity to destroy the Nashville supply installations.[60]

After the Dalton campaign began, Johnston still did little to attempt to break Sherman's communications. By the time he crossed the Oostanaula and maneuvered southward toward Cassville, the accession of Jackson's division from Polk and the return of Martin's division gave him a good opportunity. Only one time between Dalton and the Chattahoochee did Johnston even make a partial move to strike Sherman's communications. In his memoirs Johnston maintained that after crossing the Etowah, he ordered Wheeler back across on May 22 "to inflict harm upon the enemy, by breaking the railroad, and capturing or destroying trains and detachments." [61] But this is not exactly why Wheeler was sent. According to Wheeler, he was ordered, on May 23, "to ascertain the strength, location and movements of the enemy." [62] Later, on midnight of May 24, he was given orders by Johnston to reconnoiter the enemy's position in the Cassville area. Only coincidentally did Wheeler learn that night that a large Federal wagon train was on the railroad at Cassville. Though the train was destroyed, this was small compensation for the failure to break the rail line. The effort was particularly wasted since Johnston by May 22 had intelligence that Sherman was already on short rations. He left Ringgold and Cleveland with only twenty days' supply.[63]

Yet, even when hope that any outside aid would be sent seemed futile, Johnston still refused to send any of his cavalry against the railroad.

59 Bragg to Davis, June 29, 1864, in Johnston Papers, William and Mary; Army of Tennessee returns, May 7, 1864, *ibid.;* Johnston to Wigfall, February 26, 1865, in Wigfall Papers, DLC.

60 *Official Records,* XXXVIII, Pt. 4, pp. 802–803, XXXII, Pt. 3, pp. 620, 668, LII, Pt. 2, p. 651; James Sherwood to Morgan, June 6, 1864, in Morgan Papers, UNC; Saunders to Sale, July 5, 1864, Davis to Sale, July 22, 1864, in Davis Papers, Tulane.

61 Johnston, *Narrative,* 325–26.

62 *Official Records,* XXXVIII, Pt. 3, p. 947. That Wheeler's mission was mainly one of reconnaissance is further evidenced by the journal of one of Johnston's staff. See Mackall Journal May 22, 23, 1864, *ibid.,* pp. 985–86.

63 Sherman, *Memoirs,* II, 36, 42.

Such was the situation by June 27. That day Johnston received notification from Davis that since the "draft upon the Dept. of Ala. Miss. & E. La have already been too great," Johnston "may not count on aid from General Lee." [64] Yet, that Johnston went blindly on with a strategy keyed to massive breakage of Sherman's railroad was very clearly demonstrated in his July 1 conversation with Hill. He admitted that the holding of the defenses below the Chattahoochee depended on assistance which only four days earlier Davis had said he would not get. With the situation growing desperate by late June, it appeared the general had little alternative but to commit his own cavalry against the railroad. Instead, Johnston would not budge, but chose his old course of merely debating the matter with the government.

As Johnston neared the Chattahoochee, Richmond refused to believe that Johnston's army was insufficient to stop Sherman's progress. Exactly how many men Johnston had lost by the first of July is uncertain. Later, Hood claimed that Johnston lost twenty-five thousand troops between Dalton and the time of his removal. After the war, Hood obtained affidavits from staff members who recalled that Major Kinloch Falconer, assistant adjutant general under both Johnston and Hood, made such a statement.

While Hood's testimony was colored by ulterior motives, there is no doubt that Johnston had lost heavily. By July 9 his medical director, Dr. A. J. Foard, listed 9,972 infantry killed or wounded. This figure included no cavalry, nor did it include Tyler's brigade of Bate's division, any captured, deserters, or stragglers. Johnston later played down the number of those captured and deserting. He claimed that only a company of Hardee's skirmishers, some 200 of Hood's men, and a few others had been captured. In his March, 1865, Senate speech, Wigfall, supplied with Johnston's figures, estimated that the total of prisoners, stragglers, and deserters was only 2,468 men. This figure is probably much too low, since Hardee estimated the number of captured and deserters in his corps alone as 1,737. A semiofficial estimate of Johnston's losses by June 30 was prepared by his adjutant-general, Colonel B. S. Ewell. In a memo, Ewell estimated Johnston's losses to date as approximately 15,000. But Ewell's figure is grossly low, since he claimed this figure included these listed as sick. Johnston in 1865 also claimed a figure approximating Ewell's, and estimated his total sick and deserters as 4,728. Actually, Confederate hospital records indicate that by July 1, Johnston's hospitals were recording 15,241 cases of illness as being held over from June. Of these, 11,437 troops were listed as patients ill but not from battle

64 Cooper to Johnston, June 23, 1864, with notation by Davis, in Johnston Papers, Tulane. Johnston did not receive this letter until June 27.

wounds. This figure does not include those cases listed in the July 1–August 1 returns, of which a sizable number of the 24,384 cases were non-wound illnesses and were admitted during the seventeen days of July when Johnston commanded. In short, if cases of illness are counted, even Hood's original figure of 25,000 was probably too low.[65]

The argument over Johnston's number of casualties was indicative of the total confusion which had evolved by late June.

The usage of the terms "effective" as opposed to "present for duty" and "aggregate present" was convenient for both Johnston's friends and critics. The terminology could easily be manipulated to prove that Johnston either had enough men or was weak.

Richmond officials could hardly be blamed for their dubious attitude, since Johnston's roll-keeping was confusing. On June 10 he reported 50,053 effective infantry and artillery, but reported 55,745 infantry and artillery present for duty and an aggregate present of 65,176. Johnston never explained the 15,000-man difference between those he listed as effective and those as aggregate, nor the 5,000 difference between effectives and those present for duty. By June 30 matters were still confused. Johnston's effective total for infantry and artillery had slipped to only 44,476 while his total present was 59,942. By July 10 Johnston listed only 40,850 effective infantry and artillery, but 56,694 total present.[66]

Confusing also was the superabundance of cavalry evidently listed as present with the army but not fit for duty. Cavalry losses had been extremely light; Wheeler, by June 1, had lost only 550 men from all causes. With the cavalry's problem of finding horses, Wheeler, by June 30, obviously had a great many dismounted men who could have been used as infantrymen. On June 30, Johnston's cavalry listed only 10,409 as effective, yet listed another 7,000 as being with the army.[67]

Another key issue confused the government. Johnston was evidently playing both sides of the statistical game. He insisted that Sherman had overwhelming numbers and stated this in key telegrams to the govern-

[65] James O. Breeden, "A Medical History of the Later Stages of the Atlanta Campaign," *Journal of Southern History*, XXXV (February, 1969), 54–55. See also Johnston to Wigfall, February 26, 1865, in Wigfall Papers, DLC; A. J. Foard to Hood, April 1, 1866, in Hood Papers, National Archives; Affadavit of Eth. B. Wade, November 18, 1865, Affadavit of John S. Smith, June 22, 1865, in Davis Papers, Tulane; *Official Records*, XXXIX, Pt. 2, p. 829, XXXVIII, Pt. 3, p. 687; Field return of Hardee's corps in Campaign from Dalton, 8 May to 14 July (MS in Bragg Papers, Western Reserve); Returns of Hardee's corps, in Miscellaneous Field Returns, Duke; Johnston, *Narrative*, 354, 592; B. S. Ewell, "Campaigns in Virginia and Georgia in the Spring and Summer of '64 Compared, June 30, 1864" (MS in Johnston Papers, William and Mary).

[66] *Official Records*, XXXVIII, Pt. 3, pp. 677–79.

[67] Johnston to Bragg, June 27, 1864, in Johnston Papers, Historical Society of Pennsylvania; *Official Records*, XXXVIII, Pt. 3, pp. 678, 949.

ment on July 8 and July 16. Yet when Johnston needed to prove the opposite position, he argued differently. In his Marietta conversations with Wigfall and Hill, he argued that his strategy was working because Federal losses were so heavy that Sherman could not take Atlanta after crossing the Chattahoochee.

Thus, to the government Johnston gave a contradictory story. On June 27 he estimated to Bragg that Sherman had lost approximately 27,000 men. In that same note he assured Bragg that he did not believe Sherman had received any other reinforcements except a division of some 5,000 to 7,000 men and some bridge guards. The version which Hill carried to Richmond was basically the same. Sherman had lost between 25,000 and 30,000 men. His original force at Dalton had consisted of 93,000 troops. Yet, if Sherman had possessed that number at Dalton, had received only 7,000 reinforcements, and had lost 25,000 men, his total force by the end of June would be only 75,000 men. In the meantime, Johnston by June 30 was reporting his own army had 49,858 infantry and artillery present for duty, not including some 12,889 cavalry and 3,000 state troops. Yet Johnston on July 16 argued to Davis that he could not take the offensive because Sherman outnumbered him two to one.[68]

It was apparent by late June that the government simply did not believe that in comparison to Sherman's, Johnston's force was as weak as he insisted. Bragg, on June 29, reported to Davis that "every available man" had been sent to Johnston, and that the difference between Johnston's and Sherman's armies "is much less than it has ever been between those two armies." [69] The government's attitude was summed up in a later report sent by Bragg to Davis when he visited Johnston in mid-July. Bragg had accepted Johnston's version of Sherman's heavy losses and had added that Sherman's force "has always been overestimated." [70] Bragg contended that Sherman only had 75,000 men, of whom only 60,000 were infantry. Johnston deliberately gave heavy estimates of Federal losses, in order to prove his strategic success. At the same time, he gave heavy estimates of Federal strength to prove his need for more men. This double standard, coupled with the general confusion of his roll-keeping, greatly hurt his credibility in Richmond.[71]

68 *Official Records,* XXXVIII, Pt. 3, p. 678; Hill to Seddon, July 14, 1864, in Johnston Papers, William and Mary; Johnston to Davis, July 8, 16, 1864, in Johnston Dispatch Book, William and Mary; Johnston to Bragg, June 27, 1864, in Johnston Papers, Pennsylvania.

69 Bragg to Davis, June 29, 1864, in Johnston Papers, William and Mary.

70 *Official Records,* XXXIX, Pt. 2, p. 713.

71 *Ibid.* Sherman on June 30 listed over 88,000 infantry as effective, over 18,000 cavalry and almost 6,000 artillery. His total effective strength on June 30 was 106,070 men. See *ibid.,* XXXVIII, Pt. 1, pp. 116–17.

fourteen

The Removal

During the early days of July, a final impasse between Johnston and the government wrecked the army with an unexpected swiftness. On July 2, the day after Johnston assured Senator Ben Hill that he could hold Sherman north of the Chattahoochee for at least a month, the army began a fifteen-mile retreat toward the river. Within a week Johnston abandoned the north bank and fell back into the Atlanta defenses. There, on July 17, he was removed by the government.

Within those fifteen days the worst command crisis since Chickamauga occurred. Later, Johnston and his admirers broadcast the enduring charge that he was removed when the army was on the brink of victory, poised to smash Sherman crossing Peachtree Creek. The removal was characterized to be one last act in Davis' long persecution of the general, an act bordering on sheer madness. With his peculiar ability to emerge as the champion of the might-have-been situation, Johnston proved victorious in the post-campaign historiography.

By the end of June, the many disagreements between the general and Richmond had narrowed to one key issue—what did Johnston intend to do? Neither Johnston's actions nor his messages to the government gave much indication that he had the situation under control or that he would fight for Atlanta. Despite the general's post-campaign avowals that he had had a plan of action ready, his unsureness had become evident by July 5. It had rained for days in the red clay country around Kennesaw Mountain, and the oozing, muddy roads had prevented Sherman from advancing farther. Then, on July 1, the rains ceased, the weather became excessively hot, and the roads began to dry. Immediately Johnston's

391

scouts noted that the Federals appeared to be moving around Johnston's left flank, reaching for the crossings of the Chattahoochee below the main pike to Atlanta. Thus, Johnston on the night of July 2 abandoned the Kennesaw fortifications and skillfully fell back eight miles to temporary entrenchments prepared at Smyrna Station. Johnston ordered forward the three thousand Georgia militiamen under the command of General G. W. Smith to extend his left, and even placed Jackson's cavalry division in the entrenchments. Still, there were not enough men to extend the line across the parallel road from Marietta to Atlanta via the crossing at Green and Howell's Ferry. On July 4, when Sherman again began to flank the left, Johnston ordered a retreat into Shoup's fortifications on the north bank of the Chattahoochee. By the morning of July 5, Sherman had accomplished in three days what Johnston had estimated to Hill it would require a month to do.[1]

From July 5 until July 14, Johnston indicated indecision as to what to do, and confusion as to Sherman's whereabouts. He made a series of major command errors which suggest that he did not have his army under control. His first error was in losing track of Sherman's army on the north bank. From July 5 until July 9, when he fell back across the river, Johnston did not take adequate precautions to anticipate or to prevent a crossing upstream above his six railroad, pike, and pontoon bridges grouped at the crossing of the Western and Atlantic Railroad and the Atlanta Pike. Johnston admitted that he knew this was the most vulnerable point. The Chattahoochee, always swift and deep, was swollen by incessant rain until fords were at a premium. Johnston knew that there were no available fording points below the railroad bridge, whereas there were several above it.[2]

Yet Johnston expected a crossing below the bridges, since twice within three days Sherman had driven against that flank. Even before his left was threatened, Johnston had paid more attention to the downstream crossings. While at Marietta, he had ordered Shoup to extend the entrenchments he was preparing on the north bank in order to cover Mason and Turner's Ferry, the crossing of one of the parallel roads from Marietta to Atlanta downstream from the main pike bridges. Later, Johnston sent a staff officer, Major William Clare, to prepare a detailed description of all potential crossings on that section of the river twelve miles downstream from Mason and Turner's Ferry. Clare's report, sent

---

[1] Jacob Cox Diary, June 18–21, July 2, 1864, Kennesaw; James Connolly to wife, June 26, 1864, in *Three Years in the Army of the Cumberland*, 227; *Official Records*, XXXVIII, Pt. 3, pp. 970, 617.

[2] Johnston, *Narrative*, 350; Campbell Journal, July 15, 19, 1864 (typescript in Kennesaw).

on July 4, was not comforting. He warned of seven potential crossings, with the best approaches and the choicest ground for artillery positions on the north bank. Some of the crossings seemed a direct threat to both Atlanta and the railroad junction at East Point. Green and Howell's Ferry lay on a good road formed by the convergence north of the river of routes from Powder Springs and Marietta. South of the ferry, the road ran through Lick Skillet and struck the railroad on the west side of Atlanta. Farther downstream at Wilson and Baker's Ferry, a road crossed which had branched on the north bank from that road leading to Green and Howell's Ferry, and rejoined the road at Lick Skillet. Still further downstream, crossings at Sandtown Ferry and Adaholt's Ferry offered a route to strike the railroad either at East Point or between that junction and Atlanta. Then, twelve miles below Mason and Turner's Ferry, Gorman's Ferry offered routes through Campbellton to reach the West Point railroad far southwest of the rail junction at East Point.

Convinced that Sherman would move on this front, Johnston overlooked the upstream crossings. On July 5 he sent his cavalry south of the river to observe the crossings both upstream and downstream from the pike bridges. But the bulk of the troopers was sent to guard the downstream crossings. Wheeler was allotted only two of his own divisions to cover a front of nearly thirty miles upstream beyond Roswell and bending back toward the Augusta Railroad. These crossings seemed most vulnerable for two key reasons. Sherman would be much closer to his rail communications if he crossed above Johnston's fortifications on the north bank. The Chattahoochee fortifications extended only about a mile upstream from the railroad bridges, ending near Howell's Ferry. Two miles above this ferry, a key road from the railroad at Vining's Station crossed the river at Pace's Ferry. A crossing here could use the Pace's Ferry Road to cross Peachtree Creek and strike the railroad between the river and Atlanta, or could move east to Buckhead, on the north bank of Peachtree Creek and only about five miles north of Atlanta. Farther upstream, a key road from Marietta to Atlanta, via Buckhead, crossed at Power's Ferry. About two miles farther upstream, another road from Marietta via Buckhead crossed at Isham's or Cavalry Ford. Almost three miles farther north, a crossing at Power's Ferry connected with the main road leading south from Roswell through Buckhead to Atlanta. This road also was reached some two miles farther north at Philipp's Ferry, at the mouth of Soap Creek. At Roswell, twenty miles north of Atlanta, a bridge and a shallow ford provided access to the direct road south of the river to Atlanta. East of the town, there were other crossings giving access to Buckhead and to the Georgia Railroad between Atlanta and Augusta.

These crossings were the most vulnerable. Sherman's consistent strategy had been to abandon the railroad to force Johnston back, and then to return to it to secure his line of supply. The upstream crossings above Howell's Ferry lay dangerously close to the railroad as it passed through Marietta, Smyrna Station, and Vining's Station. To flank Johnston in this direction would require far less marching from the Federal supply line. The nearest crossing north of Johnston's fortifications, Pace's Ferry, was one mile from the railroad at Vining's Station. Yet the nearest crossing southwest of the terminus of Johnston's line, Green and Howell's Ferry, required a fourteen-mile march across Johnston's entire front. Too, there were fords available north of the fortifications, at Isham's Ford and near Roswell. Also, once across the Chattahoochee, Sherman would have a safer march if he crossed upstream. The long, deep Peachtree Creek flowed in a westward course north of Atlanta, and emptied into the river only slightly upstream from the Western and Atlantic Bridge. Thus, Johnston was somewhat separated from these crossings.[3]

Between July 5 and July 9 the crossings remained vulnerable. Wheeler was hampered by orders to detach one of his two available divisions, that of General John Kelly, to pay special attention to protecting the railroad to Augusta. Wheeler was further deterred by orders from Johnston on July 6 to concentrate his observations on the river to the small area northward from the railroad bridge to Pace's Ferry. The result was that the critical crossings at Power's Ferry, Isham's Ford, Johnson's Ferry, Philipp's Ferry, and the shallow ford at Roswell, all within easy striking distance from Vining's Station, were practically unguarded save for scouting parties.[4]

Johnston thus lost control of the river and in so doing, lost Sherman's army. As early as July 5 the Federals appeared in force northeast of Shoup's defensive line. They demonstrated heavily that day against Pace's Ferry, as well as downstream below the railroad bridge. On July 6 the Federals appeared in force in front of Power's, Philipp's, and Johnson's ferries.[5]

Johnston's lethargic response proved disastrous. No reinforcements were sent to Wheeler's weak river defenses. Instead, on July 7, Johnston's chief of staff, Mackall, confided that it was expected that Sherman would "be quiet" for some days yet. Within twenty-four hours, however, Sherman had gained several key crossings. By the night of July 8 Johnston had information that a contingent of Sherman's army had already crossed at Isham's Ford. Other disturbing news was received on the morning of

---

3 *Official Records*, XXXVIII, Pt. 3, pp. 617, 951; Sherman, *Memoirs*, II, 66–69.
4 *Official Records*, XXXVIII, Pt. 3, p. 951, Pt. 5, p. 967.
5 *Ibid.*, Pt. 5, pp. 863, 865–67; J. H. Kelley to Major Burford, July 5, 1864, in Wheeler Papers, Alabama; Sherman, *Memoirs*, II, 66–69.

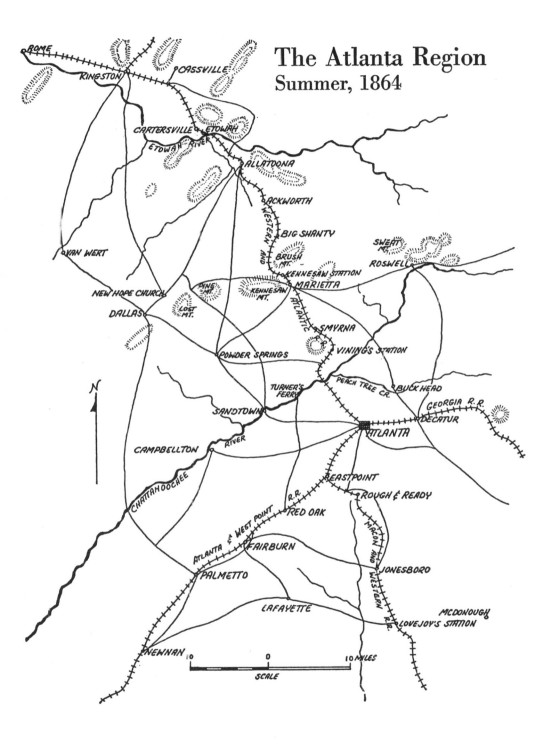

The Atlanta Region
Summer, 1864

ROME
RINGSTON
CASSVILLE
CARTERSVILLE · ETOWAH
ETOWAH RIVER
ALLATOONA
ACKWORTH
BIG SHANTY
BRUSH MT.
SWEAT MT.
ROSWELL
KENNESAW STATION
VAN WERT
PINE MT.
KENNESAW MT.
MARIETTA
NEW HOPE CHURCH
LOST MT.
DALLAS
SMYRNA
WESTERN AND ATLANTIC R.R.
POWDER SPRINGS
VINING'S STATION
N
TURNER'S FERRY
PEACH TREE CR.
BUCK HEAD
GEORGIA R.R.
SANDTOWN
DECATUR
ATLANTA
CAMPBELLTON
RIVER
CHATTAHOOCHEE
EASTPOINT
ROUGH & READY
R.R.
RED OAK
ATLANTA & WEST POINT
FAIRBURN
MACON AND WESTERN R.R.
JONESBORO
PALMETTO
LAFAYETTE
MCDONOUGH
LOVEJOY'S STATION
NEWNAN 10   0   10 MILES
SCALE

July 9. A strong force had seized Philipp's Ferry, taken without the loss of a Federal soldier. Thoughtfully, the Confederates had left a ferry boat on the opposite bank. At one nearby crossing, Cochran's Ford, the position was taken by a detachment of naked Union cavalry who swam the creek wearing only hats and cartridge boxes. The important shallow ford at Roswell was also taken.[6]

The Confederate response to these unexpected maneuvers was a confusion at Johnston's headquarters which was reminiscent of the May situation at Cassville. At Marietta, Johnston had led Shoup to believe that the purpose of the Chattahoochee fortifications was to deal with such a situation as this. Shoup had devised the entrenchments in a nonconventional manner. Not mere lines of breastworks, they were composed of a series of log redoubts packed with earth, joined by a log abatis. Shoup's idea had been that such a line could be held by as small a force as a division, thus allowing the Confederates either to strike Sherman as he attempted to cross the river, or to detach part of the infantry to the south bank and isolate any force which was crossing. With the news that part of Sherman's army was crossing, Johnston seemed to have an excellent chance to catch Union forces divided by a rain-swollen river. With six good bridges at his rear, Johnston could hold the interior line of communication.[7]

But Johnston wavered as to what he should do. Later, in his official report, he argued that he had ordered the army to withdraw to the south bank on the night of July 9 because of news that two corps had crossed above Power's Ferry. Even if two corps had crossed, the situation appeared better than ever for an ambush. Actually, Johnston's version had the advantage of hindsight. He did not know on July 9 what force had crossed, nor exactly where the crossings were being made. Johnston even contradicted himself, for on July 10, in his report to Richmond, he stated he had retreated because the two corps had crossed at Isham's Ford. Yet his own intelligence on the night of July 8 reported that only two brigades had crossed there. The following day Johnston admitted that he did not know how many troops had crossed. The scout reports from Isham's Ford, as well as from other areas, did not give any indication that two corps had crossed. Johnston's own chief of staff commented on

---

6 J. H. Kelley to "Major," July 5, 1864, in Wheeler Papers, Alabama; *Official Records*, XXXVIII, Pt. 5, pp. 869–72, Pt. 2, pp. 760–61; Mackall to wife, July 7, 1864, in Mackall, *Recollections*, 218; "Journal of the Atlanta Campaign, kept at headquarters of the Fourth Army Corps, by Lieut. Col. Joseph S. Fullerton, Assistant Adjutant General," in *Official Records*, XXXVIII, Pt. 1, pp. 893–96.

7 Shoup, "Dalton Campaign–Works at Chattahoochee River," 263.

July 9 that it was not known whether the enemy had crossed "in earnest or to see if they could plague us." [8]

The real reason Johnston crossed was because he was losing control of the army. There were many disturbing signs of this. On July 8 Johnston had called a council to discuss what should be done. Hardee had favored using Shoup's fortifications; Hood disliked the idea of fighting on the north bank and urged that the entire army should be withdrawn across the river. Shoup demurred and reminded Johnston of their Marietta discussion which had centered on detaching part of the army to the south bank to deal with such a crossing. At first, Johnston seemed to favor Shoup's idea, but on the next evening he ordered the entire army withdrawn to the south side of the Chattahoochee.[9]

That Johnston was losing control of the situation was more evident by his conduct on the south bank. Curiously, he gave Sherman an entire week to cross his army and concentrate, if he so desired. Johnston still maintained the bulk of his river guards downstream, and not in the area where the crossings were reported. Some brigades were sent on July 9 to aid Jackson's cavalry in covering the downstream fords, but Wheeler was forced to use his same thin force to observe those fords and ferries upstream from the railroad. Meanwhile, Johnston sent strong infantry brigades as far south as Green and Howell's Ferry to the area where Sherman was not even crossing. The bulk of the infantry was withdrawn some three miles from the river to an elevation overlooking Peachtree Creek; there they sat while Sherman crossed the river.[10]

Here Johnston lost probably the greatest opportunity of the campaign. For seven days after he crossed the Chattahoochee, Johnston knew that Sherman's forces were badly divided. By July 14 intelligence reports indicated that three of Sherman's corps were isolated on the south bank. Dodge's corps was reported to have crossed and halted at the ford at Roswell; Schofield and Howard were reported halfway between Roswell and the railroad, at Isham's Ford and Power's Ferry. On the following day, the situation became even more advantageous. Wheeler reported that a corps, believed to be Schofield's had advanced some three to four miles eastward from Isham's Ford and had entrenched. By July 16, the opportunity still existed for a strike against a badly divided Federal army. Sherman was reported still to be in corps strength as far south as Wilson and Baker's Ferry, six miles below the Western and Atlantic Railroad

---

[8] *Official Records*, XXXVIII, Pt. 3, p. 618, Pt. 5, pp. 869–73; Mackall to wife, July 9, 1864, in Mackall, *Recollections*, 218.

[9] Shoup, "Dalton Campaign—Works at Chattahoochee River," 264; Mackall to Wheeler, July 9, 1864, in Wheeler Papers, Alabama.

[10] Mackall to Wheeler, July 9—7:15 P.M., 1864, in Wheeler Papers, Alabama.

bridge. As early as July 14, Johnston had known that Sherman's army still held the north bank this far southwest. Thus, the Federals on both sides of the river were scattered over a front from Baker's Ferry twenty miles to Roswell. Too, by the night of July 16, Johnston knew that his opportunity was slipping away, as intelligence reported that that part of Sherman's army still on the opposite bank was moving northward toward the crossing points north of the Western and Atlantic Railroad bridge.[11]

Why did Johnston not attack? His explanations often seemed contradictory. In his official report, he claimed he did not contest the fords north of Peachtree Creek because of the broad channel of the creek, which would have divided his army. In order to smash the isolated corps, however, Johnston could have thrown his entire army north of the creek to avoid being divided. This hazard was no less than that Sherman faced—being divided by the much larger, rain-swollen Chattahoochee. On July 16, in a telegram to Davis noting the isolated condition of the force crossing at Isham's Ford, Johnston explained that since Sherman had twice his numbers, "we must be on the defensive." [12]

This brief explanation contradicts what later became Johnston's basic excuse. In his official report, and later in his memoirs, he contended that he planned to take the offensive. Johnston elaborated the basic Peachtree Creek strategy which became the touchstone for damning the government for relieving him of his command. Johnston's three corps were to occupy the high ground north of the Atlanta defenses, overlooking Peachtree

11 Johnston to Cooper, July 14, 1864, Johnston to Davis, July 16, 1864, in Johnston Dispatch Book, William and Mary; *Official Records*, XXXVIII, Pt. 5, p. 881. Johnston did not know the perilous state of Sherman's command. By July 14 Sherman was badly divided. Between July 8 and 13 Schofield's Army of the Ohio (23rd Corps) was crossing at Philipp's Ferry. By July 14, Schofield's four divisions were a mile in the advance of the ferry. General James McPherson's Army of the Tennessee was also divided. By July 12, General Grenville Dodge's corps had crossed at Roswell, but it was not joined on the east bank by General John Logan's corps until July 15. General Frank Blair's corps did not cross the river at Roswell until the morning of July 17. Meanwhile, General George Thomas' Army of the Cumberland was also divided. General Oliver Otis Howard's corps crossed at Power's Ferry on July 12 and united with Schofield's army. General John Palmer's corps did not cross at Pace's Ferry until July 17, followed by Hooker's corps. Thus, as late as July 14, there were only three Federal corps on the east bank—Schofield's, Dodge's, and Howard's. As late as the morning of July 17, there were only four Federal corps on the east bank, with the addition of Logan's corps to the three which had crossed previously. Sherman thus was left with three corps on the north bank. Sherman had decided to cross upstream both because of the weakness of the Confederate defenses on the upper crossings, and because he desired to make a circuit of the town and destroy its railroad connections before investing it. Sherman had expected "every possible resistance" to crossing the river. (Sherman, *Memoirs*, II, 68–69) .

12 Johnston to Davis, July 16, 1864, in Johnston Dispatch Book, William and Mary; *Official Records*, XXXVIII, Pt. 3, p. 618.

Creek. When Sherman began to cross the creek, Johnston was to attack him in detail. If the Confederate attack failed, Johnston was to retreat within that segment of the Atlanta fortifications on the north side of town. He was to hold these in siege until Governor Joseph Brown had time to mobilize the Georgia militia. Johnston claimed that on July 15, Governor Brown had told him that he could mobilize ten thousand men. Johnston planned to place the militia within the northern line of Atlanta defenses, pull back his three corps into Atlanta, and by a circuitous route attack Sherman on the flank as he approached Atlanta. If defeated, Sherman would be forced to retreat across the Chattahoochee at some point below the mouth of Peachtree Creek, which ran into the Chattahoochee near the railroad bridge. Since there were no usable fords on this segment of the river, Sherman thus would be entrapped.[13]

Whether Johnston actually would have promulgated such a battle plan is uncertain. Most of the evidence that he actually intended to commit his troops to such an endeavor was presented in retrospect, either after he was removed or after the war. A number of biographers sympathetic to the general not only asserted that such a plan was in the offing but that Johnston was relieved on the night of July 17 almost while proclaiming orders for the attack. One such account has Johnston, after learning on July 17 that the remainder of Sherman's army had crossed the Chattahoochee, snapping out orders for Stewart to prepare for the attack. Another version portrays Johnston as a near prophet, knowing not only that Sherman would divide his forces and send only a segment across Peachtree Creek, but that the particular units to be sent across would be General George Thomas' Army of the Cumberland. Still another claims that the details of Johnston's plan, as he later elaborated it in his official report, were well known throughout the army on July 17. Senator Louis Wigfall's Senate speech in March of 1865 denounced the removal and depicted Johnston as having his sword figuratively torn from his grasp while on the verge of crushing Sherman. Wigfall, of course, had received much of his information from Johnston himself. Johnston, in both his battle report and postwar reminiscences, strongly maintained that such a plan was in preparation.[14]

13 *Official Records*, Pt. 3, p. 618; Johnston, *Narrative*, 350–51; Johnston, "Opposing Sherman's Advance to Atlanta," 275–76.

14 Guild, *Fourth Tennessee*, 66; Johnston, *Johnston*, 267–68; Schofield, *Forty-Six Years in the Army*, 153; Du Bose, *Wheeler*, 357–58; Mackall, *Recollections*, 220; Joseph M. Brown, *The Great Retreat: Could Johnston Have Defended Atlanta Successfully . . . A Review of His Plan of Campaign* (Atlanta, n.d), 4, 13; Mrs. Burton Harrison, *Recollections Grave and Gay* (New York, 1911), 192; Johnston, *Narrative*, 598, 601, 350–51; Johnston, "Opposing Sherman's Advance to Atlanta," 275–76; *Official Records*, XXXVIII, Pt. 3, pp. 618, 620.

No solid evidence can be found that Johnston was preparing to execute any master plan when relieved on the night of July 17. When President Davis inquired on July 16 as to the details of Johnston's plans for holding Atlanta, Johnston replied not only that he must remain on the defensive but that his plan "must therefore, depend upon that of the enemy." Johnston described his plan as "mainly to watch for an opportunity to fight to advantage." Early on July 18, after learning that Johnston had been relieved, his three infantry corps leaders, Hood, Hardee, and Stewart, telegraphed Davis requesting that he temporarily delay the decision to remove Johnston from command. Some historians have misquoted the generals. They did not ask Davis to delay the removal in order to give Johnston time to attack. Nothing was mentioned of *any* plan by the Confederates to attack. Instead, because the enemy was "now in our immediate front, and making, as we suppose, a general advance," the three generals deemed it dangerous to change commanders.[15]

While Johnston may have had a general idea of striking Sherman, there were many factors which indicated his plans were not as formalized as he made them appear. Essential to his plan was the calling out of the Georgia Reserve Militia. In his official report Johnston maintained that on July 15 Governor Brown had informed him "orally" that he intended to call out the ten thousand troops Johnston planned to use to man the Atlanta defenses. Oddly, no one else mentions such a figure. Brown notified Richmond on July 10 that he intended to call out five thousand "old men and boys" for the emergency if the government could arm them. Brown did not even promise this many, but stated, "I will try to furnish that number." [16] General G. W. Smith, who commanded the state forces, considered Johnston's plan unrealistic and the figures inflated. Smith asserted that by July 18 there were still only two thousand effective militiamen in the Atlanta trenches; all these were men who had been called out previously. Smith, who was sent to organize the alleged ten thousand, argued that he never managed to assemble more than three thousand additional effective troops, and that none of these had been sent to the front by July 18. Also, in Johnston's version, Brown promised the troops only by the end of July. How Johnston planned to stall Sherman for an additional two weeks until the supposed ten thousand were assembled, he did not explain.[17]

15 Johnston to Davis, July 16, 1864, in Johnston Dispatch Book, William and Mary; *Official Records*, LII, Pt. 2, p. 708.

16 *Official Records*, LII, Pt. 2, p. 691.

17 General G. W. Smith, commanding the state troops, considered Johnston's militia plan completely unworkable. See G. W. Smith, "The Georgia Militia About Atlanta," *Battles and Leaders*, IV, 334; see also *Official Records*, XXXVIII, Pt. 3, pp. 969–70, Pt. 5, p. 878, LII, Pt. 2, p. 691.

Also essential to Johnston's Peachtree plan was a strong line of Atlanta defenses. The circular fortifications, whose construction was begun in the spring of 1864, later excited the admiration of the Federals. They were impressed by the miles of ditches, earth parapets and headlogs, and abatis which surrounded the town. The supposed strength of these entrenchments was essential to two key Johnston arguments. They were a part of his Peachtree strategy, since he argued that in case he could not defeat Sherman crossing the creek, he would retire temporarily into the fortifications and then garrison the trenches with militia while he moved out again to fight Sherman. Too, Johnston's argument that he would not have abandoned Atlanta without a fight was based almost solely upon his description of the strength of the defenses. Johnston never flatly stated that he would not give up the town, but used a lateral argument that the city's defenses should make that evident. He cited their strength as evidence he intended to hold the town and that Atlanta could be taken neither by assault nor siege.[18]

But the Atlanta defenses were not as impregnable as Johnston later claimed. Much of the formidable earthwork construction admired by the Federals was placed there during the forty-five-day siege while Hood was in command. Hood constructed both the inner line of defenses and the extension southwest to the rail junction. When Johnston crossed the Chattahoochee, the fortifications were in no condition for use in the way he later claimed to have had in mind. After crossing the river, Johnston sent his chief of artillery, General Francis Shoup, to inspect the fortifications. Shoup was shocked at their weakness, and reported to Johnston that they consisted of "a rather poor line of rifle pits with an occasional earthwork of more pretensions." [19] Not until the army was drawn back to the high ground overlooking Peachtree Creek did Johnston move to strengthen them. In fact, Johnston was conferring with his chief engineer, Colonel Stephen Presstman, as to how they could be strengthened, when he received word on the night of July 17 that he had been removed by Davis. So poor were the fortifications that Johnston realized he did not have time to work on all weak areas simultaneously. Thus, he had given Presstman orders to hurry up the job of strengthening only that portion confronting Sherman on the north side of town. Left undone was the needed extension to East Point. General G. W. Smith, well acquainted with the defenses, termed Atlanta prior to Hood's taking command as

18 *Official Records*, XXXVIII, Pt. 3, pp. 618, 620; Johnston, *Narrative*, 350–51, 358, 363; Johnston to Wigfall, August 27, 1864, February 26, 1865, in Wigfall Papers, DLC; Johnston to Beverley Johnston, August 28, 1864, in Hughes, "War Letters," 321.

19 Shoup, "Dalton Campaign—Works at Chattahoochee River," 265.

"not strongly fortified," and denied that his militia could have defended the fortifications in the manner which Johnston later claimed he planned.[20]

Other matters indicate some contradiction between what Johnston claimed his plans were and the actual situation. During Hill's visit, Johnston did not mention his Peachtree plan but insisted that outside cavalry support was essential to stopping Sherman. Later, in his reminiscences, Johnston insisted that such cavalry aid was an essential part of his Peachtree plan. Yet almost two weeks before reaching Atlanta, Johnston had received word from Davis that no such support could be sent, a statement Davis repeated as late as July 11. Still Johnston claimed he was attempting a plan which he admitted could not have succeeded without such assistance. Too, there was a contradiction concerning his and Sherman's comparative manpower. On July 16 Johnston told Davis that Sherman outnumbered him two to one, with Sherman thus having about 116,000 troops present for duty. With such a mismatch, Johnston argued that he could only maintain the defensive at Atlanta. But in August of 1864 he argued that the very thing that would have made his Peachtree plan work was Sherman's weakened condition after he crossed the Chattahoochee. Johnston now claimed his plan was infallible because there was no possibility Sherman could invest the city. He stated that "the enemy was too weak to invest it when he crossed the river." [21] By the following November, Johnston had returned to the position cited in the July 16 letter to Davis. He explained that he could not take the offensive at Atlanta because of Sherman's overwhelming numbers; Johnston also revised his statistics and now gave Sherman almost three times his own strength. Then, in February of 1865, Johnston went back to his second position. He furnished Wigfall with statistics attempting to prove that by the time Sherman crossed the river he was too weak either to invest Atlanta or to attack it.[22]

Did Johnston actually plan to fight for Atlanta? The many contradictions involved in the Peachtree strategy indicate that he probably had

[20] Smith, "Georgia Militia About Atlanta," 334; Johnston, "Opposing Sherman's Advance to Atlanta," 274, 276; *Official Records*, XXXVIII, Pt. 3, p. 618. For Federal estimates of Atlanta's fortifications, see G. W. Nichols, *The Story of the Great March* (New York, 1865), 24–25; Henry Hitchcock, *Marching With Sherman*, ed. by M. A. DeWolfe Howe (New Haven, 1927), 55; John W. Geary to "Mary," July 29, 1864, in Letters of Brevet Major General John W. Geary, Atlanta Historical Society; *Official Records*, XXXVIII, Pt. 1, pp. 31–32.

[21] Johnston to Beverley Johnston, August 28, 1864, in Hughes, "War Letters," 321; see also Cooper to Johnston, June 23, 1864, in Johnston Papers, William and Mary, Johnston to Davis, July 16, 1864, in Johnston Dispatch Book, William and Mary; *Official Records*, XXXVIII, Pt. 5, p. 875.

[22] Johnston to Beverley Johnston, November 8, 1864, in Hughes, "War Letters," 324; Johnston to Wigfall, February 26, 1865, in Wigfall Papers, DLC.

not devised a definite battle plan. At best, Johnston had a general idea of attacking Sherman, but he badly neglected those details essential for success. Perhaps Johnston did not know what he would do. During the week he was in front of Atlanta, Johnston gave orders for all stores and ordnance machinery to be removed from the town. Although he later described this as a precautionary measure, it could have been done to lighten the logistical burden in case he lost the town. As mentioned, Johnston never flatly stated that he would not have given up Atlanta, but instead argued that the town's fortifications should have made it evident he intended to hold the town. Johnston had held several other entrenched positions, however, some of which he had considered extremely strong. He eventually surrendered these—Dalton, Resaca, Cassville, New Hope Church, Kennesaw, Smyrna Station, and Shoup's Chattahoochee line. He had made declarations of intent to give battle at other places, but he eventually revised his plans. Johnston's vacillating explanations after his removal strongly indicate he really did not know what he was going to do. In August of 1864 he declared that "there is not the slightest foundation" [23] for the charge that he would have abandoned Atlanta without a fight. Characteristically, he contradicted himself within three months. In November of 1864 he seemed less certain. He wrote his brother, "If I had been left in command of that army it is very unlikely that Atlanta would have been abandoned." [24]

As he backed toward Atlanta during his last two weeks in command, he communicated no plan to Richmond. As he neared the river, Davis nervously warned him on July 7 of the potential hazards of a further retreat, both to the army's communications with Alabama, and to the Georgia-Alabama munitions area. Although Davis remarked that he was now "more apprehensive for the future," [25] and Johnston knew of reliable reports that the government was considering removing him, the general did nothing to allay Davis' fears. His July 8 reply to Davis said nothing of any intention either to cross the Chattahoochee or to fight at Peachtree Creek, though Johnston had already issued some orders preparing for the eventuality of a retreat across the river. [26]

After crossing the river, Johnston remained uncommunicative. Other than informing Richmond of his crossing, he did not communicate with Davis until July 12. This note made no mention of any plans regarding Sherman, but solely concerned the need for assistance from outside cavalry. The previous day, Johnston had not implied any optimism when

---

23 Johnston to Beverley Johnston, August 28, 1864, in Hughes, "War Letters," 321.
24 Johnston to Beverley Johnston, November 8, 1864, in *ibid.*, p. 324.
25 Davis to Johnston, July 7, 1864, in Rowland (ed.), *Davis*, VI, 283.
26 Johnston to Davis, July 8, 1864, in Johnston Dispatch Book, William and Mary.

he sent a note to Bragg recommending that the prison compound at Anderson Station, Georgia, be broken up and the prisoners redistributed to safer places. On the twelfth, Johnston sent Bragg some information regarding the enemy's position on the south bank, but made no mention of his plan to attack Sherman crossing Peachtree Creek.[27]

Once across the Chattahoochee, he received other warnings of the government's discontent. A delegation of congressmen visiting him brought such a warning. Then on July 14 a cryptic telegram from Senator Ben Hill in Richmond informed Johnston that he must fight with his available force, and added, "For God's sake do it." [28] Finally, on July 16, Davis telegraphed Johnston asking for his future plans "so specifically as will enable me to anticipate events." [29] Johnston's reply was typical in its insensitiveness to the situation. He summarized it only in four brief sentences via telegram. He would be forced to maintain the defensive, and thus the enemy would determine his plan of operations. Generally, his plan was "to watch for an opportunity to fight to advantage." Finally came the statement which perhaps sealed the general's fate. He informed Davis that he was putting Atlanta in a condition "to be held for a day or two" by the Georgia militia, so that his own movements might be "freer and wider." [30]

His reference to placing Atlanta in the hands of the militia, coming on the heels of his Andersonville request and his removal of all munitions works and stores, could easily have left the impression that he was abandoning Atlanta. While the possible interception of a telegram might have prompted him to be discreet, Johnston could have given some indication that he had a plan. Instead, he even took the opposite approach, stating that he would remain on the defensive and wait for the enemy's move. Yet he allegedly had had for weeks a plan to fight on Peachtree Creek.[31]

The need for Johnston to be more explicit with Richmond was greater because of his past performances. Several times earlier in the campaign, Johnston had uttered almost the very words he sent to Davis on the

27 Johnston to Bragg, July 12, 1864, in *ibid.*
28 *Official Records,* XXXVIII, Pt. 5, p. 879.
29 *Ibid.,* 882.
30 Johnston to Davis, July 16, 1864, in Johnston Dispatch Book, William and Mary.
31 For evidence of rising public and army discontent in the Atlanta area, see Manning to mother, July 10, 1864, in Williams–Chesnut–Manning Papers, South Carolina; Diary of Samuel P. Richards, May 29, 1864, July 10, 1864, in Atlanta Historical Society; Mackall to wife, July 11, 1864, in Mackall, *Recollections,* 219, Mackall to wife, July 7, 1864 in *Recollections,* 218; Neal to mother, May 20, July 7, 1864, in Neal Letters, Georgia Department of Archives and History; Leonidas Mackey to "Loved ones at home," July 5, 1864, in Mackey Letters, Atlanta Historical Society; Hagan, *Confederate Letters,* 50.

sixteenth—that he was looking for a good opportunity to give battle—only to continue his retreat. Now he expected Davis to accept this terse explanation again when the key to the campaign, Atlanta, was at stake. The man and the myth were apparently to separate in July of 1864. Johnston's actual field service had been limited. His reputation was based mainly upon a series of might-have-been situations. Except for the operations on the Peninsula in the spring of 1862, Johnston had never commanded anything which resembled a genuine field army, and his lack of experience was telling.

Atlanta's importance as a political symbol in the coming northern elections of 1864 seemed unknown to him. If, as he later contended, he did realize the city's political significance, why did he not make an early fight instead of leading Sherman to the city's very gates, thus buoying morale in the North?

The process by which Davis and his cabinet concluded that Johnston would not defend Atlanta and his ensuing removal present difficult historiographical questions due to the abundance of conflicting testimony. And Hood's subsequent failure to hold Atlanta magnified the government's appearance of error in relieving Johnston when they did.

Scarcely had he been removed from his command when his partisans accused Davis of fostering a long, deliberate plot against the general. On July 22 a North Carolina politician, Kenneth Rayner, claimed that the removal resulted from Davis' "long-cherished prejudice." [32] The previous day the editor of the anti-administration Richmond *Whig* attributed Johnston's removal to 'a cold snaky hate," [33] while the Richmond *Examiner* commented that for some time prior to the removal "the wretched supplejacks of the Government have been busy in blackening him." [34] On the day after the battle a correspondent of the Savannah *Republican* accused the government of failing to support Johnston in the campaign.[35] That same day another correspondent writing from Atlanta termed the removal an act of "Davis' personal hostility." [36] Johnston himself in August of 1864 asserted that he had been victimized by a Davis plot against him. In the spring of 1865 his friend Senator Louis Wigfall

[32] Kenneth Rayner to Thomas Ruffin, July 22, 1864, quoted in Thomas R. Hay, "The Davis–Hood–Johnston Controversy of 1864," *Mississippi Valley Historical Review*, XI (June, 1924) , 78n.

[33] Richmond *Whig*, July 21, 1864, quoted in Govan and Livingood, *A Different Valor*, 326.

[34] Richmond *Examiner*, July 19, 1864, quoted in Eliot, *West Point in the Confederacy*, 107.

[35] "Special Correspondent of Savannah *Republican*, behind Chattahoochee, July 18, 1864," clipping in Confederate scrapbook, Joseph Jones Papers, Louisiana State Department of Archives and History.

[36] "War correspondent Grape, from Atlanta, July 18, 1864," clipping in *ibid*.

resounded on the Senate floor that the removal was caused by the President's effort "to destroy Johnston." [37]

Davis' attitude has probably been badly misinterpreted. The insinuations of Johnston partisans that the President had deliberately held back support hoping that Johnston would fail seem puerile. So, too, are the insinuations that Davis knowingly jeopardized the fate of Atlanta by removing Johnston. Davis was too obsessed with the preservation of territory, particularly the vital munitions area, to allow a personal hatred to intervene. It had been this same obsession with territorial defense, and not a personal plot, which had motivated him to hold back reinforcements from Bragg in 1862 and 1863.

If Davis had wanted to remove Johnston, he could have done so long before the general reached Atlanta. Since Johnston had been expected to fight north of both the Oostanaula and the Etowah, Davis could have removed him then for his failure to fight. On earlier occasions Davis had removed officers for much less. Beauregard, in 1862, had been relieved on the mere technicality that he had deserted his command at Tupelo without authority when he was convalescing on a sick leave in Alabama. Davis had acquiesced to the removal of Harvey Hill as Bragg's corps commander on the grounds that he had exhibited a lack of confidence in his commander.

Too, the removal and replacement of a commanding general was no minor matter. By 1864 the South was running out of full generals. Davis had selected Johnston in December of 1863 because there seemed to be no other choice. The situation was no better in July, 1864. Robert E. Lee had already declined the command on various occasions. Kirby Smith was now commanding the Trans-Mississippi department. Beauregard's South Carolina–Georgia department had been stripped of its troops and had been sent to Lee's Virginia front, along with its commander. Bragg, now nominal general in chief of Confederate armies, had left the western army in a cloud of public criticism. Who was left among the lieutenant generals? Longstreet's miserable performance in Tennessee in 1863 had probably doomed his chances for future independent commands. Hardee in December had already indicated that he did not desire permanent command of the army. Polk was dead, and his successor, General A. P. Stewart, was a novice in high command. The only possible other choice among corps commanders seemed to be Hood, who was also a novice in this position. Davis, who had experienced anguish with the earlier turnovers of the army's high command, no doubt dreaded the difficulties of finding an adequate successor to Johnston.

Actually, Davis had been under considerable pressure from his Rich-

[37] Johnston, *Narrative*, 601.

mond advisors to remove Johnston before he reached the Chattahoochee. Secretary of State Judah P. Benjamin admitted later his conviction that Johnston would never fight before he crossed the river, and that he had badgered Davis to remove him. Secretary of War Seddon, a Johnston ally in the spring of 1863, was by August, after the fall of Vicksburg, hostile to the general, and urged Johnston's removal. Postmaster General John Reagan later recalled that private delegations and letters sent to Davis prior to Johnston's crossing the river were of the same sentiment. These and other evidences indicate that prior to the retreat across the Chattahoochee, Davis' advisors were far more anxious to eliminate Joe Johnston than was Davis.[38]

Once Johnston was across the river, however, the adverse opinions uttered by several key individuals combined with the lack of communication from Johnston apparently convinced the President. Repeatedly, Johnston was stabbed in the back by individuals who completely discredited him with Davis. By early July, Davis had received Hardee's June 22 letter depicting Johnston's losses as heavy. Hardee noted that "under present circumstances" he did not see when a battle with Sherman would occur. Cryptically, Hardee added that "if the present system continues," the army would be in Atlanta "before a serious battle is fought." Hardee's letter was followed by Senator Ben Hill's appearance in Richmond on July 9.[39]

There is evidence that Hill doublecrossed Johnston. After his meeting at Marietta on July 1, Hill promised to go immediately to Richmond and seek Davis' aid in obtaining cavalry for a strike against Sherman's railroad. For one who told Johnston that "everything hung upon it," and "I would go at once to Richmond," [40] Hill moved slowly. He did not arrive in the capital until July 10, after which he plunged into several days of discussions with Davis, Seddon, individual cabinet members, and the cabinet as a whole. Hill, who later admitted that he considered Johnston suspicious, spiteful, and jealous, considered himself to be an impartial observer. He moved in the aura of an *amicis curiae,* since he was generally a pro-administration politician, yet nominally had come to Richmond to seek aid for an old enemy of Davis'. Also, Hill's was the first detailed

38 For evidence of earlier pressure upon Davis to remove Johnston, see Seddon to Davis, June 17, 1872, in Rowland (ed.), *Davis,* VII, 320; Seddon to W. T. Walthall, February 10, 1879, in *ibid.,* VIII, 349–53; Judah P. Benjamin to Davis, February 15, 1879, in *ibid.,* VIII, 356; Jefferson Davis to Herschel V. Johnson, September 18, 1864, in *ibid.,* VI, 336, 338; John H. Reagan to Davis, February 7, 1878, in *ibid.,* VIII, 78–79; Will Gale to "Kate," July 30, 1864, in Polk Papers, Sewanee; Campbell Brown Diary, August 4, 1868, in Brown-Ewell Papers, Tennessee.

39 Hardee to Davis, June 22, 1864, in Davis Papers, Emory.

40 *Official Records,* LII, Pt. 2, p. 706.

account Davis had yet received of what was going on in Georgia since
Hood had sent his personal emissary in late May. Anxious for information, Davis warmly received Hill as an authority on what was occurring
in Georgia. He conferred with Davis on July 10, and with Seddon on
July 11. He furnished Seddon a writen statement of his conversation with
Johnston for the cabinet's use, and even attended one cabinet session in
which Johnston's removal was debated.[41]

In these various capacities, Hill damaged Johnston in two ways. Openly
advocating his removal, Hill stated that he was satisfied Johnston would
not fight for Atlanta. Even if Hill had not engaged in this duplicity,
merely his relating his conversation with Johnston proved damaging
enough. If Davis had hoped that Johnston, reticent to telegraph his plans,
would send them via Hill, he was disappointed. As related by Hill, Johnston's attitude was gloomy enough to excite alarm. Sherman would not
attack his entrenched positions; he in turn could not attack the Federal
fortifications. Meanwhile, the enemy's superior numbers enabled him
continually to force Johnston to fall back. Thus, according to Hill,
Johnston argued that the only way to get Sherman's army out of the
country was to bring cavalry from other areas and attack his communications. Three times, Hill told Davis, he asked Johnston if he understood
him to say that the only way Sherman could be defeated was with such
cavalry support.[42]

When Johnston replied in the affirmative to this question, he unknowingly had set his own trap. According to the version given the government, Johnston had said "distinctly and positively that with his army and
resources he could not repel the enemy nor protect the State" [43] without
outside cavalry aid. Hill had agreed with Johnston that not only was
outside cavalry aid essential but also had agreed on the necessity to hold
Sherman north of the Chattahoochee River long enough for the cavalry
to arrive and be effective. Yet, according to the version Hill gave Davis
and Seddon, Johnston estimated that he could hold Sherman north of the
river for a month or more. On July 10, even as Hill related his com-

41 *Ibid.*, pp. 693, 704; Hill to ———, October 12, 1878, in Davis, *Rise and Fall*,
II, 559–61.

42 For evidence that Hill in Richmond advocated Johnston's removal, see Vandiver,
Gorgas Diary, July 22, "p.m.," 1864, 127–28; James Lyons to W. T. Walthall, July 31,
1878, in Rowland (ed.), *Davis*, VIII, 215–16; Pollard, *Life of Jefferson Davis*, 372.
Hill later wrote of Hood's appointment, "Yet I do confess, and did confess at the
time, I cannot see how the President under these circumstances could do better.
Atlanta had virtually been lost when Hood took command." See Hill to Herschel
Johnson, October 13, 1864, in Herschel Johnson Papers, Duke. See also Seddon
to Hill, July 13, 1864, Hill to Seddon, July 14, 1864, in Johnston Papers, William and
Mary.

43 Seddon to Hill, July 13, 1864, in Johnston Papers, William and Mary.

mander's views to Davis, the President had the news that Johnston had reached the Chattahoochee.[44]

The implication was obvious. According to the version given Richmond, the only formula for success that Johnston could present had already failed. Particularly damaging was the recounting of his alleged statement that he could not stop Sherman with his own army. But there were other damaging statements. Hill emphasized that Johnston never specifically said that he would fight for Atlanta. Hill reported that "the only point at which my mind received the impression that General Johnston would fight" was when Johnston made a vague allusion to a "bloody fight" which would occur if Sherman crossed the river and attempted to pen him in Atlanta.[45] Hill also told the government that he, like Davis, had warned Johnston that if he crossed the Chattahoochee, the enemy could move against his railroad links into Alabama. Particularly cutting was Hill's reminder to Davis that Johnston had not even known that the Chattahoochee bridges at West Point and Columbus, Georgia, were undefended. Too, according to Hill, Johnston had assured him that from Dalton to Kennesaw Mountain he had been "willing and anxious to fight if he could only obtain a fair field" [46] but had found no place. These were almost the exact words Johnston had uttered to Davis while retreating from Dalton across the Etowah at various times. They were repeated again in Johnston's famous telegram on July 16—words that had always followed one retreat and preceded another, in Johnston's case.

Hill's report of Johnston's analysis of enemy strength no doubt also confused President Davis. To Hill, Johnston had argued that Sherman's initial force of ninety-three thousand men had suffered losses perhaps as high as thirty thousand without having received reinforcements equal to these casualties. Yet, a few days after his conversatons in Richmond with Hill, Davis received word from Johnston that he must maintain the defensive because Sherman outnumbered him two to one.[47]

Even before Hill reached Richmond, a message was en route from another old Bragg ally. During the early summer, Wheeler continued to correspond secretly with Bragg as he had done in the spring. Wheeler's letters flattered Bragg, furnished him with statistics regarding the state of the enemy confronting them, and aided in kindling the fires in Richmond for demanding an offensive by Johnston. Though he corresponded with Bragg as late as July 1, Wheeler, as the chief of Johnston's cavalry, never

44 Ibid.; see also Hill to Seddon, July 14, 1864, in ibid.; Hill to ———, October 12, 1878, in Davis, Rise and Fall, II, 560.

45 Hill to Seddon, July 14, 1864, in Johnston Papers, William and Mary.,

46 Seddon to Hill, July 13, 1864, in ibid.

47 Hill to Seddon, July 14, 1864, in ibid.; Johnston to Davis, July 16, 1864, in Johnston Dispatch Book, William and Mary.

asked Bragg to order any cavalry from Lee's or other departments to aid in striking Sherman's communications. Instead, on July 1, at a time when Johnston was stressing that the need for outside cavalry was most urgent, Wheeler took the opposite view. Johnston's repeated argument had been that he lacked enough of his own horsemen both to cover his flanks and to raid the railroad behind Sherman's column. But Wheeler told Bragg that he had begged Johnston to allow him to make the raid and he would not allow it.[48]

The influence of Hardee, Hill, and Wheeler, deliberate or otherwise, in undermining Johnston was overshadowed by the activities of Bragg in early July. Everyone had underrated Bragg since his removal from command. The anti-administration press and his enemies among the military considered him finished. Even after Davis, on February 24, appointed him commander in chief of Confederate armies "charged with the conduct of military operations in the armies of the Confederacy," many observers, including Johnston, considered Bragg scarcely more powerful than he had been during the nearly three months of inactivity between his two commands. After his April mission to Richmond, Ewell reported to Johnston that Bragg was powerless, able only to "record the President's edicts and grant small favors to persons not disliked by the President." [49] Thus, feeling pity for Bragg, Johnston went out of his way, during the early spring, to congratulate him on his new position. Even during the argument with Richmond regarding an offensive from Dalton, Johnston continued to support his conduct in early 1863. In April of 1864, Johnston told Wigfall that while he commanded the army, Bragg "had done more execution in proportion to numbers than any other in the war." [50] Though he did not consider Bragg a "great general," Johnston believed that in 1863 he was more fit to command the army "than anyone who could be expected to be chosen to succeed him." [51] On another occasion that spring, Johnston depicted Chickamauga as a more decisive victory and better fought than any Virginia campaign.[52]

Like another Johnston who once commanded the army, Joe Johnston simply was not the best judge of people, and sometimes seemed incredibly naïve—as in dealing with Hood for instance. The crippled Kentucky general had done nothing to merit the special consideration which Johnston gave his advice. A half dozen times Hood had balked or favored re-

48 See Wheeler to Bragg, February 14, 1864, in Joseph Wheeler Letters, Harvard; Wheeler to Bragg, March 3, April 16, June 5, July 1, 1864, in Bragg Papers, Western Reserve; Johnston to Wigfall, January 9, 1864, in Wigfall Papers, DLC.
49 Mackall to wife, April 30, 1864, in Mackall, *Recollections*, 208.
50 Johnston to Wigfall, April 1, 1864, in Wigfall Papers, DLC.
51 *Ibid.*
52 Johnston to Wigfall, April 5, 1864, in *ibid.*

treating from positions which Johnston believed to be strong ones. Yet Johnston confided in him more than in the other corps commanders. Even while Hood was writing treacherous notes to the government during the spring, Johnston was asserting that his presence in the army was his only comfort.

There were ample signs that Bragg had a wide influence which Johnston did not comprehend. He had taken the leading role in the correspondence with Johnston during the spring regarding the projected offensive, and had led in supplying statistics to show why Johnston could not be reinforced. It had been Bragg with whom Johnston's envoy, Colonel Benjamin Ewell, had first consulted on his April visit to Richmond. It had been Bragg's military secretary, Colonel John Sale, who in March had borne to the West the government's plan for a joint offensive between Johnston and Longstreet. Bragg had sarcastically told Johnston he need expect no more reinforcements unless he promised to take the offensive. Bragg had led the protest against Polk's wholesale reinforcement of Johnston during the crisis at Resaca in May. Yet Johnston seemed not to appreciate Bragg's influence. Nor did he appear to see anything foreboding in the fact that this same general—who had commanded the Army of Tennessee longer than any other individual, who was a warm friend of Davis' and an obvious western expert, a general often castigated by Johnston's supporters in Richmond for the past two years, a man who in essence had lost his job to Johnston—now at least nominally headed the conduct of the Confederacy's military affairs. Johnston's naïveté went further than this. With his army at Peachtree Creek, its back to Atlanta, and well apprised of Richmond's displeasure, Johnston saw nothing peculiar in the sudden appearance of Bragg at Atlanta on July 13. Johnston believed Bragg's visit was a casual one that involved no official business.[53]

Yet, it seems that Bragg in 1864 was not the stooge as general in chief which some considered him. Davis relied heavily upon him in devising the offensive plan he wanted Johnston to use. He depended upon him for the official estimates of Johnston's and Sherman's troops, of the available cavalry in Lee's neighboring department, and of the feasibility of sending Lee's cavalry to aid Johnston. It was Bragg who sealed the army's fate on June 29 with his detailed note to Davis in which he argued that every available man had been sent to Johnston.

Bragg also remained far more powerful among army people than historians have given him credit for being. A hard-core group of his supporters still were in important positions within the army. Wheeler was

[53] Johnston to Wigfall, August 27, 1864, in *ibid;* Johnston to Beverley Johnston, August 28, 1864, in Hughes, "War Letters," 321.

devoutly loyal. Significantly, his messages to Richmond behind Johnston's back were all sent to Bragg. Hood, probably for other reasons, was a strong backer of Bragg and addressed most of his letters to him. There were also loyal friends among division and brigade officers, many of whom were still in the army. These men fed Bragg's resentment at being relieved, by attributing his removal to a plot by a few in the army, and they also rekindled his desire to command. General Patton Anderson, a long-time division commander in the army, had warned Bragg the previous October of a plot to overthrow him. Now, in July of 1864, Anderson, commanding the District of Florida, wrote Bragg that while Atlanta was being contested, "you are not in the field—not at the head of this army for which you did so much but which did so little for you." [54] From Alabama, one of Bragg's former medical officers labeled his removal as the plot of a few jealous men.[55] From Augusta, one of Bragg's staff officers, Colonel H. W. Walter, wrote on July 11 that if Bragg were to return to command the army for only five days, "Atlanta would be saved." Walter added that, with the army's present commander, "it will be lost." [56] From the army itself, officers such as Wheeler, States Rights Gist, and A. P. Stewart rejoiced at Bragg's new appointment and praised the general's abilities. Stewart, now one of Johnston's corps commanders, like Wheeler and Hood was on unusually good terms with Bragg and wrote him private letters during the spring of 1864. He described himself to Bragg as being among the general's "friends" in the army and praised Bragg's new position as "far from being on the shelf." [57]

There is an importance to such statements, which some historians have overlooked. Bragg's supporters continued to impress upon him that he had not been removed because of a widespread discontent with his generalship in the army but because of the jealousies of a few generals, and he believed them. Even before he left the army in December of 1863, he was convinced of two critical facts: his removal had been a conspiracy of only a few jealous men. On December 14, he told his friend General Marcus Wright that the clamor against him was caused by a few individuals motivated by either revenge or ambition, and that the army as a whole did not support either feeling. Earlier, after the retreat from

---

[54] Anderson to Bragg, July 17, 1864, in Bragg Papers, Western Reserve. See also Anderson to Bragg, October 10, 1863, *ibid.*

[55] Nott to Bragg, December 16, 1863, in Bragg Papers, Emory.

[56] Walter to Bragg, July 11, 1864, in Bragg Papers, Western Reserve.

[57] Stewart to Bragg, March 19, 1864, in *ibid.*; see also Gist to Bragg, February 27, 1864, *ibid.*; Wheeler to Bragg, March 3, 1864, *ibid.*

Missionary Ridge, he told Davis the one problem of the army was "the vices of a few profligate men." [58]

Other beliefs tied to these were motivating Bragg toward a second and more significant belief. He considered the Army of Tennessee as his own. He took pride in how he had assumed command in 1862 of Beauregard's army, which he considered to be terribly dismembered. After his removal, Bragg remembered the halcyon days of his command, and never admitted that when he retreated from Missionary Ridge the command was shattered. Such feelings were the root of his irritation and impatience with Johnston's not taking the offensive. When Johnston pointed out the inadequacies of the army to Bragg, this probably seemed a reflection upon his own past service in the western command.

Bragg wrote, on December 2, the day he retired from the command, that he trusted "that I may be allowed to participate in the struggle which may restore to us the character, the prestige, and the country we have just lost." [59] To his friend General Marcus Wright, Bragg was even more specific. Obviously referring to Hardee, the temporary commander, he wrote that "some have found the bed of roses well set with *thorns*, and that it is easier to condemn than remedy." Bragg asserted that the army generally had not wanted his removal, and distinctly added that he believed, "I could do more good by returning to my old place than any other." [60]

This being Bragg's belief, the time during the second week of July seemed opportune. On July 9, increasingly fearful for Atlanta's safety, Davis sent Bragg to confer with Johnston, specifically with reference to military matters there. Some writers have indicated that Bragg was sent as an executioner and that Davis had already decided to remove Johnston. Thus, the visit was either to gain evidence to justify the removal or to confer with possible successors. [61]

This interpretation is probably not accurate. Obviously, Davis had considered removing Johnston, but probably he did not actually decide to remove him until after Hill's visit and after the telegram came from Johnston recommending the redistribution of the Andersonville prisoners. These developments indicated that Johnston had no plan and would not hold Atlanta. Even then, Davis delayed his final decision, evidently against the strong urgings of several cabinet members. His desire to hear something from Bragg, and the problem involved in finding a potential

[58] Bragg to Wright, December 14, 1863 in Wright Papers, UNC; Bragg to Davis, December 1, 1863, in Bragg Papers, Harvard.

[59] Bragg to Davis, December 2, 1863, in Bragg Papers, Western Reserve.

[60] Bragg to Wright, December 14, 1863, in Wright Papers, UNC.

[61] *Official Records*, XXXIX, Pt. 2, p. 695; see Govan and Livingood, *A Different Valor*, 311.

successor caused him to hold off the final decision until after he received Johnston's vague explanation of his plans on July 16. Bragg's report sent to Davis on July 15 indicates that at that time there was no hard and fast decision to remove Johnston, and he anticipated some of the difficulties "should such a measure be considered." [62] Of course, when Bragg went to Georgia, he knew that Davis was considering the step. Some cryptic telegrams sent between the two on July 14 and 15 indicate that Davis provided Bragg with a list of several possible courses, and was awaiting the general's personal inspection to see which might be most feasible.[63]

On July 12, while Bragg was en route to Atlanta, Davis telegraphed Robert E. Lee to ask for advice, citing some of the points that strongly indicated that Johnston would abandon Atlanta. Davis asserted that it seemed necessary to remove Johnston at once, and asked for Lee's recommendations regarding a possible successor. Specifically, Davis asked Lee's opinion of Hood. Like Bragg, Davis evidently had been captivated by Hood's pronouncements of the need for an aggressive policy in Georgia. That same day, Lee replied by telegram and by letter. Characteristically, though he admitted he knew nothing of the western situation, he gave advice. He mentioned the dangers involved in changing commanders, but did not protest the idea of Johnston's removal, as some historians have indicated. Instead, he noted, "if necessary, it ought to be done." Nor did Lee oppose Hood's possible selection. Though he added a brief footnote that Hardee had had more experience in managing an army, Lee's entire recommendation for a possible successor hinged on Hood. He said neither yes nor no, but did utilize those descriptive terms which a government anxious for an aggressive policy would welcome. Lee admitted that he had not had opportunity to judge Hood when the general had the entire responsibility, and admitted his doubt that Hood possessed some of the qualities necessary for a commanding general. Yet Lee considered him a "bold" and "good" fighter, zealous and very industrious on the field. Several days later, after Davis had more definitely decided upon removing Johnston, he sent Secretary of War Seddon to Lee's headquarters near Petersburg to discuss the choice of a successor. Exactly what Lee told Seddon is unknown. General Wade Hampton later claimed that Lee assured him that he had urged Seddon not to remove Johnston from command, arguing that if Johnston could not command the army, no one could. Yet Lee's notes of July 12 contain no such strong opposition to Johnston's removal. If he actually did protest as

62 *Official Records,* XXXIX, Pt. 2, p. 713.
63 *Ibid.,* LII, Pt. 2, pp. 704, 707.

strongly to Seddon as Hampton later recalled, why did he wait until after he knew the cabinet had decided to remove Johnston? [64]

More official channels for such important decision-making had broken down between the President and Johnston. Instead, Davis was relying on unofficial observers such as Hill, improper correspondence from Wheeler and Hood, advice from Ewell, Sale, Wigfall, Senator Richard Walker of Alabama, Pendleton, and others. Such sources were often unreliable and contradictory, sometimes treacherous, and never a satisfactory substitute for direct communication between a commander in chief and his general. Davis never actually demanded a point blank statement of plans from Johnston, and certainly Johnston never volunteered any.

Bragg's mission was only an extension of the same practice. Davis, apparently unsuspecting of Bragg's ambitiousness or possible weaknesses of character, naïvely expected an objective report on Johnston.

Thus, while between July 12 and 16 Davis held off the order for removal, Bragg provided the *coup de grace*. There is little doubt that Bragg lied to Johnston concerning the purpose of his mission. Later, Johnston maintained that Bragg assured him his visit was not official, asked for no comments on Johnston's future plans, gave no instructions from the government, and left Johnston convinced that he was satisfied with the state of affairs. Johnston further added that the only topics discussed concerning the Army of Tennessee were ones he introduced—reiterating that Bragg offered no advice or suggestions. [65]

There is considerable evidence that Johnston's version was no exaggeration. Johnston's own chief of staff, General W. W. Mackall, did not know why Bragg was there save that, "I don't think he has any special mission." [66] Another observer, Lieutenant Halsey Wigfall, the Senator's son and an aide to Hood, confided to his father, "What the object of his visit is I don't know." [67] There is strong evidence from Bragg himself that he was dealing in subterfuge. On July 15 Bragg claimed to Davis that he had spent practically all day July 13 talking with Johnston about the army's plans. Curiously, Bragg never mentioned to Davis Johnston's plan for attacking Sherman crossing Peachtree Creek. Instead, Bragg noted that, "As far as I can learn we do not propose any offensive op-

---

64 *Ibid.*, 692; Lee to Davis, July 12, 1864, in McWhiney (ed.), *Lee's Dispatches*, 158, 283–84; Wade Hampton to Davis, September 5, 1874, in Rowland (ed.), *Davis*, VII, 399; Govan and Livingood, *A Different Valor*, 315; Wade Hampton to Johnston (undated), quoted in Johnston, "Opposing Sherman's Advance to Atlanta," 277.

65 Johnston to Wigfall, August 27, 1864, in Wigfall Papers, DLC; Johnston to Beverley Johnston, August 28, 1864, in Hughes, "War Letters," 321.

66 Mackall to wife, July ———, 1864, in Mackall, *Recollections*, 217.

67 Halsey Wigfall to father, July 15, 1864, in Wigfall Papers, DLC.

erations." [68] That same day Bragg telegraphed Davis that he could not learn from the general "that he has any more plan for the future than he has had in the past." [69] Obviously, Bragg was guilty of one of two things. Either Bragg spent far less time in discussing with Johnston the army's military affairs than he led Davis to believe, or else he held back from Davis knowledge of Johnston's plan for attacking Sherman.

Apparently Bragg did spend less time learning the army's plans than he actually told Davis. He all but admitted this. Twice on July 15 Bragg took pains to tell Davis that certain facets of his conversations with Johnston had been limited. On one occasion he telegraphed, "He has not sought my advice, and it was not volunteered." [70] Afterwards he repeated this statement in a letter to Davis. He wrote that because Johnston "has not sought my advice, nor ever afforded me a fair opportunity of giving my opinion, I have obtruded neither upon him. Such will continue to be my course." [71] In fact, one of Bragg's most damaging telegrams sent from Atlanta was dispatched immediately after his arrival on July 13, even before he consulted with Johnston. In the telegram, Bragg noted his arrival and reported that matters there indicated that a complete evacuation of Atlanta would take place. Davis was startled by this information. After receiving it, he wrote Lee that "the case seems hopeless in present hands," and that Johnston's removal was "a sad alternative." [72]

This note was only the first in a series that damned Johnston. After sending the telegram, Bragg went to Johnston's headquarters. Though Bragg was in Atlanta from July 13 to 17, he apparently made only two visits to Johnston. The first was on July 13. Bragg wrote Davis on July 15 that he had spent most of that day with Johnston. This is not true. Shortly after noon Bragg was already back in Atlanta, as noted on the telegraph to Davis. At 1 P.M. he telegraphed Davis that Johnston's army was "sadly depleted," had lost ten thousand men since June 10, and that he found "but little encouraging." [73]

The following day Bragg met with his two supporters, Wheeler and Hood. Hood, particularly, furnished Bragg with damaging testimony. In their conversation, Hood said that since leaving Dalton he had been in favor of giving battle, but that Johnston had bypassed several opportunities to do so. Hood quoted the recently deceased Polk as having followed the same policy he did, but claimed that Hardee, whom he

68 *Official Records*, XXXIX, Pt. 2, p. 713.
69 *Ibid.*, XXXVIII, Pt. 5, p. 881.
70 *Ibid.*
71 *Ibid.*, XXXIX, Pt. 2, p. 714.
72 *Ibid.*, LII, Pt. 2, p. 692, XXXVIII, Pt. 5, p. 878.
73 *Ibid.*, XXXVIII, Pt. 5, p. 878.

possibly considered a rival for the command, favored Johnston's policy of retreat. After the conversation Hood provided Bragg with a written statement of his views. The army had had several chances to strike the enemy "a decisive blow" from Dalton to the Chattahoochee, but had failed to take advantage of them. Even without fighting such a battle, Johnston had lost at least twenty thousand men. Hood contended that the army's only hope of saving Atlanta was by attacking. He again reminded Bragg, as he had done several times previously, that he favored an offensive course. In fact, Hood described himself as being considered reckless by some of the army's officers because he had "so often urged that we should force the enemy to give us battle." [74]

Apparently Hood was making his last bid for the army's generalship. He was not the simple man some considered him to be. When he came to Dalton, he knew that Richmond expected him to keep in touch. He provided the government with a series of letters, all of which were damaging to Johnston. Johnston's aide, Lieutenant Richard Manning, who visited his South Carolina home immediately after Johnston's removal, told Johnston later of a conversation with Hood's fiancée, Sally Preston, in which she told him she had been expecting Johnston's removal and Hood's promotion for some two weeks. Though Hood later swore that he had not intrigued for Johnston's removal, there was a remarkable similarity between what Hood had written for months and what he knew the government officials wanted to hear.

He had not constantly urged giving battle. He had advocated not fighting at Adairsville, and had urged a retreat across the Etowah River even before the Cassville episode. At Cassville it was Hood who had called off the morning attack, and had that night fought against renewing the offensive. At New Hope Church he had balked at orders to renew the attack against the Federals. He had advised a retreat from Kennesaw Mountain, and had also urged a retreat from Shoup's fortifications on the north bank of the Chattahoochee. [75] At best, Hood was a chronic liar, yet the government, particularly Bragg, chose to believe him.

Bragg's letter of July 15, a total condemnation of Johnston's policies, recounted Hood's claim that Johnston had lost twenty thousand men practically without fighting. Bragg hinted that Atlanta might be abandoned since everything valuable had already been removed from the town. Also, he insisted that Johnston had always overestimated Sherman's

74 Hood to Bragg, July 14, 1864, in Bragg Papers, Western Reserve; *Official Records,* XXXIX, Pt. 2, p. 713.

75 Johnston to Beverley Johnston, November 15, 1864, in Hughes, "War Letters," 326; Judge J. P. Young to Thomas R. Hay, March 26, 1921, in Thomas R. Hay private collection of J. P. Young Papers; Edward A. Pollard, *The Lost Cause: A New History of the War of the Confederates* (New York, 1867), 567–77.

strength, which Bragg placed at sixty thousand infantry and seventy-five thousand men of all arms. Also, Bragg reminded Davis that during the campaign Hood and Polk repeatedly had implored Johnston to fight.[76]

Bragg's letter revealed some key matters regarding a possible successor. Bragg was not certain that Davis intended to remove Johnston, but apparently Davis had requested that Bragg give some recommendations if such a step were taken. Bragg's July 15 recommendation of Hood may well explain why, on July 12, Davis already had suggested Hood to Lee as a possible successor to Johnston. Other than generals then fighting in Virginia, the only serious candidates were Hood and Hardee. Bragg recommended Hood not so much because of his belief in his generalship. In a classic understatement, Bragg admitted to Davis that he was not "a man of genius, or a great general." Still Hood was praised as being "far better" in the emergency than any other available officer, a man of whom Bragg's opinion was "high," and one whom he thought would give "unlimited satisfaction." Thus, "if any change is made," Bragg thought Hood was the best man.[77]

But what of Hardee? The senior corps commander in the army, nominally the second in command, Hardee had been a corps commander in the West while Hood was commanding a regiment in Lee's army. Also, Hardee already had had experience in such army administration. He had temporarily commanded the army in December, 1863, and had done an admirable job of rebuilding. Prior to this, he had been second-in-command to Johnston in the Alabama-Mississippi department.

But Hardee was a marked man. He was one of the small group whom Bragg blamed for his ouster. The quarrel between the two generals had deep roots, back to the Kentucky campaign of the autumn of 1862. Too, Hood had succeeded in stereotyping Hardee as a passive officer who would take the offensive no sooner than Johnston would. Evidently, Hood's envoy to Richmond after Cassville, Colonel George Brewster, went with the opinion that the only high commanders in the army who wished to fight were Hood and Polk. In his conversation with Bragg on July 14, Hood labeled Hardee as one who sustained Johnston's policy of retreating and claimed he had done so since leaving Dalton. The lie was obvious, since at Cassville Hardee had been the only corps commander who favored a fight on the night the war council was held. In his note to Bragg that same day, Hood took another slap at Hardee. He maintained that he always had urged that Johnston should give battle, an opinion completely opposite to that of "the officers high in rank in this army." [78]

76 *Official Records*, XXXIX, Pt. 2, pp. 712–14.
77 *Ibid.*, p. 714.
78 Hood to Bragg, July 14, 1864, in Bragg Papers, Western Reserve.

Since only Johnston and Hardee outranked Hood, the implication was obvious.

It was Bragg's July 15 telegram that probably demolished Hardee's chances of assuming the command. As mentioned, Lee on July 12 had suggested Hardee as a possible successor, and noted that he had more experience than Hood. Davis, obviously impressed by Hood's alleged longing for an offensive operation, may have heard adverse comments about Hardee's willingness to fight from Hood's emissary in late May or comments on Hardee's shortcomings in general from Bragg. Still, Davis may have given serious consideration to Hardee as a possible successor. There is an indication that on July 14 or 15 Davis telegraphed Bragg and asked for his views on Hardee as Johnston's successor. A cryptic telegram Bragg sent Davis on July 15 could only have applied to Hardee. The context of Bragg's reply indicates that Davis not only asked for Bragg's opinion of Hardee, but that he perhaps voiced fears that some other officer he had in mind, probably Hood, would produce some objection in the army. Bragg replied that he was "decidedly opposed" to the idea, "as it would perpetuate the past and present policy which he has advised and now sustains." Though any change would produce some objections, noted Bragg, "this one could produce no good." [79] The context of Bragg's letter written that same day indicates that his allusion to the one who sustained Johnston's policy could only have been Hardee. Hood and Stewart were depicted as favoring an aggressive policy, but Hardee "generally favored the retiring policy." Moreover, Bragg did not believe that Hardee "has the confidence of the army" to the extent that Johnston did, and believed that if any change were made, Hood should be given the job.[80]

Later, in August, when Hardee, angered by Hood's appointment, asked to be relieved of his command, Davis attempted to leave the impression that Hardee had not even been considered. Davis argued that because in December of 1863 Hardee had declined the permanent offer, he believed Hood's appointment "would be satisfactory to you." [81] There are several flaws here. In the autumn of 1863 Lee also had declined the western army's command, but this did not stop Davis from offering it to him again in December of 1863. A more likely reason was that Davis knew only too well that the elevation of a junior corps commander over the senior officer would cause resentment. Actually, Davis probably was shielding both his and Bragg's preference for Hood because they believed

79 *Official Records,* LII, Pt. 2, p. 707.

80 *Ibid.,* XXXIX, Pt. 2, pp. 713–14.

81 *Ibid.,* XXXVIII, Pt. 5, p. 988; see also p. 987, LII, Pt. 2, p. 645; Hardee to Davis, August 6, 1864, Davis to Hardee, August 7, 1864, Roy's Sketch, all in Hardee Papers, Alabama.

Hood would carry out their desired policy of being more aggressive.

Thus Bragg was influential in two respects, the condemnation of Johnston and Hardee, and the praising of Hood. Probably he swayed Davis' decision more in the removal of Johnston than the rejection of Hardee. Bragg's long letter of July 15 may not have reached Richmond prior to the cabinet's decision to remove Johnston. The letter was sent by personal courier, Colonel H. W. Walter, on a night train from Atlanta on July 15. Whether it arrived in time to influence Davis is not certain; there is some evidence that it did not arrive until after the orders had gone out to relieve Johnston.[82]

Even without the letter, Bragg's reports to Richmond via telegraph were damaging enough to Johnston's case. His dispatches of July 13 and 15 which, considering Davis' lack of knowledge of what was happening in Atlanta, certainly would have motivated the President to take strong action. Bragg sent at least three telegrams on the fifteenth concerning conditions at Atlanta. Like those sent two days earlier, they strongly condemned Johnston's generalship. In one, Bragg commented that Johnston had not even sought his advice, but stated that after listening to Johnston's plans, "I cannot learn that he has any more plan for the future than he has had in the past." [83] Bragg described Johnston's future plans as only defensive, and indicated that the enemy's force contained only sixty thousand infantry. In a second note, Bragg made it seem that Atlanta was on the verge of collapse. Still not mentioning Johnston's general plans to fight along the Peachtree line, he warned Davis that nearly all the available munitions equipment and stores had been removed from Atlanta and that most of the town's citizens had left. Meanwhile, one contingent of Federals had already penetrated to near the West Point Railroad near Newman before they were driven back by cavalry. Another corps was crossing above Atlanta. In a third telegram, sent after he had penned the letter to be sent by Walter, Bragg still did not mention Johnston's plan. He merely warned Davis that one segment of the enemy advance appeared to be moving northward around Atlanta toward the Augusta railroad. That same day Bragg also sent his dispatch objecting to Hardee's being placed in command.[84]

[82] The receipt of the letter prior to Johnston's removal was not mentioned in later correspondence by Davis or his cabinet members. In an undated manuscript among Bragg's papers, which some believe the general prepared, it is asserted that the report did not reach Richmond in time. See "Notes to Gen'l Bragg; services in the cause of the Confederacy after leaving Army of Tenn. in Dec. 1863," copied from paper "apparently in Bragg's handwriting in pencil endorsed 'Notes of Movement from Dec. '63 to July 1864'" (MS in Bragg Papers, Western Reserve). See also *Official Records*, LII, Pt. 2, p. 707.

[83] *Official Records*, XXXVIII, Pt. 5, p. 881; see also LII, Pt. 2, p. 707.

[84] Johnston to Davis, July 16, 1864, in Johnston Dispatch Book, William and Mary.

Even if Bragg's letter did not arrive before the decision was made, he had done sufficient damage. The cabinet had been meeting continuously during the few days prior to Johnston's removal on July 17. Evidently Seddon, once Johnston's supporter, and Benjamin, his long-term enemy, pushed for Davis to make his final decision. Then came telegrams from Bragg which seemed to verify Davis' worst fears—that Johnston had no plan, that the Confederates had lost heavily without engaging in many direct battles, that Johnston had exaggerated Sherman's numbers, and that apparently Atlanta would be evacuated.

Until July 16 Davis wavered, evidently against the advice of the entire cabinet. That day he telegraphed Johnston to ask for his specific plans for the future campaign. Johnston's famous reply did nothing to counteract Davis' impressions, and the next day Davis issued orders authorizing Cooper to remove Johnston and replace him with Hood.[85]

Davis' decision, though it seemed quite justified on the basis of evidence given to him, was a costly error. It began once more that dreary cycle of a change of leadership on the eve of a campaign which had plagued the army since 1861. In the contest for Atlanta, three of the four ranking officers would be new in their positions. Stewart, assigned to command Polk's old corps, had not assumed his new position until the first week of July. Until General Stephen D. Lee arrived in late July to command Hood's former corps, General Frank Cheatham was given temporary command. Thus, not only was there a change of commanders, but two of the army's three corps commanders would also be new.

The dangers involved in such a drastic reorganization were immediate, and all three corps commanders seemed to realize the hazards. Johnston was handed the order relieving him from command about 10 P.M. on the night of July 17. Though probably stunned, he immediately prepared a farewell message to the army, issued the orders for the change of command, and sent a note of congratulations to Hood's headquarters. Not long after Johnston received the order, General A. P. Stewart rode to his headquarters for a conference. Upon learning that Johnston had been removed, Stewart implored him not to turn over the command until the impending clash with Sherman had occurred. Johnston declined, and a troubled Stewart rode immediately to Hardee's headquarters. Hardee, too, was surprised at the news, and probably even more surprised that he

85 Seddon to Walthall, February 10, 1879, in Rowland (ed.), *Davis*, VIII, 349, 352–53; Benjamin to Davis, February 15, 1879, *ibid.*, 356; Jefferson Davis to James Lyons, August 13, 1876, in Jefferson Davis Letters, Virginia Historical Society; Seddon to Davis, June 17, 1872, in Rowland (ed.), *Davis*, VII, 320.

had not been named the successor. He agreed to urge Johnston to disregard the order temporarily.[86]

Nor did there seem to be rejoicing at Hood's headquarters that night. In his 1 A.M. response to Johnston's note of congratulations, Hood stated that he was surprised at his appointment. This reaction was probably not altogether an exaggeration. From then on, the young Hood seemed overwhelmed at the task of assuming command under such circumstances, with enemies within the army and at the gates of Atlanta. That same night he received a note from Stewart requesting that he meet with the other corps commanders early the following morning.

Again the dreary dramas of command bitterness and disorganization were played out as Sherman neared Atlanta. About sunrise on July 18, the three corps commanders met on the road outside Johnston's headquarters. After some conversation, they agreed to prevail upon Johnston to delay his departure until the Atlanta crisis had passed. Again Johnston refused. Then the three generals sent Davis a telegram requesting that the order to remove Johnston be held up since Sherman was making a general advance. The generals urged Davis to suspend it temporarily because they deemed it dangerous to change commanders. Their reasoning seemed sound. "A few days will probably decide the fate of Atlanta," they reasoned, after which a new commander would have time to reorganize the army.[87] But Davis refused their request and argued that Johnston's reply to his telegram of July 16 had "confirmed previous apprehensions." [88] Hood still tried to postpone the change temporarily until after the Atlanta situation had been decided. He telegraphed Cooper, asking that no change be made till after the fate of Atlanta was decided. He too noted that he considered it dangerous to change commanders at that particular time, since the enemy indicated a general advance.[89]

More than confusion and reorganization was involved in the sudden transfer. Hood was now reaping some of the discontent which he had sown in his clandestine correspondence with the government. The months of Johnston's leadership had been relatively free of open feuding between

[86] Stewart to Hood, August 7, 1872, in Davis Papers, Tulane; for a later and somewhat contradictory version, see T. G. Dabney, "When Hood Superseded Johnston," *Confederate Veteran,* XXII (September, 1914), 406–407; Govan and Livingood, *A Different Valor,* 317–18.

[87] *Official Records,* LII, Pt. 2, p. 708.

[88] Davis to Hood, Hardee, and Stewart, July 18, 1864, in Hood Papers, National Archives.

[89] *Official Records,* XXXVIII, Pt. 5, p. 888, see also pp. 889, 891, 887; Stewart to Hood, August 7, 1872, in Davis Papers, Tulane.

the commander and his generals. Some of this bitterness was now to re-turn. General W. W. Mackall, a seasoned chief of staff, resigned the fol-lowing week. This step forced Hood to break in a new chief of staff, Johnston's former artillery commander, General Francis Shoup. Hardee was deeply incensed that he had been passed over for the command. By July 27, after he returned from a visit to General Stephen Lee's depart-ment, Bragg reported from Atlanta to Davis that Hardee had requested a transfer. Hood agreed in this matter and admitted that between himself and Hardee there was a lack of "cordiality and mutual confidence and support." [90] Later, in early August, Hardee formally requested a transfer. Generals W. H. T. Walker, French, Cleburne, Stewart, and others ex-pressed their disapproval of the change.[91]

Hood's appointment also wreaked bitterness among the private soldiers of the army. It was not that Hood was unpopular. Indeed, the reverse seemed true. Nor did the army totally support Johnston's policy of retire-ment. But Johnston had done much to restore the army's shattered morale. A cold, reserved person in private, he possessed a certain aura of pride, military bearing, and kindness when he appeared in public. When public disdain and scorn for the western army's failures were well known, it was Joe Johnston, the hero of Bull Run, the foe of McClellan, who gave evidence that some easterners cared for the West. It was not merely that he attempted to improve the army's logistical condition which the troops appreciated. The army was, as one correspondent observed the day Johnston left his command, "a huge ganglionic nerve," [92] quarrel-some, childish, self-conscious, but always proud. It was a long way from the flight from Missionary Ridge to the valor shown in the trenches at Kennesaw, and many troops gave the credit for the difference to Johnston.

Now Johnston was leaving, and the depressed troops in many ways showed their admiration for him. One brigade sent a note of apprecia-tion; other troops wept openly. Regiments marching past his headquar-ters lifted their hats in silent tribute, and some tearfully broke the ranks to shake his hand. Within a few hours, it was done. The army had only learned of the removal on the morning of the eighteenth. That afternoon

[90] Bragg to Davis, July 27, 1864, in Bragg Papers, Duke.

[91] Walker to "Mary," July 18, 1864, in W. H. T. Walker Papers, Duke; Hay, "Davis-Hood-Johnston Controversy," 77n.; Govan and Livingood, *A Different Valor,* 321; Stewart to Hood, August 7, 1872, in Davis Papers, Tulane.

[92] "Special Correspondent of Savannah *Republican,* behind Chattahoochee, July 18, 1864," in Confederate Scrapbook, Jones Papers, LSU.

Johnston rode into Atlanta to gather his belongings. That night he and his wife entrained for Macon.[93]

The suddenness of Johnston's departure was itself a source of much later bitterness. Hood subsequently maintained that Johnston both deceived and deserted him. According to Hood, Johnston, on the eighteenth, stoutly refused to stay with the army despite Hood's pleas. Finally, he claimed, Johnston promised that he would go into Atlanta that afternoon but would return that evening. Hood claimed that he did not learn Johnston had left until someone told him that he had gone to Macon. Moreover, Hood denied that Johnston described any detailed plans to him, though he admitted that "he may have said somewhat to me in regard to his plans." [94]

Johnston's version is different. He makes no mention of any promise to stay and give assistance. But he maintains that Hood stayed at his headquarters throughout the eighteenth from early morning until nightfall and that Johnston explained in detail his Peachtree Creek strategy. Moreover, at Hood's request, Johnston throughout the day continued to issue orders aligning the three corps for a possible attack on Sherman while his force was divided crossing Peachtree Creek.[95]

The truth probably falls somewhere between these two versions. Hood's version contains several errors. It is doubtful that Johnston made any such promise to return to the army and then deserted Hood. One of Hood's aides and a friend of the Johnston family, Lieutenant Halsey Wigfall, recalled a few days later that he rode into Atlanta on the evening of July 18 specifically to say goodbye to Johnston. Wigfall had been with Hood during the day, and would have known of such a plan. Too, Johnston probably did describe his Peachtree plan to Hood. The following month, Hood's aide and former Richmond envoy, Colonel George Brewster, told the Confederacy's chief gossip, Mrs. James Chesnut, that Hood asked Johnston for all his views and plans and that "they were freely given." [96] Also, there was too much similarity between Johnston's Peach-

---

93 Diary of Captain Alfred Fielder, 12th Tennessee, July 18, 1864, in Confederate Collection, Tennessee; William E. Sloan Diary, July 23, 1864, *ibid.;* Joel Murphree to wife, July 19, 1864, in H. E. Sterkx (ed.), "Autobiography and Civil War Letters of Joel Murphree of Troy, Alabama 1864–1865," *Alabama Historical Quarterly*, XIX (Spring, 1947), 184; Watkins, "Co. Aytch," 174; Kirwan (ed.), *Orphan Brigade*, 142; Hagan to wife, July 19, 1864, in Hagan, *Confederate Letters*, 51; *Official Records*, XXXVIII, Pt. 5, pp. 890–91.

94 Hood, *Advance and Retreat*, 141, see also pp. 127–28, 143.

95 Johnston, "Opposing Sherman's Advance to Atlanta," 275–76; Johnston, *Narrative*, 350–51.

96 Chesnut, *Diary from Dixie*, 430; see also Halsey Wigfall to mother, July 31, 1864, in Wigfall Papers, DLC.

tree plan and that which Hood utilized, for the new commander not to have known what Johnston intended.

Johnston's account also contains some discrepancies. Hood was not at his headquarters from early morning until nightfall. Johnston did not remain with the army that long. Probably he left in the late afternoon, after having two separate conversations with Hood. His most recent biographers speculate that he may have left for Atlanta as early as the late morning.[97]

Even if Johnston did spend the entire day in consultation with Hood on battle plans, which seems doubtful, there was cause for Hood's bitterness. Johnston was obviously angry at Richmond's decision. This was obvious in his telegram that morning to Cooper in which he acknowledged that he had turned over the command to Hood. Referring to the "alleged causes of my removal," [98] Johnston bitterly made one of his favorite comparisons, the treatment afforded him with that given to Lee. He contended that Sherman was much stronger in comparison to the size of Johnston's army than Grant's force was to Lee's army. Also, Lee had retreated much more quickly to the vicinity of Richmond than Johnston had to Atlanta, and Grant had penetrated much deeper into Virginia than Sherman had into Georgia. Then Johnston closed with the stinging comment that confident language by a general "is not usually regarded as evidence of competency." [99]

Johnston could have put aside his anger and injured pride and remained to assist Hood through the Atlanta crisis. Even Bragg, in December of 1863, had offered to stay on as his chief of staff under similar circumstances.

The most experienced commander would have required time to organize a staff, open proper channels of communications with his subordinates, and orient himself with the general situation. Hood had two months' experience in combat as a corps leader and none as an army general.

[97] Govan and Livingood, *A Different Valor*, 323.

[98] Johnston to Cooper, July 18, 1864, in Joseph E. Johnston Letters, United States Military Academy Library; see also Cooper to Johnston, July 17, 1864, *ibid.*

[99] Johnston to Cooper, July 18, 1864, in *ibid.* A Johnston friend who conversed with him that day remarked that while he appeared outwardly calm, it must have been at the cost of much exertion. See Halsey Wigfall to mother, July 31, 1864, in Wigfall Papers, DLC. Howell Cobb, who met with Johnston immediately after his arrival in Macon, remarked that while "he indulges in no spirit of complaint" and he spoke kindly of Hood, "he evidently feels his present unpleasant situation in being relieved from the command of the army." See Cobb to wife, July 20, 1864, in *Annual Report of the American Historical Association for the Year 1911: The Correspondence of Robert Tombs, Alexander H. Stephens, and Howell Cobb,* ed. Ulrich B. Phillips (Washington, D.C., 1913) , II, 647.

Johnston left Hood, feeling certain that Sherman, with an army twice the size of the Confederates', stood less than ten miles away, about to cross Peachtree Creek and attack Atlanta—a town of critical military, logistical, and political importance.

That evening most of Wheeler's cavalrymen were driven back across to the south bank of the creek.

PART IV

the hood-beauregard influence

fifteen

The Loss of Georgia

THE TALL, SAD-FACED JOHN BELL HOOD HARDLY LOOKED SUITED TO HIS
new role as commander of the Army of Tennessee when it faced
William Tecumseh Sherman at Atlanta. He had only one leg, and he
must manipulate his crutches with his one good arm.

His physical handicaps were no less than his emotional ones. A sensi-
tive, ambitious man, Hood's personality had suffered almost as much
from his successes as his body had from injuries.

He could look back on a military career that had been brief and
meteoric. A near failure at West Point, he came close to expulsion because of poor grades and heavy demerits. He graduated near the bottom
of his class and began his first tour of duty as a lieutenant in Albert Sidney Johnston's Second Cavalry in Texas. In April, 1861, he resigned his
commission and returned East. After he joined the Confederate army on
the Virginia Peninsula, his career, which had till then shown little
promise, progressed rapidly.

He entered the army as a cavalry captain, and by autumn of 1861
he was colonel of the new and rowdy Fourth Texas Brigade and had won
praise and honor at the battles of Seven Days and Second Manassas.
At the time of the Maryland invasion he was leading a division and in
late 1862 was promoted to major general. At Gettysburg he lost the use
of an arm; he also became a full-fledged hero of the Confederacy. It
was during his recuperation from his Gettysburg injuries that he made
his fateful trip to Georgia, which resulted in his participation in the
Battle of Chickamauga, his lasting friendship with Bragg, a lieutenant-

generalship and corps command, and even greater fame. He also lost a leg.

Now, at thirty-three—his body decimated and his emotions ravaged by the diverse experiences of failure and sudden adulation, plus the special strain of that long and agonizing courtship of Sally Preston during his convalescence at Richmond—he was a troubled man.[1]

His intense and driving ambition to save Atlanta and to maintain his image as hero must function from this "queer compound" as his friend Mrs. Chesnut had so aptly described him.[2]

Because of the notorious Confederate command system, the personality of a commanding general was a crucial matter. That basic Confederate faith in the willingness of a brother officer to accomplish a task without specific instructions placed a high premium on personal relationships in the high command. More than once, as in Kentucky in 1862 and at McLemore's Cove in 1863, opportunities were lost because of Bragg's lack of direct orders to his subordinates. Such directives as "attack when practicable," or "attack at your discretion" might have worked with Lee. But Bragg, like Hood, never achieved that rapport with his corps leaders. In short, because of this peculiarly personal touch to the western command system, the army commander needed strategic and tactical capabilities, but also needed character.

Hood simply did not have the character that was required, and he found, as Bragg also had, that his subordinates did not trust him. Essentially Hood was untruthful. He had misrepresented the condition of Johnston's force during the spring. He had lied about Johnston's unwillingness to fight and about his own readiness to contest Sherman's advance. He had played down the need for outside cavalry assistance, and then on July 19, the day after he assumed command, had telegraphed Richmond to beg for Lee's cavalry to strike Sherman's communications. Perhaps it was not insignificant that at West Point, Hood's grades in ethics ranked fifty-second in a class of fifty-five.[3]

Although Hood enjoyed imitating Lee's tactics of 1862–63, he did not display that general's willingness to accept blame. After the July and August failures at Atlanta and Jonesboro, Hood blamed his subordinate officers and seriously questioned the army's valor. He seemed totally without tact. Hood had no qualms about humiliating Hardee by blaming him for the loss of Atlanta. He stated openly that the army had become timid because under Johnston it had grown accustomed to fighting

1 Guild, *Fourth Tennessee*, 120; Dyer, *Gallant Hood*, 28–33, 45.
2 Chesnut, *Diary from Dixie*, 474.
3 Hood to Seddon, July 19, 1864, in Hood Papers, National Archives; Dyer, *Gallant Hood*, 33–34.

behind breastworks. He also compared the western army unfavorably with Lee's eastern command, and hinted that the westerners lacked the will to fight that troops in Virginia exhibited.[4]

The army knew of Hood's scorn, and eventually the officer corps lost confidence in him. This feeling was intensified because of Hood's reputation for being a reckless individual. By nature Hood was a gambler and the army knew this. There were many tales afloat concerning his gambling habits in the old army, one of which told how he put a thousand dollars on one card in a faro game and won. However, his impetuosity went much farther than a card game. His success in Lee's army, which he now pined to repeat, had been achieved with the shedding of much blood. At Second Manassas his Texas brigade had lost 42 percent of its strength. At Sharpsburg his First Texas Regiment had lost 82 percent of its strength while the entire Texas brigade came through with only 318 men who escaped death or injury. Such aggressive tactics had brought him the withered arm in the action along the Emmitsburg Road in July of 1863, and the amputation of a leg in the Chickamauga bottoms scarcely three months later.

Still, Hood had not abandoned his love of aggressive tactics. Almost to the point of being psychotic, he associated valor with casualty figures. Success or failure was to be determined by one standard—whether sufficient blood had been shed. Thus, he apologized to the government later in September for the "disgraceful effort" on the first day of the battle at Jonesboro. It was disgraceful, Hood explained, because only about fifteen hundred men had been killed or wounded. Repeatedly, from early August until mid-September, he rebuked his own troops for their cowardice. This lack of valor, he claimed, was evinced by insufficient battle deaths. There is little doubt that when Hood took command, it was well known by both friends and enemies along Peachtree Creek that the days of caution under Johnston had ended.[5]

But Hood was victimized by matters other than his own personality. He was also a victim of that peculiar Virginia syndrome which pervaded the Army of Tennessee. He was the last of that troubled set of officers sent to the West for varied purposes—none beneficial to the western army. Joe Johnston and Beauregard had been sent under a cloud of

4 See *Official Records*, LII, Pt. 2, pp. 729–30, XXXIX, Pt. 2, pp. 832, 837; Hood to Bragg, September 5, 1864, in Telegrams, General John Bell Hood's Command, July 27, 1864–January 5, 1865, National Archives, hereinafter cited as Hood Cipher Book, National Archives; Chesnut, *Diary from Dixie*, 427; Hood, *Advance and Retreat*, 162, 171, 184, 204.

5 Hood to Bragg, September 5, 1864, in Hood Cipher Book, National Archives; see also Oates, *War between the Union and the Confederacy*, 421; Wilson, *Under the Old Flag*, II, 40; Nichols, *Story of the Great March*, 18.

governmental displeasure; Kirby Smith came seeking lost glory, and Longstreet came perhaps in search of an army command. At best, Hood was searching for assurance that he could be effective without an arm and a leg. At the worst, Hood also came in search of an army command.

But there was something special about this last officer from Virginia. In two respects the war had passed Hood by. It had been a year since Hood had fought with Lee. Now the war was changing, even in Virginia, and Hood did not realize this. He came West, as he described it, as an "ardent advocate of the Lee and Jackson school" [6] of the bold offensive. But Jackson was dead, and Lee's bold offensives, stymied by growing Federal superiority, were now resorting to the same drudgery of trench warfare that Johnston had used in North Georgia.

Hood could not see this, however, and only remembered war as it had once been in Virginia. Thus, in 1864, he attempted to imitate what he knew Lee had done in 1862–63. Hood remembered Lee's success with bold flank moves, open field charges, and without miles of prepared entrenchments. In July of 1864 Hood determined to use the only tactic he knew—an open field charge against the enemy's line. To him the offensive was more than a way to defeat the enemy—it was a discipline to improve the army's morale and even to halt desertion. Thus, when he later attempted to prove the army's morale had been injured by Johnston's entrenching policies, Hood produced a postwar letter from General Stephen D. Lee, who agreed with his views. Hood considered Lee's endorsement of his views as especially important, since his "large experience in Virginia qualified him to form a correct opinion on this subject." [7] But even in Virginia the war was changing. General Robert E. Lee's entrenching policies were no less rigorous than Johnston's. Yet Hood had not seen the earthworks thrown up from the Rapidan to Petersburg.[8]

Hood brought another idea from Virginia which was almost equally harmful. By the force of his personality and character, Lee had welded a much more coordinated command system than had ever existed in the West. Corps command changes had been far less numerous. Thus, Lee could outline his plans for battle and leave their execution to his corps leaders. Hood attempted to fight this way and failed miserably. The western system was simply not that well coordinated. The constant reshuffling of important commanders frustrated such cohesion.

Hood was also a victim of the circumstances under which he assumed command. There were several unfavorable conditions, probably none

6 Hood, *Advance and Retreat*, 162.
7 *Ibid.*, 185.
8 *Ibid.*, 162, 181, 185, 192.

more significant than his own crippled physical condition. By the spring of 1864, Hood had obtained from Europe two artificial limbs, one of which was kept strapped to the saddle of his spare horse. Still, he got around only with great difficulty. He apparently never learned to walk with his artificial leg, and only hobbled without it on crutches. Two aides were required to assist Hood in mounting his horse, to which he was then strapped.[9]

There were serious problems of timing. It was no secret that Johnston had been relieved of command for not giving assurance that he would defend Atlanta and for not pursuing a more aggressive policy. Cooper's July 17 dispatch announcing his removal had charged that Johnston had failed "to arrest the advance of the enemy to the vicinity of Atlanta, far into the interior of Georgia," and that Johnston had expressed no confidence "that you can defeat or repulse him." [10] Too, that same day, Seddon's congratulatory telegram to Hood indicated what the government wanted. Seddon noted that there might still be time either to cut Sherman's communications "or find or make an opportunity of equal encounter whether he moves east or west." [11] When Bragg returned to Atlanta during the last week of July, he supported Hood's use of offensive tactics and spoke favorably of Hood's planned offensive at Ezra Church. In fact, not until August 5, after Hood had fought three battles, did Richmond question his offensive policy. Then Davis noted that Hood's losses from attacking fortifications were such that "requires you to avoid that if practicable." [12]

Hood's known stand on the offensive, the circumstances of Johnston's removal, and Richmond's scant advice caused him to think solely of the attack. In doing so, he may not have been far wrong. What else could he do? Richmond provided no instructions whatsoever, except to encourage an offensive, until Davis' August 5 note. Left to his own resources, Hood's choices seemed narrow. He could abandon Atlanta and retreat southward, which he knew the government did not want. He could fall back into Atlanta and undertake siege operations. But by July 19 Sherman had already severed one of Atlanta's three rail arteries, the Augusta road. By July 29 a single Federal cavalry division had crossed the Chattahoochee far downstream and had torn up two and

9 One observer noted that Hood was "physically handicapped, if not wholly disqualified from active service in the field," by the autumn of 1864. See Cumming Recollection, UNC; Dyer, *Gallant Hood*, 238, 354.

10 Cooper to Johnston, July 17, 1864, in Johnston Letters, West Point.

11 Seddon to Hood, July 17, 1864, in Hood Papers, National Archives.

12 *Official Records*, XXXVIII, Pt. 5, p. 946; see also Bragg to Davis, July 27, 1864, in Bragg Papers, Duke.

a half miles of track on both the West Point and the Macon, demonstrating those railroads' vulnerability. Despite Johnston's later claims, it was obvious that Sherman did have sufficient numbers to disrupt, if not control, all three rail approaches to Atlanta.

Hood's third choice would have been to attempt to force Sherman's retreat by disrupting his communications. Here Hood found himself the victim of both his own behavior and Richmond's departmental policies. His correspondence with the government had insisted that Johnston possessed ample cavalry to sever Sherman's communications if it were utilized properly. Hood recognized the fallacy in this claim, as seen in his plea the day after he took command that the government send Lee's cavalry to strike Sherman's supply line. He repeated this request in early August.[13]

Hood was now learning that Johnston's problems had been more involved than he had realized. Richmond still refused to concentrate in the West. The policy of maintaining a separate departmental command in Alabama and Mississippi was continued in the late summer even after its commander, General Stephen D. Lee, came to Hood's army as a new corps commander. By July, Lee's department had almost seventeen thousand troops. By September the Alabama-Mississippi department boasted almost twenty-two thousand men, more than half of them cavalry, and seventy-five pieces of field artillery. In addition, there were twenty-four military outposts, some of dubious value, stretched from Mobile to Clinton, Louisiana, and from Oxford, Mississippi, to Cahaba, Alabama.

The government's policy toward Hood was much like its policy toward Johnston. In late July, Bragg promised Hood an additional fifty-five hundred men from Lee's department. While some were sent—though probably not even the meager fifty-five hundred—it was a motley organization. Some were returned stragglers; others were needed workers at the Macon and Columbus munitions installations, who were only temporarily detached for the emergency. In September Hood pleaded for more men, and Davis' responses on September 5 were similar in language to those he had sent Johnston in early July—that every available man not needed elsewhere had been sent.[14]

With little hope of outside aid, Hood, in early August, sent his own cavalry to attempt to break Sherman's communications. With forty-five

[13] Hood to Seddon, July 19, 1864, in Hood Papers, National Archives; *Official Records,* XXXVII, Pt. 5, p. 951.

[14] Davis to Hood, September 5, Bragg to Hood, July 22, 23, 1864, in Hood Papers, National Archives; Hood to Davis, September 4—11:30 A.M., 1864, in Hood Cipher Book, *ibid.; Official Records,* XXXIX, Pt. 2, pp. 886, 675, Pt. 3, pp. 909, 872, XLV, Pt. 2, p. 632, XXXVIII, Pt. 5, p. 939.

hundred men, almost half of the cavalry, Wheeler was ordered northward to destroy the railroad between Atlanta and Nashville. Wheeler was to tear up the Western and Atlantic to Chattanooga, then was to cross the Tennessee River and operate against the dual rail lines leading from Middle Tennessee into North Alabama, and then to return to the army, destroying any remains of the Western and Atlantic en route.

Wheeler foolishly rode himself completely out of the campaign. After sporadically destroying sections of the Western and Atlantic between Marietta and Dalton, he disobeyed orders and launched a haphazard dash into East Tennessee. En route he stopped periodically to duel with various unimportant garrisons, and did not even cross the Tennessee River until he was some three hundred miles northeast of Atlanta, above Knoxville. From here another march of nearly two hundred miles across the difficult Cumberland Mountains was required before Wheeler struck the Nashville and Chattanooga Railroad and penetrated to near Nashville. Harassed by strong Federal pursuit, Wheeler only expended two days in operating on the Nashville and Chattanooga, before moving west to the road from Nashville to Decatur, which he did effectually damage. After a series of running battles, in which he lost one of his finest brigade commanders, General John Kelly, the Federals chased him almost to the Alabama-Mississippi border before Wheeler could recross the Tennessee at Tuscumbia in early September.[15]

Wheeler had destroyed Hood's cavalry. He later glossed over the disaster by claiming that he brought out of Tennessee twenty-eight hundred absentees and recruits. This claim is sheer fantasy. So badly cut up was Wheeler's command that he did not rejoin Hood until early October. At Tuscumbia he reported having only two thousand men with him, and his adjutant general noted that Wheeler probably could not organize five hundred effective men.[16]

The defeat of Wheeler did more than destroy any hope Hood had of breaking Sherman's communications. It illustrated a factor in the changing nature of the war which neither Johnston nor Hood seemed to grasp. Johnston and his later biographers would hold out the destruction of Sherman's railroad as the ultimate weapon needed to throw back the Federal surge on Atlanta, if only the government could be persuaded to use it.

By the summer of 1864 a combination of improved technology and growing Federal cavalry strength made this destruction impossible. By July, Sherman's railroad artery was not as weak as it had been while

15 *Official Records*, XXXVIII, Pt. 3, pp. 957–91; Dyer, *Wheeler*, 187–97.
16 *Official Records*, XXXVIII, Pt. 3, pp. 957–61; Dyer, *Wheeler*, 187–97.

Johnston's army lay at Dalton. There had been a steady perfecting of techniques both in railroad repair and protection. In January of 1864 Colonel W. E. Merrill had been appointed chief engineer of Thomas' Army of the Cumberland. Throughout the spring of 1864, Merrill designed an intricate set of railroad defenses consisting of strong infantry and artillery blockhouses. More than sixty were erected on the Nashville and Chattanooga Railroad between Nashville and Stevenson, while fifty-four were constructed on the Nashville and Decatur Railroad and its extension via the Memphis and Charleston into Stevenson. Twenty-two others were erected on the Western and Atlantic south of Chattanooga to protect water crossings. As Wheeler discovered in August of 1864, such blockhouses were almost impregnable to the ordinary cavalry raid. Of thick log construction and often reinforced with iron, these fortresses were supplied with ventilators, cellars, and water tanks.

The success of this advancement in military engineering was well demonstrated during Wheeler's raid. While his troopers destroyed some track, they did not destroy a single bridge between Chattanooga and Atlanta nor did they attack one blockhouse on this route. Between Nashville and Chattanooga, Wheeler repeatedly was frustrated in his efforts to destroy bridges. The blockhouse at Smyrna drove off his attempt to burn the Stewart's Creek bridge north of Murfreesboro, while the most vital bridges across the Stone's, Duck, Elk, and Tennessee rivers went unscathed. In fact, General Robert Milroy, who commanded the Middle Tennessee defenses, gave credit to Sherman's railroad engineers for the failure of Wheeler's raid.[17]

Other advances in technology dimmed Confederate hopes to smash the rail route from Atlanta to the Nashville warehouses. The presence in Georgia of Yankee supply trains bearing cars marked "Delaware and Lackawanna" and "Pittsburg & Fort Wayne" was symbolic of the mass rail effort Sherman was making. Already this had been demonstrated while Johnston commanded the army. Sherman had detached whole regiments of engineers for standby duty to repair broken rail links and had amassed huge shops at Chattanooga to supply the needed equipment. Johnston simply could not halt the trains. Although he burned the Oostanaula Bridge when he fell back across the river on May 15, within five days Sherman's locomotives were chugging into Kingston while Johnston's trains from Atlanta were only two miles away, near Cassville. On May 20, when Johnston fell back across the Etowah River, the long Western and Atlantic Railroad bridge was burned, and some track was

17 Merrill, "Block-Houses for Railroad Defense in the Department of the Cumberland," 389–404; *Official Records*, XXXVIII, Pt. 3, p. 83.

destroyed as the army retreated. By June 11, Sherman had repaired the bridge and track, and his trains were running as far south as the Federal line opposite Kennesaw Mountain.[18]

The only alternative seemed to be to take the offensive. There were other reasons for this besides the lack of suitable options. Again, Hood had also become entrapped in a situation which he had helped create. As late as July 14, Hood had played down Sherman's numerical superiority and had advocated an aggressive policy. It was Hood who provided Bragg with the estimate of Sherman's total force at 75,000. But now that the government demanded action, Hood lacked the men to accomplish it. During July and August the Confederates were hard pressed by outbreaks of yellow fever, smallpox, measles, typhoid, dysentery, and other diseases that greatly reduced Hood's strength. During July there were over 40,000 sick in the chain of Rebel hospitals along the railroads to Augusta, Macon, and Montgomery. Fewer than 10,000 of these were from battle wounds. An additional 21,000 new cases were admitted in August. These illnesses and Johnston's losses were affecting the muster roll of July 10, even before Hood ascended to the command. Only 35,856 infantry were listed as effective, although 51,707 were present with the army, and an additional 48,747 were listed as absent.[19]

Hood's determination to fight was tied to another key matter—the enduring influence of Bragg into July and August. Usually Bragg's conduct in the Atlanta campaign has been described in one of two ways. Some writers have belittled his influence as commander in chief and have labeled his visit to Atlanta in July as merely carrying out Davis' wishes to gather evidence on removing Johnston. Other historians have also played down the power in Bragg's new job but have admitted that he had some influence in Johnston's removal. These same writers, however, depict Bragg as skulking away into the night after his initial conferences with Johnston.

Neither version is quite accurate. Bragg's influence did not abate with Hood's appointment. Instead, in late July and August, Bragg exerted broad influence over western affairs. In effect he took emergency control of both Hood's and S. D. Lee's departments. After his Atlanta visit, Bragg proceeded to Montgomery, Columbus, and Macon. He organized defenses for Montgomery and for the West Point Railroad, conferred with Lee on strategic matters, organized defenses for Columbus, Geor-

18 *Official Records*, XXXVIII, Pt. 3, p. 83; Sherman to wife, August 11, 1864, in Sherman, *Home Letters*, 307; Dyer, *Wheeler*, 195; Sherman, *Memoirs*, II, 42.

19 Hood to Bragg, July 14, 1864, in Bragg Papers, Western Reserve; *Official Records*, XXXVIII, Pt. 3, p. 679.

gia, and funnelled some reinforcements to Hood. In addition he also worked on the problem of replacing several of Hood's officers who had been killed or who were ill. His old friend General Patton Anderson was ordered to Atlanta to replace the ailing General Thomas C. Hindman.

By July 24 Bragg was back in Atlanta for more conferences with Hood. By early August, he was again in Macon and Columbus, busily arranging for supplies to be forwarded to Atlanta, for railroad protection between Lee's and Hood's departments, and for filling vacancies in Hood's officer corps.

Through all of this activity, Bragg continued to prod Hood to take the offensive. While at Montgomery on July 18, he had suggested to Richmond that the only possible hope in Georgia was for Hood immediately to assume the offensive, a suggestion which Davis quickly urged Bragg to press upon Hood.[20]

But Bragg had something else in mind. While touring Columbus, Macon, Montgomery, and other towns, he depicted the removal of Johnston as a necessity, and gave elaborate reasons which were slanted against that general. Bragg seemed obsessed with defending the government in the removal. In so doing, he sent back to Richmond a distorted view of actual conditions in Hood's army. His reports contrasted the shambles of Johnston's organization with the superb rebuilding of the army by Hood. In fact, some of his appraisals were simply unbelievable. After Hardee's failure to break Sherman's left flank on July 22, Bragg reported to the government that Hood had won a "brilliant" victory, and that Sherman had been "badly defeated." [21] on July 27 Bragg again referred to the "signal defeat" of Sherman on July 22.[22]

There were other distortions. Hood's failure at Peachtree Creek was tossed aside as a minor loss, and Bragg erroneously reported to Richmond that in both the Peachtree Creek and the Atlanta engagements, Hood had lost a total of only three thousand men. Instead, argued Bragg, the army's strength was "increasing daily," [23] with large numbers of Georgia Militia turning out and heavy returns of stragglers being reported.[24]

20 *Official Records*, XXXIX, Pt. 2, pp. 719, 721, XXXVIII, Pt. 5, pp. 887–88, 894, 899, 904, 907, LII, Pt. 2, p. 709; Bragg to Hood, July 22, 23, 1864, in Hood Papers, National Archives.

21 *Official Records*, XXXVIII, Pt. 5, p. 908.

22 Bragg to Davis, July 27, 1864, in Bragg Papers, Duke. See also *Official Records*, XXXVIII, Pt. 5, pp. 911, 908; Johnston to Wigfall, August 27, 1864, in Wigfall Papers, DLC.

23 *Official Records*, XXXVIII, Pt. 5, p. 911.

24 Bragg to Davis, July 27, 1864, in Bragg Papers, Duke.

The bias of these reports is obvious. Hood's returns showed no substantial gain from returnees. The Georgia Militia was never the power Bragg depicted. General G. W. Smith was never able to assemble more than two thousand additional men to bolster the three thousand called out while Johnston commanded the army. The depiction of the July 22 battle as a Confederate victory was little short of a lie. Also, Bragg's repeated boasts that Hood's appointment had greatly increased the efficiency and morale of the officer corps were sheer fallacy. The week that Bragg was in Atlanta on his second visit, Hood was confronted with serious problems of organization, no small matter being the brand new corps command organization.

Still, Bragg's influence remained powerful. The government seemed to accept his view that matters in Georgia had improved. Too, even before he reached Atlanta on his second visit, he had given official governmental approval to Hood's desire to attack Sherman.

Hood's first opportunity for such an offensive came the day after he assumed command. By early morning on July 19, advanced units of General George Thomas' Army of the Cumberland began to drive back Hood's skirmish line along Peachtree Creek. By noon, Thomas was crossing on a wide front at several points on roads leading from Pace's Ferry and Buckhead to Atlanta. By nightfall, intelligence from both the Decatur and Peachtree fronts indicated that the opportunity to use Johnston's attack plan was at hand. McPherson's Army of the Tennessee was reported astride the Augusta Railroad at Decatur, and was said to be slowly advancing toward Atlanta. Schofield's Army of the Ohio, slightly to the west of McPherson, was also in the vicinity of Decatur, advancing on Atlanta by a road which paralleled the railroad.[25]

There were several factors which made the situation inviting. Thomas was separated from Schofield's right wing by a space of almost two miles. Thomas' army itself was badly extended across a six-mile-wide front, from west of the Pace's Ferry Road eastward to the upper reaches of Peachtree Creek. The creek itself offered promise. Deep and sluggish, the meandering stream was scarcely fordable. Too, the upper portion of Peachtree, between Decatur and the main road from Buckhead to Atlanta was a maze of smaller creeks. The north and south forks of Peachtree Creek ran west here, only to join near the Buckhead Road. In addition, there were smaller tributaries flowing through this swampy, thicket region. Thomas' left wing, which Hood knew lay east of the Buckhead Road, would be compelled to cross both branches of the creek

25 *Official Records*, XXXVIII, Pt. 3, p. 630; Hood, *Advance and Retreat*, 165.

on a long wheel before aligning with the right wing which lay west of the Buckhead Road.

Determined to strike Thomas while the bulk of his force was crossing Peachtree Creek, Hood called his new corps organization—Hardee, Stewart, and Cheatham—to his headquarters on the morning of July 20. There he outlined a deceptively simple plan to ensnare Thomas. Stewart's corps, which held the left wing, stretched from the Western and Atlantic Railroad on a semicircular arc to Pace's Ferry Road. Hardee's corps occupied the center, across the main Buckhead Road. Cheatham's corps extended the line toward the Georgia railroad. The extreme right, astride the railroad and the pike to Augusta, was held by General G. W. Smith's Georgia state troops, protected in front by Wheeler with twenty-five hundred cavalry.

Hood's plan was for Cheatham and Smith to immobilize McPherson and Schofield while Hardee and Stewart drove Thomas back into the pocket formed by the confluence of Peachtree Creek and the Chattahoochee River. To accomplish this, Hardee in the center would begin the attack at 1 P.M. in the characteristic manner of the western army—en echelon—beginning with his right division. Stewart would then take up the assault from right to left.[26]

No sooner had Hood explained the plan, however, than the army's new command organization fell into the familiar confusion. Haste was essential lest Thomas completely cross the creek and entrench. But Hood, though he had known of the situation since the previous night, had delayed calling a council of war until the morning of July 20, and thus had delayed the attack until the afternoon of that day. This delay gave Thomas well over twelve hours of additional time to cross his troops. Hood simply was not allotting enough time for preparation or for any of those contingencies which often upset battle plans. Such a contingency arose during the morning after the council had adjourned. Wheeler's two cavalry brigades on the Decatur Road were being steadily pushed back by mid-morning. After receiving warnings from Wheeler, Hood, by 10 A.M., was forced to shift and extend Cheatham's line a division's length eastward to cover the Augusta Railroad completely. Fearful of a gap between his right and center, Hood ordered both Hardee and Stewart to shift to the right one-half division to close the gap.[27]

As noon approached, more confusion developed. Hood did not re-

26 Hood, *Advance and Retreat*, 166; *Official Records*, XXXVIII, Pt. 3, pp. 630, 871.
27 T. B. Roy, "General Hardee and the Military Operations Around Atlanta," *SHSP*, VIII (1880), 348; E. B. Wade to Wheeler, July 20—11 A.M., 1864, in Wheeler Papers, Alabama; *Official Records*, XXXVIII, Pt. 5, pp. 894-95, Pt. 3, pp. 871, 952.

main on the field, but retired to Atlanta, some four miles distant. In his absence his design disintegrated along Peachtree Creek. Instead of shifting a division's length to the east, Cheatham throughout the morning continued a long process of shifting, halting to re-form battle lines, then shifting again toward the Georgia Railroad. By the time appointed for the attack to begin, Cheatham had moved his line eastward some two miles—a far greater distance than Hood had estimated.[28]

The strategy could have been salvaged had it not been for Hardee's peculiar attitude on July 20. Although on July 19 Hood had ordered a reconnaissance of the terrain toward the creek, not until after the July 20 council did Hardee order his staff to reconnoiter the front. And not until noon did Hardee's observers even return to his headquarters with a report for an attack to begin within an hour. Hardee's attitude throughout the day appeared to be one of sulkiness, with great reluctance to consult Hood. Not until almost noon did Hardee place his divisions in battle line. At nearly 1 P.M., the time appointed for the attack, Hardee began the shift a half division to his right to join up with Cheatham.

The result was more confusion. The shift would require a move by Hardee's three divisions on the front line. General William Bate was to move first, followed by W. H. T. Walker's division in the center and General George Maney, temporarily commanding Cheatham's division, on the left. Cleburne's division, held in reserve, would also make the shift. As Hardee slid east a half division's length, the left wing, Stewart's corps, would follow another half division's length. Stewart had placed all three of his divisions in attacking line, with no reserve. Loring's division occupied the right, Walthall's the center, and French's the left.[29]

Delay ensued. Absent from the field, Hood did not know that Cheatham was extending his line much further eastward than was planned. About one o'clock Hardee's divisions began to slide eastward. Hardee ordered a staff officer, Major Samuel Black, to post himself at the point where Maney's left brigade was to halt and assume the extreme left position of Hardee's new line. But between one and two o'clock, as Hardee began to shift eastward, he discovered that Cheatham had not carried out his orders properly, that a full two miles existed between the center and the right wings. This was obvious on Hardee's left. When Maney's left brigade approached the new position which Hardee had

28 *Official Records*, XXXVIII, Pt. 5, pp. 895–97; W. S. Featherston to Hood, December 15, 1866, in Hood Papers, National Archives; Featherston to W. W. Loring, September 1, 1866, in Wheeler Papers, Alabama.

29 Roy, "Military Operations Around Atlanta," 348–49; Hughes, *Hardee*, 220–21; *Official Records*, XXXVIII, Pt. 5, p. 894.

designated, its commander refused to halt because the remainder of the division was continuing eastward. Black sought out Hardee and reported that the corps was continuing to shift, but the general merely replied that his orders were to maintain contact with Cheatham's left. Though he admitted such a policy would prolong the delay, Hardee evidently did not bother to dispatch a courier to Hood at Atlanta to ask which of the contradictory orders was more urgent: to attack immediately or to maintain communications with Cheatham's corps. Meanwhile, the almost ludicrous situation continued. To the surprise of Stewart's brigade commanders, their shift was not a half mile, but two miles. Thus, not until three-thirty did Hardee have his lines adjusted.[30]

The results were disastrous to Hood's hopes for a swift attack. Neither Hood nor Hardee gave sufficient time to enable the two attacking corps to maneuver across the most difficult terrain along the south bank of Peachtree Creek. The country was a morass of thick woods, small tributary streams, boggy, swampy ground and rough high ground. Nor had sufficient time been given to reconnaissance. The rough country so masked the Federals that Hardee's right wing would never make contact with the enemy when the battle began. Unknown to Hood, Thomas had sent two of Howard's divisions to reinforce Schofield, creating a broad gap on Thomas' left which the Confederates never discovered. Usually a master at discerning topography, Hardee's prior preparations seemed poor.[31]

These errors became evident when Hardee was finally ready to attack about 4:00 P.M. Already the hope to surprise was gone. Hood's plan had been for each division to advance from right to left successively, then obliquely to the west as they approached the creek, driving the Union troops downstream toward the Chattahoochee. Instead, the attack was a badly handled, sporadic affair. Some of Stewart's units had already advanced as early as 2:30 P.M., due to a misunderstanding. Hardee at that time had reported to Stewart that he was ready to attack. In reality it was over an hour before Hardee's right wing got in motion.

Stewart's main attack preceded Hardee's. Stewart's right division, commanded by General W. W. Loring, moved forward toward Thomas' temporary breastworks before a single one of Hardee's divisions moved forward. When Loring reached the Union entrenchments, he overran a segment of Thomas' line but was repulsed because he lacked support

[30] S. L. Black to Roy, May 31, 1880, in Roy, "Military Operations Around Atlanta," 348; Featherston to Loring, September 1, 1866, in Wheeler Papers, Alabama.

[31] Roy Sketch, in Hardee Papers, Alabama; Lilla Mills Hawes (ed.), *The Memoirs of Charles H. Olmstead,* Collections of the Georgia Historical Society (Savannah, 1964), XIV, 149.

from Hardee. Where were Hardee's three divisions? The right division under Bate, scheduled to strike the entrenchments first, did not even find Thomas. Bate's men spent the afternoon stumbling through the thick underbrush in search of Thomas' line. Suddenly, Bate simply disappeared from sight, and Hardee did not find him until after 6 P.M., when he sent a staff officer who located the general still searching for Thomas' line in a forest of thick timber.

Meanwhile, the remainder of Hardee's corps had been badly used. Walker's division in the center had moved forward after Bate. Walker's right wing also became lost and never found Thomas' line, but his left brigades were smashed by unexpected heavy artillery resistance near the Buckhead Road. As Walker's men reeled back, Maney's division reached the breastworks, only to find that Loring's division on their left had already been repulsed. Maney also was thrown back after losing heavy casualties. Clearly, the short but hard fight was over by nightfall. After Loring's initial repulse, Stewart's center division, Walthall's, had also attacked piecemeal. The left division, French's, scarcely had made contact with the enemy when orders came from Hardee at about nightfall to break off the fight.[32]

What had gone wrong? While Hood bore the responsibility for his lack of presence on the field, Hardee handled the attack badly. Aside from the initial delay of almost three hours in moving forward, Hardee also did not have his men under control. Of his four divisions, only one full division, Maney's, made contact with the enemy. Bate's and the right of Walker's divisions never made contact. Hardee's most experienced command, Cleburne's, was never sent into action. Hardee later maintained that he was about to send Cleburne to support Maney when he received orders from Hood to send support to Wheeler's cavalry on the far right. Cheatham had failed to extend his line across the Georgia Railroad, where Wheeler's twenty-five hundred cavalrymen were confronting heavy columns of McPherson's army. Driven back to a bald knoll south of the railroad, Wheeler about, 5:45 P.M., appealed to Hood for assistance. Fearful that Atlanta could be taken by a drive through Wheeler's thin line, Hood, at some time shortly before 7:00, finally reached Hardee's front with a courier ordering that a division be withdrawn and rushed to Wheeler's support. Accordingly, Cleburne was hastily marched to the far right, some two miles north of the city limits of Atlanta.

But Hardee's attack had already dwindled before Cleburne was withdrawn. The courier from Hood did not arrive until near 7 P.M., and

32 Hughes, *Hardee*, 221–22; *Official Records*, XXXVIII, Pt. 5, p. 897, Pt. 3, pp. 698–99, 871; Buck, *Cleburne and His Command*, 231; French, *Two Wars*, 218–19.

only a few minutes remained before dark. Hardee later admitted that any renewed attack could not get under way until dark. Actually, Hardee's most veteran division, Cleburne's, had been held out of action long after Hardee knew that his right wing was not making contact with the enemy. Hardee's explanation masked the fact that he did not have control of his divisions. He lost Bate and allowed Maney and Walker to attack in piecemeal fashion. Meanwhile, Loring's and Walthall's divisions had been beaten severely in attacking the breastworks on Stewart's front. Still, Hood's casualties had been light, probably not exceeding twenty-five hundred, and within two days he had decided to try again.[33]

By the morning of July 21 Hood resolved that this time he must deal with McPherson, whose forces lay astride the Augusta Railroad. The previous night his cavalry had brought a more accurate depiction of the posture of Sherman's army. Sherman's left flank was definitely vulnerable. McPherson's left lay along the Georgia Railroad between Decatur and Atlanta. A long, encumbering wagon train was parked in the rear at Decatur. With visions of Jackson's flank move at Chancellorsville, Hood conjured the idea of a rapid night march by one of his corps and an overlapping of McPherson's line.

Clearly something must be done at once on the Decatur Road front. All day on July 21, Cleburne's division and Wheeler's cavalrymen fought desperately to control the Bald Hill eminence. Under a hot sun, the Confederates were pounded mercilessly by McPherson's rifled guns. An entire company of Texas cavalry was wiped out in one shot. Repeated waves of blue infantry assaulted the hill, with fierce hand-to-hand encounters. By the afternoon, Bald Hill was in Federal hands, and it

---

[33] *Official Records,* XXXVIII, Pt. 3, pp. 698–99; Buck, *Cleburne and His Command,* 231–33; Buck to Roy, March 27, 1880, in Roy, "Military Operations Around Atlanta," 350, see also pp. 351–53; G. A. Smith to Wheeler, July 20—4:45 P.M., 1864, A. P. Mason to Wheeler, July 20—7:15 P.M., in Wheeler Papers, Alabama; Hughes, *Hardee,* 223–24. Hood's later assertion that Hardee's delay and mismanagement cost him the opportunity to catch Thomas' army divided by Peachtree Creek is not quite accurate. Had Hood attacked early on July 20 instead of delaying the attack until the afternoon, he would have caught Thomas completely divided. However, by noon of July 20, practically all of Thomas' army was across the creek. By the morning of July 20, only a single brigade of Palmer's 14th Corps had not crossed. Hooker's 20th Corps crossed on the morning of July 20. Newton's and Stanley's divisions of Howard's 4th Corps had also crossed on the morning of July 20. The only substantial number of men not across by early in the afternoon of July 20 was Wood's division of Howard's corps and a brigade of Palmer's corps. See *Official Records,* XXXVIII, Pt. 1, pp. 635, 601, 562, 297, 202, 382, Pt. 2, p. 137; see also Errol MacGregor Clauss, "The Atlanta Campaign 18 July–2 September, 1864" (Ph.D. dissertation, Emory University, 1965), 61–63, 74, 76. Clauss's work is probably the most detailed description available of the movements of individual Federal units in the campaign.

appeared that McPherson the following day could flank Hood's entire line and reach Atlanta.[34]

To forestall this, Hood had, by the evening of July 21, prepared a bold plan. During the day, Stewart's, Hardee's, and Cheatham's men were withdrawn into a new outer line of fortifications which Hood's chief engineer, Colonel Stephen Presstman, had hastily prepared that day. The line was far less lengthy than that on Peachtree Creek, could be held by fewer men, and was on a higher elevation. This new line was to be garrisoned by Stewart, Cheatham, and the Georgia state troops. During the night of July 21, Hardee was to swing northeast around McPherson's line and attack him the following day on the flank and rear. Once McPherson was turned, then Cheatham and Stewart would take up the assault. The plan appeared to have promise. The bulk of Sherman's army, Thomas' wing, lay astride Peachtree Creek, separated by twelve miles of circuitous roads from McPherson near Decatur.[35]

Like Hood's Peachtree scheme, the plan for Hardee's flank attack exhibited the weakness of the new command structure. The selection of Hardee's corps seemed wise, since that general was the army's only experienced corps leader, and his men had been much less engaged on July 20 than Stewart's. But Hood's plan called for a daylight attack following a night march by Hardee via Cobb's Mill to McPherson's rear near Decatur, a distance of some eighteen miles over one road. Aside from the normal contingencies of delay which arose, there was the problem of Cleburne's division. Until nightfall of the twenty-first, Cleburne was forced to remain in position several miles north of Atlanta on the Georgia Railroad. It would take time for him to fall back to Atlanta and join the marching column. Even then, his men were exhausted from a long day's fight under the hot Georgia sun. This was obvious by nightfall. Hardee, at 7:30 P.M, ordered Cleburne to break off skirmishing with McPherson and fall back within the Atlanta defenses. But by 11:00 Cleburne still had not left the front. Hood would have done better to detach another division to replace Cleburne's. Again Hardee seemed not to have his troops under control. After ordering Cleburne at 7:30 to make the initial withdrawal, Hardee delayed almost four hours before again requesting his presence in Atlanta, and did not order Cleburne to be ready to march until 1:00 A.M.[36]

Even before Hardee left Atlanta, Hood was forced to change his

---

[34] Hood, *Advance and Retreat*, 173; Buck, *Cleburne and His Command*, 232–34; *Official Records*, XXXVIII, Pt. 3, p. 952.

[35] Hood, *Advance and Retreat*, 173–74.

[36] Hughes, *Hardee*, 226–27; Buck, *Cleburne and His Command*, 234–35; Roy, "Military Operations Around Atlanta," 354–59; *Official Records*, XXXVIII, Pt. 5, pp. 898–900.

original plan on the night of July 21. Sometime during the day, he had called his three corps commanders and General G. W. Smith to his headquarters to explain the plan. In this first council, Hood outlined a plan whereby Hardee would move on the McDonough Road to Cobb's Mill, and then march completely around McPherson to Decatur, where Hardee would attack the Federal rear. Hood later claimed that it was with this order that Hardee left Atlanta and that the attack's failure was due to Hardee's negligence in not marching his corps far enough to get completely around McPherson.

Some time during the evening, it seems that Hood did revise his plans to give Hardee more discretion. Hood's original order called for Hardee to move at twilight from Atlanta. But when it was obvious that the withdrawal of Cleburne would delay matters, apparently a second council was held. Hardee later argued that Hood now gave him a different plan. It was known that McPherson's army was aligned generally along the Georgia Railroad in a north-south position facing westward. To reach the rear of the army at Decatur would require an eighteen-mile night march via Cobb's Mill. Merely to reach the left flank and rear of the left wing of the army via Cobb's Mill would require a shorter march. Thus Hardee later contended that during the evening Hood changed his plans and ordered a strike via the shorter route, against McPherson's left flank.[37]

There is still a third version which contradicts both Hood's and Hardee's. Some fifteen years after the war, Hardee's wartime chief of staff, Colonel T. B. Roy, attempted to collect evidence to prove Hardee's allegation that he obeyed a revised set of orders. Cheatham's recollection jibed with neither Hardee's nor Hood's. Cheatham agreed that a second council was held, and that Hood abandoned his first plan. But Cheatham differed with Hardee concerning the revision. According to him, Hood did not now give specific orders for a flank attack. Hood still was "very decided" that Hardee should move completely to McPherson's rear at Decatur. Still, due to the late hour, Hood agreed that Hardee "should have discretion" merely to attack the left flank and rear of the left portion of McPherson's line.[38]

Actually, Hardee may not have known exactly what he was doing. The march from Atlanta toward McPherson's left was a morass of confusion reminiscent of the march from Corinth to Shiloh in 1862.

[37] *Official Records*, XXXVIII, Pt. 3, pp. 699, 631; Hood, *Advance and Retreat*, 176–78; Roy, "Military Operations Around Atlanta," 354–55, 357–58; Hughes, *Hardee*, 226.

[38] Cheatham to Roy (n.d.), quoted in Roy to Cheatham, October 15, 1881, in Cheatham Papers, Tennessee; Hughes, *Hardee*, 226.

Hardee's laxity in getting Cleburne in motion was soon obvious. Not until 3 A.M. did the last of the corps leave Atlanta for the dawn assault. Through the night, the men, weary from fighting and skirmishing from July 20–21 and entrenching on the twenty-first, toiled across Entrenchment Creek at Cobb's Mill and then turned north on the road from Cobb's Mill to Decatur. Repeated delays occurred. Some of Hardee's men had not slept for two days. Others simply fell exhausted because of the arduous labors of the previous two days and the oppressively hot July night. Some possessed inadequate ammunition, and delays of as much as two hours were required before some units could be supplied. So slow was the march that it was not until after noon of July 22 that Hardee's troops were finally aligned for attack. Meanwhile, since daylight Hood had waited with Cheatham's corps for the sound of guns toward Decatur.[39]

Hood's planning, fashioned after a well-oiled command structure in Virginia, simply was too sophisticated for the new western command. By noon of July 22 Hardee was fifteen miles from the army, a half day late in launching an attack, and completely out of touch with Hood. At Atlanta, Hood knew nothing of what was going on until he heard Hardee's skirmishers open on McPherson. Since a dawn attack was expected, Hardee should have informed Hood of the considerable delay. If he had notified Hood, pressure might well have been applied on the Union right to attract both reinforcements and attention to the front northwest of Atlanta.

In the meantime, Hardee again lost control of his divisions in the difficult terrain between the Cobb's Mill–Decatur Road and the Augusta Railroad. By about dawn the vanguard of the corps had reached the Widow Parker's, some three miles south of Decatur. There Hardee had halted and conferred with his division commanders and with Wheeler, whose cavalry was to extend Hardee's line toward Decatur. Neither Hardee nor his commanders knew exactly where they were in relation to McPherson's line, but cavalry reconnaissance had led them to believe they had at least reached the rear of McPherson's left flank. Thus from dawn until noon, Hardee busied himself in aligning the slowly arriving troops into battle formation. Cleburne's division, the last to arrive, would occupy the left wing, with its left flank resting on the road from Atlanta to Cobb's Mill. The remaining three divisions, Bate's, Walker's, and Maney's, were aligned in a northeast slant along the road from Cobb's Mill via the Widow Parker's to Decatur. Shortly before noon the army was at last ready to advance.

[39] *Official Records,* XXXVIII, 737, 747; Roy, "Military Operations Around Atlanta," 356–59; Buck, *Cleburne and His Command,* 235.

The resulting attack, known as the Battle of Atlanta, was curiously like that of Shiloh, in that the Confederate surprise attack was frustrated and broken up by difficult topography. From the road between Cobb's Mill and Decatur to the Federal line was a morass of dense woods, swamps, and a long mill pond. This terrain produced a two-mile-wide wilderness where visibility, especially on the center and right, was sometimes limited to ten paces, and on Cleburne's front to fifty yards. Since Hardee actually did not know where McPherson's left flank was supposed to terminate, his four divisions were aligned abreast with no strong reserves. This alignment further jeopardized communication, since the woods were so thick that in places Hardee's battle line was not visible for more than a hundred yards. The lateness both of promulgating plans for the attack and the march to McPherson's front had made a close reconnaissance impossible. Hardee barely knew what obstacles lay between his troops and McPherson. He had learned of the thick woods and of a long mill pond, wide and deep, which lay across his path, but he learned little else.[40]

The result was an entangling of divisions and sporadic attacks which frustrated any coordinated effort. The army was supposed to guide on General Daniel Govan's brigade, which formed Cleburne's left along the road from Atlanta to Cobb's Mill. But due to the terrain, Cleburne's men reached McPherson's line much sooner than the accompanying three divisions. As Hardee's divisions became intermingled in the thick underbrush, Bate's, Walker's, and Maney's divisions ran upon the half-mile-long mill pond which was impossible to cross. Precious time was lost as Bate and Walker veered to the left to circle the pond. On the right, Maney's situation seemed so hopeless that Hardee pulled him completely out of the battle line and ordered him to march and reinforce Cleburne.

When Cleburne first struck the Federals shortly after 1 P.M., another unexpected obstacle developed. McPherson's flank was not in the air as it had been represented to be. Instead, it extended toward Atlanta as far as Bald Hill, and veered back on a curve to encircle completely McPherson's far left. In addition, Cleburne and later Walker, who attacked to his right, discovered that McPherson's line apparently was not facing west as planned. A two-division front entrenched extension of McPherson's left was facing the Confederates with their backs apparently to the expected line.

During the early afternoon, Cleburne's division smashed into the

40 Roy, "Military Operations Around Atlanta," 359–60; *Official Records*, XXXVIII, Pt. 3, pp. 731, 737, 747–48, 751, 753, 952; Hughes, *Hardee,* 227; Buck, *Cleburne and His Command,* 235.

curved angle of the line and roared through a gap between this and the two detached divisions facing Hardee's men. For a time it appeared the Federal left might collapse. Cleburne's men carried the outer line of entrenchments and drove back the left wing to Bald Hill. In the meantime Walker's division arrived after a hard struggle through oak woods and brier thickets, and fell upon the two divisions facing Hardee from behind strong entrenchments. Like Cleburne, Walker received a galling fire and lost heavily.[41]

However, this initial attack did not have the power to carry McPherson's line, for it was unsupported by Bate and Maney, who had not arrived. Cleburne's men withstood a murderous fire as Walker advanced to their aid. The hot-tempered Walker, long bitter at being passed over for a corps command, was killed as he rode to the front. One of his brigade commanders, General States Rights Gist, was wounded. Already Walker's division was melting away in mid-afternoon when Bate finally arrived to make another uncoordinated attack on Walker's right.

Finally, about 5 P.M., Hardee managed to get all of his troops to the front. Maney, who had suffered a long march by the left flank to Cleburne's rear, appeared on the field. Hardee immediately threw Cleburne's exhausted men, fragments of Walker's decimated command, and Maney's troops against the extreme left flank and angle of McPherson's line. The Confederates overran that portion which faced Hardee and drove it back onto the main Federal line facing toward Atlanta. By nightfall, McPherson's extreme left had been squeezed back into the angle at Bald Hill.[42]

Again a bit of Hood's strategy, admirable in conception, failed in execution. The key to its success was the coordination of attack between Hardee and Cheatham. Cheatham, who held the right wing north of Atlanta, was to attack McPherson's left from the west as it was hard pressed by Hardee's attack from the east. But Hood did not order Cheatham to advance until two hours after Hardee's attack began, even though he admitted that Hardee's left was visible in its attack during the early afternoon. About 3 P.M. Hood gave orders for Cheatham to move forward. So slow was the Tennessee general in obeying that by the time he reached McPherson's front, Cleburne's assault had already been repulsed. Instead, Cheatham was enfiladed by a heavy

41 Buck, *Cleburne and His Command,* p. 235; *Official Records,* XXXVIII, Pt. 3, pp. 731–32, 737–39, 747; Roy, "Military Operations Around Atlanta," 360–64.

42 Buck, *Cleburne and His Command,* 240–41; *Official Records,* XXXVIII, Pt. 3, pp. 547, 739–40.

massing of Schofield's artillery from the Federal center and was thrown back without breaking McPherson's hold on Bald Hill.[43]

Why had Hood failed? It was not because of timidity, though Hood later hinted that the army's fear of attacking breastworks had been a deciding factor. Instead, Hardee had lost heavily. Some 3,299 Confederates in Hardee's corps were killed, wounded, or captured. The corps had lost one division commander, Walker, and two of Cleburne's brigade leaders, Gist and James A. Smith, were wounded. All but one commander of Smith's brigade were casualties, and Cleburne's entire division lost thirty field officers. General Mark Lowery's brigade lost one-half of its strength.[44]

The most obvious failure of Hood's plan could be seen in the casualty figures. Almost one-half of Hardee's losses were in Cleburne's division, which bore the brunt of the attack from early afternoon until nightfall. A lack of coordination among Hardee's four divisions had produced a circumstance similar to that of July 20, in that his men were committed piecemeal, with each division being repulsed before the next reached the front. In turn, this was matched by a lack of coordination between Hood and Hardee. Hood had expected too much of his new command structure, and did not give his orders in time for Hardee to make the difficult march completely to McPherson's rear. For his part, Hardee appeared to be in no hurry to leave Atlanta on the night of July 21. He did not seem to align his four divisions for any breakthrough. Instead, they were dispersed across a front four divisions wide with no strength at the critical point, McPherson's left flank. The results of this dispersal was an intermingling in the heavy wooded country which was reminiscent of Shiloh. In effect, Hardee's corps got lost in the woods and straggled to the front in numbers incapable of crushing McPherson's line. Once at the front, they received no help from Hood, who was angry that Hardee had not attacked at dawn.

There were some disturbing signs in the defeat of July 22. Already it was evident that the army was tightening its belt. By July 24 it was obvious to Hood that he could not hold such an extended line. Hardee was thus ordered back into the defenses on the east side of Atlanta. With the losses of July 22–24, Hood now had only thirty thousand effective infantry aside from G. W. Smith's Georgia troops. Even more serious, the army was running low on experienced officers, and the constant reshuffling of those available was telling. The command of Hood's

---

43 Buck, *Cleburne and His Command*, 241; *Official Records*, XXXVIII, Pt. 3, pp. 547, 739–40; Hood, *Advance and Retreat*, 180–81.

44 Hood, *Advance and Retreat*, 183; Roy, "Military Operations Around Atlanta," 367; *Official Records*, XXXVIII, Pt. 3, pp. 747, 732.

old corps had changed hands four times within eight days. When Hood relinquished the command on July 18, it had passed temporarily to General Carter Stevenson, the senior division commander. Then Cheatham was given the command. But by July 27 General Stephen D. Lee had arrived to take command, and Cheatham returned to his old command of a division in Hardee's corps. The death of W. H. T. Walker found the army flatly without an experienced division officer, so the division was broken up and distributed among Cheatham's, Cleburne's, and Bate's divisions. Also, the arrival of Lee to command Hood's old corps meant that the army would also have its third new arrangement of corps commanders in seven days.[45]

There were a number of other problems. General T. C. Hindman was too ill to continue in command of his division in Lee's corps. The command had been held temporarily by General John C. Brown, but a more experienced officer was needed. Consequently, Bragg in late July had ordered his old friend General Patton Anderson, then serving in Florida, to hasten back to the army. The condition of the officer material in Walker's now defunct division was also a pressing matter. One brigade commander, General Clement Stevens, had been killed at Peachtree Creek, while another, General Hugh Mercer, was considered too old and ill for further field service. Hood's chief of staff, General W. W. Mackall, had resigned and left the army by July 24. His replacement, General Francis Shoup, was hampered because Mackall had taken all of the chief of staff's records with him when he left. Meanwhile, Hardee and Hood's mutual dislike flourished. When Bragg made his second visit to Atlanta on July 25, Hardee requested that he be transferred to another command. For his part, Hood made no apologies for his statements that Hardee was responsible for the failures of July 20 and 22, particularly because he and the troops in general disliked to attack breastworks.[46]

There were other signs of a deteriorating condition. When Hood withdrew Stewart and Cheatham from the outer works on July 21, the Federals took over the Confederate defenses. By July 25 Sherman had inched forward on the Decatur front to within two miles of the center of Atlanta, and was only a thousand yards from Hood's line.

Already on July 22 the formal forty-day siege of Atlanta had been

---

45 *Official Records*, XXXVIII, Pt. 3, pp. 679–80, 762, 661–65.

46 *Ibid.*, Pt. 5, pp. 1021, 904, 907, 911, LII, Pt. 2, pp. 729, 730, XXXIX, Pt. 2, pp. 832, 837; Bragg to Davis, July 27, 1864, in Bragg Papers, Duke; "Journal of Brig. Gen. Francis A. Shoup, C. S. Army, Chief of Staff, of Operations, July 25, 1864–January 15, 1865," in Hood Papers, National Archives, hereinafter cited as Shoup Journal; Chesnut, *Diary from Dixie,* 427

heralded by the opening of Sherman's artillery, followed by day after day of incessant bombardment. The first day's shelling created a panic. During the ensuing weeks, rows of houses on Peachtree Street were struck, and an entire city block was demolished. Shells rained upon the female college, the state commissary, newspaper offices, Concert Hall, saloons, stables, the Western and Atlantic roundhouse, and private homes. Often at night the sky seemed ablaze with holiday rockets, as timed fuse shells arched skyward. As the citizenry sought refuge in basement shelters, other miseries of war flourished. Flour was selling for three hundred dollars a barrel and coffee for twenty dollars a pound. City parks had been turned into emergency field hospitals, filled with tables of groaning men and baskets of amputated arms and legs.[47]

By July 27 Hood's scouts reported disturbing new from both west and east of Atlanta. The dreaded encirclement of Hood's rail communications by Sherman's cavalry had begun. That evening, Wheeler learned that General George Stoneman was leading a cavalry force southeast of Atlanta, swinging around toward the Macon and Western Railroad at Jonesboro. By the morning of July 28 Wheeler learned that both rail lines to Alabama were threatened by three separate parties. On the night of July 27 Hood sent Wheeler's corps to intercept Stoneman, who was believed headed for Jonesboro via Flat Rock. At dawn of July 28 Wheeler intercepted General Kenner Garrard's division at Flat Rock. Garrard was driven back toward Decatur, but prisoners admitted that the twenty-two-hundred-man main column led by Stoneman was sweeping toward Covington and perhaps would eventually reach Macon. While Wheeler halted at Flat Rock, Hood's headquarters heard that General Edward McCook's division had crossed the Chattahoochee at Campbellton Ferry and was aiming for the Macon Railroad. Hood sent Jackson's cavalry division to stop McCook and ordered Wheeler to send aid.[48]

When Wheeler received this news, he quickly divided his command into three groups. General Alfred Iverson with three brigades was to pursue Stoneman toward Macon. Another brigade was left to observe Garrrad, while Wheeler with two other brigades rode toward Jonesboro with the intention of ensnaring McCook between his and Jackson's columns. The plan worked far better than Wheeler had hoped. In his finest hour as head of the army's cavalry, Wheeler turned Sherman's

[47] Cox Diary, July 22–25, 1864, in Kennesaw; Cooper, *Official History of Fulton County*, 170–73; Richards Diary, July 23, 1864, Atlanta Historical Society; Geary to wife, July 24, 1864, in Geary Letters, Atlanta Historical Society.

[48] Hood to Seddon, July 27, 1864, in Hood Cipher Book, National Archives; *Official Records*, XXXVIII, Pt. 5, p. 913, Pt. 3, p. 953.

three-pronged raid into a shambles. McCook, after destroying several miles of both the West Point and the Macon roads, was trapped between Jackson and Wheeler at Newman on July 30. McCook abandoned his artillery and ordered his brigades to disperse and cut their way through the Rebel lines. Stoneman, on July 29, had met an equally hapless fate. His troopers reached the Ocmulgee River opposite Macon, shelled the town, and then promptly were encircled by Iverson's three brigades. Ordering most of his men to cut their way out, Stoneman with a forlorn seven hundred troopers stayed behind to be captured. On August 4, a nine-hundred-man remnant of Stoneman's command reached Atlanta. Sherman had lost over forty-two hundred troopers, almost half of the army's cavalry.[49]

But even as McCook and Stoneman rode south, a new threat arose at Atlanta. Hood's headquarters was aware of a major shift in the Union position. The previous night, McPherson's Army of the Tennessee had withdrawn from its position on Sherman's left wing. By 4:15 A.M., Hood was convinced that McPherson evidently was moving to the Rebel left to mass with Thomas for an attack. Through the afternoon, Hood continued to shift his own troops toward the left until nightfall when the Confederate left, Stewart's corps, extended across the Western and Atlantic Railroad.[50]

That night Hood called a council of war where he again gave evidence of his dreams of imitating the Army of Northern Virginia. It was obvious that Sherman was sliding his command toward the Confederate left to gain the rail junction at East Point. To do so, Sherman must control a critical road junction. The Lick Skillet Road crossed the Chattahoochee at Green and Howell's Ferry and led thence into Atlanta. A critical lateral road from the Marietta Pike junctioned with the Lick Skillet Road at Ezra Church. If Hood controlled the intersection, Sherman's shift to the southwest of the town could perhaps be halted. Thus Hood outlined another bold flank attack which smacked again of Jackson at Chancellorsville. On the twenty-eight Lee's corps would advance to Ezra Church, halt, and entrench on a line facing northeast to control the cross country road from the Marietta Pike. The following morning Stewart's corps would swing around Lee's left on a pivot and strike the Federals on the flank as they faced Lee at Ezra Church.[51]

49 *Official Records*, XXXVIII, Pt. 3, pp. 953–57, Pt. 5, pp. 921, 924; Hood to Seddon, August 1, 1864, in Hood Cipher Book, National Archives; Shoup Journal, July 27–29, 31, August 1, 1864, in Hood Papers, National Archives.

50 Hood, *Advance and Retreat*, 194; *Official Records*, XXXVIII, Pt. 5, pp. 913, 916–17, Pt. 3, pp. 762, 872, 631.

51 *Official Records*, XXXVIII, Pt. 3, pp. 631–32, 762, 872; Hood, *Advance and Retreat*, 194.

But the plan went afoul on July 28. Lee advanced out the Lick Skillet Road, only to find that the Federals already controlled the intersection. The inexperienced Lee, without asking Hood if this necessitated a change of plans and without waiting for Stewart to come up on his left, wore his command out in a series of suicidal attacks against entrenchments during the early afternoon. Lee did not even wait for all of his own corps to come up, but sent his divisions into action one by one, and they were promptly repulsed.[52]

Lee's wasteful attacks were clearly a product of faulty communication with Hood. Again Hood attempted to imitate Robert E. Lee's conduct of battles in Virginia and remained at his headquarters in Atlanta. The result was a clear confusion of purpose. On the morning of July 28 Hood had ordered Lee to prevent the enemy from reaching the Lick Skillet Road but "not to attack unless the enemy exposes himself in attacking us." [53] When he heard that Lee had come in contact with the enemy, Hood sent a confusing message at about 2 P.M. Evidently Hood, far from the field, did not understand that the enemy already held the Lick Skillet Road. He ordered Lee to "hold the enemy in check," since the object was "to prevent him from gaining the Lick Skillet road." [54] Again at 4 P.M. Hood warned Lee that he should not allow the enemy "to gain upon you any more than possible." [55] From the tone of Hood's dispatches, he also did not realize that Lee was on the offensive and was losing heavily in repeated division assaults on the Union trenches.

Hood's lack of contact was reflected in other matters. Stewart apparently had no clear orders for such a contingency. On his own initiative, he drifted toward the sound of Lee's guns and also threw his divisions against the fortification. Stewart and one of his division commanders, General W. W. Loring, were wounded in the desperate afternoon fight. Actually, however, Stewart had also disobeyed orders, since his instructions were to sweep wide around Lee's left flank and strike the enemy in flank and rear. He, too, was confused by Hood's orders. About 3:30 P.M. Hood ordered him "to hold the enemy, but not to do more fighting than necessary, unless you should get a decided advantage." [56]

Because of his absence from the field, it seems highly probable that Hood knew neither that the Federals already held the Lick Skillet Road

52 *Official Records*, XXXVIII, Pt. 3, pp. 762–63.
53 *Ibid.*, Pt. 5, p. 919.
54 *Ibid.*, 919.
55 *Ibid.*, 919.
56 *Ibid.*, 920, see also Pt. 3, 872.

nor that his own two corps had taken the offensive. In the meantime, both corps lost heavily. Like Hood, General Stephen Lee had been, for the most part, out of touch with wide-scale field combat since he left Virginia in the fall of 1862. Lee also believed in the offensive, and believed that Hood's army had been injured by Johnston's policy of entrenching. Therefore, on the afternoon of July 28, with the breakdown in communications between Lee and Hood, the corps was sacrificed in a series of repeated suicidal assaults. Though Lee later blamed his own troops' timidity, the casualty figures indicated a desperate effort. General John C. Brown's division alone lost over eight hundred men. In one of his brigades, three successive commanders were wounded during the afternoon. Though Stewart only managed to bring two of his own divisions into action, losses in that corps were also heavy. Stewart was severely wounded, as was one of his division commanders, General W. W. Loring. In all, Lee and Stewart lost at least five thousand men during the repeated desperate attacks.[57]

These losses, which brought Hood's losses thus far in the campaign to over twelve thousand, were a monument to his lack of control of the army. On the afternoon of July 28, when he judged in Atlanta that something was not going well at Ezra Church, Hood did not ride to the front. Instead, he sent several couriers to find Hardee, who commanded on the north side of Atlanta. Hardee was ordered to leave his corps and ride to Atlanta to confer with Hood. Hardee received the note some time in the afternoon and immediately sought out the commanding general. Even while Hood conferred with Hardee, news arrived that Loring and Stewart had been wounded. Still Hood did not ride to Ezra Church, but sent Hardee "to look after matters." When Hardee arrived in the early evening, the fight was over.[58]

By early August, Atlanta's outlook blackened. Hood's army was weakened both by field losses and by widespread illness. Within the month since Johnston had been at Marietta, Hardee's corps' effective strength had been reduced from over 15,600 to about 11,500. By August 10 Hood's total effective strength in both infantry and artillery had slipped to 35,371, a drop of almost 8,000 since the first of July. The officer corps' morale had not improved. Already there was some talk of replacing Hood. Hood blamed the entrenching policy of Johnston for his losses,

[57] *Ibid.*, Pt. 3, pp. 872, 760, 767–68; S. D. Lee to Walthall, May 20, 1878, in Rowland (ed.), *Davis*, VII, 204–206; Connolly to wife, July 31, 1863, in Connolly, *Three Years in the Army of the Cumberland*, 246–47; Hood to Seddon, July 28, 1864, in Hood Cipher Book, National Archives.
[58] Roy, "Military Operations Around Atlanta," 370; see also Roy Sketch, in Hardee Papers, Alabama; *Official Records*, XXXVIII, Pt. 3, p. 699.

and intimated that the army was suffering from cowardice. Hardee had already applied to Bragg for relief. On August 3 he telegraphed the President to ask that he be exchanged for General Richard Taylor. Davis expressed surprise that Hardee termed his position under Hood's command unpleasant, and alluded to the general's previous statements declining the permanent command in late 1863. On August 6 Hardee replied bitterly that he had not meant to refuse the army's generalship forever by refusing it then, and that he disliked the appointment of a junior officer over his head. Still, Davis refused his request and insisted that he was needed. Another officer was relieved because of the pangs of disappointment. When Stewart and Loring were wounded, General Samuel French, no admirer of Hood, assumed command of the corps on the field. But on July 29 Hood sent Cheatham to take command temporarily. Angry, French wrote Hood a protest and asked to be relieved. On August 16 his request was granted.[59]

Meanwhile, the enemy's pressure on Atlanta mounted steadily. Throughout August, there was incessant bombardment in Atlanta. Public buildings and private homes were hit often. The Atlanta Medical College, the offices of the Atlanta *Appeal,* a coffin shop, St. Luke's Chapel—the distruction was varied. Bombardment was especially severe on August 10, when twenty-one Confederate and Union batteries engaged in a massive, day-long duel which sent great clouds of bronze-colored, evil-smelling clouds drifting through Atlanta. Then, as at other times, the citizenry sought refuge in cellars and holes dug in back lawns, only to emerge and go about their business when the guns halted. Often the shelling did not stop with twilight, but continued into the night. Fires were a common occurrence during August. In addition to Hood's mounting casualties there were personal incidents touching the lives of the town's citizens. For these people, death was not confined to Peachtree Creek or off the Cobb's Mill Road near Bald Hill. It came to a Negro barber standing by the wrong lamp post on Whitehall Street one hot August day—a small child playing with a pet dog on Ivy Street the day the Peachtree battle was fought—a lady who had fled from Sherman's seizure of Rome and was ironing in a house on Peachtree Street—an inexperienced Georgia militiaman who made one tap too many with a rock upon an unexploded shell he had picked up. Until now the war had not come so close to Atlanta.[60]

---

59 *Official Records,* XXXVIII, Pt. 3, pp. 679, 681, Pt. 5, p. 968; Hardee to Davis, August 6, 1864, Davis to Hardee, August 7, 1864, Hardee to wife, August 4, 5, 1864, in Hardee Papers, Alabama; French, *Two Wars,* 219; Chesnut, *Diary from Dixie,* 427.

60 Cooper, *Official History of Fulton County,* 171–76; William Key, *The Battle of Atlanta and the Georgia Campaign* (New York, 1958), 67, 69.

Now Sherman's preponderance of troops began to show. By August 2 Hood's scouts reported the Union right wing was beginning to slide further toward the west of Atlanta. Until August 13 both armies gradually shifted westward and then southwest until Hood's left flank now rested at the railroad junction at East Point, six miles southwest of downtown Atlanta. In so doing, Hood had completely realigned his command. Hardee's corps had been shifted from the Decatur front to East Point. Lee held the center and confronted the old battle ground at Ezra Church, while Stewart's corps and the Georgia Militia extended the thin line across the Marietta Road and to the north of Atlanta.[61]

During this time Hood played his last card. His failure in three hard battles had shown that he lacked the power to overrun Sherman's own entrenchments. On August 5 Davis had all but ordered Hood to engage in no more such operations unless a clear advantage was seen, due to the heavy casualty toll. This step meant taking a gamble on the only other seemingly available plan other than abandoning Atlanta—a strike on Sherman's communications. By August 1 reports from the debacle of McCook's and Stoneman's raids further encouraged Hood. It now appeared that Wheeler's cavalry could be detached safely with much less danger of an ensuing raid upon Hood's own communications. Consequently, on August 10, Wheeler left for Sherman's rear.[62]

Several things were wrong with this venture. Wheeler was given four thousand troopers, almost half of the army's cavalry. This left only General William Jackson's division with Hood's army, and some isolated units. Also, Hood ordered Wheeler to go too far. After destroying the Western and Atlantic Railroad, all four thousand men were to cross the Tennessee River west of Chattanooga and operate against the two railroads leading from Tennessee into North Alabama. Then Wheeler was to leave twelve hundred men to continue to destroy the Tennessee roads, while he returned to the army with twenty-eight hundred, hitting the Western and Atlantic again as he returned.

Sending such a large force turned out to be a particularly serious error because of Wheeler's bad performance. In his senseless dash into East Tennessee above Knoxville, Wheeler disobeyed orders. He also went against orders by penetrating as far north as near Nashville. Nor did he leave twelve hundred men on the Nashville and Chattanooga Railroad as Hood had ordered. Instead, he wrecked his corps, knocked

---

[61] Shoup Journal, August 2–3, 6, 8–9, 1864, in Hood Papers, National Archives; *Official Records*, XXXVIII, Pt. 3, pp. 632, 763.

[62] Shoup Journal, August 1, 1864, in Hood Papers, National Archives; *Official Records*, XXXVIII, Pt. 3, pp. 632, 957; Dyer, *Wheeler*, 187.

out Hood's reconnaissance for over two months, and ended up fleeing
from Tennessee into Alabama near the Mississippi border.[63]

Also, both from Wheeler and from Union prisoners, Hood was completely misled as to the amount of damage done to the Western and
Atlantic Railroad. Wheeler sent a glowing account of the mass destruction of the railroad around Big Shanty, Resaca, Calhoun, and Tunnel
Hill. Prisoners embellished the account by reporting that Wheeler had
burned the Etowah River Bridge and had blown up the tunnel at
Tunnel Hill. Actually, Wheeler had done little damage to the railroad,
and he certainly had burned no bridges and had destroyed no tunnel.
Most of his efforts on that segment of his raid in Georgia were directed
at less important objectives, such as capturing a few trains and mules,
attacking outposts, and other minor operations.[64]

But a combination of factors in late August convinced Hood that
Wheeler had been highly successful. On August 26 a remarkable event
was observed by Hood's scouts. The previous night, the entire Union
force on the front from the Augusta Railroad northeast of Atlanta to
the Western and Atlantic line northwest of the town had been withdrawn. More strange occurrences were in the offing. On the night of
August 26 the enemy had also disappeared from Lee's and Stewart's
fronts south of the Western and Atlantic line. Pressing his scouts for
information, Hood, by August 28, had pinpointed the unusual change in
Sherman's position. Though he still held the ferries as far north as the
railroad bridge, Sherman's main line had been vastly changed. Now his
left rested near the Chattahoochee at Sandtown Ferry, far below the
railroad bridge. Then his line extended southeast until it ended near
the West Point Railroad at a point south of its junction with the Macon
Road. By this shift, Sherman had changed his entire line until it faced
northeast toward Atlanta.[65]

What did this mean? Later, in his official report, Hardee charged that
Hood believed Sherman was in full retreat due to a lack of supplies,
ordered General Will Jackson's cavalry to pursue, and that Jackson
attempted to convince Hood that he was wrong. Several things are
wrong with Hardee's depiction. Hood on August 26 did not order
Jackson to pursue Sherman but rather ordered him to send his brigades
out to reconnoiter exactly where Sherman was going. Also, given the

63 Dyer, *Wheeler*, 187–97; *Official Records*, XXXVIII, Pt. 3, pp. 632, 957–61.

64 *Official Records*, XXXVIII Pt. 3, pp. 957–58, Pt. 5, p. 967; Shoup Diary, August 16–
18, 1864, in Hood Papers, National Archives.

65 Shoup Diary, August 26–28, 1864, in Hood Papers, National Archives; *Official
Records*, XXXVIII, Pt. 5, pp. 990, 992–94, 997; Hood to Seddon, August 26, 27, 28, in
Hood Cipher Book, National Archives.

situation between August 26 and 28, Hood could scarcely be blamed for believing that Sherman was retreating. Since early August, Hood had received reports that some of Sherman's men were ending their period of service and were being mustered out. On August 17 Hood received information that an entire division was going out of service. Too, there were reports of severe food shortages among the Union troops. Some historians later belittled Hood by claiming that Hood based this belief on the story of one elderly woman interrogated on August 18 after she had had a conversation with the Federal general Jacob Cox. Actually Hood received a considerable number of reports between August 17 and 27, some from prisoners, that Sherman was short on food and forage due to Wheeler's railroad destruction and that he was retiring to the Chattahoochee. So impressive were such reports that Hood's chief of staff, General Francis Shoup, recorded on August 26 that "the prevailing impression of the scout reports thus far indicated the enemy were falling back across the Chattahoochee." [66]

Nor did Hood seem to hold this belief as long as Hardee and others later indicated, if indeed he held it at all. He gave no hint in his dispatches to Richmond that he thought Sherman was in full retreat across the river. In fact, his dispatches of August 26–28 merely reported a change in Sherman's line. Nor was Hood so blind to Sherman's shifting of troops toward the West Point and the Macon railroads as Hardee and others later maintained. On August 27 Hood made no mention of any belief that Sherman was retreating when he telegraphed Richmond. He reported Sherman was moving troops toward the right flank. By August 28 Hood knew and reported, that Sherman's right had been further extended so that it now was anchored on the West Point Railroad south of East Point.[67]

A combination of prejudice and mythology has presented Hood as a much greater dupe during the last days of August than he actually was. Hardee's official report has stereotyped Hood as being completely fooled by Sherman, though other observers knew better. According to Hardee, Hood—and practically no one else—thought Sherman was retreating across the Chattahoochee. Consequently, he allowed Sherman to steal a march of several days around his left flank. By August 31 almost all of Sherman's army was south of Atlanta at Jonesboro, a fact which Hood would not admit.

Most of this version is apparently untrue. Hardee, Lee, and Stewart,

---

[66] *Official Records*, XXXVIII, Pt. 3, p. 700, Pt. 5, p. 992; Shoup Journal, August 7, 17–18, 20, 22, 26–27, 1864, in Hood Papers, National Archives.

[67] Hood to Seddon, August 26, 27, 28, in Hood Cipher Book, in Hood Papers, National Archives.

on August 26–28, seemed to have no better idea than did Hood as to what Sherman was doing. By August 28 Hood had received word that Sherman definitely had seized the West Point Railroad, and that the new Federal right rested between Fairburn and East Point.

But what was Hood to do? Later he was criticized for not rushing troops southward toward Jonesboro to protect the Macon Railroad. Actually he did just this on August 28 when he learned that Sherman had seized the West Point Railroad. Two infantry brigades and a cavalry regiment were rushed some seventeen miles southward to Jonesboro, where key roads from the West Point Railroad, via Fairburn and Red Oak, struck the Macon Railroad. Three other infantry brigades from Bate's old division, temporarily commanded by General John C. Brown, were halted midway between Jonesboro and Atlanta at Rough and Ready. Hardee's entire corps lay at East Point, only ten miles north of Jonesboro. In addition, the bulk of General Will Jackson's cavalry division was probing west of Hardee's position in an attempt to learn what Sherman was doing.[68]

Hood's movements on August 29–30 would also be criticized, and again his chief critic would be Hardee. Hardee later claimed that not until August 30 did Hood learn Sherman's main force was moving on Jonesboro, that Hood only then believed that two Federal corps were menacing Jonesboro. In actuality, there were six. Hardee further claimed that Hood was convinced Jonesboro was the enemy's destination only because of Hardee's perceptive warnings.

Little of this appears to be exactly correct either. On August 29 Hood had already received word that a Union force of cavalry, infantry, and artillery was moving cross-country from the West Point Railroad to Jonesboro and Rough and Ready. Because they were moving behind a large infantry screen, Jackson's thin cavalry was unable to ascertain just how many were approaching the railroad. Hardee did not know either, for, on August 29 from East Point, he requested that Lee attempt to find out just where the enemy was going. The following day, Hood had received more definite information from his scouts. According to this report, Sherman seemed to be moving toward both Rough and Ready and Jonesboro.[69]

To accuse Hood of being blind toward the danger on the Macon Road on August 30 seems incredible. By then Hood already had shifted Hardee's corps to Rough and Ready, and Lee's corps to East Point,

68 Shoup Journal, August 28–29, 1864, in *ibid.; Official Records*, XXXVIII, Pt. 5, p. 997; see also Pt. 3, p. 700.

69 *Official Records*, XXXVIII, Pt. 3, p. 700, Pt. 5, p. 999; Shoup Journal, August 29–30, 1864, in Hood Papers, National Archives.

both within ten miles of Jonesboro. Why should Hood have thrown
most of his force to Jonesboro, as Hardee by hindsight argued that he
should have done? The sparse cavalry intelligence Hood had received on
August 29 and on 30 did not pinpoint Sherman's advance squarely on
Jonesboro, but on Rough and Ready as well. To stretch three slim
corps the complete distance from Atlanta to Jonesboro would have been
impossible. Hood did the next best thing by placing two-thirds of his
infantry on the left flank at East Point and Rough and Ready.

In short, Hood seemed to do all that he possbily could do by August
30. The distance from Sherman's right wing at Red Oak to Rough and
Ready was less than eight miles, to Jonesboro, scarcely ten miles. Before
committing a mass force at Jonesboro, Hood was forced to wait and see
which front was to be the threatened point: East Point, Rough and
Ready, or Jonesboro. He was counting on Jackson's cavalry and the two
brigades at Jonesboro to hold any enemy force on the west bank of the
Flint River, which ran on the west side of the town, until help could
arrive. Hood was well aware that such a need might arise. One historian
attempted to prove that Hood, on August 30, did not think that Sherman's main force was headed toward Jonesboro. To prove this, he cited
a dispatch sent to Hardee by Hood at 1:00 P.M. of August 30. In this
dispatch Hood stated he did not think there was any need to send more
troops to Jonesboro that day.[70] Unfortunately, the historian omitted
the last phrase in Hood's sentence and thus took it completely out of
context. Hood merely said he saw no more need in sending troops
"to-day," [71] a key phrase which was deleted. Others have cited a dispatch sent by Hood at 1:20 P.M. in which he stated that he did not
think a large force was advancing upon Jonesboro. A third oft-quoted
note, a 2 P.M. telegram to Hardee, indicated that Hood did not think
the enemy would attack at Jonesboro on August 30.[72]

Hood's critics who have freely cited these dispatches have neglected
to point out other things which put the notes in a completely different
context. Though Hood, at 1 P.M., was not planning to further reinforce
Jonesboro that day, within forty-five minutes he had sent Hardee a note
at Rough and Ready indicating that more reinforcements might have
to be sent to Jonesboro that same day. Also neglected in citations of the
later 2 P.M. dispatch to Hardee was his statement that Hardee was
"to take whatever measures you may think necessary" [73] on the after-

[70] Clauss, *Atlanta Campaign*, 288.
[71] *Official Records*, XXXVIII, Pt. 5, p. 1000.
[72] *Ibid.*, 1000, 1005.
[73] *Ibid.*, 1000.

noon of August 30 to prevent a takeover of either Rough and Ready or Jonesboro.

Two key factors emerge here. Hood was not alone in not knowing where Sherman's advance was aimed that day. One searches in vain for any telegrams from Hardee or Lee which indicate they knew the main Federal advance would be upon Jonesboro. In fact, Hardee, about 1 P.M. of August 30, had reported to Hood from Rough and Ready that the enemy was advancing on him there. Another point often overlooked is that on the afternoon of August 30, Hood assigned Hardee to command the entire front from East Point to Jonesboro, with full authority to send his corps to any part of the line. Yet throughout the afternoon, though later he claimed he knew the enemy was approaching Jonesboro in massive strength, Hardee kept his own infantry corps aligned between East Point and Rough and Ready. If he knew what he later claimed he knew, why had he not shifted his corps southward? [74]

The events of the following day are also clouded in controversy. In the early evening of August 30, Hood had received intelligence from his detachments at Jonesboro that a sizeable force was approaching Flint River. Urging that they hold until reinforcements arrived, Hood summoned Lee and Hardee to his Atlanta headquarters. Hardee was given orders to move with both corps to Jonesboro, attack the enemy, and drive him across Flint River if possible.[75]

But Hardee moved slowly. Though he arrived about daylight by train from Atlanta, Hardee's corps did not arrive until much later. This situation could have been avoided if he had known what he claimed to know. Not until 9:00 A.M. was his corps arrayed in battle line. Lee moved so slowly that his main column did not arrive at Jonesboro until 11:00, and all of his troops were not on the field until 1:30 P.M. of August 31. Finally, about 2:00, Hardee had readied his men for the attack on the Union entrenched position between Jonesboro and Flint River. Cleburne, commanding Hardee's corps, would open the battle on the left. When Lee observed that Cleburne was seriously engaged, he would advance on the right wing.[76]

Still Hardee delayed the advance, and not until 3:00 P.M. did Cleburne advance. A curious, badly managed battle ensued. Lee, mistaking some of Cleburne's skirmish fire for the main attack, disobeyed orders and advanced about 2:20 P.M. The attack was a feeble one which

74 For evidence of Hardee's authority, see *ibid.*, 1000; see also p. 1002, Pt. 3, p. 700.

75 Shoup Journal, August 30, 1864, in Hood Papers, National Archives; *Official Records*, XXXVIII, Pt. 5, pp. 1001–1005.

76 *Official Records*, XXXVIII, Pt. 3, pp. 700, 764.

brought even the scorn of some officers who participated. Although General Patton Anderson's division, on Lee's front line, suffered moderate casualties, many of the supporting units merely refused to advance. Meanwhile, on the left wing, Hardee's own corps got out of control. At about 3:00 Hardee's front line, Cleburne's and Bate's divisions, finally advanced. These divisions soon became jammed with Brown's and Maney's, and only isolated and unsuccessful attacks were made. The only success came on the far left where Cleburne's division, temporarily commanded by General Mark Lowery, not only carried the Union entrenchments and drove the far Union right into the river, but disobeyed orders and crossed the river in pursuit.[77]

Later in the afternoon, Hardee at last managed to bring some coordination to the field. After separate repulses of Brown, Maney, and Bate, and after Lowery's men recrossed the river, Hardee finally sought a coordinated attack with Lee. But Lee demurred, arguing that his corps was simply too demoralized to attack. When Hardee in the early evening learned that the enemy seemed to be massing against Lee for a possible counterattack, he called off any plans for an offensive and fell back to his original line facing westward, along the Georgia Railroad.[78]

Again Hardee seemed to have badly managed a stint at independent command. The delay in reaching Jonesboro had been his fault, since the previous day Hood had given him *carte blanche* to use the troops on the left at whatever point he deemed threatened. Hardee was also slow in getting the troops into formation. Save for two brigades, Lee's column had arrived by 11 A.M. Yet Cleburne, who had been on the ground since mid-morning, did not attack until 3 P.M. Too, Hardee disobeyed Hood's orders. Twice during the early morning of August 31, Hood sent specific orders to attack and drive the Federals into the Flint River. Instead, after two partial assaults, Hardee at his own discretion and without informing Hood took up a defensive position.[79]

Hardee later attempted to justify this move by asserting that he had

---

[77] *Ibid.*, Pt. 3, pp. 700, 764; Hughes, *Hardee*, 236–37; Buck, *Cleburne and His Command*, 250–52.

[78] *Official Records*, XXXVIII, Pt. 3, pp. 700–701, 773–74, 764–65. For evidence that Lee's troops did seem too demoralized to attack the Union entrenchments, see *ibid.*, pp. 773–74; Watkins, *"Co. Aytch,"* 201.

[79] At 3 A.M., Hood had written, "as soon as you can get your troops into position . . . you must attack and drive the enemy across the river." *Official Records*, XXXVIII, Pt. 5, p. 1006. At 3:10 A.M., Hood telegraphed, "you must not fail to attack the enemy as soon as you can get your troops up." (p. 1006.) At 3:20 A.M., Hood telegraphed that "the necessity is imperative. The enemy must be driven into and across the river." (p. 1006.) At 10 A.M., Hood telegraphed that he "desires the men to go at the enemy with bayonets fixed, determined to drive everything they may come up against." (p. 1007.)

faced overwhelming numbers at Jonesboro. Hardee subsequently contended that his Jonesboro contingent was facing six corps while Hood, completely duped, believed the main strength of the army was still near Atlanta. On the surface, there seems to be some justification for Hardee's accusations. At the conference with Lee and Hardee on the evening of August 30, Hood had expressed the belief that two corps, or at most three of the Federal army's weaker corps, were marching for Jonesboro. Later, when it was discovered that Sherman actually had moved on Jonesboro with six corps, some asserted that Hood had been duped.[80]

Such accusations come more from hindsight than knowledge. Actually, Hardee had contended on August 31 with a much weaker force than the two or three corps supposedly on the field. That morning, unknown to Hardee, Howard had only two infantry corps and a single cavalry division, all together no more than seventeen thousand men, on the east bank of Flint River. Hardee and Lee had twenty-four thousand troops. If Hood's pre-dawn orders had been obeyed—attack quickly and drive the enemy into the river—this weakness might have been telling. Instead, it appears that to justify his own lack of success on August 31, Hardee pointed to information which he actually did not have—that six corps were at Jonesboro.

Again, the old breakdown of communication between Hardee and Hood was partially at fault. At 6 P.M., some six hours before he knew of Hardee's fight at Jonesboro, Hood, by courier, ordered Lee's corps to return to Atlanta. Exactly what Hood had in mind is unclear. In his dispatch to Hardee, ordering the transfer, he indicated that he feared an attack at Atlanta on September 1. Yet, in his official report, Hood, also with the aid of hindsight, explained that he knew Sherman was shifting his whole force toward Jonesboro, and thus he hoped to use Lee in an attack on the Federal left flank while it was in motion. Regardless of his motive, Hood ordered the change, and during the night of August 31, Lee's men trudged northward to rejoin Stewart at Atlanta.[81]

On August 31, Hood obviously did not realize that Sherman had shifted almost all of his strength to the area between the West Point and the Macon railroads. But he must not bear all of the responsibility. If Hardee knew that such a large force was approaching Jonesboro, why did he not tell Hood? Evidently Hardee did not know. Telegraph communication with Atlanta was cut by the afternoon of August 31.

80 *Ibid.*, Pt. 3, pp. 633, 700.
81 Shoup to Hardee, August 31—6 P.M., 1864, in Hardee Papers, Alabama; *Official Records*, XXXVIII, Pt. 3, p. 633.

Thus, until September 3, Hardee did not report to Hood but, rather directly to Richmond via wire. Although he later ridiculed Hood for ordering Lee's corps back to Atlanta on the night of August 31, Hardee did not seem particularly concerned. After the battle, before Lee's corps was recalled, Hardee reported to Davis that he could hold Jonesboro "unless the enemy cross Flint River below me." [82] No mention was made to Davis of any six corps being near Jonesboro until a telegram was sent by Hardee on September 2. In this wire, describing the battle on September 1, Hardee stated that prisoners reported there were six corps on his front. In his official report, Hardee deftly inserted this prisoner report in his commentary on the August 31 battle without specifically saying that he received this news that day. Actually, it seems Hardee did not learn of it until the evening of September 1.[83]

If Hardee considered his situation at Jonesboro so perilous, why did he not tell Hood? His behavior was reminiscent of his and Polk's tight-lipped attitude toward Bragg in Kentucky in 1862. Since Hood's courier could reach him, Hardee likewise could have reached Hood if he believed his situation was so dangerous. But on August 31 he sent back to Atlanta no estimates of heavy Federal strength, and he did not protest Lee's withdrawal to Atlanta.

Actually, if one considers the intelligence Hood possessed on the night of August 31, the recall of Lee's corps does not appear as irrational as some have indicated. There had been no word from Hardee to alter the opinion that two or three corps at the most were moving on Jonesboro. Nor had Hardee sent any requests for reinforcement. On the other hand, there was a new threat between East Point and Rough and Ready. On August 30 Hood had sent his reserve cavalry, not even two regiments strong, commanded by General John T. Morgan, to protect the Macon Railroad between East Point and Rough and Ready. By early afternoon on August 31, Morgan's position at Mt. Gilead Church, about a mile west of the railroad, was overrun. Morgan was driven back, Rough and Ready was taken, and the railroad was cut. So strong was the attack that Morgan notified Hood that evening that apparently the enemy would attack East Point on September 1 in strong force. Determined to hold Atlanta to the last, Hood had brought back Lee because he feared such an attack against Stewart from the southwest, via Rough and Ready.[84]

As Lee trudged toward Atlanta by a circuitous route east of the railroad, Hood was moving toward a decision to abandon Atlanta. About midnight of August 31, Hood had learned that Hardee had failed to

[82] Official Records, XXXVIII, Pt. 3, p. 696.
[83] Ibid., 696, 701.
[84] Ibid., 633, Pt. 5, pp. 1007, 1009.

break the Federal hold on the Macon Railroad by not driving the
enemy at Jonesboro across Flint River. Now all railroads into Atlanta
had been seized—something which Johnston had insisted Sherman could
not do the previous month. Too, by noon on September 1, the threat of
an attack on East Point seemed much closer. Federal activity also
threatened Stewart's right flank, along the Marietta Road.[85]

Because there seemed no other choice, on the afternoon of September
1, Stewart's corps was ordered to move southward to McDonough,
twenty-eight miles distant on the pike to Macon. Couriers were sent to
intercept Lee's corps, approaching Atlanta on the same road, with orders
for him to return to assist Hardee. Stewart was to follow as soon as
possible.[86]

There was little need to send reinforcements to Hardee, since by
September 2 he had been forced to abandon the Jonesboro position.
After Lee's departure, Hardee's line was thinned as it spread out to
cover Lee's abandoned temporary entrenchments. Fortunately for Hardee, the Federals did not launch an all-out attack on September 1. Such
an attack would have decimated his corps. Instead, through the morning
and early afternoon, there were sporadic flashes of musketry and artillery
fire, with an occasisonal dash at Hardee's works. But by 4 P.M. the situation had become more grave. A fresh Union corps from the north had
come up opposite the right wing and promptly had attacked. Hardee's
right was smashed, and one of his brigade commanders, General D. C.
Govan, and several hundred members of the brigade were swept away
as prisoners. Although determined charges by Cleburne closed the gap,
by nightfall there was more disturbing news. Another Federal corps
had lapped his line on the right and actually was penetrating toward his
communications with Hood and with Atlanta.

It was obvious that Hardee must retreat, since prisoners revealed
that he was facing all of Sherman's army save a single corps at Atlanta.
Thus, about midnight of September 1, Hardee's men sullenly abandoned
the hard-fought ground at Jonesboro and trudged through the night
down the Macon Railroad toward Lovejoy's Station. The Confederates
arrived at Lovejoy's early on September 2. By mid-morning, Sherman's
advance units had arrived and skirmishing had begun. Then, about
4 P.M., another strong attack was launched against the hastily dug entrenchments. Hardee's men beat back this attack.[87]

85 *Ibid.*, Pt. 3, p. 633, Pt. 5, pp. 1007, 1009; Shoup Journal, August 31, September 1,
1864, in Hood Papers, National Archives.

86 Shoup Journal, September 1-2, 1864, National Archives.

87 *Official Records*, XXXVIII, Pt. 3, pp. 701–702; Hughes, *Hardee*, 239–40; Buck,
Cleburne and His Command, 253–58; Lowery, "An Autobiography," *SHSP*, XVI (1888),
373.

On September 2 the Confederate army was once more on the brink of disaster. Hood ordered Hardee to hold his position at Lovejoy's until aid arrived. But Hood's army was spread over almost thirty miles between Atlanta, McDonough, and Lovejoy's Station. Not until the morning of September 3 did Stewart's corps arrive to relieve Hardee's men, who had withstood another strong attack the previous afternoon. Later in the day, Lee's men arrived. Fortunately for Hardee, Sherman had not renewed the attack on the morning of September 3, but gave Hood an opportunity to regroup his battered columns at Lovejoy's. Instead of attacking, Sherman halted for three days confronting the Confederates. Then on September 5 he began withdrawing toward Jonesboro.[88]

Atlanta had been defended at an awful cost to the army. By September 10 Hood had only about 23,000 effective infantry and a total effective force of infantry, cavalry, and artillery of slightly over 39,000. Since taking command, Hood had lost over 12,500 killed and wounded. Exactly how many had been taken prisoner, had deserted to Sherman, or simply had gone home was difficult to ascertain. Through the entire campaign from May until mid-September, Sherman's commands reported receiving almost 13,000 prisoners and deserters. That many more men had left the army because of either sickness or desertion was obvious. Even after the fighting from Dalton to New Hope Church, Johnston by early June still had an aggregate present of over 82,000 men; by September, this total had dropped to barely 60,000. The total of effective troops had dropped even more sharply. After New Hope Church, Johnston still had over 45,000 effective infantry. Now in September, Hood had only 23,000. Because of conflicting statistics and a lack of adequate returns for sick and deserters, it is difficult to determine just how many men the army lost from Dalton to Jonesboro. Yet, including killed, wounded, prisoners, deserters to the enemy, and those struck by illness in July and August, a conservative estimate would be 50,000.[89]

The army also had been bled logistically. Staggering losses in small arms, artillery, and ammunition were evident by September. Like Albert Sidney Johnston in his evacuation of Nashville in 1862, Hood had simply waited too late to get many of his stores out of Atlanta. The army's ordnance and commissary trains had been sent with Hardee to Jones-

---

[88] Shoup Journal, September 3–6, 1864, in Hood Papers, National Archives; Cox Diary, September 4–6, 1864, Kennesaw.

[89] *Official Records*, XXXVIII, Pt. 1, pp. 85, 172, Pt. 3, p. 677, XXXIX, Pt. 2, p. 828; Hood, *Advance and Retreat*, 220–21; Returns of Hardee's corps, in Miscellaneous Field Returns, Duke; Hardee to Davis, September 27, 1864, in Hardee Letters, Harvard; Foard to Hood, April 1, 3, 11, 1866, in Hood Papers, National Archives; Roy sketch, in Hardee Papers, Alabama.

boro, but the reserve ordnance train had remained at Atlanta. Although Hood ordered the ordnance train sent southward at dawn on August 31, due to a confusion of orders it remained in Atlanta after the Macon Railroad was seized. Thus when Hood left Atlanta on September 1, detachments were left behind to destroy those stores which remained. The losses were staggering. Twenty-eight car loads of ammunition were blown up—the army's entire reserve supply. Eighty-one cars and five locomotives, thirteen siege guns, large quantities of quartermaster stores, and ordnance equipment were abandoned.

This was only the beginning. Huge amounts of foodstuffs gathered in the commissary warehouse had to be left behind. The doors to the warehouse were thrown open, and hungry citizens crowded in to seize hams, barrels of syrup, sacks of sugar, and other foodstuffs. Also, a large amount of the machinery and equipment for manufacturing war materiel was abandoned or destroyed. The Western and Atlantic roundhouse was blown up full of equipment, the cannon foundry was destroyed, and valuable materials at the Confederate Arsenal, the Confederate Rolling Mill, the Atlanta Machine Works, Winship's Railroad Foundry, the Novelty Iron Works, and other installations were abandoned.[90]

The disruption of the manufacture of war materiel at Atlanta was made more serious by the heavy losses of equipment since May. In four months the army had lost forty-eight pieces of artillery captured by the enemy. Over thirteen thousand small arms had been captured by Sherman. With the loss of the Atlanta Arsenal, the Augusta and Macon arsenals were now strained to provide both small arms and artillery ammunition. So heavy was Hood's need that in September the Augusta arsenal alone was called upon for a half million rounds of small arm ammunition, and four thousand rounds of artillery ammunition.[91]

Above all, there was the threatened dislocation of the entire Confederate munitions area by Hood's loss. Slowly the Heartland was shrinking. Already those installations in Tennessee, Kentucky, and North Georgia were gone. Now Atlanta's demise threatened the axis from Augusta via Macon to Columbus. In August there had been serious interruptions due to Hood's impressment of munitions workers to man the Atlanta defenses. When Atlanta fell the Confederacy's largest powder mill and one of its finest arsenals at Augusta were laid bare to invasion from the west. The vast complex at Macon was so endangered that in

---

90 *Official Records*, XXXVIII, Pt. 3, pp. 684–86, 991–92; Cooper, *Official History of Fulton County*, 176–77; Frank Vandiver, "General Hood as Logistician," *Military Affairs*, XVI (Spring, 1952), 4–5.

91 *Official Records*, XXXVIII, Pt. 1, pp. 124–26; Vandiver, "General Hood as Logistician," 7.

September the Ordnance Bureau pondered whether to dismantle the equipment there and ship it either to Columbia, Savannah, or some other more safe place.[92]

Too, there was a deeply symbolic loss. The Confederates were not unaware of the political importance of a possible seizure of Atlanta in the fall elections of 1864. Indeed, they had helped to make it so. Editorials in Richmond and Atlanta newspapers, reprinted widely in northern periodicals, stated the importance of Rebel success in the field to the hopes of McClellan's supporters. In an editorial that epitomized this goading, the Atlanta *Register* had suggested that the Democrats should utilize the ballot box while the army used the cartridge box, and together they would defeat Lincoln. The northern press had responded in kind. After Atlanta's fall, a host of northern journalists in the New York *Daily Tribune, Harper's Weekly,* and others proclaimed loudly that Lincoln's chances for reelection had been greatly enhanced. Lincoln probably believed this as well. On September 7, as Hood's corps began the slow process of counting losses and bringing in stragglers, Lincoln ordered 100-gun salutes from Washington to New Berne, and from Pensacola to New Orleans.[93]

In short, the struggle for Atlanta had become a national trauma for North and South. Both Sherman and the Confederates had subordinated military operations against the enemy to its retention or seizure. Though obviously designed to bolster morale, the many September editorials of Rebel newspapers on the Atlantic seaboard may have contained some truth in their assertions that too much was being made of the seizure of Atlanta. Some newspapers recalled that in 1861–62, the South's key munitions region in the upper Heartland, together with its key western city, Nashville, had been swept away without squelching the rebellion.[94]

Now, relieved of its long commitment, what was the army to do? Should the army be reinforced for an attempt to drive Sherman from central Georgia or to attack his communications? Or did a shifting to either South Carolina or Alabama offer more promise? No doubt there was a feeling of change in the air by late September. Obviously, too, change and bitterness again colored the high command. It took no prophet to recognize that when President Jefferson Davis, a harbinger of some discord among the high command in times past, arrived at Hood's headquarters on September 25, there was new trouble in the West.

92 Vandiver, "General Hood as Logistician," 4.
93 Clauss, *Atlanta Campaign*, 366–72.
94 *Ibid.*, 373–78.

sixteen

Dreams of Glory

IT WAS NOT AN UNFAMILIAR SIGHT. ON A RAINY SEPTEMBER 25 JEFFERSON Davis and an entourage of advisors stepped from a train at Palmetto, Georgia, into the red clay mire that coated Hood's encampment. Twice before, in December of 1862 and in October of 1863, the President had come to the West to solve the army's problems. Now he came again to heal the army's internal wounds, bolster the morale of the populace, and plot new strategy.

But never had the outlook seemed this dreary. Several thousand of Hood's troops were without shoes. Flour and other foodstuffs were scant due to the loss of commissary stores at Atlanta. There were dire shortages of gunpowder, artillery shot, and small arms ammunition. Already losses from desertion and straggling were high, and it seemed to Richmond that the army was falling apart. On September 4 Hood had begged for reinforcements lest the country be overrun. He also had warned of the army's dwindling morale and even of near mutiny. Cryptically he stated that "there is a tacit if not expressed determination among the men of this army, extending to officers as high in some instances as colonel, that they will not attack breast-works." [1] The next day Hood further warned of eroding morale and characterized the Jonesboro fight as a "disgraceful effort." [2] Hardee, on September 4, had also warned the government that unless the army was reinforced, the Georgia-Alabama region would be overrun. In his warning, he spoke of an impending "calamity." [3]

[1] Hood to Bragg, September 4, 1864, in Davis Papers, Duke.
[2] Hood to Bragg, September 5, 1864, in Hood Cipher Book, II, Hood Papers, National Archives.
[3] *Official Records*, XXXVIII, Pt. 5, p. 1018.

The greatest calamity appeared to be among the officer corps. The situation was reminiscent of Chickamauga. On September 14, at the request of several officers whom he did not name, General Samuel French warned Davis that the army's morale was low, and urged Davis to send some staff members to learn the facts for themselves. Meanwhile, the embers of the Hood-Hardee controversy flared up.

Through August, Hardee had continued sulking because he had been superseded by Hood. Then on September 4 Hood, in a letter to Bragg, had indirectly blamed the loss of Atlanta on Hardee's Jonesboro defeat. Four days later Hood laid his cards on the table. On September 8 he applied to the government to have Hardee exchanged for General Richard Taylor. Then on September 13 he informed Davis that he placed the blame for the losses at Peachtree Creek, Atlanta, and Jonesboro squarely on Hardee. Again on September 17 Hood appealed to Davis for Hardee's transfer. By then, Hood was even willing to substitute General Frank Cheatham, who had temporarily commanded his old corps before Lee's arrival.[4]

Even before Davis left Richmond, he seemed to realize that the Georgia situation had become intolerable. The dispute between the pro- and anti-administration forces relative to Johnston's dismissal had flared up again with each Hood defeat. Also, from within the army the government had evidently learned of widespread dissatisfaction among the generals with Hood, and of their desires to have him removed and replaced by either Johnston or Beauregard. To replace Hood with Johnston was too strong an antidote for Davis, since it would involve a clear confession that he had been wrong. Instead, prior to leaving Richmond he sounded out the possibility of the least undesirable choice—Beauregard. In mid-September, Davis asked Robert E. Lee whether Beauregard would consider a command in Georgia. Exactly what Davis intended is unclear. He may have intended for Beauregard to replace Hood—this was the impression Lee received—though there is slim evidence to support such an intention. From the outset, Davis probably intended to give Beauregard a feeble command in order to silence antiadministration critics—a broad theater command with little power.

Whatever his original intent, it was obvious by September 25 that some change must be made. Davis remained with the army for three days, conferring with Hood and his generals, and reviewing the troops, who sometimes greeted his appearance with cries demanding the return of Johnston. But the pleas of the officers were more telling. Hardee in pri-

4 *Ibid.*, 1987, XXXIX, Pt. 2, p. 832; Hood to Bragg, September 4, 1864, in Davis Papers, Duke; Hughes, *Hardee*, 246–47; Hardee to wife, August 17, 1864, in Hardee Papers, Alabama.

vate counsel struck hard at Hood's duplicity while Johnston commanded the army. Hardee argued that Hood actually had consistently counselled retreat. Hardee also insisted that the army wanted a change of commanders. When questioned as to the army's preference, Hardee first suggested Johnston. When Davis demurred and brought up Beauregard's name, Hardee stated that he also would be acceptable to the army. But Hardee was adamant on one point—either he or Hood must be relieved. From Stewart and S. D. Lee in a separate conference, Davis detected this same basic belief—that Hood should be replaced by Johnston or Beauregard, in that order of preference.[5]

As he had after Chickamauga, Davis refused to admit his mistake, even though it would again cost him valuable officers. By September 28 he had gone on to visit other areas of Hood's and Taylor's departments. On that day, from Opelika, Alabama, he sent a note to Hood in which he gave his decision. Hood was to be sustained, though he had offered to resign and though his staying meant the loss of Hardee, the only corps commander who had more than three months' experience at the post. That same day, Davis relieved Hardee and ordered him to take command of the Department of South Carolina, Georgia, and Florida.

To placate his critics and at the same time avoid admitting his own mistake, Davis, by September 28, had also conceived the idea of another western supracommand. Evidently he had already discussed this plan with Hood at Palmetto but did not reach a final decision until he had left the army. Beauregard, who was then at Charleston, was instructed to meet with Davis at Augusta, Georgia, about October 2. By October 3 both had arrived and entered into a long conference. When it was finished, Davis dictated Beauregard's new orders and a new command structure for the West. Beauregard would head a new organization optimistically called the Military Division of the West, which would embrace at least parts of five states—about one third of the Confederacy's territory. Beauregard would oversee two departments, Hood's Department of Tennessee and Richard Taylor's Department of Alabama, Mississippi, and East Louisiana.[6]

It was clear that Beauregard's appointment was in the tradition of Johnston's theater command of 1862–63, and not a position of real authority. Little more than an advisor, he could only take immediate command of troops whenever he was present with a particular army. This was

5 Hughes, *Hardee*, 247–48; Stewart to Johnston, February 11, 1868, in Johnston, *Narrative*, 368; Horn, *Army of Tennessee*, 372; Hood, *Advance and Retreat*, 253–54.

6 Roman, *Beauregard*, II, 278–79; Williams, *Beauregard*, 241; Davis to Beauregard, October 2, 1864, in Hood Papers, National Archives; *Official Records*, XXXIX, Pt. 2, p. 800, Pt. 3, p. 782.

to be done, however, only "whenever in your judgments the interests of your command render it expedient." [7] In short, only in time of genuine peril was Beauregard to interfere with the operations of a field commander, and even then only for that period of time he considered his presence necessary.[8]

This type of assignment, which only portended confusion, was complicated by Davis' further definition of terms. Beauregard did not understand his new status exactly, and shortly thereafter inquired of Davis if, when he visited an army, he actually was expected to take the field command. Could he not merely give orders to the army through the commanding general? Davis' reply on November 1 was a masterpiece of confusing terminology Beauregard when present with an army was to exercise "immediate command" but "not relieve the general of the particular army"—the second interpretation of Beauregard's position within less than a month.[9]

There were other problems involved in Beauregard's appointment than the mere confusion of terms. The Louisianian seemed weary, less vigorous, and more amenable to the powerless appointment than he would have been once. This seeming docility, indicated in his letter to Davis asking if he actually would be *required* to take command of one of his two armies, might aid in explaining the ensuing tangle over Hood's strategy for Tennessee. Why did Beauregard take the position? He could scarcely have forgotten his own bitter experience of 1862 in the West, and should well have remembered Johnston's unfortunate status in Tennessee and Mississippi in 1862–63.

Probably Beauregard accepted the task in order to escape the very thing he was to confront when he came to the West—a general ignoring of his advice and policies by the administration. Not since 1862, had Beauregard actually held a position commensurate with either his ability or his experience. Deliberately or not, he had been kept in an isolated status by the administration. After Davis relieved him of command of the Army of Tennessee in the summer of 1862, Beauregard had been exiled to the Department of South Carolina, Georgia, and Florida for almost two years. There his defense of Charleston and other coastal points had been outstanding, although Davis slighted the general by giving the credit to others. Beauregard's duties consisted chiefly of garrison defense of coastal towns and providing a source of reinforcement for other departments.

During this period, Beauregard had become strategist without port-

7 Davis to Beauregard, October 2, 1864, in Hood Papers, National Archives.
8 Williams, *Beauregard,* 241; Roman, *Beauregard,* II, 279.
9 Davis to Beauregard, November 1, 1864, in Beauregard Letters, University of Texas Library, microfilm in Louisiana State University, Department of Archives.

folio. He sent detailed plans of concentrated action to Bragg, Johnston, Richmond friends such as Pierre Soulé and Louis Wigfall, novelists such as Augusta Jane Evans, and others. Between June of 1861 and December of 1863, Beauregard had presented six major strategic plans to the government either directly or through generals or friendly political allies. In addition he maintained a voluminous correspondence with Johnston, Bragg, William Porcher Miles, Soulé, Charles Villeré, Mansfield Lovell, Wigfall, and others concerning strategic matters.

Although many of his ideas were applauded by individuals, Beauregard's advice was ignored by the government for several reasons. Since 1862 Beauregard had been clearly identified with the antiadministration bloc. Too, Beauregard's strategic ideas grated against governmental strategic policy. For example, his three plans presented in the spring, autumn, and winter of 1863 called for a reduction of the Virginia force, a massed concentration in the West, and a temporary abandonment of less essential territory—all matters not pleasing to Davis. His May, 1863, plan had called for a reinforcement of the West by twenty-five thousand to thirty thousand men, with a large percentage being derived from Lee's army. His October, 1863, plan had again called for a concentration on Bragg's front with twenty-five thousand men being sent from Virginia. His December plan had called for forty thousand men to be stripped from his own department, Virginia, North Carolina, and the Alabama-Mississippi department to be concentrated under Johnston at Dalton. Half of these were to come from Lee. Always Beauregard's argument was the same—that the Confederacy had ample troops, but that they had been misapplied and scattered to defend too much ground.[10]

There was another critical reason why the government ignored Beauregard's advice and often ignored Beauregard. Beauregard's career, since leaving the Army of Tennessee in 1862, had seen no letup in his feuding with Jefferson Davis. Somehow Beauregard seemed ill starred in such matters. He had an almost uncanny ability to become embroiled with the government in controversy. Part of the problem may have been the machinations of his long-time chief of staff, General Thomas Jordan. Jordan, an unctious Virginian who had once been Sherman's roommate at West Point, had dabbled in intrigue since entering the Confederate service in May of 1861. Appointed by Beauregard as chief of staff at Manassas Junction in June, 1861, Jordan later served as the general's

10 For examples of Beauregard's correspondence on strategy, see Beauregard to Pierre Soulé, December 8, 1863, Beauregard to Augusta Jane Evans, February 21, 1863, in Beauregard Papers, National Archives; Beauregard to W. P. Miles, January 5, 1863, Beauregard to F. W. Pickens, November 11, 1862, in Beauregard Papers, DLC; *Official Records*, XXVIII, Pt. 2, pp. 173–74, 399–400.

staff officer in the Shiloh campaign and during the siege of Charleston in 1863–64. Also, he was Bragg's chief of staff during the Kentucky campaign.

Probably part of the government's dislike of Jordan was transferred to Beauregard. At best, it does seem that Jordan sometimes took the lead in penning vituperative letters which enraged the government. It was this chronic troublemaker who, in the spring of 1861, established the liaison of spies in Washington which included Mrs. Rose Greenhow. Frequently employed by Beauregard to correspond with the government, he, in his letters, was often sarcastic and faultfinding. Some Richmond observers believed that Jordan, who hated Davis, often led Beauregard into controversy with the President. There is other evidence that in 1864, Jordan even issued orders and wrote letters in Beauregard's name without the general's knowledge. For whatever reason, Jordan seemed a Machiavellian type, who enjoyed prodding the government from his position as Beauregard's chief of staff. Probably justly did Longstreet's chief of staff, Colonel Moxley Sorrel, depict Jordan as a man with "something lacking in his make-up as a whole that disappointed his friends." [11]

Regardless of Jordan's part in the matter, feuding between Beauregard and the government over a wide number of issues had continued from 1862 to 1864. By the autumn of 1864 Beauregard seemed anxious to leave the Atlantic Coast. During the avalanche of proposals sent to Richmond in early 1864 regarding western strategy, Beauregard evidently had hoped to be rid of his tiresome duties at Charleston and to obtain a new field command. Instead, in April of 1864, he was given command of the Department of North Carolina and Southern Virginia, and by the early summer found himself actually under Lee's command in the defense of Richmond.

Beauregard's experience on the Richmond-Petersburg line was indeed a miserable one, and probably was a factor which prompted his going West. There was continuing tension between Beauregard and the government. Both Davis and Bragg turned down a May strategic proposal by Beauregard for a concentration of troops under him at Petersburg to deal with General Benjamin Butler. Through the summer, Beauregard, as a full general, was unhappy to remain under Lee's command. Because he disliked such an idea, he had, in late May, delayed moving his troops out of the Bermuda Hundred line to reinforce Lee north of the James River. When Lee himself moved into the region south of the James in mid-June, Beauregard in effect had become neither an army nor department com-

[11] Sorrel, *Recollections of a Confederate Staff Officer*, 15–16. See also Chesnut, *Diary from Dixie*, 102–103, 365, 445; Mary E. Massey, *Bonnet Brigades* (New York, 1966), 91.

mander. Instead, he was a mere corps commander appended to Lee's command. The result was obvious—Beauregard desired to return to some independent command. He had wanted to lead the force which Lee sent under General Jubal Early to threaten Washington, but had been passed over. He had also wanted Johnston's command, but had been passed over for Hood.

By late summer Beauregard seemed almost desperate to leave Virginia. This factor might explain why he was so amenable to the almost ridiculous new Military Division of the West in October. He had even been willing to accept a position as commander of the Wilmington defenses, or to return to his old position at Charleston. Then, in late September, he received the telegram from Davis which requested his presence in Augusta on October 2.

Beauregard was desperate to escape serving under Lee and Bragg at Richmond. Also, one senses that Beauregard had been burned badly by past experience, even to the point of almost giving up. Thwarted on every hand by the government in attempts to regain a field command, his many strategic proposals were ignored by Richmond. He was battered by repeated petty and serious brushes with the government, and tainted by having been once relieved from an army command. Thus, by late 1864, Beauregard, with some justification, seemed to have lost some of his former élan. After joining the defense of Richmond, Beauregard, in May and June, seemed unusually cautious about making a mistake. For example, on June 3, after a long controversy over whether he should send reinforcements to Lee north of the James, Beauregard took pains to protect himself by filing with Bragg his entire correspondence on the matter and by appending a letter explaining his hesitation at sending Lee more reinforcements. Then, when attempting to get clarification from Davis about his new western command assignment, Beauregard made it evident that he actually did not desire to take command of an army in the field, but merely to pass orders through the commanding general.

The nebulous state of Beauregard's new command structure was one of the major reasons why Davis had come to the West—to help plan the army's new strategy. Actually, much of the plan had been decided before Beauregard was appointed. Even before Davis arrived in Georgia, Hood had decided upon a course of action which appeared strategically admirable. By the second week in September, realizing that his army could no longer engage in pitched battles with Sherman, he had to determine a course of action. To remain at Lovejoy's on the Macon Road only invited disaster. Hood was too weak even to think of investing Atlanta or risking another full fight. Yet to remain idle would invite trouble. He feared the army would be demoralized by inaction and would erode by those natural processes which always accompanied a static encampment—loss of men via furloughs, extra duty details, and desertion. Worse, such a policy would give Sherman the initiative with two ready choices. The Federals could rest in Atlanta, replenish and re-equip their ranks, and then move to eliminate Hood. Or Sherman could keep Hood at a distance while he moved southwest along the West Point Railroad into the munitions heart of Alabama, and simultaneously destroyed adjacent facilities at Augusta.

Hood's only recourse seemed to be an attempt to demolish Sherman's line of communications with Tennessee. By September 6 he had advanced this far in his thinking and informed the government that he would soon move his army to a new base on the West Point Railroad in order to be in a position to strike Sherman's supply line. Some historians have criticized Hood for initiating this eventual swing to the north of Atlanta, but he had no choice. In September his sources of intelligence indicated that Sherman would move next upon south Alabama, probably upon Columbus or Montgomery, in order to establish contact with Mobile. If Hood remained south of Atlanta, such a move would sever him from his foodstuff sources in Alabama, from Lee's department, and from the Alabama munitions works. Also, even before he began to slide toward the West Point Railroad, it appeared that a new strategy of operating against the Tennessee communications would work. On September 10 Hood received a grossly misleading report from Wheeler in which he bragged about destroying fifty miles of track on the Nashville and Chattanooga Railroad and several key river bridges as well. By September 14 Hood had learned that Wheeler had recrossed the Tennessee River at Florence, Alabama, and evidently was preparing for another expedition. What Hood did not know was that Wheeler's corps was practically destroyed and that only slight damage had been done to the railroad.[12]

On September 19 Hood shifted his base to Palmetto Station on the West Point Railroad, and almost immediately began to develop his plans further. In a brief dispatch three days later to the government, Hood first dimly outlined his plans. He would recross the Chattahoochee to the region west of Marietta, on the road from Powder Springs to Rome. To protect his communications, Sherman could only follow and either give battle or leave Hood behind and move farther south. In the event of the latter, Hood would follow and attack his rear.[13]

After Davis arrived at Palmetto on September 25, the two discussed and improved upon Hood's plan. Hood would cross the Chattahoochee

12 Shoup Journal, September 10, 14, 1864, in Hood Papers, National Archives; *Official Records*, XXXIX, Pt. 2, p. 864.
13 *Official Records*, XXXIX, Pt. 2, p. 862; Shoup Journal, September 19, 1864, in Hood Papers, National Archives.

and seize the Western and Atlantic Railroad. Under the circumstances, this seemed the best available plan. Intelligence indicated that Sherman was having supply difficulties at Atlanta, that he was deficient in wagon transportation, and that his cavalry had not recovered from its August disasters. It was also known that his army had been weakened by the departure of groups whose term of service had ended. In short, Hood was probably not far wrong when, on September 22, he stated, "Sherman is weaker now than he will be in the future, and I as strong as I can expect to be." [14] Too, on September 16, an intelligence report from Marietta indicated that Sherman was building up large supplies at Marietta prior to abandoning the railroad to Tennessee and cutting loose for a move on south Alabama. If Hood were going to halt Sherman's drive at all, this appeared to be his last chance. [15]

Within three days the new strategy was formulated. Hood was to seize the Western and Atlantic Railroad north of the Chattahoochee, and thus force Sherman to move north to protect his communications. Such a move would probably weaken Sherman if he desired to leave troops to hold Atlanta and the surrounding territory. But even if Sherman appeared too strong, Hood would retreat through the mountains to Gadsden, Alabama. Here, on a new base fed via the Alabama and Tennessee Rivers Railroad from Selma to Blue Mountain, Hood would again offer battle in country highly advantageous to the defender. If, however, Sherman returned to Atlanta, Hood would follow, even if he were forced to pursue him toward the Atlantic, via an interior line of march through Augusta. In this matter Davis and Hood evidently differed. Hood expected Sherman's move to be toward the Gulf, but Davis feared he intended to move toward Charleston or Savannah. Regardless, when the President left Hood's headquarters on September 27, he had secured from Hood an agreement that he would pursue Sherman toward the ocean if he turned back from Gadsden. [16]

Some historians have read into this agreement more than probably was intended. Davis' frequent speeches made at Macon, Augusta, Columbia, Montgomery, to Hood's regiments, and elsewhere have been cited to prove that the President knew on his visit that Hood planned to invade Tennessee and march toward the Ohio River. For two reasons Davis' speeches were foolish. Although he admitted he came to the West to aid

14 *Official Records*, XXXIX, Pt. 2, p. 862; see also Davis to Northrop, September 25, 1879, in Rowland (ed.), *Davis*, VIII, 415.

15 Shoup Journal, September 16, 1864, in Hood Papers, National Archives.

16 Davis to Northrop, September 25, 1879, in Rowland (ed.), *Davis*, VIII, 415, Davis to Northrop, April 9, 1879, *ibid*, p. 376; W. T. Walthall to S. D. Lee, November 17, 1879, in Stephen D. Lee Papers, UNC; Thomas R. Hay, *Hood's Tennessee Campaign* (New York, 1929), 27.

in rebuilding morale, he did little good by his repeated public attacks on Johnston, Governor Joseph Brown, and others. Davis also gave away the information that Hood planned to operate on Sherman's communication. In his speech delivered at Columbia a few days after he left Hood, Davis stated that the general "hopes soon to have his hand fixed upon Sherman's line of communications, and to fix it where he can hold it." [17] In his speech at Macon on September 28, Davis predicted Sherman would reap the same fate as Napoleon before Moscow, that he "cannot keep up his long line of communication, and retreat, sooner or later, he must." [18] Also, in his speech to the First Tennessee Regiment at Palmetto, Davis promised that "we will flank Sherman out of Atlanta, tear up the railroad and cut off his supplies, and make Atlanta a perfect Moscow of defeat. . . . With his communications all cut off, and our army in the rear, he will be powerless." [19]

There is little in Davis' several messages to indicate that any plan was in the making for leaving Sherman behind and invading Tennessee and the Ohio Valley. Occasionally, Davis did make some grandiose allusions to the future in an attempt to restore the morale of the border troops. He made such statements as, "I believe it is in the power of the men of the Confederacy to plant our banners on the banks of the Ohio," [20] and "we must beat Sherman, we must march into Tennessee. . . . We must push the enemy back to the banks of the Ohio." [21]

But such comments had been made often by Confederate leaders attempting to whip up the western morale. These allusions to the Ohio were little more than a continuation of that long-standing dream which had plagued the government since Bragg's Kentucky failure—that Kentucky still was rightfully Rebel territory. There seems little difference between Davis' remarks here and the varied comments by Richmond officials and others in early 1864 when they speculated upon the possible success of a Johnston invasion of Tennessee.

While Hood made preparations to cross the Chattahoochee, Davis hurried to the meeting with Beauregard at Augusta. In some ways, it was a melancholy reunion of two comrades. Hardee, who was leaving the army, rode to Augusta with Davis after a poignant farewell given him by his corps in their camp at a pine forest at Palmetto. Hardee and Beauregard had worked together during the first great concentrated effort at

---

17 "Speech of President Davis in Columbia," in Rowland (ed.), *Davis*, VI, 353.
18 "Speech of President Davis in Macon, Georgia," *ibid*, p. 341.
19 Watkins, "*Co. Aytch*," 205.
20 "Speech of President Davis in Columbia," in Rowland (ed.), *Davis*, VI, 355.
21 "Speech of President Davis at Augusta," *ibid*, 358.

Corinth in 1862. Now Davis, who greatly respected the scholar-general, took him to Augusta to give his views on the proposed offensive.[22]

Although Hood already knew of Davis' intention to assign Beauregard to the new theater command, the Louisiana officer, at first, did not. Davis first discussed Hood's proposed strategy at length, to sound out whether Beauregard agreed. Beauregard sensed the logistical problem involved, since Hood would have to transfer his supply route to the railroad from Selma to Blue Mountain, and establish his supply base ten miles northeast of Jacksonville, Alabama, on the pike from Gadsden to Rome via Cedartown. Still, he favored the plan, possibly because he envisioned himself as leading the expedition.[23]

But when Davis offered him, instead, the theater command with its vague powers, Beauregard seemed eager enough to accept. Even while the two men conferred, Hood was already swinging northwest of Atlanta. He had crossed the Chattahoochee on September 29–30 at Moore's Ferry, then had veered northeast to strike the Western and Atlantic Railroad. Between October 2 and 6, Hood's infantry busied themselves destroying the railroad at different points between the Etowah and Chattahoochee rivers, and in so doing they captured the Federal garrisons at Big Shanty and Acworth. The plan seemed to be working. By the sixth, Hood's intelligence indicated that, as they had hoped, Sherman was recrossing the Chattahoochee. Already by October 5, one segment had reached the old battleground at Kennesaw.[24]

But now Hood began the first in a long series of confusing revisions of the original plan. He and Davis agreed that the army was to strike the railroad between Chattanooga and Atlanta and force Sherman out for a fight. If Hood did not think his army had a chance for success, he was to retreat further northwest to Gadsden, Alabama, and again offer Sherman battle. However, by October 8, Hood had abandoned both of these projects. Without first informing the government, he quickly marched his army across the old battleground at New Hope Church, and by that afternoon was almost seventy miles northwest of Atlanta at Cedartown, Georgia, on the Alabama border.

There, on October 8, he telegraphed Richmond his new plan. He had abandoned the first alternative of fighting Sherman on the railroad north of Atlanta. Hood never explained why, save in a vague note in his

22 Roy Sketch, in Hardee Papers, Alabama; Davis to Northrop, September 25, 1879, in Rowland (ed.), *Davis*, VI, 416.

23 Rowland (ed.), *Davis*, VI, 416; see also Roman, *Beauregard*, II, 277–78; Williams, *Beauregard*, 241–42.

24 Shoup Journal, September 29–October 6, in Hood Papers, National Archives; *Official Records*, XXXIX, Pt. 1, p. 802.

memoirs that he changed plans because "the effect of our operations so far surpassed my expectations that I was induced to somewhat change my original plan." [25] Too, Hood had abandoned the alternative of moving to Gadsden and again offering Sherman battle. Instead, he would strike the railroad again north of the Etowah River. If Sherman did not follow him but fell back to Atlanta, Hood would follow his rear. But if Sherman pursued, Hood's plans now said nothing about halting and fighting. Instead, he vaguely stated that in that event, he would move "to the Tennessee River." [26]

Hood's offensive now seemed to be in trouble. The weaving, twisting pattern of his march thus far and his plans for the future indicated more of a raid than a shift of position for a major army. The supply problem alone was enormous. Hood's new line of supply via the railroad to Blue Mountain and thence by wagon to Jacksonville, Alabama, was yet to be established. Yet already he planned to abandon this and strike across country "to the Tennessee River." Hood's wagon transportation simply could not stand this. By late September, Hood still had over forty thousand effective infantry, artillery, and cavalry, and was issuing rations for sixty-five thousand men. His wagon transportation was in poor condition. Though prior to leaving Palmetto, Hood estimated that he needed six hundred supply wagons for his expedition, he had only three hundred available.[27]

Why did the government allow Hood to revise his strategy? The command chain was extremely tangled in early October. In Richmond, Bragg, to whom Hood reported, knew little of the Georgia situation. Davis was still campaigning across Georgia on October 8. Beauregard, the new theater commander, on that date, was en route to find Hood and ascertain what he was doing.

On October 9 Beauregard at last caught up with Hood ten miles northwest of Cedartown at Cave Spring, a spa nestled in a small range of mountains near the Alabama border. The conversation between Hood and Beauregard there is remarkable for its lack of clarity. Beauregard frankly did not understand what Hood was doing. Evidently Hood, either deliberately or not, misled him. Apparently, at Cave Spring, Hood told Beauregard nothing of his plan to push beyond Gadsden to the Tennessee River. Hood stressed that he planned again to strike the Western and Atlantic Railroad, this time between Dalton and Resaca. But Hood left the impression that he still intended to operate from his Jacksonville base, within the immediate area of Gadsden, some ten miles distant. Hood,

25 Hood, *Advance and Retreat*, 258.
26 *Official Records*, XXXIX, Pt. 3, p. 804.
27 *Ibid*, Pt. 2, pp. 850, 875; Black, *Railroads of the Confederacy*, 264.

clearly left the impression that he would stick closely to Sherman. If Sherman pursued him north of the Oostanaula as he destroyed the railroad, Hood would look for an opportunity to give battle. If Sherman retired, Hood would follow him back toward Atlanta.[28]

The weakness of the new command system was at work. If Hood actually planned to fight Sherman, the time seemed opportune. Hood's intelligence indicated that Sherman had moved north from Atlanta with only forty thousand men and had left an entire corps at Atlanta. By early October Hood had thirty-three thousand infantry and artillery alone. Also, Beauregard was appalled at the lack of preparation for supplying the army. The railroad extended only as far as Blue Mountain, and thus a rough twelve-mile wagon haul to Jacksonville was necessary. Hood had made no preparations either to extend the railroad or to establish a supply depot at Jacksonville. Yet Beauregard seemed entrapped in red tape partly of his own making. Technically, he did not assume command of his new Military Division of the West until October 17. Thus, at Cave Spring, he admitted he did not feel that he could yet order Hood to discontinue his present course, but could only advise him. Why Beauregard did not assume command of the Military Division at Cave Spring is unclear. He admitted that he was almost totally ignorant of the terrain in which Hood was maneuvering.[29]

During the next few days, the command situation became even more ludicrous. Beauregard hastened to Jacksonville to prepare a supply depot, since he assumed Hood now would permanently operate from the Jacksonville area. Meanwhile, as Beauregard expected, Hood, on October 10, struck northeast against the Western and Atlantic Railroad between Dalton and Resaca. The Dalton garrison surrendered to Hood on October 13, the railroad between Tunnel Hill and Resaca was heavily damaged, and over a thousand men were taken prisoners. Again Hood's plan seemed to be working. By October 13 his intelligence indicated that the main body of Sherman's army was pursuing toward Dalton and that the advance had already reached Resaca. Protected by the Oostanaula and by the encompassing ranges surrounding Dalton, Hood seemed in an excellent position.[30]

But again Hood revised his now well-patched strategy. Upon Sherman's approach, Hood drew back into the old terrain over which Bragg and Rosecrans had maneuvered almost exactly a year ago. On October 15–16

28 Roman, *Beauregard*, II, 281; Williams, *Beauregard*, 242–43; *Official Records,* XXXIX, Pt. 1, pp. 795–96.

29 *Official Records*, XXXIX, Pt. 1, pp. 795–96; see also Roman, *Beauregard*, II, 283.

30 Shoup Journal, October 10–13, 1864, in Hood Papers, National Archives; Hood, *Advance and Retreat*, 262–63.

Hood halted about nine miles south of La Fayette, beneath Pigeon Mountain. Again, however, he passed up the avowed plan to halt and fight Sherman, who was known to be moving westward in pursuit toward La Fayette. Instead, while Wheeler, who had just rejoined the army, skirmished with Sherman's advance west of La Fayette, Hood reassessed the situation and made two critical decisions. After conferring with his corps commanders and division leaders, Hood decided that the army lacked both sufficient morale and numbers to fight a pitched battle with Sherman. Consequently, he determined to withdraw westward into northeastern Alabama.[31]

This withdrawal may have been necessary, but Hood went further and totally disobeyed orders. While encamped south of La Fayette, he decided to abandon completely the Georgia front. Instead, he would cross the Tennessee River northwest of Gadsden at Guntersville, destroy Sherman's rail communications in the Stevenson-Bridgeport area, rout any defending forces in Tennessee, capture Nashville, and invade Kentucky. Then he would continue into northeastern Kentucky, threaten Cincinnati, and await Sherman. If Sherman did not come, Hood either would send detachments to aid Lee or would march directly through the Cumberlands of Kentucky and threaten Grant's rear.

In his explanation of this project after the war, Hood was blatantly dishonest. He asserted in his memoirs that from the outset he had planned to defeat forces accumulating in Tennessee under the command of Generals George Thomas and John Schofield. Yet Hood did not even know such forces were accumulating until more than two weeks after he left the La Fayette area. He then moved to Gadsden where, if he met Beauregard, he intended to submit his plan to him. Actually, Hood planned to move into Tennessee without even informing Beauregard if necessary. On October 19, two days before he met Beauregard at Gadsden, Hood informed the government that within three days he planned to move toward the Tennessee River. The next day, still before conferring with his superior, Hood was already making arrangements for the move with the new Alabama department commander, General Richard Taylor. He asserted that, "I will move to-morrow for Guntersville, on the Tennessee." [32]

After making arrangements at Jacksonville for a new supply depot, Beauregard had moved thirty-six miles northeast to Blue Pond, Alabama, on the road from La Fayette to Jacksonville, where he expected Hood's army to be. Beauregard found only Wheeler and his cavalry. To the Cre-

---

[31] Hood, *Advance and Retreat*, 262–63; see also Shoup Journal, October 15–16, 1864, in Hood Papers, National Archives.

[32] *Official Records*, XXXIX, Pt. 3, p. 835, also p. 831; Hood, *Advance and Retreat*, 268.

ole's chagrin, he was informed that Hood had already begun his march, and had shifted westward to Gadsden, on the north bank of the Coosa River. An irritated Beauregard continued his pursuit of Hood, and after a twenty-seven-mile ride, caught up to him at Gadsden on October 21.

That day, for the first time, the commander of the entire western theater learned that Hood was already in motion for a strike across the Tennessee River. Into the night of October 21, Hood and Beauregard pored over maps, debating the proposed campaign. Though Beauregard later maintained he had many objections to the proposal, the tone of his correspondence with Richmond, in which he explained the decision to send Hood, seemed almost enthusiastic. Essentially, Hood's plan was much like some of the proposals advocated by Beauregard from 1862 through early 1864, which embraced a drive into the Ohio Valley. Though more of a realist about logistics than Hood, Beauregard was not immune to the old Confederate dream of reaching the Ohio River.

Beauregard was concerned about the matter of timing. Hood's intelligence continued to report that Sherman was short of both food and forage due to the destruction of the Chattanooga-Atlanta Railroad. Intelligence also indicated that his wagon transportation was not in good condition, and that at least five weeks would be needed to repair the railroad. Hood must move with celerity and cross at Guntersville, forty miles distant, and destroy the railroad on the north bank before Sherman could complete repairs south of Chattanooga. This would force Sherman to continue to move northward across the river to protect his line of communications. An additional problem was the matter of Hood's supplies. His move would force a change of base from Jacksonville to Tuscumbia, in northeast Alabama. This would involve using the Mobile and Ohio Railroad from central Mississippi northward to Corinth, and then the Memphis and Charleston eastward. But the Mobile and Ohio, frequently peppered by Federal raiders, was constantly in a state of disrepair. Worse, the Memphis and Charleston had been almost totally destroyed in northern Alabama. A portion, not in use and overgrown with underbrush, did run east thirty-two miles from Corinth to Cherokee, Alabama. Since Hood had delayed in revealing his plans to Beauregard for at least a week, not until October 23 did Beauregard order the railroad to be put in a state of use.

Even if Beauregard had opposed the plan, it is doubtful he would have stymied it. Undoubtedly Hood had seen fit twice to change his plans without informing Beauregard. Hood also communicated directly to the government—that same evil pattern of command responsibility evident among Bragg, Pemberton, and Johnston. In fact, Hood's brief notes to the government on October 19–20, announcing his decision, all but hinted that he considered Beauregard's counsel more of a formality. There were many dispatches in the ensuing weeks which Beauregard would not even see. Most of the slim correspondence between the two generals directly concerned more unimportant matters. Twice during November, Beauregard called for a written review by Hood of his past operations and future plans, only to be ignored. On more than one occasion in December, Beauregard complained that he had heard nothing from Hood. Whether Hood resented Beauregard's appointment is uncertain. It appears clear that Hood seemed to scorn Beauregard's authority, and considered him commander in name only, useful for advice not necessarily to be heeded. For example, Hood depicted Beauregard's appointment as satisfactory to him because "it afforded me at least an opportunity to confer with an officer of distinction." [33]

Thus Beauregard agreed to Hood's plan, and, on October 22, the army marched toward Guntersville. But on the first day out of Gadsden, Hood revised his strategy again without informing Beauregard. Now he determined not to attempt crossing the river at Guntersville, but to move west to another crossing point. His reasons for this and his new destination seem curiously confused. In his memoirs, Hood explained that the night after leaving Beauregard at Decatur, he learned that General Nathan Bedford Forrest's cavalry division was in West Tennessee, unable to join him for the expedition. The only bit of authority exercised by Beauregard at Gadsden had been to insist that Wheeler's worn corps should remain in Georgia to operate on Sherman's communications. Save for General W. H. Jackson's two brigades, this left Hood with no cavalry, so Beauregard had dispatched orders to Forrest in West Tennessee to cross the river and join Hood. Beauregard apparently did not know that on October 16, Forrest had begun a new invasion of West Tennessee in which he operated against gunboats on the Tennessee River and the Union supply depot at Johnsonville, Tennessee. Time would be required to bring him into Middle Tennessee, where he then would have to travel almost one hundred miles from the Tennessee River crossing to join Hood's column. Beauregard believed that Forrest was on the east bank of the river, operating on the Northwestern Railroad between Johnsonville and Nashville. [34]

But Hood's explanation in his memoirs seems dubious. Forrest was not at Jackson, but was operating along the west bank of the Tennessee River. Exactly how Hood learned of Forrest's inability to join him, conveniently

---

[33] Hood, *Advance and Retreat*, 258; see also Hay, *Hood's Tennessee Campaign,* 38–39; *Official Records,* XXXIX, Pt. 3, pp. 831, 835.

[34] *Official Records,* XXXIX, Pt. 3, pp. 797, 870–71; Hood, *Advance and Retreat,* 270.

on that night, he did not elaborate. It was not the story he gave Beauregard when the latter again caught up with him near Decatur. Then Hood explained that while en route to Guntersville he had learned that the crossing was too heavily guarded, and had turned westward. Exactly what Hood had in mind is uncertain, but the story regarding Forrest seems to be pure fabrication. Forrest, on October 23, was not even ordered by his department commander, General Richard Taylor, to join Hood. Taylor misunderstood Beauregard's wishes and first ordered Forrest to proceed on his West Tennessee raid. Not until October 26 did matters become clarified, and Taylor ordered Forrest to join Hood as soon as he completed his raid. Thus, the message to Forrest was not even sent until three days after Hood maintained that Forrest said he would be delayed in joining him.[35]

Equally confusing was Hood's newly proposed crossing point. This was no minor change, since an essential part of Hood's plan was to destroy the Nashville-Chattanooga Railroad in the Bridgeport-Stevenson area. Now he was marching away from it and did not appear to know where he was going. After the war Hood claimed that upon abandoning the Guntersville project, he immediately determined to march to northwestern Alabama and cross at Florence, where he could be near Forrest.[36]

But this explanation seems erroneous and calculated to excuse the various delays and changes of plan Hood promulgated before he reached Florence. Beauregard had followed Hood toward Guntersville, only to be forced to continue his pursuit to Decatur. On October 27 an irritated Beauregard finally located Hood. Hood was preparing to lay siege to the strong garrison at Decatur, which lay on the south bank of the river. For a day and a half Hood delayed at Decatur, while he and Beauregard debated whether the garrison was too strong to invest.

Finally, on the afternoon of October 28, the expedition's plans were again changed. Reconnaissance indicated the garrison was too strong to carry, but engineers reported another favorable crossing point lay twenty miles west at Courtland. By October 29 Hood's army was again in motion.[37]

Not until October 31 did Hood finally reach what he deemed a suitable crossing point. He had explained to an astounded Beauregard that his army was too poorly supplied to cross the river at Courtland. He convinced Beauregard that the only desirable crossing lay at Tuscumbia, almost a hundred miles west of the original destination near Guntersville. Hood asserted that at Tuscumbia, he would be within ten miles of the

35 Hay, *Hood's Tennessee Campaign,* 56; Roman, *Beauregard,* II, 203.
36 Hood, *Advance and Retreat,* 270.
37 Roman, *Beauregard,* II, 293.

Memphis and Charleston Railroad, which had been repaired to Cherokee, Alabama.

Such a drastic shift westward completely altered the campaign's strategy. By November 3 Beauregard had agreed to a new Hood proposal. To strike the Nashville and Chattanooga Railroad now seemed impossible, since Hood had almost reached the Mississippi border. Now the army would move into Middle Tennessee, join Forrest's cavalry, and then decide where to go.[38]

Beauregard evidently agreed to this change of strategy for two key reasons. There was growing friction between the two generals. Beauregard was ill at ease in his new, dubious command, and Hood knew it. More than once Hood had ignored Beauregard's requests to forward reports of his operations since leaving Jonesboro. Although he was angry over Hood's constant revisions in planning, Beauregard avoided taking command. In his November 3 report to Richmond he even depicted Hood's moves thus far as successful and explained that he would only "assist as far as practicable." [39]

Hood sensed Beauregard's discomfort but did little to soothe matters. The slowness in completing the railroad to Tuscumbia, and the difficulties in crossing the rain-swollen Tennessee at Florence continually delayed Hood's advance. Beauregard pressed repeatedly for a commitment on when he would advance, but Hood remained tightlipped. He even decided, without informing Beauregard, that he would await Forrest at Florence rather than join him in Middle Tennessee.

By November 13 any working relationship between the two generals had broken down completely. When Beauregard the previous day informed Hood that he desired to review Stewart's corps, a petty quarrel ensued. On the thirteenth, Hood abandoned his Tuscumbia headquarters and slipped across the river to a new headquarters at Florence. Unaware of Hood's flight, Beauregard on the thirteenth sent his adjutant, Colonel George Brent, to request a meeting with Hood before the latter invaded Tennessee. By now Beauregard was so disinclined to exercise any authority over his subordinate that he merely asked "when and where it would be most convenient" for him to call on Hood.[40]

The situation became more ridiculous. Brent scoured Tuscumbia, but found no Hood. Learning that Hood had crossed the river, Brent informed Beauregard that he "went in pursuit." Though Brent finally

---

[38] *Official Records*, XXXIX, Pt. 3, p. 858, XLV, Pt. 1, p. 648; Hood, *Advance and Retreat*, 71. Hood argued that he had intended all along to cross at Florence. See p. 270.

[39] *Official Records*, XXXIX, Pt. 3, p. 879.

[40] Roman, *Beauregard*, II, 607, see also p. 606.

caught up with the general, Hood would not be enticed back to the south bank. Two days later, Beauregard tried again. He still refused to order Hood to confer with him, but urged a conference. When Hood remained implanted on the north bank, a disgusted Beauregard, on November 17, left for Corinth, where he hoped at least to hasten preparations to supply the army.[41]

An erroneous opinion of Sherman's location and intentions may also have motivated Beauregard to agree to the Tennessee invasion. Later, some critics would accuse Beauregard and Hood of abandoning Georgia to Sherman's march to the sea. The matter would be further simplified: Hood and Beauregard supposedly made the decision to invade Tennessee because Sherman had abandoned his pursuit of Hood and had detached Thomas and Schofield to protect Tennessee. And the Tennessee invasion would be described as a romantic and bold race between Hood's and Thomas' forces to gain Middle Tennessee.

Yet at Tuscumbia, Beauregard and Hood had no such information concerning Sherman or Thomas. Until mid-November, Rebel intelligence reported that the original strategy to draw Sherman north was working. By November 13 Beauregard's information indicated that Sherman with practically his entire army was moving into Tennessee. Sherman was reported to be moving with several corps toward Bridgeport. By November 15 intelligence sources placed Sherman at Pulaski, Huntsville, and Decatur. Now that Sherman seemed almost astride Hood's planned line of march into Middle Tennessee via Columbia, Beauregard feared that the Confederate right flank might be endangered while marching near Pulaski. It was in order to discuss this danger that he had sent Colonel George Brent on the mission to search for Hood.[42]

Beauregard and Hood soon learned that their estimate of Sherman's location was in error. Contradictory reports were being received by November 15. Scouts reported that it was rumored in Sherman's camps that he was not marching north, but toward Savannah or Mobile. The following day General Richard Taylor relayed a disturbing message from Wheeler, who had returned to Georgia. The railroad north of Atlanta had been destroyed, and on the morning of the fifteenth a force of undetermined strength had left Atlanta, marching south toward Jonesboro. Finally, on November 17, as Beauregard was leaving for Corinth, Wheeler

41 *Ibid.*, 607; Beauregard to Hood, November 15, 1864, in Telegrams Received, Hood's Command, National Archives.

42 *Official Records*, XXXIX, Pt. 3, pp. 878, 882–83, 887, 891, 904, 908, 917–18; Beauregard to Hood, November 15, 1864, in Telegrams Received, Hood's Command, National Archives.

again sent news from Lovejoy's. Sherman was definitely leading three corps southeast from Atlanta.[43]

When he learned on November 17 of Sherman's real location, Beauregard saw that it would be fruitless to pursue. Hood's army now lay almost three hundred miles to the west. The Rebel wagon transportation simply could not support a winter march through the Alabama and Georgia mountains. Instead, that same day, Beauregard ordered Hood to invade Tennessee, defeat the Federals believed gathered there under Thomas, and attempt to draw Sherman back from Georgia. Since Hood's march to north Georgia had forced Sherman to follow him previously, such a plan did not seem unrealistic to Beauregard.

Yet Beauregard wavered in this commitment. In a curious departure from his own viewpoints on concentration, he ordered Hood to return Jackson's cavalry division to Georgia to aid Wheeler in slowing Sherman's march. When Hood flatly refused, Beauregard simply abdicated all further decision-making to Hood. On November 18 he informed Hood that he could follow one of two alternatives. He could invade Tennessee with his entire force, or he could divide his army and send part back to Georgia. Beauregard's offer to let Hood make the decision indicated how powerless he felt. Still, however, Beauregard was adamant on one key point—that any Tennessee invasion should be designed to defeat Thomas and thereby threaten Sherman's communications. On November 18 Hood telegraphed his decision—to take the offensive with his entire army. Believing this to be the strategy, Beauregard left Corinth to arrange for the defense of the Georgia munitions area.[44]

Unfortunately, the government and Hood had other ideas about the planned invasion. Davis later blamed the Tennessee disaster on Beauregard, and argued that the general had changed the plans made at the Augusta conference. Yet in November, when he learned that Hood now planned to invade Tennessee, Davis offered no protest. Instead, he dangled before Hood the old Ohio dream. On November 7 he vaguely suggested that Hood beat Sherman "in detail" [45] and then advance to the Ohio River. Even when he learned that Hood did not plan to keep his army in touch with Sherman's, Davis offered no protest. On November 30 the President offered the alternatives of concentrating against Sherman or destroying his Tennessee communications. Davis implied that he pre-

[43] Roman, *Beauregard*, II, 300, 608–609; *Official Records*, XXXIX, Pt. 3, p. 918, XLV, Pt. 1, pp. 1220, 1224.

[44] *Official Records*, XXXIX, Pt. 3, pp. 1220, 1225, 1242–43; Roman, *Beauregard*, II, 300.

[45] Davis to Hood, November 7, 1864, in Beauregard Papers, Texas.

ferred the latter, and hinted that Hood should not be content with invading Tennessee or Kentucky but instead move into the enemy's country "proper." [46]

Hood's objectives in the march were clouded. Apparently the general himself was not certain where he was going. Since his stay in northwestern Georgia, he had harbored a dream of invading Kentucky and threatening Cincinnati. If Sherman failed to pursue, Hood would then push through West Virginia to join Lee. Beauregard apparently knew little or nothing of this long-range objective.[47]

Hood was no more certain of his immediate objective than of this mysterious long-range plan. Romanticists have depicted Hood's march as a race for Nashville from Tuscumbia and Pulaski. Probably Hood was aiming for the seizure of Nashville, though Beauregard evidently did not know this either. Hood knew far less of the location of the Federals in Tennessee than some have indicated.

Clearly Hood was not racing into Middle Tennessee to forestall a build-up of troops at Nashville under Thomas. Evidently all Hood knew was that Schofield with the Fourth Corps and part of the Twenty-third Corps, fifteen thousand strong, lay seventy miles south of Nashville at Pulaski. Save for vague warnings of Federal troops at Memphis and Paducah, Hood possessed no other intelligence of a Federal concentration in Tennessee. Probably he did not even know that any sizeable force was concentrating at Nashville, awaiting Schofield's arrival from Pulaski.[48]

In short, when he left Florence, Hood seemed to think that the Pulaski force was his only impediment to capturing Nashville. Later he claimed that he knew that Thomas was at Nashville, separated from Schofield by the Duck River at Columbia. Thus he and others created the impression of a race for Columbia that probably was more fiction than reality.

Hood certainly did not march from Florence as if he desired to cut Schofield off at Columbia. With his own staff and his general officers well-studded with Tennessee officers, Hood chose a most peculiar route of march for one aiming to intercept Schofield. If he desired to crush Schofield separated from Thomas, as he later claimed, why did he not march toward Pulaski? If he were aiming for Schofield, why did he make the seventy-mile march from Florence to Columbia? The quickest route would have been the Florence-Columbia road as far as Lawrenceburg, where a good road led only eighteen miles to Pulaski. Not until Hood had already passed through Lawrenceburg en route to Columbia, did he even learn that Schofield had left Pulaski for the same destination.

46 Davis to Beauregard, November 30, 1864, in Davis, *Rise and Fall*, II, 569.
47 Hood, *Advance and Retreat*, 366–67.
48 *Official Records*, XLV, Pt. 1, p. 1214.

The order of Hood's march further indicated his lack of interest in a race for Columbia. Only a single corps marched on the main road via Lawrenceburg and Mount Pleasant. The left wing, Cheatham's corps, moved by a circuitous 103-mile route through the rugged Highland Rim country around Waynesboro. Hood kept his headquarters with Cheatham's corps, on a route over thirty miles farther to Columbia, and almost completely isolated from the other two corps.[49]

Too, if Hood intended to isolate Schofield from Thomas, he moved extremely slowly. By November 25 Hood's headquarters was only twelve miles from Columbia at Mt. Pleasant, while Forrest's cavalry corps and Lee's infantry corps were within eleven miles of Columbia. Since the previous day, Forrest had been fighting Schofield's approaching Federals on the outskirts of the town. Though Hood's other two infantry corps were not far southwest of Mt. Pleasant, he placed none of his infantry into position around Columbia until November 27. By then, Schofield had reached the town, and that night had crossed to the north bank of the Duck River.[50]

The design behind Hood's curious behavior became somewhat more clear on the night of November 27. It was bitterly cold, and snow was falling as his infantry and cavalry corps commanders were summoned to his headquarters on the Pulaski Pike. There he outlined a bold plan which probably was to be much misunderstood. He intended that Forrest's cavalry would move up the Duck River the following day and seize several fords within a space of twelve miles. Then Forrest could drive back any Federal cavalry to permit Hood to lay a pontoon bridge at Davis' Ford.

On November 29 Hood, with Cheatham's and Stewart's corps, would cross the river and march on Davis' Ford Road to Spring Hill, thirteen miles north of Columbia on the main pike to Nashville. One of Lee's divisions would accompany Hood. The other two would remain at Columbia with the army's artillery and trains, and would demonstrate heavily to hold Schofield on the north bank opposite Columbia.[51]

Hood's intention in seizing Spring Hill may have been distorted by his subsequent claims. Later his move would be depicted as an ingenious march to entrap Schofield between Spring Hill and the Duck River.

Yet Hood may not have moved to Spring Hill with such an intention.

49 Hood, *Advance and Retreat*, 281–82.

50 Shoup Journal, November 24–27, 1864, in Hood Papers, National Archives; Henry, *Forrest*, 385–87.

51 Henry, *Forrest*, 387. For further evidence of vague planning see Stephen D. Lee, "From Palmetto, Ga. to Defeat at Nashville," *Confederate Veteran*, XVI (June, 1908), 257.

There is evidence that he was more interested in gaining the pike at Schofield's rear in order to outrace the Federals to Nashville. He said this, in effect, to Bishop Charles Quintard that night after the council had met. Quintard recorded in his diary that "Hood detailed to me his plan of taking Nashville & calling for volunteers to storm the key of the works about the city." [52] On the following day he again told Quintard that the army "will press forward with all possible speed and told me just now *confidentially* that he would either beat the enemy to Nashville or make them go there double quick." [53] Before daylight, on November 29, as the army moved toward Davis' Ford, Quintard again met with Hood. After the Bishop offered a brief prayer, Hood thanked him and asserted that "the enemy must give me a fight, or I'll be in Nashville before tomorrow night." [54]

Hood's unrealistic remarks to Quintard were very meaningful. Why would Hood interpose only two corps of infantry between Schofield and the gathering army at Nashville under Thomas? His motive in this might well explain his later willingness to lay "siege" to Nashville, defended by seventy thousand Federals, with barely twenty thousand troops. Evidently he still knew little of Thomas' strength at Nashville, and perhaps he even still considered Schofield's army the only real obstacle to the city's capture.

But Hood's motives went deeper than this. His determination to outrace Schofield to Nashville might explain the almost total lack of planning for the Spring Hill venture. Hood's corps leaders, Stewart and Cheatham, marched without any specific orders, without most of the army's artillery, and without their ammunition trains.

In short, Hood's plans at Columbia were scarcely less vague than his strategy at Florence. Ignorance of Thomas' power was only one cause. By November of 1864 Hood was tired, sick, and no longer the idol of the Confederacy. His four battle defeats in Atlanta and the loss of that city had tarnished his reputation. In Tennessee he groped for some grandiose scheme—the capture of Nashville, a march on Cincinnati, a crossing of the Ohio. Repeatedly, since reaching North Georgia in October, he had changed his objective, not because of unexpected Federal moves as much as because he had no real objective save that long-lasting Confederate dream that victory—and perhaps fame as well—lay along the Ohio River.

At Columbia the whole army seemed to cherish this old dream. Thirsty

52 War Diary of Chaplain (Later Bishop) Charles Todd Quintard, November 27, 1864, Sewanee.
53 *Ibid.*, November 28, 1864.
54 *Ibid.*, November 29, 1864.

for victory and anxious to regain the homeland, the Tennessee army and the populace were moved by this last pathetic hope of invasion. A flood of familiar sights and faces in the Columbia area stirred emotions. The road from Mt. Pleasant to Columbia was lined with the spacious mansions of the Pillow and Polk clans. Here was tiny St. John's Church, where the now-dead Bishop-General Polk once preached. Nearby were the homes of Generals Lucius Polk and Gideon Pillow. For several days prior to Schofield's abandonment of Columbia on November 27, Hood and his generals, intoxicated by the acclaim bestowed on them, were feted at parties and receptions, serenades and religious gatherings. Meanwhile Hood's infantry, barely twenty-six thousand strong and with thousands barefoot, waited through the cold November weather for the new move to redeem Tennessee.[55]

55 *Ibid.*, November 25–28, 1864; Halsey Wigfall to "Lou," December 5, 1864, in Wigfall Papers, DLC; Foard to S. H. Stout, October 4, 1864, copy of letter in Kennesaw; E. Shapard, "At Spring Hill and Franklin Again," *Confederate Veteran*, XXIV (March, 1916), 138.

seventeen

The Ohio Dream Fades

BY THE LATE MORNING OF NOVEMBER 29, THE EFFECTS OF HOOD'S VAGUE strategy were becoming evident. Forrest had completed the Duck River crossing that morning, and had taken the Federal cavalry corps out of the campaign altogether. General James Wilson's Union troopers had been pushed back along the Franklin–Lewisburg Pike, which was parallel to the Columbia–Spring Hill Road to the west. By 11:00 Wilson was in retreat toward Franklin, and Forrest turned his command onto the Mt. Carmel Pike which led to Spring Hill.

But Forrest was surprised to find strong Federal resistance at Spring Hill. An initial attack by his lead division, Chalmers', was sharply repulsed before noon. Heavy Federal reinforcements were arriving from Columbia as Forrest deployed his remaining two divisions on the east side of Spring Hill. Confused by this unexpected strength, Forrest was probably unsure of what to do. If Hood had actually intended to seize the pike and entrap Schofield opposite Columbia, Forrest could have skirted the village and held the pike to the north. Instead, without specific orders, a puzzled Forrest aligned his divisions facing westward, and until nearly 3 P.M. wasted his men in sporadic assaults on the village.

Forrest probably did not know how close he had come to capturing Spring Hill. As he had approached from the east via the Mt. Carmel Pike, the two Federal garrison regiments at Spring Hill were in the very act of being reinforced. The able commander of the Fourth Corps, General David Stanley, was marching into Spring Hill from the south with the lead brigade of General George Wagner's division. By the time Forrest had deployed his cavalry for a direct attack, Spring Hill was no longer a weakened position. By 2 P.M. Wagner's infantry, nearly six thousand

494

strong, was well entrenched on a long, semicircular line covering the high ground around the east and south sides of the village. Stanley's troops, backed by Schofield's reserve artillery, extended from the Alabama Railroad northwest of the village, eastward to the east side of Spring Hill, and then back southwest toward the Columbia Pike.[1]

Hood did not realize that he had already lost the race to Spring Hill. About 3 P.M., Hood and Cheatham, riding in the van of Cleburne's division, reached the crossing of Rutherford Creek southeast of Spring Hill. Here Davis' Ford Road intersected Rally Hill Pike, which led two and one-half miles to Spring Hill. Apparently Hood possessed no genuine plan nor did he understand the heavy strength of Stanley's position. Forrest remained two miles away, engaged in his sporadic assaults. In fact, Hood began to move his infantry forward without even consulting Forrest on the situation. Instead, he ordered Cleburne to take the responsibility of learning from Forrest the enemy's position.[2]

Hood's late afternoon orders illustrated his lack of planning and his lack of intelligence of Stanley's position. He issued no orders for an attack on Stanley, but gave choppy directives aimed at seizing the Columbia Pike south of the village. Shortly after 3 P.M. Hood personally led Cleburne's division a short distance across Rutherford Creek, and then sent Cleburne on with orders to take the pike. Cheatham was to await the arrival of Bate's division at the creek crossing and then lead the division to Cleburne's support. Hood would then remain at the creek to send forward Cheatham's final division, that of General John C. Brown.[3]

Within an hour the situation had become almost ludicrous. Cleburne failed to make personal contact with Forrest, and consequently walked into a trap. Oblivious of Stanley's strength or position, Cleburne left the Rally Hill Pike and veered west toward the Columbia Pike. Suddenly, within a mile of the road, Cleburne's right brigade ran squarely into Stanley's position southeast of the village. Cleburne disobeyed orders and swung his division northward toward Spring Hill. As he approached the village he was again ambushed by a galling artillery barrage from Schofield's guns.[4]

---

[1] Henry, *Forrest*, 387–89; Wilson, *Under the Old Flag*, II, 46–47; J. P. Young, "Hood's Failure at Spring Hill," *Confederate Veteran*, XVI (January, 1908), 27–31.

[2] Young, "Hood's Failure at Spring Hill," 31; Hood, *Advance and Retreat*, 284.

[3] "Statement of Captain L. H. Mangum, Assistant Adjutant General of Cleburne's Division," copy in J. P. Young Papers, in possession of Thomas R. Hay; Govan to Young, May 5, 1897, copy in *ibid*; B. F. Cheatham, "The Lost Opportunity at Spring Hill—General Cheatham's Reply to General Hood," *SHSP*, IX (1881), 524–25.

[4] Govan to Young, May 5, 1897, in Hay Collection; Young, "Hood's Failure," 31–32.

496

Meanwhile, Hood and Cheatham were busily reversing each other's orders. Cheatham disobeyed orders and did not personally conduct Bate to the front. Had he done so, Cheatham would have learned that Cleburne had not followed instructions and that Stanley was strongly entrenched in the village. Thus Bate wandered north along the Rally Hill Pike until he met Hood returning from sending forward Cleburne. Hood ordered Bate to advance on Cleburne's supposed left and get onto the Columbia Pike. About 5:30 P.M., an hour after sunset, Bate did penetrate to within two hundred yards of the pike on the Cheairs farm, a mile south of Spring Hill. Skirmish firing erupted as Bate observed a Federal division marching northward toward the village. But as he was preparing to advance and seize the road, Bate received contradictory orders from Cheatham. Bate was ordered to pull back from the pike, and march northeast to form on Cleburne's left facing Spring Hill.

Without informing Hood, Cheatham had altered his plans to seize the pike. After Bate's departure Cheatham had moved to Cleburne's front, learned of his difficulties, and ordered Bate to his support. Then, as General John C. Brown's division moved up, Cheatham ordered it also to form facing northward, on Cleburne's right flank.[5]

Hood knew none of this. He had sent all three divisions forward to seize the pike. Brown was sent by Hood to form on Cleburne's right, a move which the commander assumed would place all three divisions facing westward on the Columbia Road. It was not all Cheatham's fault, however. As at Atlanta, Hood did not remain on the field to ascertain if his orders were carried out. Instead, he now retired to his headquarters on the Thompson farm, over two miles distant from Cheatham's position.[6]

Meanwhile, Cheatham continued both to alter Hood's orders and to fail to keep his commander informed. Without Hood's knowledge Cheatham, by 5:00 P.M., had prepared a full-scale assault of Spring Hill with his corps. Brown would begin the attack on the right, to be followed by Cheatham and Bate. While Cheatham made his preparations, Hood impatiently waited for news of the successful seizure of the pike south of Spring Hill. Hearing nothing, about 5:00 he sent his personal aide, Governor Isham Harris, to learn from Cheatham what was occurring.[7]

Again Hood's orders were disobeyed. Harris stumbled upon General

5 Cheatham, "The Lost Opportunity," 525–26; Young, "Hood's Failure," 32; W. T. Crawford, "The Mystery of Spring Hill," *Civil War History*, I (June, 1955), 114.

6 Young, "Hood's Failure," 33–34; Crawford, "Mystery of Spring Hill," 115; Cheatham, "The Lost Opportunity," 526.

7 Young, "Hood's Failure," 33; John C. Brown to Cheatham, October 24, 1881, quoted in Cheatham, "The Lost Opportunity," 538; Buck, *Cleburne and His Command*, 268; Conversation with Governor Isham Harris, April, 1888 (MS in Campbell Brown reminiscences, microfilm in Tennessee State Archives).

John C. Brown, who had delayed the attack because his line was badly outflanked. Harris then located Cheatham and explained Brown's predicament. Cheatham now cancelled all orders for any advance, though Hood's original order had been for his corps to move toward the Columbia Pike. Instead, the troops remained idle as Cheatham and Harris, at about 6:00 rode toward Hood's headquarters.[8]

More confusion now foiled the seizure of the Columbia Pike. Stewart had arrived at Rutherford Creek late in the afternoon, but had strangely been held there by Hood until about dark. Puzzled, Stewart rode to headquarters to inquire why his corps had not been deployed. Hood's response indicated his almost total lack of knowledge of the situation. He explained that Stewart was being held in reserve to pursue any retreating Federals who might try to escape via the Rally Hill Pike. Still, by 6:00, Hood apparently did not know either that Cheatham was not aligned on the Columbia Pike or that a strong Union force occupied Spring Hill.

Had Hood known these facts, he would not have given the curious order to Stewart which followed. Hood had received a note from Harris indicating that Brown was outflanked. Harris' note was misleading, for he recommended that Stewart march on Brown's right and seize the road north of Spring Hill. Believing that Cheatham's line fronted the pike, Hood now ordered Stewart to march on a road parallel to the Rally Hill Pike. With a local guide furnished by Hood, Stewart was off by 6 P.M.[9]

More confusion erupted when Cheatham and Harris reached headquarters shortly after Stewart's departure. Though Cheatham now requested that Stewart's corps be placed on Brown's overlapped right flank, he did not explain to Hood that his line did not front the Columbia Pike. Apparently Hood still believed Cheatham to be advancing westward from the Rally Hill Pike instead of northward toward Spring Hill. Certainly he had not known this before Cheatham's arrival, since the path he directed Stewart to take would move him squarely within artillery range of the guns on the eastern side of Spring Hill.[10]

Hood's new orders for Stewart also illustrated this fatal misconception. A staff officer was now dispatched to halt Stewart and return his corps to

[8] Harris Conversation in Brown Reminiscences, Tennessee; excerpt of article by Major Henry Vaulx, from *New York Evangelist*, May 2, 1889, quoted in Young, "Hood's Failure," 33–34; Brown to Cheatham, October 24, 1881, in Cheatham, "The Lost Opportunity," 538; Statement of Captain Mangum, in Hay Collection; Govan to Young, May 5, 1897, in Hay Collection.

[9] Stewart to Cheatham, February 8, 1881, in Cheatham, "The Lost Opportunity," 535; Crawford, "Mystery of Spring Hill," 117–18; Isham Harris Conversation in Brown Reminiscences, Tennessee; Young, "Hood's Failure," 39.

[10] Harris Conversation in Brown Reminiscences, Tennessee; John K. Shellenberger, "The Fighting at Spring Hill, Tenn.," *Confederate Veteran*, XXXVI (April, 1928), 143.

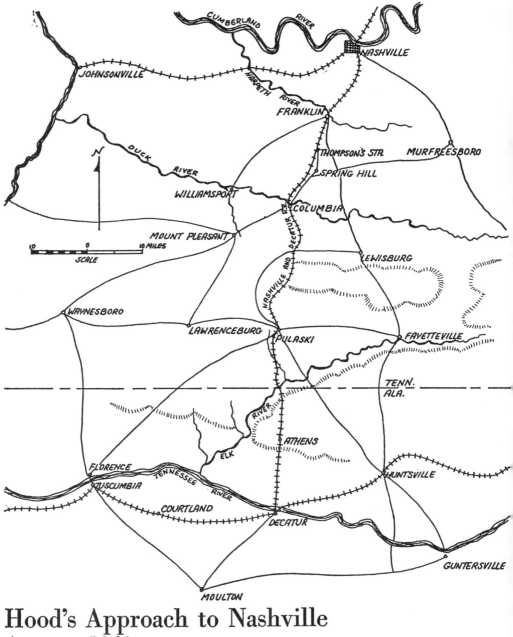

Hood's Approach to Nashville
Autumn, 1864

align on Brown's right. Obviously Hood did not understand that this new position would place Stewart nowhere near the Nashville Pike. Hood seemed to believe Stewart's new line would curve around toward the pike north of Spring Hill. As soon as he saw his new line, however, Stewart comprehended the mistake. About 7 P.M. the courier found Stewart lost on a country road east of Spring Hill. Within an hour the new line had been located. Unable to see how such a position would achieve his initial order to get on the pike, a puzzled Stewart rode back to Hood's headquarters at about 8 P.M.[11]

Hood's reactions to his conversations with Cheatham and Stewart were curious. After his talk with Stewart, Hood apparently knew for the first time that his troops were aligned in the wrong direction, and that he had not yet seized the Columbia Pike.

Yet Hood showed no sense of urgency. Cheatham already had been told to bivouac his troops, at least until news from Stewart had arrived. When Stewart reported that his new position did not cross the pike to Franklin and Nashville, Hood did not order him to resume his march to gain the road. He merely asked Stewart if he could not spare a brigade to block the pike. With equal disinterest, Stewart demurred, arguing that his men were tired and hungry. Hood accepted this, and about 11 P.M. ordered Stewart to go ahead and bivouac his corps.[12]

Hood now turned to Forrest, who had accompanied Stewart. The cavalryman also was asked if he could not place a brigade on the pike. But two of Forrest's divisions had exhausted their ammunition, and only Jackson's division had a modest supply captured from the enemy. Stewart could not supply any, since his trains were with Lee at Columbia. Still, Forrest promised that he would do what he could with Jackson's men, and on that flimsy hope of success, Hood staked the capture of the Nashville Pike.[13]

That Hood assigned this mission to a poorly equipped cavalry division of such little promise was curious. Why did Hood not now order either Cheatham or Stewart to advance and take possession of the Columbia Pike? Apparently Hood held another important misconception on November 29. Ignorant of the region's terrain, he assumed that Schofield would have no less difficulty in reaching Spring Hill than he. Lee's artillery, too, was heard periodically during the afternoon and evening. Thus Hood seemed to believe that Schofield would not reach Spring Hill

11 Cheatham, "The Lost Opportunity," 526; Young, "Hood's Failure," 39; Harris Conversation in Brown Reminiscences, Tennessee.

12 Harris Conversation in Brown Reminiscences, Tennessee; Young, "Hood's Failure," 39; Henry, *Forrest*, 393.

13 Henry, *Forrest*, 393–94; Harris Conversation in Brown Reminiscences, Tennessee.

that evening, and certainly could go no farther north than the village. Instead, Hood seemed confident that the next morning would still find Schofield between Spring Hill and Columbia.

Hood's future plans probably went scarcely farther. He still was more concerned with outracing Schofield to Nashville. Thus he told Stewart to bivouac his troops and resume the march toward Franklin the next morning. To another officer that night he boasted that morning would find the Confederates between Schofield and Franklin. With practically no artillery and no reserve ammunition and with almost a third of his infantry at Columbia, twenty-five miles distant via Davis' Ford Road, he probably did not seriously consider a halt to give battle.[14]

Still, Hood could have taken steps to insure that Schofield would not bypass him that night. No troops were ordered to the pike, nor did he go personally or even send a staff officer to observe conditions there. His failure to do this was partially an outgrowth of his overconfidence regarding Schofield. Also, by midnight of the twenty-ninth, Hood may have been in no condition to make military decisions. His old leg wound may have been irritated by the long, damp ride over rough roads, and there is some evidence that he was generally exhausted as well.

Hood was ignorant that the Federals were moving on the Spring Hill Pike. He apparently received only two warnings that night. About midnight, General William Bate came to report that Federals had been moving on the road about 5 P.M. when Cheatham recalled him. Then, at some time between midnight and 2 A.M., a private soldier roused Hood at the Thompson farm to report that infantry and wagons were passing on the pike. Because Bate's report was of a movement hours old and no one else bothered to warn him of any such move, Hood took the early morning report lightly. He directed that orders be sent to Cheatham to send a regiment to the pike and fire on passersby.[15]

But when daylight came, Hood was enraged to learn that he had underestimated what Schofield could do. During the night the Federals had marched through Spring Hill, within sight of Bate's campfires.

The Spring Hill incident was an object lesson in the breakdown of command responsibility and communication. Hood was partially responsible. He had come to Spring Hill with no plan save to outrace Schofield to Nashville. His absence from the field made him ignorant of several crucial matters. When he finally had learned by midnight that the Rebel

---

14 William Bate to Cheatham, November 29, 1881, in Cheatham, "The Lost Opportunity," 541; Stewart to Young, April ——, 1895, in Young, "Hood's Failure," 39.

15 Bate to Cheatham, November 29, 1881, in Cheatham, "The Lost Opportunity," 541; Harris Conversation in Brown Reminiscences, Tennessee.

line was not facing the pike, he still shunned personal observation, being too confident of Schofield's position.

His corps leaders had not served him well, either. Stewart had shown little interest in blocking the road, though his men were relatively fresh. Forrest behaved in a disinterested fashion. As promised, Forrest had sent Jackson's division to the pike north of Spring Hill. During the night Jackson observed long infantry columns and wagons fleeing toward Franklin. Jackson struck the pike, but could hold it only a few minutes before being driven off. None of this was reported to Hood.[16]

Cheatham was particularly at fault. Repeatedly during the late afternoon, he contradicted Hood's orders to seize the pike and did not inform his commander of the change of direction. Without authority Cheatham, about 6 P.M., had broken off all activity. In his conversation with Hood, Cheatham remained so uncommunicative that apparently he did not even tell the commanding general that his troops were not aligned adjacent to the pike.

During the night Cheatham remained uncommunicative. At some time after midnight, he received Hood's order to send a regiment to fire at anyone marching on the pike. Curiously, the officer who wrote the order, Major Pen Mason, contended later that he fell asleep before sending it to Cheatham. This incident of the unsent dispatch has been overblown by some writers. Actually Cheatham received the order. Even had he not received it, Hood's order called for no blocking of the pike. The importance of the episode was Cheatham's reaction. Already one of his staff had warned him of troops moving on the pike. Hood was not notified, nor did Cheatham move to the pike. He only sent General Edward Johnson to fire on stragglers. When Johnson returned with news that all was quiet, Cheatham let the matter drop. No information went to Hood, and no regiment was left on the pike.[17]

Though the Spring Hill matter was significant as an exercise in poor command, probably its military importance has been greatly overrated on two counts. Even had Hood placed his entire command astride the Columbia Pike, Schofield would still have held three alternate routes to Franklin or Nashville. Schofield could have used the roadbed of the Alabama Railroad which passed west of the village. Better, the Carter's Creek Turnpike farther west was a good road to Franklin. Farther west, Schofield could have avoided Franklin and marched by country roads of

16 Henry, *Forrest*, 394.

17 Isham Harris to James Porter, May 20, 1877, in *Annals of the Army of Tennessee and Early Western History*, I (May, 1878), 49–50; Harris Conversation in Brown Reminiscences, Tennessee; Cheatham, "The Lost Opportunity," 527.

the caliber of the Davis' Ford Road to reach the old pike to Nashville from Hillsboro.

Nor did Hood have the superior numbers at Spring Hill indicated by some. By 7 P.M., when Stewart still was at Rutherford Creek, Schofield had two divisions and his reserve artillery at Spring Hill. Two additional divisions were only a few miles south with their advance at the Cheairs farm. Shortly after midnight, all Federal troops had either reached Spring Hill or had passed on toward Franklin.[18]

Hood probably could not have brought up his column that evening in time for any significant action. Sunset came at 4:30, and it was dark within an hour. Many troops had been pushed to the limit by the exhausting trek over the miserable Davis' Ford Road. In short, Schofield probably had won the race to Spring Hill.[19]

The real importance of the fiasco was its effect on Hood's behavior. His obvious rage on November 30 was a bursting forth of his frustration. For months he had sought to make the army into what he believed Lee's army had been during his old days in Virginia. More than once, Hood had come to grief by attempting to imitate Lee's tactics and command policies. The Spring Hill maneuver, as Hood later admitted, was fashioned upon the well-oiled command relationship of Lee and Jackson. Hood did not understand that such maneuvers demanded a well-coordinated and seasoned command staff.

Failing to understand this, he sought to rationalize. He had done so in Georgia by blaming his subordinates for command errors and accusing the army of fearing to attack fortified positions. Now, at Spring Hill, all of his months of frustration welled up within Hood. Sick, tired, and distraught, he was too emotionally unhinged to continue to command. He lashed out at Cheatham, Cleburne, and others, arguing that the war's greatest opportunity had been lost.[20]

Worse, Hood now sought to discipline his army by means of a frontal assault. Through the morning the army pushed on toward Franklin on the route of Schofield's retreat. Shortly after 2 P.M. Hood's infantry had

18 Young, "Hood's Failure," 39; Crawford, "Mystery of Spring Hill," 124; James Wilson to Jacob Cox, August 7, 1882, in Carman Papers, New York Public Library.

19 Hood to S. D. Lee, April 18, 1879, in S. D. Lee Papers, UNC; the writer is indebted to Mr. Stanley Horn for pointing out the time factor. See Stanley Horn, "The Spring Hill Legend—A Reappraisal," Civil War Times, VIII (April, 1969), 20–32.

20 Isham Harris to Charles Quintard, December 29, 1894, in Quintard Papers, Duke; Gale to wife, January 14, 1865, in Gale-Polk Papers, UNC; James Harrision to Lily Harrison, December 6, 1864, in James Harrison Letters, in Gale-Polk Papers, UNC; John C. Brown to Cheatham, October 24, 1881, in Cheatham, "The Lost Opportunity," 589; Harris Conversation in Brown Reminiscences, Tennessee; Harris to Porter, May 20, 1877, in Annals of the Army of Tennessee, I, 49–50.

reached the southern slope of Winstead Hill, a high, cedar-covered eminence overlooking Franklin and the Harpeth River Valley. As they slowly came up, Hood, Cheatham, Forrest, and others climbed to the summit.

Below them spread the panorama of the river valley and of Schofield's awaiting army at Franklin. Situated in a curve of the Harpeth River, Franklin on the west, north, and east was a natural fortress. Since 1862 the Federals had maintained a line of earthworks, now heavily reinforced, which protected the southern approach, from the river above the town extending nearly to the river below Franklin. These works, with deep outside ditches and headlogs, were fronted by *chevaux-de-frise* and abatis. The works were open to admit the passage of the Columbia Pike. Now, a few yards northward, a second line of works closed off that road. Across the river on a high eminence, Fort Granger bristled with artillery.

Even to reach such formidable defenses would be difficult. Because of the curvature of the river, several approaches from the south—the Lewisburg, Columbia, and Carter's Creek pikes—jammed into a narrow space on the outskirts of the town. The distance between the Lewisburg and Carter's Creek routes at Winstead Hill was three miles; at Franklin they converged into a space half a mile wide. Such constriction would both slow and disorganize an advance. Too, there would be no protection from Schofield's artillery within the parapets and at Fort Granger. Continual military occupation had stripped the rolling bluegrass valley of trees, leaving only open ground for two miles in front of Franklin.

Despite the power of the Franklin defenses, Hood quickly ordered his astonished subordinates to prepare for a frontal assault. Cheatham, Forrest, and others quickly protested. There was much wrong with this idea; it appeared suicidal. Forrest knew the country well and attempted to convince Hood that he could cross at one of several upstream fords and flank Schofield from Franklin. But Hood's irrational mind would not entertain the idea. He dogmatically prepared for the attack. So anxious was he that he would await neither Lee's corps nor the artillery. Instead, nineteen thousand infantrymen without artillery support would make the attack. So thin were Hood's lines, which he spread between the Carter's Creek and Lewisburg pikes, that he had not a single reserve. His deployment of cavalry also marked his irrational behavior. He granted Forrest only a single division to attempt to flank Schofield. The remaining two divisions were placed on the army's flanks.[21]

Why did Hood order such a foolish assault? His continued anger and frustration were only partly responsible. Probably he intended the assault,

21 Sims Crownover, "The Battle of Franklin," *Tennessee Historical Quarterly*, XIV (December, 1955), 11–13; Henry, *Forrest*, 397; Buck, *Cleburne and His Command*, 280.

in his own tormented way, as an exercise of discipline for the army. He later admitted that he utilized frontal assaults for such a purpose, and reveled in the shedding of blood as a booster of morale. For him, the Franklin attack would be a last great effort to mold the army into his image of the Virginia army as he had known it.[22]

If he desired casualty lists as evidence of valor, Hood was not to be disappointed. It had turned unseasonably warm, and a balmy breeze blew against Winstead Hill as Cheatham and Stewart readied their troops. Chalmer's cavalry division occupied the extreme left, anchored on the Carter's Creek Pike. Cheatham's corps extended the line eastward across the Columbia Pike. On the east side of the road, Cleburne's division merged with Stewart's three divisions, which then extended to the Lewisburg Pike. Jackson's cavalry division occupied the narrow space between the pike and the river.

About 4 P.M., the signal came to advance. The columns lurched forward, displaying the last great spectacle of the war. In near-perfect formation, eighteen infantry brigades, banners flapping in the wind, moved across the open plain. Save for the sound of regimental bands and occasionally shouted orders, there was little noise except the flurry of rabbits and quail escaping the steadily moving Confederates. Half a mile south of Franklin the columns halted and shifted into a formation of two battle lines. Then came the order to charge, and thousands of yelling Confederates moved forward.[23]

It was less a battle than a slaughter. Because of the need to adjust to the constriction of the terrain, Cheatham's left wing and Stewart's corps did not strike the parapets until Brown's and Cleburne's divisions, astride the Columbia Pike, had been repulsed. Brown and Cleburne first overran an advanced Federal division posted on a stretch of high ground along the Columbia Pike. The Federals fled along the pike and through the gap left open in the parapets. Behind them came Brown's and Cleburne's men. The Federals in the entrenchments at first held their fire, lest they hit their retreating comrades.

Then, when within several hundred yards of the earthworks, Cleburne and Brown were met with a withering artillery and small-arms fire. The fire was so severe that hundreds of Confederates reached the outer ditch and lay there until after dark, afraid to either advance or retreat. Several hundred breached the gap in the main line, overrunning Federal batteries

22 Hood, *Advance and Retreat,* 292, 294, 297, 290, 162, 181.
23 Hardin P. Figuers, "A Boy's Impressions of the Battle of Franklin" (MS in Figuers Memoir, Tennessee State Archives) ; Henry A. Castle, "Opdycke's Brigade at the Battle of Franklin," in *Papers Read before the Minnesota Commandery of the Military Order of the Loyal Legion of the United States* (Minneapolis, 1909), VI, 396.

on each side of the road. A weird hand-to-hand fight ensued around the Carter farmhouse and nearby cotton gin, as Federal gunners swung axes and cannon rammers to drive off Cheatham's men. Then, a strong counterattack by a Federal reserve brigade drove back the intruders by sheer physical force. For the remainder of the afternoon, Brown's and Cleburne's troops either huddled in the outer ditch or launched repeated suicidal charges against the earthworks.[24]

Cheatham's attack had already been broken up when Stewart struck the earthworks. Because of the curve in the river, Stewart had been slowed by the necessity to halt and change direction. Additional delay had occurred when Stewart's center and right divisions, Loring's and Walthall's, struck a deep railroad cut. This, too, forced a change of front toward the left.

As Stewart's men scrambled around the railroad cut, they were struck by a murderous fire from three fronts. An unexpected barrage came from a battery of ten guns masked on the opposite side of the river from the railroad cut. As Stewart's men swung to the left, their entire flank was exposed to this barrage, and a severe bombardment from Fort Granger as well. Then, as they picked their way through the massive abatis in front of the parapets, they were met with a terrible small-arms fire. Walthall's division particularly suffered from the rapid fire of Federal units armed with repeating rifles. It was too much to withstand. Stewart's men also either hid in the outer ditch or reeled back in disorganized fashion to continue the fight in isolated, sporadic assaults.[25]

Elsewhere on the field, Hood's attack was also blunted by lack of coordination. Bate's division, on Cheatham's left, had difficulty locating the Federal line, which bent back sharply toward the river. Only a single brigade made contact. A more resourceful officer would have discovered that the fortifications west of the Carter's Creek Pike were only weak barricades—a condition Bate later admitted to exist. Instead, as at Peachtree Creek, Bate scarcely touched the Federal line. On the other end of the line, Forrest crossed the Harpeth River three miles above Franklin with Jackson's division. Quickly Forrest was overwhelmed and driven back across the river by Wilson's cavalry corps.[26]

If Hood had been in closer touch with the field, the slaughter, which continued until the firing ended about 9 P.M., might have been stopped. But Hood remained at Winstead Hill, where little could be seen in the intense smoke and gathering darkness. He sent no orders for Stewart and

24 Crownover, "Battle of Franklin," 17–22.

25 *Ibid.*, 23–24; Park Marshall, "Artillery in the Battle of Franklin," *Confederate Veteran*, XXIII (March, 1915), 101.

26 Crownover, "Battle of Franklin," 25; Henry, *Forrest*, 398.

Cheatham to withdraw. Instead, when General Edward Johnson's division arrived after dark, Hood sent it forward in another isolated assault. Hood was so ignorant of the situation that when the attack finally died out, he was planning to assault the works again the next morning.

But there would be no further assault. The morning of December 1 found Schofield on his way to Nashville. Only with daylight did the awful cost of the attack become evident. Fewer than 16,000 infantry had actually gone into action. Hood had lost over 6,200 men; of these, 1,750 were killed. He had suffered more battle deaths than did the Union army at Fredericksburg, Chickamauga, Chancellorsville, Shiloh, or Stone's River. His army was destroyed.[27]

The heaviest loss was among the officer corps, where talent in Cheatham's and Stewart's corps was almost extinguished. The greatest single loss was in the death of General Patrick Cleburne, the Irish individualist. In Cleburne's division, the veteran brigade commander General Hiram Granbury had been killed as well. Losses in Brown's division were even more severe. Brown was severely wounded, and all four of his brigade commanders were either killed or captured. On December 1 a colonel was the ranking division officer. Losses in Stewart's corps were also heavy. Three brigade and twenty-four regimental commanders were killed, wounded, or captured.

In leadership, as well as in numbers, the army was destroyed at Franklin. Six generals had been killed, five were wounded, and one was captured. Fifty-four regimental commanders were also killed, wounded, or captured. Even with the arrival of the remainder of Lee's corps, Hood now had fewer than eighteen thousand effective infantrymen.[28]

The carnage was continued by a further deterioration of Hood's mental condition. Disappointed that he could not renew the attack, Hood now gave orders to pursue Schofield to Nashville. There Hood planned to lay siege to the city.[29]

Hood's behavior was caused by a combination of ignorance and irrationality. All of his plans to aid Lee or to force Sherman's withdrawal were cast aside in his obsession to capture Nashville. Hood later argued that his reasoning was sound. He maintained that he was aware of Thomas' overwhelming strength at Nashville. He planned to take a defensive position south of Nashville, await reinforcements he anticipated from the trans-Mississippi region, and force Thomas to attack him.[30]

There is strong evidence that Hood's explanation was an afterthought.

27 Hood, *Advance and Retreat*, 295, 330; Henry, *Forrest*, 399–400.
28 Henry, *Forrest*, 399–400.
29 Hood, *Advance and Retreat*, 299–300.
30 *Ibid.*

Hood knew little of Thomas' strength other than his knowledge, on December 7, that fifteen thousand Federal troops were passing upriver from Memphis. There is little to indicate that Hood knew that Thomas had seventy thousand troops, and much to indicate that Hood simply marched into a trap. Also, Hood had not received the slightest hope from either the government or from Beauregard of any planned reinforcement from Kirby Smith's department.

There is other evidence to indicate that Hood was either ignorant of the situation or was operating with delusions of victory. If Hood knew of Thomas' power, why did he, on December 6, detach Bate's division, Forrest with two cavalry divisions, and other infantry, altogether sixty-five hundred men, to seize the Federal garrison at Murfreesboro? Too, if he planned to await Thomas on the defensive, Hood could have remained behind the protecting Harpeth River at Franklin, where he could draw supplies via the Alabama Railroad from the Duck and Elk River valleys. By early December the railroad was in operation from Franklin southward into northern Alabama.[31]

Hood's correspondence with his superiors also indicated his clouded thinking—if not his dishonesty. Already on December 1 he had congratulated the army for the "victory" of the previous day. Two days later, Hood's report to Beauregard and Richmond mentioned nothing of his casualties save to list the general officers he lost, and again the fight was depicted as a victory. Lest someone might wonder how an army could lose so many officers amidst a victory, Hood provided the answer in a Richmond telegram of December 5. Here again he did not report his loss of sixty-two hundred men, but instead said the loss of officers "was excessively large in proportion to the loss of men." Of the number of wounded Hood said nothing save that there was "a very large proportion of slightly wounded men."[32] Until his final report in January, Hood would continue to keep the government ignorant of his real losses at Franklin.

By December 7 Hood had brought his army to the hilly bluegrass country south of Nashville, where he planned to assume a defensive position. Hood's decision not to again take the offensive was prudent. Situated in a curve of the Cumberland River, Nashville was one of the most strongly fortified cities in the country. Twenty miles of extensive breastworks, trenches, and abatis led from the river above to below the town. These

31 *Official Records,* XLV Pt. 2, pp. 653, 659; Henry, *Forrest,* 403.
32 Hood to Seddon, December 5, 1864, in Hood Papers, Duke; see also Hood to Seddon, December 3, 1864, *ibid;* Hood to Beauregard, December 3, 1864, in Confederate Archives—Army of Tennessee, Duke; *Official Records,* XLV, Pt. 2, p. 628.

were further protected by a half dozen forts atop commanding elevations.[33]

But Hood's deployment for the defensive was less prudent. With the detachment for the expedition against Murfreesboro, Hood was left with only fifteen thousand infantry. Had he tried, Hood could not have aligned his troops on a worse position. There were seven main pikes leading south, southeast or southwest from Nashville, and Hood attempted to cover most of them with a line of entrenchments five miles in width. Cheatham's corps was placed on the right wing, with his own right anchored in a railroad cut just east of the Nolensville Pike. Cheatham's line then led west to join Lee's corps, who extended the line across the Franklin Pike. Stewart's corps then extended the line westward across the Granny White Pike to the Hillsboro Pike. There Stewart's thin line bent at right angles southward along the Hillsboro Pike for almost two miles.[34]

It is not clear why Hood selected such a poor location. His line covered only three road approaches out of Nashville. Cheatham could be flanked on the east via the Murfreesboro Pike, and Stewart on the west by the Harding and Charlotte pikes. There simply were not enough men to cover the wide front from the Hillsboro Pike to the Cumberland River, so Hood posted Chalmer's division there in observation. Thus it was a half-way job which not only failed to cover all approaches, but stretched Hood's strength to the breaking point.

Hood could have found a far better line a mile to the south. The massive, high Overton Hill range extended from the Franklin Pike toward the Hillsboro Pike, where it blended into the equally rugged Harpeth Hills. A defensive line along these ridges would have been of great strength, and would have covered the direct approaches on Franklin via the Franklin, Granny White and Hillsboro pikes.

It was soon obvious that Hood's defensive position had placed the army in jeopardy. The mercury suddenly dropped on December 8, and a mixture of sleet, rain, and snow fell during the night. By the next day, the trees and hills glittered under sheets of ice and snow, and the ground was frozen hard. With the temperature at ten degrees, Hood's wagon transportation to Franklin stalled, and the army suffered for lack of shoes, blankets, tents, hats, and winter clothing. It was almost impossible to dig entrenchments in the frozen ground. By the morning of December 13, the temperature was still only thirteen degrees.[35]

[33] Stanley Horn, *The Decisive Battle of Nashville* (Baton Rouge, 1956), 24–29.
[34] *Ibid.*, pp. 34–36.
[35] John B. Lindsley Diary, December 10–13, 1864, in Tennessee State Archives; Captain A. J. Brown Diary, December 9–12, 1864, in Evans Memorial Library, Aberdeen, Mississippi; Wilson, *Under the Old Flag,* II, 99–101.

The thaw that began that same afternoon brought only more trouble. By December 14 Hood's supply route to Franklin was a sea of mud, and his Nashville entrenchments were far from complete. Too weak in numbers to fight, and possessing too poor a transportation system to withdraw, the army could only await the expected onslaught.[36]

Hood received word on the night of the fourteenth that an attack could be expected via the undefended country west of the Hillsboro Pike. Probably the reason that he did not send reinforcements to Stewart early on the fifteenth was because Thomas deceived him with a feint against Cheatham. By 8 A.M., as a heavy fog was lifting, Federal troops in division strength fell upon Cheatham's far right near the Nolensville Pike. Not until noon did Cheatham's men, entrenched in a railroad cut east of the pike and atop a high hill on the west side of the road, beat off the attackers.

The persistence of this limited assault, and distance as well, drew Hood's attention away from Stewart's position. Again Hood was out of touch with his command. His headquarters at the Overton farm, Traveler's Rest, was over six miles from the critical angle in Stewart's line at the Hillsboro Pike, and over eight miles distant from Chalmers' cavalry. Apparently Hood did not know that Chalmers, by 9 A.M., was being overrun in a massive wheeling maneuver by about forty thousand Union troops, with their pivot on the Hillsboro Pike north of Stewart's position.

Stewart first learned of his own impending disaster about 11 A.M. A few days previous, Hood had sent the remnants of Ector's infantry brigade, seven hundred strong, to support Chalmers. Now Ector's men streamed across the Hillsboro Road, warning of the massive wheeling move. About noon, Stewart called to Hood for reinforcements, and awaited the onslaught.[37]

Before Hood could send aid, Stewart was overrun by a massive attack from the north and west. For three hours Walthall's division stubbornly held on behind a rock fence east of the Hillsboro Pike, as Hood slowly funnelled reinforcements from Lee and Cheatham. By 4:30 P.M., as darkness approached, the angle held by Loring's division at last gave way, and the Confederates streamed in confusion southeast toward the Granny White Pike.[38]

That night Hood placed the army on an even more precarious line, two miles to the south. Here, almost a mile north of the Overton Hill

36 Lindsley Diary, December 13–14, 1864, Tennessee.
37 Stephen D. Lee, "From Palmetto, Ga. to Defeat at Nashville," 259; M. B. Morton, "Battle of Nashville," *Confederate Veteran*, XVII (January, 1909), 18; Horn, *Decisive Battle of Nashville*, 73–76, 92–93, 95–96.
38 Horn, *Decisive Battle of Nashville*, 93–103.

Range, Hood deployed in the Brown's Creek Valley. Lee's corps now occupied the right, with their flank anchored on Peach Orchard Hill, just east of the Franklin Pike. Stewart was now placed in the center, between the Granny White Pike and Lee's position. Stewart's new line, located on rolling farmland, was chiefly posted behind a rock fence which formed the northern boundary of the Lea farm. Cheatham's corps, which had already been shifted to reinforce Stewart, formed the new left. Cheatham extended the line several hundred yards west of the Granny White Pike to Shy's Hill. Here his line bent back abruptly southward, several more hundred yards to an adjacent small hill, and then was re-fused so that the extreme left actually faced southward.

There were several fatal errors in Hood's new deployment. Amidst the darkness and confusion he failed to take into account the Overton Hill range, which commanded the two direct routes to Franklin, via the Granny White and Franklin pikes. Though Bate's division had returned from Murfreesboro, Hood still had only fifteen thousand infantry to man a line over three miles in width. Too, his line was deployed in the wrong direction. Less than a division front of Cheatham's command actually faced westward. Meanwhile, two thirds of the army's infantry was across the Granny White Pike, facing northward, and the freshest corps, Lee's, was fartherest removed from the danger point.

The greatest error, however, was in the deployment of Cheatham's corps. Hood's weakest point, Cheatham's angle atop Shy's Hill, was opposite the center of Federal power. The Union line lay both west and north of Shy's Hill. To the west, across Sugartree Creek, the Federal right wing was implanted on a high ridge. To the north, the Federals held a neighboring hill only three hundred yards distant from Shy's Hill. The proximity of Thomas' lines only promised deadly enfilading artillery fire on December 16.

Worse, Cheatham was also confronted by Federals on the south. Hood was now operating without cavalry. Forrest with two divisions was absent at Murfreesboro, while Chalmers' division had been driven southwest along the Harding Pike and almost out of the campaign. Thus Hood did not know that Wilson's cavalry corps, by the night of December 16, had seized the Granny White Pike at Cheatham's rear. Wilson occupied Granny White Gap, where the pike broke through the Overton Hills, thus blocking one of Hood's two lines of retreat to Franklin. Hood's ignorance of this was obvious in orders he issued in case the army was forced to retreat. Cheatham was expected to take the route now held by Wilson's corps.[39]

39 Park Marshall, "Shy's Hill—Whence the Name," *Confederate Veteran*, XX (No-

By the morning of the sixteenth, it was obvious that Hood's defeat was certain. All day long, Cheatham's position on Shy's Hill, and to the south, withstood a fierce bombardment from several directions. Late the previous night Stewart's line had been re-fused several hundred yards to take advantage of the sheltering rock wall on the Lea farm. On the sixteenth, Thomas' artillery opposite Stewart thus enfiladed Cheatham's position from the east. Other batteries kept up a bombardment from the hill just north of Shy's Hill. One battery alone fired almost six hundred rounds on Cheatham here during the day. From the west, artillery on the ridge across Sugartree Creek also pounded Shy's Hill. Then, by 8 A.M., Wilson's troopers emerged from the south and began pressing the extreme left of Cheatham's line.[40]

Hood seemed less concerned with Cheatham's plight than with matters on Lee's front. Limited attacks were made upon Lee's flank on Peach Orchard Hill at 10 A.M. and again at noon. Hood seemed convinced the Federals would attack in strength here. Thus he further weakened Cheatham during the afternoon by withdrawing Cleburne's old division, now commanded by General James A. Smith, and sending it to Lee's support. Again at 3 P.M. the Federals made a limited assault on Lee's position on both sides of the Franklin Pike.[41]

Hood had been misled, however. At 4 P.M. as darkness approached, a cold drizzle fell. Through the mist, long waves of the Federal infantry of the Twenty-third Corps poured across Sugartree Creek from the west, while the Sixteenth Corps attacked from the north. From the south came Wilson's cavalry, over ten thousand strong.

Within a few minutes, the battle of Nashville was over. Bate's regiments atop Shy's Hill were practically annihilated, and the remnants of Cheatham's corps fled for the Granny White Pike. When they realized that Wilson held their line of retreat, Cheatham's men further panicked. The corps melted into a disorganized rabble that tossed away small arms, abandoned artillery, and scurried for the Franklin Pike. Stewart's corps was caught up in the rout as well.

Only Lee's corps retained any organization. Stunned to see the army evaporating before his eyes, Lee skillfully pulled back his troops to the Overton Hills. While a young drummer beat the long roll, Lee held firm until his entire corps could be put in retreat. Still, the end had come so

vember, 1912), 522; Horn, *Decisive Battle of Nashville,* 108–109; Wilson, *Under the Old Flag,* II, 118; *Official Records,* XLV, Pt. 2, p. 696.

40 Horn, *Decisive Battle of Nashville,* 110–11, 118–20.

41 S. D. Lee, "From Palmetto, Ga. to Defeat at Nashville," 259; Stephen D. Lee's report of Tennessee campaign, January 30, 1865, in Hood, *Advance and Retreat,* 345–46.

swiftly that sixteen of Lee's guns were captured before the artillery horses could be brought up from the rear.[42]

There would be no stand at Columbia as Hood had envisioned. The road from Nashville was strewn with abandoned wagons, artillery, baggage, and small arms. Thousands of men were barefoot and dressed in thin cotton clothing. With a rearguard commanded by Forrest, the army marched on to the Tennessee River, bound for Hood's supply bases at Tupelo and Corinth. The weather changed again on December 21, and a driving snow pelted the miserable column while icy roads slashed the bare feet of thousands. On Christmas Day they began crossing the Tennessee River near Florence.[43]

Not until almost a month after the disaster at Nashville would either the government or Beauregard learn that the army had actually been destroyed. In fact, the authorities learned only indirectly that Hood had retreated from Tennessee. On Christmas Day Colonel George Brent, at Montgomery, telegraphed Beauregard, then at Charleston, and warned that he had received a note from General Lee at Florence. Brent surmised if Lee were in Alabama, some reversal must have occurred. Six days later Brent telegraphed more third-hand information. Now General Richard Taylor had spoken with an officer from the army, who had said that Hood had crossed the Tennessee River on December 26–27. The government knew little more than Beauregard. Richmond's only word on the campaign was a cryptic Christmas Day telegram from Governor Isham Harris which alluded to a disaster in Tennessee.[44]

Efforts to learn the truth from Hood were unsuccessful. He ignored Beauregard's order of January 1 to send a written report and to advise by a telegram as to what had happened. Troubled, Beauregard left Charleston and started for Tupelo. Beauregard made the trip for two reasons. He wanted to learn Hood's army's condition, and he wanted to organize and send troops eastward to help stop Sherman in the Carolinas. Oblivi-

---

[42] For descriptions of the rout see James M'Neilly, "With Hood before Nashville," *Confederate Veteran*, XXVI (June, 1918), 253; Louis F. Garrard, "General S. D. Lee's Part in Checking the Rout," *ibid*, XII (July, 1904), 350–51; Frank S. Roberts, "Spring Hill–Franklin–Nashville, 1864," *ibid.*, XXVII (February, 1919), 60; W. D. Gale to wife, January 19, 1865, in Polk Papers, Sewanee; Halsey Wigfall to "Lou," December 19, 1864, in Wigfall Papers, DLC; see also W. S. Featherston to Hood, December 15, 1886, in Hood Papers, National Archives; Hood, *Advance and Retreat*, 303.

[43] Henry, *Forrest*, 412–14; "Reminiscences of Thomas S. Wilson (MS in Confederate Collection, Tennessee); Carter, *First Tennessee*, 237; William Garrard to L. F. Garrard, April 3, 1902, in U.D.C. Bound Typescripts, IV, Georgia Department of Archives and History; Wilson, *Under the Old Flag*, II, 138, 142–43.

[44] *Official Records*, XLV, Pt. 2, pp. 731–32, 749.

ous of the plight of Hood's army, Richmond officials and Beauregard were assuming that he was capable of sending heavy reinforcement to Hardee in South Carolina. However, Beauregard suspected trouble, and before he left Charleston, he obtained Davis' permission to remove Hood and appoint General Richard Taylor to command the army if such a replacement appeared needed.[45]

En route to Tupelo, Beauregard was further confused. At Macon on January 3, he received contradictory and misleading notes from Hood. One, dated December 17, informed him the army was retreating with the loss of fifty guns. Another, dated January 3, however, said that the army had retreated "without material loss since the battle of Nashville." [46] On January 4 Hood further exaggerated and telegraphed that the army had suffered no material loss since Franklin. A few days later Beauregard received another misleading report from Hood depicting his Nashville losses in killed and wounded as small, and stating that in the entire Tennessee campaign, only ten thousand casualties had been suffered.[47]

As Beauregard approached Tupelo, he received a report from General Taylor, who had visited the army on January 9. Only then did Beauregard learn the stunning truth. Hood had only about fifteen thousand infantrymen remaining with the army. Of these, fewer than half were still equipped or considered effective. A large part of the army's artillery had been captured, abandoned, or destroyed. Some thirteen thousand small arms were missing, and wagon transportation had been annihilated on the long march. By January 14, when Beauregard arrived at Tupelo, the army was practically without food, and still had no winter clothing and had few blankets to withstand the unusually cold Mississippi winter.[48]

The day before Beauregard arrived, Hood finally admitted the truth by applying to the government to be relieved. Two days later Richmond formally authorized Beauregard to replace Hood with Taylor. Still dreaming of glory, Hood on January 23 left the army for Richmond to discuss the possibility of his bringing twenty-five thousand troops from the trans-Mississippi.

Taylor would not command for long. Although he and Beauregard

45 Ibid, pp. 738, 749, 751, 753, 772; Brent to Hood, January 3, 1865, in Hood Papers, National Archives; Davis to Beauregard, January 7, 1865, in Rowland (ed.), Davis, VI, 445; Williams, Beauregard, 249.

46 Official Records, XLV, Pt. 2, p. 757, also p. 699; see also Hood to Beauregard, January 3, 1865, in Hood Cipher Book, II, Hood Papers, National Archives.

47 Hood to Beauregard January 4, 1865, in Roman Papers, DLC; Official Records, XLV, Pt. 1, p. 660.

48 Ibid, Pt, 2. pp. 756–58, 772, 774–75, 782, 786, 788; Noll, Quintard, 129; Jones, War Clerk's Diary, II, 401; Taylor, Destruction and Reconstruction, 218; A. Welch to Basil Duke, January 17, 1865, in Duke–Morgan Papers, UNC.

insisted that the army was in no condition to move eastward, Davis was adamant. On the fifteenth, Beauregard was ordered to leave Taylor in command of the Alabama-Mississippi department and move with such troops as could be spared to aid Hardee. On January 12 Davis had explained to Taylor what portion of men could be spared. Taylor was to retain Stewart's corps and the cavalry. Lee's and Cheatham's corps were to be sent to the East.[49]

Thus the President of the Confederacy succeeded where General Thomas of the Union had failed—he completely dispersed the western forces. More men were left in the Alabama-Mississippi department than went to the Carolinas. Earlier Davis had insisted that Beauregard had gone to Tupelo with wide powers of discretion. However, the only revision he allowed Beauregard was to obtain Stewart's diminished corps. Taylor still controlled probably ten thousand infantry and cavalry of the Army of Tennessee, including four thousand of its best-equipped troops sent to Mobile. In all, scattered from eastern Louisiana to the Georgia border, Taylor probably retained thirty thousand men, well over twice the number of troops which went with Beauregard.[50]

Actually, the three small corps did not even go with Beauregard. Insistent upon hasty reinforcement, Davis did not allow the Carolina-bound units to remain concentrated. By late January they were strung from Tupelo to South Carolina. Without any new commander, the remnants of the army moved eastward and into a new area of command confusion, where lines of authority were entangled between Beauregard, Hardee, and Bragg. Meanwhile, with visions of saving Richmond by a grand reinforcement of Texans, Hood hurried to the capital. There, General Joseph E. Johnston was biding his time among his old congressional allies.

49 *Official Records*, XLV, Pt. 2, pp. 768, 772, 778, 785, 789, 792, 800, 804–805; Taylor to Brent, February 17, 1865, in George Brent Papers, Duke; Hood to Seddon, January 13, 1865, in Hood Cipher Book, II, National Archives; Hood to S. D. Lee, January 15, 1865, in S. D. Lee Papers, UNC.

50 *Official Records*, XLV, Pt. 2, pp. 757, 791–93, 800, 802; Davis to Beauregard, December 30, 1864, in Rowland (ed.), *Davis*, VI, 434; Horn, *Army of Tennessee*, 422–23; Marcus Wright, "Strength of the Confederate Army (At the Close of the War)" (MS in Marcus Wright Papers, University of Georgia).

EPILOGUE

the return of joe johnston

epilogue

The Return of Joe Johnston

IT WAS A FAMILIAR CLAMOR. BY MID-JANUARY OF 1865, EVEN BEFORE Hood resigned, the public was crying for his replacement by Joseph E. Johnston. Open meetings were held at Tupelo by officers and enlisted men alike asking for Johnston's return.

As the news of the Tennessee debacle reached Richmond, the demand for Johnston's appointment to a third assignment in the West heightened.[1] On January 14 the Senate had passed a resolution introduced by Senator Gustavus Henry of Tennessee which stated that Johnston's return to command would produce "the most salutary effect." [2] Two days later, Senator Allen Caperton of Virginia offered a similar resolution that passed both the Senate and House.[3]

Davis remained silent while the Johnston mania heightened. The Virginia legislature requested that Davis restore Johnston. Longstreet warned Robert E. Lee that nothing but the restoration of Johnston to command would save the army. On February 4, two days before Davis appointed Lee as general-in-chief, fifteen senators petitioned the Virginia general, "earnestly but respectfully" recommending Johnston's reappointment.[4]

At first Lee hedged on such a recommendation. He evaded the issue by replying on February 13 to the fifteen petitioners that his position did not carry such authority. Moreover, Lee warned that "continual change of

1 Jones, *War Clerk's Diary*, II, 380; *Official Records*, XLV, Pt. 2, p. 784; Noll, *Quintard*, 126; Vandiver, *Gorgas Diary*, 169; Chesnut, *Diary from Dixie*, 474.

2 Confederate *Senate Journal*, IV, 453.

3 *Ibid*, 458; Confederate *House Journal*, VII, 463.

4 Landon Haynes *et al.*, to Lee, February 4, 1865, in Wigfall Papers, DLC; Chesnut, *Diary from Dixie*, 474; Govan and Livingood, *A Different Valor*, 341.

commanders is injurious." Instead, Lee hoped that Beauregard could weld together a force in Georgia and the Carolinas to stop Sherman.[5]

By late February, however, it appeared that Beauregard could not halt Sherman's advance. With no real central command authority, Beauregard was unable to unite the scattered detachments that were available, and by late February, the scattered and confused elements of Confederate resistance were in flight for a new concentration point at Greensboro, North Carolina. Sentiment in Richmond and elsewhere demanded that some officer with central authority be sent to North Carolina. Beauregard had drawn increasing criticism from both Lee and Davis, who believed the general, suffering from recurring illness, had not done well in his efforts to halt Sherman in South Carolina. Thus, on February 21, Lee requested that Johnston be returned to duty. Two days later Davis submitted, and Johnston was ordered to assume command of both the Army of Tennessee and the troops in Hardee's old Department of South Carolina, Georgia, and Florida.[6]

Why did Davis allow the West to flounder for two months with no central command authority? Probably personal and political reasons were closely intermingled. To appoint Johnston would be a double blow to the President's pride. It would involve reinstating a man he had replaced with Hood, and would be almost a tacit admission of Davis' error in appointing the Kentuckian at Atlanta. Too, many of the more vocal advocates for Johnston's reappointment were not on the best of terms with Davis. A bevy of individuals, such as Alexander Stephens, Louis Wigfall, William Porcher Miles, and General James Longstreet, pressed both Davis and Lee to appoint Johnston.[7]

Perhaps even the advice from these—some of them sworn enemies of Davis—might have been heeded in other times. But in January and February of 1865, Johnston's appointment was closely tied to two key political issues in Richmond. Since early January, Congress, especially the Senate, had been pressing Davis to create the position of general-in-chief and to appoint Lee. Always, the name of Johnston came up in the debates. Therefore, Senator Henry's January 13 resolution calling for John-

5 Lee to "Gentlemen," February 13, 1865, in Wigfall Papers, DLC.

6 Lee to John C. Breckinridge, February 19, 1865, in Dowdey and Manarin (eds.), *Wartime Papers*, 904; Lee to Davis, February 19, 1865, *ibid.*, 905–906; Lee to Breckinridge, February 21, 1865, *ibid.*, 906; Lee to wife, February 21, 1865, *ibid.*, 907; Lee to Davis, February 23, 1865, *ibid.*, 909–10.

7 Govan and Livingood, *A Different Valor*, 341–43; Landon Haynes *et al.*, to Lee, February 4, 1865, in Wigfall Papers, DLC; Chesnut, *Diary from Dixie*, 474–91; William Porcher Miles to A. G. Magrath, January 15, 1865, in A. G. Magrath Papers, South Carolina.

ston's appointment to the Army of Tennessee was linked to a plea for the appointment of Lee as general-in-chief.

The two generals were linked in other such pleas. In mid-January the Virginia State Legislature petitioned Davis to restore Johnston to command and to appoint Lee as commander in chief. This move occurred almost as Senator Caperton of Virginia offered his resolution supporting Johnston, while the entire Virginia delegation warned Davis of a congressional revolt if he did not take action.[8]

When Davis yielded on February 6 and appointed Lee, he still made no motion toward appointing a western commander. This continued refusal was probably motivated by another political matter, his old struggle with the anti-Davis congressional bloc. New bitterness had flared in December after Johnston had forwarded his report of the Georgia campaign to the War Department. Davis wrote a blistering endorsement, indicating for all purposes that Johnston was a liar. Davis also warned that, with the report which he planned to forward to Congress, he would include certain dispatches and reports designed to refute Johnston.

When Johnston learned of Davis' endorsement, he hastened to Richmond to marshal his forces. He lobbied with the anti-Davis men in Congress, and was even given a seat of honor on the floor of the Senate. Later, in January, other bitter words were exchanged when the War Department seemed tardy in sending Johnston's report to the Congress.

By February the old dispute was as lively as ever. Johnston's friends were angry when Davis appointed Lee and ignored Johnston. Led by Wigfall, they bitterly denounced the administration on the Senate floor. More fuel was added on February 15, when Hood forwarded his alleged report of the army's operations under his command. The rambling, angry document was less a report than a vicious attack on Johnston's policies in Georgia.[9]

Davis and Johnston were miles from agreement. At first, Johnston asserted that he would refuse the appointment if it were offered. He reiterated his old argument that no general could be successful without the support of the government. As to his hopes for this support, he remarked that as long as Davis was President, "no friend of mine or the country ought to wish to see me restored to the command."[10] Later, with his own peculiar ability to bear the double standard, Johnston complained that Lee had waited too late to reappoint him.[11]

[8] Confederate *Senate Journal,* IV, 453; Vandiver, *Gorgas Diary,* 166.

[9] Hood, *Advance and Retreat,* 317–37; Govan and Livingood, *A Different Valor,* 333–35, 343–45.

[10] Johnston to Mackall, January 27, 1865, in Mackall, *Recollections,* 226.

[11] Johnston to Wigfall, March 14, 1865, in Wigfall Papers, DLC.

Davis was equally adamant. In February he prepared a massive document of almost five thousand words which he planned to send to Congress. The document, a review of Johnston's career from his early service in the Shenandoah Valley until the Georgia campaign, was intended as a strong argument against reappointing a man he considered to be a failure. The document was for some reason never sent to Congress, and Johnston did not learn of its existence until after the war, but it was indicative that Davis' opinion of Johnston had not mellowed.[12]

In late February, however, even the stubborn Davis could no longer withstand the pressure. By February 19 the situation in the Carolinas had completely deteriorated. Charleston had fallen, and the South Carolina–Georgia departmental troops under Hardee were being swept northward by Sherman, and were completely isolated from those Beauregard was assembling at Augusta. With only a vague authority and plagued with ill health, Beauregard seemed unable to draw together any defenses.

Under these circumstances, governmental attitudes changed rapidly. Six days after he rejected the congressional petitioners, Lee on February 19 began to move toward approval of Johnston's appointment. In a letter classic in its hedging, Lee told John C. Breckinridge that should a replacement for the West be desired, Johnston would be the only satisfactory choice. When Breckinridge told Lee that he did not understand what he meant, Lee went further on February 21 and applied for Johnston to be assigned to the West. Lee's opinion made it almost unanimous. Reluctantly, Davis conceded, and on February 23 Johnston received the orders for his third career with the Army of Tennessee.[13]

The delay in appointing Johnston proved disastrous for the West. Johnston was no genius at strategy. But if he had been appointed earlier, he might have wrought some order, and concentration might have been effected. Instead, for almost two critical months in 1865, the Confederacy confronted Sherman in the Carolinas with nothing but chaos.

The West's problem in early 1865 was not as much a lack of men as it was the dispersal of available troops under the legalistic departmental system. By February this disorganization seemed beyond repair. After leaving Tupelo in mid-January, Beauregard hurried to Augusta, Georgia, to confer with Hardee, who commanded the South Carolina–Georgia department. Beauregard's command status was vague. Except for superintending the three small corps being sent from Hood's army, the Creole's authority actually ended at Augusta, on the South Carolina border.

Both Hardee and Beauregard seemed confused as to what direction

12 Govan and Livingood, *A Different Valor*, 345.
13 Lee to Breckinridge, February 19, 1865, in Dowdey and Manarin (eds.), *Wartime Papers*, 904–905; Lee to Breckinridge, February 21, 1865, *ibid.*, 906.

Sherman would take after his capture of Savannah in late December. Since the generals believed that Sherman would aim for either Augusta or Charleston, no concentration was effected of the thirty thousand available regular and militia forces. Instead, during the first week of February, Hardee and Beauregard met at Augusta and agreed upon a disastrous policy of a dispersed line. At Charleston, Hardee would command the old Savannah garrison and Wheeler's cavalry corps. Lee's old corps from the West, temporarily commanded by General Carter Stevenson, would occupy the center below Columbia, aided by South Carolina militia. At Augusta, Beauregard had a medly of troops—Georgia Militia, some scattered forces of the Army of Tennessee, and a makeshift division of workers from the Macon and Augusta factories.[14]

Confused by Sherman's destination and continually pressured by Davis to hold Charleston, Beauregard and Hardee remained dispersed. Not until February 17, did Davis yield and allow Hardee to abandon Charleston for a concentration with Beauregard at Columbia.

By then it was too late. Sherman entered Columbia that same day, and the Rebel defenses in South Carolina were cut in two. Beauregard gathered Stevenson's corps, scattered remnants of other commands, and some militia and desperately fell back toward a newly intended point of concentration at Greensboro, North Carolina. Hardee, with ten thousand infantry and Wheeler's cavalry, was in poor condition to concentrate either with Beauregard or the two arriving corps from Hood's army. Hardee was on Sherman's right flank and must cross the entire Federal front to join Beauregard. Too, Hardee was in danger on his own right flank. The newly appointed commander of the Federal Department of North Carolina, General John Schofield, had troops at Wilmington. Thus, when Johnston took command on February 25, Hardee's men were still racing northward between Cheraw and Florence, South Carolina, almost seventy miles from Johnston's newly intended point of concentration at Fayetteville.[15]

The remainder of Johnston's command was, by the first of March, equally scattered. Stevenson's corps had reached Charlotte with Beauregard. Stewart's corps was southwest at Newberry, South Carolina, and Cheatham was still between Augusta and Newberry.

There were other troops available but not under Johnston's command. General Braxton Bragg, with fifty-five hundred infantry of the Department of North Carolina, was at Goldsboro. But Johnston had no author-

14 Hughes, *Hardee*, 273–77; Williams, *Beauregard*, 249–50.
15 Joseph E. Johnston, "My Negotiations with General Sherman," *North American Review*, CXLIII (August, 1886), 183–84; Hughes, *Hardee*, 278; Williams, *Beauregard*, 250–52.

ity over North Carolina, and would not be given command of Bragg's column for two more weeks. In Alabama and Mississippi, Taylor had retained almost fifteen thousand cavalry and infantry from Hood's army, as well as probably fifteen thousand additional scattered units. General Howell Cobb, with probably five thousand troops, was, in early April, assigned to command Hood's old department, which optimistically embraced Tennessee and that portion of Georgia west of the Chattahoochee River.[16]

Due to the western command vacuum in January and February, Sherman easily had pushed aside the scattered Rebel commands in South Carolina as he moved toward the Old North State. The problem was one of both cause and effect. Johnston, the new commander, had neither time nor authority to concentrate these divided forces which had not halted Sherman's march. Even without Taylor's Alabama-Mississippi forces, an earlier concentration of all Confederate troops in Georgia and the Carolinas would have provided over forty thousand men.

Johnston himself did not alleviate this problem very much. Never did he concentrate all of his available troops in North Carolina alone during March and April. On March 4 he had moved his headquarters from Charlotte eastward to Fayetteville, on Sherman's supposed line of march from Columbia. Johnston was convinced that Sherman was aiming for both a concentration with Schofield and an eventual union with Grant. Yet Johnston was equally unsure what route Sherman would take once he reached Fayetteville. Would Sherman move sixty miles northeast to Goldsboro for an immediate concentration with Schofield, or sixty miles north to gain the state capital and the railroad at Raleigh? [17]

Whatever Sherman's destination, Johnston knew that his army was divided into two wings and was now moving more slowly as he approached the North Carolina border. Excessive rainfall had bogged down Sherman's transportation. And Johnston's cavalry did a splendid job of impeding his march. Wheeler's corps had been joined by General M. C. Butler's small one-thousand-man division, and all cavalry had been placed under the able General Wade Hampton, who knew the roads north of Columbia well. From Hampton, Johnston received the intelligence that Sherman had divided his army into two wings on the march from Columbia. General Oliver Howard's two corps formed the left wing and was marching toward Fayetteville via Camden and Cheraw. General Henry Slocum with two other corps formed the left wing, and he was marching

16 Johnston, "My Negotiations with General Sherman," 184; John G. Barrett, *The Civil War in North Carolina* (Chapel Hill, 1963), 285; Williams, *Beauregard*, 250–51; Marcus Wright, "Strength of the Confederate Army," Georgia.

17 Johnston, *Narrative*, 378.

on Fayetteville via Winnsboro and Rocky Mount. Due to poor roads and flooded streams, the two wings were estimated to be separated by at least a full day's march.[18]

Johnston planned to strike one of these exposed wings as it crossed the Cape Fear River near Fayetteville, but there were two faults in such planning. Johnston's admitted grand strategy, in March and early April, was for Lee, after he abandoned Richmond, to join with Johnston in an attack on Sherman. This concentration Johnston later characterized as his "ultimate" objective, while he depicted his attack on one of Sherman's two wings as his "immediate" objective. Actually, Johnston's determination to attack Sherman was probably more an outgrowth of his failure to reach an agreement with Lee for combined operations. As such, there seemed little correlation between the two aims. Johnston realized that alone he was too weak to crush Sherman. Thus, his decision to give battle without awaiting Lee must have been a desperate move growing from a lack of definite word from the government.[19]

There was an additional flaw in Johnston's planning to strike either Howard or Slocum. In order to reach one of Sherman's wings, Johnston of necessity must take position somewhere between the routes from Fayetteville to Goldsboro and Raleigh. By the time he arrived at Fayetteville on March 4, Johnston had already chosen the village of Smithfield, forty-five miles northeast of Fayetteville, as the point of concentration. Before leaving Charlotte, Johnston had ordered Beauregard to send the remaining two corps from Hood's army on to Smithfield when they arrived at Charlotte.

But Johnston's much heralded concentration at Smithfield was more theory than fact. Instead of pulling in his scattered units, he allowed them to be wasted in piecemeal efforts to obstruct Sherman's march. Hardee had arrived at Fayetteville on March 9 but was not sent on to concentrate at Smithfield. Instead, Hardee was to place his small force in front of Sherman's army at Fayetteville. If Sherman marched toward Raleigh, Hardee would fall back on that point. If the Federals moved toward Goldsboro or Wilmington, Hardee would retreat northeast to join other Johnston forces at Smithfield.[20]

The result was a waste of scarce manpower. Sherman reached Fayetteville the following day, March 10, and his left wing pushed northeast on the road to Goldsboro via Averasboro and Bentonville. Instead of falling back as ordered, Hardee, strangely, halted on March 16 at Averasboro and gave battle to Slocum. After a hard day's fight, Hardee continued his

18 *Ibid.*, 376–78.
19 Johnston, "My Negotiations with General Sherman," 184.
20 *Ibid;* see also Hughes, *Hardee,* 280–81.

retreat toward Smithfield, but he had lost seven hundred valuable men.[21]

To the east, other manpower was wasted. For some reason, Bragg's command, slightly over five thousand strong, was not pulled west for the concentration, but was kept at Goldsboro, twenty-one miles east of Smithfield. On March 6 Bragg informed Johnston that Schofield's army was definitely aiming for Goldsboro and had already reached a point nine miles east of Kinston. Bragg desired to fight, and even requested that Johnston send him such troops from the Army of Tennessee as had arrived at Smithfield. Why Johnston allowed this further scattering of his troops in the face of Sherman's advance is uncertain, save that Bragg argued victory was possible. Bragg, at Goldsboro, must march almost thirty miles across the front of Sherman's right wing to meet Schofield at Kinston. Two divisions of Lee's old corps which had already reached Smithfield would require a march of over fifty miles across the front of both of Sherman's wings to reach Schofield. If disaster befell Bragg, Johnston's small command would probably be cut in two.[22] It was a foolhardy plan.

Still Johnston assented and ordered the remnants of the two divisions from Lee's corps to aid Bragg. Ironically, the command of the corps had been passed from General Carter Stevenson to the ranking officer available at Smithfield, Bragg's hated foe General Harvey Hill, who urged his men eastward to aid the man who had destroyed his career. The resulting battle at Kinston, on March 8–10, was an ironic affair, with the men of Lee's old corps attacking entrenchments held by the old nemesis of Spring Hill, Wagner's division. It was also fruitless and wasteful. Bragg with eight thousand men could scarcely have hoped for any lasting success. However, he inflicted twelve hundred casualties and lost only two hundred men, before he was forced to fall back to Goldsboro.[23]

Elsewhere Johnston's troops were scattered and wasted. When he took command at Charlotte, Johnston was embarrassed that he must replace Beauregard, who had come under increasing criticism in Richmond for failing to halt Sherman. Johnston visited Beauregard at Charlotte and secured the general's assurance that he would continue in a subordinate position. Johnston assigned Beauregard the last link of rail supply, the line from Greensboro and Charlotte to Chester, South Carolina. Beauregard would also protect this line to preserve the last rail link with Lee northward via Danville, Virginia.

Unfortunately, Beauregard almost created a separate command within Johnston's own command. During March and the first week of April, two

---

21 Barrett, *Civil War in North Carolina*, 319–25; Hughes, *Hardee*, 281–84.
22 Barrett, *Civil War in North Carolina*, 285–87; Johnston, *Narrative*, 378–79.
23 Johnston, *Narrative*, 379; Barrett, *Civil War in North Carolina*, 286–90.

full divisions of Cheatham's old corps, at least two brigades of Stewart's corps, and other assorted commands were held by Beauregard at Greensboro, Raleigh, Charlotte, Danville, and other points. All told, Beauregard probably controlled between six thousand and eight thousand troops scattered from Danville to upper South Carolina. Johnston did not press for these, probably because he realized Beauregard's embarrassing position and was concerned for keeping open communication with Lee. Not until early April would Johnston attempt to bring these to his main force.[24]

So scattered were Johnston's forces that he could not bring them all together in an organized fashion in time to confront Sherman. Early on March 18 the reliable Wade Hampton furnished Johnston with solid intelligence that Sherman definitely was moving on Goldsboro to unite with Schofield. On March 13 Johnston had ordered Bragg's command back from Goldsboro to Smithfield. By March 18 Bragg had united there with four thousand sad remnants of the Army of Tennessee.[25]

With the arrival of Hardee's troops in the Smithfield-Bentonville area on the morning of March 19, Johnston's strength was boosted to probably twenty-three thousand—infantry, artillery, and cavalry. Within this skeleton force were several veteran generals who had commanded either the army or one of its corps. Johnston's command was loosely organized into three units of unequal size, all led by former commanders of the army. Bragg, a full general, now commanded the North Carolina departmental troops, sixty-five hundred strong, merely a good division in numbers. Hardee, a lieutenant general and former commander of the Army of Tennessee, led the remnants of the Carolina-Georgia department, seventy-five hundred infantry. Wheeler had commanded the Army of Tennessee's cavalry corps in its halcyon days, when often fifteen thousand troopers were present with the army. Now Wheeler's command, part of Hampton's cavalry, could muster only four thousand men.[26]

In those remaining elements from the Army of Tennessee, was found this same attrition. Only four thousand men were present, a testament to the attrition of the Tennessee campaign and the ensuing long march to North Carolina. General Stephen Lee, wounded during the Nashville retreat, had been left behind in Georgia. His "corps" was commanded by another veteran corps commander of the army, Harvey Hill. General A.

24 Williams, Beauregard, 253; Govan and Livingood, A Different Valor, 348.

25 John B. Sale to D. H. Hill, March 13, 1865, in Carter Stevenson Papers, National Archives; Johnston, Narrative, 384–85.

26 Bragg to Davis, March 26, 1865, in Bragg Letters, Harvard; Barrett, Civil War in North Carolina, 326; Wade Hampton, "The Battle of Bentonville," Battles and Leaders, IV, 701; Johnston, Narrative, 384.

P. Stewart's promotion to the army's command placed his men under General W. W. Loring. Cheatham trailed behind with General John C. Brown's division at Salisbury, North Carolina, and the remains of his corps were led by General William Bate.

That all three of Johnston's makeshift corps were commanded by men who had led the Army of Tennessee—Hardee, Bragg, and Stewart—was only one indication of the army's decline. Within the ranks there were other signs of this reduced force. Walthall's entire division numbered two brigadier generals and fewer than 100 men. The First Tennessee Regiment had begun the war with 1,250 men, and now possessed barely 65. The Thirteenth Tennessee had marched forth in 1861 with 1,200 men. Now it did well to muster 50.[27]

With this meager army Johnston by March 18 had determined to attack Sherman's left wing as it marched on the road from Fayetteville to Goldsboro via Bentonville. By the early noon of March 19 Johnston, at Hampton's suggestion, had concentrated to make the fight two miles south of the village of Bentonville, where the single road to Goldsboro bisected a patch of dense woodland and thickets. Bragg's troops occupied the left wing, with his line astride the Goldsboro Road. Hardee's corps, which has not yet arrived, was to form the center *en echelon* to Bragg's troops. Stewart's corps were placed to extend Hardee's line. Stewart's line, hidden in a dense thicket, curved until it lay almost at right angles to the Goldsboro Road. With Hampton's cavalry placed to further extend Stewart's line, practically the entire Confederate line was parallel to the Goldsboro Road over which Slocum's troops were expected.[28]

Johnston's plan was probably his best tactical move of the war. Assuming that Hardee's troops could arrive in time, Johnston would have over eighteen thousand infantry and cavalry hidden to strike Slocum's flank as he approached Bragg's right wing, which blocked the narrow, wooded road. But Hardee was late in arriving, so late that Johnston's plan miscarried. By mid-morning, all of Johnston's troops were on the field, save for Hardee's corps which had just arrived at Bentonville, two miles north, at about 9 A.M. By 9:00 Slocum's advance skirmishers were appearing in front of Bragg's position. An impatient Johnston could do little more than fill the empty space between Bragg and Stewart with two batteries of horse artillery.[29]

27 Johnston, *Narrative*, 384; Watkins, "*Co Aytch*," 227; Vaughan, *Thirteenth Tennessee*, 35.

28 Johnston, *Narrative*, 385–86; Barrett, *Civil War in North Carolina*, 328–29; Hughes, *Hardee*, 287.

29 Johnston, *Narrative*, 386–87; Hughes, *Hardee*, 287. Hampton, "Battle of Bentonville," 703.

By 10:00 Slocum's lead division had advanced, and had attacked Bragg's position astride the Goldsboro Road. Though this initial attack was more a reconnaissance in force than a wholesale assault and was easily thrown back, Bragg nervously appealed to Johnston for reinforcements. Now Johnston weakened his chance of success with his planned right flank attack. By midday, the head of Hardee's column, General Lafayette McLaw's division, was coming up. Instead of hurrying Hardee's troops to their designated position on the right and center, Johnston both delayed and divided them. McLaw's entire division was sent to aid Bragg, who had easily repulsed the 10:00 assault. This left only a single division to join Stewart in the planned surprise assault. Too, this shift delayed Johnston's plans. Not until almost 3:00 P.M. was Hardee's remaining division, that of General William Taliaferro, in position on Stewart's left. Hardee had orders to take charge of the entire assault. He was to advance with his and Stewart's corps to strike the Union left flank. Then Bragg would advance against the center. Thus, shortly after 3:00 Hardee ordered the right and center to advance.[30]

Within two hours Johnston's hope of crushing the Federals' Fourteenth Corps had evaporated. Hardee's attack had been delayed long enough for two of the corps' three divisions to deploy. General William Carlin's division, which had duelled with Bragg that morning, had been strengthened on its right flank by General J. D. Morgan's division. When Hardee and Stewart burst from the woods, Morgan was completely taken in flank, routed, and driven southward along the Goldsboro Road. Had Bragg attacked promptly, this combined drive on Morgan's lone remaining division would have swept it away. Instead, Bragg delayed his assault until the original drive by Hardee and Stewart across the Goldsboro Road had lost its momentum. Still, Morgan could not possibly have held had Hardee not unwisely divided his force, sending Taliaferro's division and Bate's corps to pursue Carlin. This detachment soon struck the approaching Twenty-Third Corps coming up in relief. Hardee allowed these troops to be wasted the remainder of the evening in fruitless attacks upon an entire Union corps, and even ordered reinforcements for them.[31]

Johnston's plan, though well designed, had failed because of mediocre execution by Hardee and Bragg. By nightfall the opportunity to crush a detached Union corps had faded. Curiously, Johnston did not begin to withdraw. He did not do so even the following day when intelligence from Wheeler's cavalry on the far left indicated that Sherman's right wing was approaching from the direction of Goldsboro, behind Bragg's

30 Hughes, *Hardee*, 287–88; Hampton, "Battle of Bentonville," 703.
31 Barrett, *Civil War in North Carolina*, 329–35; Johnston, *Narrative*, 387–88; Hampton, "Battle of Bentonville," 704; Hughes, *Hardee*, 288–90.

left. This move threatened Johnston's only line of retreat to Raleigh, a bridge over rain-swollen Mill Creek.[32]

By March 21 the situation had worsened, and still Johnston would not withdraw. The previous afternoon he was aware of the arrival of the two corps of Sherman's other wing opposite Bragg's new position west of the Goldsboro Road. This union of Sherman's wings meant that the Federals had at least sixty thousand troops. Johnston had lost over two thousand men on March 19 and now had only about sixteen thousand infantry. Hard rain continued to fall, and the new threat on his left worsened by late afternoon. Skirmishing flickered along the entire line on the twenty-first, until about 4 P.M. when a strong attack against Johnston's far left almost seized the Mill Creek bridge before Hampton's cavalry beat it back.[33]

That night Johnston finally admitted the situation was hopeless. More intelligence received from the far left indicated that Schofield's army had reached Goldsboro, only twenty miles east of Bentonville. A union of Sherman and Schofield, would, according to Johnston's intelligence, give Sherman over 100,000 men. There was little to do save to retreat. Before dawn on March 22, amidst a driving rain, Johnston's small army quietly left its entrenchments, crossed Mill Creek, and marched toward its new encampment at Smithfield.[34]

Johnston had chosen Smithfield for two reasons. Still convinced that Sherman was set on marching to join Grant, Johnston held to his belief that such a move would come via Raleigh or Goldsboro. A position at Smithfield, halfway between these two points, would place the Confederates in a better position to maneuver against Sherman or to unite with Lee.

Johnston's continuing hope for a junction with Lee was the main reason for taking the position at Smithfield. This enduring hope might also explain why Johnston fought at Bentonville. What had Johnston hoped to accomplish? Even had he decimated entirely Sherman's left wing under Slocum, an obvious impossibility, this would not have prevented a junction of Sherman's right wing with Schofield at Goldsboro. Nor did Johnston have much hope of any lasting success in a fight against Slocum. His only chance lay in the first element of surprise. Also, if Johnston's overall strategic design, as he explained, was eventually to join Lee, why waste his small army in an attack on Sherman? Such a policy did not effect the overall concentration against Sherman which

[32] Johnston, *Narrative*, 389; Barrett, *Civil War in North Carolina*, 336.

[33] Barrett, *Civil War in North Carolina*, 338–39, 343; Hampton, "Battle of Bentonville," 705; Johnston, *Narrative*, 389–92.

[34] Johnston, *Narrative*, 392; Barrett, *Civil War in North Carolina*, 340.

Johnston desired, but was an attack by one of the two small armies the general hoped to unite against Sherman.

Probably Johnston's decision to fight at Bentonville was an outgrowth of his inability to receive any commitment from Lee and Davis as to what the overall Rebel strategy should be. Since January, Lee and Davis had continued that same blindness to western problems which had characterized their behavior in the Confederacy's more prosperous years. By the time Johnston was appointed in late February, Lee's opinions seemed fixed. In January he played down Sherman's strength and insisted that several of the western Federal corps were in Virginia. He overrated both the size of Hardee's South Carolina–Georgia army and the number of reinforcements being sent by Hood. In one breath Lee spoke of how Sherman could be checked if Hardee concentrated his forces. Yet in the same dispatch, he urged that Hardee hold Charleston, a posture which would discourage concentration.[35]

Lee's obvious lack of understanding of the debacle in the Carolinas was evident, also, in February. On several occasions, though warned by Beauregard, he flatly refused to believe that Sherman could either march from South Carolina for a junction with Grant at Petersburg or even unite with Schofield at Goldsboro. Thus, when he appointed Johnston, Lee seemed almost naïve in his directions for the general to "drive back Sherman." The same day he sent Johnston these instructions, Lee expressed his belief to Davis that Sherman might still be driven back.[36]

The height of Lee's naïveté and the greatest understatement of the war came on March 9, when, in a dispatch to Breckinridge, he stated that Johnston's army in North Carolina "is believed . . . to be inferior to that of the enemy." [37] Five days later he again showed his ignorance of the North Carolina situation. In another classic understatement, he referred to Johnston's army as "inferior in number to the enemy." [38]

Lee's ignorance of the problem Johnston faced and his own obsession with the defense of Richmond probably colored his attitude toward hopes for a united effort. At first he seemed to favor a junction with Johnston.

35 Lee to Davis, January 8, 1865, in McWhiney (ed.), *Lee's Dispatches*, 312–14; Lee to Davis, January 10, 1865, *ibid.*, 315; Lee to Davis, January 21, 1865, *ibid.*, 327; Lee to Davis, January 30, 1865, *ibid.*, 331.

36 Govan and Livingood, *A Different Valor*, p. 347; see also Lee to Davis, February 22, 1865, in Dowdey and Manarin (eds.), *Wartime Papers*, 909; Lee to William Porcher Miles, January 19, 1865, *Wartime Papers*, 885–86, Lee to Breckinridge, February 19, 1865, *Wartime Papers*, 904–905. Lee to Davis, February 19, 1865, *Wartime Papers*, 905.

37 Lee to Breckinridge, March 9, 1865, in Dowdey and Manarin (eds.), *Wartime Papers*, 913.

38 Lee to Davis, March 14, 1865, *ibid.*, 915.

In his February 23 instructions to Johnston, he stated that he was willing
to concentrate with Johnston for an attack on Sherman before he joined
Grant. Yet Lee hesitated. He insisted that he would not entertain such a
possibility until Sherman crossed the Roanoke River near Weldon, almost
on the Virginia–North Carolina border. Even then Lee did not promise
to do this. He hinted that he might decide, instead, to turn and attack
Grant.[39]

This first flicker of interest by Lee was probably the high tide in
Johnston's effort to secure any cooperation. Fired by the hope of such a
union, Johnston leveled with Lee. He admitted on February 23 that he
simply could not accumulate enough troops to drive back Sherman. Instead, Lee must come when Sherman neared the Roanoke. Thus, Johnston by March 11 twice proposed a new plan. Could not Lee leave half of
his army in the Richmond lines and spare at least half to join Johnston
near the Roanoke?

Lee's reaction to this and subsequent appeals by Johnston must have
confused the general. On March 15 Lee again mentioned the possibility
of combining against Sherman. But he insisted that for morale and material reasons he should remain in Virginia as long as possible, and dangled the possibility of Johnston's moving to the Richmond lines to unite
in an attack on Grant. Yet a few days later, immediately after Bentonville, Lee returned to the matter of uniting against Sherman and asked
Johnston to suggest a possible rendezvous.[40]

Scarcely had Johnston suggested on March 24 that they meet south of
the Roanoke when Lee again changed his mind. Discouraged by news
that Johnston was reporting fewer than fourteen thousand effective infantry, Lee by March 26 seemed to abandon the idea. He informed Davis
that Johnston's army was so weak that an attack by their combined forces
against either Grant or Sherman would be fruitless.[41]

Unfortunately, no one bothered to tell Johnston that the concentration
scheme had been abandoned. At Smithfield he vainly waited for word
from Lee. In the meantime the remainder of Hood's men arrived and
Johnston made one last reorganization of the army on April 9. His infantry, which numbered slightly over sixteen thousand effectives, was
completely incorporated into the Army of Tennessee. Johnston's ability
to maintain this level of effective troops after the Bentonville casualties

[39] Lee to Johnston, February 23, 1865, quoted in Govan and Livingood, *A Different
Valor*, 351–52; Lee to Davis, February 23, 1865, in Dowdey and Manarin (eds.),
Wartime Papers, 909.

[40] Govan and Livingood, *A Different Valor*, 351–53, 357.

[41] *Official Records*, XLVII, Pt. 3, p. 682; Lee to Davis, March 26, 1865, in Dowdey
and Manarin (eds.), *Wartime Papers*, 917.

and subsequent straggling and desertion was due to unexpected reinforcement. General Stephen Lee had recovered from his wounds sufficiently to lead several thousand troops from the army northward from Augusta. Lee had, while recuperating there from his wound, collected scattered detachments as they drifted toward the Carolinas.

Thus, in General Orders Number 13, the last of dozens of reorganizations of the army was made. Johnston resumed the title of commander of the Army of Tennessee. His three corps commanders were veterans. Hardee's first corps included the division of Bragg's North Carolina troops commanded by General Robert Hoke, and the veteran divisions of Cheatham and John C. Brown. Stewart reverted to command of the second corps, and his three division leaders were rich in long service with the army. Back was General Patton Anderson, who assumed control of Taliaferro's division. Walthall took control of the division of General Lafayette McLaws, while Loring constituted the third division. S. D. Lee, commanding the third corps, had two division leaders with mixed experience in the army. Harvey Hill, long castigated by the government for alleged misconduct at Chickamauga, was back for the last roll as a division commander. General Carter Stevenson, another veteran, led Lee's second division.[42]

But the organization was not even completed when it became clear it would no longer be necessary. Anxious for a junction with Lee, Johnston telegraphed him on April 1 to suggest a conference at his Virginia headquarters.[43] Lee thought such a plan was advisable, but in his reply did not tell Johnston he had abandoned the plan to unite. Three days went by, and at Smithfield, Johnston heard nothing. Then, on April 5, he learned from a newspaper dispatch that Lee had abandoned Richmond. Since no one in the government had bothered to inform him, Johnston assumed that Lee was now moving to make the junction, and telegraphed the government for information.[44]

Still Johnston was kept in the dark. That same day Davis replied to his query with an admission that Lee had abandoned his lines and was concentrating toward Amelia Courthouse. Davis mentioned nothing of a uniting with Johnston, and blandly stated that "your knowledge of General Lee's plans will enable you to infer future movements and his wishes in regard to your forces."[45]

Though Davis promised to communicate any information "which will

[42] *Official Records*, XLVII, Pt. 3, pp. 713, 748–49, 764.
[43] *Ibid.*, 737.
[44] *Ibid.*, 755; Govan and Livingood, *A Different Valor*, 359–60.
[45] *Official Records*, XLVII, Pt. 3, p. 755, also pp. 737, 759.

be valuable to you," [46] Johnston heard nothing further on April 5–7. Finally, exasperated, Johnston again asked the government on April 8 for instructions as to how he could unite with Lee. All he learned was that Lee was retreating westward across the Appomattox River, but no one seemed sure where he was going. On April 9 Johnston again attempted to learn where he could concentrate with Lee. The matter seemed urgent, since Johnston had learned that Sherman was planning a march toward Raleigh on April 10. Then, early on the tenth, Johnston began moving his three corps toward Raleigh, anxious for the long-sought junction. As yet, Johnston not only did not know that Lee had abandoned his plan of a junction, but also did not know that Lee's abandonment of Richmond lines had been forced—that he had been driven from his lines. Johnston still assumed that Lee's departure was voluntary, a precipitate action prior to a junction with his own troops.[47]

On the night of April 10, Johnston encamped fourteen miles east of Raleigh at the crossing of the Neuse River. There, at 1:30 A.M., he received a confusing and ominous telegram from Davis at Greensboro. The cipher message was so unclear that Johnston immediately asked Davis to repeat it. A few anxious minutes elapsed, and then the unexpected news was clarified. Unofficial reports, which Davis believed reliable, had reported that on April 9 Lee had surrendered his army at Appomattox Courthouse. Johnston was to press on toward Greensboro, where Davis wished to see him.[48]

Early in the afternoon of April 10, Johnston completed the agonizing ride to Raleigh where he hoped to hear more news from the Virginia front. Still he was kept uninformed. When he arrived at Raleigh, Johnston received another telegram from Davis which mentioned nothing of Lee save that the President had received "no official report" from the Virginia army. In a long, rambling telegram, Davis still spoke of a concentration at Greensboro and of his desire to meet somewhere with Johnston. Exasperated, Johnston, at 1:30 P.M., telegraphed to see if he should go to Greensboro and confer with Davis. Three hours later he finally received another confusing reply which said nothing of Lee, only that "it is probably better that you come here." [49]

How lonely the midnight train ride to Greensboro must have been for Johnston! He now feared that his small army alone still faced over 250,000 Federals in Virginia and North Carolina. At Greensboro, on

46 *Ibid.*, 755.

47 *Ibid.*, 773–74, 760, 765, 767; Johnston, *Narrative*, 395–96.

48 Govan and Livingood, *A Different Valor*, 360; Joseph B. Cumming, "How I Knew that the War Was Over," *Confederate Veteran*, IX, 18. Cumming, a member of Johnston's staff, gave a vivid portrayal of the night's events.

49 *Official Records*, LXVII, Pt. 3, p. 788, also p. 787; Johnston, *Narrative*, 396.

April 11, the situation seemed even more bleak. There was no official word from Lee, and the situation appeared hopeless. Selma had fallen, and there were reports of either the capture or the eventual seizure of Columbus, Macon, Augusta, and Montgomery. With news of disaster everywhere, Johnston met his old comrade Beauregard, and together they went to Davis' headquarters.

There they found the sick, frail President desperately grasping for some shred of hope. Already his opinions had been evidenced in an April 4 message to the people of the Confederacy, penned after Richmond's fall. Davis had spoken of continuing the fight in a style which sounded like guerilla warfare. Then, in his dispatches to Johnston on April 11, Davis had spoken vaguely of Johnston's effecting a concentration with other troops at Salisbury or Charlotte before continuing the fight.[50]

In the April 12 conference with Beauregard, Johnston, and cabinet members John Reagan, Judah P. Benjamin, and Stephen Mallory, the President was less willing to listen to reports of the army's condition. He was more interested in talking of continuing the fight even if Lee had surrendered. He spoke of a mass recruiting effort to build a new army, and tossed aside Johnston's explanation that for him, either a fight or a retreat would be disastrous. Nothing was settled. Davis was insistent that they must await news from Breckinridge, who had not arrived from Virginia. The meeting adjourned until the Secretary of War arrived.[51]

That night, Breckinridge reached Greensboro and confirmed that Lee had surrendered. Prior to meeting Breckinridge, Johnston conferred with Beauregard, and both agreed that the war was lost. That night Johnston then sought out Breckinridge and explained his and Beauregard's position. The Kentuckian promised that he would make sure Johnston would be allowed to present his views at the cabinet meeting planned for the following day.

On April 13 Johnston and Beauregard were summoned to the residence of Colonel John Taylor Wood, where Davis' war cabinet was having its final meeting. The two generals were admitted just as Breckinridge concluded his report of the disaster in Virginia. Again Davis called on Johnston for his views. With Lee's surrender, Johnston argued, the situation was hopeless. The Virginia army had vanished, practically all key munition centers were destroyed, and Johnston's force was outnumbered

[50] Davis to People of the Confederate States, April 4, 1865, in Rowland (ed.), *Davis*, VI, 529–31, Davis to Lee, April 9, 1865, *ibid.*, 541–42; *Official Records*, XLVII, Pt. 3, pp. 787–88.

[51] John Reagan to Davis, December 12, 1880, in Rowland (ed.), *Davis*, 535–36, George Davis to Davis, October 15, 1880, *ibid.*, 504–505; Johnston, *Narrative*, 396–97.

more than 10 to 1 by the Federals under Grant and Sherman alone. Beauregard echoed Johnston's advice that terms should now be obtained from Sherman. All cabinet members present save Judah P. Benjamin concurred. Not until April 22 did Benjamin publicly admit that further struggle was hopeless.[52]

Although Davis refused to admit defeat, he reluctantly allowed Johnston to initiate surrender negotiations. He dictated a letter to Sherman, sent under Johnston's name, which requested a cessation of hostilities until the civil authorities could discuss surrender terms. On April 14 the letter was sent out toward Raleigh unde a flag of truce. While awaiting Sherman's reply, Johnston marched his small army to encampments around Greensboro.[53]

Sherman replied on April 16 that he was empowered to act for the civil authorities in any surrender negotiations. Johnston ordered General Wade Hampton to arrange a suitable point near Durham midway between the lines. Then, he sought out Davis. Even in this last hour, the Army of Tennessee was slighted by its government. The President had apparently broken his ties with the army, and had left Greensboro without informing Johnston. On April 15 Davis had moved with his entourage to Charlotte, preparatory to his quixotic flight toward the Southwest.[54]

But the Army of Tennessee had often carried out orders with little support from the government, and on April 17 a warm, moist breeze brought the mingled scent of pine, apple blossom, and lilac as Johnston rode quietly out the pike toward Raleigh. Somewhere ahead, beyond the modest James Bennett farmhouse, Sherman slowly approached his old adversary.

Nine days later, it was done. On April 26 the Army of Tennessee, veteran of combat in every Rebel state east of the Mississippi River except Virginia and Florida, was formally surrendered. Many private soldiers expressed surprise or disgust that "Old Joe" desired to fight no longer. Some did not even wait for the formalities of accepting paroles and stacking arms, but drifted off in small bands, bound for home or some imagined new field to the Southwest.[55]

By May 3, with paroles and the stacking of arms complete at Greens-

52 *Ibid.*, 398–99; Williams, *Beauregard*, 255; Govan and Livingood, *A Different Valor*, 361–62.

53 Govan and Livingood, *A Different Valor*, 362; Johnston, *Narrative*, 399–400.

54 John Reagan to Davis, December 12, 1880, in Rowland (ed.) , *Davis*, VIII, 537; Govan and Livingood, *A Different Valor*, 362.

55 Guild, *Fourth Tennessee*, 145; Wise, *End Of An Era*, 453–54; Hardee to Beauregard, April 17, 1865, in Louisiana Historical Collection, Civil War Papers, Tulane.

boro, the army prepared to disband. There was to be one last march in the old corps formation to Salisbury, fifty miles to the southwest. There the roads would divide for the long journey across the Appalachians.

To march to Salisbury was not easy. The small, solemn band carried many lingering memories. Who could forget the sound of Hardee's regimental bands as his stubborn corps marched from the cedar thicket at Murfreesboro for one last dash against the angle . . . the peculiar roar of the autumn wind on the rolling hills at Perryville . . . the hoarse cheers in the gathering dusk at Chickamauga, when Longstreet's and Polk's wings reunited . . . the smartly dressed ranks in that last glimpse of a vanishing war at Franklin?

But there were bitter memories, too. They would not forget Zollicoffer lying dead in the fog and rain at Mill Springs . . . Sidney Johnston bleeding to death in the blooming Shiloh peach orchard . . . the sheer panic when Thomas' men scampered atop Missionary Ridge . . . the senseless, bullish slaughter that hot July day at Ezra Church . . . the sharp ice and pelting snow on the barefoot march from Nashville.

Lingering too was that constant frustration which tormented the army—the feeling that the government and others neither understood nor appreciated them. Some believed the government saw things through Lee's eyes only and considered the hills around Gettysburg more important than those at Perryville or Chickamauga. Who would remember that the Army of Tennessee defended an area almost ten times the size of that in which Lee fought? Who would remember that the western army had a double burden—to defend the geographical West, and to protect the Rebel heartland of raw materials, munitions, and foodstuffs which often supplied Lee as well.

Some in the Confederacy had never fully known of the enduring turmoil which disrupted the western army. No other army in the war had experienced such a high degree of command change and disorganization or had seen such bitter infighting among its generals.

Well scarred by internal turmoil, the army had also been scarred by continual defeat. The public's reaction to the army's problems must have tried the patience of the men in the ranks. The army was characterized by some as an aggregation of raw westerners who could not face the enemy. One of their own commanders, the tormented Hood, later accused them of cowardice. It was true that they bore the blemishes of the debacles of Fort Donelson, Missionary Ridge, and the Nashville rout. But they returned to fight again, often under generals whom they distrusted or hated. For through all its troubles and defeats, the army possessed a greatness deep in the ranks—at Greensboro, while Johnston surrendered nearby to Sherman, General John C. Brown drilled his division.

Even in death the army echoed with the turmoil of western command disputes from Mill Springs to Atlanta. The army could not make peace with itself. Joe Johnston's *Narrative of Military Operations* would be an indictment of Davis' war policies, as well as an attack upon Bragg and Hood. Hood's *Advance and Retreat* characteristically was a blind, charging attack upon Johnston. In articles and through his selected biographer, Alfred Roman, Beauregard would criticize his old enemy Davis, and Bragg as well. Longstreet in *From Manassas to Appomattox* would bitterly denounce Bragg's policies in the Chickamauga-Chattanooga campaign. Others, such as Kirby Smith and Hardee, would prepare meticulous private notes and memoranda for attack and defense on several campaign matters. Even those who failed to survive the war, Sidney Johnston and Polk, had postwar biographies compiled by their sons to plead their causes.

Gradually, these last salvos began to dim as fading memories, a sense of loneliness, and dwindling ranks cooled the old hatreds. Steadily the old leaders faded, often in poignant scenes: Joe Johnston entering a railroad car in the Virginia valley to bid farewell to a dying Hardee; Jefferson Davis at the bedside of the dying Bedford Forrest on an autumn day in Memphis; Simon Buckner and Phil Sheridan standing together in Riverside Park at Grant's funeral.

By the eighteen nineties the ranks were becoming sparse. Johnston died in 1891 after contracting a severe cold at Sherman's funeral, where he stood bareheaded because he insisted his old enemy would have done the same for him. Two years later, Beauregard died in New Orleans where he had become a successful businessman, and Kirby Smith died after spending eighteen years as a professor on the mountain at Sewanee. In 1906 small Joe Wheeler, then a general in the United States Army, died, followed two years later by the educators, Stephen Lee and A. P. Stewart.

In 1914, as warclouds gathered in Europe, the Army of Tennessee's one remaining corps commander died. Simon Buckner's endurance to the last capped a stormy career that included Fort Donelson and Chickamauga, a career that typified the army's basic command turmoil. As a Kentuckian he was also a representative of that persistent dream that had bedeviled the western leaders—reaching the Ohio River.

Now he was gone. While heroes' monuments sprouted in the East at Gettysburg, the Green River flowed near Buckner's homeplace and past Bragg's old earthworks of 1862, now covered with grass.

Bibliography

All manuscript sources consulted are cited here. Because of the vast number of printed sources relating to the Army of Tennessee, the printed sources cited here are a supplementary to those listed in the previous volume, *Army of the Heartland,* and contain only sources not cited in that volume.

MANUSCRIPTS

Alabama State Department of Archives and History, Montgomery
  Lieutenant General William J. Hardee Papers
  Joseph Wheeler Papers
  Sterling A. Wood Papers
  Earl Van Dorn Papers

Atlanta Historical Society
  Civil War Collection
  James Crew Letters
  Telamon Cuyler Collection
  Brevet Major General John W. Geary Letters
  Leonidas Mackey Letters
  Samuel P. Richards Diary

Beauvoir, Biloxi, Mississippi
  Jefferson Davis Papers

Chattanooga Public Library
  Nathan Bedford Forrest File
  Joseph Wheeler File

Chickamauga-Chattanooga National Military Park Library
  August Bratnober Diary
  Robert Sidney Reminiscences
  Typescript Diary of A. M. Brinkerhoff

Typescript Diary of John Ely
Captain Joab Goodson Letters
G. E. Goudelock Letters
Typescript Letters of John W. Nesbitt
Typescript Journal of Hulbert H. Palmer
Axel H. Reed Diary
Typescript Diary of J. J. Reed
John W. Tuttle Diary

Chicago Historical Society
John C. Breckinridge Papers
George W. Brent Journal, December 8–19, 1864
Benjamin Franklin Cheatham Papers
Nathan Bedford Forrest Papers
William Hardee Papers
Leonidas Polk Papers
Joseph Wheeler Papers

Cincinnati Historical Society
William Lytle Papers

Columbia University Library, New York, N.Y.
York-Beauregard Papers

Duke University Library, Durham, N. C.
P. G. T. Beauregard Papers
Braxton Bragg Papers
George William Brent Papers
John Buie Letters
Clement C. Clay Papers
Confederate Archives: Army of the Mississippi Papers, 1861–65
Confederate Archives: Army of Tennessee Papers, 1862–65
Confederate Archives: Department of South Carolina and Georgia Letters
    and Papers, 1862–65
Confederate Archives: Miscellaneous Soldiers' and Officers' Letters
Jefferson Davis Papers
Nathan Bedford Forrest Papers
Georgia Portfolio: Scrapbook of Charles Colcock Jones
John Bell Hood Letters, 1864
Joseph E. Johnston Papers, 1855–84
Edmund Kirby Smith Papers
James Longstreet Letters, 1848–1904
Miscellaneous Archives: Field Returns, 1861–64
Miscellaneous Archives: Ordnance Reports and Requisitions, 1861–65
McKinney Family Papers
Munford-Ellis Papers (G. W. Munford Division)
Hypolite Oladowski Papers, 1862–65
William Nelson Pendleton Letters and Papers, 1861–82
Gideon J. Pillow Papers
Leonidas Polk Papers, 1828–71
Orlando Metcalfe Poe Papers
C. T. Quintard Papers

    Daniel Ruggles Papers
    Tennessee Rolls and History, 3rd Tennessee Regiment
    C. B. Tompkins Papers

Emory University Library, Atlanta, Ga.
    Army of Tennessee: Miscellaneous Papers
    Army of Tennessee: Quartermaster Papers
    P. G. T. Beauregard Papers
    Braxton Bragg Papers
    Joseph E. Brown Papers, 1859–77
    James Chesnut Military Letterbook, 1864–65
    Jefferson Davis Papers
    James Longstreet Papers
    Samuel H. Stout Papers
    A. H. Wilbur Papers

Evans Memorial Library, Aberdeen, Miss.
    A. J. Brown Diary

Filson Club Historical Society, Louisville, Ky.
    J. Stoddard Johnston Military Papers
    J. Stoddard Johnston Papers

Georgia Department of Archives, Atlanta
    Joseph E. Brown Letterbook, 1861–65
    Joseph E. Brown Letters Received
    Confederate Diaries and Letters: U.D.C. Bound Typescripts
    I. V. Moore Diary
    A. J. Neal Letters

University of Georgia Library, Athens
    J. F. Brown Papers
    Marcus Wright Scrapbook

Houghton Library, Library of Harvard University, Cambridge, Mass.
    Braxton Bragg Letters
    John C. Breckinridge Letters
    Simon Bolivar Buckner Letters
    Jefferson Davis Letters
    William J. Hardee Letters
    Thomas C. Hindman Letters
    Joseph E. Johnston Letters
    James Longstreet Letters
    John Hunt Morgan Letters
    Leonidas Polk Letters
    Joseph Wheeler Letters

Henry E. Huntington Library, San Marino, Calif.
    Simon Bolivar Buckner Papers, 1830–1912
    Joseph Eggleston Johnston Papers, 1861–65

Kennesaw Mountain National Battlefield Park Library, Marietta, Ga.
    General Jacob Cox Diary (typescript)

M. H. Dixon Diary
G. W. Hunnicutt Diary, December, 1863–August, 1864
A. J. Neal Letters
W. H. Montgomery Letters
Typescript Recollections of George A. Williams

Kentucky State Archives, Frankfort
D. Howard Smith Papers

University of Kentucky Library, Lexington
Thomas Hines Papers

Library of Congress, Washington, D. C.
P. G. T. Beauregard Papers
Leonidas Polk Papers
Alfred Roman Papers
Earl Van Dorn Papers
Wigfall Family Papers

Department of Archives, Louisiana State University, Baton Rouge
P. G. T. Beauregard Papers,
P. G. T. Beauregard Papers, copy of correspondence in University of Texas
    Library
Charles J. Johnson Family Papers
Joseph Jones Papers
Liddell (St. John and Family) Papers
Confederate Collection

Miami University Library, Oxford, Ohio
Joseph E. Johnston Papers

Mississippi State University, State College
Nannie Rice Papers

Missouri Historical Society, St. Louis
William K. Bixby Collection of Braxton Bragg Papers

National Archives, Confederate Records Division, Washington, D. C.
P. G. T. Beauregard Papers
Bushrod R. Johnson Papers, 1862–65
St. John R. Liddell Papers
Gideon Pillow Correspondence, 1861–65
Leonidas Polk Papers, 1861–64
Thomas C. Hindman Papers
John Bell Hood Papers
Joseph Wheeler Correspondence, 1863–64
E. C. Walthall Papers
Samuel G. French Correspondence, 1861–65
Letters and Telegrams Sent, General James Chalmers' Command, 1862–65,
    Ch. II, Vols. 288–90.
Letters, Telegrams and Orders Received and Sent, General John C. Breckin-
    ridge's Command, 1861–65, Ch. II, Vol. 311
Letters and Telegrams Sent, General P. G. T. Beauregard's Command, 1862–
    64, Ch. II, Vol. 35

Correspondence of the Western Department and the Army of the Mississippi, 1861–65, Ch. II, Vol. 271

Letters, Orders and Circulars Sent and Received, Medical Director's Office, Army of Tennessee, 1862–65, Ch. VI, Vol. 748

Letters Sent, Ordnance Officer, Army of Tennessee, 1862–64, Ch. IV, Vols. 141–43

Communications Received by Major General P. R. Cleburne's Division, 1862–64, Ch. II, Vol. 265

Orders, Army of Mississippi, Western Department No. 2, and Army of Tennessee, 1862–63, Ch. VIII, Vol. 342

Extracts of Special Orders Issued by Adjutant and Inspector General at Richmond, Virginia, and forwarded to General Polk's Command, 1862–63, Ch. II, Vol. 53½

Letters Sent, Department of East Tennessee, 1862, Ch. II, Vol. 237

Letters Sent, Chief of Engineers, Western Department, 1861–62, Ch. III, Vol. 8

Register of Letters Received by General Polk's Corps, Army of Tennessee, 1861–62, Ch. II, Vol. 12

Index to Letters Sent by General Polk's Command, 1861–62, Ch. II, Vol. 13½

Special Orders and Index, Commands of Generals Leonidas Polk, D. H. Maury, S. D. Lee, and Richard Taylor, 1862–64, Ch. II, Vol. 15

Special Orders, Letters Sent and Battle Reports, First Division, Western Department; and First Brigade, First Division of General William J. Hardee's Corps, 1861–63, Ch. II, Vol. 18

Letters and Telegrams Sent, Department of East Tennessee, March–November, 1862, Ch. II, Vol. 51

Endorsements on Letters Received, Department of East Tennessee, 1862–63, Ch. II, Vol. 51½

Letters and Telegrams Sent, Department of East Tennessee, 1862, Ch. II, Vol. 52

Endorsement Book, Polk's Command, 1861–63, Ch. II, Vol. 52½

Letters and Telegrams Sent and Special Orders, Department of East Tennessee, 1862, Ch. II, Vol. 52½

Register of Letters Received, Western Department and Army and Department of Mississippi, 1861–63, Ch. II, Vol. 158½

Special Orders, Army of the Mississippi, Department No. 2 and Department and Army of Tennessee, 1862–64, Ch II, Vol. 221

Letters and Telegrams Sent, Headquarters, Confederate Forces at Chattanooga and Department of Western Virginia, 1862–63, Ch. II, Vol. 233

Orders and Circulars, Army of Tennessee and Subordinate Commands, 1863–64, Ch. II, Vol. 53

Miscellaneous Records, Army of Tennessee, 1863–65

Letters Sent, Department of the West, 1863, Ch. II, Vol. 18¼

Letters Sent, Polk's Command, 1862–64, Ch. II, Vol. 13

Letters Sent and Endorsements on Letters Received, Army of Tennessee, 1863–64, Ch. II, Vol. 158¼

Polk's Command, Telegrams Received, 1862–64, Orders and Circulars, 1863–64

Selected Letters and Telegrams Sent, Polk's Command, 1861–64

Letters Sent, Orders and Circulars, Hood's Corps, Army of Tennessee, 1864–
  65
Dispatches from the Front Received by Polk's Corps, 1863
James Nocquet Military Service Record
William J. Hardee Military Service Record

New York Historical Society
  John C. Breckinridge Letter
  Alexander Chisholm Letters

New York Public Library
  Ezra Carman Papers
  Century Collection: D. H. Hill Letters
  Century Collection: James Longstreet Letters
  Century Collection: Thomas Jordan Letters
  Century Collection: Joseph E. Johnston Letters

North Carolina Department of Archives and History, Raleigh
  Patton Anderson Papers
  Daniel Harvey Hill Papers

Southern Historical Collection, University of North Carolina, Chapel Hill
  James Alcorn Papers
  E. P. Alexander Papers
  Irving A. Buck Letters
  J. F. H. Claiborne Papers
  Alexander Donelson Coffee Papers
  Major Joseph B. Cumming Papers
  Duke-Morgan Papers
  Gale-Polk Papers
  Daniel C. Govan Papers
  William A. Graham Papers
  James Iredell Hall Papers
  James Harrison Papers
  G. A. Henry Papers
  Daniel Harvey Hill Papers
  J. A. Hinkle Papers
  Edmund Kirby Smith Papers
  H. C. Lockhart Papers
  W. W. Mackall Papers
  Lafayette McLaws Papers
  John Hunt Morgan Papers
  Samuel H. Stout Papers
  Charles Scott Venable Papers
  Marcus J. Wright Papers
  Charles William Dabney Papers: Thomas J. Jackson Series

Historical Society of Pennsylvania, Philadelphia
  Braxton Bragg Letters
  Simon Bolivar Buckner Letters
  William Hardee Letters
  Joseph E. Johnson Letters

Fondren Library, Rice University, Houston, Texas
  Don Carlos Buell Papers

University of the South Library, Sewanee, Tenn.
  Joseph E. Johnston Letters
  Leonidas Polk Papers
  Charles Quintard Diary

South Caroliniana Library, University of South Carolina, Columbia
  Williams-Chesnut-Manning Papers
  A. G. Magrath Papers

Tennessee State Library and Archives, Archives Division, Nashville
  Brown-Ewell Papers
  Benjamin F. Cheatham Papers
  Sherrell Figuers Papers
  Isham G. Harris Papers
  Confederate Collection:
    George Thompson Blakemore Diary
    W. J. Brigham Letters
    Terry H. Cahal Letters
    David Clark Letters
    W. E. Coleman Letters
    Thomas H. Deavenport Diary
    James C. Edenton Diary
    George P. Faw Letters
    Alfred Fielder Diary
    Hardin P. Figuers Memoir
    Thomas Julian Firth Letters
    W. D. Gale Letters
    James L. Gee Memoir
    Dr. D. G. Godwin Letters
    John Harris Letters
    Gustavus A. Henry Letters
    Stephen A. Jordan Diary
    F. B. Kendrick Memoir
    John Berrien Lindsley Diary, typescript, Vol. I
    James C. Malone Letters
    James Ollar Letters
    Leonidas Polk Letters
    James Rains Letters
    Andrew Rice Letters
    W. W. Searcy Letters
    S. R. Simpson Letters
    William E. Sloan Diary
    S. T. Williams Letters
    J. F. Wheless Reminiscence
    Thomas B. Wilson Reminiscence
    George Winchester Diary
    Marcus Wright Diary, printed copy
    Miscellaneous File

Regimental Papers: Fifth, Thirteenth, Fifteenth, and Fifty-fifth Tennessee Infantry, Fifth Tennessee Cavalry

Howard-Tilton Memorial Library, Tulane University, New Orleans
The Mrs. Mason Barret Collection of Albert Sidney and William Preston Johnston Papers
Jefferson Davis Papers, Louisiana Historical Association Collection
Army of Tennessee Papers, Louisiana Historical Association Collection
Samuel Rankin Latta Papers

Western Reserve Historical Society, Cleveland, Ohio
William P. Palmer Collection of Braxton Bragg Papers
William P. Palmer Collection of Confederate Papers

United States Military Academy Library, West Point, N.Y.
Braxton Bragg Papers
Joseph E. Johnston Papers

Virginia Historical Society, Richmond
George Binford Letters
Leonidas Cochran Letters
Jefferson Davis Letters

Virginia State Library, Richmond
Daniel Harvey Hill Papers

College of William and Mary Library, Williamsburg, Va.
Joseph E. Johnston Papers

J. P. Young Papers, in possession of Thomas R. Hay, Locust Valley, New York

SUPPLEMENT TO NEWSPAPERS

Augusta *Chronicle and Sentinel*
Knoxville *Register*
Richmond *Enquirer*
Richmond *Whig*

SUPPLEMENT TO PRINTED PRIMARY SOURCES, PUBLIC DOCUMENTS, AND REMINISCENCES

Austin, J. P. *The Blue and the Gray.* Atlanta, 1899.

Bickham, William D. *Rosecrans' Campaign with the Fourteenth Army Corps, or the Army of the Cumberland.* Cincinnati, 1863.

Blackford, Susan Leigh (ed.). *Letters from Lee's Army or Memoirs of Life in and Out of the Army in Virginia During the War Between the States.* New York, 1947.

Brooks, R. P. (ed.). "Howell Cobb Papers." *Georgia Historical Quarterly,* VI (December, 1922).

Connolly, James. *Three Years in the Army of the Cumberland.* Ed. Paul M. Angle. Bloomington, 1959.

Cox, Jacob. *Military Reminiscences of the Civil War.* 2 vols. New York, 1900.

Cumming, Kate. *Gleanings from the Southland,* Birmingham, 1896.

Davis, Varina. *Jefferson Davis, Ex-President of the Confederate States.* 2 vols. New York, 1890.

De Leon, T. C. *Four Years in Rebel Capitals: An Inside View of Life in the Southern Confederacy from Birth to Death.* Mobile, 1890.

Dorsey, Sarah A. *Recollections of Henry Watkins Allen.* New York, 1866.

Dowdey, Clifford, and Louis Manarin (eds.). *The Wartime Papers of R. E. Lee.* Boston, 1961.

Fitch, John, *Annals of the Army of the Cumberland.* Philadelphia, 1864.

French, Samuel G. *Two Wars.* Nashville, 1901.

Gammage, W. L. *The Camp, the Bivouac and the Battle Field: Being a History of the Fourth Arkansas Regiment.* 2nd ed., Little Rock, 1958.

Gay, Mary A. H. *Life in Dixie During the War.* Atlanta, 1897.

Gordon, John B. *Reminiscences of the Civil War.* New York, 1903.

Hagan, J. W. *Confederate Letters of John W. Hagan.* Ed. Bell I. Wiley. Athens, Ga., 1954.

Harrison, Mrs. Burton, *Recollections Grave and Gay.* New York, 1911.

Hawes, Lilla Mills. *Memoirs of Charles H. Olmstead.* Volume Fourteen of *Collections of the Georgia Historical Society.* Savannah, 1964.

Heartsill, William. *Fourteen Hundred and Ninety-One Days in the Confederate Army.* Ed. Bell I. Wiley. 2nd ed., Jackson, Tenn., 1954.

Hood, John Bell. *Advance and Retreat: Personal Experiences in the United States and Confederate States Armies.* Ed. Richard N. Current. 2nd ed., Bloomington. 1959.

Howe, M. A. DeWolfe (ed.). *Home Letters of General Sherman.* New York, 1909.

————. *Marching With Sherman: Passages from the Letters and Campaign Diaries of Henry Hitchcock, Major and Assistant Adjutant General of Volunteers, November, 1864–May, 1865.* New Haven, 1927.

Hughes, Robert M. (ed.). "Some War Letters of General Joseph E. Johnston." *Journal of the Military Service Institution of the United States,* L (May–June, 1912), 319–28.

Johnston, Joseph E. "'Jefferson Davis and the Mississippi Campaign." *North American Review,* CXLIII (December, 1886), 585–98.

————. "My Negotiations with General Sherman." *North American Review,* CXLIII (August, 1886), 182–97.

Kelley, William M. "A History of the Thirtieth Alabama Volunteers (Infantry) Confederate States Army." *Alabama Historical Quarterly,* IX (Spring, 1947), 115–89.

Kirwan, Albert (ed.). *Johnny Green of the Orphan Brigade: the Journal of a Confederate Soldier.* Lexington, 1956.

Lee, Susan P. *Memoirs of William Nelson Pendleton.* Philadelphia, 1893.

Longstreet, James. *From Manassas to Appomattox.* Philadelphia, 1896.

Mackall, William W. *A Son's Recollections of His Father.* New York, 1930.

Maury, Dabney H. *Recollections of a Virginian in the Mexican, Indian and Civil Wars.* New York, 1894.

Military Historical Society of Massachusetts. *Papers Read Before the Military Historical Society of Massachusetts.* 12 vols. Boston, 1881–1912.

Military Order of the Loyal Legion of the United States, Kansas Commandery. *War Talks in Kansas.* Kansas City, Mo., 1906.

————, Minnesota Commandery. *Glimpses of the Nation's Struggle: Fourth Series.* (Saint Paul, 1898) ; *Sixth Series.* (Minneapolis, 1909) .

————, Ohio Commandery. *Sketches of War History, 1861–1865.* 6 vols. Cincinnati, 1888–1908.

Morgan, Mrs. Irby. *How It Was: Four Years Among the Rebels.* Nashville, 1892.

Morton, John W. *The Artillery of Nathan Bedford Forrest's Cavalry.* Nashville, 1909.

Nichols, G. W. *The Story of the Great March.* New York, 1865.

Oates, William C. *War between the Union and the Confederacy and Its Lost Opportunities with a History of the Fifteenth Alabama Regiment.* New York, 1905.

Phillips, Ulrich B. (ed.) . *Annual Report of the American Historical Association for the Year 1911: The Correspondence of Robert Toombs, Alexander H. Stephens, and Howell Cobb.* 2 vols. Washington, 1913.

Pryor, Mrs. Roger A. *Reminiscences of Peace and War.* New York, 1904.

Reagan, John. *Memoirs with Special Reference to Secession and the Civil War.* ed. Walter McCaleb. New York, 1906.

Review of Certain Remarks made by the President When Requested to Restore General Beauregard to the Command of Department No. 2. Charleston, 1863.

Ross, Fitzgerald. *Cities and Camps of the Confederate States.* ed. Richard B. Harwell. Urbana, 1958.

Scribner, B. F. *How Soldiers Were Made; or The War as I Saw It Under Buell, Rosecrans, Thomas, Grant and Sherman.* New Albany, Ind., 1887.

Shanks, William. "Lookout Mountain, and How We Won It." *Harper's New Monthly Magazine,* XXXVII (June, 1868) .

Smith, Mrs. E. D. *The Soldiers' Friend: Four Years Experience & Observation in the Hospitals of the South.* Memphis, 1867.

Schofield, John M. *Forty-Six Years in the Army.* Washington, 1897.

Sherman, William T. *Memoirs of General William T. Sherman.* 2 vols. in one. 2nd ed., Bloomington, 1957.

Sterx, H. E. (ed.) . "Autobiography and Civil War Letters of Joel Murphree of Troy, Alabama, 1864–1865." *Alabama Historical Quarterly,* XIXX (Spring, 1947) , 170–208.

Wilson, James Harrison. *Under the Old Flag.* 2 vols., New York, 1912.

Wise, John S. *End of An Era.* Boston, 1899.

Wright, Mrs. D. Giraud. *A Southern Girl in '61—the War-Time Memories of a Confederate Senator's Daughter.* New York, 1905.

United States. 58th Congress 2nd Session. *Senate Document Number 234. Journal of the Congress of the Confederate States of America, 1861–1865,* Vols. III, IV, Washington, 1904, Vols. VI, VII, Washington, 1905.

SUPPLEMENT TO SECONDARY SOURCES

Annals of the Army of Tennessee and Early Western History. Nashville, 1878.

Avery, I. W. *History of the State of Georgia from 1850 to 1881.* New York, n.d.

Barrett, John G. *The Civil War in North Carolina.* Chapel Hill, 1963.

Bassler, R. S. *Stratigraphy of the Central Basin of Tennessee,* Tennessee Division of Geology *Bulletin 38.* Nashville, 1932.

Bearss, Edwin C. "Cavalry Operations in the Battle of Stone's River, Part One." *Tennessee Historical Quarterly*, XIX (March, 1960), 23–53; "Part Two" (June, 1960), 110–44.

Breeden, James O. "A Medical History of the Later Stages of the Atlanta Campaign." *Journal of Southern History*, XXV (February, 1969), 31–59.

Bridges, Hal. *Lee's Maverick General*. New York, 1961.

Brown, Andrew. "The Chickamauga Campaign and Geology." *Geotimes*, VIII (March, 1964), 17-21.

Brown, John C. *Old Frontiers*. Kingsport, 1938.

Brown, Joseph M. *The Great Retreat: Could Johnston Have Defended Atlanta Successfully?* Atlanta, n.d.

Bryan, T. Conn. *Confederate Georgia*. Athens, 1953.

Chickamauga and Chattanooga National Military Park Commission. *The Campaign for Chattanooga*. Washington, 1902.

Childress, David T., Jr. "Cavalry in the Western Confederacy: A Military Analysis." M. A. Thesis, Mississippi State University, 1961.

Clauss, Errol MacGregor. "The Atlanta Campaign 18 July–2 September, 1864." Unpublished Ph.D. Dissertation, Emory University, 1965.

Cooper, Walter G. *Official History of Fulton County*. Atlanta, 1934.

Crawford, W. T. "The Mystery of Spring Hill." *Civil War History*, I (June, 1965), 101–26.

Crownover, Sims. "The Battle of Franklin." *Tennessee Historical Quarterly*, XVI (December, 1955), 1–32.

De Leon, T. C. *Joseph Wheeler: The Man, the Statesman, the Soldier*, Atlanta, 1899.

Du Bose, John W. "Chronicles of the Canebrake." *Alabama Historical Quarterly*, IX (Winter, 1947), 475-613.

Dodson, William C. *Campaigns of Wheeler and His Cavalry*. Atlanta, 1899.

Dyer, John P. "Some Aspects of Cavalry Operations in the Army of Tennessee." *Journal of Southern History*, III (May, 1942), 210–25.

Eckenrode, H. J. and Conrad, B. *James Longstreet*. Chapel Hill, 1936.

Eliot, Ellsworth, Jr. *West Point in the Confederacy*. New York, 1941.

Flint, Roy Kenneth. "The Battle of Missionary Ridge." Unpublished M.A. Thesis. University of Alabama, 1960.

Goetzmann, William E. *Army Exploration in the American West, 1803–1863*. New Haven, 1959.

Gonzales, John E. "'Henry Stuart Foote, Confederate Congressman and Exile." *Civil War History*, XIX (December, 1965), 384–95.

Hannah, Howard M. *Confederate Action in Franklin County Tennessee*. Sewanee, 1963.

Hartje, Robert. *Van Dorn: The Life and Times of a Confederate General*. Nashville, 1967.

Hay, Thomas R. "Davis, Bragg, and Johnston in the Atlanta Campaign." *Georgia Historical Quarterly*, VIII (March, 1924), 38–47.

———. "Joseph Emerson Brown, Governor of Georgia, 1857–1865." *Georgia Historical Quarterly*, XIII (June, 1929), 89–109.

———. "The Davis-Hood-Johnston-Controversy of 1864." *Mississippi Valley Historical Review*, XIX (June, 1924), 54–84.

Johnston, Bradley T. *A Memoir of the Life and Public Service of General Joseph E. Johnston*. Baltimore, 1891.

Key, William. *The Battle of Atlanta and the Georgia Campaign.* New York, 1958.

Massey, Mary E. *Bonnet Brigades.* New York, 1966.

Meade, Robert Douthat. "The Relations between Judah P. Benjamin and Jefferson Davis: Some New Light on the Working of the Confederate Machine." *Journal of Southern History,* V (November, 1939) , 468–78.

McElroy, Robert. *Jefferson Davis: The Unreal and the Real.* 2 vols. New York, 1937.

McWhiney, Grady. *Braxton Bragg and Confederate Defeat,* Vol. I. *Field Command* (New York, 1969) .

Patten, Carter. *Signal Mountain and Walden's Ridge.* n.p., 1962.

Pemberton, John C. *Pemberton, Defender of Vicksburg.* Chapel Hill, 1942.

Pittard, Mabel Baxter. "The Coleman Scouts." Unpublished M.A. Thesis. Middle Tennessee State College, 1953.

Pollard, Edward A. *Life of Jefferson Davis, with A Secret History of the Southern Confederacy.* Philadelphia, 1869.

Proctor, Ben H. *Not Without Honor: The Life of John H. Reagan.* Austin, 1962.

Seymour, Digby Gordon. *Divided Loyalties: Fort Sanders and the Civil War in East Tennessee.* Knoxville, 1963.

Shaw, Arthur Marvin. *William Preston Johnston: A Transitional Figure of the Confederacy.* Baton Rouge, 1943.

Sims, Carlton C. (ed.) . *A History of Rutherford County.* Murfreesboro, 1947.

Tucker, Glenn. *Chickamauga: Bloody Battle in the West.* Indianapolis, 1963.

———. *Lee and Longstreet at Gettysburg.* Indianapolis, 1961.

Vandiver, Frank. "General Hood as Logistician." *Military Affairs,* XVI (Spring, 1952) , 1–11.

Walker, Robert Sparks. *Lookout: The Story of a Mountain.* Kingsport, Tenn., 1941.

Yearns, Wilfred B. *The Confederate Congress.* Athens, Ga., 1960.

Index

549